Gustav Stresemann

Portrait of Dr Gustav Stresemann by Augustus Edwin John
(1878–1961), March 1925. Oil on canvas, 43" x 31".
*Albright-Knox Art Gallery, Buffalo, New York, Fellows for Life
Fund, 1926.* © *Courtesy of the artist's estate/Bridgeman Art Library.*

OXFORD

UNIVERSITY PRESS

Great Clarendon Street, Oxford OX2 6DP

Oxford University Press is a department of the University of Oxford.
It furthers the University's objective of excellence in research, scholarship,
and education by publishing worldwide in

Oxford New York

Auckland Bangkok Buenos Aires Cape Town Chennai
Dar es Salaam Delhi Hong Kong Istanbul Karachi Kolkata
Kuala Lumpur Madrid Melbourne Mexico City Mumbai Nairobi
São Paulo Shanghai Taipei Tokyo Toronto

Oxford is a registered trade mark of Oxford University Press
in the UK and in certain other countries

Published in the United States
by Oxford University Press Inc., New York

© Jonathan Wright 2002

British Library Cataloguing in Publication Data

Data available

Library of Congress Cataloging in Publication Data
· Data available

ISBN 0-19-821949-0

3 5 7 9 10 8 6 4 2

Typeset in 10.5 on 14 pt Jansen text
by Kolam Information Services Pvt. Ltd, Pondicherry, India
Printed in Great Britain
on acid-free paper by
T.J. Interrnational Ltd,
Padstow, Cornwall

Gustav Stresemann

WEIMAR'S GREATEST STATESMAN

Jonathan Wright

Millennium Centre
Bury College Learning Resources

OXFORD
UNIVERSITY PRESS

For Susan
Sadie, Katie and Ben

ACKNOWLEDGEMENTS

My interest in Stresemann goes back over twenty years. In this time I have accumulated many debts of gratitude and it is a pleasure to acknowledge them here. I should like to thank first the librarians and archivists who have assisted my work in Britain and Germany, particularly Dr Ludwig Biewer of the Politisches Archiv of the Auswärtiges Amt. I am grateful to Dr Markus Huttner for his expert advice on questions relating to Stresemann's university education and for answering a stream of incidental queries on other matters. I also benefited from the advice of Dr Jan Palmowski on the Wilhelmine period, from the research assistance of Patrick Cohrs and from Hartmut Mayer's kind help with the proofs. Dr Karl Gutzler applied his rare skill at deciphering superseded shorthand systems to passages in Stresemann's diaries and papers. I have also benefited greatly from the generous assistance of Professor Peter Krüger and for access to the papers in his possession of Stresemann's secretary of state at the Auswärtiges Amt, Carl von Schubert. I am very grateful to Dr Ludwig Richter, who generously allowed me to consult his authoritative study of the Deutsche Volkspartei before publication. I also gained valuable insights from a conference on Stresemann organized by the Friedrich Naumann Foundation and Professor Karl Heinrich Pohl in March 2001. Others who have been kind enough to send me material or answer queries include Peter Alter, Herbert Behrendt, Hannelore Braun, Alan Cassels, John Dunbabin, Jürgen Frölich, Richard Grayson, Martin Grossel, Ulrich von Hehl, Gaynor Johnson, Gerd Krüger, Walter Mühlhausen, Gottfried Niedhart, Jeremy and Lesley Noakes, Rafał Pankowski, Peter Parsons, Michael Prinz, Hartmut Pogge von Strandmann, Jim Read, Michael Rudloff, Christiane Scheidemann, Richard Sheppard, Brendan Simms, Holger Starke, Ronald Truman, Joachim Wintzer, Peter-Christian Witt, and Clemens Wurm. I have also received much friendly encouragement from successive history editors at Oxford University Press, most recently from Ruth Parr and Kay Rogers, and it is a pleasure to be able to thank them at last in print.

I was fortunate enough to be able to talk about Stresemann both with his elder son, Dr Wolfgang Stresemann—who also allowed me to consult his collection of family papers concerning his father—and with

Professor Theodor Eschenburg, who as a young man had become part of Stresemann's circle and himself wrote perhaps the best critical appreciation of Stresemann as a politician. More recently, Mrs Jean Stresemann kindly allowed me renewed access to the papers and responded willingly to further requests for information.

My work in Germany has been sustained and advanced over the years by many friends and in particular on countless occasions by Albrecht and Lore Tyrell, and Eckhart and Doris Hellmuth.

It is a particular pleasure to acknowledge the support I have received from the Alexander von Humboldt Foundation, that most generous and friendly of organizations, which it may be noted here was created with the support of the Auswärtiges Amt in 1925, reflecting the interest which Stresemann took in encouraging foreign students to come to Germany.[1] His last speech to the Reichstag contained an eloquent defence for maintaining the budget for this purpose despite the increasing difficulty of the financial situation.[2] I am also grateful to my college, Christ Church, for its support and for providing me with a congenial climate in which to teach and study, and pupils whose cheerful scepticism has forced me constantly to re-examine assumptions I might otherwise have too easily taken for granted. I should also mention my colleagues in the department of politics and international relations, who have shown great forbearance as successive research assessment exercises have found this book still in progress. It is also a pleasure to acknowledge a special debt to two Oxford colleagues who have recently retired. Anthony Nicholls first guided my interest in the history of the Weimar Republic, and the seminars organized by him and German visitors at St Antony's College have provided an invaluable focus for the study of modern German history. I also owe an enormous debt to Peter Pulzer, who nobly agreed to read and comment on the whole work in draft. He has made many helpful suggestions and saved me from many errors—those that remain are mine alone. My greatest debt is, as in everything, to my wife Susan who has meant more to me than I can put into words, and to Sadie, Katie, and Ben. This book is also theirs.

J.W.

---

[1] Volkhard Laitenberger, *Akademischer Austausch und auswärtige Kulturpolitik: Der Deutsche Akademische Austauschdienst 1923–1945* (Göttingen: Musterschmidt, 1976), 19–21.

[2] Speech on 24 June 1929: *Verhandlungen des Reichstags*, vol. 425, p. 2881.

CONTENTS

LIST OF ILLUSTRATIONS

Frontispiece Portrait of Dr Gustav Stresemann by Augustus John, March 1925

(*between pp. 174–175*)

Plates 1–8. Stresemann and his family

1. Stresemann's father Ernst
2. Stresemann's mother Mathilde
3. Stresemann as a boy
4. Stresemann's class at the Andreas *Realgymnasium*
5. Stresemann in the uniform of his *Burschenschaft*
6. Käte Stresemann with elder son Wolfgang
7. Stresemann and his sons Wolfgang and Joachim
8. Stresemann and Käte on their silver wedding anniversary, 20 October 1928

Plates 9–18. Stresemann's Career

9. Syndic of the Association of Saxon Industrialists
10. At the Café Scheurer, Locarno, October 1925
11. The treaty of Locarno, London, 1 December 1925
12. The treaty of Berlin, 24 April 1926
13. On the train to Paris for the signing of the Kellogg–Briand Pact, August 1928
14. With journalists in the Reichstag, 1929
15. During the Reichstag debate, 24 June 1929
16. Addressing the League of Nations, 9 September 1929
17. German People's Party poster for the Reichstag elections, May 1928
18. Stresemann at the Hague Conference, August 1929

(*between pp. 366–367*)

Plates 19–24. Stresemann in Liberal Caricature

19. Stresemann as the leader of the National Liberal Party, October 1917
20. Stresemann as a tramp collecting recruits for the German People's Party from the rubbish dump of the Democratic Party, May 1920
21. Stresemann as the lion in A *Midsummer Night's Dream*, roars 'No' while making it clear to the audience that he is not a real lion, May 1921

Note: Details of provenance and copyright for the illustrations are given with the captions. I have tried to trace copyright in all cases, but if I have inadvertently infringed in any instance I hope the holders will accept my apologies. J.W.

LIST OF MAPS

ABBREVIATIONS

ADAP	*Akten zur Deutschen Auswärtigen Politik*
BAB	Bundesarchiv Berlin
BAK	Bundesarchiv Koblenz
BH	Bayerisches Hauptstaatsarchiv Munich
BVP	Bayerische Volkspartei (Bavarian People's Party)
Centre	Centre Party
DBFP	*Documents on British Foreign Policy*
DDP	Deutsche Demokratische Partei (German Democratic Party)
DNVP	Deutschnationale Volkspartei (German National People's Party)
DVFP	Deutschvölkische Freiheitspartei (German Racial Freedom Party)
DVP	Deutsche Volkspartei (German People's Party)
GA	Geschäftsführender Ausschuß
KPD	Kommunistische Partei Deutschlands (German Communist Party)
MICUM	Mission Interalliée de Contrôle des Usines et des Mines
Nl.	Nachlaß: refers to Nachlaß Stresemann unless identified by another name, e.g. Nl. Bernhard
NLC	*Nationalliberale Correspondenz*
NSDAP	Nationalsozialistische Deutsche Arbeiterpartei (National Socialist Party)
PA	Politisches Archiv, Auswärtiges Amt, Berlin
SPD	Sozialdemokratische Partei Deutschlands (German Social Democratic Party)
USPD	Unabhängige Sozialdemokratische Partei Deutschlands (Independent German Social Democratic Party)
ZS	Zeitgeschichtliche Sammlung

GLOSSARY

Abitur school-leaving examination
Anschluß union of Germany with Austria
Arbeitsgemeinschaft deutscher Landsmannschaften association representing German minorities in areas lost by the Versailles treaty
Auswärtiges Amt German Foreign Ministry
Bauernbund League of small farmers or peasants
Beamte state official, public employee
Bund der Auslandsdeutschen Association of Germans Overseas
Bund der Industriellen Association of Industrialists (representing exporters and manufacturers)
Bund der Landwirte Agrarian League
Bundesrat Federal Council representing the states of the German Empire
bündnisfähig capable or worthy of being an ally
Burschenschaften student fraternities
Central Verband Deutscher Industrieller Central Association of German Industrialists (representing large-scale and heavy industry)
Deutsche Vaterlandspartei German Patriotic Party (First World War)
Deutscher Bühnen-Klub German Theatre Club
Deutscher Reichsverein National Liberal Party association
Deutscher Staatspartei German State Party
Deutscher Volksbund association of the German national minority in Poland
Fraktion parliamentary party
Freikorps volunteer units used to suppress revolution in 1919
Geschäftsführender Ausschuß standing committee of the National Liberal Party and of the German People's Party, to act in place of the national executive
Handlungsgehilfen Verbände unions of white-collar employees or 'clerks'
Jungdeutscher Orden Young German Order
Korps aristocratic student fraternity
Kulturkampf conflict between church and state
Land, Länder German federal state, states
Landbund Farmers' Association electoral list
Landesverband state association
Landtag state parliament

Ministerrat   Council of Ministers: a meeting of the cabinet with the Reich president presiding

Parteivorstand   small executive committee of the German People's Party

Privatangestellten   white-collar employees

Realgymnasium   secondary school with an emphasis on 'modern' subjects rather than the classical languages of a *humanistisches Gymnasium*

Reichsausschuß   Reich Committee of the German People's Party, including party officials of the central and provincial organizations

Reichsbank   Reich Bank

Reichsgeschäftsstelle   central office of the German People's Party

Reichslandbund   Reich Farmers' Association

Reichsrat   Reich Council representing the federal states in the Weimar Republic

Reichsverband der deutschen Industrie   Reich Association of German Industry

Reichswehr   German defence forces, German army. 'Black' Reichswehr: unofficial armed forces (in excess of the numbers permitted under the Versailles treaty)

Reichszentrale für Heimatdienst   head office of the Reich government's information service

Rentenbank   bank established in November 1923, secured by a mortgage of agricultural land and industrial assets

Rentenmark   currency issued on the security of the Rentenbank

Rundschreiben   circular

Staatsrat   State Council representing the Prussian provinces

Stahlhelm   anti-republican, ex-servicemen's organization

Verband Sächsischer Industrieller   Association of Saxon Industrialists

Verein für Sozialpolitik   Association for Social Policy

Vernunftrepublikaner   pragmatic republican

Volksgemeinschaft   community of the nation

Vorstand   executive committee

weiss   Berlin 'white' beer

Wirtschaftspartei   Business Party, representing artisans and small businessmen

Zentralvorstand   national executive of the National Liberal Party and of the German People's Party

INTRODUCTION

In 1930, a year after Stresemann's death, the British historian John Wheeler-Bennett wrote:

With the possible exception of M. Aristide Briand, no figure since the war has so dominated European affairs as did Herr Stresemann; and no statesman has shown so unwavering a devotion to what he conceived to be the right course for his country. By a fortunate coincidence it was also the right course for the world. Herr Stresemann may be said to have been the first of the Europeans.[1]

It is easy to see that between the lines this praise is double-edged. Stresemann followed his concept of Germany's national interest first, and only as a result of 'a fortunate coincidence' could he claim to be a European statesman.

The ambiguity of Stresemann's achievement, suggested by Wheeler-Bennett, became the central theme in discussion of his career. Was his policy of rapprochement with the West, of the Locarno pact and German participation in the League of Nations, a temporary ruse until Germany should have recovered its economic and military power and again be in a position to dominate the Continent? Had Briand been duped by Stresemann, as French politicians on the right feared? Or had Stresemann developed from the feverish advocate of victory and annexation during the First World War to a position where he saw German and European interests as congruent not simply as a short-term expedient but permanently? The question becomes therefore not whether Stresemann put German national interests first, which is not in doubt, but how he defined

---

[1] John W. Wheeler-Bennett and Hugh Latimer, *Information on the Reparation Settlement: Being the Background and History of the Young Plan and the Hague Agreements 1929–1930* (London: Allen & Unwin, 1930), 137. Aristide Briand (1862–1932) played a leading role in French politics from before the First World War. During the 1920s he was the French political leader who worked most closely with Stresemann both as the French premier (1925–6, 1929) and as foreign minister (1926–9).

them and whether this definition was compatible with the interests of other European countries.

Thomas Mann, in an evocative biographical sketch compressed into two sentences, also written in 1930, put the view that Stresemann grew out of his limited nationalism and developed a genuinely European mentality:

The history of this extraordinary man belongs to the most remarkable of German lives. Coming from a right-wing bourgeois background, with the spiritual and political traditions of this origin in his blood, as a patriotic middle-class businessman, even if above average in education and intellectual curiosity, identified with the idea of an expansion of German power and still during the war a convinced advocate of imperial conquest, he was able through a power of understanding which was simultaneously full of vitality and refined by illness, directed and driven by an exemplary will to live although physically already marked by death, to grow out from and above all the traditions he had inherited, faster and faster—a man who was both driven and gripped, who did not have much time—into the world of a European society of nations in thought, conviction, and deed, which no one would have dreamt possible on the basis of his early adulthood.[2]

The opposite view, that Stresemann remained an unreconstructed nationalist, was held by the left-wing British journalist Claud Cockburn, who started his career in *The Times* office in Berlin in 1927 and was taken by the Berlin correspondent Norman Ebbutt to drink beer with Stresemann in the garden of the Foreign Ministry. He wrote later of his disenchantment with Stresemann and with the whole concept of 'a new democratic peaceful European community' on which Liberals pinned their hopes:

Personally I found that Stresemann was entertaining provided that you did not believe in him. He was one of those Germans who had, at a fairly early date, discovered that the way to get away with being a good German was to pretend to be a good European. He had a wonderful act in which he pretended to be not only fat, which he was, but good-hearted and a little muzzy with beer into the bargain. In reality he was as quick and sharp as a buzz-saw, and if being a sharp, fast-moving buzz-saw was not enough, he would hit you from behind with a hammer.[3]

As Cockburn's criticism suggests, the question of Stresemann's sincerity is bound up with a wider question which extended beyond Stresemann's

---

[2] Quoted by Felix Hirsch, *Stresemann. Ein Lebensbild* (Göttingen: Musterschmidt, 1978), 307.
[3] Claud Cockburn, *In Time of Trouble: An Autobiography* (London: Hart-Davis, 1957), 97–8.

time. Did German and perhaps other European statesmen only invoke 'Europe' as a cover for their own national interests?[4] Was the idea of a peaceful, democratic Europe of nation states an illusion? The dilemma was keenly felt in France, where Germany's larger population and resources were a constant source of concern. On Stresemann's death there were many tributes, but doubts soon surfaced, especially after the publication of selections from his papers in 1932.[5] The French journalist Jules Sauerwein, who acted as an intermediary between Stresemann and Briand, argued that there had never been a genuine understanding between the two but only a relationship in which each tried to get the better of the other 'poorly camouflaged by effusive sentimentality'.[6] In the same way André François-Poncet, the French ambassador to Germany from 1931 to 1938, wrote of Stresemann's 'fundamental duplicity and hypocrisy', but also wondered whether it had been less Stresemann's character than the situation which had been responsible for this 'double game': 'The French certainly wanted rapprochement but one which cost nothing. The Germans certainly wanted rapprochement but one which paid. Only Stresemann's skill enabled him to keep his balance on this unstable ground'.[7]

This perspective, which seemed to rule out a lasting settlement of Franco-German differences, was much less common in Britain. British governments were more easily persuaded that if Germany was allowed to recover Europe would become, as Keynes argued, more stable and prosperous, and that French attempts to maintain its supremacy on the Continent following the war were to be resisted.[8] Austen Chamberlain, the foreign secretary from 1924 to 1929, saw himself as recreating the concert of Europe like Castlereagh after the Napoleonic Wars.[9] Although himself

---

[4] For a subtle analysis of this theme for the period since 1945, see Timothy Garton Ash, *In Europe's Name: Germany and the Divided Continent* (London: Jonathan Cape, 1993). He quotes Bismarck's pithy comment, 'I have always found the word "Europe" in the mouths of those politicians who wanted from other powers something they did not dare to demand in their own name': ibid. 20.

[5] Henry Bernhard (ed.), *Gustav Stresemann. Vermächtnis*, 3 vols., (Berlin: Ullstein, 1932); Eng. edn. by Eric Sutton (London: Macmillan, 1935–40).

[6] Jules Sauerwein, *30 ans à la une* (Paris: plon, 1962), 183.

[7] André François-Poncet, *De Versailles à Potsdam: La France et le problème allemand contemporain 1919–1943* (Paris: Flammarion, 1948), 106, 132.

[8] J. M. Keynes, *The Economic Consequences of the Peace* (London: Macmillan, 1919, 1971), 169–70; the 1971 edn. is cited throughout.

[9] Chamberlain to his half-sister Ida, 28 Nov. 1925: Robert C. Self (ed.), *The Austen Chamberlain Diary Letters* (Cambridge: Cambridge University Press, 1995), 285.

a Francophile, he knew that Germany would have to be included in the concert. It is not surprising that Stresemann was able to look to the British ambassador from 1920 to 1926, Lord D'Abernon, for support, and that over time he was also able to win Chamberlain's confidence. Nor was this trust confined to the Foreign Office. In an editorial to mark Stresemann's death, *The Times* saw no incompatibility between the nationalist and the good European—a view that was to become typical of a particular strand of British thinking about European integration after the Second World War:

He [Stresemann] remained intensely nationalist; but the necessities of Europe and the interdependence of its states led him to the wider nationalism that sees in co-operation the only escape from chaos...It is intelligent and practical patriots—not vague idealists who cannot first serve their own countries—who make the 'good Europeans' of today. Stresemann did inestimable service to the German Republic; his work for Europe as a whole was almost as great.[10]

The historiographical debate about Stresemann has revolved around the questions of his sincerity and the conditions for a peaceful and stable Europe. Stresemann's early biographers believed in his good faith, and set out to explain his evolution from German nationalist to European statesman.[11] After the war there was a reaction as the vast collection of his unpublished papers became available to historians. Annelise Thimme drew a perceptive portrait of him as a man torn between romantic nationalism and a realism imposed by circumstance.[12] This was an important corrective to the temptation to promote Stresemann in the early years of the Federal Republic as a pioneer of European unity rather than simply a peaceful Europe of nation states—although Konrad Adenauer, the leading German exponent of European integration, had himself always regarded

[10] *The Times*, Friday, 4 Oct. 1929.

[11] Rudolf Olden, *Stresemann* (Berlin: Rowohlt, 1929; Eng. edn. London: Methuen, 1930); Antonina Vallentin, *Stresemann. Vom Werden einer Staatsidee* (Leipzig: List, 1930; Eng. edn. London: Constable, 1931). Of more recent biographies, two are also part-memoir and are both informative and sympathetic: Hirsch, *Stresemann*, and Wolfgang Stresemann, *Mein Vater Gustav Stresemann* (Munich: Herbig, 1979).

[12] Annelise Thimme, *Gustav Stresemann* (Frankfurt am Main: Goedel, 1957). Another scholar who made a major contribution to a more rounded picture of Stresemann, from the evidence of his papers, was Hans W. Gatzke, *Stresemann and the Rearmament of Germany* (Baltimore: Johns Hopkins University Press, 1954; New York: Norton, 1969). Thimme later reviewed the controversy which their work provoked: 'Einmal um die Uhr. Die Stresemann-Kontroverse von 1927–1979', in Hartmut Lehmann (ed.), *Historikerkontroversen* (Göttingen: Max Planck Institut für Geschichte, 2000), 31–85.

Stresemann with suspicion.[13] There then followed a long period of accumulating detailed monographs on different aspects of Stresemann's foreign policy.[14] More recently, there has appeared the first comprehensive biography by Christian Baechler.[15] This traces Stresemann's career in great detail and reaches the conclusion that there was a genuine development in his outlook from Wilhelminian imperialist to believer in collective security through the League. This conclusion is all the more striking coming from a French historian.

Parallel to the debate about Stresemann's intentions ran a debate about the history of German foreign policy and the forces that sustained it. Were there fundamental continuities from the Wilhelminian empire to the Third Reich in the prevailing view of Germany's place in the world, the elites which made policy, and the social and political forces they represented?[16] Or was there rather, as Peter Krüger argues, a discontinuity during the Weimar Republic as the constraints of conducting a purely peaceful foreign policy took hold in the Auswärtiges Amt, establishing a style which had more in common with that of the Federal Republic than the Third Reich?[17] In this debate too the interpretation of Stresemann plays a pivotal role.

While it is natural that attention should have concentrated on Stresemann's foreign policy, it is easy to forget that he also played a central role in the domestic politics of the Weimar Republic. Indeed at his death in

---

[13] The different ways in which Stresemann has been portrayed in public debate and school books in Germany since his death are analysed by Andreas Körber, *Gustav Stresemann als Europäer, Patriot, Wegbereiter und potentieller Verhinderer Hitlers* (Hamburg: Krämer, 1999).

[14] Martin Walsdorff, *Westorientierung und Ostpolitik. Stresemanns Rußlandpolitik in der Locarno Ära* (Bremen: Schünemann, 1971); Michael-Olaf Maxelon, *Stresemann und Frankreich. Deutsche Politik der Ost–West-Balance* (Düsseldorf: Droste, 1972); Werner Weidenfeld, *Die Englandpolitik Gustav Stresemanns. Theoretische und praktische Aspekte der Aussenpolitik* (Mainz: Hase & Koehler, 1972); Manfred J. Enssle, *Stresemann's Territorial Revisionism: Germany, Belgium, and the Eupen-Malmédy Question 1919–1929* (Wiesbaden: Franz Steiner, 1980); Manfred Berg, *Gustav Stresemann und die Vereinigten Staaten von Amerika. Wirtschaftliche Verflechtung und Revisionspolitik 1907–1929* (Baden-Baden: Nomos, 1990); Piotr Madajczyk, *Polityka i Koncepcje Polityczne Gustawa Stresemanna Wobec Polski (1915–1929)* (Warsaw: Instytut Nauk Politcznych Polskiej Akademii Nauk, 1991); Constanze Baumgart, *Stresemann und England* (Cologne: Böhlau, 1996); Wolfgang Michalka and Marshall M. Lee (eds.), *Gustav Stresemann* (Darmstadt: Wissenschaftliche Buchgesellschaft, 1982).

[15] Christian Baechler, *Gustave Stresemann (1878–1929): De l'impérialisme à la sécurité collective* (Strasbourg: Presses Universitaires de Strasbourg, 1996).

[16] Marshall M. Lee and Wolfgang Michalka, *German Foreign Policy 1917–1933: Continuity or Break?* (Leamington Spa: Berg, 1987).

[17] Peter Krüger, *Die Aussenpolitik der Republik von Weimar* (Darmstadt: Wissenschaftliche Buchgesellschaft, 1985).

1929 he was widely seen by admirers and critics alike as the master of the parliamentary game and as the person who maintained the precarious balance of the political system. This was an extraordinary achievement for someone whose political career had been written off after the First World War, because he had supported victory and the High Command to the end. Spurned by the republican parties in 1919, he became their unanimous choice as chancellor in August 1923 at the height of the crisis caused by the French occupation of the Ruhr. When his government fell in November 1923 he remained as foreign minister and continued to hold that office in the seven administrations which followed until his death in October 1929. This required skill and courage as well as luck. His development from the discredited monarchist of 1919 to the greatest of the pragmatic republicans (*Vernunftrepublikaner*) was first described by Henry Turner in a concise and authoritative study in the 1960s.[18] There remain, however, interesting questions. What light does Stresemann's career throw on the structure of Weimar politics? On what did his power rest, other than his own ability? Could one speak of a 'Stresemann system'?

There are pitfalls in a biographical approach to these questions—most obviously too close a focus on the person. But there are also advantages. A biography requires domestic politics and foreign policy to be considered together in a way which is surprisingly rare. It is a truism that in the Weimar Republic, a regime born out of defeat and humiliation, burdened with reparations, and with part of its territory under foreign occupation, foreign policy was also domestic politics to an unusual degree. Yet it is also easy to forget as historical studies separate into specialist disciplines— political, social, economic, cultural—and the history of foreign policy is itself regarded as a separate domain.

In a biography one is reminded of the unity of history and of the complexity of the elements of which it is composed. In Stresemann's case these elements included a forceful personality, one that inspired dislike and distrust as well as respect and admiration. Theodor Heuss, a political contemporary to the left of Stresemann in the German Democratic Party (DDP) and subsequently the first president of the Federal Republic, admitted that he 'could not stand him', while Theodor Eschenburg, the leading political scientist of his generation in the Federal Republic, came to know Stresemann as a graduate student and never lost his

---

[18] Henry Ashby Turner, *Stresemann and the Politics of the Weimar Republic* (Princeton: Princeton University Press, 1963).

admiration for him.[19] A biography of Stresemann must also take account of contradictions, not simply between his early and later careers but also within the later career—for instance, despite his genuine commitment to liberalism and parliamentary government, the exaggerated respect he showed for the Crown Prince which puzzled friends and even his own family.[20] There are also the occasional nationalist outbursts which seemed to reveal another self—usually kept well hidden—even if these outbursts served a political purpose. A biographer must heed as a warning the comment Stresemann quoted approvingly from the Swiss poet Conrad Ferdinand Meyer: 'I am not a carefully constructed book, I am a human being with human contradictions.'[21]

There is much else to understand in a life which spanned careers in both business and politics, as well as a useful sideline in journalism; which experienced extraordinary reversals of fortune even for a period in any case marked by war, defeat, and revolution; which demonstrated both driving ambition and opportunism but also in other moods the ability to reflect from a basis of liberal beliefs, enriched by a deep interest in history, literature, and the performing arts; a life supported by a close family and marked by indomitable energy and resilience despite the effects of illness; and by the end a life which had acquired a certain moral stature in a society riven by increasingly bitter divisions. Each of these is part of Stresemann's biography. Each also has a place in understanding his role in German and European politics. No biography could do justice to all the links between them. If this book succeeds in indicating just some of the elements which made Stresemann the outstanding German politician of his era, it will have been worthwhile.

[19] Theodor Heuss, *Erinnerungen 1905–1933* (Tübingen: Rainer Wunderlich, 1963), 247; Theodor Eschenburg, 'Gustav Stresemann', in id., *Die improvisierte Demokratie* (Munich: Piper, 1963), 143–226; repr. in Theodor Eschenburg and Ulrich Frank-Planitz, *Gustav Stresemann. Eine Bildbiographie* (Stuttgart: Deutsche Verlags-Anstalt, 1978); Theodor Eschenburg, *Also hören Sie mal zu. Geschichte und Geschichten 1904 bis 1933* (Berlin: Siedler, 1995), 219–31.

[20] Interviews with Dr Wolfgang Stresemann, Berlin, Apr. 1983 and Professor Eschenburg, Tübingen, 4 Sept. 1998.

[21] Bernhard (ed.), *Vermächtnis*, vol. i, p. ix.

1

'The Child is father of the Man'

1878–1901

Stresemann opened an autobiographical sketch, which he wrote shortly before becoming chancellor in August 1923, by using Wordsworth's words as an introduction to his early life.[1] It was a typical literary touch, and he went on to explain that in his last year at school he had intended to study literature and history rather than, as later became his degree subjects, political economy and economics. Throughout his life he maintained his interest in literature and history, and sometimes regretted that he had not followed his first inclinations.[2] The problem had been to know how he could combine them with a career. As he explained, in an essay about himself written when he was 18 as part of the school-leaving examination (*Abitur*), he would have liked to become a teacher, but because of the kind of school he had attended he would have been eligible to teach only modern languages or natural sciences.[3] He also already had a keen interest in politics, which he clearly did not think it advisable to refer to in the essay, but is clear from correspondence with an older friend from school, Kurt Himer, to whom he wrote for advice at the

[1] Bernhard (ed.), *Vermächtnis*, i. 1–8.
[2] For instance, Stresemann to the author Rudolf Presber, 12 July 1928: (PA, Nl. 290).
[3] Arnold Harttung (ed.), *Gustav Stresemann Schriften* (Berlin: Berlin Verlag, 1976), 1–10. Stresemann's school was a *Realgymnasium*, introduced to encourage education in modern subjects, rather than one of the prestigious 'humanities' (*humanistischen*) *Gymnasien* where there was more emphasis on classical languages.

same time.[4] The political interest seemed to point to a career in journalism, since political journalism was one of the few ways that existed of making a living from politics.[5]

Stresemann told Himer that he had come to consider journalism both because of his aptitudes and, half-joking, because of the lack of suitable alternatives:

I cannot become a civil servant: I should find it intolerable to perform the same task day in day out . . . always under the thumb of a superior, nothing more than a small cog in a large machine. Being a businessman would suit me better if I had the prospect of becoming independent later, but for that hundreds of thousands are necessary and they are not at my disposal. I would very gladly become a lawyer, indeed that would represent in a certain way the summit of my wishes, but for that other conditions are necessary which make it impossible for me to carry out this plan, above all the length of training, made longer still by the year that I would need to complete the *Gymnasium Abitur*. . . . If I were to become a student of language and literature, I should have to wait until I was 96 to be appointed to a position and I do not want to become a bank official.[6]

By the time he wrote his essay for the *Abitur*, however, he also had doubts about journalism, particularly since 'there are so few really independent editorial posts. I could never, however, subordinate my own opinion to that of someone else or write anything against my convictions.'[7] His dream was to set up as a novelist, but he knew that this was not a practical option without other means of support and he doubted whether he possessed the ability.[8]

This mixture of idealism, self-assertion, and uncertainty about the future might be regarded as typical of an 18-year-old about to start university. In Stresemann's case, however, there were particular elements in his background which made his situation unusual. He was born in Berlin on 10 May 1878 into a lower-middle-class, Protestant family, the youngest of

---

[4] 'From my early youth I have occupied myself with politics as with other things that were not at all appropriate to my age then': Stresemann to Herr [Kurt] Himer, 24 Nov. 1896. Himer later recalled that at school it was rumoured that Stresemann was active in politics, which was 'strictly forbidden', and even took part in progressive meetings. 'Jugenderinnerungen an Stresemann', *Hamburger Anzeiger*, 7 Oct. 1929. Dr Detlev Himer kindly sent me this reference and copies of the correspondence between Stresemann and his father.

[5] See e.g. Max Weber, 'Politics as a Vocation', in H. H. Gerth and C. Wright Mills (eds.), *From Max Weber: Essays in Sociology* (London: Routledge, 1967), 96–7.

[6] Stresemann to Himer, 24 Nov. 1896: Himer correspondence (Wright collection).

[7] On the low status of journalists in the Wilhelmine empire, see Kurt Koszyk, *Geschichte der deutschen Presse*, ii: *Deutsche Presse im 19. Jahrhundert* (Berlin: Colloquium, 1966), 224–6.

[8] Stresemann to Himer, 24 Nov. 1896: Himer correspondence (Wright Collection).

seven surviving children, one having died as an infant. His father ran a small business making and distributing bottled Berlin *weiss* beer, which he bought in casks from a brewery. The family home in the Köpenicker Straße, in the south-east of the old city, also served as a bar, and parts of the house were let to produce additional income. It was a modest but relatively comfortable existence, although in the 1890s the large breweries started to sell bottled beer direct and undercut the small distributors.[9]

This background was important for Stresemann in several ways. It was completely undistinguished—his paternal grandfather had been a coach-man, and on his mother's side the family came from a poor agricultural area in the Oder marshes.[10] Nevertheless his parents had built up a business which meant that, in an unfashionable area of Berlin, they were regarded as well off.[11] When their youngest child proved to be intelligent and successful at school, they had the means as well as the aspiration for him to stay on at school and go to university. Gustav therefore enjoyed the unusual luxury, from his background, of wondering what profession he should follow.

In his essay for the *Abitur* Stresemann wrote of his early life that, despite being a member of a large family, he had been lonely.[12] His elder siblings soon left home, a sister died when he was 8, and an elder brother aged 22 committed suicide two years later, leaving only his youngest sister at home with him and their parents.[13] His mother and father were encouraging and supportive, but both they and his sister were too preoccupied with running the family business to have much time for him, and 'under these circumstances I scarcely experienced a real family life'.[14] He was left to himself and turned to reading, telling Kurt Himer that 'I completely isolated myself from my contemporaries and lived only for my books.'[15] His only diversion was to travel to the mountains or the sea during the

---

[9] At one time Stresemann's father had supplied some 200 regular customers, but by the time of his death in 1905 the house carried mortgages to a total of 103,000 marks: Nl. 125. Wolfgang Stresemann, *Mein Vater*, 23–5; Kurt Koszyk, *Gustav Stresemann. Der kaisertreue Demokrat* (Cologne: Kiepenheuer & Witsch, 1989), 31–3.

[10] The best account of Stresemann's family history is Koszyk, *Stresemann*, 26–31.

[11] A contemporary recalled that at the local dancing class where the parents were mostly tradesmen, shopkeepers, and petty officials, the Stresemann family was regarded as 'very prosperous': Georg Schwidetzky, 'Kreise um den jungen Stresemann', *Kölnische Zeitung*, 8 Oct. 1929.

[12] Harttung (ed.), *Schriften*, 1–2.

[13] Koszyk, *Stresemann*, 30. Stresemann referred to a brother having committed suicide in a newspaper article, 'Unter der Herrschaft der Orthodoxie', *Dresdner Volks-Zeitung*, 9 Aug. 1896.

[14] *Abitur* essay: Harttung (ed.), *Schriften*, 1.

[15] Stresemann to Himer, 24 Nov. 1896: Himer Correspondence (Wright collection).

holidays, particularly to the North Sea or the Baltic, where he could indulge a fondness for melancholy dreaming looking out to sea. The mood of introspection had been especially marked the previous year when his youngest sister had left home and his mother, whom he 'loved passionately', had died, leaving him grieving and listless.[16] However, loneliness had one advantage. It was to his love of books that Stresemann attributed his success at school. He told Himer that he had acquired a good knowledge of literature and history and also 'a stylistic skill and ease of expression' which earned him high marks in those subjects and in religion.[17] That gave him confidence that he would be successful in the school-leaving examination, despite a weakness in mathematics.

Stresemann received a good education at school and remained a grateful pupil in later years.[18] In the *Abitur* essay he described—no doubt with an eye to pleasing his teachers—the subjects that had made the greatest impression on him.[19] Of these German literature came first, particularly Schiller's *Wallenstein* and, in the upper school, Goethe's poetical works. He also recorded his interest in the poetry, sometimes with political themes, of the period after Goethe—Freiligrath, Lenau, and Uhland—and he attended evening lectures given by university teachers on these and others, including Hoffmann von Fallersleben and a later favourite, Georg Herwegh.[20] The political theme of the revolutionary movements of the 1830s and 1840s was also important in the work of a later novelist, who was still active in the 1890s, Friedrich Spielhagen. According to Stresemann, Spielhagen 'exercised an unquenchable influence on me. I admired almost everything about him: the flaming heat of the description, the poetry of his language, the often sheer oppressiveness of his wealth of ideas, the richly moving treatment, and that, in the finest sense of the word, liberal attitude which is the basis of all his works.'[21] Spielhagen was one of the very few authors to offer a critical view of the German society of his time in the manner of Dickens or Balzac.[22] Stresemann also read

---

[16] *Abitur* essay: Harttung (ed.), *Schriften*, 3–4.

[17] Stresemann to Himer, 24 Nov. 1896: Himer correspondence (Wright collection).

[18] Stresemann to the headmaster of the Andreas Realgymnasium, Fritz Johannesson, 15 Apr. 1922, thanking him for his teaching of English and enclosing a gift of 10,000 marks: Harttung (ed.), *Schriften*, 10–12.

[19] Ibid. 2–8.

[20] His lecture notes are in Nl. 362.

[21] *Abitur* essay: Harttung (ed.), *Schriften*, 7.

[22] Fritz Stern, 'Subtle Silence and its Consequences', in Henning Tewes and Jonathan Wright (eds.), *Liberalism, Anti-Semitism and Democracy: Essays in honour of Peter Pulzer* (Oxford: Oxford University Press, 2001), 2.

foreign authors at school, including Dickens and Macaulay, as well as Shakespeare, and some French and American literature.

The theme of liberalism recurred in his account of his attitude to religion. Although he was careful to pay tribute to the religious education he had received from a Conservative clergyman who was also a court chaplain, he made it clear that he did not share the same views. He had read the criticisms of the historical truth of the Gospels by Ernst Renan and David Strauss and attended a conference of the association of liberal Protestant theologians, the Protestantenverein, in 1896. He declared his belief in God and in 'Jesus Christ as "God's son" inasmuch as in him the divine being has been revealed in its purest and noblest form', but he did not believe that at the Last Judgement, if there was one, it would matter whether one had been a member of a particular church or subscribed to a particular dogma. He thought there should be 'the greatest possible tolerance in all matters of faith', though this would not prevent his attacking 'the anti-national character of Catholicism in its degenerate form as Ultramontanism'. Naturally he opposed any attempt by the Church to restrict the freedom of theological enquiry in universities—a reference to controversies at the time over the Apostles' Creed.

Compared to the sections on literature and religion, Stresemann said relatively little about history. He had enjoyed studying different examples of the conflict of ideas—between pope and emperor and absolutism and constitutionalism. Beyond that his interest had been fired by particular people—Frederick the Great, Joseph II, and Napoleon.

It is noticeable that, although Stresemann felt able to be open about his religious beliefs in the essay, he made no direct comment on his political interests—presumably because they would have been frowned on. For the origins of these interests we have only his later autobiographical account, in which he says that at home there was a collection of literature from the 1848 revolution.[23] He mentions some items, including a work on the Bonn professor and revolutionary Gottfried Kinkel and the record of the trial of the Prussian liberal Benedikt Waldeck, and pamphlets celebrating his acquittal. These details suggest that the memory was genuine, although he was mistaken in thinking that the collection came from his paternal grandfather, who died in 1840.[24] The Berlin in which he grew up was in any case strongly Left Liberal, and Stresemann's attitudes were typical of this background.

---

[23] Bernhard (ed.), *Vermächtnis*, i. 2.   [24] Koszyk, *Stresemann*, 28–9.

By the time he wrote the school-leaving essay, he had in fact already developed an active political commitment and tried his hand as a journalist. Starting in December 1895, he wrote a number of 'Berlin letters' for a Dresden Left-Liberal weekly newspaper, the *Dresdner Volks-Zeitung*, without of course revealing his age to the editor.[25] He covered a variety of subjects—scandals, new publications, theatre premieres, the Berlin exhibition of 1896 celebrating the achievements of German business and technology, and also a number of political themes. His targets included the Prussian Conservatives and their allies in the Protestant Church, the anti-Semitic ex-court chaplain Adolf Stöcker, the three-class Prussian franchise which weighted votes according to taxable income and was about to be introduced in Saxony, the Agrarian League's (the Bund der Landwirte) campaign against margarine against the wishes of ordinary consumers, and even the plight of striking women confectionery workers who were paid starvation wages and driven to prostitution. He deplored what he saw as the growth of reactionary views among the middle class and particularly among university students, where anti-Semitism and anti-liberalism were on the increase. He noted that these circles even disputed the contribution the liberal movement had made to national unification:

Truly, there is little to make one happy wherever one looks, a perceptible decline of Left-Liberal opinion in all areas, and with this a middle class so little conscious of its high position within the state and far too often acting as the direct ally of political reaction and ecclesiastical orthodoxy, so that one could really lose heart. One thinks back all the more fondly to the period which was the springtime of nations, where not the proletariat but the middle class, the representatives of property and education, won freedom in bloody battles on the barricades.[26]

Stresemann conceded that the Left Liberals were in a 'serious crisis', having lost half their seats in the Reichstag elections of 1893 and being squeezed by the competition from the German Social Democratic Party (SPD) on one side and the Conservatives and anti-Semites on the other.[27]

---

[25] Stresemann wrote fourteen 'letters' and also published three other articles between Dec. 1895 and Dec. 1896, when he cancelled his contract to concentrate on working for the *Abitur*. Stresemann to Himer, 24 Nov. 1896: Himer correspondence (Wright collection). Koszyk located the 'letters' and gives a good account of them: Koszyk, *Stresemann*, 56–66. The Dresden Stadtarchiv has copies of the newspaper.

[26] 'Berliner Briefe', VII, *Dresdner Volks-Zeitung*, 22 Mar. 1896.

[27] 'Die beiden Volksparteien', *Dresdner Volks-Zeitung*, 1 Mar. 1896. Stresemann's article refers to the two major groups of Left Liberalism, the Freisinnigen and the regional Deutsche Volkspartei in Württemberg. German liberalism was notoriously fissiparous. It split in 1867 between

His remedy was that 'we must free ourselves from all tepid half-measures and be just purely democratic', and he quoted Spielhagen on the need for liberals to espouse the principles of freedom not only in theory but in practice.

Consistent with these Left-Liberal views, it is interesting to see that at this date Stresemann did not spare the National Liberal Party (National-liberale Partei) or the colonial society (the Deutsche Kolonialgesellschaft) his criticism. The first he mocked as a home for all causes, however contradictory, and the colonial society for the way its delegates outdid each other in proposing spending on the fleet without regard for where the money was to come from.[28] Stresemann was even sceptical about the founding of the National Social Union (Nationalsozialer Verein) under the Protestant pastor Friedrich Naumann—which he was later to be influenced by—fearing that it would in practice remain too close to Stöcker's Christian Social Movement (Christlich-Soziale Arbeiterpartei).[29] In sum, Stresemann appeared completely committed to the Left-Liberal position, and it seems likely that he was a member of the Left-Liberal Waldeck youth club in Berlin, to which he referred in one of the articles.[30]

The different sources give a coherent picture of the 18-year-old Stresemann. He emerges as a young man with liberal views and strong political interests. He showed no sign of a powerful or original mind. He was successful at school but not outstanding.[31] But he had an enquiring and critical intelligence and had already shown the ability and the energy to put it to use. His Left-Liberal views reflected the milieu from which he came, and his rejection of the conservative trend in the upper middle class is striking for someone who would soon be in a position to join their ranks.

the National Liberals who put support for Bismarck's policy of unification above constitutional principle and the Progressives (*Fortschritt*) who did not. In 1881 the National Liberals themselves split over the principle of free trade, and the free traders joined the Progressives in a united Left Liberal Party (Deutsche Freisinnige Partei) in 1884. This split again in 1893 between those who opposed increased military expenditure under Eugen Richter and those who supported a large army and colonies under Theodor Barth. For the Wilhelmine period, Alastair Thompson, *Left Liberals, the State, and Popular Politics in Wilhelmine Germany* (Oxford: Oxford University Press, 2000) is informative and original.

[28] 'Berliner Briefe', V, VI, *Dresdner Volks-Zeitung*, 16 Feb., 1 Mar. 1896.

[29] 'Berliner Briefe', XI (in fact the twelfth letter but misnumbered), *Dresdner Volks-Zeitung*, 11 Oct. 1896.

[30] 'Berliner Briefe', IV, *Dresdner Volks-Zeitung*, 2 Feb. 1896.

[31] Fritz Johannesson, 'Aus Stresemanns Schulzeit', *Mitteilungen des Vereins für die Geschichte Berlins*, 47/4 (1930), 121–32.

In April 1897 Stresemann enrolled as a student in the University of
Berlin, which had been founded in 1810 during Prussia's war of liberation
against Napoleon, and was by the 1890s at the height of its fame and
influence. He was persuaded by a businessman whom he met through his
student association to take political economy as his main subject rather
than literature.[32] This meant that he was thrown into the debates which
were raging at the time between the so-called 'academic socialists', such as
Adolf Wagner and Gustav Schmoller, who had established a dominant
position in the university, and their critics outside, particularly in the
Conservative Party (Deutschkonservative Partei), where the Saar industrialist Freiherr von Stumm-Halberg took the lead in attacking professors
whom he saw as peddling socialist propaganda. Public agitation led to the
appointment of an extra professor, Karl Reinhold, to present a different
point of view. Stresemann recalled these controversies in his autobiographical sketch in 1923, but in a way which suggested that though he
had attended the lectures of both sides, he had been there as an interested
observer not as a committed supporter of one or the other.[33]

The attempt by Stumm-Halberg to make political capital out of the
issue in any case gave a thoroughly misleading impression of the main
school of thought among Stresemann's teachers. The principal figures
were social reformers but not Social Democrats. The emphasis of their
teaching was historical—an attempt to produce an overall view of the
development of economic life from the earliest times. Even the lectures
on economic theory were in effect the history of economic thought. The
Verein für Sozialpolitik (Association for Social Policy), of which Schmoller
was one of the founders, became an influential forum for social history—
attracting historians and sociologists as well as economists. Schmoller
believed that social history should serve an ethical purpose, but he was
concerned with the conditions of all social groups, including the problems
created by industrialization for the lower middle class not simply the
labour movement. In the same way, the lectures on economic thought
contained criticisms of Marxism along with other social theories. Underlying this comprehensive approach was pride in Germany's achievements,
evident also in support from members of the faculty for the fleet and
colonies, and a desire to create a German tradition of political economy

[32] Autobiographical sketch, 1923: Bernhard (ed.), *Vermächtnis*, i. 4.
[33] Ibid. For the background, see Rüdiger vom Bruch, *Wissenschaft, Politik und öffentliche Meinung. Gelehrtenpolitik im Wilhelminischen Deutschland (1890–1914)* (Husum: Matthiesen, 1980), 145–8, 304–5.

which could rival those of France and England.[34] Through the lectures on political economy Stresemann was exposed to a powerful and coherent view of German society from people who, like Schmoller, believed in reform for the general good rather than revolution.

His lecture notes show that Stresemann was, at least at first, an assiduous and energetic student.[35] In his first term he attended, among others, Max Lenz's lectures on German history in the nineteenth century. Lenz was a leading figure in the tradition of Ranke, whose main theme was the development of Germany's national history from Luther to Bismarck, which he saw as based on the Protestant belief in the value of the individual. He was also a supporter of imperial expansion. At the same time, he sought to convey a more objective view, and one closer to the sources, than the Prussian—centred interpretation of Heinrich von Treitschke—who had died the previous year.[36] Given Stresemann's own view of the importance of the contribution of the liberal movement to German unification, Lenz's interpretation was no doubt sympathetic to him.

In the same term he attended two sets of lectures by Schmoller, one on economic theory and the other on types of employer, from the paterfamilias to trusts and cartels. He also heard the distinguished historian Otto Hintze, then at the beginning of his career, lecture on theories of state and society, covering political thought from Aristotle to Treitschke.[37] In addition, he found time for other lectures on both history and literature.

The following two terms in Berlin continued along the same lines though, judging from his lecture notes, with a more relaxed attitude. There was another course by Schmoller on economic practice, one on social policy by another of the 'academic socialists', Ignaz Jastrow, a course in statistics, which took as its starting point the various uses of

[34] Rüdiger vom Bruch, 'Gustav Schmoller', in Wolfgang Treue and Karlfried Gründer (eds.), *Berlinische Lebensbilder. Wissenschaftspolitik in Berlin* (Berlin: Colloquium, 1987), 175–93. Mark Hewitson, *National Identity and Political Thought in Germany: Wilhelmine Depictions of the French Third Republic 1890–1914* (Oxford: Clarendon Press, 2000), 5–6, 35.

[35] The notes are contained in a collection of small exercise books (Nl. 362). Stresemann took notes in shorthand, but it is possible to follow the subjects of the lectures from names and literature which appear in longhand. He seems to have learned shorthand in his last year at school, perhaps with a view to becoming a journalist (a suggestion I owe to my wife Susan). Unfortunately the system he used (Stolzeschen) is now obsolete, and it is a difficult process even for experts to decipher it.

[36] Rüdiger vom Bruch, 'Max Lenz', in *Neue Deutsche Biographie* (Berlin: Duncker & Humblot, 1985), xiv. 231–3.

[37] Brigitta Oestreich, 'Otto Hintze', in Michael Erbe (ed.), *Berlinische Lebensbilder. Geisteswissenschaftler* (Berlin: Colloquium 1989), 287–309.

statistics rather than mathematics, and lectures on German legal history by Otto Gierke and on Roman legal history by Alfred Pernice.

One reason for the slackening pace of Stresemann's studies was his growing involvement in the student fraternities, the *Burschenschaften*. In his later account of his time at university he gave more space to this activity than to his academic work. The experience was clearly important in developing his confidence from the shy and lonely person he had been at school. He recalled that through the *Burschenschaften*, 'I first found friendship, the first training in working together and perhaps the first training in leadership'.[38]

The *Burschenschaften* had been founded after the Napoleonic Wars as a middle–class student movement for a liberal, united Germany in contrast to the aristocratic *Korps*. However, by the 1880s the *Burschenschaften* had themselves become increasingly conservative, behaving like second–class *Korps*, adopting the practice of duelling, and moving towards excluding Jews. In 1883, in reaction against this trend, Dr Konrad Küster founded a small breakaway movement, the Allgemeine Deutsche Burschenbund or *Reformburschenschaften*, to maintain the original ideals of the movement.[39] Stresemann immediately joined its tiny Berlin branch—the Neo-Germania—and in his second term was elected their 'spokesman'.[40] Through Dr Küster he also became the editor for a year from April 1898 of the fortnightly newspaper of the *Reformburschenschaften* throughout Germany, the somewhat grandly named *Allgemeine Deutsche Universitäts-Zeitung*.

Stresemann used his first editorial to make a political statement.[41] He took as his theme the fiftieth anniversary of the 1848 revolution and the way in which liberals had allowed the occasion to be appropriated by the Social Democrats. He criticized the Left Liberals as a sad and passive group who no longer wished to be reminded of their 'youthful follies'. He also, however, criticized the 1848 liberals for having ignored the social question which, he said, had now become central. By continuing to try to avoid the question liberalism was opening itself to 'a devastating accusation' and making genuine liberals, who believed in social liberalism, politically homeless.

[38] Autobiographical sketch, 1923: Bernhard (ed.), *Vermächtnis*, i. 7–8.

[39] Norbert Kampe, *Studenten und 'Judenfrage' im Deutschen Kaiserreich* (Göttingen: Vandenhoeck & Ruprecht, 1988), 196–9.

[40] Autobiographical sketch, 1923: Bernhard (ed.), *Vermächtnis*, i. 3–7.

[41] 'Vor fünfzig Jahren', *Allgemeine Deutsche Universitäts-Zeitung*, 12/7, 1 Apr. 1898.

In the same number, Stresemann published another article on the political role of the *Burschenschaft*.[42] He pointed out that the universities had played an important part in the liberal movement of the 1840s and that the Frankfurt parliament of 1848 could be described, with a grain of salt, as more like a meeting of the Verein für Sozialpolitik than like their current parliaments. Stresemann argued that the *Burschenschaften* had a duty not to engage in party politics but to maintain their original ideals, in particular:

to stand up for the equality of all citizens and to protest against anti-Semitism and disguised class rule. Just as they could not accept that being an adherent of the Jewish religion was a reason for rejection from state employment, so equally they could not accept without protest the contempt shown from above for the intelligence of the entire middle class, by the preferential treatment of the aristocracy in the officer corps, senior administrative appointments etc.

The *Burschenschaften*, he said, were the sworn enemies of absolute rule. They should oppose discriminatory legislation against political or labour movements (a reference to attempts to reintroduce a ban on the SPD) and restrictions on freedom of belief or academic enquiry. The article concluded: 'If there are today associations which call themselves "*Burschenschaften*" but are anti-Semitic and reactionary then...that only shows that these *Burschenschaften* have inherited only one thing from the old *Burschenschaften*, the name.'

Despite his comments on the *Burschenschaften* not engaging directly in party politics, in June 1898 Stresemann felt free to discuss whether a student could support any of the existing parties in the forthcoming Reichstag elections.[43] The Conservatives were naturally ruled out—as enemies of education and freedom of opinion, supporters of absolutism and champions of the privileges of the nobility. He again dismissed the National Liberals as not a party at all but a refuge for every kind of opinion—protectionists and free traders, philo-Semites and anti-Semites, large-scale capitalists and professors—to call oneself a National Liberal, he said, was to risk ridicule. The Left Liberals, on the other hand, were

---

[42] 'Burschenschaft und Politik', *Allgemeine Deutsche Universitäts-Zeitung*, 12/7, 1 Apr. 1898. This was the text of a paper he had given to an evening discussion group of the Neo-Germania, a traditional activity which had fallen into neglect but which he claimed to have revived with a paper on Thomas More's *Utopia*: Bernhard (ed.), *Vermächtnis*, i. 4.

[43] 'Zu den nächsten Reichstagswahlen', *Allgemeine Deutsche Universitätszeitung*, 12/12, 15 June 1898.

stuck in the dogma of laissez-faire and lacked any social ideas. The Social Democrats were unacceptable because they were anti-national and because of their plans for a communist future which would stifle individual freedom. Finally, neither the anti-Semites nor the fanatical (Catholic) Centre Party could conceivably be supported. There was therefore no party to which 'a modern, liberal human being' could turn. The best they could hope for was the success of certain individuals, such as Friedrich Naumann, and that from the present stagnation there would come a movement of younger liberals to produce the 'social liberal party' which would be 'the party of the future'.

These and other articles support Stresemann's later recollection of incidents from his time in the *Burschenschaft*—that he persuaded them to allow him to lay a wreath on the graves of the revolutionaries who had died in March 1848 and that he successfully opposed a move to exclude Jews from his own Neo-Germania, arguing that what mattered was not racial background but whether someone accepted the ideas of the *Burschenschaft*.[44] His liberal attitudes, however, were combined with nationalism. He organized a rally of the *Reformburschenschaften* in Frankenhausen at the foot of the Kyffhäuser mountains, which had legendary associations with the Emperor Frederick Barbarossa, and made a rousing speech in which he celebrated the contribution of the *Burschenschaften* to German unification and proposed a toast to the Kaiser, as the representative of the German people, 'not from a byzantine sense of slavery but from free hearts'.[45] He also drew a clear line against the SPD, opposing a resolution to identify the *Burschenschaft* with the Social Democrats, which was defeated unanimously.[46]

Stresemann's political attitudes had developed from the Left Liberalism of the 'Berlin letters' of two years before. His growing interest in how the state should respond to the problems produced by industrialization was prompted by his study of political economy and made him receptive to the ideas of Friedrich Naumann. At Naumann's death in 1919, Stresemann wrote, 'How we young students cheered him then in his struggle against the narrowness and pig-headedness of German party politics.' He explained why none of the parties at the time attracted them and continued,

[44] Autobiographical sketch, 1923: Bernhard (ed.), *Vermächtnis*, i. 4–5.
[45] 'Der Bundestag der A.D.B.- Burschenschaften in Frankenhausen', *Allgemeine Deutsche Universitäts-Zeitung*, 12/13, 1 July 1898.
[46] 'Vom XV. A.D.B.-Tag', *Allgemeine Deutsche Universitäts-Zeitung*, 12/14, 15 July 1898; Bernhard (ed.), *Vermächtnis*, i. 7.

Then came Friedrich Naumann and threw into this time of ferment, searching for new ideas, the great concept of uniting the Kaiser and the German working class. He gave his proposals the social content which the liberalism of that period lacked . . . 'An expanding nation like ours must believe in its masses if it is not to die of its masses.' This remark . . . characterized all his efforts up to the time of the collapse of the National Social Union. In it were found all those who believed . . . with him that it was decisive for our future to educate a national-minded working class.[47]

The need for such a movement was all too clear from the success of the SPD, which in Reichstag elections had steadily increased its share of the vote (despite the anti-socialist legislation from 1878 to 1890) from 3 per cent in 1871 to 27 per cent in 1898, a larger share than any other party.

In the winter term of 1898 Stresemann transferred to Leipzig University, leaving home for the first time. He again became the spokesman of the local *Reformburschenschaft*, Suevia, but one purpose of the move was to enable him to concentrate on completing his academic studies for a doctorate.[48] In Leipzig he heard the lectures of two further members of the Verein für Sozialpolitik, Karl Bücher and Wilhelm Stieda, and joined Bücher's seminar.[49] Bücher persuaded Stresemann to take as his thesis topic the development of the Berlin bottled beer industry, both because he was in a good position to know about it and because this kind of detailed study fitted the research interests of his group. The topic was the subject of ribald comment later, and Stresemann was sensitive about it, explaining that he would have liked to take a large theoretical topic—he had written a paper for the seminar on what determined the value of silver and why it had not been able to maintain itself as a currency standard beside gold—but that this idea did not find favour with Bücher.[50]

The thesis gave Stresemann the opportunity to carry out empirical research into one example of the general problems facing small businesses.

[47] 'Friedrich Naumann', repr. from *Deutsche Stimmen*, 31 Aug. 1919, in Rochus von Rheinbaben (ed.), *Stresemann. Reden und Schriften*, 2 vols. (Dresden: Carl Reissner, 1926), i. 241–51, quotations pp. 244–6. For Naumann and his influence, see Theodor Heuss, *Friedrich Naumann. Der Mann, das Werk, die Zeit*, 3rd edn., ed. Alfred Milatz (Munich: Siebenstern, 1968) and Peter Theiner, *Sozialer Liberalismus und deutsche Weltpolitik. Friedrich Naumann im Wilhelminischen Deutschland (1860–1919)* (Baden-Baden: Nomos Gesellschaft, 1983).

[48] Autobiographical sketch, 1923: Bernhard (ed.), *Vermächtnis*, i. 6.

[49] Walter Goetz, 'Karl Bücher' and 'Wilhelm Stieda', in id., *Historiker in meiner Zeit* (Cologne: Böhlau, 1957), 277–85, 286–95.

[50] Autobiographical sketch, 1923: Bernhard (ed.), *Vermächtnis*, i. 6.

Under Bücher's direction he was ingenious about sources, using newspaper advertisements, trade directories, and production statistics for historical material and a survey of current producers for contemporary
evidence.[51] The writing was enlivened by humorous social observation.
He drew parallels between, on the one hand, the traditional Berlin *weiss*
beer, which required elaborate preparation and careful and leisured consumption, and the traditional deliberate and unhurried life of the pipe-
smoking Berliner, and, on the other, between the increasingly popular
Bavarian bottled beer, which could be drained in an instant on a building
site and which suited the new bustle of the metropolis where at the same
time cigars and, even more, cigarettes were ousting the pipe. His conclusions were not sentimental: the decline of small firms, such as his father's,
was natural given that the big breweries could supply bottled beer more
efficiently. At the same time he was not fatalistic. He recommended that
the small firms should coordinate their activities and organize their own
brewery, an experiment which had already been tried and failed, but which
he believed could succeed with better management.

As a diversion from his thesis Stresemann also wrote an article about
the controversial topic of department stores, which was published in a
prestigious academic journal.[52] Again it offered an unprejudiced explanation for the success of the department store, looking at French and
British as well as German experience. Stresemann argued that the stores
were a product of their time and offered gains to both employers and
consumers, which had to be set against the losses of small shopkeepers. He
described how department stores had succeeded in making shopping a
social outing by providing displays and restaurants and even musical
entertainment. Again his conclusions were balanced. The department
stores were putting many small shopkeepers out of business, and this
trend in the modern economy 'has brought us no sufficient substitute
for the valuable middle-class life which it has destroyed'. On the other
hand, he was against proposals for legislation since that would simply
produce a deluge of demands from every kind of small trader for similar
protection. There was no point in trying to stop a development as inevitable as the railway.

---

[51] Gustav Stresemann, *Die Entwicklung des Berliner Flaschenbiergeschaefts* (Berlin: R. F. Funcke
[1901]). Stresemann's research notes for the thesis are in Nl. 362.

[52] Gustav Stresemann, 'Die Warenhäuser. Ihre Entstehung, Entwicklung und volkswirtschaftliche Bedeutung', *Zeitschrift für die gesamte Staatswissenschaft*, 56 (1900), 696–733. The journal
was edited by Albert Schäffle, a friend and colleague of Bücher's.

In view of Stresemann's later career it is of interest that he also took a course in international law. The professor with whom he studied, Karl Fricker, was not famous, but he had a reputation for taking pains with his lectures and with the students who, like Stresemann, also attended his seminar.[53] Fricker's post was in the faculty of philosophy where he taught as part of Stresemann's course in political economy (*Staats- und Cameralwissenschaften*), and not, as was becoming normal, in the separate law faculty. Fricker, like his colleagues in the Verein für Sozialpolitik, took a broad view of the law as an aspect of social history. Stresemann decided to offer international law as one of the three subjects for his oral examination, and prepared by carefully transcribing his shorthand notes on Fricker's lectures.[54]

From these notes it is clear that Fricker provided his students with a sophisticated introduction to the subject. His definition of international law was 'the law of a community that is in the process of coming into being', linking the growth of international law to the growth of an international society in the tradition of the seventeenth-century Dutch jurist Hugo Grotius. The historical part of the course paid special attention to the nineteenth century, with references to the concert of Europe and subjects like the growth of embassies, the regulation of the slave trade, and the protection of shipping. The analytical part of the course dealt with the principles of international law, 'balance of power and the principles of legitimacy and nationality', and the way it operated through 'arbitration courts and the practice of intervention, collective action and congresses'. Further lecturers considered the role of states as the subjects of international law, the nature of treaties, state formation and change, the rights of foreigners including asylum seekers, the role of international bodies to secure passage along the Danube or through the Suez canal or to supervise the finances of individual states (Turkey, Egypt, and Greece), the nature of alliances and collective guarantees, such as those for the German states in the treaty of Westphalia, and war and its rules on land and sea. Fricker would today have been regarded in international relations theory as a 'realist'—that is he rejected as 'obsolete' the idea that international law could be based on concepts such as world citizenship or human rights. The literature recommended included classical authors—Grotius, Vattel, Wolff, Kant, and Hegel—as well as legal texts. Stresemann may not have

---

[53] Karl Bücher, 'Karl Viktor Fricker', *Zeitschrift für die gesamte Staatswissenschaft*, 64 (1908), 193–200.
[54] Nl. 362.

read the books, but he became familiar with the main theories, later for instance referring to Kant's argument that international law could be built only on a federation of free nations.

Stresemann submitted his thesis in January 1901, and it was examined by Bücher and Stieda.[55] Both thought well of it, though Bücher commented that the detailed examination of current conditions was more successful than the historical part, and that the whole was too long. However, he praised the way in which Stresemann had tackled the wider aspects of his theme, such as the dependence of the beer producers on the changing tastes of an urban public. The thesis received a II from a scale of pass marks consisting of I (which was seldom given), IIa, II, IIb, and III. In the subsequent oral examination, in which Stresemann had to answer questions about political economy from Bücher, international law from Fricker, and statistics from Stieda, he was also given a II. Bücher thought his performance 'thoroughly satisfactory', as did Fricker, who would have been prepared to go as far as a IIa, but Stieda was not impressed by Stresemann's answers on statistics, observing that 'the candidate spoke with great eloquence but was not always clear' so that a II was as high as he was willing to go.

Stresemann's time at university was important to him in various ways. He gained a thorough knowledge of both political history and the development of a modern industrial economy and the social theories which sought to explain and reform it. He learned to work systematically and weigh the gains and losses of economic development and the problems of state intervention. He also acquired from his teachers in the Verein für Sozialpolitik a particular view of German society as a whole and a sense of the responsibility of an educated elite towards it. This was accompanied by pride in Germany's achievements and its still growing importance in the world. From Fricker he had also learned something about the practice and limits of international cooperation.

As a student, he was not involved directly in party politics—he later recalled that the only political meeting in which he took part was to support the fleet.[56] Through his work with the *Burschenschaften*, however, he acquired political experience in a wider sense and greater social confidence. There was also a significant development in his political attitudes.

[55] The examination records are in the Universitätsarchiv Leipzig, Phil. Fak. Prom. 853, 1–5. I owe this reference to Dr Markus Huttner, who generously also provided me with information about Stresemann's university teachers.

[56] Autobiographical sketch, 1923: Bernhard (ed.), *Vermächtnis*, i. 6–7.

His early Left Liberalism remained in his criticism of discrimination by class and religion in government appointments, his rejection of the Conservative Party, Protestant and Catholic intolerance, and anti-Semitism. But he had also become critical of the failure of Left Liberalism to offer any constructive solutions to social problems. He did not himself suggest what those solutions might be, though he read a number of books on the subject.[57] He was not tempted to join the SPD because he saw it as both potentially intolerant and unpatriotic. He recognized the power of Marxism as an explanation of history, but he agreed with those who thought it one-sided. The social order, he wrote, was not the result only of the means of production but also of 'customs and habits, beliefs and settled ideas'.[58] Like many students of his generation, he was a natural convert to Naumann's ideal of winning over the working class by social reform and imperial expansion. How this was to be done, however, remained unclear.

[57] His notes include references on this theme to (?)Martin Behrend, *Die Verjungung des Liberalismus*, and Ignaz Jastrow, *Socialliberal*. He also reviewed a book on land reform in the *Allgemeine Deutsche Universitäts-Zeitung*, 13/7, 1 Apr. 1899.

[58] Review of Diederich Bischof, *Maurertum und Menschheitsbau. Freimaurerische Gedanken zur sozialen Frage* in *Allgemeine Deutsche Universitäts-Zeitung*, 14/19, 1 Oct. 1900. Stresemann took the quotation from Eugen von Philippovich's, *Grundriss der Nationalökonomie*; he also made detailed notes on Werner Sombart's *Sozialismus und soziale Bewegung* recording both the importance and shortcomings of Marxism (Nl. 362).

2

'A hunger for power'

Business and Politics, 1901–1914

Between 1901 and 1914 Stresemann established his reputation in two areas: as the organizer of manufacturing industry in Saxony, in which his success created a model for other parts of the Reich and, secondly, as a young politician of unusual gifts in the National Liberal Party. The two areas were closely connected, for Stresemann saw in manufacturing industry a natural partner for the left wing of the National Liberal Party with which he became associated.

When he started his professional life as a syndic or promoter of the interests of manufacturing industry in Saxony, Stresemann found a situation in which his clients were both poorly organized and disadvantaged. Compared to the interests of agriculture organized predominantly in the Agrarian League and the interests of heavy industry, particularly the coal and steel giants of the Ruhr, which dominated the Central Association of German Industrialists (Central Verband deutscher Industrieller), the corresponding manufacturers' interest group, the Association of Industrialists (Bund der Industriellen), founded in 1895, was weakly organized and uninfluential.[1] Yet the manufacturers' interests were distinct from those of agriculture and heavy industry in important ways. Both the agrarians and the coal and steel industries were protectionist, the alliance of 'rye and

---

[1] Hans-Peter Ullmann, *Der Bund der Industriellen* (Göttingen: Vandenhoeck & Ruprecht, 1976).

iron' which backed Bismarck's adoption of tariffs in 1879. The interests of
manufacturing, on the other hand, depended to a much greater extent on
exports, and the precise terms of trade treaties were therefore vitally
important to its different branches. Because of their size and organization
agriculture and heavy industry were able to influence Reich governments
to put their interests first in foreign trade negotiations and make, in
return, concessions damaging to the manufacturers.

There were also other conflicts of interest and of outlook between the
two groups. Manufacturers were consumers of Ruhr coal and therefore
vulnerable to its cartel pricing policies. In addition, the Agrarian
League and the heavy industrialists' Central Association were ultra-
conservative on political and social questions. The Agrarian League
campaigned mainly through the German Conservative Party while
heavy industry was strongly represented in the right wing of the National
Liberal Party, particularly in its Prussian section.[2] Its spokesmen were
anti-democratic and anti-trade union. Stresemann saw the interests of the
manufacturers, by contrast, in using democratic institutions to achieve
fairer representation and break the grip of 'rye and iron'. He also saw it as
in the interests of his clients to negotiate with trade unions, whose influence in the long term they were too weak to resist. He therefore promoted
within the manufacturers' association a distinctive progressive platform
which quickly brought him into conflict with Conservative groups in both
business and politics.[3]

The National Liberal Party which Stresemann joined in 1903 was only
a shadow of its former glory.[4] Founded in 1867 to support Bismarck's
policy of unification at the price of accepting a constitution which fell
short of Liberal demands, it had enjoyed its heyday in the 1870s as the
strongest single party in the Reich with about 30 per cent of the total vote,
while the Left Liberals or Progressives (the Deutsche Fortschrittspartei),
who continued to oppose Bismarck, accounted for another 8 per cent. The
National Liberals hoped that over time a full system of parliamentary

    [2] James N. Retallack, *Notables of the Right: The Conservative Party and Political Mobilization in Germany 1876–1918* (Boston: Unwin Hyman, 1988), 100–12, 131–47; Hartwig Thieme, *Die nationalliberale Fraktion des Preußischen Abgeordnetenhauses 1914–18* (Boppard am Rhein: Harald Boldt, 1963), 34–7.

    [3] His views were laid out in a collection of his speeches from 1902–10; Dr Gustav Stresemann, *Wirtschaftspolitische Zeitfragen* (Dresden: F. Emil Boden, n.d. [1910]; 2nd expanded edn., 1911).

    [4] James J. Sheehan, *German Liberalism in the Nineteenth Century* (London: Methuen, 1982), 181–271; Dieter Langewiesche, *Liberalism in Germany*, Eng. edn. Basingstoke: Macmillan, 2000), 121–249.

government would develop from their support for the chancellor. But in 1879 Bismarck reasserted his independence, breaking with the National Liberals and abandoning free trade for protection. This split the party, and those who were most opposed to Bismarck's new course seceded to the Left Liberals. In the 1890s and 1900s the Liberal vote kept pace with the expansion of the electorate, as population expanded, but not with a steep rise in electoral participation which overwhelmingly benefited the SPD. As a result the Liberal share of the vote fell to about 25 per cent, of which the National Liberals won some 13–14 per cent. The SPD, by contrast, rapidly increased its share to a high point of almost 35 per cent in 1912. In terms of Reichstag seats, elected on a system of universal male franchise, this meant that the National Liberals had fallen from their peak of 152 in 1874 to forty-five by 1912 (with a further forty-one Left Liberals). The National Liberals after 1874 were weaker than the Catholic Centre Party, which had about 19 per cent of the vote and 100 Reichstag seats. The Centre Party won a higher proportion of seats for its vote because its strength was regionally concentrated, and this gave it an advantage under the electoral system (single-member constituencies with election by an absolute majority after a second round where necessary) over the National Liberals, whose vote was dispersed. Perhaps more worrying for the National Liberals was that the main competitors on the right for their overwhelmingly Protestant vote, the Conservative and Free Conservative parties (Freikonservative Partei) and their allies, retained support equal to that of the National Liberals and (again because of regional concentration) a larger number of seats (about seventy) in the Reichstag.[5]

The decline in the electoral fortunes of the National Liberals was in a sense inevitable once national unification had been achieved, and new issues divided both the electorate and the party. It never recovered from the split in 1881 when it lost whole regions to the Left Liberals. In the 1890s it suffered further losses to the right as the Agrarian League and the anti-Semites exploited rural discontent at the reduction in agricultural tariffs introduced by chancellor Caprivi. The issue of tariffs continued to divide the party as a new round was negotiated in 1902–6. As economic

---

[5] A detailed and sophisticated analysis of the complex voting trends which produced this result is provided by Jonathan Sperber, *The Kaiser's Voters. Electors and Elections in Imperial Germany* (Cambridge: Cambridge University Press, 1997), 108–53. The Free Conservative Party was founded in 1860, giving consistent support to Bismarck's policies, in contrast to the main Conservative Party.

life became more highly organized into interest groups, so these conflicts became more intense. The interests of trade unionists, white-collar workers, agriculture, manufacturing, commerce, and heavy industry conflicted, and the party was torn by these conflicts. Even on the issue of constitutional reform it was no longer united, as the right wing—fearful of the growth of the SPD—opposed strengthening the Reichstag and liberalization of the 'three-class' franchise in Prussia. The different levels of the party system—municipal, *Land*, and Reich—with their own electoral systems, and regional differences for instance between the Liberal *Länder* of the south-west and Conservative provinces of Prussia, complicated the picture further. The party leadership at Reich level had the awkward task of managing these divergent elements. The party was also slow to reform its organization, although this was difficult given its reliance on local notables and ties of deference to hold its divergent groups together. The decline in its fortunes was indeed to some extent masked by the continuing success of National Liberals in municipal politics, where they benefited from restricted franchises.[6]

By the turn of the century the National Liberals depended mainly on the Protestant middle class, professional and business, and Protestant peasant proprietors, though they also won a significant minority of Catholic votes in southern Germany.[7] They won Reichstag seats in small cities, towns, and agricultural villages, not in the great industrial centres or areas dominated by large agricultural estates. They represented a potentially volatile electorate, whose divisions on economic and political issues made nationalism and imperialism the natural basis of party unity and electoral success.

As a minority party the National Liberals had to seek allies to be effective. The damage the Conservatives and National Liberals could inflict on each other by competing in the same constituencies, and the emphasis on nationalism which they had in common, made an electoral pact between them a natural tactic and one which was adopted successfully in 1887 and 1907. The domestic policies of the Conservatives, however, opened up the divisions within the National Liberal Party, making it impossible to maintain cooperation between the two parties for very

---

[6] An authoritative study of urban liberalism and the reasons why it was not able to transfer its success in the cities to the state (*Land*) and national levels is provided by Jan Palmowski, *Urban Liberalism in Imperial Germany. Frankfurt am Main, 1866–1914* (Oxford: Oxford University Press, 1999).

[7] Sperber, *The Kaiser's Voters*, 141–6.

long in the Reichstag. On the other hand, cooperation with the other major groups was more difficult to achieve: differences between National Liberals (the party of the *Kulturkampf*) and the Catholic Centre Party, particularly over education, ruled out a formal partnership between them, and the gulf between National Liberals and the SPD at Reich level was even wider (though they worked together at a *Land* level in Baden from 1908 to 1913 against the Centre Party).[8]

Given its position in the party system, squeezed between right and left, the leadership of the National Liberal Party had constantly to manoeuvre for influence. It also had to conceal, as far as possible, its deep internal divisions. It had to bridge the gap between the ultra-conservative Westphalian representatives of heavy industry and the organization of Young Liberals (Jungliberaler Reichsverband), which grew rapidly after 1900 and advocated constitutional reform and a progressive social policy. The party leadership, under Ernst Bassermann from 1898, preserved the precarious unity of the party by emphasizing its ideology as a middle party, a pragmatic party which preferred cooperation with government to opposition, and giving priority to its traditional preserve, the issues of defence and foreign and imperial policy. In support of this general approach, the leadership was able to rely on a majority of upper-middle-class professional men (especially lawyers), businessmen, and officials, the alliance of 'property and education' which dominated the higher levels of the party, the Reichstag party (*Reichstagsfraktion*), and the national executive (Zentralvorstand). Indeed, in the absence of a unifying programme, the party leader played a crucial role in rallying the party and setting its direction.[9]

Stresemann's rapid rise in the world of Wilhelmine business and politics was remarkable. In 1901 when he started work in Dresden he had neither wealth nor social connections. The girl whom he had adored since he was 17 and to whom he now eagerly proposed refused him on her mother's advice that his prospects were too uncertain.[10] But what he lacked in social standing he made up for in ambition, drive, and determination. He was also sensitive, and retained a measure of critical detachment from the

---

[8] On the question of SPD–Liberal cooperation, see Beverly Heckart, *From Bassermann to Bebel: The Grand Bloc's Quest for Reform in the Kaiserreich, 1900–1914* (New Haven: Yale University Press, 1974).

[9] Oscar Stillich, *Die politischen Parteien in Deutschland*, ii: *Der Liberalismus* (Leipzig: Werner Klinkhardt, 1911), 280–1.

[10] Stresemann's autobiographical short story 'Die Barre', written in 1924; Bernhard (ed.), *Vermächtnis*, i. 553; Georg Schwidetzky, 'Kreise um den jungen Stresemann', *Kölnische Zeitung*, 8 Oct. 1929; Hirsch, *Stresemann*, 28–9.

world in which he moved. He saw the opportunities with which the inequities of the Wilhelmine empire presented him—manufacturers who were under-represented and a leader of the National Liberal Party, Bassermann, who needed support in holding the party together against the overbearing influence of heavy industry.[11] His own abilities and convictions were perfectly matched to these opportunities. He seized his chances with the ruthless energy of a young man determined to make his mark. By 1914 he had established a successful business career and by 1917 he was already, aged 39, Bassermann's heir apparent for the leadership of the National Liberal Party.

The Organization of Manufacturing Industry

While finishing his doctorate Stresemann briefly resumed his activities as a journalist, writing on a voluntary basis for a Berlin newspaper, the *Deutsche Warte*, attending discussions between leading politicians such as August Bebel of the SPD, Adolf Stoecker, and the Left Liberal leader Eugen Richter, held in a Berlin brewery (the Bockbrauerei) and frequenting the Café Orient where politicians and journalists, such as Kurt Eisner of the SPD and the distinguished independent publicist Maximilian Harden, met and talked into the small hours.[12] Journalism, however, did not provide a living, and through a contact on the *Deutsche Warte* he was offered and accepted his first salaried post with the association of chocolate manufacturers in Dresden, starting in March 1901 immediately after receiving his doctorate.[13]

Stresemann was confronted in Dresden with a situation in which the chocolate manufacturers were suffering at the hands of a cartel of sugar growers and refiners.[14] The chocolate manufacturers had already decided to break the cartel by building their own sugar refinery (just as Stresemann

[11] Ludwig Richter, '"Auseinanderstrebendes Zusammenhalten". Bassermann, Stresemann und die Nationalliberale Partei im letzten Jahrzehnt des Kaiserreiches', in Wolfram Pyta and Ludwig Richter, *Gestaltungskraft des Politischen. Festschrift für Eberhard Kolb* (Berlin: Duncker & Humblot, 1998), 55–85.

[12] Paul Schweder, 'Stresemann als Journalist' in *Neue Zeit* (Berlin-Charlottenburg [1929]); PA, Nl. Konsul Bernhard, Zeitungsausschnitte über Reichsaussenminister Gustav Stresemann, vol. 14.

[13] On the connections between the *Deutsche Warte* and the manufacturers' association, see Ullmann, *Bund der Industriellen*, 249, 279.

[14] Donald Warren, *The Red Kingdom of Saxony: Lobbying Grounds for Gustav Stresemann 1901–1909* (The Hague: Martinus Nijhoff, 1964), 30–1.

had recommended in his thesis that the Berlin beer retailers should build their own brewery).[15] The new factory was founded in September 1901 and Stresemann became secretary to the directors and then a director himself. The sugar refiners' cartel was destroyed in any case by a new international agreement on sugar in 1902, creating temporary difficulties for the chocolate manufacturers' separate refinery as well.[16] But Stresemann had attracted attention. The manufacturers of the district of Dresden and Bautzen had already decided to form a Saxon branch of the Association of Industrialists in 1901.[17] According to his own account, it was left to Stresemann to put this idea into practice. In January 1902 he was appointed secretary to the Dresden branch and persuaded another branch in Leipzig to join to form the Association of Saxon Industrialists (Verband Sächsischer Industrieller). From a membership of just 180 firms at the start, it grew rapidly to reach 5,740 firms by 1914, employing over half a million people. It represented over two-thirds of all Saxon industry, making the association much the largest of its kind.[18] Its success was identified with Stresemann's leadership and it became the vehicle not only of his business but also his political career.

The reason for the rapid growth of the association was that industry in Saxony had distinctive interests, and Stresemann articulated those interests for the first time in a way that was politically effective.[19] In 1900 there

---

[15] Holger Starke, 'Dresden in der Vorkriegszeit: Tätigkeitsfelder für den jungen Stresemann', in Karl-Heinrich Pohl (ed.), *Politiker und Bürger. Gustav Stresemann und seine Zeit* (Göttingen: Vandenhoeck & Ruprecht, 2002) 89–90. (I am grateful to Herr Starke for giving me an advance copy of his paper.) This corrects the claim by Stresemann's secretary and nephew Franz Miethke that Stresemann was himself responsible for the decision: Franz Miethke, *Dr. Gustav Stresemann der Wirtschaftspolitiker. Eine Skizze* (Dresden: Sächsische Verlagsanstalt, 1919), 6–7.

[16] Miethke, *Stresemann*, 6–7.

[17] Starke, 'Dresden', 89–90.

[18] Gustav Stresemann, 'Zehn Jahre Verband Sächsischer Industrieller', in *Festschrift zur Feier des zehnjährigen Bestehens des Verbandes Sächsischer Industrieller Dresden, am 11. und 12. März 1912* (Dresden: F. Emil Boden [1912]), 35–8; Ullmann, *Bund der Industriellen*, 343.

[19] Warren, *The Red Kingdom of Saxony*, and Ullmann, *Bund der Industriellen*, remain the basic studies for this phase of Stresemann's career. However, the fall of the GDR stimulated a rapid growth of regional research which has provided new perspectives on the society in which Stresemann made his name. For evaluations of this work, see James Retallack, 'Society and Politics in Saxony in the Nineteenth and Twentieth Centuries: Reflections on Recent Research', *Archiv für Sozialgeschichte*, 38 (1998), 396–457 and id., 'Saxon Signposts: Cultural Battles, Identity Politics, and German Authoritarianism in Transition', *German History*, 17/4 (1999), 455–69. Particularly relevant for Stresemann are the publications of Karl Heinrich Pohl, including 'Sachsen, Stresemann und die Nationalliberale Partei. Anmerkungen zur politischen Entwicklung, zum Aufstieg des industriellen Bürgertums und zur frühen Tätigkeit Stresemanns im Königreich Sachsen vor 1914', *Jahrbuch für Liberalismusforschung*, 4 (1992), 197–216; id., 'Die Nationalliberalen in Sachsen vor 1914. Eine Partei der konservativen Honoratioren auf dem

were some 3,400 factories in Saxony, most of which had been founded after the unification of the Reich in 1871. They were mainly small-scale and dependent on exports, with textiles and metal works particularly important among them. Three-quarters of the population of 4.5 million lived from trade and industry, making Saxony the most densely populated German state apart from the Hanseatic city states. Yet the interests of the industrial sector were virtually unrepresented in the provincial parliament (Landtag), ignored by the Saxon government, and also discounted by the Reich authorities. This created the perfect opportunity for Stresemann to exploit.

The constitutional system of the Kingdom of Saxony in 1900 was almost a caricature of the divisions of German society. The Landtag had two chambers: the upper chamber overwhelmingly represented the landed nobility and large estates, with only one or two representatives of trade and industry appointed by the king. The second chamber had been elected on a fairly liberal suffrage from 1868, but the success of the SPD, as industry expanded, led the Conservative Party to introduce a restricted franchise on the Prussian model in 1896, with votes allocated according to classes of taxable income and also its source, which gave agricultural areas disproportionate representation. The great majority of the National Liberals in the Landtag supported the reform from fear of the SPD. The polarization of Saxon politics between left and right (made more complete by the absence of a significant Catholic population and hence, unlike Prussia, the absence of the Centre Party in the middle of the spectrum) meant that the National Liberal Party was in danger of being squeezed and reduced to a mere echo of the Conservatives. The injustice of the new franchise, which the Saxon government admitted made the votes of 80 per cent of the electorate 'illusory' was clearly a recipe for civil strife.[20]

Wege zur Partei der Industrie', in Lothar Gall and Dieter Langewiesche (eds.), 'Liberalismus und Region. Zur Geschichte des deutschen Liberalismus im 19. Jahrhundert', *Historische Zeitschrift*, Supplement, 19 (1995), 195–215; id., 'Politischer Liberalismus und Wirtschaftsbürgertum: Zum Aufschwung der sächsischen Liberalen vor 1914', in Simone Lässig and Karl Heinrich Pohl (eds.), *Sachsen im Kaiserreich. Politik, Wirtschaft und Gesellschaft im Umbruch* (Cologne: Böhlau, 1997), 101–31; id., 'Sachsen, Stresemann und der Verein Sächsischer Industrieller: "Moderne" Industriepolitik zu Beginn des 20. Jahrhunderts?', *Blätter für deutsche Landesgeschichte*, 134 (1998), 407–40.

[20] Centralbüro der Nationalliberalen Partei Deutschlands (ed.), *Politisches Handbuch der Nationalliberalen Partei* (Berlin: Buchhandlung der Nationalliberalen Partei, 1907), 907; Richard J. Bazillion, 'Liberalism, Modernization, and the Social Question in the Kingdom of Saxony, 1830–90', in Konrad H. Jarausch and Larry E. Jones (eds.), *In Search of a Liberal Germany* (New York: Berg, 1990), 87–110.

In 1905 the SPD retained only one seat in the Landtag although in 1903 they had won twenty-two of the twenty-three Saxon seats in the Reichstag.

The grip of the Conservative landowning interest was not confined to the constitutional system. In 1902 a new tariff system was adopted by the Reich which raised agricultural tariffs and was therefore unpopular with most Saxon businessmen, since dearer food would raise their costs by putting pressure on wages and might also provoke retaliatory tariffs against German exports. Despite the opposition, the Saxon representatives to the upper chamber of the Reich legislature, the Bundesrat, were ordered by the king to vote for the tariff. Resentment against the tariff and the new trade treaties with Russia and the United States, which followed in 1904–7, was a powerful incentive to local industry to join the Association of Saxon Industrialists. The different branches of manufacturing were in fact internally divided over their attitude to tariffs, depending on the terms of trade for each sector at the time, but they were generally united in feeling that their interests had been inadequately represented, both locally and nationally, compared to the dominant lobbies of agriculture and heavy industry.[21]

Stresemann was quick to mobilize this sentiment in what he later called the 'Sturm und Drang' period of the Association of Saxon Industrialists.[22] Since the association lacked the contacts in government enjoyed by its rivals, it had to rely on public pressure.[23] Stresemann made the grievances of manufacturing industry into a political issue. He held meetings, made contacts with the press, and founded his own journal, *Sächsische Industrie*, in 1904. Most importantly, he intervened in elections, supporting candidates in return for their commitment to the manufacturers, helping with their election expenses—the association provided some 60,000 marks for the Landtag elections in 1909—and wherever possible securing the adoption of candidates who were themselves members of the association.[24]

The success of these tactics (all but the last of which had been pioneered by the Agrarian League in the 1890s) was startling. A proposed tax exemption for working capital invested in agricultural enterprises, passed by the Landtag in 1902, provided an issue around which to rally opinion

[21] Stresemann, *Wirtschaftspolitische Zeitfragen* (2nd edn), 165–6.
[22] Stresemann, 'Zehn Jahre Verband', 43.
[23] Warren, *The Red Kingdom of Saxony*, 53–6; Ullmann, *Bund der Industriellen*, 143–61.
[24] The election expenditure was mentioned by Stresemann in a letter to Bassermann, 16 Sept. 1909 (Nl. 137); Warren, *The Red Kingdom of Saxony*, 56.

and was eventually withdrawn in 1906.[25] In 1904, Stresemann won his first victory when the Landtag defeated a proposal for a new tax on manufacturing, since twelve Conservatives defected as a result of Stresemann's lobbying.[26] In the Landtag elections in 1905 four members of the association were elected, and in 1907 their number rose to twenty-five, of whom twenty-one were National Liberals, from a total Landtag membership of eighty-two. The Conservative *Kreuzzeitung* complained that the Landtag had become 'just a local branch of the Association of Saxon Industrialists'.[27]

Stresemann also campaigned for proper representation for trade and industry in the upper chamber and for a reform of the franchise for the lower chamber.[28] In doing so he took the risk that the SPD would also benefit, but this was consistent with his general view that attempts at exclusion, such as the 1896 Landtag franchise, were bound to fail. In the long run he believed that in politics, as in business, a more intelligent approach was to seek accommodation, drawing the SPD by stages into working within the political system and away from revolution.[29] Stresemann was unsuccessful in his attempts to reform the upper chamber as— perhaps usefully for him—it showed its contempt for small business by rejecting reform, while Stresemann's bloc in the lower chamber successfully voted down the cosmetic concessions they were offered.[30] The franchise he advocated was a modest improvement on the existing one, eliminating the distinction between agricultural and industrial income, but retaining an advantage for those on higher incomes—such as his own members—through a system of 'plural' votes.[31] The franchise bill was lost in 1905 when popular demonstrations divided the National Liberals and frightened the majority back into alliance with the Conservatives—to Stresemann's chagrin.[32] It passed eventually in 1909, and as a result, although five of the association's members lost their seats, its influence increased because Conservative losses were balanced by SPD gains, making the National Liberals the pivotal party able to influence the key committees. In Stresemann's words, Saxon industry had set 'its hand on the latchkey to legislation'.[33]

---

[25] Warren, *The Red Kingdom of Saxony*, 36, 75–6.   [26] Ibid. 55.

[27] Ullmann, *Bund der Industriellen*, 145.   [28] Warren, *The Red Kingdom of Saxony*, 59–61.

[29] Pohl, 'Die Nationalliberalen in Sachsen vor 1914', 210–12.

[30] Warren, *The Red Kingdom of Saxony*, 75.   [31] Ibid. 65.   [32] Ibid. 67–70.

[33] Ibid. 79. On the electoral reform of 1909, see Gerhard A. Ritter, 'Das Wahlrecht und die Wählerschaft der Sozialdemokratie im Königreich Sachsen 1867–1914' in id. (ed.), *Der Aufstieg der deutschen Arbeiterbewegung* (Munich: Oldenbourg, 1990), 84–8.

When one considers that Stresemann was only 23 when he started in Dresden, his achievement is the more remarkable. Clearly he could not have done it unaided. Saxon industrialists were suffering from both an economic depression and blatant discrimination. There was a readiness to adopt the radical measures suggested by the dynamic young man, recently arrived from Berlin. But the degree to which he was encouraged by leading businessmen and a minority of National Liberals, disaffected by the passivity of the main party, is still a subject for research.[34] In a speech to celebrate the tenth anniversary of the association, Stresemann was careful to remember those who had supported them in the early days—the first chairman, Franz Hoffmann, the owner of a photographic business in Dresden, whom Stresemann described as an optimist who suffered many disappointments, the chairman of the Dresden chamber of commerce, Adolph Collenbusch, and its syndic, Paul Schulze, who was also a member of the Landtag, and the manager of a chemical factory, Dr Kolbe, whom Stresemann described as the finest speaker of all the industrialists he knew, and whose support for the association led to Conservative pressure on him to prevent his becoming its deputy chairman.[35] Stresemann needed this support for there was also opposition to the new course, leading him on one occasion to draft a letter threatening resignation.[36]

But if Stresemann needed support, there can be little doubt that he was the author of the new course. He brought to the task a simple view that those who were suffering from the increasing organization of some sections of the economy—agriculture, heavy industry, and trade unions—should defend themselves by the same methods. Saxon—and other—industrialists should have the self-confidence to compete in the modern world of economic and political organization and not accept the passive role of victims.[37] To this he added the idealism of challenging a ludicrously unrepresentative power structure in the interest of firms whose exports were vital to Germany's future. The task suited both his talents and convictions. He was making a career and a name for himself

[34] Pohl, 'Politischer Liberalismus', 119. Starke, 'Dresden', 111–12.

[35] Stresemann, 'Zehn Jahre Verband', 35, 40–2. On Kolbe, see Warren, *The Red Kingdom of Saxony*, 51, 70.

[36] Warren, *The Red Kingdom of Saxony*, 69.

[37] See e.g. his speech commending what had been achieved in Saxony to the south German branch of the manufacturers' association in Mannheim on 16 May 1908: 'Industriepolitik' in Stresemann, *Wirtschaftspolitische Zeitfragen* (2nd edn.), 162–92.

and remaining true to the Liberal convictions of his youth. He was 'the right man at the right time in the right place'.[38]

Stresemann was not afraid to cause offence. He campaigned against the Agrarian League (rejoicing in the defeat of one of its leaders, Georg Oertel, by the SPD in the Reichstag elections of 1903), organized opposition to the Conservative Party leader in the Landtag, Paul Mehnert, and ridiculed a prominent Conservative industrialist, Friedrich Jencke, a leading member of heavy industry's Central Association of German Industrialists and the only industrialist to be appointed to the upper chamber by the king, writing that Jencke 'feels as though he is a voluntary government commissar'.[39] A Saxon industrialist from the conservative wing of the National Liberal Party, Konrad Niethammer, thought that the dispute between the Central Association and the Association of Saxon Industrialists was largely a result of Stresemann's ambition, writing of Stresemann's undoubted ability, energy, and knowledge but also of his 'ample self-confidence and a striving for reputation and recognition'.[40]

Inevitably, Stresemann clashed with the powerful secretary of the Central Association of German Industrialists, Heinrich Bueck. Their aims had already been opposed when Bueck represented the sugar refiners against the chocolate manufacturers.[41] A more serious clash occurred when the textile workers of Crimmitschau, some 7,000 strong, went on strike for a ten-hour day in 1903. Bueck, seeing in this conflict a decisive battle between trade unions and employers, organized a fund from all over Germany which broke the strike. Afterwards, he naturally expected the mill-owners to join the Central Association. By playing upon the protectionist policies of heavy industry and their close cooperation with the Agrarian League, Stresemann was able to persuade the textile manufacturers to join his association instead, though he had to accept that they would also join Bueck's new anti-strike organization.[42]

[38] Pohl, 'Politischer Liberalismus', 119.

[39] Stresemann to Ernst Clauss, 22 Dec. 1905 (Nl. 115); Warren, *The Red Kingdom of Saxony*, 51–60. On Mehnert's attempts to block Stresemann's candidacy for the Reichstag, see Ullmann, *Bund der Industriellen*, 348.

[40] Niethammer to a colleague in Württemberg, Hermann Voith, 3 Dec. 1908: Michael Rudloff, 'Von den Nationalliberalen zur Deutschen Volkspartei. Der Umbruch im sächsichen Parteiensystem im Spiegel der Korrespondenz des Kriebsteiner Unternehmers Dr. Konrad Niethammer', in Manfred Hettling, Uwe Schirmer, and Susanne Schötz (eds.), *Figuren und Strukturen. Historische Essays für Hartmut Zwahr zum 65. Geburtstag* (Munich: Saur, 2002), 704–5. (I am grateful to Dr Rudloff for sending me an advance copy of this paper.)

[41] Warren, *The Red Kingdom of Saxony*, 30.

[42] Ibid. 43–6.

Before long, however, Stresemann developed an alternative method of protection against strikes. After an attempt to found an independent organization at Reich level for manufacturing industry failed (because it was soon taken over by groups favourable to the Central Association), Stresemann founded his own organization which was later extended to other parts of the Reich.[43] As befitted manufacturers, who were too weak to resist trade union organization altogether, Stresemann put the emphasis on providing an employers' strike insurance scheme which would enable employers to negotiate on equal terms with trade union officials and thereby avoid strikes. He took the pragmatic view that trade unions were a fact, which could not be wished away, and that they were indeed useful because they would persuade employees to accept an agreement reached by negotiation.[44] His lack of class antagonism towards trade unions is noticeable, perhaps reflecting his own modest background as well as the moderate stance of most German trade unions. In the same way, Stresemann argued that employers' interests were best served by supporting 'justified' demands for social legislation and helping to shape it rather than opposing it in principle.[45]

Stresemann helped to promote similar associations in other parts of the Reich—Württemberg, Baden, Thuringia, Hessen, and Hessen-Nassau—though attempts to break into the Prussian heartland of the Central Association failed.[46] The regional manufacturers' associations were to a large extent autonomous despite the existence of a central organization in Berlin, the Association of Industrialists, to which they were affiliated. Stresemann's success in Saxony together with discontent at the ineffective leadership of the central organization (which was felt to have failed to protect the manufacturers' interests in the new tariff and trade treaties) led to a storm of criticism of the central leadership in 1905 and the gradual adoption thereafter of Stresemann's tactics of public pressure.[47]

[43] Warren, *The Red Kingdom of Saxony* 73–4; Ullmann, *Bund der Industriellen*, 197–9.

[44] Speech to the Association of Saxon Industrialists, 5 Dec. 1904, 'Der Zusammenschluß der deutschen Arbeitgeber', in Stresemann, *Wirtschaftspolitische Zeitfragen* (2nd edn.), 22–46; Miethke, *Stresemann*, 12–17; Karl Heinrich Pohl, 'Der Verein Sächsischer Industrieller und "sein" Industrieschutzverband. "Fortschrittliche" Unternehmerpolitik zu Beginn des 20. Jahrhunderts?', in Ulrich Hess and Michael Schäfer (eds.), *Unternehmer in Sachsen* (Leipzig: Leipziger Universitätsverlag, 1998), 145–56.

[45] Speech to the Association of Saxon Industrialists, 16 Feb. 1910, 'Industrie und Gesetzgebung', in Stresemann, *Wirtschaftspolitische Zeitfragen* (2nd edn), 231–5; Stresemann, 'Zehn Jahre Verband', 50–1.

[46] Ullmann, *Bund der Industriellen*, 53–65.

[47] Ibid. 134–5.

Stresemann himself joined the central organization in 1910 (and moved with his family from Dresden to Berlin, though he also kept a base in Dresden),[48] and after pressure from the regions in 1911 he became its effective, though not sole, director.[49] His views had already prevailed in 1908 when the Association of Industrialists broke with another organization, the Interessengemeinschaft der deutschen Industrie, which was supposed to represent the interests of German industry as a whole, because of the usual differences with heavy industry.[50] This was followed in 1909 by a major new development when the Association of Industrialists joined in the foundation of the Hansa Association which linked it with banking and commerce in a broad front (in which for the first time heavy industry was on the defensive) specifically founded to combat the Agrarian League and the Conservative Party.[51]

The occasion for this new departure was the successful resistance of the Conservative Party to death duties and its simultaneous ditching of its Reichstag partners, the Liberal parties, in favour of an alternative majority with the Catholic Centre Party and a programme of taxes on consumption and trade. This blatant class selfishness and anti-industrial bias provoked a widespread reaction organized in the Hansa Association to make business politically effective and to break the monopoly of power apparently enjoyed by the agrarian right.[52] Stresemann was delighted, seeing in the Hansa Association a natural extension of his campaign in Saxony to the Reich as a whole. He spoke of creating an organization with the support of 'a class, a million strong, of those employed in business', and of the general acceptance of the ideas which the Association of Saxon Industrialists had promoted, 'often in opposition to the industrial groups to our right'.[53] Addressing the first Reich conference of the Hansa Association in Berlin, he said that industry could no longer afford to have 'blind faith in the power of petitions' and, adapting lines from Goethe's *Faust*, he added that a political anthem might be a nasty anthem but it was a necessary one.[54]

---

[48] Starke, 'Dresden', 105–6.   [49] Ullmann, *Bund der Industriellen*, 73–4.   [50] Ibid. 209–11.

[51] Siegfried Mielke, *Der Hansa-Bund für Gewerbe, Handel und Industrie 1909–1914* (Göttingen: Vandenhoeck & Ruprecht, 1976).

[52] Geoff Eley, *Reshaping the German Right: Radical Nationalism and Political Change after Bismarck* (New Haven: Yale University Press, 1980), 297–302.

[53] Speeches on the occasion of the foundation of the Dresden group of the Hansa Association, 1 Sept. 1909, and to the Association of Saxon Industrialists, 16 Feb. 1910, in Stresemann, *Wirtschaftspolitische Zeitfragen* (2nd edn.), 193–213, 235; Ullmann, *Bund der Industriellen*, 213.

[54] 'Industrie und Hansabund', 12 June 1911: *Veröffentlichungen des Verbandes Sächsischer Industrieller*, 13 (Dresden, 1911), 246–52 (notes for the speech, Nl. 128).

Stresemann hoped that the new organization would attract a mass membership by recruiting individuals unlike the existing organizations, which were limited to firms. In particular he hoped for support from the white-collar or salaried employees (*Privatangestellten*) of business, state, and local government and of public corporations like the churches, who neither had the rights of state officials (*Beamten*) nor were part of the industrial working class. This large group, about 2 million strong, dubbed by Schmoller 'the new middle class', had their own 'clerks' unions' (*Handlungsgehilfen Verbände*). Stresemann hoped to win them over, both to provide industry with a wider base of support and to prevent them being drawn into the Social Democratic trade unions. As evidence of industry's good faith on their behalf, he took a leading role in promoting a special state pensions and sickness insurance scheme for them and committed the Association of Saxon Industrialists to it, despite the costs that would fall on employers as a result.[55]

Stresemann mastered the details of this complicated subject, and his persistent lobbying was instrumental in the adoption of the scheme in 1911 over the objections of opposition which ranged from the federal states in the Bundesrat, the Conservatives, and heavy industry, to the SPD (which objected to privileged treatment for white-collar workers).[56] Stresemann used his twin positions in the manufacturers' association and, from 1907, as a National Liberal member of the Reichstag, to persuade both his association and his party and then the government, in the person of Clemens von Delbrück (state secretary of the interior from 1909), that the scheme was affordable. His standing as a 'business expert' gave him influence with his party and government, and his standing as a politician gave him influence with his business colleagues. His success added to his reputation as an effective lobbyist, someone to be reckoned with by friends and opponents alike.

The idea of a broad anti-Conservative business front to enable particularly the smaller firms to achieve proper consideration by government did not, however, enjoy the same success at Reich level as in Saxony. For this

---

[55] See e.g. his speech to the manufacturers' association, 15 Oct. 1906, 'Die Stellung der Industrie zur Frage der Pensions-Versicherung der Privatangestellten', and to the conference of the National Liberal Party, 6 Oct. 1907, 'Die Pensions-Versicherung der Privatbeamten', in Stresemann, *Wirtschaftspolitische Zeitfragen* (2nd edn.), 47–60, 71–102. Ullmann, *Bund der Industriellen*, 215–21.

[56] On this subject I am indebted to a brilliant paper by Michael Prinz, 'Magier oder Zauberlehrling? Gustav Stresemann als Sozialpolitiker', in Pohl (ed.), *Stresemann*, 114–42.

there were many reasons. The manufacturers' association was internally divided. The decline of export prices after 1908 with growing protection of foreign markets against German exports (particularly in the United States) led the textile firms of Saxony and Thuringia to support protection and cooperation with heavy industry. The light engineering industry of south Germany, however, and other regions argued as before for a reduction of tariffs. Stresemann responded flexibly by trying to find a middle way. He pointed out to the dissatisfied south Germans that the manufacturers' association was not 'as homogeneous, as it may seem in your eyes'. It had its own right wing and left wing, its own so-called heavy industry in Saxony and Thuringia, its own supporters of high tariffs as well as free traders, and it required 'great diplomatic tact' to steer the ship.[57] Despite his efforts, the south German branch decided to leave in October 1913, although the decision did not take effect before it was overtaken by the outbreak of war.[58]

The polarization of German politics after the 1912 Reichstag elections when the SPD won over a third of the votes also worked against Stresemann's idea of an independent business lobby in the middle ground of politics. There was an instinctive tendency among the different industrial groups to concert their forces against the advance of Social Democracy. In addition, Stresemann's independent policy and public methods had made him powerful enemies. The industrial barons of the Ruhr resented his attacks on them and regarded him as an arrogant upstart with dangerous views. Their representatives, men like the Central Association's managing director Ferdinand Schweighoffer, its chairman Max Roetger—who was also chairman of the board of directors of Krupp—and Alfred Hugenberg, who succeed Roetger as Krupp chairman, counter-attacked by checking Stresemann's influence wherever possible. Hugenberg said he would not sit at the same table as Stresemann.[59] This personal antagonism made Stresemann vulnerable, particularly as the right wing of the manufacturers' association favoured closer cooperation with heavy industry. Although Stresemann moved to accommodate the opposition by accepting the basic principle of an industrial tariff and offering to work with the Central

---

[57] Stresemann to the Württemberg branch of the manufacturers' association, 15 Aug. 1913 (Nl. 122); Ullmann, *Bund der Industriellen*, 74.

[58] Ullmann, *Bund der Industriellen*, 75–9.

[59] Dirk Stegmann, 'Hugenberg contra Stresemann: Die Politik der Industrieverbände am Ende des Kaiserreichs', *Vierteljahrshefte für Zeitgeschichte*, 24 (1976), 329–78; Lothar Dohn, *Politik und Interesse. Die Interessenstruktur der Deutschen Volkspartei* (Meisenheim am Glan: Anton Hain, 1970), 103.

Association on matters of common interest, this did not satisfy his opponents.[60]

With the outbreak of war in 1914 the manufacturers' association joined the Central Association in a joint industrial war committee, but it soon proved too weak to defend its interests in the new body. Stresemann's election to the executive of the new committee was successfully blocked, and this was repeated after the war when the committee took a permanent form as the Reich Association of German Industry (Reichsverband der deutschen Industrie) and Stresemann was again excluded from its executive. Stresemann wrote bitterly to an old friend in the manufacturers' association, reviewing his work over the previous sixteen years and the enemies it had made him. He refused to attend the 'comedy' of a planned ceremony in his honour since the association had been too weak to insist on his election to the new body; instead he announced his resignation from the association.[61] The cooperation of the manufacturers in a joint body with the Central Association marked the end of their influence as they were too weak to resist what Stresemann called heavy industry's 'tendency to dominate'. It also marked the end of Stresemann's career as an industrial organizer, which had in any case already been eclipsed in importance by his career as a politician.

National Liberal Politics

When Stresemann started work in Dresden in 1901 he was still a member of Naumann's National Social Union and he represented the Dresden group at a national conference the same year.[62] However, his membership was short-lived. He disagreed with the leadership over tariff policy. Although he was in favour of lower rather than higher tariffs, he did not regard free trade as a matter of principle. Within manufacturing industry there was a range of views on the subject—Stresemann joked about the 946 articles of the German tariff—and as a representative of

---

[60] Ullmann, *Bund der Industriellen*, 226–31.

[61] Stresemann to [Max] Hoffmann, 26 Nov. 1919 (Nl. 114), printed in Harttung (ed.), *Schriften*, 133–7. In 1919 Stresemann's candidacy also suffered from his wartime reputation as an annexationist and from his being seen as an obstacle to a united liberal party. Dohn, *Politik und Interesse*, 99–108. At the end of March 1919 he had already resigned from the Association of Saxon Industrialists: Miethke, *Stresemann*, 3.

[62] Heuss, *Naumann*, 178.

manufacturing industry he could not afford to be dogmatic.[63] When Naumann adopted free trade and, following the failure of the National Social Union to win any seats in the 1903 Reichstag elections, merged it with Theodor Barth's group of Left Liberals, Stresemann was bound to look elsewhere. He may in any case have already come to the conclusion that the Union had no future. He wrote later that it had been 'an army of officers' and that Naumann's importance had been as a prophet not a politician.[64]

In his student journalism Stresemann had made fun of the National Liberals because of the contradictory elements within the party. Yet it was to the National Liberals he now turned. In addition to his disagreement with the Left Liberals over tariffs, that party was only weakly represented in Saxony. The National Liberals, on the other hand, were the natural party of the Saxon business class to which he now belonged. And in the Dresden party, the Deutscher Reichsverein, he found a congenial group who opposed cooperation with the Conservatives and had kept their distance from the provincial party in protest against the introduction of the three-class franchise in 1896.[65] Writing in 1917, Stresemann recalled how they had gradually won support by exploiting the resentment of industrialists at the way the ruling cartel ignored their interests.[66] Their leading spirit, Paul Vogel, was elected to the Landtag in 1901, followed by Stresemann's colleague from the Association of Saxon Industrialists, Paul Schulze, in 1903. This was the springboard for further successes over the following six years when, as we have seen, the National Liberals broke the Conservative hegemony in the Landtag. Stresemann was himself elected to the Dresden town council in November 1906, but his career as a councillor was soon overshadowed by his surprise elevation to the national stage.[67]

In October 1906 Stresemann attended the National Liberal Party conference as a Saxon delegate charged with introducing a resolution,

---

[63] Stresemann, *Wirtschaftspolitische Zeitfragen* (2nd edn.), 165–6.

[64] Rheinbaben (ed.), *Reden und Schriften*, i. 242, 246. On the National Social Union, see Theiner, *Sozialer Liberalismus*, 53–127.

[65] Pohl, 'Die Nationalliberalen in Sachsen vor 1914', 199–204.

[66] Stresemann's introduction to the entry on Saxony in Hermann Kalkoff (ed.), *Nationalliberale Parlamentarier 1867–1917 des Reichstages und der Einzellandtage. Beiträge zur Parteigeschichte herausgegeben aus Anlaß des fünfzigjährigen Bestehens der nationalliberalen Partei Deutschlands* (Berlin: Schriftenvertriebsstelle der nationalliberalen Partei Deutschlands, 1917), 296–9.

[67] On Stresemann's activity as a councillor, a position he held until 1910, see Starke, 'Dresden', 95–9.

criticizing the Reichstag party for supporting an increase in postal charges and the tax on railway tickets. He turned this trivial issue into a general attack on the Reichstag party for not showing more independence towards the government.[68] He urged the party to reassert its liberalism and to show 'a hunger for power'. He warned of the danger that the National Liberals would be ground between the millstones of the Conservatives and the Catholic Centre, who would be driven together against the rising tide of the SPD. To prevent this, the National Liberals would have to reach out to new sources of support beyond the narrow circle of professors and businessmen of some party branches and become 'people's parties' (*Volksvereine*). And to do this they needed the Reichstag party to be willing to give a lead in criticizing the government where it deserved it—abuses in the civil service, in the military, and in the colonies—and to emphasize 'the resolutely liberal element' of the party as well as the national. Stresemann's speech was greeted with 'stormy, continuous applause' as well as some dissent, and the party leader, Bassermann, was stung into an immediate reply.

Stresemann had made an impact. Later the same day he was invited by another Saxon delegate to become the candidate for the Reichstag constituency of Annaberg-Schwarzenberg. This was a poor area in the mountainous Erzgebirge where over 80 per cent of the population was involved in trade and industry, but much of this was still provided by cottage industries such as lace-making.[69] The Social Democrats held the seat in the Reichstag and Stresemann's prospects looked remote. He was lucky. Almost immediately, in December 1906, chancellor Bülow called a snap election after allegations of corruption in the colonial administration and criticism of the methods used by German troops to suppress a rebellion in South-West Africa. The attacks had come not only from the SPD but also the Centre Party on whom Bülow's majority depended. With government support, the elections produced a new majority of Conservatives and Liberals of all shades, the 'Bülow bloc'. Social Democratic representation in the Reichstag fell from eighty-one to forty-three, although its total vote increased. It apparently suffered from the mobilization of a new

[68] *Neunter allgemeiner Vertretertag der nationalliberalen Partei am 6. und 7. Oktober 1906 in Goslar a./H.* (Berlin: Centralbüro der nationalliberalen Partei [1906]), 46–54. The charges were a popular source of discontent: Thompson, *Left Liberals*, 18.

[69] Ritter, 'Das Wahlrecht', 65. On the conditions of cottage industry in another region of Saxony, see Jean H. Quataert, 'The Politics of Rural Industrialization: Class, Gender, and Collective Protest in the Saxon Oberlausitz of the Late Nineteenth Century', *Central European History*, 20/2 (1987), 91–124.

anti-Socialist and anti-Catholic vote on the colonial issue, aided by populist organizations such as the Navy League (Deutscher Flottenverein).
The desertion of the Left Liberals to the new majority also damaged the
SPD in the run-off elections (which occurred if no party gained an
absolute majority in the first round).[70]

Stresemann—whatever his doubts about abuses in the colonial administration—believed in the need for colonies. He threw himself into the
campaign, travelling through the constituency and making fifty-two
speeches in six weeks.[71] He defeated his Social Democratic opponent in
the run-off by 2,000 votes with the help of the Left Liberals.[72] Stresemann's was one of six National Liberal gains in Saxony, but, given the
poverty of his constituency, it was an eye-catching victory. Aged 28, he
entered the Reichstag for the first time in 1907 as its youngest member.

Stresemann's politics were clearly not those of the traditional National
Liberal 'notable'. He belonged to a new class of those whom Max Weber
termed professional politicians.[73] The term has many senses. In Stresemann's case it applies most obviously to his understanding of the need for
political organization. It would have been impossible to win in Annaberg
without organizing an active campaign to counter the Social Democrats.
He had already shown his belief in the power of organization in building
up the Association of Saxon Industrialists and intervening through it in
local politics. This activity reached a high point for the 1907 elections. A
'national committee' was organized in Dresden bringing together all
kinds of anti-socialist groups: the Pan-German League (Alldeutscher
Verband), *Burschenschaften*, citizens' and district associations, the Navy
league (Deutscher Flottenverein), the Dresden lawyers' association, the
clerks' union (Deutschnationaler Handlungsgehilfenverband), various
Protestant associations, the Society for the Eastern Marches (Ostmarken-
verein; dedicated to promoting German settlement in the eastern provinces of Prussia to counter Polish influence), the Association for Land
Reform (Verein der Bodenreformer), the Reich Association Against Social

---

[70] Sperber, *The Kaiser's Voters*, 240–54.

[71] Stresemann, *Wirtschaftspolitische Zeitfragen* (2nd edn.), 68.

[72] Ritter, 'Das Wahlrecht', 65.

[73] Another example was Matthias Erzberger on the left wing of the Centre Party. Three years
older than Stresemann, he had already entered the Reichstag in 1903 and established a reputation
for himself as a financial expert and critic of the abuses of the colonial administration. Like
Stresemann he came from a modest background, was able, ambitious, and caused offence. Klaus
Epstein, *Matthias Erzberger and the Dilemma of German Democracy* (Princeton: Princeton University Press, 1959), 38–60.

Democracy (Reichsverband gegen die Sozialdemokratie), and the electoral association of white-collar workers.[74] There was no doubt a great
deal of overlapping membership among these groups, but the list gives a
sense of their common aims. The committee organized meetings, placed
advertisements, and 'corrected' SPD allegations, and on election day some
900 volunteers helped to get people to the polls supported by a fleet of
twenty cars lent by the automobile club of Saxony. Some 400,000 pamphlets were distributed in the old town of Dresden alone.[75] Not surprisingly
turn-out was up—in the run-off elections in Stresemann's constituency to
91.7 per cent.[76] The membership figures of the National Liberal Party
also rose dramatically from 1,530 in 1895, to 6,500 in 1906, and to over
20,000 in 1911. The increase in membership also produced a new social
balance: in Dresden 30 per cent upper-class, 20 per cent upper-middle-
class, 40 per cent lower-middle-class, and 10 per cent working-class.[77]
The National Liberals were on their way to becoming the 'people's party'
of Stresemann's dreams.

The election campaign of the Saxon 'national committee' in 1907 was
part of a wider movement of radical nationalism among the Protestant
electorate. There were two sides to the movement. There was the resentment of parts of the middle class against the political establishment—its
arrogance, privilege, and unwillingness to incorporate interests not its
own—felt for instance by the businessmen who joined the Association of
Saxon Industrialists. There was also the anti-socialism of a class which felt
threatened by the SPD. These two elements combined in an ideology of
radical nationalism which was critical of both the government for the
moderation it showed in foreign and imperial policy and the SPD for its
lack of patriotism.

Stresemann was in some ways a perfect example of this new movement.
He was an active member of a range of nationalist groups and in demand
as a speaker. He was on the executive committee of the Association for
Training Merchant Seamen (Deutscher Schulschiffverein), a member of
the provincial executive of the Navy League, and a supporter of its radical
wing under Major-General August Keim against the more moderate
Catholic Bavarian wing.[78] Keim for his part supported Stresemann's
campaign for the 1907 elections. Stresemann was also a member of the

[74] Pohl, 'Sachsen, Stresemann und die Nationalliberale Partei', 203–4.   [75] Ibid.
[76] Ritter, 'Das Wahlrecht', 65.   [77] Pohl, 'Politischer Liberalismus', 111.
[78] Pohl, 'Sachsen, Stresemann und die Nationalliberale Partei', 203; Eley, *Reshaping the German Right*, 257–8, 274, 279.

Pan-German League, though he distinguished between its 'sensible parts' and the rest.

In speeches to these and other audiences he developed the economic case for colonies and the navy.[79] Germany's population was rising rapidly by nearly a million a year, and the new jobs to support this increase could come only from expansion of trade and industry and, in particular, from the exporting industries which were the most dynamic sector. Without large colonial markets, Germany had to depend on the quality of its exports to win customers. But as competition became fiercer, so did the resentment against Germany. Demands for protection against German goods were increasing, for instance Joseph Chamberlain's campaign for tariff reform in Britain, and trade rivalries were leading to international tension. In these circumstances, Germany needed naval power for self-protection: in a war Britain could simply impose a blockade of German ports and cut off supplies of raw materials. Dependence on imports was indeed Germany's 'Achilles heel'.[80] Its industry needed cotton, copper, and rubber from abroad, and even in peacetime this put it at a disadvantage in trade negotiations with, for instance, the United States. Germany's only asset was the size of its home market, to which others wanted access. But to safeguard its future it needed to expand its colonial territories on the model of the British empire. The necessary naval expenditure should not be grudged because the money spent—contrary to criticism from the SPD—in fact flowed back through employment to German industry and workers. Stresemann hoped that it might be possible to conduct colonial policy in cooperation with Britain since neither had an interest in war and 'an entente of that kind in mutual world economic policy would lead to a détente in the relations between nations'.[81] But he did not shrink from war, describing the idea of eternal peace as an illusion.[82]

Stresemann was also aware of the potential of the colonial issue to bring about a revival in the fortunes of the National Liberal Party—particularly

[79] He included a section on the importance of the navy and colonies in almost every speech but the theme was particularly central in his speech to the Cologne congress of the Navy League in May 1907, published as 'Flotte, Weltwirtschaft und Volk' in Stresemann, *Wirtschaftspolitische Zeitfragen* (2nd edn), 61–70; also his speech to a local branch of the Protestant Nationaler Arbeiterverein in Apr. 1908, published as 'Die Arbeiterschaft und die nationalen Fragen der Gegenwart', ibid. 114–42.

[80] Stresemann, 'Zehn Jahre Verband', 57.

[81] Speech to the Reichstag, 15 Mar. 1910; printed in Gerhard Zwoch (ed.), *Gustav Stresemann. Reichstagsreden* (Bonn: az studio, 1972), 20–42, quotation p. 26.

[82] Stresemann, *Wirtschaftspolitische Zeitfragen* (2nd edn.), 66.

after the 1907 elections, in which he estimated that a third of his own vote had come from the working class.[83] In September 1908 he wrote to Bassermann:

In questions of colonies, the navy, and a keen foreign policy we must take the lead without fail so that we win over the wide circles who are organized in the Navy League and the colonial societies and the sensible parts of the Pan-German League...The preservation of the world economic position of the German Reich is an enduring principle, independent of chance currents of opinion, and one which will secure us enthusiastic support, while in the area of economic issues, as a middle party, we will still have to reckon with the greatest difficulties in the future.[84]

Nationalism provided the best unifying issue for the party, a stick with which to beat the SPD, and from June 1909, when Bülow was replaced as chancellor by Bethmann Hollweg, an issue on which the National Liberals could also assert their independence of a government which they saw as too timid in the defence of German interests. However, nationalism was not the whole of Stresemann's politics. He was also concerned to assert what he had called at the party conference in 1906 'the resolutely liberal element' of the party tradition. This distinguished his politics from those in the Conservative Party and the right wing of the National Liberals, who favoured authoritarian solutions to the problem posed by the SPD. It also distinguished his politics—and those of the more liberal elements within the radical nationalist camp in general—from the extreme racist elements.

One significant factor in this difference was a personal one. In October 1903 Stresemann married Käte Kleefeld, the 18-year-old sister of a friend from his Leipzig *Burschenschaft*. Her father was a Berlin manufacturer of Jewish descent who had become a Protestant. The Kleefelds were well-to-do and the wedding was celebrated in the Kaiser Wilhelm Gedächtniskirche in a fashionable quarter of Berlin. In the perspective of the time, Stresemann had married above himself 'but Jewish'.[85] There was nothing surprising in this. As a student Stresemann had opposed anti-Semitism and the attempts to exclude Jews on racial grounds from the *Burschenschaft*. The marriage was by all accounts a very happy and successful one. Stresemann admired his father-in-law, both as a businessman

[83] Reichstag speech, 12 Apr. 1907; Zwoch (ed.), *Reichstagsreden*, 4.

[84] Unusually, there is no copy of this letter among Stresemann's papers. It was quoted from Bassermann's papers (which no longer survive) by Theodor Eschenburg, *Das Kaiserreich am Scheideweg. Bassermann, Bülow und der Block* (Berlin: Verlag für Kulturpolitik, 1929), 117.

[85] Interview with Theodor Eschenburg, 4 Sept. 1998.

and for his interest in literature, art, and music.[86] Käte had two children, both sons. The elder, Wolfgang, had a pronounced musical talent, to the pleasure of his father.[87] At the same time the marriage deepened the division between Stresemann and racist groups. The chairman of the Pan-German League, Heinrich Claß, referred to Stresemann and Bassermann (whose wife was also of Jewish descent) as 'Jewish affiliated' in a well-known anti-Semitic text.[88]

The personal source of division was reinforced by political differences. The 'Bülow bloc' of Left Liberals, National Liberals, and Conservatives with which Stresemann had been elected in 1907 soon fell apart, as it became clear that the Conservatives were unwilling to make the least concession to their Liberal partners.[89] A Left Liberal proposal for the introduction of universal male suffrage for elections to the Prussian Landtag prompted an offer of marginal changes from the government but, out of deference to the Conservatives, these did not go far enough to satisfy even the National Liberals who supported only a modest reform to a plural suffrage—on the model Stresemann had helped to introduce in Saxony.

This was ominous for the continued cooperation of the bloc parties when the issue of taxation reform had to be faced in 1908 because of the rapid growth of expenditure, particularly on defence. The National Liberals were ready to support an increase in indirect taxation, which was the major source of revenue raised by the Reich (direct taxation being regarded as the preserve of the individual states since 1871), only if it was combined with a tax on property. The property tax was a sticking point for the Liberals who argued that indirect taxes penalized trade and industry by taxing consumption and it was essential that property, including agricultural estates, should also contribute. In the words of Bassermann, the National Liberals were not prepared to be made a 'fig leaf' to hide the agrarian interests of the Conservative Party.[90]

---

[86] Hirsch, *Stresemann*, 37.

[87] 'Wolfgang performs his sonata. A great concept full of talent.' Diary entry, 17 Apr. 1921 (Nl. 361). For Wolfgang's career, see his memoirs: Wolfgang Stresemann, *Zeiten und Klänge. Ein Leben Zwischen Musik und Politik* (Berlin: Ullstein, 1997).

[88] Daniel Fryman [Heinrich Claß], *Wenn ich der Kaiser wär—Politische Wahrheiten und Notwendigkeiten*, 2nd edn. (Leipzig: Theodor Weicher, 1912), 205. The book continued to be reprinted in the Weimar Republic, its 7th edn. appearing in 1925.

[89] Eschenburg, *Das Kaiserreich am Scheideweg*, 131–236; Heckart, *From Bassermann to Bebel*, 44–87; Thompson, *Left Liberals*, 158–82.

[90] *Elfter allgemeiner Vertretertag der Nationalliberalen Partei am 3. und 4. Juli 1909 in Berlin* (Berlin: Buchhandlung der Nationalliberalen Partei [1909]), 14. Peter-Christian Witt, *Die*

Bülow offered a compromise, with 80 per cent of revenue to come from indirect taxes and the remainder from an extension of inheritance taxes. This was, however, unacceptable to the Conservatives. Their opposition was strengthened by the existence of an alternative Reichstag partner to the Liberals in the Centre Party which, anxious to break the Conservative–Liberal alliance, was willing to join the Conservatives in opposing death duties. Bülow's position was further weakened by losing the support of the Kaiser by offering him only muted defence in the Reichstag against a storm of criticism, which had been aroused by a *Daily Telegraph* report of alarmingly indiscreet remarks made by the Kaiser while on a visit to England. Having lost both his Reichstag majority with the defeat of his tax proposals in June 1909 and the support of the Kaiser, Bülow resigned. It was the end of the hopes for a new Conservative–Liberal patriotic era.

Stresemann's bitterness at what he saw as the selfish defection of the Conservative Party was long-lasting. In 1928, in an introduction to Eschenburg's study of the Bülow bloc, he wrote that the Conservatives 'were never more guilty' than at that time.[91] By failing to support Bülow they had weakened his position in relation to the Kaiser and thus helped to cut short what Stresemann called 'the first fumbling attempt to create a Reichstag tradition which would have led to a kind of parliamentary system'. They had also failed to restrain the headstrong and impulsive nature of the Kaiser, which was to have dire consequences in Germany's isolation during the war. In addition, by their 'orgies of egoism' on the tax issue they had destroyed a process which had brought the Left Liberals into cooperation with the government for the first time since unification.

Looking back after the war, Stresemann overestimated the significance of the breakdown of the bloc. German isolation was as much the result of Bülow's colonial and naval policy, which had Stresemann's full support, as of the Kaiser's erratic behaviour. Stresemann had an exaggerated respect for Bülow who never intended to bring about a shift from monarchical to parliamentary government, although once he had lost the support of the Kaiser he had no alternative but to rely on the Reichstag and on occasion, at least, gave the impression of favouring constitutional change.[92] The

---

Finanzpolitik des Deutschen Reiches von 1903 bis 1913 (Lübeck and Hamburg: Matthiesen, 1970), 289–311.

[91] Eschenburg, *Das Kaiserreich am Scheideweg*, pp. vii–xii, quotations pp. viii–ix.

[92] See the contrasting interpretations of Katharine A. Lerman, *The Chancellor as Courtier: Bernhard von Bülow and the Governance of Germany 1900–1909* (Cambridge: Cambridge University Press, 1990), and Terence F. Cole, 'The *Daily Telegraph* Affair and its Aftermath: The Kaiser,

failure of the Reichstag to exploit the *Daily Telegraph* affair was also not simply the fault of the Conservatives but, as Stresemann knew, of Bassermann's unwillingness to force a conflict with the Crown.[93]

At the time Stresemann could not foresee the disasters which lay ahead, but his anger with the Conservatives was deeply felt. He saw that their repudiation of inheritance taxes would make it harder to keep alive the patriotic enthusiasm which had brought victory against the SPD in the 1907 elections. And, as he told the National Liberal Party conference immediately after the collapse of the bloc in July 1909, 'We are nothing if we do not have the wide basis of that great crowd of the workers, middle class and farmers, in which just at the present time national and liberal feelings are beginning to stir again.'[94]

The obvious tactic for the National Liberals was to exploit the unpopularity of the Conservatives over both inheritance taxes and their opportunistic alliance with the Centre Party. The formation of the Hansa Association in 1909 with close links to the National Liberals encouraged the hope that a broad front of trade and industry would rally to the Liberal cause and drive pro-Conservative groups in heavy industry on to the defensive. This was particularly welcome to Stresemann, who had been engaged in a running battle with heavy industry on behalf of the Saxon manufacturers and had enraged the Ruhr coal-owners by attacking their price cartel in the Reichstag and suggesting government intervention to regulate it.[95] Stresemann's brother-in-law, Kurt Kleefeld, was one of two deputy managers of the Hansa Association, and in 1912 Stresemann himself became a member of its central organization.[96] Stresemann's campaign for a separate social insurance scheme for white-collar workers would also, he hoped, secure the support of this rapidly growing class for the new organization. He also supported a new farmers' organization

Bülow and the Reichstag, 1908–1909', in John C. G. Röhl and Nicolaus Sombart (eds.), *Kaiser Wilhelm II: New Interpretations* (Cambridge: Cambridge University Press, 1982), 249–68. For the argument that Bülow was forced to take account of the wishes of the parties and that therefore the bloc marked a significant stage in the growth of parliamentary power, see Manfred Rauh, *Föderalismus und Parlamentarismus in Wilhelminischen Reich* (Düsseldorf: Droste, 1973), 298–352.

[93] Eschenburg, *Das Kaiserreich am Scheideweg*, p. xi. On the issue of constitutional reform, see Heckart, *From Bassermann to Bebel*, 73–7.

[94] *Elfter allgemeiner Vertretertag*, 45. On the revival of the Liberal vote after 1900 and the degree of working-class support for the Liberal parties, see Sperber, *The Kaiser's Voters*, 146–53.

[95] Speeches to the Reichstag, 26 Nov. 1907 and 3 Mar. 1908; *Verhandlungen des Reichstags*, vol. 229, pp. 1806–9, vol. 231, pp. 3574–81.

[96] Mielke, *Der Hansa-Bund*, 72–3.

(the Deutscher Bauernbund) to carry the campaign into the countryside and win over the small farmers from the pro-Conservative Agrarian League.[97]

The shift by the National Liberal leadership to an anti-Conservative policy naturally aroused the hostility of the party's right wing in Prussia. Three members of the Reichstag party who voted with the Conservatives against death duties were expelled, leading to the defection of a group in Hessen. Ruhr heavy industry, which was strongly represented in the Prussian party, showed its discontent with the new course by stopping its contributions to the national party in April 1910, launching a press campaign for Bassermann's resignation and withdrawing from the Hansa Association in 1911.[98] Bassermann easily beat off this challenge in 1910, winning an ovation at the party conference which frightened his opponents into silence. He rejected criticism of him as a south German 'democrat' who ostensibly wanted to see a Liberal–Social Democratic bloc, such as existed in Baden against the Centre Party, extended to the Reich as a whole. The slogan 'From Bassermann to Bebel', he said, was a fantasy of Naumann's which neither he (Bassermann) nor Bebel believed in. He reaffirmed his desire for a new Liberal–Conservative bloc, but insisted on the independence of the National Liberals from both right and left: 'we are and we must remain a middle party, whose concern it must be to find a compromise between right and left'.[99]

Stresemann, who had won Bassermann's good opinion since 1907, identified himself completely with the party leader.[100] He warned that the SPD, which had been doing well in by-elections, might become strong enough to deprive the government of a majority in the next Reichstag. Unlike the Baden party and the Young Liberals who were prepared for limited cooperation with the SPD, he said that, coming from Saxony (where the SPD was their main opponent), they would not understand any attempt to compromise with the ideology of Social Democracy even

[97] George S. Vascik, 'The German Peasant League and the Limits of Rural Liberalism in Wilhelmian Germany', *Central European History*, 24/2 (1991), 147–75.

[98] Dirk Stegmann, *Die Erben Bismarcks. Parteien und Verbände in der Spätphase des Wilhelminischen Deutschlands. Sammlungspolitik 1897–1918* (Cologne: Kiepenheuer & Witsch, 1970), 222–4. Thieme, *Nationaler Liberalismus in der Krise*, 44–50.

[99] *Zwölfter allgemeiner Vertretertag der Nationalliberalen Partei am 1. und. 2. Oktober 1910 in Cassel* (Berlin: Buchhandlung der Nationalliberalen Partei [1910]), 5–27, quotations pp. 20, 27; Eschenburg, *Das Kaiserreich am Scheideweg*, 272.

[100] On Ernst Bassermann and his background, see Lothar Gall, *Bürgertum in Deutschland* (Berlin: Siedler, 1989), 401–65.

with its revisionist wing.[101] However, he was also critical of the Conserva-tives, accusing them of abandoning 'active Conservatism' to become simply the agents of the Agrarian League. He blamed them for the resur-gence of the SPD and warned that ideas of restricting the Reichstag franchise would simply play into the hands of the radical wing of the SPD. It was essential, as Bassermann had said, for the National Liberals to retain their independence to be able to carry out their main task 'to resist political radicalism in Germany'.[102]

The hopes that the National Liberals would be able to maintain their support by distancing themselves from the Conservatives came to noth-ing. The swing to the left benefited the SPD alone, which in the 1912 Reichstag elections won 34.8 per cent of the vote and became the largest party, with 110 seats. Stresemann was defeated together with five other National Liberals in Saxony. He lost on the first round to his SPD opponent, who won an absolute majority.[103] Unlike in 1907, he had an electoral pact with the Left Liberals, whose different groups combined in 1910 to form the Progressive People's Party (Fortschrittliche Volkspartei), but not the Conservatives—although his Conservative opponent did not win enough votes to affect the result.

The success of the Social Democrats in the 1912 elections made it inevitable that the National Liberal right wing would renew its opposition to Bassermann. Stresemann had watched the activities of this group carefully since his election to the Reichstag, particularly since it had a personal edge in his conflict with the representatives of the Ruhr. In 1908 he warned Bassermann against the hostile manoeuvres (Kesseltreiben) of Bueck, the secretary of the Central Association of German Industrialists, in both organizing a separate electoral fund and having the intention of forming an 'employers' party' to steer industry into the Conservative camp.[104] Stresemann urged the formation of a National Liberal industrial association to forestall the proposed 'employers' party'. Nothing came of

[101] *Zwölfter allgemeiner Vertretertag*, 69–79. The following year he took the same stand, saying that the division with the SPD could only be healed when it accepted the values of the nation state: *Dreizehnter allgemeiner Vertretertag der Nationalliberalen Partei am 19. November 1911 in Berlin* (Berlin: Buchhandlung der Nationalliberalen Partei [1911]), 61. On the Baden party and the Young Liberals, see Heckart, *From Bassermann to Bebel*, 91–121, 133.

[102] Gustav Stresemann, 'Die letzte Reichstagssession', *Nationalliberale Blätter*, 23/3 (15 Jan. 1911).

[103] Ritter, 'Das Wahlrecht', 65.

[104] Stresemann to Bassermann, 11 Apr. 1908 (Nl. 137) and 5 Sept. 1908: Eschenburg, *Das Kaiserreich am Scheideweg*, 114–17.

the idea before it was overtaken by the formation of the Hansa Association in 1909. The swing to the Social Democrats in 1912, however, galvanized the right into a new bid to change the direction of the party.[105]

The issue on which they struck was the voting by members of the Reichstag party to elect Social Democrats to positions in the Reichstag presidency. This was a complex issue—the result both of the Social Democrats becoming the largest party and of tactical considerations, including maintaining cooperation with the Progressives.[106] A storm of protest was organized by the party central office in Berlin, where members of the organization were themselves opposed to Bassermann's leadership. Stresemann imprudently defended his chief in a speech in which he pointed out that Eugen Schiffer, whom right-wing newspapers were promoting against Bassermann, had in fact also voted for a Social Democrat for the vice-presidency.[107]

This was the signal for the right wing and the central office to teach Stresemann a lesson. The official party news service defended Schiffer in a statement which appeared to disown Stresemann without consulting him. Stresemann's anger turned to bitterness when Bassermann, instead of standing up for him, asked him to make peace with Schiffer since as party leader he had to work with Schiffer. Stresemann replied sharply that he doubted whether Bassermann's political career would come to a happy conclusion if he saw the right tactics as always giving in.[108] The row had immediate consequences for Stresemann. At a meeting of the national executive in March 1912, the right forced a vote on elections to the standing committee (Geschäftsführender Ausschuß), and Stresemann was voted off it. He received only thirty-nine votes from a body with at least 112 present. The senior official from the central office, Paul Breithaupt, noted with satisfaction that Stresemann's 'meddling and vanity' had made him more enemies than he realized.[109]

---

[105] Richter, '"Auseinanderstrebendes Zusammenhalten"', 57–66. Stegmann, *Die Erben Bismarcks*, 305–16.

[106] Heckart, *From Bassermann to Bebel*, 198–205; Thompson, *Left Liberals*, 206–7.

[107] Klaus-Peter Reiß (ed.), *Von Bassermann zu Stresemann 1912 bis 1917. Die Sitzungen des nationalliberalen Zentralvorstandes 1912–1917* (Düsseldorf: Droste, 1967), 92–3. See also the typescript extracts from the Schiffer diaries (unfortunately undated and not in chronological order), BAK, Rep. 92, 1, Part (*Heft*) 1, fo. 66; part 2, fo. 42.

[108] Bassermann to Stresemann, 1 Mar. 1912; Stresemann to Bassermann, 2 Mar. 1912 (Nl. 136).

[109] Memorandum by Breithaupt, which came into Stresemann's possession (Nl. 136); Reiß, *Von Bassermann zu Stresemann*, 93.

Stresemann was depressed, exhausted by the election campaign and bitter at the double blow of losing his Reichstag seat and being snubbed by the national executive. His hopes for a revival of popular Liberalism and with it his career prospects, which had been developing so rapidly until 1912, both lay in ruins. When August Weber, the party treasurer and someone who shared Stresemann's outlook—he had represented another Saxon constituency and also lost his seat in 1912—defended himself for trying to mediate with the right wing for the sake of unity and because the party needed the money, Stresemann refused to be mollified. He wrote that the party was being bought by the Central Association of Industrialists, who would oust Bassermann and his supporters as soon as they had a candidate for the leadership. He predicted that the next party conference would be the last at which Bassermann would get a majority and if the right wing was not resisted and the 'dictatorship' of the Central Association continued, then the left wing would defect to the Progressives and the remainder would sink to unimportance beside the Conservatives. Stresemann said he would not himself go to the Progressives, but nor would he remain in what would be left of the National Liberals. He accepted Weber's implied criticism that he should not allow himself to be swayed too much by his feelings (*Gemüt*). But he suggested that Weber should consider that politics was not simply a game of chess and that, unlike the nonentities in the right wing who thought in those terms, Bassermann stood for something which had a following of hundreds of thousands in the country at large. It would be better for Bassermann to resign than to allow himself to be humiliated and misused for an illiberal policy only to be discarded later.[110]

Bassermann, to whom Stresemann had also protested about his willingness to appease the opposition and who had himself had to put up with receiving thirty blank ballot papers in his election as chairman of the standing committee, steadily soothed the battered nerves of his protégé. He agreed with Stresemann's analysis of the aims of the right wing and assured Stresemann that he would stand firm on policy.[111] He had already taken Stresemann into his confidence in 1910, discussing other party members with him and describing him as 'part of the future of the

---

[110] Weber to Stresemann, 28 Mar. 1912; Stresemann to Weber, 29 Mar. 1912 (Nl. 120). Stresemann modified his position slightly in a second letter, dated 3 Apr. 1912, saying that he did not rule out cooperation with the right-wing and moderate Conservatives in the future, but he did not think it was the right time to come to an understanding with them then: Nl. 118.

[111] Bassermann to Stresemann, 18 and 28 Mar. 1912 (Nl. 136).

party and indeed a great part'.[112] He now told him that he missed him in the Reichstag and tried to help him find another seat. At the same time, he warned his temperamental colleague to keep cool and not to alienate the centre of the party.[113]

Stresemann responded to the advice of his mentor and supported Bassermann in finding a resolution to the divisions.[114] Bassermann cleverly side-stepped the issue on which the right wing had focused—whether the Young Liberals could organize as a separate group—in order to concentrate on defending his control of policy in the Reichstag party. Stresemann proposed a commission to find a compromise over the Young Liberals, which defused the issue, and Bassermann got overwhelming support at the party conference with a speech reaffirming his policy of independence towards both the Conservatives and the SPD.[115]

Stresemann continued to think that Bassermann tended to be too conciliatory to the right wing, which organized an 'Old National Liberal' Association (Altnationalliberales Reichsverband) after the party conference, paid for by the Central Association to oppose the influence of the Hansa Association in the party.[116] Nevertheless, he remained Bassermann's faithful lieutenant, defending his reputation against the criticism of the right. For instance, he rejected the insinuation by the 'Old National Liberals' that Bassermann had departed from the tradition of the party's first leader, Rudolf von Bennigsen. Characteristically, he took the trouble to read Hermann Oncken's two-volume life of Bennigsen to prepare his case.[117] He was able to show that Bennigsen, like Bassermann, had led the party from the middle, had supported a number of liberal causes, including the principle of ministerial responsibility to parliament, and had described a government based on the Conservatives and the Centre Party as 'a mortal

[112] Bassermann to Stresemann, 14 July 1910 (Nl. 137).

[113] Bassermann to Stresemann, 1 and 8 Mar., 1 June, 26 July 1912 (Nl. 136); 3 Jan., 28 Jan. 1913 (Nl. 135).

[114] Stresemann to the Young Liberal leaders Dr Köhler and Dr Fischer, 26 and 30 Apr. 1912; Stresemann to the newspaper editor Alexander Wyneken, 30 Apr. 1912; (Nl. 118).

[115] Heckart, *From Bassermann to Bebel*, 222; *Vierzehnter allgemeiner Vertretertag der Nationalliberalen Partei in Berlin am 12. Mai 1912* (Berlin: Buchhandlung der Nationalliberalen Partei [1912]), 27–39; Richter, '"Auseinanderstrebendes Zusammenhalten"', 61.

[116] Stresemann to Bassermann, 30 May 1912 (Nl. 136); Richter, '"Auseinanderstrebendes Zusammenhalten"', 62–6.

[117] 'Um Bennigsens Erbe', published in various newspapers including the *National-Zeitung*, 149–150, 28–9 June 1912. A draft and Stresemann's notes on the biography are in Nl. 128; Hermann Oncken, *Rudolf von Bennigsen. Ein deutscher liberaler Politiker*, 2 vols. (Stuttgart and Leipzig: Deutsche Verlags Anstalt, 1910).

danger'. Stresemann reminded what he called the 'coup d'état thirsty, Conservative desperado politicians' of Bennigsen's warning that if ever parliament were removed by the Crown, the effect would be to legitimate revolution. When Bassermann, whose health was not strong, considered resigning on his sixtieth birthday in July 1914, Stresemann persuaded him to continue and composed a warm tribute to his achievements in keeping the party together.[118]

An immediate result of the divisions in the party was that Bassermann, with Stresemann's encouragement, put a new emphasis on German imperialism.[119] Nationalism was the traditional unifier of the party and it also found a ready response in the climate of international crisis which built up from 1912 to 1914. Bassermann and Stresemann, who both regarded Bethmann Hollweg as a weak man, joined in the criticism of his handling of the Morocco crisis of 1911 and interpreted the outcome, in which France established a protectorate over Morocco, as a defeat.[120] Stresemann took up the theme with relish. In his speech to the party conference in 1912, he attacked Bethmann Hollweg for accusing the National Liberals of making electoral capital out of the Morocco crisis and added that they all felt they would 'have to fight again for the continued existence of this German Reich', and that it was their main task to win over SPD voters to this view.[121] He also warned against Bethmann Hollweg's attempts to relax the policy of Germanizing the Polish areas of Prussia, saying they should not be 'lulled by the litany of reconciliation' and should remember the example of Austria-Hungary where German influence had been driven back—Prague had once been a German city.[122] To those who criticized Bassermann for not cooperat-

---

[118] Stresemann to Bassermann, 6 Mar. 1914, Bassermann to Stresemann, 4 June 1914 (Nl. 135); Gustav Stresemann, 'Ernst Bassermann. Zum 60. Geburtstag', *Niedersächsisches Wochenblatt*, 11, 25 July 1914 (Nl. 135).

[119] Richter, '"Auseinanderstrebendes Zusammenhalten"', 61–2.

[120] Heckart, *From Bassermann to Bebel*, 176–85.

[121] Stresemann's comment about a future war was not simply a public pose. He had made a similar remark in a speech at the reception for the marriage of his sister-in-law Eva to a Prussian officer on 24 Oct. 1905: Stresemann family papers, Berlin.

[122] *Vierzehnter allgemeiner Vertretertag*, 86–97. The policy of discrimination against the Polish population of Prussia's eastern provinces started with Bismarck. Measures were imposed to exclude Polish clergy from schools and against the use of the Polish language in schools and other public bodies. In 1886 there followed a scheme to buy estates from Polish landowners, divide them into small farms, and encourage Germans settlers to buy them. The hostility aroused among the Polish population and the disappointing results of the settlement policy led to harsher measures being adopted under Bülow, including a decree in 1908 which allowed expropriation of

ing with the government, Stresemann: replied 'Bethmann is not Bismarck.'[123]

Stresemann's tone became increasingly strident. In 1913 he suggested that in the Reichstag debate on new military expenditure Bassermann should repeat a phrase he (Bassermann) had used to the national executive—that the result of world events was that 'other nations got a part of the world, but we only got a new army bill'. Stresemann referred to a newspaper article saying that, despite the strength of the German army, it had no influence on events because no one believed it would attack. He added that he had found spontaneous approval for this kind of remark in recent speeches—'Here the whole people is behind us, if we represent this point of view energetically.'[124]

Stresemann was certainly energetic. In a series of speeches he rammed home the need for an expansionist imperial policy even at the risk of war—in an age of protection, Germany's place in the world economy depended on pursing 'world policy'.[125] He pointed out that socialist belief in the international proletariat had not prevented wars between Russia and Japan, Britain and the Boers, the United States and Spain, or the Balkan wars. 'Germany in the heart of Europe [is] the most threatened', he declared, and therefore it needed the best military equipment.[126] He saw the main source of conflict as economic and imperial rivalry with Britain. Germany's position had deteriorated as a result of this conflict—the triple entente of Britain, France, and Russia was stronger than the alliance of Germany, Austria-Hungary, and Italy. Germany was threatened 'from the west and the east and the North Sea'. He hoped it would still be possible to reach agreement with Britain but, on one occasion, he said, 'The vital questions of the nations will always be decided by the sword. The division of the world does not follow from paragraphs in conferences.'[127] In a review of Norman Angell's *The Great*

Polish estates in certain circumstances. Martin Broszat, *200 Jahre deutsche Polenpolitik* (Munich: Ehrenwirth, 1963), 96–131.

[123] 'Um Bennigsens Erbe'.

[124] Stresemann to Bassermann, 4 Apr. 1913 (Nl. 135).

[125] e.g. speech to the Bund der Industriellen, 11 Sept. 1913, 'Probleme der deutschen Industrieentwicklung', *Veröffentlichungen des Bundes der Industriellen*, 6 (Nov. 1913), 38–9. Further examples in the notes for his speeches during 1911–13 (Nl. 128).

[126] Notes for a speech in Greiz, 6 Dec. 1912 (Nl. 128).

[127] Notes for speeches in Dresden, 9 Apr. 1913; to the Bund der Industriellen, 15 Apr. 1913, on the taxation to pay for the new army bill (printed in *Veröffentlichungen des Bundes der Industriellen*, 5 (May 1913), 9–23); and in Elberfeld, 20 Apr. 1913 (Nl. 128).

Illusion, he rejected its arguments that there was no relationship between empire and wealth, and that victory in a future war would be unprofitable. Stresemann pointed out that German trade with the British empire was only one-tenth of the size of Britain's trade with the empire. He also predicted that the defeated in a future war would lose their world trade, see their merchant fleet destroyed, and have to pay reparations.[128]

In July 1914 Bethmann Hollweg asked himself why Germany's position had become critical. He listed among the reasons the pressure of 'the "national" parties which with their racket about foreign policy want to preserve and strengthen their party position'.[129] Stresemann's was only one voice among many, but he had certainly contributed his full share to the 'racket'.

The belligerent tone of his speeches did not mean that Stresemann had abandoned liberalism. He saw no conflict between nationalism and liberalism. It was after all the Conservatives who had refused inheritance duties as a way of financing the defence budget. Stresemann looked back to the contribution of the pre-Bismarck liberal movement to national unification and further back to the example of the Prussian reformers of the war of liberation against Napoleon. By comparison, he was critical of the ethos of their own times. Had they made progress, he asked a National Liberal audience, referring to the centenary celebrations for Prussia's victory over Napoleon in 1813, in the ideas of dedication to the state and trusting the people?[130] The names of the Prussian reformers such as Stein were not mentioned; official celebrations were often court occasions, and government policy too often lacked contact with the people. But, he added, popular participation in the legislative process could not be permanently prevented by the three-class franchise and people must not only have a sense that they were being ruled but also that they were themselves contributing to decisions.

One of Stresemann's targets was the Auswärtiges Amt, which he had criticized in the Reichstag for its aristocratic character and its lack of commercial expertise, a speech which also helped to broaden his reputation

---

[128] 'Normann Angells falsche Rechnung', *Nationalliberale Blätter*, 25/18, 4 May 1913.

[129] Entry for 20 July 1914 in the diary of Hollweg's assistant, Kurt Riezler: Karl D. Erdmann, *Kurt Riezler. Tagebücher, Aufsätze, Dokumente* (Göttingen: Vandenhoeck & Ruprecht, 1972), 188.

[130] Notes for a speech in Elberfeld, 20 Apr. 1913 (Nl. 128). See also the interesting discussion of the limits to the political effectiveness of nationalism as a tool of the right in Thompson, *Left Liberals*, 219–30.

from being primarily an expert on social policy.[131] He was also scandalized by the Zabern incident in Alsace in November 1913, where the insults of a Prussian lieutenant provoked disorder which was then suppressed by the military, riding roughshod over the competent civilian authorities, behaviour upheld by a military court and evoking only a lame defence from Bethmann Hollweg in the Reichstag. The National Liberal Party joined the Reichstag majority in protest and Stresemann defended its actions, replying to a critic that the verdict of the military court would breed more Social Democrats than a thousand party meetings, and that the military should remember that 'we live in a state under the rule of law (*Rechtsstaat*)'.[132]

Stresemann also criticized the middle class for its lack of pride and its desire to ape the aristocracy, telling a meeting of the Hansa Association that what was required was a renewal of the 'sense of power and of a free citizenship' of the era of the Hanseatic League.[133] One of the key changes needed was that they must rid themselves of the 'philistine view that government and citizens are opposites' and learn from the English example, where one might attack a Conservative government or a Liberal government but not the government as such.[134]

There were, however, clear limits to Stresemann's liberalism. It did not include respect for the rights of the Polish population in Prussia's eastern provinces, and he remained suspicious of Catholicism and Social Democracy.[135] German nationalism was the basis of the state, and only those who

[131] Speech to the Reichstag, 15 Mar. 1910: Zwoch (ed.), *Reichstagsreden*, 27–34. The government agreed to the formation of an economic advisory committee of businessmen. Gustav Stresemann, 'Ein wirtschaftlicher Beirat für das Auswärtige Amt', *Nationalliberale Blätter*, 22/29, 17 July 1910. Stresemann's nephew and secretary Franz Miethke wrote to him on 25 July 1910, commenting on invitations to speak on German foreign policy which had been prompted by the Reichstag speech: Stresemann papers, Berlin.

[132] Stresemann to Max Rüger, 11 Jan. 1914 (Nl. 138); Thompson, *Left Liberals*, 223–4.

[133] Notes for the speech in Blumenthal, 23 Aug. 1913 (Nl. 128).

[134] Speech to the National Liberal Party conference, 12 May 1912: *Vierzehnter allgemeiner Vertretertag*, 96. Stresemann's admiration for Britain as a model of parliamentary government, national consensus, and empire was common among German liberals. Max Weber, for instance, in his inaugural lecture at Freiburg University in 1895, also contrasted the attitudes of the German and British working class to the state, putting the emphasis on the educative effects of empire. Wolfgang J. Mommsen, *Max Weber and German Politics 1890–1920* (Chicago: University of Chicago Press, 1984), 88.

[135] Erzberger's views make an interesting comparison with Stresemann's. Both favoured the growth of parliamentary power for similar reasons. Erzberger, however, saw both Liberalism and Social Democracy as subversive, because they lacked a basis in religious authority, while Stresemann saw both the Centre Party and the SPD as suspect in terms of national loyalty. Epstein, *Erzberger*, 89–95.

accepted this basis were regarded as full citizens. In this attitude he
followed a tradition of German liberalism which linked citizenship to
the nation state.[136] The criteria of exclusion were not rigid and therefore
not entirely clear. They were not simply racial or religious or ideological.
Patriotic Jews, Catholics, and Social Democrats could qualify for membership, but their membership was not automatic.

Stresemann's Liberalism also faced an obvious problem in the way of
constitutional development. It would be hard in a democratic system to
prevent the SPD, as the largest party, having a say in government. Yet until
the SPD accepted the nation state, Stresemann regarded such an outcome
as dangerous. He was clear that existing constitutional rights should not
be taken back, as some Conservatives wanted—that would open the door
to anarchy and revolution. He also at least implied that he favoured a
gradual extension of democracy—the replacement of the three-class franchise in Prussia by a plural franchise and the strengthening of the powers
of the Reichstag—in the belief that this would encourage a wider public to
feel a sense of responsibility for government and help the moderate wing
of the SPD.[137]

It was, however, quite unclear how this process of evolution was to be
brought about against the opposition of the court, the Conservatives, and
even the right wing of the National Liberals. After the success of the SPD
in the 1912 Reichstag elections, Stresemann himself trimmed to the right.
In his speech to the party conference that year, he defended the measures
for social insurance passed by the previous Reichstag but called for a long
pause to allow industry to absorb the costs before any new measures were
proposed. He also warned against cooperation with the SPD, as advocated
by a delegate from Baden, saying that at the level of the Reich there was as
yet no basis for cooperation. And he attacked SPD unions for violating
the rights of members of the 'national' unions.[138] The *Hamburger
Nachrichten*, which reflected the views of the Central Association of

[136] Peter Pulzer, *Jews and the German State: The Political History of a Minority* (Oxford: Blackwell, 1992), 32–4. Following Nipperdey's categorization of German nationalism after 1890 into
three main types, 'national patriotism', 'normal nationalism', which is subdivided between its
'governmental' and its 'autonomous' forms, and 'radical nationalism', Stresemann may be said to
have belonged to the 'autonomous' type of normal nationalism, since he did not share the anti-
democratic and racist views which increasingly set the tone of radical nationalism. Thomas
Nipperdey, *Deutsche Geschichte 1866–1918*, ii: *Machtstaat vor der Demokratie* (Munich: C. H.
Beck, 1992), 595–609.

[137] See e.g. 'Die letzte Reichstagssession', *Nationalliberale Blätter*, 23/3, 15 Jan. 1911, and 'Um
Bennigsens Erbe', *National- Zeitung*, 149, 28 June 1912.

[138] *Vierzehnter allgemeiner Vertretertag*, 90–3.

German Industrialists, commented sarcastically that since Stresemann had lost his seat he seemed to have changed his politics—his speech would entitle him to become a spokesman for heavy industry.[139]

This was an exaggeration. Stresemann wanted to keep industrial support for the National Liberal Party through the Hansa Association and he needed to reflect a hardening of attitudes among employers, for instance towards strikes, even though this would mean moving the Hansa Association to the right.[140] He also exploited the creation of a new body linking the Central Association and the Agrarian League in a so-called Cartel of the Productive Estates (Kartell der schaffenden Stände), dubbed by Stresemann the 'Cartel of Grabbing Hands', to strengthen the position of the Hansa Association.[141] He claimed that in contrast to this lobby for ever higher tariffs and extreme Conservative views, the manufacturers from the middle class were 'still today culturally and politically in the moderate Liberal camp'.[142] Nevertheless, the increased polarization between right and left made it more difficult to see how the Wilhelmine empire could develop peacefully into a constitutional democracy. There is no evidence that Stresemann thought the political problems of the Wilhelmine empire insoluble, but he did give the impression of fighting a rearguard action both within the party and the Hansa Association to maintain support for Bassermann against the Central Association and the 'Old National Liberals'.[143]

From 1912 to 1914 Stresemann was also desperately searching for a new constituency. After a number of disappointments he was finally successful in December 1914, when he was returned for Aurich, a farming area in the extreme north-west of the Reich, where the sitting National Liberal member had died and Stresemann's election was uncontested because of the wartime truce between the parties.[144]

[139] Hamburger Nachrichten, 13 May 1912 (Nl. 118).

[140] Stresemann to Bassermann, 30 May 1912 (Nl. 136) and 31 Oct. 1913 (Nl. 135). Mielke, Der Hansa-Bund, 126–7.

[141] Speech to the Bund der Industriellen, 'Probleme der deutschen Industrieentwicklung', 11 Sept. 1913: Veröffentlichungen des Bundes der Industriellen, 6 (Nov. 1913), 24–40 (notes in Nl. 128). Fritz Hauenstein, 'Die ersten Zentralverbände', in id. (ed.), Der Weg zum industriellen Spitzenverband (Darmstadt: Hoppenstedts Wirtschafts-Archiv, 1956), 71; Ullmann, Bund der Industriellen, 157, 227–32.

[142] Stresemann to Hermann Vogel, 6 Sept. 1913 (Nl. 122).

[143] Stresemann to Bassermann, 7 Nov. 1912 (Nl. 136).

[144] Stresemann was defeated twice and did not pursue two other possibilities—one because Naumann would not withdraw in his favour, another for financial reasons and because it would have meant relying on SPD support in a rural constituency which, he observed wryly, would have

Stresemann's dilemma before 1914 was that of the moderate middle ground of German politics as a whole. Historians differ as to whether the Wilhelmine empire had reached a dead end, in which the only outcome was revolution, or a stable crisis where the government angled its policies towards the middle, consisting of the Liberal parties supported on some issues by the Centre Party and even the SPD, notably succeeding in passing inheritance taxes to pay for national defence in 1913.[145]

There is a similar ambivalence about the direction of the National Liberal Party before 1914. Did Stresemann's strategy of a people's party that was both national and liberal have the potential to become the instrument of peaceful change—a Protestant 'third way' between the increasingly polarized camps of the nationalist right and the Social Democratic left? Or was radical nationalism at risk of merging with the more extreme forms of racist populist politics which were to prove explosive in the Great Depression a generation later? Either future can be read back into the Wilhelmine period but, before the traumas precipitated by war and defeat, neither outcome was predetermined.[146]

There is a persuasive argument that in his first political career in Saxony, Stresemann showed many of the qualities which later made him a pragmatic Republican (*Vernunftrepublikaner*).[147] He was willing to adjust to political realities and rely on modern forms of political organization. He believed in conciliation and compromise, not legal discrimination or force. He tried to find the middle ground between the Conservatives and the Social Democrats, around the twin ideals of liberalism and nationalism. There was more than pragmatism, however, to Stresemann's politics. He was a Liberal from a Left-Liberal background, and he remained a natural critic of discrimination and intolerance in Wilhelmine society. He was also a nationalist from conviction, a position only strengthened by his view of the international economy as a competition of empires and the

been 'rather complicated for me'. In another constituency, Heidelberg, his selection was opposed by the Central Association. The costs of standing he bore partly himself and the rest was put up by the Association of Saxon Industrialists, the Hansa Association, and the party, but his second defeat left him in some financial embarrassment. Stresemann to Bassermann, 13 May, 17 July 1913, 21 July 1914; Bassermann to Stresemann, 13 July 1914 (Nl. 135); Stresemann to Weber and to Bassermann, 29 Jan. 1913 (Nl. 123); Stresemann to Friedrichs, 24 July 1913 (Nl. 122).

[145] Nipperdey, *Deutsche Geschichte*, ii. 748–57. On the financial constraints on Reich governments in relation to defence spending, see Niall Ferguson, 'Public Finance and National Security: The Domestic Origins of the First World War Revisited', *Past & Present*, 142 (1994), 141–68.

[146] On the complex legacy of the war for the Weimar Republic, see Richard Bessel, *Germany after the First World War* (Oxford: Clarendon Press, 1993).

[147] Pohl, 'Politischer Liberalismus', 127–30.

imperative for the National Liberal Party to find a theme around which it could unite. Each kind of conviction also remained important to him, as we shall see, after 1919.

By 1914 Stresemann could look back on a decade of substantial achievement. It had brought him both material success and recognition. In addition to his work with the Association of Saxon Industrialists and the manufacturers' association, he held a number of directorships. Through the Hansa Association, he came into contact with Albert Ballin, the managing director of the Hamburg–America Line, the world's greatest steamship company. Stresemann had visited the United States and Canada in the autumn of 1912, when his political career was in the doldrums, and together with Ballin he founded the German-American Economic Association in 1914 and became a salaried member of its executive.[148] There are only fragmentary sources on Stresemann's income but he was clearly prospering. His original salary with the chocolate manufacturers had been 1,000 marks per annum; his annual salary from the German-American Economic Association alone was 15,000 marks. For tax purposes in 1917, he declared capital with a net value of 167,214 marks on behalf of Käte and himself.[149] In Berlin, he and his family lived in a fashionable area, close to the Kaiser Wilhelm Gedächtniskirche. A sign of his acceptance into the higher reaches of a particular kind of Wilhelmine society was Ballin's invitation to join him at the Kiel naval regattas. At the same time, this also marked one of the forms of exclusion within that society: when the Kaiser visited Ballin's ship, he asked not to have Bassermann and Stresemann presented to him.[150]

Despite the reverses he had suffered in 1912, Stresemann's career had brought him to the centre of the industrial and political worlds and he had made an impact. He had seized the opportunity offered to make a career in business and politics out of the resentment of those disadvantaged by some of the more obvious inequities of the Wilhelmine system.

---

[148] Hirsch, *Stresemann*, 55–9.

[149] Stresemann's notes and a copy of the tax form for his property as at 31 Dec. 1916 (Nl. 124). The total was made up of three-eighths of the value of his father's house (47,515 marks), government securities—possibly war loans—(33,000 marks), mortgages issued to others on their property (56,700 marks), shares (69,800 marks), and life insurance policies (24,449 marks), less mortgages taken out by them (44,250 marks) and a bank loan (20,000 marks). In addition, Stresemann declared for war tax purposes 5,000 marks spent on a luxury item—objects to do with Goethe.

[150] This happened two years running and was recalled in a letter from Stresemann to Frau von Roon (née Bassermann), 22 Nov. 1928 (Nl. 290).

Representing Saxon manufacturers and trying to make the National Liberal Party into an effective instrument of change satisfied his ambition and idealism alike. His basic conviction that the National Liberals should maintain their independence from the Conservatives was upheld by Bassermann even in the more difficult climate after 1912. The hostility Stresemann had incurred from the Central Association and the Old Liberals was a form of recognition—they saw him as a threat. At the same time, Stresemann learned from Bassermann, as well as from his own difficulties in holding the manufacturers' association together, to contain his impatience and practise the art of compromise. If the National Liberal Party was to fulfil its traditional function of mediating the conflicts between right and left, it had first to be able to manage its own internal conflicts.

Stresemann's views were neither original nor particularly radical. He gave expression to the discontent of industrial society in Saxony and then extended the same approach to the Reich. Some on the left wing of the National Liberals and among the Young Liberals were prepared to go further, for instance in cooperation with the SPD.[151] Stresemann, though sometimes critical of Bassermann, was careful not to isolate himself from the centre of the party. His nationalism and imperialism were the classic cement of party unity and part of the standard fare of Wilhelmine rhetoric.[152]

Where Stresemann was unusual was in his energy and his ability to organize. A sense of his hectic life—and of a certain self-importance—emerges from a brusque reply in 1908 to his sister, who had written complaining about his management of their father's estate and asking to see him: 'I am indeed tomorrow in the Reichstag, but must go back to Dresden the day after tomorrow for the meeting of the town council, on Friday I am in Düsseldorf, on Saturday and Sunday in Herford and on Monday I have a meeting with the coal syndicate in Dresden.'[153]

For all his reputation as a modernizer, Stresemann's political career was also still bounded by the conventions of Wilhelmine politics. He was an able speaker, who had made a reputation for himself in the Reichstag as an expert on social policy and on the economic aspects of foreign policy. He

---

[151] This was also true of the Hansa Association, which was prepared to support SPD candidates in run-off elections in 1912 to defeat the alliance between the Conservatives and the Centre Party. Mielke, *Der Hansa-Bund*, 162–5.

[152] Nipperdey, *Deutsche Geschichte*, ii. 629–50.

[153] Stresemann to Elise Plagge, 2 Jan. 1908 (Nl. 125).

was in demand as a speaker, particularly for the Hansa Association and the National Liberal Party in different parts of the country.[154] He carried his audiences with him by presenting his arguments clearly, putting technical subjects into a larger context, showing respect for his opponents, and by shafts of humour, sentiment, and the occasional memorable phrase, such as 'a hunger for power'. But his speeches were essentially designed to rouse support, not as a serious programme for government. When representing the manufacturing interest against the coal syndicate, he knew what he was talking about. But on the theme of Germany's need for colonies he went no further than outlining Germany's disadvantage compared to the major colonial powers. He made no serious study of where Germany might profitably seek colonies, though he did praise Bülow's colonial secretary, Bernhard Dernburg, for his interest in their commercial exploitation.[155] Stresemann was no mere demagogue. He was capable of mastering a brief—for instance in his successful campaign for social insurance for white-collar workers—and he could hold his own in the different arenas of the Reichstag, party conferences, business meetings, and electioneering. His views, even if sometimes superficial, were also genuine, as his initial indignation at Bassermann's temporizing showed. But for all his desire that Germans should feel responsible for the decisions of government, he was still essentially playing the role allotted to him under the Wilhelmine system—campaigning at one remove from power in the hope of influencing the government but without any prospect of one day being able to enter it.

[154] See the notes for his speeches in 1911–13 in Nl. 128.
[155] Gustav Stresemann, 'Das Ende der Aera Dernburg', *Nationalliberale Blätter*, 22/25, 19 June 1910.

3

'For the greater, freer Germany of the future'

War, 1914–1918

The two central themes of Stresemann's political career before 1914, nationalism and liberalism, were both given new impetus by the war. The combination was expressed in the title he gave to a volume of his speeches in 1917, 'Power and Freedom'.[1]

Like most Germans, Stresemann was convinced that Germany was not responsible for the war. He blamed it on the enmity of Britain for any power which was capable of challenging British mastery of the seas and her unique empire. Britain, he claimed, had forged the coalition of Continental powers which had fallen on Germany 'like the thief in the night',[2] just as a hundred years before it had organized a Continental coalition against Napoleon. It followed for Stresemann that German war aims must include guarantees against the renewal of such a coalition in the future.[3] That meant inevitably a 'greater Germany' which could dominate the Continent, preventing a renewal of the Franco-Russian alliance, and also occupying the Channel ports as a deterrent against British attack. In a

[1] Gustav Stresemann, *Macht und Freiheit* (Halle: Carl Marhold, 1918).
[2] Notes for a speech in Aurich, 4 Oct. 1914 (Nl. 140).
[3] The best account of Stresemann's war aims is still the study based on his papers by Marvin L. Edwards, *Stresemann and the Greater Germany 1914–1918* (New York: Bookman Associates, 1962).

sentence, Calais should become a 'German Gibraltar'. On the issue of war aims, Stresemann became known as one of the leading 'annexationists'. At first his views were shared by politicians in all parties except the SPD. However by the summer of 1917, still with no real prospect of victory after three years of war, the Centre Party and the Progressives combined with the SPD to form a majority in the Reichstag behind a programme of peace without annexations. Stresemann and the National Liberals distanced themselves from this resolution and continued to hold out for a 'victorious peace' which would allow Germany to keep much of the territory it had conquered. His commitment to victory aligned him with the Conservatives and the High Command, leading to the jibe that he was 'Ludendorff's young man'.[4] When on Germany's defeat power passed to the parties of the Reichstag majority, the reputation he had acquired on war aims became a political liability.

His disagreement with the majority parties over war aims did not, however, prevent Stresemann advocating greater power for the Reichstag and reform of the Prussian franchise. The sense of national unity in August 1914 and the vote by the SPD for war credits convinced him of the patriotism of all parties and of all sections of the population. Germany had 'no enemies at home', he declared in October 1914.[5] It followed, particularly as the war became protracted and the sacrifices endured by the whole population rose immeasurably, that political rights should be shared more equally. Stresemann, therefore, led the National Liberal Party into cooperation with the other parties of the Reichstag majority on constitutional reform, despite his opposition to their war aims. He had no time for those on the right who hoped to exploit victory to shore up the old regime. On the contrary, he warned against repeating the error of Frederick William III, who had promised Prussia a representative assembly at the end of the Napoleonic Wars only to retract the promise under pressure from the tsar.[6] Stresemann hoped to see victory used to cement the mood of August 1914 and to overcome Germany's political divisions in a more equal society.

Stresemann's attitudes were a natural development from his support for both imperial expansion and, albeit cautious, constitutional and social change before the war. The combination of expansionist war aims and domestic reform was also not unique to him. Liberal intellectuals,

---

[4] Olden, *Stresemann*, 54.
[5] Notes for a speech in Aurich, 4 Oct. 1914 (Nl. 140).
[6] Speech to the Reichstag, 18 Jan. 1916: Rheinbaben (ed.), *Reden und Schriften*, i. 104.

including Max Weber, Friedrich Naumann, and the historian Friedrich Meinecke, also came to the conclusion during the war that constitutional reform was essential to maintain support—and even desirable to give Germany more effective government—though they differed over the extent to which the Reichstag's powers should be increased.[7] They also shared Stresemann's view that the war could not have been avoided and advocated greater or lesser extensions of German power to guarantee her security in the future.[8] Stresemann's enthusiasm for Ludendorff was also shared at times by others who hoped for strong, popular leadership, including the Jewish industrialist and intellectual Walther Rathenau.[9] On war aims, however, Stresemann's desire to see Germany take Britain's place as the global sea power, and after that proved impossible, his support in 1917–18 for the High Command's programme of a vast empire in the east, aligned him with those who resisted constitutional reform and hoped that victory would make it unnecessary. He also stuck to his belief in victory until the summer of 1918, where cooler heads had come to the conclusion a year earlier that the war could not be won. As a result, by October 1918 Stresemann found that by his reckless commitment to both victory and reform he had become stranded in a political no man's land.

War Aims

Stresemann had been rejected on health grounds from the normal requirement of compulsory military training in 1901, being classified as fit only for the territorial reserve. He was again rejected as unfit for the reserve in 1914 and thereafter exempted.[10] This left him free to devote himself entirely to politics, apart from advising manufacturing industry on how to adapt to wartime conditions. Stresemann's war was therefore a

---

[7] Klaus Schwabe, *Wissenschaft und Kriegsmoral. Die deutschen Hochschullehrer und die politischen Grundfragen des Ersten Weltkrieges* (Göttingen: Musterschmidt, 1969), 125–65; Mommsen, *Max Weber*, 244–66; Heuss, *Naumann*, 379–90; Theiner, *Sozialer Liberalismus*, 260–1.

[8] Schwabe, *Wissenschaft, passim*; Mommsen, *Max Weber*, 190–227; Heuss, *Naumann*, 361–70, 390–439; Theiner, *Sozialer Liberalismus*, 225–6, 236–58.

[9] Hartmut Pogge von Strandmann (ed.), *Walther Rathenau. Industrialist, Banker, Intellectual and Politician. Notes and Diaries 1907–1922* (Oxford: Clarendon Press, 1985), 212–32.

[10] Hirsch, *Stresemann*, 62. Application for a life insurance policy, 21 June 1906 (Nl. 124); application for exemption from call up, 16 Apr. 1915 (Nl. 119). In May 1915 Stresemann again applied to serve and this time was passed fit. He expected to be called up in July, but for whatever reason he was not required: Stresemann to Hauptmann Dirr, 14 May 1915 (Nl. 146).

politician's war: it was as a politician that he tried to make his contribution to victory.

The central task, as he saw it, was to educate public opinion in the causes of the war and what, as a consequence, should be the aims of victory. His overriding fear was that victory, if won, would be squandered: public uncertainty about the right war aims might allow Bethmann Holl- weg to follow his instinct for cautious compromise rather than the bold vision which Stresemann thought the occasion demanded. Stresemann's tireless propaganda for a 'greater Germany' in west and east was intended to counter the SPD's campaign for a 'peace of understanding' which would restore the status quo of July 1914.

Stresemann believed that this political task was particularly vital be- cause the government was still composed of imperial administrators who were trying, he joked, to fight the war 'in strict confidence'.[11] Their failure to give political leadership, as he thought, weakened Germany in com- parison to the democracies where men such as Briand and Lloyd George were masters of the art of mobilizing public opinion. Stresemann con- trasted the German government's maladroit handling of the propaganda war with the successes of the Entente in turning international opinion against Germany. He considered Bethmann Hollweg's admission of the wrong done by Germany to Belgium in violating its neutrality in 1914 as a particularly bad blunder, which had lost the war diplomatically before it had begun.[12] In a speech to the Reichstag in January 1916, he argued that instead of being embarrassed by a campaign for far-reaching war aims, the chancellor should welcome the efforts of those who, following Goethe, 'aspired to the impossible'. It was the task of military leaders and statesmen to decide what was realistic but they would achieve more if they could call on public support than if they preferred to do without it.[13]

Stresemann was aware that his dreams for a 'greater Germany' de- pended not only on public opinion but on victory. He also admitted at times that some of his war aims might not be feasible. But as a politician Stresemann saw his contribution to victory as helping to maintain the morale of the home front. This meant persuading a population mourning unprecedented casualties and suffering severe shortages of food and other necessities as a result of the British blockade, to go on believing in victory

[11] Reichstag speech, 26 Oct. 1916: Zwoch (ed.), *Reichstagsreden*, 52.
[12] 'Eine Atempause im Weltkriege', *Deutsche Stimmen*, 29/1, 10 Jan. 1917.
[13] Reichstag speech, 18 Jan. 1916: Rheinbaben (ed.), *Reden und Schriften*, i. 103.

and 'stick it out'.[14] He did not accept the criticism of those on the left that, by holding out for victory, Germany was letting slip the chance of a negotiated peace and courting the danger of defeat. He countered that the Reichstag's resolution for a compromise peace in July 1917 had made no impression on Germany's enemies. He quoted General Haig on the dependence of the armies on the nerves of the people and urged that their nerves must hold out until victory had been won.[15]

There is nothing surprising in these attitudes, which were common to nationalist politicians in all countries at war. The desire to make Germany safe from any future Franco-Russian-British coalition was the German equivalent of the Entente's aim to make the world safe against German aggression. On both sides, the assumption that the other was responsible for the war led to demands for future security, which could only be achieved by a complete change in the distribution of power on the Continent.

Although unsurprising, Stresemann's war aims were not realistic. Even had Germany won in the west as it did in the east, there is every reason to doubt whether 'greater Germany' in the form Stresemann wanted, based on a liberal political system at home, could have been established on a lasting basis. The opposition of the SPD to a war of conquest and the resentment of subject nationalities would have created permanent tension. A dictatorial regime might have sustained such an empire, but not a liberal one. Stresemann conceived of 'greater Germany' primarily in terms of security. But, as he was the first to argue, policies could not succeed without public support. It was galling that the security needs of Germany's enemies could be combined with the best propaganda lines—national independence and the right of self-determination. He was particularly bitter at what he saw as British (and American) hypocrisy endorsing democracy in Europe the better to secure their dominion overseas. Blinded by his desire for both victory and reform, he refused to see the contradiction between 'greater Germany' and liberal Germany.

Stresemann first developed his arguments in speeches to his new constituency, Aurich, at the end of 1914.[16] Among Germany's enemies, he singled out Britain as bearing the major responsibility for the war. French

[14] Gustav Stresemann, *Warum müssen wir durchhalten?* (Berlin: Kriegs-Presse-Amt [1917]).

[15] Reichstag speech, 10 Oct. 1917: Zwoch (ed.), *Reichstagsreden*, 69–80.

[16] One of these, given on 4 Dec. 1914, was published as a pamphlet, *Deutsches Ringen, deutsches Hoffen* (Berlin: Reichsverlag, 1914), repr. in Gustav Stresemann, *Michel horch, der Seewind pfeift...!* (Berlin: Reichsverlag Hermann Kalkoff, [1916]), 7–20.

motives of revenge for defeat in 1871 and the loss of Alsace-Lorraine he understood, though by allying with Britain they were deserting the tradition of Napoleon. As for Russia, Stresemann pointed to the contradiction of the tsar aligning himself with the assassin of an Austrian archduke. Elsewhere he suggested that Russia had found in the war a diversion from its domestic divisions and an opportunity to satisfy its drive for expansion.[17] But whereas at the beginning of the war he had noted in his diary 'Yesterday bad news from the east. Will we be able to withstand the Russian millions?', by the end of the year he was able to speak confidently of the success of German troops under Hindenburg despite being outnumbered four to one by the Russians.[18]

For Stresemann, as for many Germans, Britain was the real enemy. Behind this attitude lay a deep confusion. Britain as the global power was the standard towards which Germany aspired. Before the war Stresemann had seen the economic rivalry between 'the Germanic nations'—Britain, Germany, and the United States—as a source of tension, though he continued to hope that it could be resolved peacefully.[19] He never admitted, however, that Germany posed any kind of threat to British security, comparing only the relative sizes of their colonial empires. He conveniently overlooked the threat which the German fleet posed to Britain, seeing it simply as necessary to protect Germany. In his view, Britain had no reason for war other than the desire to crush an economic rival whose competition it had been unable to match in peace. Britain's motive was therefore peculiarly reprehensible, a desire to cheat Germany of its proper destiny. Future historians, he said, would see in the war above all a contest between Britain and Germany, between a power which enjoyed world dominion and a power which claimed equal rights. As Bülow had said, Britain always regarded the second strongest power as its enemy because it saw the world as its exclusive, God-given property. This justified for Stresemann feelings of hatred towards Britain with whom, unlike France and Russia, post-war reconciliation would be impossible. He ended one speech with a patriotic hymn of hate against Britain.[20]

---

[17] Notes for another speech in Aurich, 4 Oct.1914 (Nl. 140); 'Englands Wirtschaftskrieg gegen Deutschland', in Stresemann, *Michel, horch*, 22.

[18] Entry for 25 Aug. 1914 from some sheets apparently transcribed from a diary (Nl. 138); *Deutsches Ringen*, 9.

[19] Notes for a speech entitled 'Die germanischen Völker im Kampf um den Weltmarkt', 16 Mar. 1914 (Nl. 140).

[20] *Deutsches Ringen*, 10–20.

Stresemann's extraordinary animosity towards Britain, which was widely shared in Germany, betrayed deep fears and hopes. His unspoken fear was that Germany which he accepted was 'the second strongest power', while it might defeat Russia and France, would not be the equal of Britain. His hope, conversely, was that the German challenge to British supremacy would now be carried to a successful conclusion. He quoted lines from one of his favourite poets of the 1840s, Georg Herwegh, in which he exhorted Germany 'to win the world', concluding:

> You are the shepherd of the great herd of nations,
> You are the great nation of hope for the earth,
> So cast anchor.

Already, in December 1914, Stresemann explained to his constituents his view of what this should mean in practice. 'Greater Germany' was to include not only the Baltic provinces of Russia and the major towns of Belgium, which he asserted were German by history and culture, but also part of the northern coast of France as far as Calais. This last was necessary to prevent Britain from launching a new war. On this basis Germany could move from 'Continental policy to world policy'.[21]

Stresemann also had the opportunity to present his views directly to the chancellor. He was a member of the war aims subcommittee of the joint war committee of German industry (which represented both the Central Association and the manufacturers' association). He took part in drawing up the list of demands which this body thought should be imposed in the event of victory and he and Max Rötger, the chairman of the Central Association, met Bethmann Hollweg on 8 December 1914 to put their case.[22] Their combined aims included the detachment of the coastal region of northern France as far as Calais, the 'correction' of the Franco-German frontier to give Germany the coal and iron mines of Longwy and Briey and the Vosges fortresses which the military wanted,

---

[21] *Deutsches Ringen*, 16–19.

[22] Memorandum of the meeting of the subcommittee, 7. Nov. 1914, and Stresemann's account of the meeting with Bethmann Hollweg, 8 Dec. 1914 (NI. 139). Edwards, *Stresemann and the Greater Germany*, 52–5; Fritz Fischer, *Germany's Aims in the First World War*, Eng. edn. (London: Chatto & Windus, 1967), 165. In the meeting of the industrialists Stresemann disagreed with Hugenberg in a way which was characteristic of both. Hugenberg argued that annexation of foreign territory would be necessary to counteract the increased power of the working class after the war by providing psychological diversion and 'scope for fantasy'. Stresemann replied that satisfying the demands of trade unions depended on the state of the economy whether there was a war or not, and that if the economy expanded strongly then of course the working class would demand a share.

and all French rights in Morocco. The list continued with Belgium, which had to be 'attached' to Germany, possibly in the manner of a British colony. In the east, Russia was to lose Poland, Courland, and Estonia. In addition, the memorandum declared that it would be desirable to create a closer economic association or customs union between Germany, Austria, France, Switzerland, Belgium, and the Scandinavian countries. This was to compensate for the loss of overseas markets which was expected to continue after the war. The whole programme, they explained, was based on the assumption that Russia and France were defeated but that the outcome with Britain remained indecisive.

Bethmann Hollweg was polite but evasive, saying that since neither France nor Britain had been defeated it was too early to adopt such a programme. Stresemann defended their efforts, pointing out that unlike the wars of unification there was no agreement about what the aims should be. That meant that the government would not be able to rely on public opinion in future peace negotiations. The purpose of their memorandum was to influence opinion and assure the chancellor of at least the backing of industry.

Stresemann was already anxious about the chancellor's intentions and he became increasingly dissatisfied. Although Bethmann Hollweg promised that his views did not differ very much from those of the committee, he also made clear his desire for reconciliation with France. Stresemann thought the right strategy should be, on the contrary, to secure a separate peace with Russia in order to concentrate on the war in the west, particularly against Britain.[23] He was strengthened in his doubts about Bethmann Hollweg by Bassermann, who wrote to him from his position in the military government of Belgium describing the chancellor variously as 'this weakling' and 'a tall but small man'.[24] When Stresemann wrote explaining the programme of the industry committee and added enthusiastically, 'The great moment of world history has come, we will push forward to the sea lanes of the world', Bassermann replied with resignation, 'Dear Stresemann, with Bethmann and Wahnschaffe [under-secretary of state at the Reich Chancellery] we will not conquer the world.'[25]

[23] Stresemann to Hans von Capelle, 4 Jan. 1915: Harttung (ed.), *Schriften*, 146–8. Hans was the younger brother of Eduard von Capelle, who became secretary of state for the navy on Tirpitz's resignation in 1916: Berg, *Gustav Stresemann und die Vereinigten Staaten*, 53.

[24] Bassermann to Stresemann, 24 Dec. 1914 and 6 Apr. 1915 (though misdated in original as 1914; Nl. 135).

[25] Stresemann to Bassermann, 30 Dec. 1914: Harttung (ed.), *Schriften*, 143–6; Bassermann to Stresemann, 5 Jan. 1915 (Nl. 134).

Stresemann was particularly indignant at official attempts to censor the publication of the annexationist case while foreign newspapers were openly discussing the future division of Germany.[26]

Stresemann reacted to official disapproval by redoubling his efforts. In 1915 he published a new pamphlet claiming that the nation instinctively recognized that it was engaged in a life-and-death struggle with Britain— 'the most gigantic economic struggle of all time'—comparable to the Punic wars.[27] When Ballin, to whom he had sent a copy of the pamphlet, criticized his arguments saying that he was convinced that Britain had not planned the war, Stresemann ignored the criticism.[28] To another correspondent, however, he admitted that the question of who had caused the war 'will always be difficult to answer', but he fell back on the explanation that Germany had been forced into a preventive war:

The underlying reason lay certainly in Britain's effort to bring a powerful coalition of states into being against us, in order to force us down. We pre-empted this by not allowing any doubt about our willingness to strike out at once after the murder at Sarajevo. One cannot object to that when one considers that every additional year would have reduced the possibility of victory for us or perhaps in two years would have made it impossible.[29]

After the war he was prepared to concede that German diplomats had not behaved any more cleverly than those of other countries in the July crisis, but he remained of the view that the deeper cause was the creation of 'this great world coalition against Germany'.[30]

In 1915 Stresemann helped to organize further petitions on war aims of the leading industrial and agricultural associations.[31] With Bassermann he founded a discussion group, the Wednesday Society, of industrialists, politicians, academics, churchmen, and others to influence

[26] Stresemann to Hans von Capelle, 4 Jan. 1915, and to Friedrich Uebel, 16 Jan. 1915: Harttung (ed.), *Schriften*, 146–51.

[27] *Englands Wirtschaftskrieg gegen Deutschland* (Stuttgart: Deutsche Verlagsanstalt, 1915), repr. in Stresemann *Michel, horch*, 21–51.

[28] Ballin said he knew that the British Foreign Secretary, Edward Grey, had tried to the last to avoid the war and that the charge against him was rather that he had hesitated too long to make his position clear: Ballin to Stresemann, 23 Mar. 1915 (Nl. 146).

[29] Stresemann to Senator Biermann, 9 June 1915 (Nl. 146); Edwards, *Stresemann and the Greater Germany*, 31.

[30] Speech to the first party conference of the Deutsche Volkspartei, 13 Apr. 1919; Gustav Stresemann, *Von der Revolution bis zum Frieden von Versailles* (Berlin: Staatspolitischer Verlag, 1919), 160–1.

[31] Petitions dated 10 Mar. and 20 May 1915 (Nl. 146); Edwards, *Stresemann and the Greater Germany*, 59–64.

elite opinion.[32] Bassermann and Stresemann were determined to counter the influence of anti-annexationist groups, which included some university professors, Progressives such as Theodor Wolff, the editor of the influential *Berliner Tageblatt*, and Social Democrats. What Stresemann called 'the battle for the chancellor's soul' continued with deputations of the annexationist parties and of the economic associations pressing their views on him in further meetings in May 1915.[33]

Bethmann Hollweg moved to accommodate this pressure, telling the Reichstag on 28 May of the need to persevere until 'real guarantees' against a renewal of the war had been secured, but Bassermann and Stresemann were not satisfied. The mutual resentment between them and the chancellor flared up in July 1915. Their criticisms of the chancellor at a party meeting in the Rhineland were in error reported to the press. Bethmann Hollweg arranged a meeting with Bassermann and some other National Liberal politicians who were known to be moderate on war aims, presumably in the hope of rallying support. The day before the meeting, however, he learned from the mail censor of a telegram which Bassermann had sent trying to influence the king of Bavaria to prevent the Kaiser issuing a proclamation on the anniversary of the outbreak of war, which was alleged to contain the words that Germany did not seek an extension of its territory. Bethmann Hollweg thereupon withdrew his invitation to Bassermann but proceeded with his meeting with the other National Liberals and appealed to them for support. Robert Friedberg, the leader of the Prussian party, was persuaded to issue a statement denying that the party leadership lacked confidence in the chancellor. The upshot was a meeting of the national executive on 15 August at which Bethmann Hollweg's supporters were routed. A resolution was approved by an overwhelming majority affirming that

the result of the present war can only be a peace, which with the extension of our frontiers in east and west and overseas, secures us militarily, politically and economically against a new assault and justifies the immense sacrifice which the German people have made...

[32] Stresemann to Bachem, 21 Nov. 1915 with a list of other invitees to the first meeting (Nl. 148). There is an interesting account in Walter Görlitz, *Stresemann* (Heidelberg: Ähren, 1947), 67–8. He points out that it was a varied group, including Walther Rathenau and Graf Keßler among others, and he suggests that the contact with people who did not share his views on war aims may have been important for Stresemann's later development.

[33] Edwards, *Stresemann and the Greater Germany*, 61. The quotation comes from Stresemann's memorandum of the meeting of the Zentralvorstand, 15 Aug. 1915: Reiß (ed.), *Von Bassermann zu Stresemann*, 201.

Stresemann wrote a brief account of these events.[34] He added his own indictment of Bethmann Hollweg, describing him as a man who had failed to understand British hostility before the war until it was too late, and who now associated mainly with those 'who advocated a policy of concessions', although he was also capable under pressure from the annexationists of taking the opposite view. Stresemann described the chancellor as someone 'torn with inner doubts, who went around with the pro and contra of every case for so long that he was finally incapable of taking any decision'. In view of the organization of their opponents, it was essential that the annexationists maintain their pressure on him so that 'at least he is kept in the middle'.

Unrestricted Submarine Warfare

The question of how to win the victory on which his hopes for the future depended worried Stresemann increasingly. Despite Germany's success in 1914 in carrying the war into France and driving the Russians back out of East Prussia and further successes on the eastern front in 1915, Stresemann knew that victory was still far from assured. In particular, Germany had failed to strike at the heart of Britain, in his view its arch-enemy. Britain had not only been able to transport and maintain an army in France, it had also imposed a naval blockade to strangle Germany's economy by depriving it of food and raw materials. The result was, in Stresemann's words, that Germany might 'win victories to death' on land but still find itself without the economic resources to continue.[35] There was only one means of hitting back at Britain directly, the submarine. But, because of its fragility, the submarine could only be used effectively if it was allowed to attack without warning, regardless of the loss of life which followed. Whereas the British blockade operated by forcing neutral ships into sea lanes where they were searched for goods which might find their way to Germany, the German blockade of Britain operated simply by sinking as much shipping as possible bound for British ports. Naturally such a tactic inflamed international opinion in a way the British blockade did not. In particular, it inflamed opinion in the most powerful of the

[34] Stresemann's memorandum of the Zentralvorstand meeting and the events leading up to it: Reiß (ed.), *Von Bassermann zu Stresemann*, 195–203.

[35] Stresemann's report to the meeting of the Zentralvorstand, 23 Sept. 1917: Reiß (ed.), *Von Bassermann zu Stresemann*, 309–51; quotation, 317.

neutral countries, the United States. In deference to American protests, the German government therefore restricted the operation of submarines in 1915 after the sinking of the *Lusitania* with American casualties on 15 May. Further incidents were followed by fresh protests and new restrictions, culminating in the resignation of Admiral Tirpitz as secretary of state for the navy on 10 March 1916.

Stresemann followed this policy of German concessions to American pressure with growing dismay. He regarded President Wilson's protests as hypocritical, since the United States had interpreted its neutrality in a one-sided way and continued to supply Germany's enemies not only with food but weapons.[36] Wilson's protests against German submarine warfare carried the threat of war, but the protests which he made against the illegal aspects of the British blockade carried no such threat.[37] Stresemann allowed himself to be convinced that in unrestricted submarine warfare Germany possessed the means to win the war by crippling British imports. He dismissed the warnings of Max Weber against gambling everything on the success of a single weapon, preferring instead to trust the naval experts.[38]

The issue was debated both within the National Liberal Party and in the finance committee of the Reichstag.[39] Bassermann led the discussion at the committee, arguing that the crucial question was whether submarine warfare could inflict sufficient damage on British shipping for Britain to be unable to continue the war. He asserted that the German admiralty's calculations showed that this could be achieved by unrestricted use of the submarines which would destroy 600,000 to 700,000 tonnage of shipping per month. He accepted the risk that the United States might declare war in retaliation, though he did not think it was inevitable and in any case American aid to Britain would be mainly financial since it did not possess the ships to transport an army to Europe. He rated the chance of forcing Britain to conclude peace higher than the dangers of an American declaration of war.

---

[36] Berg, *Stresemann und die Vereinigten Staaten*, 48–52.

[37] As Stresemann pointed out to the finance committee of the Reichstag: confidential National Liberal report of the proceedings, 28–31 Mar. 1916 (Nl. 153).

[38] Berg, *Stresemann und die Vereinigten Staaten*, 58–60. Stresemann's critique of Weber is printed in Mommsen, *Max Weber*, 515–20.

[39] Minutes of the meeting of the Zentralvorstand, 21 May 1916: Reiß (ed.), *Von Bassermann zu Stresemann*, 228–82; confidential National Liberal report of the proceedings of the finance committee, 28–31 Mar. 1916 (Nl. 153) and the less detailed official minutes, Reinhard Schiffers and Manfred Koch (eds.), *Der Hauptausschuß des Deutschen Reichstags 1915–1918*, 4 vols. (Düsseldorf: Droste, 1981), ii. 399–402, 416; Berg, *Stresemann und die Vereinigten Staaten*, 60–9.

Bethmann Hollweg put the opposite view: unrestricted submarine warfare would definitely provoke an American declaration of war, and Britain could survive the projected losses by using ships from other countries and armed convoys: 'The attempt to starve Britain by the submarine war was an illusion.' The chancellor received some support from the new secretary of state for the navy, Eduard von Capelle, who also doubted whether Britain would be forced to submit.

Stresemann then amplified Bassermann's arguments on the economic consequences to be expected. He did not think that America's financial support for Britain would be decisive and the loss of German shipping in neutral ports abroad (to which the chancellor had referred) would happen in any case. He argued that a favourable consequence for Germany would be increased supplies from Holland and Denmark since these countries would be unable to export to Britain. He also doubted whether America would declare war, given the opposition of a strong minority in Congress and the fact that it was a presidential election year when both candidates would want the votes of the Irish and German communities. Like Bassermann, he argued that the damage inflicted on the British economy would in any case be more important than the, admittedly serious, consequences of an American declaration of war. The chancellor thought the whole debate had been started because they had an exaggerated notion of the size of Germany's submarine fleet. But, Stresemann declared, although he knew exactly how many submarines there were, this was not the crucial issue. What mattered was the monthly total of British shipping that could be sunk: on the admiralty's figures this would be the equivalent of 25–30 per cent of the total British merchant fleet. He agreed with the chancellor that this would not 'force Britain to its knees' but it would make Britain willing to have a negotiated peace. The rise in the cost of living in a country which depended on imports for 85 per cent of its food and the destruction of a third of its merchant navy—which was the foundation of its world power—would have an enormous effect, and if it did not break Britain in the first six months the war had only to be continued until it did.

Stresemann referred to the views of twelve experts from industry and commerce—not 'pan-German utopians' but 'cool, calculating business-men'—who agreed with his assessment.[40] He also referred to the difficul-

[40] The original has 'altdeutschen', but this is clearly a typing error. The experts included representatives of heavy industry, such as Paul Reusch and Hugo Stinnes, and a number of bankers.

ties of Germany's own economic position, which was deteriorating month by month, and the lack of an alternative strategy for forcing Britain to conclude peace. He pointed out that the neutrals, including the United States, had accepted a ban on sending ships to German ports: with what right therefore could they protest against a German ban on British ports? He concluded that unrestricted submarine warfare alone offered the promise of success.

There was no majority on the committee since the National Liberals and Conservatives were opposed by the SPD and the Progressives with the Centre Party holding the balance—in principle in favour but leaving the timing open. The committee therefore decided on a compromise resolution, leaving the question open, to avoid a public debate in the Reichstag. In October 1916 the matter was again discussed in committee and this time the Centre Party joined the Conservatives and National Liberals in passing a resolution that unrestricted submarine warfare should be adopted at the discretion of the High Command. This abdicated any influence the Reichstag might have had to Hindenburg and Ludendorff, who had taken over the military direction of the war at the end of August 1916. It also showed the lack of confidence of the Reichstag majority in Bethmann Hollweg. By December Hindenburg and Ludendorff had come to the conclusion that unrestricted submarine warfare was essential and threatened resignation if it were not adopted. Bethmann Hollweg, who had launched a peace initiative in December to try to persuade the United States to remain neutral in the event of an extension of the submarine war, tried to get the decision postponed but capitulated on 9 January, after intense pressure from the military and naval leadership on the Kaiser.

Stresemann was well informed of these developments and had tried, through Bassermann, to influence Ludendorff.[41] In an article published the day after the decision had been taken, he argued that the submarines should be allowed to cut Britain off like a fortress in the way the British blockade had been used against Germany.[42] In the main committee of the Reichstag, he rejected arguments in principle against the use of unrestricted submarine warfare, saying that 'he himself would accept the deployment of a poison bomb and the death of half a million inhabitants of London if that would bring peace and save the lives

---

[41] Bassermann to Stresemann, 23 Sept. 1916 (Nl. 134).
[42] 'Eine Atempause im Weltkriege', *Deutsche Stimmen*, 29/1, 10 Jan. 1917.

of half a million Germans'.[43] He ridiculed the idea that the German aim should be simply to return to the status quo of August 1914, as Philipp Scheidemann, a leading member of the SPD, had suggested. Stresemann argued that without the Flemish coast, Germany could not protect its overseas trade or colonies and, if they had to bear the whole cost of the war, German exporters would be unable to compete with the United States.

The initial effects of the submarine war seemed to confirm Stresemann's predictions. British and neutral losses from February to April 1917 produced a crisis in London, where it was recognized that unless an answer could be found Britain would be defeated.[44] The British admiralty's belated conversion to armed convoys, which it had previously considered impracticable for merchant ships, saved the situation by the autumn. In addition, the entry of the United States into the war on 5 April 1917 meant that if Britain and France could hold out on the western front until an American army could join them, their victory was assured.

In retrospect, it was clear that unrestricted submarine warfare was one of the crucial blunders of the war. Stresemann had been wrong to follow the German naval experts in discounting the effects of the convoy system—even though at the time their judgement agreed with that of the British admiralty. After the war he described how Capelle had told the Reichstag committee that the chances of the United States being able to transport an army to Europe were 'Nil, nil, nil'.[45] He had also been wrong to play down the risk of the United States entering the war— indeed he suffered the embarrassment of the news of America's declaration of war reaching a meeting of the national executive at the same time as he was giving assurances that it would not happen.[46] Unabashed, he argued at the next meeting that it had been not so much the decision for unrestricted submarine warfare but an intercepted telegram from

---

[43] Minutes of the meeting, 1 Feb. 1917: Schiffers and Koch (eds.), *Der Hauptausschuß*, iii. 1107. The budget committee was renamed the main committee from the autumn of 1916 to reflect the expansion of its business: ibid., vol. i, p. vii.

[44] Arthur J. Marder, *From the Dreadnought to Scapa Flow: The Royal Navy in the Fisher Era, 1904–1919*, iv: *1917: Year of Crisis* (London: Oxford University Press, 1969), 147–9.

[45] Stresemann's evidence to the committee of investigation established by the National Assembly in 1919: Walter Schücking and Johannes Bell (eds.), *Das Werk des Untersuchungsausschusses der Verfassunggebenden Deutschen Nationalversammlung und des Deutschen Reichstages 1919–1928*, 4th series: *Die Ursachen des Deutschen Zusammenbruches im Jahre 1918*, vol. vii (Berlin: Deutsche Verlagsgesellschaft für Politik, 1928), 307.

[46] Reiß (ed.), *Von Bassermann zu Stresemann*, 312.

the state secretary at the Auswärtiges Amt, Arthur Zimmermann, to Mexico offering it Texas, New Mexico, and Arizona if it would join an alliance with Germany, that had provoked a congressional majority for war.[47]

After the war Stresemann criticized the failures of the naval leadership, but he was still prepared to defend his record, saying that had unrestricted submarine warfare been adopted six months earlier, it would have had quite different results from even the near defeat of Britain achieved in summer 1917.[48] This argument, which depends on Stresemann's assertion that in August 1916 Britain had developed hardly any countermeasures, is not very convincing, since there seems no reason to suppose that the prospect of defeat would not have led to the adoption of convoys then as it did later.

Stresemann's miscalculation over unrestricted submarine warfare had lasting consequences. It aligned him squarely with the High Command and the political right among those who had gambled on a German victory rather than accepting that the war could not be won and looking for a compromise peace. This separated him not only from the SPD but also from the Progressives and, increasingly, the Centre Party, and even a minority of National Liberals who were pessimistic about the war in the west and looked for a way of ending it. Had Stresemann, like the Centre Party politician Matthias Erzberger, shifted in 1916–17 from his early annexationist stand through rejection of unrestricted submarine warfare to promoting a compromise peace, he would not have been discredited in the eyes of the Left–Centre coalition which took power after the war.[49] On the other hand, not to have seized any chance of victory so long as it appeared feasible would have been contrary to Stresemann's character and convictions. In addition, if he had argued for a compromise peace in 1917, he would have had great difficulty in carrying the National Liberal Party with him. A two-thirds majority within the Reichstag party and an overwhelming majority in the national executive supported Bassermann's and Stresemann's pursuit of a 'lasting peace' through victory.[50]

---

[47] Minutes of the meeting of 23 Sept. 1917: Reiß (ed.), *Von Bassermann zu Stresemann*, 312–13.

[48] Stresemann to an American critic Phelan Beale, 9 Feb. 1921: Harttung (ed.), *Schriften*, 276–8.

[49] Epstein, *Erzberger*, 96–117, 182–90.

[50] Reiß (ed.), *Von Bassermann zu Stresemann*, 32, 281–2. Stresemann set out the requirements of a 'lasting peace' in 'Deutschlands Siegeswille' repr. from the *Leipziger Illustrierten Zeitung*, 22 June 1916, in *Michel Horch*, 141–6.

Constitutional Reform

Stresemann had been critical of aspects of the political system before 1914, but the war convinced him of the need for reform. He had been deeply impressed by the patriotism shown by all sections of the population. As Bassermann said, the nation had displayed the spirit of Bismarck which unhappily, by its lack of leadership over war aims, had been missing in government.[51] In a speech to the Reichstag in January 1916, he attacked the use of censorship to prevent debate on war aims, saying that of course there would be differences of opinion in a nation of 70 million, and that there was no danger in allowing them to be voiced, provided each side recognized the patriotism of the other.[52] On the contrary, there was great danger in restricting debate, because 'The world war can only be won anyway with public opinion.' He promised the left support in measures to increase the power of the Reichstag, since 'We can only imagine the greater Germany we hope for, built on a free, self-respecting nation which participates in the affairs of state in a decisive way.'

In October 1916 the National Liberals joined the SPD, Progressives, and Centre Party in proposing a standing committee to discuss foreign policy with the government. Stresemann eloquently explained his party's position in the Reichstag winning applause from the left.[53] The main purpose, he said, was to strengthen the rights of the national assembly and to achieve a closer connection between it and the government. He criticized the government for its lack of enthusiasm for the measure, challenging it to take the lead in 'a great policy of liberal reorientation'.[54] Stresemann held up the debates in the British House of Commons as a model which, through the openness of their criticism, revealed the strength of the nation. He traced the comparative lack of power of the

---

[51] Stresemann's summary of Bassermann's speech to the Zentralvorstand, 15 Aug. 1915: Reiß (ed.), *Von Bassermann zu Stresemann*, 195.

[52] Reichstag speech, 18 Jan. 1916: Rheinbaben (ed.), *Reden und Schriften*, i. 81–104. Stresemann was replying to those Progressives and moderate National Liberals who supported Bethmann Hollweg and feared that constitutional reform would allow a demagogic debate over war aims which would tear the nation apart. Schwabe, *Wissenschaft und Kriegsmoral*, 124–30; Heuss, *Naumann*, 379–83; Theiner, *Sozialer Liberalismus*, 229–30.

[53] Reichstag speech, 26 Oct. 1916; Zwoch (ed.), *Reichstagsreden*, 43–56. Stresemann had already foreshadowed this demand in a speech to the National Liberal Party in Thuringia on 3 Sept. 1916: *NLC*, 43/113, 3 Sept. 1916; Richter '"Auseinanderstrebendes Zusammenhalten"', 75.

[54] Stresemann was playing on the fact that the state secretary for the interior, Clemens von Delbrück, had referred to the government's intentions to bring about a 'reorientation': Thieme, *Nationaler Liberalismus*, 93.

Reichstag to the dominating influence of Bismarck, but astutely quoted Bismarck himself, after his dismissal, calling for a stronger Reichstag to balance the government. Stresemann added another consideration: the war had speeded up the growth of political consciousness by the equivalent of decades of peace and he expected as a result a quite different position for the Reichstag after the war. In an article on the same theme he argued that Germany was seriously lacking in the 'mutual interchange between government and parliament'.[55] In countries where politicans knew they might soon become ministers, they behaved with a greater sense of responsibility, and ex-ministers brought expertise to parliamentary debates.

Stresemann temporarily accepted Bassermann's lead that major constitutional change should not be attempted in wartime. But in 1917 his position changed. Bassermann became ill in February and died in July. This increased Stresemann's influence in the Reichstag party, though he succeeded to the leadership only in September. More important, the political situation changed dramatically. Popular discontent at the third wartime winter, with no prospect of victory and severe shortages of food and coal, increased the pressure on the government to make political concessions. It became clear in March that the SPD would not continue to vote for war credits unless there were political reforms, the main focus of discontent being the Prussian franchise. Bethmann Hollweg accepted in speeches to the Reichstag and the Prussian Landtag that reforms would be necessary after the war, but this concession came too late to stop the radical current which was given new impetus by the Russian revolution. At the end of March the Progressives took the lead, putting down a resolution in the Reichstag for the introduction of universal male franchise throughout the Reich.

The resolution forced the National Liberals to review their position that reforms should be postponed until after the war. The Reichstag party was divided. To avoid making these divisions public it was agreed to propose that the Reichstag should establish a constitutional committee to review the question. According to Stresemann, in a letter defending the new policy to a doubtful Bassermann, all those who spoke at the party meeting agreed that the policy of postponing change in the Prussian franchise could no longer be upheld.[56] Postponing the issue made it

---

[55] 'Ein ständiger Ausschuß für auswärtige Angelegenheiten', *Nationalliberale Blätter*, 28/19, 3 Oct. 1916.

[56] Stresemann to Bassermann, 31 Mar. 1917 (Nl. 133). This letter followed a telephone conversation in which Bassermann had expressed unease at the new course.

look as though the party was secretly opposed to change, and that would bring defeat at the next elections. Stresemann added the tactical calculation that this was probably the last opportunity to steer through a plural rather than a universal suffrage for Prussia.

Stresemann had already appealed to the National Liberals not to be frightened of change in a speech to mark the party's fiftieth anniversary in February 1917. He predicted that, after the war, Germany would experience 'a great wave of democratic sentiment', and he recommended that parliamentary institutions should be strengthened, that Prussia should follow the example of Saxony in adopting a plural voting system, and that Social Democrats should be given positions in government.[57] But he left the question of when these reforms should take place open.

In his speech to the Reichstag on 29 March proposing the setting up of a constitutional committee, Stresemann explained that the party had now decided that, in view of the length of the war and the unprecedented demands it was making on the population, the time had come for action: 'The new era demands new rights.' He scornfully rejected criticism of the Reichstag from the aristocrats of the Prussian upper chamber, contrasting their slogans with the progressive ideas of the heroes of the war of liberation against Napoleon, warning that talk of military absolutism was dangerous, and that in a modern state a monarch could no longer rule personally but was dependent on his advisers. Stresemann admitted that his party contained different views on the question of parliamentary government, but he went on to praise Britain's success in uniting public opinion and winning international support. By comparison, Germany's lack of political success in recent decades despite its enormous achievements in other areas showed that there must be 'a fault in the political system'. German ministers might have great professional expertise in their departments but they lacked political sense both in handling other nations and their own. The best way to forestall demagogic opposition from parliament was to give it more power. He appealed to the chancellor to reform the Prussian franchise since on that depended the future relationship with the SPD, and he added that his party welcomed the appointment of Social Democrats to administrative positions since it believed that all public positions should be open on the basis of merit alone.[58]

---

[57] 'Zum fünfzigjährigen Bestehen der Nationalliberalen Partei', 28 Feb. 1917, Stresemann, *Macht und Freiheit*, 23–37, quotation, p. 29.

[58] *Verhandlungen des Reichstags*, vol. 309, pp. 2849–57. The main part of the speech dealing with constitutional reform is repr. in Rheinbaben (ed.), *Reden und Schriften*, i. 172–92. Stresemann's

These were strong words which inevitably aroused the opposition of the right wing of the party.[59] Bassermann, from his sick bed, was worried that Stresemann had gone too far, and Stresemann wrote to him at length defending himself.[60] He referred to the reduction of the bread ration, the first signs of serious industrial unrest, and the impact of the Russian revolution added to American propaganda that the war was being fought against the autocratic system of government in Germany: 'After all', he added, 'we and Austria are the only countries in the whole inhabited earth which allow a monarch that kind of influence.' He declared his total opposition to a system where the Kaiser could appoint as chancellor whomever he liked, even though the fate of 65 million people depended on the choice. Bassermann himself had said that the Kaiser and chancellor were leading Germany to ruin: was William II to be given a vote of confidence after the war? A parliamentary system did not have to mean full parliamentary government, but at least the Reichstag must have the power to exert pressure on a chancellor to resign by a vote of no confidence. After the experience of the war, he concluded, he could not defend the present system.

Stresemann's conviction that Germany's political system was dangerously obsolete was reinforced by his reading of the political situation in 1917. The crumbling of morale convinced him that a dramatic shift of public opinion was taking place. If the National Liberals were not to be left isolated with the Conservatives, they had to associate themselves with the demand for reform. Stresemann's calculations in this respect were similar to those of Erzberger, who led the Centre Party at the same time on the same course.[61] As Stresemann warned Bassermann, 'The nation is eminently politicized. The driftwood must not be allowed to float away to the left or we may be lost at the next elections, especially as people have the feeling in any case that they should choose new parties for themselves.'[62]

By taking the lead in proposing constitutional reform, Stresemann hoped to ride the movement for change. The fact that the proposal for a

arguments followed similar lines to those developed by Max Weber shortly afterwards in articles in the *Frankfurter Zeitung* in May–June 1917. Mommsen, *Max Weber*, 156–63; Schwabe, *Wissenschaft und Kriegsmoral*, 134–42.

[59] Richter '"Auseinanderstrebendes Zusammenhalten"', 77–82.

[60] Stresemann to Bassermann, 9 Apr. 1917 (Nl. 133); reproduced in part in Harttung (ed.), *Schriften*, 167–70.

[61] Epstein, *Erzberger*, 189–90.

[62] Stresemann to Bassermann, 31 Mar. 1917 (Nl. 133).

constitutional committee was passed by a majority of 277 to 33 in the Reichstag and was followed by the Kaiser's 'Easter message' on 7 April promising reform after the war was seen by Stresemann as confirming his judgement.[63] The National Liberals had been true to Bennigsen's maxim 'to recognize the signs of the times and to satisfy their demands'.[64] Stresemann's initiative was too much for a group of Old Liberals, who voted against the proposal and organized opposition in newspapers financed by Wilhelm Hirsch, a representative of Westphalian heavy industry and a member of both the Reichstag and the Prussian Landtag.[65] Stresemann organized a meeting of the standing committee of the national executive with the chairmen of the provincial parties and, despite some 'very lively discussion', was able to secure a measure of unity, though he had to concede that they rejected 'parliamentary rule on a foreign model'.[66]

These events marked an important stage in Stresemann's development. For the first time he had emerged from Bassermann's shadow and taken the lead on a major issue. He wrote to a colleague that Bassermann's style of compromise was in many cases right for 'a party with such a complicated construction as ours', but 'there are moments in which one must have the courage by taking the helm to give the ship a definite, even if new, direction'.[67] Stresemann was not yet the leader of the Reichstag party. During Bassermann's illness a senior figure, Prince Heinrich zu Schönaich-Carolath, became acting leader with Stresemann as one of three deputies.[68] Nevertheless, Stresemann was already the leading candidate for the succession, if only because of his ability in debate. By his outspoken stand in favour of reform he could have jeopardized his prospects, and he was clearly concerned that he might lose Bassermann's support.[69] But he was convinced that reform was necessary and that the party could not afford to stand aside. He hoped that it would be able to unite behind the

---

[63] Stresemann to Bassermann, 9 Apr. 1917 (Nl. 133).

[64] Reichstag speech, 26 Oct. 1916: Zwoch (ed.), *Reichstagsreden*, 48.

[65] Stresemann to Bassermann, 15 and 18 Apr. (Nl. 133); Richter, '"Auseinanderstrebendes Zusammenhalten"', 76–80.

[66] Stresemann to Bassermann, 19 June 1917 (Nl. 133); Richter, '"Auseinanderstrebendes Zusammenhalten"', 80–1.

[67] Stresemann to Friedrich List, 9 Apr. 1917 (Nl. 170).

[68] Stresemann to Bassermann, 22 Feb. 1917 (Nl. 133).

[69] Stresemann asked Bassermann to counter the rumours that 'our personal and political relations had suffered as a result of the recent disputes', referring to the confusion this was causing in relation to the question of the next leader. Stresemann to Bassermann, 9 June 1917 (Nl. 133).

twin aims of victory and reform—'for the greater... for the freer Germany of the future'.[70]

It has been suggested that Stresemann's continued strong support for expansionist war aims may have been partly designed to keep the right wing of the party in line while he was identifying himself with the campaign for reform.[71] He was clearly aware of the advantages of a balanced ticket, writing to Bassermann that 'the overwhelming majority of the party is united behind us on war aims' and that concerns that they were moving to the left, which always followed 'a liberal action', had largely evaporated.[72] But he would probably have supported the same war aims in any case, both from conviction and to maintain public support for victory.

On the issue of which aims could be achieved, he still deferred to the judgement of the military leadership. But, even in this respect, there was worrying news which underlined the need for reform. He warned Bassermann in April 1917 that if the submarine war did not bring a decision before the economic situation became catastrophic they would have to have SPD representation in government. He claimed that the High Command supported this view. In addition, the chief of the General Staff on the eastern front, General Hoffmann, had told Erzberger and their National Liberal colleague Hartmann von Richthofen that if the military situation did not improve they would have 'to seek an honourable peace' and only a committee of parliamentary ministers—not the appointee of an absolute monarch—would be in a position to do this.[73]

The Crisis of July 1917

It was one thing to maintain the electoral credibility of the party by identifying it with the majority for reform. It was another to remain master of the consequences. The political crisis which came to a head in July did not follow the course Stresemann intended. The majority for reform settled on the demand for a 'peace of understanding' from which the National Liberals dissociated themselves. Stresemann exploited the

[70] Speech to celebrate the party's fiftieth anniversary: Stresemann, *Macht und Freiheit*, 37.

[71] Eberhard Kolb, 'Probleme einer modernen Stresemann-Biographie', in Otmar Franz (ed.), *Am Wendepunkt der europäischen Geschichte* (Göttingen: Musterschmidt, 1981), 118–19.

[72] Stresemann to Bassermann, 9 June 1917 (Nl. 133).

[73] Stresemann to Bassermann, 10 Apr. 1917 (Nl. 133).

situation to bring about the fall of Bethmann Hollweg, using the reservations felt by parts of the new Reichstag majority towards the chancellor as one of his levers. But Bethmann Hollweg was replaced not, as Stresemann hoped, by Bülow but by an obscure official, Georg Michaelis, who was wholly dependent on the Kaiser and the High Command. Instead of a closer connection between government and Reichstag, the gap between them grew wider than ever.

By taking their stand for constitutional reform and against the peace resolution, the National Liberals were increasingly caught in a dilemma of their own making. As the nation polarized between the alternatives of either peace and reform or victory and no reform, Stresemann was caught in the middle. He cooperated with the Reichstag majority of Social Democrats, Progressives, and the Centre Party on reform while trying to loosen their united front on peace. He enjoyed some success, particularly in March 1918 when the Reichstag accepted the dismemberment of the Russian empire by the treaty of Brest-Litovsk. But defeat in October 1918 left him isolated, rejected by both left and right since he had belonged fully to neither. His manoeuvres had first provoked the accusation that he was two-faced in 1917; in 1918 he paid the price.

The crisis of July 1917 had unexpected consequences, at least in part because of the confused aims of its instigators. The Reichstag had to meet to vote war credits. The SPD, facing competition from the Independent Social Democrats (Unabhängige Sozialdemokratische Partei Deutschlands; USPD) who had broken away from the main party in April 1917, demanded political concessions and a clear statement on war aims renouncing annexations as the price of their continued support. Bethmann Hollweg was unable to satisfy them because of the pressures on him in the reverse direction from the High Command, the Kaiser, and the Conservative Party, and it was clear when he met party leaders on 2 July that he had nothing to offer and could only appeal for unity.[74]

The opposition of the SPD to war credits would not by itself have proved fatal to the chancellor. What raised the crisis to a new level was a speech by Erzberger to the main committee of the Reichstag on 6 July in which he declared that Germany would not get a better peace the following year, that unrestricted submarine warfare had been completely misjudged, and that the Reichstag should promote a resolution for a

---

[74] Erich Matthias and Rudolf Morsey (eds.), *Der Interfraktionelle Ausschuß 1917/18*, 2 vols. (Düsseldorf: Droste, 1959), vol. i, pp. xxiv–xxvi; Stresemann's account of the events, 'Gedanken zur Krisis', *Deutsche Stimmen*, 29/14 (23 July 1917), repr. in Stresemann, *Macht und Freiheit*, 60–81.

compromise peace. The importance of this development, which Stresemann called 'the defection of Erzberger to Scheidemann', was that it
carried the threat of a new majority, composed of the SPD, Progressives,
and Centre Party.[75] This offered the prospect of a direct conflict between
the chancellor and a Reichstag majority, unless—as Stresemann at first
thought possible—Erzberger had been acting with Bethmann Hollweg's
approval, in which case the chancellor himself was looking for support for
a compromise peace.

The first meeting of the inter-party committee of all those, including
the National Liberals, who favoured reform met on the afternoon of 6 July
after Erzberger's sensational démarche.[76] Differences soon became apparent. On the Prussian franchise, the SPD and Progressives wanted an equal
system whereas the National Liberals and Centre Party, out of deference
to their Prussian Landtag parties, only wanted to go as far as a plural
franchise. There was agreement on parliamentary government, at least in
the form that leading politicians should be given public office. However,
there were differences of view on how to press for it and over what priority
it should be given.

Stresemann, seeing a chance to get rid of Bethmann Hollweg, argued
that only a change of system and new people would make a peace resolution, such as Erzberger had proposed, effective.[77] However, in subsequent meetings of the inter-party committee it became clear that the other
parties wanted to put the peace resolution first. This posed a dilemma for
the National Liberals. The majority would not swallow the peace resolution, but Stresemann and the minority did not want the party to be
excluded from a change of government which might result. Since the
other parties also wanted to have National Liberal support if possible—
the Centre Party at first made its support for the peace resolution conditional on the National Liberals voting for it—attempts were made to
bridge the gap.[78]

While these discussions were proceeding, Stresemann acted independently to undermine Bethmann Hollweg's position. He had already been in
touch with the High Command, through Colonel Bauer who acted as
Ludendorff's confidant for questions of domestic politics, and he had

---

[75] Stresemann's report to the Zentralvorstand meeting, 23 Sept. 1917: Reiß (ed.), *Von Bassermann zu Stresemann*, 327.

[76] Matthias and Morsey (eds.), *Der Interfraktionelle Ausschuß*, i. 3–12.

[77] Ibid. 6.

[78] Records of the meetings, 7–11 July 1917: ibid. 13–36.

visited military headquarters and spoken to Hindenburg and Ludendorff in June.[79] When they heard of Erzberger's initiative, Hindenburg and Ludendorff hurried to Berlin to see if they could exploit the situation to bring Bethmann Hollweg down. They had wanted to get rid of him since the conflict over unrestricted submarine warfare in January but had been hesitant to act so long as he had majority support in the Reichstag. Ludendorff carefully avoided giving the impression that they were opposed to reform, although they were in fact resisting Bethmann Hollweg's proposals for change.[80]

Ludendorff asked to see Stresemann on his arrival in Berlin on 7 July and Stresemann told him what he wanted to hear—that the main thing was the removal of the chancellor.[81] Stresemann criticized Bethmann Hollweg for having no programme to satisfy the SPD and no answer to Erzberger's calculations about the effectiveness of the submarine campaign. The lack of leadership from the chancellor had created the opportunity for Erzberger because no one knew what government policy was. As well as a change of chancellor, Stresemann said, the Prussian franchise should be reformed and politicians should be appointed as ministers.

On the same day Stresemann made sure of Erzberger's support, asking him point blank whether he was acting in collusion with Bethmann Hollweg. Erzberger convinced Stresemann that he was not, and they agreed that Bethmann Hollweg should be replaced by Bülow.[82] The intrigue then took a comic turn when Bethmann Hollweg, deeply resenting the presence of Hindenburg and Ludendorff in Berlin to conspire against him, succeeded in convincing the Kaiser that there was no crisis, and the Kaiser promptly ordered the generals to return to headquarters.

Stresemann was not prepared to let the matter rest and on Monday, 9 July, he launched a wounding personal attack on Bethmann Hollweg in the main committee of the Reichstag.[83] He accused him of repeated

[79] Wilhelm Deist (ed.), *Militär und Innenpolitik im Weltkrieg 1914–1918*, 2 vols. (Düsseldorf: Droste, 1970), ii. 759, and Stresemann to Bassermann, 19 June 1917 (Nl. 133). Stresemann recorded the visit with evident pride in his diary entry for 14 June: 'With Hindenburg und Ludendorff!!' (Nl. 362). On Bauer, see Adolf Vogt, *Oberst Max Bauer. Generalstabsoffizier im Zwielicht 1869–1929* (Osnabrück: Biblio, 1974).

[80] Deist (ed.), *Militär und Innenpolitik*, vol. i, pp. lxiii–lxiv.

[81] Stresemann's account, 'Zur Kanzlerkrise' (Nl. 172): Matthias and Morsey (eds.), *Der Interfraktionelle Ausschuß*, i. 74–80.

[82] Ibid. 76.

[83] Stresemann's summary: ibid. 77. The official minutes give a detailed account: Schiffers and Koch (eds.), *Der Hauptausschuß*, iii. 1575–82.

failure and of having no programme in either foreign or domestic policy. He argued that offering reforms 'drop by drop' was the worst possible tactic and he blamed the chancellor for a situation where, after three years of war, party leaders had still not been given a chance to inform the Kaiser of the public mood. He warned that, in place of the hopes of August 1914 for a new period of popular monarchy (*Volkskaisertum*), there were ugly views being expressed about the way the Kaiser was sealed off from the people. He also cast doubt on the chancellor's repeated claims that he was in agreement with the High Command, asking for a joint meeting with the High Command to clear up differences over who had been responsible for decisions over Poland and the forced requisition of Belgian labour and also the question of whether the High Command opposed constitutional reform. Even if the High Command had forced its views on the chancellor that would not excuse him because if he was unable to get his way he should resign. In a bid for support from the peace resolution parties, Stresemann cleverly suggested that there could be different views about the wisdom of seeking peace at that moment, but he suggested that Bethmann Hollweg would in any case be incapable of concluding peace because of the way he had alienated opinion abroad, especially in the United States. It was a brutally effective intervention, which showed both the force of Stresemann's personality and his mastery of the tactics of parliamentary demolition. Bethmann Hollweg's attempt to play down the crisis to the Kaiser had made matters worse by causing resentment among the Centre Party and the SPD. Only the Progressives spoke up in the chancellor's defence.

Even so, Stresemann thought, Bethmann Hollweg would probably have survived, particularly as he finally wrested the Kaiser's consent to the introduction of equal suffrage in Prussia and the inclusion of politicians in the Reich and Prussian governments, which was made known on 11 July. However, at this point a new intrigue was started against him by the Crown Prince, who saw a number of party leaders, including Stresemann, selected for him by Colonel Bauer to maximize the impression that Bethmann Hollweg had lost the support of the Reichstag.[84] In addition both the National Liberals and the Centre Reichstag parties passed formal resolutions that the chancellor should go. Armed with this evidence the Crown Prince was ready to persuade the Kaiser that Bethmann Hollweg had lost control of the situation.

[84] Matthias and Morsey (eds.), *Der Interfraktionelle Ausschuß*, i. 56.

The coup de grâce was provided by Hindenburg and Ludendorff after an incident where Stresemann provoked the state secretary of the interior, Karl Helfferich, by telling him that he knew that Hindenburg and Ludendorff would resign if Bethmann Hollweg stayed.[85] Helfferich angrily retorted that the chancellor would demand from Ludendorff a categorical confirmation or denial of this rumour. Stresemann saw that the High Command was informed of what had happened, whereupon Hindenburg and Ludendorff telegraphed their resignation to the Kaiser saying they could no longer work with the chancellor. On 13 July, the Kaiser received Hindenburg and Ludendorff together with the Crown Prince and told them that he had already accepted Bethmann Hollweg's resignation.

Stresemann had achieved his objective. He had helped to bring about the fall of the man whom he considered unfit to be chancellor. He was motivated not simply by Bethmann Hollweg's lukewarm stance on war aims but by his lack of resolution, as Stresemann believed, about everything.[86] He had lost the confidence of the High Command by his hesitation over unrestricted submarine warfare, and he had failed to produce the positive programme of domestic reforms which was necessary to keep the SPD behind the war. Stresemann made no attempt to understand Bethmann Hollweg's difficulties. He simply wanted to force him out. He admitted at the time that it had been 'the most intensely exciting period of my political life'.[87] He wrote to the ailing Bassermann that he hoped the news would give him pleasure.[88] Stresemann's satisfaction was understandable. He had moved adroitly to associate the supporters of the peace resolution with his campaign against Bethmann Hollweg by arguing that the chancellor was too compromised by his previous statements on war aims to be able to make peace. In view of Stresemann's own insistence six months earlier that war with the United States would not be decisive, his new line was understandably resented by government supporters as flagrant opportunism.[89]

[85] Stresemann's account, 'Zur Kanzlerkrise': Matthias and Morsey (eds.), *Der Interfraktionelle Ausschuß*, i. 79–80.

[86] Richter points out that the standard interpretation that Stresemann was motivated simply by the desire to remove an opponent of expansionist war aims is too simple; '"Auseinanderstrebendes Zusammenhalten"', 81.

[87] Stresemann to Admiral Foss, 14 July 1917 (Nl. 172).

[88] Stresemann to Bassermann, 14 July 1917 (Nl. 133).

[89] Zimmermann described Stresemann's behaviour as 'outrageous' and the Progressives' leader, Conrad Haußmann, referred to him as 'this political double-dealer': Matthias and Morsey (eds.), *Der Interfraktionelle Ausschuß*, i. 67; Reiß (ed.), *Von Bassermann zu Stresemann*, 338. Stresemann's party colleague Schiffer was also scandalized by the way Bethmann Hollweg had been brought down, writing in his diary at the time: 'I was overcome with disgust at this underground

There can be no doubt that Stresemann manoeuvred to create the broadest possible opposition to Bethmann Hollweg. There were, however, other motives besides opportunism for his cooperation with the parties of the peace resolution. The National Liberal Reichstag party was itself divided on the issue, with a sizeable minority in favour of starting negotiations, arguing, like Erzberger, that Germany's prospects were not going to improve. Party unity was preserved only by the device of passing a resolution of its own.[90] This was more optimistic than the resolution adopted by the other parties, but it declared that they were not driven by a 'lust for conquest' and expressed readiness for a peace 'which guarantees Germany's and its allies' existence and full development and which by compromise makes possible lasting reconciliation between the nations'.[91]

Stresemann's own view of what was possible followed the lead of the High Command. After his visit to headquarters, he told Bassermann of his complete agreement with Ludendorff's war aims: Courland, Lithuania, Longwy, Briey, 'and the military, political and economic subordination of Belgium', though he added that Austria-Hungary's desire for peace was a danger.[92] In the summer of 1917 Stresemann still hoped that Germany would be able to keep basically the territory it occupied, but he was more cautious than in the heady days of 1914 and was not expecting further conquests.[93]

The peace resolution of the majority parties, passed by the Reichstag on 19 July by 214 to 116 votes, also spoke of fighting if necessary until Germany's own and its allies' 'right to life and development is secured'. Stresemann was justified in claiming that the differences over war aims between the National Liberals and the majority parties were not as

---

plot which I had to witness and was unable to prevent.' Looking back in 1920, he again described the events as a 'disaster' and the conspiracy as one marked by 'deepest untruth and insincerity' because of the fundamental differences between Erzberger and his supporters on one side and 'Stresemann, the High Command and heavy industry' on the other. Diary transcripts, undated but July 1917, and 16 May 1920: BAK, Nl. Schiffer, 1, part 2, fo. 35; Nl. Schiffer, 5, pp. 1374–6.

[90] Stresemann's report to the Zentralvorstand, 23 Sept. 1917: Reiß (ed.), *Von Bassermann zu Stresemann*, 328–9. The minority included two of the party's representatives on the inter-party committee, Hartmann von Richthofen and Johannes Junck. The *Berliner Tageblatt* (no. 349, 11 July 1917) estimated that as many as fifteen National Liberals might support the peace resolution of the majority parties: Reiß, *Von Bassermann zu Stresemann*, 329.

[91] *Verhandlungen des Reichstags*, vol. 310, p. 3585.

[92] Stresemann to Bassermann, 19 June 1917 (Nl. 133).

[93] 'Gedanken zur Krisis': Stresemann, *Macht und Freiheit*, 78–9.

absolute as they might appear. The real difference was between those, mainly among the SPD and Progressives, who opposed annexations in principle, and those, like Stresemann and a majority of the National Liberals, but also including sections of the Centre Party and the Progressives, who had no objection in principle but in practice accepted that annexation had to be limited to what was realistic. Stresemann defended the tactic of cooperation with the inter-party committee as strengthening the moderate elements within the other parties against their more radical colleagues and the SPD.[94]

Stresemann's party and parliamentary tactics may well have been correct. He appeared to have achieved all his aims. Bethmann Hollweg had been overthrown, the Kaiser had agreed to constitutional reform, and despite the peace resolution the High Command was in effect able to conduct the war as it pleased. In fact, however, he had made several serious misjudgements. Bethmann Hollweg had probably exhausted his ability to defuse conflicts between left and right over war aims by July 1917 in any case, but Stresemann never fully recognized how important his achievements had been in maintaining peace on the home front.[95] Consumed by the desire to overthrow Bethmann Hollweg, Stresemann had overlooked his inability to control the Kaiser's choice of successor. In 1927 he defended himself to a parliamentary committee of investigation, saying that as the candidate to succeed Bethmann Hollweg, Bülow had not only his support but that of the Progressives and Erzberger and that there was no opposition to him from the High Command.[96] Stresemann had also got the brother of the empress, the duke of Schleswig-Holstein, to press Bülow's claims on the Kaiser. But Wilhelm had not forgiven Bülow for 'leaving him in the lurch' over the *Daily Telegraph* affair and would have none of him. The fact, as Stresemann pointed out, that no one had thought of Michaelis, who was completely inexperienced in foreign affairs, only showed how dependent the politicians who had staged the coup still were on the arbitrary power of the Kaiser.

[94] Stresemann's report to the Zentralvorstand, 23 Sept. 1917: Reiß (ed.), *Von Bassermann zu Stresemann*, 334–6.

[95] 'Gedanken zur Krisis': Stresemann, *Macht und Freiheit*, 69–72. On Bethmann Hollweg's position, see Konrad H. Jarausch, *The Enigmatic Chancellor: Bethmann Hollweg and the Hubris of Imperial Germany* (New Haven: Yale University Press, 1973), 349–80.

[96] Schücking and Bell (eds.), *Das Werk des Untersuchungsausschusses*, 304–5. Stresemann's version of these events is supported by the vivid account, based on conversations with many of those involved, in John W. Wheeler–Bennett, *Hindenburg: The Wooden Titan* (London: Macmillan, 1967; reissue of 1936 edn.), 101–9.

Even more important, Stresemann had been wrong in thinking that the High Command would not oppose constitutional reform.[97] In fact, it opposed both the reform of the Prussian franchise and the introduction of parliamentary government until defeat in October 1918, when it reversed its position so that the Reichstag would be burdened with the responsibility of negotiating the peace.

Stresemann had hoped in April 1917 that constitutional reform would reunite the nation and divert the growing demand for peace into a different channel. At that time the SPD was the only party in the Reichstag to demand peace without annexations, although the same view had supporters in other parties. Stresemann calculated that if all parties, including the SPD, were allowed into government confidence would be restored and the pressure for 'a Scheidemann peace' would be defused.[98] Again, when Erzberger led the Centre Party to join the SPD and the Progressives in proposing the peace resolution, events took a different course from the one Stresemann had anticipated. By continuing to support parliamentary government, he appeared to be propelling into power a Reichstag majority with whose views on the war he, as well as the High Command, disagreed.

To critics on the national executive, he admitted that he did not regard the new majority as a 'workable' one, nor did he recommend that the National Liberals join it.[99] He held out the hope, however, that it might be possible in the future to construct a new majority from the Conservatives to the Progressives, since he anticipated that the issue of post-war taxation would again isolate the Social Democrats from the bourgeois parties. He therefore warned against attacking the existing majority as unpatriotic, as the so-called German Patriotic Party (Deutsche Vaterlandspartei) launched by Admiral Tirpitz in July 1917 to rally opinion against the peace resolution, was doing. Instead Stresemann recommended the tactic of maintaining contact with the Reichstag majority in order to strengthen moderate opinion within it and with the aim of drawing back like-minded elements in the Centre Party and the Progressives to the side

[97] Stresemann to Bassermann, 10 Apr. 1917 (Nl. 133); Stresemann's memorandum, 'Zur Kanzlerkrise': Matthias and Morsey (eds.), *Der Interfraktionelle Ausschuß*, i. 75.

[98] Stresemann to Major Schmidthals, 21 Apr. 1917 (Nl. 170); Richter, '"Auseinanderstrebendes Zusammenhalten"', 81. Stresemann referred to Bassermann's idea of a coalition government of all the parties in 'Die Herbstkrisis', *Deutsche Stimmen*, 29/22, 25 Nov. 1917, repr. in Stresemann, *Macht und Freiheit*, 143-4.

[99] Stresemann's speech to the Zentralvorstand, 23 Sept. 1917: Reiß (ed.), *Von Bassermann zu Stresemann*, 347-8.

of the National Liberals. Given the situation that had developed in July 1917 this was a sensible tactic, but it was a much less favourable situation than Stresemann had hoped for in the spring when he had taken up the demand for constitutional reform.

Stresemann's failure to predict the future accurately was not surprising. The Kaiser's whimsical choice of chancellor could hardly have been foreseen, though his opposition to Bülow was well known. Ludendorff concealed his views on parliamentary government from others apart from Stresemann, and the Centre Party's sudden change of course under Erzberger caused a political sensation. Nevertheless, each of these meant that his fundamental aim of achieving a closer connection between Reichstag, government, and High Command was further from realization. Initially German victory in the east held the rival centres of authority in the Reichstag and the High Command together, but from the failure of the German offensive in the west in the summer of 1918 they drew apart and the polarization which Stresemann had tried to prevent became inescapable.

For Victory and Reform

When the parliamentary session resumed in September 1917 Stresemann was elected chairman of the Reichstag party. He had accepted, however, after Bassermann's death in July that it would be wise not to push his claims to the leadership of the national executive, given the opposition of the right wing. As a result a compromise was reached for Robert Friedberg, the leader of the party in the Prussian Landtag, to become chairman, with Stresemann as vice-chairman. Both elections followed by acclamation. Since Friedberg was 66 years old and Stresemann 39, it was clear that Stresemann was the heir presumptive.[100]

The meeting of the national executive showed, however, that Stresemann's support for reform was still contentious. He presented a lengthy report, stoutly defending the actions of the Reichstag party.[101] But despite earning 'stormy, sustained applause', the meeting passed a resolution which signalled the reservations felt by a majority of delegates.[102] There

---

[100] Reiß (ed.), *Von Bassermann zu Stresemann*, 32–3, 295–7; Richter, '"Auseinanderstrebendes Zusammenhalten"', 81–2.

[101] Minutes of the meeting, 23 Sept. 1917: Reiß (ed.), *Von Bassermann zu Stresemann*, 309–51.

[102] Ibid. 378–9, 423–9.

was common ground in condemning the Reichstag peace resolution and renewing the demand for expansion 'east, west and overseas'. The national executive also rejected the idea of 'taking over the parliamentary system'—which was in part a protest against President Wilson's refusal to accept that the government spoke for the people—but it then also rejected, by 52 votes to 50, an amendment to limit the rejection to a 'parliamentary system on a foreign model'. The resolution also spoke of preserving the federal character of the Reich, another implied criticism of the Reichstag party for endorsing reform of the Prussian franchise, and concluded by declaring that victory must have priority over reform. It was clear that though Stresemann's ability had given him an uncontested claim to the leadership, his policy was distrusted by a substantial section of the party.

Stresemann did not allow himself to be intimidated by the opposition. He continued to work with the Reichstag majority parties for reform while at the same time maintaining his commitment to victory. He led the party from the left on reform and from the right on war aims. This helped to keep the different wings together and it also reflected Stresemann's beliefs. The right wing of the National Liberals would rather have associated the party with the victory and no reform stand of Tirpitz's Patriotic Party, a policy which Stresemann predicted would simply bind the Reichstag majority parties closer together and leave the National Liberals out on a limb with the Conservatives.[103] The extreme left wing of the Reichstag party would rather have associated the party more fully with the Reichstag majority both on reform and war aims. Stresemann clung doggedly to what he saw as the middle way.

Stresemann's twin policies of victory and reform were helped by the success of German armies in the east and the Kaiser's promise of reform. The unity of the peace resolution parties was already weakened in September when the Centre and Progressives did not insist that the German reply to an attempt at mediation by the papacy should mention the restoration of Belgium.[104] Stresemann saw this as a vindication of his policy of seeking influence with the majority parties.[105]

---

[103] 'Die Herbstkrisis': Stresemann, *Macht und Freiheit*, 153–5. The ambiguity of the stance of the National Liberal Party under its new leader was satirized in a cartoon in the *Berliner Tageblatt*'s humorous supplement, *Ulk*, 40, 5 Oct. 1917; see Plate 19.

[104] Matthias and Morsey (eds.), *Der Interfraktionelle Ausschuß*, i. 119–209.

[105] Stresemann's report to the national executive, 23 Sept. 1917: Reiß (ed.), *Von Bassermann zu Stresemann*, 334–5.

Chancellor Michaelis made a tentative start on broadening the political basis of the government, appointing a Social Democrat to the War Food Office and a National Liberal, Eugen Schiffer, as under-secretary in the Reich Treasury.[106] Michaelis also met party leaders to discuss the government's reply to the papal peace note, the first example of formal consultation. However, Michaelis's lack of skill in handling the Reichstag quickly proved his undoing. In October he accused the Independent Social Democrats of endangering the state, following unrest in sections of the fleet. This provocation was made worse by the fact that the government did not have the evidence to bring a prosecution and the admiralty secretary, Capelle, referred in the Reichstag to the testimony of leaders of the demonstration who had already been executed and could not therefore be cross-examined. Both the Social Democratic parties erupted in fury and were supported by the Progressives, the Centre Party, and by Stresemann for the National Liberals.[107]

The majority parties and the National Liberals agreed to press for Michaelis's resignation.[108] When he proved resistant, they gave their views to the Kaiser's private secretary, Rudolf von Valentini. The parties were unable to agree on a candidate to succeed Michaelis, though Stresemann and Erzberger again favoured Bülow. There was agreement, however, that the Kaiser's nominee should meet the parties to discuss a programme before finally accepting the position. They also agreed on a programme, of which the most important points were acceptance of the principles of the German reply to the papal peace note and equal suffrage for Prussia.

The first objective was achieved when Michaelis resigned the chancellorship on 26 October. The Kaiser asked the elderly minister president of

---

[106] The appointment of Schiffer, which automatically under article 9 of the Reich constitution meant that he had to resign from the Reichstag, had the side effect of removing a possible rival to Stresemann for the leadership of the National Liberals, though in fact Schiffer had already spoilt his chances by identifying himself too closely with Bethmann Hollweg. Thieme, *Nationaler Liberalismus*, 102–3; typescript of Schiffer diary extracts: BAK, Nl. Schiffer, 2, part 1, p. 211. Stresemann wrote to Schiffer congratulating him on his appointment and suggesting that he should seek re-election to the Reichstag, saying that the constitutional change required should be made. At the same time he put out a feeler for Schiffer's support for the leadership of the party, expressing the hope that they would work together in the situation created by Bassermann's death where mistrust about the direction of the party required 'a very skilful policy'. Stresemann to Schiffer, 9 Aug. 1917 (Nl. Schiffer, 12).

[107] *Verhandlungen des Reichstags*, vol. 310, pp. 3794–5.

[108] Matthias and Morsey (eds.), *Der Interfraktionelle Ausschuß*, i. 213–599; Stresemann's memorandum, 11 Nov. 1917, ibid. 569–84; 'Die Herbstkrisis', Stresemann, *Macht und Freiheit*, 130–55.

Bavaria, Count Hertling, to take over as chancellor but proposed to keep Michaelis as minister president of Prussia. This idea was naturally opposed by the Reichstag majority and after Hertling withdrew from the nomination, the inter-party committee discussed possible alternatives. From these discussions emerged the plan of giving the future chancellor, who was expected to be a south German, a Prussian deputy both as chancellor and minister president of Prussia. Further, at Stresemann's suggestion it was decided to approach Friedberg, as the leader of the National Liberals in the Prussian Landtag and someone who accepted that an equal franchise could no longer be postponed, to take on the post. Stresemann calculated that by in effect leading the Prussian government, Friedberg would be responsible for introducing the equal suffrage bill and this would swing a sufficient number of National Liberals behind the measure to give it a narrow majority.[109] Tortuous negotiations followed until Friedberg was finally persuaded and Hertling, who had once again allowed himself to be nominated for the chancellorship, accepted him as his deputy in Prussia, while the Progressive leader, Friedrich von Payer, became his deputy as chancellor.

The change of government in October 1917 brought the Reichstag majority parties and the National Liberals closer together. They had forced the resignation of Michaelis, and with the appointments of Friedberg and Payer they could expect the new government to work with them. However, content to have placed some of their nominees in power, the inter-party committee did not press Hertling on the crucial next stage—to allow ministers to remain members of the Reichstag. Instead attention focused on the battle for the Prussian franchise.

Stresemann was determined see franchise reform enacted, regardless of the opposition of the right wing. He opposed Friedberg's desire to resign as party chairman in view of his government post, saying that would mean the ruin of their recent policy.[110] Despite Friedberg's position in the Prussian government, a majority of National Liberals in the Landtag remained opposed to the equal franchise bill.[111] To bring pressure to bear on them special meetings of the national executive and of the Prussian party were held, both of which produced majorities for equal franchise. Stresemann warned that if the reform were not passed during the

---

[109] Records of the inter-party committee meeting, 30 Oct. 1917: Matthias and Morsey (eds.), *Der Interfraktionelle Ausschuß*, i. 368–9, 372–3.
[110] Minutes of the meeting of the Geschäftsführender Ausschuß, 18 Jan. 1918 (BAK, R 45 I/5).
[111] Thieme, *Nationaler Liberalismus*, 108–21.

war, the demand for it after the war would be like an 'avalanche'.[112]
Thousands of soldiers wearing the iron cross would demonstrate and
they could not be put down by the police. If they opposed the measure,
the National Liberals would be swept away and a radical majority would
be confirmed in power for years to come. In a speech to the Reichstag, he
had already referred to the Prussian franchise as so contrary to a natural
sense of justice that it should have been dropped long ago.[113] These
efforts were enough to produce a majority in favour among the National
Liberals in the Landtag, but not an overall majority, and the measure
languished until October 1918 when it was again revived but then overtaken by the revolution.

Though he cooperated with the Reichstag majority parties over the
Prussian franchise, Stresemann was soon again standing apart over war
aims. The issue became immediate in November 1917 when, after their
coup d'état, the Bolsheviks declared their readiness for peace without
annexations or indemnities on the basis of self-determination. The division between the Reichstag majority, which wanted the principle of
self-determination observed to a greater or lesser extent, and the High
Command and Conservatives, who wanted to annex the vast territories
occupied by German armies soon became apparent. The government, in
the persons of Chancellor Hertling and the state secretary at the Auswärtiges Amt, Richard von Kühlmann, were caught in the middle and
followed a policy of concessions to the military while trying to appease
the Reichstag with soothing words. The majority parties were not anxious
to undermine a government they had so recently helped into power and
were reluctantly forced to accept a series of faits accomplis. Stresemann,
however, adopted the arguments of the High Command and withdrew
from the inter-party committee.

Stresemann's views on war aims in the east were not as consistent as his
hopes for the west. The priority for him lay in the west—control over
Belgium to open the way for German seapower. In the east, he had hoped
from the beginning of the war that it would be possible to detach the
Baltic provinces with their German minorities from the Russian empire,
but he would have welcomed a separate peace with Russia which enabled
Germany to concentrate on the west. Until the summer of 1917, he
thought that if Russia would surrender the Baltic province of Courland,

[112] 'Politische Umschau', *Deutsche Stimmen*, 30/17, 28 Apr. 1918.
[113] Reichstag speech, 27 Feb. 1918; repr. in Stresemann, *Macht und Freiheit*, 175–202, here
p. 194.

which Germany had occupied in 1915, a separate peace should be concluded. Stresemann was critical of those who advocated the reverse strategy—the SPD, the Progressives and, he suspected, Bethmann Hollweg—seeing them as motivated by a preference for the democracies. Despite his own preference for parliamentary government, Stresemann did not allow this to affect his view that the conflict with Britain for control of the seas was the fundamental war aim. In January 1916 he even wrote approvingly of the 'strong monarchy' of Russia. In an unusual anti-Semitic comment, he added that the eastern strategy was supported by influential Progressive newspapers such as the *Berliner Tageblatt* and the *Frankfurter Zeitung* because they were in Jewish hands and for them Russian anti-Semitism was the decisive consideration. He wrote that such circles had for decades shown an 'ape-like' attraction towards France and Britain.[114]

While he realized that it might not be possible to defeat Britain, Stresemann wanted to keep control of Belgium in preparation for a future war. He considered ways of offsetting the loss of overseas markets by a 'Continental Reich, in which we are economically dominant, an economic territory that, summarized in a slogan, could reach from Antwerp to Baghdad'.[115] However, he admitted that this was more a direction for the future than a real possibility for the present.[116] Even the first step in such a scheme, an economic association with Austria-Hungary, offered only marginal advantage since Germany already supplied a high proportion of

[114] 'Die militärische und politische Lage des Deutschen Reiches', with the date 'beginning of 1916' added in a different hand (Nl. 159). (There are many examples of handwritten additions of this kind in Stresemann's papers. There is no reason in general to doubt their accuracy, but they may have been added much later when Stresemann's private secretary Henry Bernhard was ordering the papers.)

Another example of Stresemann's vulnerability to the rising tide of anti-Semitism during the war was his support in October 1916 for a 'Jewish census', a survey of the people involved in the wartime procurement agencies which would include their religious denomination. He defended this proposal (which came from Erzberger) as a way of countering the criticism that the agencies were in the hands of a Jewish clique, but by accepting that there was a case to answer, the proposal appeared to endorse the anti-Semitic campaign. Wright, 'Liberalism and anti-Semitism in Germany', 106–8.

[115] Stresemann's report, printed in the 'Vertraulicher Bericht über die Sitzung des vom Vorstande des Bundes der Industriellen eingesetzten Sonderausschusses zur Beratung der durch den Krieg geschaffenen handels- und wirtschaftspolitischen Lage' (Berlin, 9 Jan. 1915), 53–4 (Nl. 150).

[116] Record of the discussion, ibid. Stresemann's ideas developed in a similar way to those of Friedrich Naumann, who in Oct. 1915 first published his best-selling pamphlet *Mitteleuropa*, but Stresemann saw that central Europe could not readily provide a substitute for Germany's overseas trade. Heuss, *Naumann*, 361–79; Theiner, *Sozialer Liberalismus*, 240–8.

Austro-Hungarian imports.[117] Once, by the end of 1915, the route to Turkey was open, Stresemann looked forward to carrying the war against Britain to the Suez canal and Egypt—in Bismarck's words the 'neck' of the British empire.[118] Stresemann saw the possibility of a closer economic association with Austria-Hungary and south-eastern Europe as important faute de mieux, but not as a real substitute for overseas markets.[119] The Continental strategy remained secondary to the ultimate goal of defeating Britain.

For the same reason, Stresemann thought it had been a mistake for the German and Austro-Hungarian governments to offer Russian Poland, which they had occupied in 1915, independence from Russia in November 1916. This decision destroyed any hope of a separate peace with Russia and also had worrying implications for Germany's own Polish provinces. The National Liberal Reichstag party wrote formally to Bethmann Hollweg opposing the decision, and Stresemann roundly condemned it at the meeting of the national executive in September 1917. He pointed out that the hope of raising a Polish army to fight with the Germans had proved illusory, and he warned that the Poles might indeed fight with Germany's enemies in a future war.[120]

When, however, the Russian armies collapsed and the Bolsheviks offered peace in November 1917, Stresemann's position changed completely. He now joined the High Command in demanding German control of large parts of the former Russian empire to secure Germany's position in the east for the final offensive in the west. He wrote immediately to Kühlmann, saying that Germany should take control not only of Courland but also Livonia and Estonia.[121] Having offered the Poles independence it would, he said, be an insult to German national feeling to leave the Baltic Germans under Russian rule. Although a minority, they were the leading intellectual and economic group and had made the Baltic a 'land of German culture'. He warned against making the Baltic provinces independent, both because the German communities would be swamped by the ethnic majorities and because it would create another

---

[117] Stresemann's report, 55–62 (Nl. 150).

[118] Stresemann, on behalf of the Association of Saxon Industrialists, to the Saxon minister of internal and foreign affairs Graf Vitzthum von Eckstädt, 9 Sept. 1915 (Nl. 152).

[119] Speech to a meeting of the German–Austro-Hungarian Economic Association (Deutsch-Österreichisch-Ungarischer Wirtschaftsverband), 28–9 Nov. 1915 (Nl. 151).

[120] Minutes of the meeting of the national executive, 23 Sept. 1917: Reiß (ed.), *Von Bassermann zu Stresemann*, 331–2.

[121] Stresemann to Kühlmann, 14 Nov. 1917 (Nl. 178): Harttung (ed.), *Schriften*, 173–5.

region of instability like the Balkans, and one where Britain might establish a naval presence.

Given his views it was not suprising that Stresemann was soon in conflict with the majority parties. They wanted to see the principle of self-determination upheld to demonstrate their good faith to the Western powers in preparation for a future peace settlement. Stresemann, on the other hand, was still working for victory. He saw his task as to create a new Reichstag majority by winning over the Centre Party and the Progressives to support whatever the High Command deemed necessary. He was also carried along by a revival of popular enthusiasm among the National Liberal Party in the country.

Stresemann was given confidential information by Kühlmann and the High Command about the German peace terms.[122] He immediately took an independent line at the meetings of the inter-party committee. He warned that if plebiscites were held in the east the Western powers would demand the same for Alsace-Lorraine. He also argued that since the new Polish state might be the cause of a future war, Germany should take military control of Lithuania.[123] The break came on 4 January when the majority parties decided to demand a meeting with Hertling to express their dissatisfaction with the position taken by the German negotiators at the Brest-Litovsk peace talks. Stresemann refused to join them, declaring that the appearance of a lack of confidence in the government had to be avoided at all costs.[124] The Reichstag party issued a statement expressing its agreement with the party in the country that the views of the High Command should be decisive in determining future frontiers.[125]

Stresemann's tactics were to encourage a split among the majority parties. When mass strikes broke out in Berlin at the end of January 1918 and the SPD leaders joined the strike committee, he saw his chance. He did not respond to an invitation to the inter-party committee and recommended to his Reichstag colleagues that the party should stay away, since the SPD had failed to condemn the strike despite the harm it would have caused to their brothers at the front.[126] This was less than fair to the SPD leaders, whose motive had been to mediate between the strikers and the government. It seems clear that Stresemann was simply looking for a

---

[122] Matthias and Morsey (eds.), *Der Interfraktionelle Ausschuß*, i. 638–9.

[123] Minutes of the meetings of 20 Dec. 1917, 2 Jan. 1918: ibid., i. 632, ii. 57–8.

[124] Minutes of the meeting, 4 Jan. 1918: ibid. ii. 67–8.

[125] Statement dated 8 Jan. 1918: ibid. ii. 68.

[126] Stresemann to Junck and to the Reichstagsfraktion, 4 Feb. 1918: ibid. ii. 188–91.

pretext to drive a wedge between the majority parties. He told his contact in the Progressive People's Party, Otto Fischbeck, that the National Liberals would be happy to meet the other bourgeois parties.[127] At the same time, Stresemann did not push the Reichstag party, which was divided on the issue, into a final break with the inter-party committee. His preference was in any case to subvert it from within, not to be isolated on the outside.

The cooperation of the SPD with the Centre Party and the Progressives was put under severe strain both by the strikes and by the peace settlement in the east. That it survived was largely due to the tolerance extended by the SPD to their bourgeois partners in order to maintain cooperation in the future.[128] All the majority parties, including the SPD, welcomed the separate peace with the Ukraine which ensured supplies of food for Germany and her allies. The Centre Party and the Progressives also voted for the treaty of Brest-Litovsk, which provided for Russian evacuation of Finland, Livonia, and Estonia, recognition of the independence of the Ukraine, and cession of territory to Germany's ally Turkey in the Caucasus. These terms could, it is true, be regarded as giving independence to subject nationalities, but that was to overlook the determination of the German authorities to retain control. Erzberger, speaking for the Centre Party, put the best interpretation on events, declaring that the treaty was completely consistent with the peace resolution of July 1917 provided that the principle of self-determination was put into practice.[129] The SPD was more critical and abstained.

Stresemann did not think that the treaty went far enough, since he objected to even the limited independence which the government foresaw for Livonia and Estonia.[130] However, he was gratified by the support of the Centre Party and the Progressives for the treaty. He claimed that the National Liberals had succeeded in bringing all the bourgeois parties to vote for a treaty which contradicted the peace resolution and he ridiculed Erzberger's claim that the two were consistent.[131]

Despite the differences among its members, the inter-party committee remained in being. At the end of March, Stresemann accepted the fact and

---

[127] Stresemann to Fischbeck, 11 Feb. 1918: Matthias and Morsey (eds.), *Der Interfraktionelle Ausschuß*, ii. 222–3.

[128] Susanne Miller, *Burgfrieden und Klassenkampf. Die deutsche Sozialdemokratie im Ersten Weltkrieg* (Düsseldorf: Droste, 1974), 364–5.

[129] Epstein, *Erzberger*, 232–6.

[130] Reichstag speech, 19 Mar. 1918: *Verhandlungen des Reichstags*, vol. 311, pp. 4457–9.

[131] Speech to the national executive, 10 Mar. 1918: *NLC* 45/53, 10 Mar. 1918; 'Politische Umschau', *Deutsche Stimmen*, 30/15, 14 Apr. 1918.

made a tentative approach for the National Liberals to rejoin the committee for the discussion of domestic politics.[132] The suggestion was naturally received with some caution. Erzberger pointed out that it was 'somewhat odd' coming from Stresemann, who had not only tried to break up the majority but had boasted of doing so.[133] Nevertheless he saw some advantage in adding the National Liberals to their number, since even a military dictatorship would not be possible against all four parties. Members of the committee were also interested in making the National Liberals share responsibility for what were bound to be unpopular taxes to pay for the war. However, in view of the National Liberal stand on war aims and Stresemann's position 'in the front rank of the annexationists', it was agreed to consult them only over taxation.[134]

Defeat and Rejection

The collapse of the Russian front temporarily increased Stresemann's authority, appearing to confirm his judgement that the war could be won. The majority parties were thrown on to the defensive and Stresemann rubbed home their embarrassment. However, the situation was quickly reversed by the failure of the German offensive in the west which was clear by the summer. The prospect of victory melted away and those whom he had made uncomfortable were able to settle the score.

Stresemann adjusted gradually to the new situation.[135] In the spring, he hoped that Germany would soon be in a position to impose a peace settlement in the west. Commenting on the SPD's abstention on Brest-Litovsk, he said Germans found it difficult to free themselves from dogma but added hopefully, 'The great *realpolitiker* war in the end tears apart the cords in which theoretical wisdom is tied up.'[136] In April he wrote that he was thankful to have witnessed the great events in the west, and compared Hindenburg to the legendary figures of Siegfried and Roland. He said it was laughable to imagine that the German working class would oppose

---

[132] Stresemann to Fischbeck, 27 Mar. 1918: Matthias and Morsey (eds.), *Der Interfraktionelle Ausschuß*, ii. 345–6.

[133] Minutes of the meeting of the inter-party committee, 22 Apr. 1918: ibid. 362–3.

[134] Ibid. 363–6. The remark about Stresemann came from an SPD member, Eduard David.

[135] Baechler, *Stresemann*, 167–70.

[136] 'Wochenschau', *Deutsche Stimmen*, 30/13, 31 Mar. 1918.

taking over the French iron ore fields, setting up an independent Flanders or imposing an indemnity to reduce the burden of paying for the war.[137]

When, at the end of June, Kühlmann told the Reichstag that peace could not be secured by military decisions alone, Stresemann joined the Conservatives and Centre Party in angry protest. He criticized Kühlmann for his 'depressing and shattering' statement and, borrowing a phrase from Lloyd George, reaffirmed his faith in 'Ludendorff's hammer'. However, Stresemann went on to say that the National Liberals would support peace once the political and military leadership thought that the necessary guarantees had been achieved, without binding himself to particular war aims.[138] This slight concession probably reflected his awareness that, despite the initially rapid German advance, it had not achieved its objectives.

While the outcome in the west still hung in the balance, Stresemann became involved in discussions over the economic clauses of the peace settlement with Russia which had been left unsettled by the main treaty.[139] Through a business associate, a naturalized German of Russian birth, Paul Litwin, he met the Soviet representatives, Adolf Joffe and Leonid Krassin. They were anxious to regain control of the vast areas occupied by German troops beyond the limits set by the treaty of Brest-Litovsk. They held out the prospect that the economic resources, which this further advance had been intended to secure, would be better protected by agreement with the Soviet government and that Soviet forces would then be able to drive the Allied army of intervention out of northern Russia.

Stresemann was convinced by these conversations that Germany should reach a settlement with the Bolsheviks rather than, as Ludendorff wanted, continue the German advance and restore a constitutional monarchy. In a letter to Colonel Bauer, Stresemann pointed out that the Soviet government was willing to recognize effective German control of Livonia and Estonia and the independence of Georgia and pay an indemnity of 6 billion marks. He argued that Germany would not get such good terms from the monarchists, who were more likely to revive Russia's alliance with the Western powers. Given the mounting strength of the enemy in

---

[137] 'Politische Umschau', *Deutsche Stimmen*, 30/15, 14 Apr. 1918.

[138] Reichstag speech, 25 June 1918: *Verhandlungen des Reichstags*, vol. 313, pp. 5648–60. Stresemann received a message of congratulations on his speech from Ludendorff (diary entry, 29 June; Nl. 201) and Kühlmann was forced to resign on 9 July by the High Command.

[139] Hans W. Gatzke, 'Zu den deutsch-russischen Beziehungen im Sommer 1918', *Vierteljahrshefte für Zeitgeschichte*, 3 (1955), 67–98; Winfried Baumgart, *Deutsche Ostpolitik 1918. Von Brest-Litowsk bis zum Ende des Ersten Weltkrieges* (Munich: Oldenbourg, 1966), 283–4, 287–8.

the west and the importance of demonstrating that Germany could not be defeated by economic means, Stresemann urged acceptance of Soviet terms.[140] The rapid deterioration in Germany's military position in any case forced Ludendorff to change policy, and the supplementary treaties with Russia were signed on 27 August.

Stresemann, of course, had no sympathy for the Bolsheviks. He said that negotiating with them was like being seen with a prostitute on Unter den Linden, but he was quick to appreciate the importance of their break with the Western powers.[141] As Germany's position deteriorated in the west, he was tempted to look east for compensation. On 6 September he wrote to a friend 'Perhaps in future Germany will turn rather more to the east and we will find there some substitute for what we will not be able to obtain for the time being in competition overseas.'[142] It was the admission that the western priority he had advocated for so long would have to be given up, while he still hoped to retain Germany's quasi-empire in the east.

The realization of the scale of Germany's defeat was a slow process for Stresemann, as it was for most Germans after four years with their armies deep in enemy territory and in 1918 occupying an area far larger than Germany itself. Stresemann knew from the second half of June that the situation was difficult, but it was only in August that it became common knowledge that the war in the west could no longer be won.[143] On 21 August the new state secretary at the Auswärtiges Amt, Paul von Hintze, told party leaders that Germany needed to get peace negotiations started.[144] On the same day, Stresemann wrote an article admitting that the submarine war had not achieved its objectives: neither preventing the United States landing a million men in France nor crippling the British economy.[145] However, it was still generally believed that while Germany could no longer win in the west, she could hold out for a long time and therefore had considerable bargaining power for peace negotiations. Stresemann thought that the economic agreements with the Soviet Union

[140] Stresemann to Bauer, 8 Aug. 1918: Gatzke, 'Zu den deutsch-russischen Beziehungen', 92–4.
[141] Ibid.
[142] Stresemann to Stollwerck, 6 Sept. 1918: ibid. 77; Baumgart, *Deutsche Ostpolitik 1918*, 146–7.
[143] Stresemann's report to the post-war parliamentary committee of investigation: Schücking and Bell (eds.), *Die Ursachen des Deutschen Zusammenbruches*, 306.
[144] Memorandum by Stresemann, 26 Aug. 1918: Matthias and Morsey (eds.), *Der Interfraktionelle Ausschuß*, ii. 473–4.
[145] 'Politische Umschau', 21 Aug. 1918; *Deutsche Stimmen*, 30/34, 25 Aug. 1918.

would enable them to survive the blockade and that a defensive war in the west, falling back on the Meuse and then the Rhine, could prolong the war for months.[146]

It was obviously in Germany's interest to get peace negotiations started before the military situation grew worse. Stresemann now canvassed the idea of forming a new government to conclude peace in the autumn. Hintze, who was clearer about the gravity of the situation than Hertling, had complained about the ageing chancellor's failing powers to Stresemann. Stresemann, who also thought that Hertling was no longer equal to the task, suggested to Erzberger and others that Hintze should take over as chancellor with representatives of the Conservatives, the National Liberals, and the Centre Party, and he declared his readiness to join such a government.[147] Although he did not expressly mention the Progressives, he probably assumed that they would continue to be represented by the vice-chancellor, Payer. In a letter to a party colleague at the same time he also expressed his willingness to participate in a 'united front', in other words including the SPD, provided it was truly representative of the whole nation.[148]

The reaction of the inter-party committee to this suggestion showed how the political situation had been transformed since the spring. Over Brest-Litovsk, the Centre Party and the Progressives had danced to Stresemann's tune. As late as the end of August 1918, they confirmed that policy by approving the supplementary treaties with the Soviet government against the opposition of the Social Democrats.[149] But from the second half of August, as the military situation deteriorated, they no longer feared Stresemann and the National Liberals. Stresemann's conversion to the need for peace in the west was greeted with contempt by his old adversaries on the inter-party committee. Erzberger described him as a 'tree frog', who showed only which way the wind was blowing.[150] When, in the middle of September, the National Liberals enquired whether they could return to the inter-party committee, Scheidemann described Stresemann as a 'political bankrupt' trying to join a going concern.[151] The

---

[146] Schücking and Bell (eds.), *Die Ursachen des deutschen Zusammenbruches*, 306.

[147] Memorandum by Erzberger, 29 Aug. 1918: Matthias and Morsey (eds.), *Der Interfraktionelle Ausschuß*, ii. 521.

[148] Stresemann to Erwin Gugelmeier, 26 Aug. 1918: ibid. 473–6.

[149] Baumgart, *Deutsche Ostpolitik 1918*, 293–5.

[150] Minutes of the meeting of the inter-party committee, 12 Sept. 1918: Matthias and Morsey (eds.), *Der Interfraktionelle Ausschuß*, ii. 520.

[151] Memorandum by Erzberger about the meeting, 16 Sept. 1918: ibid. 611.

committee decided to demand from the National Liberals public accept-ance of the peace resolution of July 1917 before the question of their return could be considered, in effect a demand that Stresemann should accept public humiliation which was bound to be rejected.[152]

Stresemann defended himself at a meeting of the Reichstag's main com-mittee. He admitted that the National Liberals had changed their position but argued boldly that they deserved recognition for carrying out a difficult 'political retreat' rather than 'scorn and derision'.[153] He pointed out that other parties had also changed their position during the war. He seemed unable or unwilling to understand, however, the hostility that he had aroused by his deliberately disruptive tactics towards the inter-party com-mittee, or the way this now endangered his political career. Stresemann's left-wing party colleague Hartmann von Richthofen, who was close to Erzberger, wrote privately that Stresemann's person would be the biggest obstacle to the National Liberals being allowed back, and that many of his party colleagues 'would have to become a Paul from being a Saul'.[154]

The attitude of the inter-party committee was not simply governed by spite. It decided to press for peace and a full parliamentary system of government under a new chancellor.[155] In view of the consistent stand he had taken against the peace resolution, Stresemann was understandably regarded as unacceptable. It was also essential that the SPD should join the new government if revolution was to be averted, and it was unani-mously opposed to Stresemann. Equally important was the damage which Stresemann's reputation as an arch-annexationist would do abroad, since the committee hoped to appeal to President Wilson with a programme in line with the principles of the 'Fourteen Points' which he had set out as the basis for peace in January 1918.

Some right-wing members of the committee nevertheless spoke strongly in favour of including the National Liberals to broaden the base of the new government. The committee therefore decided that the National Liberal members of Hertling's government could remain in office, but no further National Liberals should be appointed, and they

[152] Account of the meeting of 16 Sept. 1918 by the SPD member Albert Südekum: Matthias and Morsey (eds.), *Der Interfraktionelle Ausschuß*, ii. 607.

[153] Minutes of the meeting, 25 Sept. 1918: Schiffers and Koch (eds.), *Der Hauptausschuß*, iv. 2311–12.

[154] Richthofen to Schiffer, 14 Sept. 1918: Matthias and Morsey, (eds.), *Der Interfraktionelle Ausschuß*, ii. 588–91.

[155] Minutes of the meeting, 30 Sept. 1918: ibid. 751–69.

should be given no opportunity to influence the programme of the committee but simply be presented with it to accept or reject.

On 2 October the party leaders were told that the High Command insisted that Germany ask for an immediate armistice, destroying any prospect of negotiating with the threat of a protracted defensive war. Stresemann was shattered, admitting that the news fell like a blow from a club.[156] That afternoon he received a second shock. Prince Max von Baden, who succeeded Hertling as chancellor and accepted the programme of the majority parties, told Stresemann that he 'needed him and his party in opposition, not in the government'.[157] Stresemann was mortified. He had assumed that the National Liberals would be wanted as usual to bolster the government against opposition from the right, and he had expected to be offered a ministerial post himself. The opportunity for which he had waited when ministers would retain their seats in the Reichstag in a full parliamentary system had arrived. But by his reckless commitment to German victory, he had disqualified himself. The double blow of defeat and exclusion from office seemed to mark the end of his political career.

---

[156] 'Politische Umschau', *Deutsche Stimmen*, 30/44, 3 Nov. 1918.

[157] Prinz Max von Baden, *Erinnerungen und Dokumente* (Stuttgart: Deutsche Verlags-Anstalt, 1927), 343; Eng. edn. (London: Constable, 1928), ii. 12.

4

'We are and remain independent towards the right and the left'

Accommodation and Opposition, October 1918–June 1920

The central challenge to a biographer of Stresemann is to interpret his development from wartime annexationist to the European statesman of 1925–9. The years between the end of the war and his appointment as Reich chancellor in 1923 provide the link. Historians have been divided between those who argue that his aims and outlook changed fundamentally and those who see an essential continuity of aim behind a skilful change of tactics. The period between defeat and the elections of June 1920 which saw Stresemann's new party become once again a significant political force marked the first phase of a painful process of adjustment.

Lessons of Defeat: October 1918

Any explanation must start with the defeat of 1918. Stresemann was bitter at the collapse of the High Command, on whose judgement he had relied, but he adjusted quickly. Refusing to accept the opposition role which Prince Max had assigned to him, the National Liberals accepted the programme of the majority parties on 3 October and offered the government their full support.[1] The programme represented the end of Stresemann's hopes—reaffirming the peace resolution, promising to restore the independence of Belgium, offering to renegotiate the eastern treaties and promising autonomy to Alsace-Lorraine. He admitted as much, but wrote that there was no alternative once the High Command had decided that an armistice was necessary.[2] In his diary he noted beside Prince Max's offer of peace: 'Feeling: finis germaniae.'[3]

Stresemann knew that the moment might already have passed when Germany would be offered peace on these terms. Acting on information from Colonel Bauer that Ludendorff had suffered a nervous collapse, he pressed the government to consult other military commanders before agreeing to evacuate the occupied territories.[4] He hoped that if the terms offered to Germany were unacceptable, it might still be possible to continue the war for a time to secure an improvement. However, he did not oppose the government's decision on 10 October to accept the Fourteen Points and evacuate the occupied territories as he was told this had general support among the military. The government was glad after all not to face opposition from the National Liberals, and the party was welcomed back into the inter-party committee on 12 October.[5]

Ironically, by 16 October Ludendorff recovered his nerve and wanted to fight on, though he resigned a few days later. Stresemann thought that the right policy was to defer a decision on renewing the war until the armistice terms were known. He wrote to Friedberg, who had remained vice-president of Prussia in the new government, saying that Ludendorff's resignation was probably for the best given his nervous exhaustion.[6] But he warned that the National Liberals would not accept the dismissal of Hindenburg—even the abdication of the Kaiser would be preferable. He expressed his suspicion of Wilson who would, he predicted, try to draw Germany from concession to concession until it was defenceless. Even the Fourteen Points might mean the loss of Alsace-Lorraine (with its iron ore),

---

[1] Stresemann to Fischbeck, 4 Oct. 1918: Erich Matthias and Rudolf Morsey (eds.), *Die Regierung des Prinzen Max von Baden* (Düsseldorf: Droste, 1962), 69–70.

[2] 'Politische Umschau', *Deutsche Stimmen*, 30/41, 13 Oct. 1918, and 30/44, 3 Nov. 1918; repr. in Gustav Stresemann, *Von der Revolution*, 15–17, 24.

[3] Diary entry, 5 Oct. 1918 (Nl. 362).

[4] Stresemann to Wilhelm von Radowitz, under-secretary of state in the Reich Chancellery, 10 Oct. 1918: Matthias and Morsey (eds.), *Max von Baden*, 123–4.

[5] Minutes of the cabinet meeting, 11 Oct. 1918, and of the inter-party committee, 12 Oct. 1918: ibid. 133–4, 148.

[6] Stresemann to Friedberg, 26 Oct. 1918: ibid. 382–4.

of Prussia's Polish provinces (with the Upper Silesian coalfield), and a huge indemnity—terms which would 'cripple us for the next century'. If the Western powers refused to give a commitment to even that programme, Germany might be reduced to total impotence and broken up into separate states again. Only a complete collapse could justify accepting such a result—it would be cowardice to do so while German armies were still in France and Belgium. The government should insist on a commitment from the Allies not to go beyond the Fourteen Points in return for an armistice.

Stresemann's concern that Germany was delivering itself up to an uncertain future at the hands of the Allies was well founded. His belief that the war could be continued, however, was unrealistic. The superiority of the Western powers and the desire of the troops for an end to the war made acceptance of the armistice inevitable. The outbreak of revolution on 9 November finally put paid to the idea of prolonging resistance.

Stresemann's overriding motive in October was to save what could still be saved. He supported the entry of the SPD into Prince Max's government and praised them publicly for their willingness to accept responsibility despite the opposition of the Independent Social Democrats (USPD) on their left.[7] On the other hand, he spoke out strongly in favour of keeping the institution of the emperor as a symbol of German unity, as the SPD moved towards demanding the Kaiser's abdication.[8] Again the revolution ended Stresemann's hopes that Prince Max's parliamentary government could ensure continuity and save Germany from 'the chaos of Bolshevism'.[9]

Stresemann's attempts in October 1918 to prevent matters getting worse are not evidence of a change of heart, though he did have to make some adjustment. He admitted to moments of doubt as to whether he had completely misjudged matters, but in public he remained defiant.[10] He did not apologize, saying that if it had been a crime to believe in German

---

[7] 'Politische Umschau', *Deutsche Stimmen*, 30/41, 13 Oct. 1918: *Von der Revolution*, 11.

[8] Minutes of the meetings of the inter-party committee, 4 and 5 Nov. 1918; statement by the National Liberal Reichstag party, 8 Nov. 1918: Matthias and Morsey (eds.), *Max von Baden*, 501, 520–1.

[9] 'Politische Umschau', 6 Nov. 1918, *Deutsche Stimmen*, 30/45, 10 Nov. 1918: *Von der Revolution*, 38.

[10] He referred to such doubts in the first meeting of the Zentralvorstand on 12 Apr. 1919; Eberhard Kolb and Ludwig Richter (eds.), *Nationalliberalismus in der Weimarer Republik. Die Führungsgremien der Deutschen Volkspartei 1918–1933*, 2 vols. (Düsseldorf: Droste, 1999), 81. On 16 Sept. 1918 he had written to his old friend Gustav Slesina, 'Who can say whether I have always found the right way? But in the end what matters for us is the saying: He who strives to achieve, we can save' (a quotation from Goethe's *Faust*); Görlitz, *Stresemann*, 86.

victory, he shared that crime with millions of the best and men of all parties.[11] He also defended Hindenburg and Ludendorff, saying that their achievements would be remembered long after their critics had been forgotten.[12] At the same time he did not adopt the convenient tactic of blaming strikes or the SPD for defeat. He defended Prince Max's government against such allegations, which in the hands of Ludendorff and others were to become the myth of the 'stab in the back'. Stresemann acknowledged in print in October 1918 that it 'was not the democratic and socialist elements of the new government, but the High Command' who had been 'at the head of the efforts to stop the war'.[13]

The most vivid picture of Stresemann's disillusionment with the old regime comes from a speech he made to a meeting of the leaders of the provincial organizations of the National Liberal Party on 13 October, recorded only in the notes of one of those present.[14] He said the decision to ask for the armistice had been forced on the parties by the 'total collapse' of the High Command. He blamed them further for failing to recognize the power of the enemy and the importance of technical innovation, especially tanks, and for their failures in arms procurement. The most incompetent had been the admiralty, which had commissioned fewer submarines than industry could deliver. Capelle had been a total failure, declaring that American intervention would have no effect and that all its troop transports would be sunk: in fact not one had been. Stresemann went on to condemn the Kaiser's zigzag course and his political interference before the war and the behaviour of the whole imperial family. The Crown Prince, he alleged, had had generals moved to other positions because they refused to greet his mistresses. Now the Kaiser was on his knees, praying. Only the Kaiser, he added, could have brought off an alliance against Germany of Britain and Russia—'these natural opponents'—together with France. The only people for whom Stresemann had a good word were the government of Prince Max and the SPD, whose attitude he described as 'exemplary', praising in particular Friedrich Ebert. Stresemann's conclusion was that 'the old system was utterly bankrupt, could no longer be saved and also did not deserve to survive longer'.

Stresemann's purpose was to convince the delegates from the provinces that the Reichstag party was right to support Prince Max's government

[11] 'Politische Umschau', *Deutsche Stimmen*, 30/41, 13 Oct. 1918: *Von der Revolution*, 17.
[12] 'Politische Umschau', *Deutsche Stimmen*, 30/44, 3 Nov. 1918: ibid. 28–9.
[13] *Von der Revolution*, 25.
[14] Matthias and Morsey (eds.), *Max von Baden*, 178–80.

but, even so, these were strong words. They reflected a further stage in his rejection of the Wilhelmine system. During the war he had admired the diplomacy and political leadership of the parliamentary democracies. He had also been impressed by examples of their efficiency. In October 1918, he recalled that when he had asked at a meeting in the Reich Ministry of the Interior in 1916 why German production had fallen behind that of its enemies, he had been told it was because 'we have not had a Lloyd George'.[15] In a Reichstag debate in March 1917, he had acknowledged Lloyd George's achievements and objected to dismissive references to him as 'a plebeian'.[16] It would have been surprising if Stresemann had not seen similarities between his own talents and background and those of the British prime minister and reflected on the different opportunities open to them under the German and British systems of government. Defeat brought home to him the failure of the most prestigious imperial institutions of all: the leadership of the armed forces. It was unlikely that he would ever trust the judgement of a military expert again.

Stresemann's attitudes in October 1918 were more complex than the opportunism with which his opponents charged him. His desire to join the government was in part to maintain the credibility of the National Liberals and cover up his mistakes. But he also saw it as a patriotic duty to prevent the situation deteriorating further. His forthright analysis of the failures of the High Command and his praise for the SPD showed the qualities of realism and intellectual honesty which were to be distinguishing marks of his later career.

The Shock of Revolution

Stresemann saw the revolution coming and tried to head it off by supporting the SPD's demands for franchise reform in Prussia and even, on 8 November, the abdication of the Kaiser and the Crown Prince.[17] It was too late, however, for such concessions to be effective. The revolution, which had started with naval mutinies in Kiel on 28 October, spread rapidly through the German industrial towns of the north-west with the formation of Workers' and Soldiers' Councils (Arbeiter- und Soldatenräte). On 8

---

[15] 'Politische Umschau', *Deutsche Stimmen*, 30/44, 3 Nov. 1918: *Von der Revolution*, 30.

[16] Reichstag speech, 1 Mar. 1917: *Verhandlungen des Reichstags*, vol. 309, p. 2472.

[17] Statement by the National Liberal Reichstag party and minutes of the meeting of the inter-party committee, 8 Nov. 1918: Matthias and Morsey (eds.), *Max von Baden*, 603–10.

November a Bavarian socialist republic was proclaimed in Munich and the king of Bavaria abdicated. It was inevitable that the same cry would be raised in Berlin, even if the Kaiser had not made matters worse by delaying his abdication until the revolution had in fact broken out in Berlin.

Stresemann experienced the alarming sense of events moving out of the control of the government and even of the Social Democratic leaders on 9 November.[18] He went to the Reichstag as usual, was told that revolution was breaking out and that the majority parties should be ready to participate in a new government. Looking out of his window he saw crowds of workers, men, women, and girls, streaming out of the factories and forming up into columns of demonstrators. A meeting of the inter-party committee was held but adjourned at his suggestion to the Reich Chancellery since the Social Democrats were absent. Prince Max had no time to spare for the leaders of the bourgeois parties and so they just waited to see what would happen. They were eventually given a sheet of paper which announced, Stresemann claimed later to their astonishment, that the Kaiser and Crown Prince had abdicated and that the chancellor had asked Ebert to take over the government.

Returning to the Reichstag they now saw cars of revolutionary sailors waving red flags. To the sound of cheering crowds outside, the National Liberal Reichstag party met and decided that it would, if asked, be prepared to join the new government on condition that it was regarded as provisional until a new National Assembly (which Prince Max had proposed) was convened to decide on Germany's future constitution. Stresemann stayed on in the Reichstag until the late afternoon when he was told to leave by armed workers. He tried to return in the evening for a further party meeting but could not get in, and in any case the meeting had been superseded since the SPD and USPD had by then formed a government of 'People's Representatives' (Rat der Volksbeauftragten) and there was no question of other parties being asked to join them. The bourgeois parties met again the following day in a private house, while bullets whined around government buildings in the centre of Berlin, but agreed that there was nothing they could do until a National Assembly had been elected.

His account of these events gives a convincing impression of the helplessness Stresemann felt, even though it was written a year later when he found it necessary to justify his inability to take any action to preserve the

[18] 'Zum Jahrestag der Revolution', *Deutsche Stimmen*, 31/45, 9 Nov. 1919: *Von der Revolution*, 186–8.

monarchy.[19] Power now lay with the competing socialist groups in the Workers' and Soldiers' Councils. To Stresemann this development towards 'Russian conditions' away from the parliamentary democracy which had already been won in October 1918 was anathema.[20] However, he continued to work on the assumption that the revolution would return to constitutional paths and that elections to a National Assembly would be held. Preparations for the elections started immediately among all parties even though the decision to hold them was only taken by the provisional government on 30 November and confirmed by a national congress of Workers' and Soldiers' Councils on 16 December. The election campaign faced Stresemann with a new and fundamental challenge, whether his party and his political leadership could survive in view of a sudden surge of support for a Liberal union.

A United Liberal Party?

The idea of a merger between the National Liberals and the Progressives had obvious attractions. Little seemed to separate the two parties since defeat had put an end to their differences over war aims and right-wing opponents of a democratic franchise were expected to secede in any case. The need to strengthen the Liberal camp to withstand the forces of socialism and the revolution was an additional incentive. The idea of union was enthusiastically supported by most of the provincial organizations, especially in south Germany where the differences between the two parties had always been less marked than in the north.

Stresemann was from the beginning sceptical of the alleged advantages of union. In October he wrote that he expected the Progressives to become increasingly an 'appendage of the Social Democrats' while the Conservatives would lose influence and therefore 'the task of balancing a precipitate democracy will lie in the hands of the two middle parties, namely the National Liberals and the Centre'.[21] He was no doubt aware that his own future would be more secure if the party system developed that way, than if the National Liberals moved to the left to join the Progressives.

[19] *Von der Revolution*, 188–90.

[20] 'Politische Umschau', *Deutsche Stimmen*, 30/46, 17 Nov. 1918, and speech to the party conference, 13 Apr. 1919: *Von der Revolution*, 40, 136.

[21] Stresemann to Professor Binder, 16 Oct. 1918: Nl. 194; Wolfgang Hartenstein, *Die Anfänge der Deutschen Volkspartei 1918–1920* (Düsseldorf: Droste, 1962), 10.

The revolution, however, divided the SPD from the Progressives and added weight to the argument that Liberal unity was necessary to resist socialism. Stresemann had to bow to the strength of this feeling in the Reichstag party. On the day of the revolution, 9 November, he raised the question of an electoral alliance and the possible fusion of the two parties with the Progressives' chairman, Fischbeck.[22] Before the two party delegations met to discuss the matter, it became known that a separate group round Theodor Wolff, the editor of the *Berliner Tageblatt*, intended to announce the formation of a new Democratic Party. Stresemann was bound to be hostile to this group of radical intellectuals who wanted to make a complete break with the past; he had frequently clashed with the *Berliner Tageblatt* on war aims and must have guessed that he would be unacceptable to any party formed under its auspices. The National Liberals discussed the forthcoming announcement of the Democratic Party, which two members of the left wing of the Reichstag party had been asked to sign. Stresemann was no doubt opposed to their doing so—he mentioned a sharp exchange of views—but again he had to give way.

Stresemann's tactics were to negotiate with the Progressives and exclude the new Democratic group, using the argument that the aims of the Democrats would be achieved by a fusion of the existing parties. He remained suspicious even of the Progressives, writing to a colleague on 15 November that he favoured an electoral alliance but would like to postpone union until the National Assembly met, to ensure a fair share of the constituencies for the National Liberals and not just their left wing.[23] When the Progressive and National Liberal delegations met later the same day agreement was soon reached on an electoral alliance and there was support for unity from both sides. On the question of leadership,

---

[22] The main source for these events is (as so often) Stresemann's contemporary account published as Reichsgeschäftsstelle der Deutschen Volkspartei (ed.), *Die Entstehung der Deutschen Volkspartei*, 3rd edn. (Berlin: Staatspolitischer Verlag, 1920). The typescript, including some passages cancelled in the published version, is in Nl. 186. Except where otherwise indicated, I have followed this account. Major secondary accounts include Hartenstein, *Die Anfänge*, 11–33, Lothar Albertin, *Liberalismus und Demokratie am Anfang der Weimarer Republik. Eine vergleichende Analyse der Deutschen Demokratischen Partei und der Deutschen Volkspartei* (Düsseldorf: Droste, 1972), 59–72; Turner, *Stresemann*, 13–26; Larry Eugene Jones, *German Liberalism and the Dissolution of the Weimar Party System 1918–1933* (Chapel Hill: University of North Carolina Press, 1988), 15–29; Baechler, *Stresemann*, 204–14; and, most recently, Kolb and Richter (eds.), *Nationalliberalismus*, 9*–30*, and Ludwig Richter, 'Von der Nationalliberalen Partei zur Deutschen Volkspartei', in Dieter Dowe, Jürgen Kocka and Heinrich August Winkler (eds.), *Parteien im Wandel. Vom Kaiserreich zur Weimarer Republik* (Munich: R. Oldenbourg, 1999), 135–60.

[23] Stresemann to Peter Stubmann, 15 Nov. 1918: Nl. 187; Hartenstein, *Die Anfänge*, 14.

raised by Stresemann, it was agreed that the two delegations would form a provisional leadership until a future party conference could decide on a chairman. However, the tactics to be adopted towards the Democratic Party, which had meanwhile announced its formation and intended to make a fresh start independent of the old parties, caused disagreement. The Progressives were unhappy at the idea of a challenge on their left and wanted the new group brought into the proposed union. Again Stresemann had to give way.

The deep resentment Stresemann felt at having to submit to these talks is clear from a letter he wrote to Otto Hugo, the General Secretary of the party, shortly before the meeting on 18 November.[24] He suggested that they should together build a new group in the National Assembly of those who were National Liberals 'without utterly surrendering their past and their feelings'. He said that his agreement to union with the Progressives had meant 'a huge sacrifice' which he had made only for the sake of the party. He denied that he feared for his position as leader, saying he had always been able to get any position he wanted, but he feared that he would not feel 'the same enthusiasm which is the precondition of all success'. On the other hand, he explained, if they refused to cooperate they would lose the whole of south Germany and the new mass of democratic young voters and, he added, the country would say that union had failed 'because I had wanted to remain in a leading position'.

Stresemann then indicated what he hoped would happen: that the Progressives would split with their left wing joining the Democrats and the others the National Liberals. He added that there was no alternative for the National Liberals in cooperation with the Conservatives as that would destroy the party. Confessing his isolation, he appealed to Hugo for support saying that he had found almost no one in the Reichstag party who would stand by him. If, he concluded, he was forced to work with people who were alien to him, he would prefer to leave politics altogether and return to business and have time for his literary interests. However, he added pathetically, he was remaining on board the National Liberal ship to see that at least if the imperial colours were lowered they would be replaced by the flag of 1848 and not 'the red or reddish banner of an international democracy'.[25]

---

[24] Stresemann to Hugo, 18 Nov. 1918 (Nl. 187): Harttung (ed.), *Schriften*, 195–7.

[25] Arguing that Stresemann was not responsible for the failure of the attempts at unification, Kolb and Richter see this letter as evidence of Stresemann's hopes for a united party, rather

The meeting with the Progressives and Democrats confirmed Stresemann's worst fears. The main spokesman for the Democrats, the Heidelberg sociologist Alfred Weber (brother of Max), dismissed Fischbeck's invitation that they should join a union of the two Liberal parties, describing them as 'bankrupt', and making it clear that the Democrats would not tolerate in leading positions politicians who were 'compromised by annexationism'. The National Liberals were told that their reputation would be 'fatal' to the Democrats and that not only must their right wing be excluded but that the 'break must come much further to the left'. The situation was given added poignancy by the presence of Stresemann's brother-in-law, Kurt von Kleefeld, in the Democratic delegation and his claim, which Stresemann noted ironically, that they represented 'a new political ethic'.[26] Weber's remarks provoked protests from the other parties and the National Liberals subsequently withdrew, although the Progressives made it clear that they would have to continue the talks.

In the long run Weber's undiplomatic outburst played into Stresemann's hands, designed as it was to split the parties in exactly the way Stresemann hoped.[27] But this was not immediately apparent. The enthusiasm for Liberal unity in the provinces put enormous pressure on the party leadership to agree, making the Democrats, as the most intransigent group, the arbiters of the situation. At its foundation on 20 November, the Democratic Party (DDP) had already won over the main body of the Progressives and four members of the National Liberal Reichstag party.

Instead of the Democrats being isolated, as Stresemann had hoped, the National Liberals were isolated and crumbling. 'Deeply depressed at the defection of former friends', Stresemann tried to rally the party.[28] Together with Friedberg and Hugo he drafted a declaration which appeared on 21 November explaining that the DDP was not in accord with 'the

than—as I read it—of his reluctant acquiescence in the process: Kolb and Richter (eds.), *Nationalliberalismus*, 16*.

[26] *Die Entstehung der deutschen Volkspartei*, 5–7, an account based on Stresemann's notes of the meeting (Nl. 187). Stresemann had earlier noted that Kleefeld had referred to him as 'my poor, unfortunate, misguided brother-in-law' (diary entry, 15 Nov. 1918: Nl. 362). Kleefeld had been raised to the rank of von Kleefeld through the good offices of his aristocratic employer, the prince of Hohenlohe-Öhringen, by the prince of Lippe on 12 Nov. 1918, the same day the prince abdicated: Koszyk, *Stresemann*, 81, 183. Stresemann may have been struck by the irony of Kleefeld's claim to democratic credentials only days later.

[27] Eberhard Demm, *Ein Liberaler in Kaiserreich und Republik. Der politische Weg Alfred Webers bis 1920* (Boppard: Harald Boldt, 1990), 265–9.

[28] Diary entry 20 Nov. 1918 (Nl. 362).

convictions of our electorate'.[29] The National Liberal Party would there-fore have to remain independent, though it would need a new programme and possibly a new name. The programme which followed accepted 'the democratic form of state created by the upheaval' and the idea of a League of Nations while asserting Germany's right to equality and col-onies. It also opposed 'nationalization of all means of production' and 'the abolition of private property'. This rather lame attempt to assert the democratic bona fides of the party (it is noticeable that the word 'liberal' was dropped), while distinguishing it from radical socialism, ended by proposing a German People's Party (Deutsche Volkspartei, DVP) 'on a national-democratic basis'.

A circular, dated 22 November, rejected the Democrats' insinuation that the negotiations had broken down because of the leadership ambi-tions of Stresemann and Friedberg, saying that they would have been prepared to withdraw for a time. The reason for the breakdown was rather that the Democrats intended to destroy the National Liberal Party by excluding its core electorate which would have been made 'politically homeless' and might as a result have swung to the right.[30] The following day, the formation of the DVP was announced with the names of two Progressive Reichstag members in its committee. There followed the bold claim that liberal unification had been achieved in the DVP.[31]

The reality was quite different. Although the provincial organizations in Hanover and Hamburg joined the DVP, elsewhere the appeals of the leadership fell on deaf ears. Stresemann said later that party headquarters had been flooded with telegrams demanding unity at any price.[32] The leadership responded by holding out the hope of further negotiations on 25 November but pleading with the provinces not to 'go over to the Democratic Party with flags flying' but to join the DVP to improve its bargaining position.[33]

Developments in Berlin were equally threatening. Stresemann and Friedberg found support for the view that they should not knuckle under to the dictatorship of the Democrats, but a 'stormy' meeting of

[29] NLC 45/222, 21 Nov. 1918.
[30] Rundschreiben, dated 22 Nov. 1918: BAK, ZSg.1, 74/7 (8). The circular was not in fact sent out until 25 Nov. 1918, by which time the situation had changed again.
[31] NLC 45/224, 23 Nov.1918.
[32] Speech to the meeting of the Zentralvorstand, 12–13 Apr. 1919 (Nl. 203): Kolb and Richter (eds.), Nationalliberalismus, 75–6.
[33] 'An die Parteifreunde', 25 Nov. 1918, also enclosing the Rundschreiben, 22 Nov. 1918; BAK, ZSg. 1, 74/7 (8).

the Berlin party association on 25 November was equally clearly against division into two camps.[34] The Young Liberals and a group of professional associations, including the Hansa Association and Stresemann's old clients the white-collar workers, also pressed for unity. They proposed that if the Democrats would make concessions on policy, Stresemann should agree to his exclusion from the central committee of the new party.[35] Equally ominous, an attempt to raise money for the DVP from Berlin businessmen failed: Friedberg was told that a lot of money would be forthcoming but only for a united party.

In these circumstances there was no way to avoid resuming negotiations with the Democrats. It was agreed that Friedberg should demand that the National Liberals be given adequate representation in the leadership of the DDP and that its views on policy on national and economic questions should be reflected in the programme. Stresemann made the inevitable sacrifice, authorizing the negotiators to say that he refused to accept election to any committee of the DDP. He then left for Dresden for a meeting of the Association of Saxon Industrialists.

Stresemann's feelings were a mixture of self-pity, resignation, and defiance, reminiscent of the doldrums of his political career in 1912. He talked of withdrawing from politics for a time and of the 'undignified collapse' of the National Liberal Party together with that of the German Reich.[36] In Dresden he told a meeting of the local party, the same National Liberal Reichsverein through which he had first become a member of the party, that he expected the negotiations in Berlin to succeed. However, already looking for a comeback, he also suggested that they should retain their organization intact in case the cooperation between the National Liberals and the DDP did not last.[37]

Meanwhile, Friedberg was unable to gain the hoped for concessions. The Democrats, now represented by Fischbeck and Hjalmar Schacht (formerly a Young Liberal), were prepared to make only marginal concessions on representation and none on policy. Friedberg, weary of negotiating from a position of weakness and convinced that there was no alternative, decided to put an end to the business by accepting surrender.

---

[34] Diary entry, 25 Nov. 1918 (Nl. 362).   [35] Albertin, *Liberalismus*, 68–9.

[36] Stresemann to the General Secretary of the Rhineland party, Otto Brües, 29 Nov., and to Dr Brüss (Leipzig), 3 Dec. 1918: BAK, R 45 II/1; Albertin, *Liberalismus*, 70–1.

[37] 'Die Entstehung der Deutschen Volkspartei' (Nl. 186); this passage was cancelled before the published version. In fact the Dresden organization was the only one in Saxony to follow his lead into the DVP: Rudloff, 'Von den Nationalliberalen zur Deutschen Volkspartei', 723.

Undeterred by the objections of his co-negotiator, Professor Leidig, and telephone messages of protest from Stresemann, he announced the successful conclusion of the negotiations to the press on his own authority on 3 December without even waiting to consult a meeting of party members he had called for later that afternoon.

Stresemann was scandalized. His son could still recall the sound of his father's fury on the telephone some sixty years later.[38] His sense of betrayal was natural. He noted in his diary on 3 December: 'Friedberg completes capitulation to the Democratic Party.'[39] Friedberg had clearly exceeded his mandate by acting unilaterally. Yet Stresemann seemed nonplussed, perhaps for the only time in his political career. He and Leidig boycotted the meeting of party members, suggesting that they saw no chance of reversing the decision. The fact that Friedberg, who had long been associated with the right wing of the party, had concluded the agreement made it particularly difficult for Stresemann to oppose. It was bound to look as though he was motivated by personal ambition and spite. It seemed to be the end of the road.

During the next two weeks it became clear, however, that the Democrats had again overreached themselves and Friedberg's impetuous submission rebounded to Stresemann's advantage. The initiative came from the provincial organization in Hanover, where Hugo, who had been in Berlin and witnessed the dramatic events of the previous days, organized the resistance. Stresemann was called to Hanover for a meeting on 6 December, where the party executive decided unanimously to remain in the DVP. The party in Bremen, Hamburg, Pomerania, East Prussia, and Westphalia followed the example of Hanover.[40] Back in Berlin, Stresemann won over a majority of the Berlin organization after repeated public recriminations with Friedberg at a meeting on 12 December, and on 15 December he also won a narrow majority of 33 to 28 of the sixty-one members of the national executive (from a total of 229) who were able to attend the meeting. This was a symbolic victory providing a thread of continuity from the most important national committee of the old party to the DVP. But Stresemann was obviously prepared to go ahead in any case on the basis of the provincial organizations loyal to him. On the evening of 15 December the DVP was formally founded at a meeting in the Savoy hotel, attended by about 100 party members. According to some later

---

[38] Wolfgang Stresemann, *Mein Vater*, 159.   [39] Nl. 362.
[40] Kolb and Richter (eds.), *Nationalliberalismus*, 26*.

accounts, Stresemann was unanimously elected party leader; in any case given Friedberg's defection he would automatically have taken his place as chairman of the national executive.[41]

The continued division of German Liberalism into two camps and the arguably serious consequences of this division in weakening the Weimar Republic, gave rise to the question then and later of whose fault it had been that unity failed in 1918–19. The Democrats were quick to blame Stresemann, and Stresemann counter-attacked, accusing the *Berliner Tageblatt* intellectuals of 'brutality' and aiming not at unity but at excluding the core of the National Liberals.[42] The truth was that neither wanted an all-Liberal union. Stresemann, partly because he saw the threat to his leadership and partly because he believed there were fundamental differences between the National Liberals and the left-wing Democrats, was more than content for the division to continue. Even if a temporary unity had been reached for the 1919 elections, he expected it to break down later. He also thought that the DDP in Berlin vastly overestimated the strength of the Party in the country at large. He expected old voting habits to reassert themselves once the shock of defeat had receded.[43]

Naturally there was in this view a considerable degree of wish-fulfilment. Stresemann had no desire to deny his own past and he expected the majority of National Liberal voters to feel the same. But the fact that Stresemann's prediction came broadly true in the elections of June 1920, when the DVP polled as well as the National Liberals had in 1912 and the DDP was cut to below the Progressive equivalent, shows that it was not mere wishful thinking. The reaction against the treaty of Versailles no doubt helped, but that showed that the loyalty of National Liberal voters who had switched to the DDP in 1919 was insecure, particularly since the DDP itself refused to vote for the treaty and resigned from the government. Stresemann's argument that without the DVP many National Liberals might have defected further to the right—or as has recently been suggested into abstention—deserves to be taken seriously.[44]

---

[41] Kolb and Richter (eds.), *Nationalliberalismus*, 28*, and report on the meeting in the *Hannoverscher Kurier*, 16 Dec. 1918, ibid. 8–10.

[42] 'Politische Umschau', *Deutsche Stimmen*, 30/50, 15 Dec. 1918: *Von der Revolution*, 55; Harttung (ed.), *Schriften*, 202.

[43] 'Politische Umschau', *Deutsche Stimmen*, 30/50, 15 Dec. 1918: *Von der Revolution*, 58; Harttung (ed.), *Schriften*, 205.

[44] Baechler, *Stresemann*, 214. In one district of Saxony, Plauen, right-wing National Liberals defected in any case to the DNVP, declaring that Stresemann was 'also inwardly a Democrat': Rudloff, 'Von den Nationalliberalen zur Deutschen Volkspartei', 727.

The return of Liberal voters to their traditional ways by June 1920 does not, however, show that Liberal unity was bound to fail. On the contrary, had the National Liberals been offered a common platform and adequate representation in November or December 1918, there is good reason to suppose that union would have been achieved. The question would then have been whether a united Liberal Party with the *Berliner Tageblatt* group as its extreme left wing (as it had previously stood on the left of the Progressives) could have adjusted to the changed circumstances of 1919–20. Could it have followed the drift back to the right among the Liberal electorate as a whole without breaking up again? This is debatable. The *Berliner Tageblatt* rapidly lost influence within the DDP, and in July 1919 Stresemann's former mentor Naumann was elected chairman.[45] The DDP programme for the elections to the National Assembly in January 1919 was revised to be almost identical with that of the DVP. There was therefore more truth in Stresemann's claim that it was the radical intellectuals, such as Weber and Wolff, who had prevented unity than was comfortable for his other view that the natural divisions between right and left Liberals were bound to resurface.

However, in the longer term Stresemann was probably right. There remained important differences between the DVP and the DDP in their attitudes to the Republic and in their willingness to form electoral alliances or government coalitions with the parties to their left and right. The divisions were not caused simply by a clash of personalities in Berlin: they had deep roots in the provincial parties. Indeed the division between left and right in the German party system can be seen as running between the DDP and the DVP.[46] The dividing line was not rigid and efforts continued from both sides to achieve Liberal union. Stresemann remained sceptical of a one-sided union with the DDP. His goal became instead to make the DVP the natural party of the Protestant middle class—a Protestant equivalent of the Centre Party—by drawing in both the right wing of the DDP and the pragmatic elements of the former Conservative Party and its allies, now organized in the German National People's Party (Deutschnationale Volkspartei; DNVP).

---

[45] Albertin, *Liberalismus*, 72–9, 100.

[46] I owe this point to Peter Pulzer. Rudloff points out that the dividing-lines in Saxony also ran within the National Liberal Party: Rudloff, 'Von den Nationalliberalen zur Deutschen Volkspartei', 732–5.

Opposition

The shock of the revolution and the attempt to exclude him as a 'compromised' politician had the effect of driving Stresemann to the right. In November 1918 he adopted the role of opposition politician which he had refused in October. A new tone entered his political vocabulary. In reply to a Democrat who said they should welcome liberation from the old rotten system of the empire, he wrote that 'much—not all—was rotten' about it and that what they had seen since could not claim to be better.[47] He now wrote and spoke more kindly of the Kaiser's strengths and weaknesses and significantly he blamed the failures of the empire on the 'satiated' middle class which had been too weak to provide a counterweight to the Kaiser's personal rule.[48] He saw the conversion of parts of the middle class to the Republic as further evidence of this moral failure. There were suddenly innumerable republicans, he mocked. 'Byzantine' monarchists now became 'Byzantine' republicans and those who had been proud of their 'By appointment' coats of arms were the first to wrap them in red flags.[49] Equally unworthy was the lack of dignity in defeat of those who attempted to win influence with Wilson by dissociating themselves from Germany's past.[50]

Having kept his distance from the imperial regime before, Stresemann now found a new loyalty to it. There were millions, he wrote, who would not change their convictions like a handkerchief, though he added that just as there had previously been republicans who did their duty to the Kaiser so there would be monarchists who put themselves at the service of the Republic.[51] A family anecdote catches the change in Stresemann's sympathies: up to 1918 he had asserted the family's independence by ordering a special black–red–gold flag (the colours of 1848) for the summer holiday sand castles; after the revolution when black–red–gold was adopted by the Republic, the Stresemanns flew the imperial colours, and he was delighted that no republican flags were to be seen on the beach.[52]

---

[47] 'Politische Umschau', *Deutsche Stimmen*, 30/48, 1 Dec. 1918: *Von der Revolution*, 51.

[48] 'Politische Umschau', *Deutsche Stimmen*, 31/6, 9 Feb. 1919: *Von der Revolution*, 101–3; speech to the first party conference of the DVP, 13 Apr. 1919: ibid., 133–5.

[49] 'Politische Umschau', *Deutsche Stimmen*, 30/50, 15 Dec. 1918: *Von der Revolution*, 60; speech in Osnabrück, 19 Dec. 1918: ibid., 68.

[50] Speech 22 Feb. 1919: *Von der Revolution*, 117–19.

[51] 'Politische Umschau', *Deutsche Stimmen*, 30/50, 15 Dec. 1918: *Von der Revolution*, 60.

[52] Wolfgang Stresemann, *Mein Vater*, 150. Stresemann criticized the government for changing the flag, not because he had any objection to the 1848 colours, but because he argued it was unworthy in defeat to reject the flag which represented Germany's past and an affront to the

Stresemann also adjusted his explanation for Germany's defeat. Defending the High Command, he argued that though the war could no longer have been won, the army could still have fought a defensive campaign for better terms if it had not been for the revolution. For that reason the anniversary of the revolution would never become a national day of commemoration.[53] With this version of 'the stab in the back', Stresemann defended his own record, saying that the crucial element in defeat had been the failure to maintain morale at home. He contrasted his consistent support for victory with the attitude of the doubters, the SPD, Erzberger, and the *Berliner Tageblatt*.[54] On the subject of war aims he had no difficulty in showing that representatives of all parties had at one time or another supported some annexation.[55] He admitted that he had held longer to such aims than others and had overestimated Germany's will to resist, but that simply brought him back to the responsibility of the majority parties for the collapse of the home front. He was on stronger ground when he replied to critics of his 'illusions' that their trust in Wilson would prove the greater illusion.[56] The armistice terms confirmed him in his view that the aim of the Allies had always been Germany's destruction and that no compromise peace had been possible.

The shift to the right reflected Stresemann's anger at what he saw as the unjust accusations of his opponents and betrayal by his friends. But it also suited his political tactics. To counteract the headlong rush to the DDP, it was inevitable that the DVP would have to rally a Liberal constituency on the right. At the first meeting of the DVP national executive, Stresemann was proposed as chairman precisely because he represented their position as an 'opposition party towards the left'.[57] Reversing the position he had occupied on the left of the National Liberal Party before the war, he now became the symbol of Liberal resistance to the new order. The anger he aroused was shown in an election meeting in

memory of those who had died fighting under it. Speech to the party conference, 13 Apr. 1919: *Von der Revolution*, 156–7.

[53] 'Zum Jahrestag der Revolution', *Deutsche Stimmen*, 31/45, 9 Nov. 1919: *Von der Revolution*, 193–4.

[54] 'Politische Umschau', *Deutsche Stimmen*, 31/15, 13 Apr. and 31/26, 29 June 1919: *Von der Revolution*, 129, 174–5.

[55] 'Politische Umschau', *Deutsche Stimmen*, 30/50, 15 Dec. 1918: *Von der Revolution*, 64–6.

[56] Speeches, 22 Feb., 13 Apr. 1919: *Von der Revolution*, 117–19, 161–2; 'Politische Umschau', *Deutsche Stimmen*, 31/20, 18 May 1919: ibid. 166–8; Harttung (ed.), *Schriften*, 253–5.

[57] Proposal by the chairman of the Hessen party organization, Arthur Osann: minutes of the meeting, 12–13 Apr. 1919 in Kolb and Richter (eds.), *Nationalliberalismus*, 28.

his constituency in January 1919, when he was interrupted by shouts of 'Bloodhound, mass-murderer, submarine-warmonger', attacked with chairs and knives, and had to run for his life to a nearby house before eventually escaping in disguise.[58]

The elections to the National Assembly on 19 January brought the DVP a modest start. Under the new system of proportional representation, the DVP gained overall 4.4 per cent of the votes and twenty-two seats in the Assembly.[59] This made it, together with the USPD, the smallest of the national parties, compared to the DNVP with forty-four and the parties that formed the new government, the SPD with 163 seats, the Centre ninety-one and the DDP seventy-five. Nevertheless, Stresemann described the result with some justification as a success.[60] The unfavourable circumstances in which the DVP had been founded and the lack of time for it to organize meant that the result underestimated its real strength.[61] It had contested only twenty-one of the thirty-seven new multi-member constituencies under its own name, in three others it presented a joint list with the DNVP, and in one a joint list with the DDP. Where it had lost its entire organization—West Prussia, Silesia, western Saxony, Bavaria, Württemberg, and Baden—it did not enter the election. Where it did compete under its own name, it won on average 7.8 per cent of the vote. This was still a poor result compared to the 13.6 per cent National Liberal share in 1912, showing the shift to the DDP among erstwhile National Liberal voters.[62] Nevertheless the DVP had weathered the taunts of its opponents who had predicted that it would be only a 'miniature Stresemann party' not large enough to form a separate group in the Assembly.[63]

Finding the Middle Ground

Although it had survived a difficult birth, the DVP was still a long way from establishing itself as the main Protestant party of the centre ground

---

[58] 'Die Schande von Nordhorn', *Osnabrücker Zeitung*, 17 Jan. 1919; PA, Nl. Bernhard, Zeitungsausschnitte, 5; Wolfgang Stresemann, *Mein Vater*, 165–7.

[59] Hartenstein, *Die Anfänge*, 67.

[60] 'Politische Umschau', *Deutsche Stimmen*, 31/5, 2 Feb. 1919: *Von der Revolution*, 95.

[61] Richter, 'Von der Nationalliberalen Partei zur Deutschen Volkspartei', 154–9.

[62] On the other hand, in some constituencies, including the Berlin suburbs, the DVP improved on the National Liberal share of the vote in 1912: ibid. 158.

[63] *Von der Revolution*, 94–6; 'Eine Privatpartei Stresemann?', *Berliner Börsenzeitung*, 6 Dec. 1918: PA, Nl. Konsul Bernhard, Zeitungsausschnitte, 4.

like the National Liberals. This was the task to which Stresemann now devoted himself. He had to win back voters from the DDP by attacking the government of which it was part, while at the same time preventing the DVP being seen as simply a pale reflection of the larger opposition party, the DNVP. This required skilful management. Stresemann did not always show that skill, partly because his judgement was clouded by emotion, partly because there was an inherent contradiction between rallying the Liberal constituency on the right and leading it back to the centre. But his aim remained constant. Indeed he hoped that it might be possible to improve on the National Liberal vote by extending the DVP's support into the former Progressive camp on the left and into the space on the right, which he expected to be vacated by the declining appeal of Conservatism. This was a bold and imaginative strategy whose importance has not been sufficiently recognized. It provided a strong underlying element of continuity with his earlier career, despite the turmoil of defeat and revolution, and it was also the basis from which he was later to lead the DVP into government.

In his speeches to the first meeting of the national executive on 12 April 1919 and to the party conference the following day, Stresemann set out the goal.[64] The first essential, he said, was to preserve their 'full independence': 'we are and remain independent towards the right and towards the left'. He admitted to the national executive that it was difficult to know how to draw the boundary on the right since the DNVP had cleverly avoided giving the impression that it was a reactionary party and it was unclear how the different groups within it (Conservatives, Christian Social Party, anti-Semites, and even some former Liberals) would influence its overall stance. But, he argued, although the DVP would often join the DNVP in opposition to the government on 'national questions', its historic task was different. It was to see that the 'hundreds of thousands, yes, millions, who went over to the Democrats completely misunderstanding the real position, not knowing what they were doing, come streaming back to us'. Stresemann was encouraged by signs that local Democratic groups were already defecting to the DVP saying that this showed 'we are on course to become...the old middle party which is

[64] Minutes of the Zentralvorstand meeting, 12–13 Apr. 1919: Kolb and Richter (eds.), *Nationalliberalismus*, 73–96, esp. pp. 78–81; speech to the party conference, 13 Apr. 1919: Reichsgeschäftsstelle der Deutschen Volkspartei (ed.), *Bericht über den Ersten Parteitag der Deutschen Volkspartei am 13. Apr. 1919 in den Akademischen Rosensälen in Jena* (Berlin: Staatspolitischer Verlag, 1919), 10–34; repr. in *Von der Revolution*, 132–65, here esp. pp. 158–9.

indispensable to the life of the state'. Looking ahead, he predicted that the DNVP would not be able to form part of a government for the foreseeable future as there would be no majority on the right. On the other hand, he thought the DVP might be required in a government very soon. He expected the existing coalition to break down as the SPD became increasingly torn between its ideals and the reality of government leading, he thought, to the defection of its left wing to the USPD. The DVP should be prepared under those circumstances for the historic task of assisting in Germany's recovery.

Stresemann did not take a prominent role in the National Assembly, declining the leadership of the party there in order to concentrate on re-establishing the national organization for the next elections.[65] He may also have wanted to avoid the accusation that the DVP was simply a vehicle for his ambition. In any case he found the National Assembly—which met in Weimar because its security could not be guaranteed in Berlin after a left-wing 'Spartacist' revolt there at the beginning of January—depressing. He wrote to Käte that government ministers were unfit for their positions and he criticized even Ebert for opening the Assembly with a party political speech instead of speaking for Germany.[66] Instead he immersed himself in the work of the national executive and its standing committee in formulat-ing the party programme, in major speeches to party rallies in the prov-inces and to the two national conferences in April and October 1919, and in his regular political commentaries for the *Deutsche Stimmen*.[67] The strain of the events of 1918–19 also took their toll on his health. Suffering from nervous and physical exhaustion, he was forced to take a complete rest during the summer months.[68]

Outside the National Assembly, Stresemann was unsparing in his criti-cism of the government. One of his most effective themes was the gulli-bility of those who had hoped that the Republic would be treated well by the Allies. When the Versailles peace terms became known in May, he felt

---

[65] Stresemann to Käte ('Katerchen'), 5 Feb. 1919: Stresemann family papers, Berlin.

[66] Stresemann to Katerchen, 6 Feb. 1919, ibid.; speech in Berlin 22 Feb. 1919: *Von der Revolution*, 108.

[67] The *Deutsche Stimmen* succeeded the *Nationalliberale Blätter* as the title of the main National Liberal weekly. Stresemann acquired it in 1917 as his own political organ and continued to edit it until he became chancellor in August 1923. In 1919 he founded the *Staatspolitischer Verlag* for DVP publications, including the *Deutsche Stimmen* and the *NLC*. Heinz Starkulla, 'Organisation und Technik der Pressepolitik des Staatsmannes Gustav Stresemann (1923 bis 1929)', unpub-lished Ph.D., Munich, 1951, 25; Döhn, *Politik und Interesse*, 373–4.

[68] Wolfgang Stresemann, *Mein Vater*, 168; Koszyk, *Stresemann*, 212–17.

vindicated. He described the proposed treaty as 'a moral, political and economic death sentence' and when all parties, except the USPD, united in condemning the proposals, he wrote that the National Assembly had shown a moment of greatness.[69]

The mood of near unanimity, however, soon gave way to more sober calculation of the risks of acceptance and rejection. Against the humiliation of accepting the terms and the loss of territory and economic burdens they involved, had to be set the risk of Allied invasion and the prospect of a continuation of the blockade. These considerations, forcefully presented by Erzberger, persuaded the Centre Party and the SPD that the treaty had to be accepted. The DDP, however, remained opposed and withdrew from the government, rejoining it only in October 1919. Stresemann wrote bitterly of the collapse of the united front for rejection and added a savage diatribe against Erzberger for conducting private diplomacy with the Allies and undermining the negotiating position of the leader of the German delegation at Versailles, Count Brockdorff-Rantzau.[70] Stresemann ended his attack with words which were to prove truer than he intended: 'The 22nd of June', the day the Assembly authorized the government to sign the treaty, 'was his [Erzberger's] greatest personal victory. Only it seems doubtful whether he will survive the consequences of this victory.' In fact, Erzberger became the victim of a vitriolic campaign of denunciation from the right, was forced to retire from politics in 1920 and was assassinated in 1921.

Given that the treaty was not going to be rejected by a united front, Stresemann regarded its acceptance by a clear majority, which allowed the DVP to vote against without affecting the outcome as the next best thing. The DVP was determined to vote against in order to reap, with the DNVP, the advantage of opposing an unpopular peace. The situation which appeared to obtain on 22 June, when the government got a majority for signing the treaty of 237 to 138, therefore suited him. He wrote to his sons almost with satisfaction, saying that the majority for the treaty was firm and the he was glad to be there to do his patriotic duty by voting 'No'.[71] He particularly enjoyed the embarrassment of

[69] 'Politische Umschau', *Deutsche Stimmen*, 31/20, 18 May 1919: *Von der Revolution*, 170–1. Also his speech to the National Assembly, 12 May 1919: *Verhandlungen der verfassunggebenden Deutschen Nationalversammlung*, vol. 327, pp. 1100–2.
[70] 'Politische Umschau', *Deutsche Stimmen*, 31/26, 29 June 1919: *Von der Revolution*, 172–5; Epstein, *Erzberger*, 305–13.
[71] Stresemann to the boys, midsummer day 1919: Stresemann family papers, Berlin. Turner argues that Stresemann would have been prepared to sign the treaty if, as he expected, the Allies

the Democrats, writing that they had now 'dreamed their Wilson dream
to the end'.[72]

The situation took a dramatic turn, however, on 23 June which forced
the DVP out of its corner.[73] The government had declared that it would
not sign the clauses of the treaty which impugned Germany's honour—
those concerned with war guilt and war criminals. Predictably the Allies
demanded an unconditional signature and gave Germany twenty-four
hours to decide. This produced consternation in Weimar; many members
of the Assembly had gone home assuming that the matter had been
settled. The Centre now swung against acceptance and it appeared possible that the treaty would be rejected. The DVP stuck to rejection, but it
did not carry this attitude to the logical conclusion of doing its utmost to
prevent the treaty passing. It refused to form a government of the parties
opposed to ratification, saying that those who had got themselves into the
mess would have to deal with it. In fact no such government was possible
since neither the Centre nor the DDP would have formed a coalition with
the DNVP. There was therefore a real impasse, making it possible that the
issue would be decided by a chance majority of a single vote and that
Germany would have to face the ensuing crisis without being able to form
a majority government.

The prospect of chaos concentrated the minds of the opposition. The
leader of the DVP in the Assembly, Rudolf Heinze, provided the way out.
Instead of taking a new vote, he suggested that there should instead simply
be a vote to confirm that the decision taken the previous day authorized
the government to sign unconditionally. Further in order to overcome the
reluctance of the Centre Party to being held responsible, Heinze proposed
that the opposition should acknowledge the patriotic motives of those
who voted for the treaty. These initiatives saved the situation and the
SPD–Centre majority was reaffirmed.

Not surprisingly the conduct of the DVP in the Assembly aroused
criticism from the constituencies. The DNVP emerged as the more
determined opponents. It is not known what part Stresemann played in

made important concessions, but the evidence he quotes—a letter from Stresemann on 11 June—
shows only that he expected there to be a majority for the treaty, not that the DVP would itself
vote for it. Stresemann to Grashoff, 11 June 1919 (Nl. 205); Turner, *Stresemann*, 38.

[72] *Von der Revolution*, 175.

[73] There is a good account of these events in the memoirs of Friedrich Payer, *Von Bethmann
Hollweg bis Ebert* (Frankfurt am Main: Frankfurter Societäts-Druckerei, 1923), 295–304; Albertin,
Liberalismus, 341–4.

the compromise on 23 June. He was taken ill soon afterwards and did not attend the meeting of the standing committee on 29 June when the matter was discussed. But it is safe to assume that Heinze had his support.[74] This is confirmed by the way Stresemann dealt with the subject in his speech to the party conference in October.[75] He claimed that the DVP had been consistent in its opposition even when the outcome on 23 June was uncertain. But he went on that although a 'Yes' would bring 'long years without political freedom', a 'No' would bring conflict for which Germany lacked the weapons. In this situation, he added, he personally refused to make moral criticisms of those who voted for acceptance. Adroitly linking the question to his earlier warnings, he said that Germany's fate had been sealed when it accepted the armistice, not on the day it concluded the treaty.

The DVP also opposed the new Constitution, which was passed by the National Assembly on 31 July. Again, the DVP's vote was essentially one of principle, this time against Germany becoming a republic. Stresemann, who was absent at the time, defended the decision as an act of loyalty to the past, to Bismarck and the institution of the Kaiser as 'the symbol of German unity'.[76]

Defining the DVP's attitude to the new state caused some difficulty. Stresemann had to strike a balance between appealing to old loyalties and accepting that the past could not be brought back. He was eventually to strike this balance by referring to 'the old Germany we loved and the new Germany we live for', but at first his attitude was not so clear.[77] In January and February 1919, he still thought that the political situation was far from stable. From Weimar he wrote to Käte that 'we are being driven towards Bolshevism' and that it was possible that the state would have to declare itself bankrupt; in further letters he wrote that he hoped the army would be preserved to keep order 'if hunger drives people onto the street' and that he expected there to be a second revolution.[78] In these circumstances Stresemann believed, or claimed to believe, that although a

[74] No suggestion was made that Stresemann had disagreed with the tactics adopted, which were defended by Jacob Rießer at the committee: Kolb and Richter (eds.), *Nationalliberalismus*, 159–63.

[75] Reichsgeschäftsstelle der Deutschen Volkspartei (ed.), *Bericht über den Zweiten Parteitag der Deutschen Volkspartei am 18., 19. u. 20. Oktober 1919 im Kristallpalast in Leipzig* (Berlin: Staatspolitischer Verlag, 1920), 12–13.

[76] Ibid. 15–16.

[77] He adopted this phrase in his speech to the party conference in 1926: *NLC*, Sonderausgabe, 'Siebenter Reichsparteitag am 2. und 3. Oktober 1926 in Köln'.

[78] Stresemann to Katerchen, 5, 8, 12, 28 Feb. 1919: Stresemann family papers, Berlin.

restoration of the monarchy would be impossible without civil war and this had to be avoided to preserve the Reich, the time might soon come 'in which the nation after the present desperate conditions will itself summon back the monarchy by an overwhelming majority'.[79]

In its first declarations after the revolution the DVP steered clear of the subject of the monarchy, presumably feeling there were no votes to be won by taking it up, but at the end of January 1919 Stresemann changed tack. On behalf of the DVP he sent a telegram to the Kaiser on his sixtieth birthday asserting that 'millions of Germans will hold high with us their profession [Bekenntnis] of monarchism in the new circumstances and on the new basis of the state form'.[80] This demonstrative gesture aroused concern that Stresemann had committed the party to work for the restoration of the Hohenzollerns. He immediately retreated, claiming that the text had been corrupted over the telephone and that the purpose had been only to express loyalty not to promote 'a royalist movement'. The DVP, he said, 'accepts the existing facts and will cooperate on the basis of the German Republic', but no one could demand that those who had been convinced monarchists for more than half a century should now 'step out as republicans'.[81] The most likely explanation for the incident is that he had not chosen his words with sufficient care, although it is possible that the ambiguity was intentional to test the reaction.[82] His claim that the text had been distorted was an invention: the draft in his papers and the published version are identical.

Another consideration led him in April to take a cooler view of the prospects of a Hohenzollern restoration. The dissolution of the Austro-Hungarian empire left a German state in Austria which in February 1919 returned a clear majority in favour of joining Germany (Anschluß) in accordance with the principle of self-determination. It appeared possible to nationalists on both sides that this victory at least could be snatched from the jaws of defeat. Stresemann was enthusiastic. The

---

[79] Stresemann to Theodor Boehm, 6 Jan. 1919: Nl. 182; Hartenstein, Die Anfänge, 108.

[80] Hartenstein, Die Anfänge, 108–12.

[81] He said that the text should have read 'millions of Germans, while recognizing the new circumstances and the new basis of the state form, will hold high with us their profession of monarchism' (ibid. 110). 'Politische Umschau', Deutsche Stimmen, 31/6, 9 Feb. 1919: Von der Revolution, 103–4.

[82] There is an interesting discussion of this incident in Baechler, Stresemann, 227–8. He suggests that the telegram may have been intended to reassure monarchists who had been dismayed by the DVP's acceptance of the Republic and also to appeal to the sentiments of National Liberals who had defected either to the DNVP because of their loyalty to the old regime or to the DDP despite it.

name Deutsche Volkspartei had been chosen partly to emphasize the link with Austrian nationalist groups.[83] In a speech in December, he declared that union would create 'the great block of 70 million Germans' of which Bismarck had said that it would lie 'like a knot of wood in the middle of Europe and no one could bypass it'.[84] In February, he even hoped that Germany might acquire the Sudetenland as well as Austria.[85] However, the restoration of the Hohenzollerns would be fatal to these hopes as the dynasty would be unacceptable to the two largest Austrian parties—the Social Democrats, who supported union, and the Christian Social Party, who were divided on the issue. This gave Stresemann an additional reason for letting the matter rest, and in his speech to the first party conference in April he said that while they would honour the memory of the great days of the Hohenzollern past they were not counter-revolutionaries—both because restoration could only be achieved by civil war and because 'Great Germany can only be created on a republican basis'.[86]

This stance was confirmed by the party programme in a tortuous compromise, acceptable to both the conservative Prussian and liberal south German wings of the party. It committed the DVP to cooperate in the existing state for the recovery of the Reich, but also maintained that the 'most suitable form of state' was the monarchy created by 'a free decision of the people in a constitutional way'.[87] Stresemann explained that it was a statement of principle but not an urgent matter, that the task of recovery required the support of republicans, and reconciliation should not be prevented by 'a sharp emphasis on monarchism'.[88]

Its tactics over the treaty of Versailles and the question of republic or monarchy showed the difficulty of coming to terms with reality. There was a rapid emotional adjustment to be made. As Stresemann wrote to his sons on midsummer day 1919 he felt it was more like Remembrance Sunday:

For the old great, mighty Germany, which was the epitome of the yearning of our ancestors and our pride when one could still hold one's head high at being a

---

[83] Stresemann's explanation to the Zentralvorstand meeting, 12 Apr. 1919: Kolb and Richter (eds.), *Nationalliberalismus*, 122. The Austrian Deutsche Volkspartei was one of a group of nationalist parties in the Austrian National Assembly: ibid.

[84] Speech in Osnabrück, 19 Dec. 1918: *Von der Revolution*, 86.

[85] Speech in Berlin, 22 Feb. 1919: ibid. 120.

[86] Speech, 13 Apr. 1919: ibid. 141–2.

[87] Minutes of the Geschäftsführender Ausschuß (GA) meeting, 19 July 1919: Kolb and Richter (eds.), *Nationalliberalismus*, 171–3; Reichsgeschäftsstelle der Deutschen Volkspartei (ed.), *Grundsätze der Deutschen Volkspartei* (Berlin: Staatspolitischer Verlag, 1920), 4.

[88] 'Zum Parteitag', *Deutsche Stimmen*, 31/42, 19 Oct. 1919.

German, is going under. One cannot say: it is long gone because it is not long at all but already it sounds to our ears like a fairy tale from a distant time.[89]

There was also a political balance to be struck between rallying the National Liberal constituency by appealing to past loyalties and becoming a potential party of government in the Republic. Stresemann tried to resolve these conflicts by distinguishing between loyalty to the past and present necessities. But though the distinction was clear in the abstract, in practice his attitude remained on occasion both ambiguous and volatile.

Anti-Semitism

One example of an issue on which Stresemann's attitude was less than straightforward was anti-Semitism.[90] He accused the left-wing Democrats of having 'cosmopolitan ideas' in contrast to the 'consciously German outlook' of the DVP.[91] This division, like that between 'fire and water', became one of his standard themes.[92] Applied always to the DDP, which had the reputation of being the Jewish party, and specifically to the Jewish-owned *Berliner Tageblatt* and *Frankfurter Zeitung*, the accusations clearly carried anti-Semitic overtones, although he also included a wider group of German intellectuals and pacifists in his condemnation.[93]

In discussing the party programme in September 1919, Stresemann was explicit about his reasons.[94] Explaining a reference to 'international tendencies to disintegration' under the heading 'Nationality and Family', he argued that they must take a stand in some form on 'the Jewish question'. He said it was clear that they could not take part in the widespread movement of anti-Semitic agitation. But he went on to blame Jews for not having the courage to take a public position against the 'baseness of the Jewish press'. 'The "Ulk" of the Mosse publishing house and the "Weltbühne" of Herr Siegfried Jacobson [*sic*] and others smear everything

---

[89] Stresemann to the boys, midsummer day 1919: Stresemann family papers, Berlin.

[90] Wright, 'Liberalism and Anti-Semitism', 108–13.

[91] Speech to the first party conference, 13 Apr. 1919: *Von der Revolution*, 158–9.

[92] e.g. speech to the second party conference, 18 Oct. 1919: *Bericht über den Zweiten Parteitag*, 22–3.

[93] On Jewish influence in the DDP, see Albertin, *Liberalismus*, 79–80; on the Democratic press, see Modris Eksteins, *The Limits of Reason: The German Democratic Press and the Collapse of Weimar Democracy* (Oxford: Oxford University Press, 1975) and Pulzer, *Jews and the German State*, 170–1.

[94] Minutes of the meeting of the GA, 13 Sept. 1919: Kolb and Richter (eds.), *Nationalliberalismus*, 189–90.

which is holy to national-minded Germans in the most disgraceful way.'
He added that there were many non-Jews involved in such activities as
well, describing the pacifists Quidde, Schücking, Gerlach, and Förster as
an 'equal cancer'. He also referred to other abuses 'in many cases Russian
conditions, with bribery part of the agenda', adding again 'Unfortunately
it was not only Jews who were involved.'

In common with other right-wing parties, the DVP included in its
programme a clause against Jewish immigration from the east under the
euphemism of opposing 'the flooding of Germany since the revolution
with people of foreign origin'.[95] In his speech to the second party conference, which adopted the programme, Stresemann lumped communist
agitation and foreign immigration together: 'We want our German
people to remain German. We do not want to become a playground for
the perverse, theoretical passions of creatures who have neither home nor
fatherland.'[96]

The party's position was modified when Jacob Rießßer, one of its few
prominent Jewish members, persuaded the standing committee that in
answer to questions about anti-Semitism it would reply that the DVP
refused to generalize from the 'relatively considerable number of Jews' in
revolutionary movements and stood by its programme of 'equal rights for
all citizens', while at the same time it was wholly opposed to the idea of
'world citizenship' in place of the 'profession of the national state'—all
who accepted this programme, whatever their faith, were welcome in its
ranks.[97]

This attempt to define a patriotic but not overtly anti-Semitic stance
distinguished the DVP from radical anti-Semites. Nevertheless, Stresemann's handling of the issue showed that he did not scruple to play on
anti-Semitic feelings as part of his campaign against the republican
parties. The fact that Käte came from a baptized Jewish family and that
he was himself attacked on this score may have made him defensive. In a
letter of protest to the DNVP chairman Oscar Hergt, he said that the
allegation that he was married to a Jew was 'untrue'.[98] But in reply to an
enquiry about the DVP's position from the Central Association of
German Citizens of the Jewish Faith, he referred to his marriage with a

[95] *Grundsätze der Deutschen Volkspartei*, 6–7.
[96] *Bericht über den Zweiten Parteitag*, 17.
[97] Minutes of the meeting of the GA, 28 Jan. 1920: Kolb and Richter (eds.), *Nationalliberalismus*, 219–20.
[98] Stresemann to Hergt, 22 Dec. 1919 (Nl. 208).

Jew.[99] He was able to take both positions by playing on the difference between Jewish descent and Jewish faith. But it was clearly an uncomfortable situation both politically and personally. The DVP had to face attacks from the DNVP that it was unsound, and an official party publication sought to show that there was in fact no difference between the two parties on the 'Jewish question'.[100] One of Stresemann's own party colleagues, Paul Moldenhauer, later wrote in his memoirs 'Basically we were all racially minded and against the Jews and we found it disturbing that the party leader was married to a Jew.'[101]

Although personal considerations and party tactics may have played some part in shaping Stresemann's attitude on the subject, it was in any case quite consistent with his hostility towards those he saw as Germany's detractors. He never endorsed and probably had no sympathy with anti-Semitism on racial or religious grounds. But he did not hesitate to attack those whom he saw as a danger to the nation by associating them with the anti-Semitic feelings of his audiences.

Independence towards the Left

As well as appealing to voters with emotive and symbolic issues, Stresemann also attacked specific measures of the government and the so-called 'republican' parties—the parties of the Reichstag majority of 1917—which composed it. He opposed the plans for nationalization and factory councils. Characteristically unwilling to be content with mere opposition, however, he declared that the idea of the councils—that people should have a greater say in their lives than could be achieved just by belonging to political parties—was a healthy one.[102] He took up the call for an economic parliament, representing employers as well as employees, agriculture, and the different branches of industry, and with the power to submit draft legislation direct to the Reichstag. In the form of the Reich Eco-

[99] Stresemann to the Zentralverein Deutscher Staatsbürger jüdischen Glaubens, 28 Jan. 1920 (Nl. 220).

[100] *Archiv der Deutschen Volkspartei* 1/1, 18 Feb. 1920, 35–8.

[101] Paul Moldenhauer, 'Politische Erinnerungen'. This section of the memoirs was composed between 1937 and 1940 and may have reflected the climate of the Third Reich: BAK, Nl. Moldenhauer, 1, pp. 119–20. For Moldenhauer's career, see Horst Romeyk, 'Paul Moldenhauer (1876–1946)', *Rheinische Lebensbilder*, 7 (Cologne, 1977), 253–69.

[102] Speech to the Zentralvorstand meeting, 12 Apr., and to the party conference, 13 Apr. 1919: Kolb and Richter (eds.), *Nationalliberalismus*, 88–92; *Von der Revolution*, 145–51.

nomic Council (Reichswirtschaftsrat) this proposal, which had wide support, became law.[103]

Stresemann attacked the Democrats alternately for sympathizing with socialist measures, such as nationalization, and failing to prevent them and thus failing to provide the 'wall against Social Democracy' which their middle-class voters had expected.[104] He exploited the divisions within the DDP and enjoyed the spectacle of Friedberg criticizing the first draft of the Constitution which was the work of his new DDP colleague, Hugo Preuß.[105] The most controversial feature of this draft was the proposed break-up of Prussia, which was opposed by the DVP together with, among others, the Prussian SPD and DDP, and was subsequently dropped.[106] Stresemann also criticized the Constitution for its 'formal democracy', which he contrasted with 'liberalism'.[107] As an example, he gave the absence of an effective second chamber as a check on the Reichstag majority. The task for Liberals, he declared, was no longer to defend the freedom of the individual against a Conservative state but 'against mechanical democratization and against Bolshevism'.[108] Stresemann also attacked the, in practice very modest, attempts of the republican parties to appoint sympathetic officials to the administration, giving the impression that a wholesale republican purge was in progress which would undermine the 'objectivity' of German *Beamten*.[109]

On the whole, Stresemann spared the Centre Party his polemics— perhaps because he saw it as the natural partner for the DVP in the middle of the political spectrum in the future. He poked fun at its 'adaptability' in joining the government after first fighting an election campaign in many areas with the DVP against the left. More seriously he criticized its 'unreliability' in border areas, threatened with plebiscites and secession by the treaty of Versailles, comparing it unfavourably in this respect with the SPD, whose members he pronounced 'a hundred times more national'.[110] There was one major exception to his general tolerance of the

---

[103] Ludwig Preller, *Sozialpolitik in der Weimarer Republik*, repr. of 1949 edn. (Düsseldorf: Droste, 1978), 251–2.

[104] Speech to the party conference, 19 Oct. 1919: *Bericht über den Zweiten Parteitag*, 20–2.

[105] Speech in Berlin, 22 Feb. 1919: *Von der Revolution*, 109.

[106] 'Politische Umschau', *Deutsche Stimmen*, 31/5, 2 Feb. 1919: *Von der Revolution*, 93–4.

[107] *Bericht über den Zweiten Parteitag*, 26–8. See also 'Liberalismus oder Demokratie', in *Von der Revolution*, 58–60.

[108] Minutes of the Zentralvorstand meeting, 12 Apr. 1919: Kolb and Richter (eds.), *Nationalliberalismus*, 95.

[109] *Bericht über den Zweiten Parteitag*, 27–8.

[110] Ibid. 23–4.

Centre Party, Matthias Erzberger, but Stresemann attacked him more as an individual than as a member of the party in an effort to isolate him.[111]

Stresemann's vicious attack on Erzberger's role in securing a majority for the treaty of Versailles has been described above. As Reich finance minister, he provoked a new storm of criticism by reforming the taxation system and introducing a series of new taxes which were as unpopular as they were necessary to pay for the war.[112] His most controversial proposal, a levy on capital, was criticized by Stresemann both because industry needed capital to restart its peacetime operations and because he feared that if the tax was successful, the Allies would take the proceeds as reparations. The DVP proposed instead a property tax and a compulsory loan from industry, which it claimed would raise an equivalent amount and which had the support of business lobbies. Stresemann alleged that Erzberger had swept aside this proposal, saying that, since he had a majority, he had no need to make concessions to the opposition. Stresemann presented Erzberger as arrogantly ignorant of the world of finance, and was once again able to make use of Friedberg who had called Erzberger 'the most bloody dilettante who was ever Finance Minister'.[113]

Only after Erzberger's assassination in August 1921 did Stresemann pay tribute to the remarkable qualities of his former opponent in a perceptive article which praised among other things Erzberger's 'sovereign command' of Reich finance and his achievements in establishing the supremacy of the Reich over the *Länder* in taxation.[114] Looking back over fourteen years of parliamentary activity, during which they had not always been on opposite sides, Stresemann wrote of the complexities of Erzberger's character and career. He added that the passions aroused by the revolution had led to the conflict of political leaders being portrayed only at the level of caricature. It was an accurate comment on a process to which both Stresemann and Erzberger, by their mutual antagonism, had contributed.

In his campaign against the republican parties, Stresemann made no allowance for the immense difficulties under which they operated, nor did he give them credit for the moderation they showed in practice. He exploited his chances with the ruthless determination of the leader of a party only twenty-two strong which had to make significant gains at the

---

[111] *Bericht über den Zweiten Parteitag*, 24, 31.   [112] Epstein, *Erzberger*, 328–48.

[113] Speech in Halberstadt, 19 Dec. 1919: *Halberstadter Zeitung*, 1 Jan. 1920; PA, Nl. Bernhard, Zeitungsausschnitte, 1.

[114] 'Politische Umschau', *Deutsche Stimmen*, 33/36, 4 Sept. 1921, repr. as 'Erzberger', in Rheinbaben (ed.), *Reden und Schriften*, i. 378–88.

next election if it was not to be doomed to irrelevance. At the same time he was careful to protect the party from the alternative threat to its future from the right—namely absorption by the DNVP in a common front against the Republic.

Independence towards the Right

Stresemann was alive to the danger that by its assault on the republican parties, the DVP would naturally invite the question of why it did not ally with the DNVP. This question was raised from within both parties in 1919–20. Stresemann had already set out his view at the first party conference that only by remaining independent could the DVP hope to win back Democrat voters and in time become part of a government. Nevertheless the idea of a single nationalist, anti-republican party continued to attract support.

In June 1919 the DVP leader in the Assembly, Rudolf Heinze, discussed the matter with DNVP leaders and then brought it to a joint meeting of the DVP members of both the National Assembly and the equivalent Prussian Assembly. The meeting decided overwhelmingly against a merger with the DNVP but agreed that the idea of a new party was worth pursuing.[115] Press reports that the DVP was considering a merger led Stresemann to air the matter in the *Deutsche Stimmen*.[116] He wrote that one could not entirely dismiss the idea, but that such a party would be divided on social and economic issues. He added that German Protestants were not united by religion in the same way as German Catholics, and a party such as the DVP, for those who were both national and liberal, was bound to arise. In a subsequent issue he repeated emphatically that the DVP would maintain its independence.[117]

Stresemann raised the matter again at the second party conference in October.[118] He warned that the old Conservative Party remained strong within the DNVP, the same party that had sabotaged the Bülow bloc in 1909 and thereby prevented the peaceful development of a parliamentary system. He declared that there was no room for such ideas in the new

---

[115] Rießer's report to the meeting of the GA, 29 June 1919, from which Stresemann was absent: Kolb and Richter (eds.), *Nationalliberalismus*, 159–60.
[116] 'Politische Umschau', *Deutsche Stimmen*, 31/24, 15 June 1919.
[117] Ibid. 31/26, 29 June 1919: *Von der Revolution*, 176.
[118] *Bericht über den Zweiten Parteitag*, 24–6.

Germany, and said he would remain sceptical of the DNVP so long as he did not know whether its character had changed.

As the prospect of new elections came closer in the winter of 1919–20—since the National Assembly had completed its work of concluding the peace and passing a new Constitution—Stresemann again showed his anxiety to draw the line clearly against the DNVP. He engaged in an open correspondence with the racist DNVP deputy, Albrecht von Graefe. Stresemann argued that it was undesirable to divide the German people into two parts, one of which was called 'national' and the other not. Since in any case a 'national party' would not have a majority, it was inevitable that they would have to join a coalition and they should not, he said, shrink from entering a government with Social Democrats 'who accepted the basis of an orderly recovery'.[119]

When Graefe demanded that the DVP should agree to form a common Reichstag group with the DNVP after the elections and suggested in public meetings that only Stresemann's opposition prevented a merger (a remark which should be seen in the context of DNVP propaganda about Käte being of Jewish descent), Stresemann brought the matter to the standing committee.[120] He criticized a party rally in Westphalia for making friendly overtures to the DNVP and said that DVP voters did not want them to remain in opposition but to pursue 'positive policies' as soon as possible. He indicated that this would be feasible only if they were willing to cooperate with the SPD and warned against a right wing establishing itself once again in the party with control over their policy. If they stayed in opposition for the next four years he predicted that they would lose the support of government officials (*Beamten*) and would eventually face the same fate as the royalist party in France. He returned to the attack at the next meeting in March, saying that they should not conduct 'irresponsible opposition' like the DNVP and that to bind themselves to join a coalition only with the DNVP would reduce the DVP to 'a farce'.[121] He also suggested that the growing influence of former Conservatives within the DNVP might lead them to form an independent party and then the other groups would join the DVP.

Stresemann's views were supported by almost all those who spoke at the standing committee. The unscrupulous agitation of, among others, Paul

[119] Hartenstein, *Die Anfänge*, 138–40.
[120] Minutes of the meeting of 28 Jan. 1920: Kolb and Richter (eds.), *Nationalliberalismus*, 213–18.
[121] Minutes of the meeting, 4 Mar. 1920: ibid. 222–9.

Fuhrmann, who had helped to organize the 'Old National Liberals' before the war and now went round the constituencies saying that a merger of the DVP and DNVP was imminent, was particularly resented. Only the party treasurer Albert Vögler, himself director of one of the great Ruhr firms, opposed Stresemann. He said he could think of no greater misfortune than a government without the DNVP and that the DVP should make it clear that it saw its future with the DNVP. Another Westphalian delegate, Carl Cremer, while supporting the party's independence, warned that if they entered a coalition without the DNVP, that party would exploit against them every concession they made to the coalition.

Stresemann's firm stand against alliance with the DNVP had important consequences. His judgement was proved right when the DVP succeeded in June 1920 in recapturing an important part of the Democratic vote. His complementary hope that the DNVP would break up and that the more moderate elements within it would also join the DVP, however, remained unfulfilled. Individual politicians came over and the DNVP remained divided between pragmatists and extremists, but as an electoral force it proved more resilient than Stresemann had expected. Instead of the DVP becoming the dominant Protestant party, it had always to face competition from its larger rival on the right.

Stresemann's decision to work for a coalition with the republican parties including the SPD also had important consequences. His policy suited his instinct for conciliation. He did not want to see the SPD return to its pre-war stand of opposition and revolution. Just as during the war he had seen the importance of maintaining SPD support by constitutional reform, so he now saw the danger of governing against them, predicting it would mean 'staggering from one general strike to another'.[122] The virtue of Stresemann's policy was to direct German politics towards consensus at a time when the bitterness between right and left might otherwise have led to civil war. The disadvantage, however, was that government from the middle of the political spectrum helped to frustrate the alternation in power between right and left which might have allowed each in time to forge stronger bonds with the parliamentary system. Given Stresemann's view of the DVP as, like the National Liberal Party, an essential element of balance in the political system, his tactics were logical. Given the internal divisions which still existed within the DVP between the conservative and liberal wings, Stresemann also had to find ways of maintaining party unity. The ideology

---

[122] Stresemann to Graefe, 23 Jan. 1920: Hartenstein, *Die Anfänge*, 124.

of National Liberalism as a responsible party of government became once again under his leadership a means of integration.

Preparing for Government

By December 1919 Stresemann felt confident enough to speak openly of his future plans for coalition. The growth in DVP organization—the party claimed an increase in membership from 100,000 in January to 500,000 in October—suggested that it would gain substantially in the next elections. Stresemann expected the main gains to be at the expense of the DDP and pitched his rhetoric accordingly to attract voters disillusioned with the republican government. At the same time he was worried that coal and food shortages might spark another revolution during the winter, and there were also rumours of a military coup.[123] This confirmed him in his view of the need to consolidate the parliamentary system by what he called 'a concentration of all reasonable elements from Social Democracy to the right'.[124] In a speech on 19 December 1919 he balanced a polemical attack on the government with the declaration that the DVP was equally opposed to 'revolution from the left' and 'a coup from the right', and wanted peaceful cooperation of all productive forces, including the SPD.[125] He expressed the hope that a pragmatic wing of the SPD would arise from the 'collapse of socialist illusions and Marxist dogma', that the Democrats would free themselves from 'cosmopolitan influences', and that the Centre Party would throw off Erzberger's 'demagogy'. The DVP, he said, wanted power, but it knew that it was an illusion to think that 'we on the right will get a majority on our own'. 'Politics' he continued, 'is the art of the possible, is the necessity of reaching an understanding with others'. Stresemann admitted that the DVP had first to increase its strength by showing up the mistakes of the government, but he also wanted to hold the way open for future cooperation.

What the policies of a future coalition might be Stresemann left obscure, though his attacks on the republican parties suggested that he

---

[123] Speech in Osnabrück, 31 Aug. 1919, *Osnabrücker Tageblatt*, 1 Sept. 1919: PA, Nl. Bernhard, Zeitungsausschnitte, 1. Minutes of the GA, 19 Jan. 1920: Kolb and Richter (eds.), *Nationalliberalismus*, 204.

[124] Report of the Osnabrück speech in the *Vossische Zeitung*, 1 Sept. 1919: PA, Nl. Bernhard, Zeitungsausschnitte, 1.

[125] Speech in Halberstadt: *Halberstadter Zeitung*, 1 Jan. 1920.

expected a new government to move substantially to the right to accommodate the DVP. He talked in vague terms of the continuity of parliamentary government, the creation of an impartial administration, and overcoming class conflict in the interests of economic recovery. Only on the last point did he go into more detail, arguing that Germany must have a government which could attract foreign capital and had the courage to restore the eight-hour (instead of seven-hour) day in the mines. Such a government—one which did not threaten the capitalist economy with extinction—would be able to buy raw materials and take advantage of the enormous post-war demand for goods of all kinds.

By appealing for an end to socialist experiment and a return to hard work, Stresemann was able to combine anti-republican rhetoric with a willingness to share in government. He was still sensitive, however, to the suggestion that the DVP was in fact accommodating itself to the Republic. When Scheidemann asserted that though not 'republicans by conviction' they would become 'republicans by reason' (*Vernunftrepublikaner*), a description Stresemann was later to accept, he rejected the idea, saying that on the contrary since the revolution many republicans had become 'monarchists by reason'.[126]

Foreign Policy

Stresemann also saw no need to make concessions to the republican parties in foreign policy. The idea of international brotherhood was, as far as he was concerned, the great myth of the Socialist and Democratic parties which he had taken the lead in exposing. The first two party conferences were suffused with nationalist rhetoric. In April, before the terms of the treaty were known, Stresemann recklessly committed himself to the view that even 'Alsace and large parts of Lorraine are German land with German blood' and it was for the DVP to see that they remained German.[127] By the time of the second conference in October delegates from each of the provinces threatened with secession by the treaty expressed their loyalty to Germany to warm applause.[128] In his speech

---

[126] Speech to the National Assembly, 8 Oct. 1919: *Verhandlungen*, vol. 330, p. 2915; *Rede des Abgeordneten Dr. Stresemann zu Magdeburg am 3. November 1919* (Magdeburg [1919]), 29: PA, Nl. Bernhard; Zeitungsausschnitte, 1.

[127] *Von der Revolution*, 163.

[128] *Bericht über den Zweiten Parteitag*, 62–84.

Stresemann took satisfaction from the confidence of Germans in the eastern provinces, which had been allocated to Poland, that the new Polish state would not last. For good measure he added that Livonia, Estonia, and Finland were also not viable.[129] On other occasions, he declared that the treaty of Versailles represented the 'Egyptianization' of Germany—a reference to international controls over the economy—and that the economic clauses could not be fulfilled.[130] He condemned the League of Nations as a 'farce' and as 'an American-English world cartel for the exploitation of other nations'.[131]

In order to keep hope alive, however, he advised his DVP colleagues not to 'preach evermore' that 'we are the Entente's slaves for decades'.[132] Adopting the language of Norman Angell (which he had criticized before the war), he asserted that the war had no victors except the United States.[133] He also predicted that the treaty of Versailles would not mark the beginning of 'a new world epoch which will define the frontiers and opportunities of nations for decades'. Rather he suggested that it was one incident in a great period of ferment, like that which started with the French Revolution, and that the effects of the spread of social conflict to the victors, including Britain and America, had yet to be seen. Other unsolved problems to which he pointed were the conflict of interest in the Pacific between Japan and the United States and, nearer to home, the question of who would rebuild the Russian economy. He declared that despite the victors' attempt to isolate Germany from Russia by constructing a line of border states between them, 'State frontiers...are not economic frontiers. That is where we must look.'[134]

---

[129] *Bericht über den Zweiten Parteitag*, 32.

[130] Speech to the National Assembly, 12 May 1919: *Verhandlungen*, vol. 327, p. 1101; speech in Brandenburg, 11 Dec. 1919, *Brandenburger Anzeiger*, 110/219, 12 Dec. 1919, and speech in Magdeburg, 3 Nov. 1919, *Rede zu Magdeburg*, 23: PA, Nl. Bernhard, Zeitungsauschnitte, 1.

[131] Minutes of the GA, 24 Aug. 1919: Kolb and Richter (eds.), *Nationalliberalismus*, 179–80; speech in Halberstadt, 19 Dec. 1919: *Halberstadter Zeitung*, 1 Jan. 1920.

[132] Minutes of the GA, 19 Jan. 1920: Kolb and Richter (eds.), *Nationalliberalismus*, 203.

[133] Speech to the National Assembly, 8 Oct. 1919: *Verhandlungen*, vol. 330, p. 2918; speech in Halberstadt, 19 Dec. 1919; *Halberstadter Zeitung*, 1 Jan. 1920.

[134] Stresemann drew on the ideas of Werner von Rheinbaben, who had been entrusted with drafting the DVP's foreign policy programme. Rheinbaben had experience both of the diplomatic service and the Auswärtiges Amt. His views are set out in *Das außenpolitische Programm der Deutschen Volkspartei. Vortrag gehalten in Halberstadt am 19. Dezember 1919 bei der Parteibeamtenbesprechung von dem Legationsrat a.D. Freihr. v. Rheinbaben* [1919]; BAK, ZSg. 1 42/1 (14). In this interesting lecture he argued that economic cooperation between Russia and Germany was bound to follow because of their complementary needs. At the same time he warned against either an eastern or western orientation since Germany was not strong enough to pursue foreign policy

Stresemann believed that only if Germany accepted that power politics was continuing as usual would it be able to recover and exploit its opportunities. He made this clear in a meeting of the standing committee in August 1919. Discussing the question of how to refer to the League of Nations in the party programme, he said:

we are united that we must again attain a respected position in the world and this goal can only be reached by power politics [*Machtpolitik*]. We will not let ourselves be deceived by the talk of a League of Nations. Already we see the Triple Alliance of Britain, America, France, navies are being built— what is this except a return to the old system! We have already been proved more right in our view than we anticipated. So there will be power groups again in the future, and the task for us is to become alliance-worthy [*bündnisfähig*] again.[135]

Quite how the principle of power politics was to be applied in practice was still unclear, but in the winter of 1919–20, Stresemann started to suggest ways in which Germany might improve her position. He was quick to seize on two ideas in particular—the importance of the German economy for the whole of Europe and the possibility of exploiting Allied fears of Soviet communism—both of which were to play an important part in his later foreign policy. Adopting arguments similar to those subsequently made popular by Keynes, he wrote 'The great question of our recovery is this, whether we will succeed in bringing about an international understanding which prevents the collapse of Germany and therefore the collapse of Europe'.[136] Germany had to persuade the victors to make it possible for her to trade again in world markets, since her economy depended on the import of raw materials and autarky was impossible. Germany had therefore to win back the moral and economic credit of the world or it would be lost. But equally France, in particular, was forgetting that its existence depended on German recovery as well. He then applied the argument to Russia, saying that at some time the Bolshevik economic system would collapse and it would need German help.

---

except in cooperation with her former enemies. The same applied to the idea of playing off one opponent against another. Stresemann later explained his foreign policy in similar terms. Werner Freiherr v. Rheinbaben, *Kaiser Kanzler Präsidenten. Erinnerungen* (Mainz: Hase & Koehler, 1968), 201–51.

[135] Minutes of the meeting of 24 Aug. 1919: Kolb and Richter (eds.), *Nationalliberalismus*, 179.

[136] 'Politische Umschau', *Deutsche Stimmen*, 32/1, 4 Jan. 1920. The 1st edn. of J. M. Keynes, *The Economic Consequences of the Peace*, was published in Dec. 1919. Stresemann referred to the book in Sept. 1920, warning against assuming that it was representative of British opinion: 'Politische Umschau', *Deutsche Stimmen*, 32/37, 12 Sept. 1920.

This could provide an opportunity for Germany to recover its economic and political importance.

In a subsequent article, written as war was threatening between Poland and the Soviet Union, Stresemann expanded his ideas of how Germany might exploit events in the east.[137] He explained that French hatred concealed its real fear of Germany. An important French visitor with whom he had talked had been full of pessimism at the prospect of an understanding between Russia and Germany which would enable Germany to raise a new army and throw itself against France. Britain, which had achieved all its war aims, would no longer support France, and Poland could not survive a German–Russian rapprochement.[138] Stresemann saw that this French 'nightmare' and also the threat of Bolshevism to the British empire, together with American withdrawal into isolation, gave Germany potential leverage. He argued that if the Soviet Union expanded west, France and Britain would need German cooperation to contain it and in return they would have to revise the Versailles treaty.[139]

The extent to which Stresemann felt by the autumn of 1919 that public opinion had again turned away from the republican parties was evident when he supported the idea of approaching Hindenburg to stand for election as Reich president. Ludendorff was also considered as a DVP candidate for the Reichstag, and his wartime political confidant, Colonel Bauer, was offered a constituency.[140] In a speech in Dortmund in November 1919 Stresemann contrasted 'the Siegfried figures, Hindenburg and Ludendorff' with the 'sad epigones in their wretchedness' who had been appointed by the National Assembly to carry out an investigation into the causes of Germany's defeat.[141]

Stresemann was keen to see elections held at the beginning of 1920, judging that the time was ripe to recapture support from the DDP. The National Assembly had, in his view, completed its work. In addition, he argued that the government would be unable because of its left-wing

---

[137] 'Politische Umschau', *Deutsche Stimmen*, 32/7, 15 Feb. 1920.

[138] The French visitor was probably Professor Émile Haguenin, the head of the French trade mission in Berlin. Maxelon, *Stresemann und Frankreich*, 89.

[139] Similarly, at a meeting of the standing committee Stresemann said it was still possible that Bolshevism would expand and that could alter the situation completely, bringing about a revision of the treaty of Versailles by itself. Minutes of the meeting of 19 Jan. 1920: Kolb and Richter (eds.), *Nationalliberalismus*, 203.

[140] Minutes of the meetings of the GA, 24 Aug., 13 Sept., 16 Oct. 1919: ibid. 185–7, 191–3.

[141] *Kölnische Zeitung*, 17 Nov. 1919: PA, Nl. Bernhard, Zeitungsausschnitte, 1. Also 'Der Untersuchungsausschuß', *Deutsche Stimmen*, 31/47, 23 Nov. 1919.

policies to raise a loan abroad, and the loan was essential to avert economic catastrophe.[142] The government parties, however, also judged that the elections would not be to their benefit and therefore refused to call them, saying that the budget for 1920 should be decided first. Their fear at the suggestion that Hindenburg might be a candidate for the Reich presidency also led them to consider a constitutional amendment to enable the Reich president to be elected by the National Assembly rather than directly. The DVP and DNVP launched a campaign accusing the republican parties of manipulating the constitution to shield themselves from the electorate.[143]

The Kapp Putsch

The situation was transformed by a military putsch in Berlin on the night of 12–13 March.[144] The background to this event was the agreement which had been reached immediately after the revolution between the provisional government and the High Command that the army would defend the government if its structure was left intact. Volunteer *Freikorps* troops were recruited from the demobilized men and officers and used to crush the Spartacist uprising in Berlin in January and the short-lived Bavarian Soviet Republic in April–May 1919. Friction between the troops and the government grew from the signing of the Versailles treaty in June, and plans were discussed for a right-wing dictatorship among circles which included Ludendorff and the former leader with Tirpitz of the German Patriotic Party, Wolfgang Kapp.[145]

The putsch was precipitated by the government's decision to start disbanding the *Freikorps* following the Versailles treaty's stipulation that the army should be reduced to 100,000 men. General von Lüttwitz, the commanding officer of the area of north Germany which included Berlin, presented the government with an ultimatum on 10 March demanding among other things the preservation of the *Freikorps* and the elections for which the DNVP and DVP were campaigning. When to his surprise the government refused and dismissed him, he had no alternative but to carry

---

[142] Speech to the party conference, 18 Oct. 1919: *Bericht über den Zweiten Parteitag*, 31; minutes of the GA, 19 Jan. 1920: Kolb and Richter (eds.), *Nationalliberalismus*, 204.

[143] Johannes Erger, *Der Kapp-Lüttwitz-Putsch* (Düsseldorf: Droste, 1967), 84–5.

[144] There is a full account of these events ibid.

[145] On the German Patriotic Party, see above p. 95.

out the putsch or give in. Although far from clear about what he intended to achieve, he occupied Berlin with the *Freikorps* Brigade Ehrhardt and asked Kapp—who had much more far-reaching plans for a dictatorship— to become Reich chancellor. The legal government escaped to Dresden and then Stuttgart leaving only a few representatives in Berlin including Stresemann's former colleague Schiffer, now one of the DDP members of the government and vice-chancellor.

The putsch took Stresemann by surprise although he knew something of the background. There had been rumours since the autumn, and Stresemann had warned that a putsch would be an 'incalculable catastrophe'.[146] He was therefore not a natural confidant for the leaders. Lüttwitz had explained his intention to give the government an ultimatum at a meeting on 4 March with the DNVP leader Hergt and Heinze, who represented the DVP as Stresemann was absent from Berlin. Both Hergt and Heinze tried to dissuade Lüttwitz, promising a parliamentary campaign instead. On 9 March the two parties introduced a joint resolution into the National Assembly for new elections and for keeping the direct system of presidential elections, and let it be known that the army was in a dangerous mood. There is no evidence, as was later alleged by Democratic newspapers, that Stresemann had inside knowledge of the plot. Rather it seems that, like the government, he did not take Lüttwitz's threats too seriously.[147] Lüttwitz himself had not thought out any coherent plan. He told Hergt and Heinze that he would delay his ultimatum until the end of April, but went back on this to prevent the disbandment of the Brigade Ehrhardt on 10 March. Only when the ultimatum was rejected did he commit himself to the putsch.

The afternoon of 12 March happened to be the date of Wolfgang Stresemann's confirmation, and his father decided that evening that for once he would not be disturbed by politics and disconnected the telephone.[148] He therefore learned nothing of the putsch until he reconnected it in the morning and it immediately started ringing. Wolfgang Stresemann's memory of some of his father's comments as he heard the news—'That is frightful, total madness, that can lead to civil war'—is entirely plausible.

---

[146] Speech in Osnabrück, 31 Aug. 1919: *Osnabrücker Tageblatt*, 1 Sept. 1919; PA, Nl. Bernhard, Zeitungsauschnitte 1.

[147] Stresemann's report to the GA, 28 Mar. 1920: Kolb and Richter (eds.), *Nationalliberalismus*, 273; Erger, *Kapp-Lüttwitz*, 132–5.

[148] Wolfgang Stresemann, *Mein Vater*, 178–80; Stresemann's diary for 12 Mar. 1920 (Nl. 142).

A meeting of the available members of the DVP parties in the National and Prussian assemblies and of the standing committee was hastily
summoned. There is only a short minute of this meeting, which records
that there was general agreement that the 'violent overthrow' of the
government 'should be condemned most sharply' but also that the fault
lay with the 'old government' for refusing elections.[149] Those present
decided that they should first try to discover the intentions of the 'new
authorities' (*Machthaber*) and that the DVP should press for elections to be
held immediately to restore Germany to a constitutional basis. One of
those present, Professor Leidig, wrote that there was a general feeling that
they should accept the new government de facto in the same way as they
had the government established by the revolution of November 1918,
although they naturally felt more sympathy for the 'national goals' of the
new regime.[150]

The DVP leaders met again in the afternoon of 13 March to hear the
report of a deputation (which did not include Stresemann) which had been
to see Kapp. Kapp had declared that the new government's aims were very
close to those of the DVP, that he had no intention of restoring the
monarchy, and that elections would be held as soon as possible.[151] Kapp's
obvious attempt to win DVP support received a mixed response at
the afternoon meeting.[152] Oskar Maretzky (who later left the DVP for
the DNVP) wanted to support the new government. Rießer on the other
hand took the view that Kapp's administration would in effect be composed of the DNVP, that it had reopened the wartime division between
the civil and military authorities, and that it would lead to civil war.
Stresemann tried to find a middle way. He pointed out that there was
also a danger that the Reich would be divided between the new government in Prussia and the old one in Dresden. 'Therefore', he went on, 'we
must follow a course, which on the one hand creates no difficulties for the
new government but which leaves us the opportunity, if the circumstances
arise, to be mediators between Berlin and Dresden.' Those present agreed
to issue a public statement which blamed the republican government for
the breakdown of 'organic development' and accepted the existence of 'a
new government', but went on to say that the party's 'liberal principles'

[149] Kolb and Richter (eds.), *Nationalliberalismus*, 233–5.
[150] 'Meine Teilnahme an den Ereignissen des 13. bis 18. März 1920' (Nl. 217).
[151] Report of the meeting by one of the DVP delegation, Hugo Garnich: Kolb and Richter
(eds.), *Nationalliberalismus*, 236–41.
[152] Minutes of the meeting on the afternoon of 13 Mar.: ibid. 241–50.

were not affected and demanded that 'the present provisional govern-ment', should be converted into a 'legal' one by elections.

This statement, which may have been drafted by Stresemann, signal-ly failed to condemn the putsch. It was naturally angrily attacked by the republican parties and has been the subject of much criticism by histor-ians.[153] Stresemann was later embarrassed by it and claimed that he had tried to get criticism of the violent breach of the constitution included in it.[154] This claim is not supported by the minutes of the afternoon meeting, though there is a reference of this kind in the short minute of the morning session. Why did Stresemann, after he had repeatedly opposed a military coup in public, at the very least consent to the weak statement on behalf of the DVP on 13 March?

His attitude is partly explained by the simple fact that his loyalty to the republican constitution did not go very deep. Such loyalty as he felt was instrumental: it provided a framework for recovery and protection against civil war. He was not so much shocked by the putsch as afraid that it would provoke a second revolution. His main aim therefore was to find a peace-ful way out of the crisis.

He also feared for the future of the army. Like most of his class he saw the army as the last defence against revolution. Yet the putsch could undermine the position the army had come to occupy since 1918 as the semi-independent guarantor of the government against revolution from the left. Stresemann expressed this fear in the next meeting of DVP leaders on 14 March when he said a collapse of the putsch would not matter so far as it affected Kapp but it would as far as the troops were concerned.[155] This was also a concern for senior officers in the Defence Ministry, who disapproved of the putsch, and indeed for some members of the republican government.[156]

[153] Hartenstein, *Die Anfänge*, 156–9; Turner, *Stresemann*, 52–3, 65–7. Baechler, *Stresemann*, 255–65, is less critical, pointing out the speed with which Stresemann adjusted to a rapidly changing situation.

[154] Draft circular 'An die Wahlkreisvorsitzenden und Parteisekretäre' (Nl. 217). According to one source Stresemann was already unhappy with the declaration the same day—and considered trying to prevent its publication—after a member of the Centre Party, Karl Herold, told him its effect would be 'downright catastrophic': Kolb and Richter (eds.), *Nationalliberalismus*, 250.

[155] Minutes of the meeting, 14 Mar. 1920: Kolb and Richter (eds.), *Nationalliberalismus*, 253. Stresemann returned to this theme in his subsequent account, 'Die Märzrevolte', *Deutsche Stim-men*, 32/12–13, 28 Mar. 1920, also published separately as G. Stresemann, *Die Märzereignisse und die Deutsche Volkspartei* (Berlin: Staatspolitischer Verlag, 1920), 7.

[156] Erger, *Kapp-Lüttwitz*, 139–47.

These considerations do not fully explain the bias towards the Kapp regime in the statement of 13 March. Stresemann had been frustrated at the refusal of the republican government to call elections and, even according to his son's account, could not altogether suppress his pleasure at its predicament.[157] Kapp seemed to be willing to hold elections. Stresemann did not therefore want to see the new government capitulate before an agreement over elections had been reached. If the putsch collapsed there was also a danger that the republican parties would recover lost ground with the electorate.[158]

When the DVP leaders met again on 14 March, it was clear that the putsch was regarded with growing scepticism.[159] Stresemann said there was no news that it had support outside Prussia and criticized it for not even preparing a list of ministers in advance, describing it as 'devoid of ideas'. He now proposed that the DVP should work on Kapp and the representatives of other parties in Berlin to find a settlement. He suggested an agreement might take the form of calling elections, the resignation of both governments, and their replacement by a transitional administration of non-political experts. It was decided to nominate two delegations, one to approach Kapp and the other to establish contact with politicians of other parties.

Initially, neither approach had much success. When the DVP leaders met again on 15 March, Stresemann reported that he had found some support from the Centre Party politician Eduard Burlage, but Burlage had been critical of the DVP's statement of 13 March.[160] The delegation to Kapp reported that he was not willing to use the DVP's good offices for mediation as he did not believe there was any willingness for concessions from the other side. It was then learned that the general strike which had been called by the SPD on 13 March was spreading and that the union of *Beamten* had decided to give it its backing. Against this background, Heinze, who was attending for the first time and who had been instrumental in winning over the military authorities in Dresden to find a modus vivendi with the republican government there, defended his actions and asked how they could expect to lead the masses back to the rule of law if they did not distance themselves from 'this madness'. Stresemann intervened to

---

[157] Wolfgang Stresemann, *Mein Vater*, 180.

[158] Stresemann later referred to the danger that the putsch would deprive the DVP of its 'political harvest': *Die Märzereignisse*, 25.

[159] Minutes of the meeting, 14 Mar. 1920: Kolb and Richter (eds.), *Nationalliberalismus*, 251–7.

[160] Minutes of the meeting, 15 Mar. 1920: ibid. 263–72.

try to forestall the division these remarks were bound to cause, arguing that both Heinze and the Berlin party had acted correctly given the different circumstances they faced. He defended their action in Berlin, saying that if they had come out against Kapp there would have been bloodshed and also that to be able to mediate they had to be in a position to negotiate with both sides. He proposed that they should continue to work for a broad coalition to take over from both existing governments and that they should try to get the parties in Berlin to present a united front to Lüttwitz to force Kapp's resignation. This appeared to command the consent of the meeting. At the same time they heard that the commanding officer in Dresden, General Maercker, was taking terms for a settlement from Kapp and Lüttwitz to the legal government, which had moved to Stuttgart.

Stresemann now tried energetically to bring about an agreement in Berlin.[161] The prospects improved as politicians from the republican parties in Berlin, including Schiffer and the chairman of the Centre Party Carl Trimborn, were anxious to find a peaceful solution, fearing that otherwise the collapse of the putsch would be followed by revolution.[162] The problem was that the legal government in Stuttgart feared that a negotiated settlement would play into the hands of the USPD making it more likely that the general strike would become a revolutionary move-ment. They were therefore unwilling to countenance any negotiations with Kapp or Lüttwitz.

This situation created an opportunity for Stresemann to act as a go-between in Berlin, since the republican politicians there wanted a settle-ment but were inhibited by their colleagues in Stuttgart. On 16 March Stresemann agreed with DNVP leaders that they should try to find an honourable way out for Lüttwitz and his troops on the basis of concessions which the republican politicians had indicated they were willing to make— new elections, direct election of the Reich president, and a reconstruction of the government. The DNVP leaders and Stresemann also agreed to propose an amnesty for all political offences committed since November 1918, whether from the left or the right, to clinch the deal.[163]

Stresemann contacted Colonel Bauer, who was acting as an adviser to Lüttwitz, and he agreed to talks. Leidig passed this news on to Schiffer, who was in turn prepared to meet Bauer. This meeting was overtaken by

---

[161] Hartenstein, Die Anfänge, 170–3; Erger, Kapp-Lüttwitz, 238–44.

[162] Schiffer wrote a detailed account of the events: BAK, Nl. Schiffer 16.

[163] Erger, Kapp-Lüttwitz, 258–63. Stresemann's account is in Die Märzereignisse, 17–23. Also Leidig's memorandum, 'Meine Teilnahme an den Ereignissen des 13. bis 18. März 1920' (Nl. 217).

another development in which Stresemann was also involved. On the evening of 16 March, Lüttwitz called for Stresemann at his home and taking him to the Reich Chancellery sounded him out on the DVP joining his government. Stresemann refused and persuaded Lüttwitz and Kapp instead to agree to a settlement on the terms he proposed. Lüttwitz thereupon sent another officer, Major Pabst, to negotiate with Schiffer. Although Schiffer agreed to support a settlement on these terms with his personal authority despite the opposition of the government in Stuttgart, this was not enough to satisfy Lüttwitz.

Stresemann was again summoned to the Reich Chancellery the following morning, 17 March, to be told by Lüttwitz that Kapp had resigned at the insistence of the Berlin security police, who had said they could no longer be responsible for public order if he remained. Lüttwitz announced that he was taking charge since conflict could soon break out with Spartacist groups. Stresemann then went round to the Ministry of Justice where politicians from the republican parties had gathered. Here, amid confusion and fear that civil war was already breaking out in Berlin, it was agreed on Stresemann's suggestion that a 'committee of parties' should be formed to conduct negotiations as a means of bypassing the Stuttgart government. Stresemann and a DNVP politician then returned to the Reich Chancellery and persuaded Lüttwitz to come with them to the Ministry of Justice. In the meantime, however, Schiffer had been rebuked by his party colleague, the minister of the interior Erich Koch, to whom he had spoken on the telephone, and no longer felt able to talk to Lüttwitz. Stresemann's pleas that the situation was too serious for such 'formalities' and Schiffer's desire for a settlement led to an even more ingenious solution. It was agreed that the talks would be conducted by Hergt and Stresemann for the DNVP and DVP, Trimborn for the Centre and a representative of the DDP. The SPD would not take part but would wait in a neighbouring room to comment from this safe distance. Schiffer made available his senior departmental official to advise the committee but remained with the SPD members outside the talks.

Agreement was quickly reached on the main terms, new elections, direct elections of the Reich president, and a reconstruction of the government, but the question of how the party leaders could guarantee an amnesty caused problems. They promised their personal support and expressed confidence that it would pass.[164] The SPD members, including

---

[164] This was to cause Stresemann trouble later. Although an amnesty was issued in August it excluded the putsch leaders, and Stresemann went back on the idea of an amnesty for all since it

ministers in the Prussian government, were asked for their opinion and indicated that ways could be found of letting it through. A secret protocol was drawn up on this point which assumed the consent of Schiffer to introduce appropriate legislation, although he denied giving it.[165] After some hesitation, Lüttwitz was persuaded to resign and a notice announcing the terms of the agreement (except the amnesty) was prepared for the press, according to Stresemann in Schiffer's presence and with his help.

The Kapp putsch has been described as 'one of the least creditable episodes' in Stresemann's career.[166] He was effectively satirized in the *Berliner Tageblatt*, whose comic supplement carried a mock advertisement: 'Seek a modest little place on the basis of the facts as they are at the time and request continuous and very rapid information to the Deutsche Volkspartei for the attention of Dr Stresemann.'[167]

Stresemann never allowed that, having been democratically elected, the republican government had a right to his loyalty. It was only after the putsch was over on 18 March that the DVP belatedly issued a declaration which included the words 'We must decisively condemn...every act of violence against the constitution.'[168] Even in retrospect Stresemann denied that those who had benefited from the revolution of 1918 had the right to complain.[169] He also warned the DVP against proclaiming the 'sanctity' of the Constitution in reaction to the putsch since that would detract from the stand they had taken against the Constitution. He even looked forward to a time when if a new Bismarck should rebuild a great

would include 'ringleaders from the left' involved in the Ruhr uprising following the putsch. Lüttwitz and Pabst were naturally indignant. Stresemann found other employment for Pabst and the Reichstag finally agreed to an amnesty on 12 Aug. 1925. Erger, *Kapp-Lüttwitz*, 343–4; Turner, *Stresemann*, 61; Vogt, *Bauer*, 276; and below, pp. 363, 437.

[165] According to Schiffer, the protocol was drawn up without his knowledge. However while they were still celebrating the successful outcome of the talks, Stresemann drew him to one side and, using all his powers of persuasion, induced Schiffer to agree to support the amnesty not in his capacity as a minister but as a DDP member of the Reichstag. Schiffer recorded that, 'From the way Stresemann's eyes lit up, I knew immediately that I had made a mistake.' According to Schiffer, Stresemann then made it known that he had agreed to support an amnesty. This led to renewed criticism of his role during the putsch from party colleagues, particularly Koch, and as a result he decided to resign from the government. Typescript dated 23 Mar. 1920 (BAK, Nl. Schiffer 5, pp. 1121–4), and memoir of the Kapp putsch (Nl. Schiffer, 16).

[166] Turner, *Stresemann*, 65.

[167] *Ulk*, 2, Apr. 1920; Gotthart Schwarz, *Theodor Wolff und Das 'Berliner Tageblatt'* (Tübingen: J. C. B. Mohr, 1968), 178.

[168] *Die Märzereignisse*, 27–8.

[169] Ibid. 8, and speech to the GA, 28 Mar. 1920: Kolb and Richter (eds.), *Nationalliberalismus*, 275–6.

Germany without observing all the paragraphs of the Constitution, the DVP would indemnify him as the National Liberals had done for Bismarck.[170]

It is also true that Stresemann sought to exploit the situation to extract concessions from the republican government—especially the promise of new elections. He was attracted by the idea of getting both the Kapp and republican governments to resign in favour of a broad coalition government, which would include the DVP, before the elections were held. Had the Stuttgart government been forced to concede this demand, it would have been a shattering blow to its prestige. The DVP would have been able to present itself as the saviour of the country from the disaster to which republican misgovernment had almost brought it. Not surprisingly the republican parties—even those politicians in Berlin who wanted a settlement—showed no inclination to accept this proposal and Stresemann let it drop, asking only for an early reconstruction of the government. The Stuttgart government in any case disowned the agreement reached in Berlin, and it looked as though Stresemann's efforts to profit by mediation had been in vain.

Stresemann also had other motives for mediation, however. It was a way of maintaining party unity in a situation where members were divided between sympathy for the putsch and fear of the consequences. It was also a genuine attempt to find a way out of a situation which appeared more threatening in Berlin than elsewhere. Once he had decided on the policy, he pursued it with characteristic determination to a conclusion. The putsch collapsed independently of his efforts, but he helped Lüttwitz to accept the inevitable. Although Stresemann's claim that the DVP had helped 'to avoid endless bloodshed and to make possible the reinstatement of constitutional government' was exaggerated, it is undeniable that the republican parties in Berlin had found his intervention helpful.[171]

Not surprisingly it was this aspect which Stresemann emphasized in retrospect. He claimed that their efforts had helped to preserve the army and to prevent the situation sliding towards communism.[172] Shrugging off attempts in the Democratic press to establish his complicity in the putsch, Stresemann turned the attack back on the DDP for siding with the general strike. The trouble with a general strike he said, again alluding to Russia,

[170] Copy from part of the original (lost) record of the GA meeting, 28 Mar. 1920: ibid. 285.

[171] Die Märzereignisse, 26; Erger, Kapp-Lüttwitz, 249–50, 262, 269–71.

[172] Die Märzereignisse, 11.

was that one never knew when and in whose hands it would end.[173] This was an effective thrust at the government parties at a time when they were alarmed and divided by the strike, which had acquired a momentum of its own. The trade union leadership in Berlin imposed political conditions for ending the strike, and in the Ruhr it turned into a spontaneous uprising which was brutally suppressed by the army. These events frightened middle-class opinion and seemed to bear out Stresemann's warnings.

The Elections of June 1920

After the putsch the government decided that the demand for elections should no longer be resisted, and they were set for 6 June. Stresemann confidently expected to gain support both from the DNVP, embarrassed by its connections with the putsch, and from the DDP, embarrassed by the general strike. He told a meeting of the standing committee that the middle class positively 'thirsted' for a party which opposed both reaction and socialism.[174] This claim seemed to be confirmed when a prominent member of the DNVP, Siegfried von Kardorff, defected to the DVP accusing the DNVP of moving further to the right. A whole series of defections from the DDP followed, one of the reasons being the DDP's support for the strike.[175]

Stresemann set the course for the election campaign at a meeting of the 200 members of the national executive on 18 April.[176] Adjusting his message to the events in the Ruhr, he declared that the whole civilized world faced the great question of how to come to terms with socialism and Bolshevism. He reasserted his view that the DVP should be willing to form a coalition with the SPD as, if they were excluded from power, the working class would be driven to the radical extreme. But he also maintained that the power of the SPD within the coalition should be reduced from their leading role to that of equality with the bourgeois parties. He

[173] Ibid. In his speech to the GA on 28 Mar. 1920, Stresemann drew a parallel between Ebert and Kerensky and the Kapp putsch and the Kornilov plot, pointing out that the last had led to the arming of the proletariat and the Bolshevik revolution, a danger that he believed still threatened from the general strike. Kolb and Richter (eds.), *Nationalliberalismus*, 278.

[174] Minutes of the meeting, 28 Mar. 1920: ibid. 280.

[175] Hartenstein, *Die Anfänge*, 195–203. See Plate 20.

[176] Minutes of the meeting of the Zentralvorstand, 18 Apr. 1920: Kolb and Richter (eds.), *Nationalliberalismus*, 290–7.

dismissed the DDP as mere 'stirrup holders' for socialism. He repeated his view that the SPD was losing support to the USPD and the Communist Party (Kommunistische Partei Deutschlands; KPD) because of the contradiction between their ideals and their policies in government and because they lacked the courage to say that their ideals would not work in practice. A future government would have to be prepared to use force to maintain the state against the growing radicalism of the masses. Turning to foreign policy, he again used the threat of Bolshevism as his starting point. Unless the Versailles treaty was revised, Germany would go under, and then 'the whole of Europe will go up in flames together'. He expressed the hope that France would realize that there was no alternative to an economic understanding with Germany and that, despite difficult years ahead, 'reason and a feeling for the common interests of Europe' would prevail.

Although he stressed that the party would retain its independence of the DNVP, he urged his supporters to fight the election from the position that 'The enemy is on the left!'. His aim remained unchanged: to join the coalition by replacing the DDP as the major Protestant Liberal party. He also hoped to take advantage of the expected loss of SPD support to the left to shift the balance of the coalition towards the middle-class parties. To support this aim he presented very little in the way of policy. His criticism of the government was essentially polemical, taking advantage of its loss of the ideological initiative since January 1919.

Stresemann's tactics made good electioneering, and success was essential if the party was to become a significant force. But his concept of the future of coalition politics glossed over serious problems. If, as he expected, the SPD were to have less influence in a future government, there was no obvious reason why it should be willing to take part, since its role would be mainly to defend unpopular measures in which it did not believe. If, on the other hand, the new government would in practice continue the moderate policies of its predecessors, then it was unclear how the DVP would retain the support of an electorate mobilized on an anti-left platform.

The elections brought the DVP the breakthrough. It won 13.9 per cent of the vote and almost tripled in size from twenty-two seats in the National Assembly to sixty-five in the new Reichstag. This achievement seems to have been mainly the result of recapturing the old National Liberal vote from the DDP.[177] The DVP did well in the traditional

---

[177] Hartenstein, *Die Anfänge*, 224–53; Albertin, *Liberalismus*, 153–8; Ludwig Richter, *Die Deutsche Volkspartei 1918–1933* (Düsseldorf: Droste, 2002), 120–3.

National Liberal strongholds: the independent peasant farmers of the north and west and the urban middle class, especially in commercial and administrative centres and in university towns. It remained comparatively weak, however, in much of south Germany where the DDP vote held up better than in the north. But overall the DDP share of the vote fell from 18.5 per cent to 8.4 per cent and its representation from seventy-five seats to thirty-nine. Stresemann savoured his triumph, describing the result as 'a catastrophic defeat' for the DDP.[178] He was particularly gratified at the DVP's success in the Berlin region where, despite the attacks of the Democratic press, it took five seats to the DDP's two. Had it not been for Jewish fears of the alleged 'blood-thirsty anti-Semitism' of the DVP, he wrote, the DDP would not have won any Berlin seats at all.

Stresemann's prediction that the SPD would suffer losses to the USPD and KPD was also fully confirmed. The SPD sank from 165 seats to 103 while the USPD shot up from twenty-two to eighty-three and the Communist KPD entered the Reichstag for the first time with four members. Facing this challenge on its left, however, the SPD was not inclined to fall in with Stresemann's plan for it to enter a coalition in which the bourgeois parties would have the greater say. Instead Germany was faced with the prospect of minority government and the SPD returning to opposition.

In another important respect, the election did not have the result for which Stresemann had hoped. There was no evidence that the DVP had succeeded in cutting into the DNVP vote on its right. Stresemann had assumed at the end of the war that the fortunes of the Conservative Party would decline in the new democracy because of its opposition to reform of the Prussian franchise. Indeed one reason for dropping the name National Liberal had been the feeling that it had been discredited by the opposition of the Prussian National Liberals to franchise reform.[179] The DNVP increased its share of the vote, however, to 14.4 per cent and its representation from forty-two to seventy-one seats. It achieved this by extending from the old Conservative base in Prussia into new areas both socially and geographically. Its alliance with the Christian Social Party and the anti-Semites enabled it to establish itself in most parts of the Reich, particularly in large towns. This was not a comfortable development for Stresemann as he prepared to enter a coalition without the DNVP.

---

[178] 'Wahlausfall und Regierungsbildung', *Deutsche Stimmen*, 32/25, 20 June 1920.
[179] Stresemann's explanation to the Zentralvorstand, 12 Apr. 1919: Kolb and Richter (eds.), *Nationalliberalismus*, 122.

The election victory of 1920 was deceptive. The government had lost its majority, with the DDP and SPD suffering badly and the Centre Party also losing ground.[180] But despite its gains the DVP had not extended its natural base. There was also no obvious consensus between the SPD and the bourgeois parties which could form the basis of a majority government. Rather, the strength of the extremes both on the left and the right threatened to pull the centre apart. Stresemann had made a successful comeback from the nadir of 1919, but he was a long way from realizing his twin dreams of the DVP as the natural home of the Protestant middle class, eclipsing the DNVP as well as the DDP, and forming with the Centre Party and the SPD a stable, majority coalition.

[180] The total vote for the Centre Party suffered only a small decline, but it was weakened by the defection of its Bavarian wing to form the Bavarian People's Party (Bayerische Volkspartei; BVP) on its right, so that instead of ninety-one seats in the National Assembly the Centre held sixty-four seats in the Reichstag and the BVP twenty-one. Alfred Milatz, *Wähler und Wahlen in der Weimarer Republik* (Bonn: Bundeszentrale für politische Bildung, 1965), 115.

5

'The latchkey to power'

Building a Coalition of the Centre, June 1920–December 1922

The elections of June 1920 were a watershed both for the Republic and the DVP. The coalition of SPD, Centre, and DDP, which had seemed to promise a secure future for the Republic in January 1919, lost its majority, and it was unclear how a new government was to be formed. This faced the DVP with a critical decision, one which was to recur repeatedly in the years that followed. Would it remain in opposition, thus protecting its right flank from the DNVP, or would it form a minority coalition with the parties of the middle, or even a so-called 'great coalition' which included the SPD in a majority government?

Stresemann had never been in any doubt that the proper place for the DVP was in government, and his success in the elections gave him the chance to put this policy into practice. He faced opposition from the DNVP, which naturally made the most of his willingness to form a coalition with the DDP and Centre Party in June 1920 and the readiness he expressed to see this extended to the SPD. He also faced opposition from within the DVP, which did not find it easy to make the transition from a party of middle-class protest to a party of government. The DVP followed his leadership, though with increasing reluctance, until his death in October 1929. This was an essentially personal achievement, a mark of his skill and authority within the party. He was able to appeal to an ideology of service to the state among middle-class professional groups and also the prospect of influence in government which was important to the industrial wing. However, there was an electoral cost. The DVP lost a third of its vote in the next elections in May 1924, support it never recaptured.

Had Stresemann chosen to continue a policy of opposition after June 1920 there would also have been difficulties. The danger of the DVP losing its identity by too close an association with the DNVP was a real one. His argument that voters who had switched back from the DDP wanted positive policies also had substance. For the party that claimed to be the party of balance in the political system, remaining outside government would have had its difficulties. What would prevent the divisions of the pre–1914 and wartime eras breaking out again? In government there was at least the ideology of working for national recovery to hold the party together. On the other hand, had Stresemann decided to continue the policy of opposition—anti-socialist and anti-republican while also distinct from the conservatism of sections of the DNVP—most of the DVP would probably have followed him with equal or greater enthusiasm. His commitment to a coalition of the centre was his main contribution to the stability of the Republic, one which did not long survive his death.

Stresemann's Political Strategy

During the period from June 1920 to November 1922 Stresemann spent much of his time persuading the DVP either to join or to remain in government. In this he was only partially successful, mainly because the Allies' attempts to enforce the Versailles treaty made the DVP increasingly unwilling to share responsibility for unpopular decisions. As a result, having joined the government in 1920, the DVP left again in May 1921 and only returned in November 1922.

Stresemann argued the case for coalition in meetings of the Reichstag party and the national executive and in major speeches to the two party conferences in December 1920 and October 1921. His arguments showed both the originality of his political views and a keen awareness of the way in which the future of the party system could be influenced by the tactics of the DVP. He saw more clearly than most the possibilities and the dangers for a minority party of the centre right. His view was informed by his own experience and also his interest in the history of the party system. In 1921 he gave a series of lectures on German politics to an adult education college, the Lessing Hochschule, and he also addressed the new school for the study of politics founded by the publicist Ernst Jäckh.[1]

Stresemann was unusually open-minded towards the SPD. This was a natural development from his pre-war and wartime attitudes but one which made him stand out from his party. To carry the DVP with him he appealed to the values of liberalism. He blamed the SPD's rise on the failure of the empire to give equal rights to all citizens.[2] More specifically, he blamed the 'satiated, liberal middle class' which had preferred to tolerate the privileges of the Conservatives rather than 'opening the door wide to cooperation with the Social Democrats which would have taught them to take responsibility'.[3] When attacked by the DNVP leader Count Westarp for his willingness to contemplate coalition with the SPD, Stresemann replied that he did not believe that it was desirable 'to perpetuate the battle between Social Democracy and the middle class'.[4] He warned the DVP party conference in December 1920 that if the bourgeois parties refused in principle to consider a coalition with the SPD, it would reunite with the USPD.[5]

In 1929 a liberal journalist recalled how Stresemann had broken with social convention in the autumn of 1922 by asking to meet leading Social Democrats over lunch to discuss their opposition to coalition with the DVP.[6] Where the right instinctively looked for protection against socialism, Stresemann instinctively looked for conciliation through the democratic process. His claim that he had always advocated the idea of the

---

[1] His diary for 12 Jan. 1921 refers to his first lecture to the Lessing Hochschule in Berlin, recording that there were about 150 people in his audience; see also diary entries for 2 and 9 Feb. 1921 (Nl. 362). The Lessing Hochschule, founded in 1901 and under the direction of Ludwig Lewin from 1914 to 1933, organized lectures on contemporary developments in the arts and sciences and mainly appealed to a well-educated, middle-class audience. (I am grateful to Jochen Fetzer of the Hochschule for this information). Ernst Jäckh, *The New Germany: Three Lectures* (London: Oxford University Press, 1927), 64–5; Antonio Missiroli, *Die Deutsche Hochschule für Politik* (Königswinter: Friedrich Naumann Stiftung, 1988). According to Jäckh the lectures drew a wide audience, including university students, officials, professional people, journalists, and businessmen.

[2] Speech to the party conference in Nuremberg, 3 Dec. 1920: BAK, R 45 II/26.

[3] Obituary notice for Robert Friedberg, *Deutsche Stimmen*, 32/26, 27 June 1920: Stresemann presented Friedberg as a representative figure for such attitudes in the old National Liberal Party, a criticism which he defended by saying he was not speaking ill of the dead, only the truth!

[4] 'Politische Umschau', *Deutsche Stimmen*, 32/39, 26 Sept. 1920.

[5] Speech to the party conference, 3 Dec. 1920: BAK, R 45 II/26.

[6] Max Reiner, 'Stresemanns Aufstieg zur europäischen Größe', *Vossische Zeitung*, 6 Oct. 1929: PA, Nl. Bernhard, Zeitungsausschnitte, 16.

'community of the nation' (*Volksgemeinschaft*) with 'energy and tenacity', and that this idea, which 'runs through all Dr Stresemann's speeches like a red thread is perhaps the essence of his political philosophy', may have been exaggerated but it represented an important element in his thinking.[7] In a deeply divided society he genuinely believed in the need for consensus.

In practice, however, in 1920 there was no likelihood of the SPD agreeing to coalition with the DVP. The DVP was seen as 'the industrialists' party' and a party whose loyalty to the Republic was still in doubt after the Kapp putsch. In addition the SPD could not ignore the challenge of the USPD on its left. Stresemann was also careful to keep his distance. Although declaring his willingness to see the SPD join the coalition, he pointed out that the bourgeois parties would remain the major influence within it. He also continued to distinguish in public between the working class, whom he regarded as fundamentally patriotic, and the SPD leadership, whom he still described as unable to admit that their ideology had failed.[8] As well as the differences over policy, there was also a tactical motive for such statements. Stresemann had to carry the DVP in what he called the 'difficult work' of changing fronts from an election campaign against the left to coalition with the SPD's erstwhile partners, the Centre and the DDP.[9] It probably suited him quite well that the SPD was as yet unwilling to join the coalition since that would have made the task of winning over the DVP more difficult.

The tactics to be adopted towards the SPD were closely tied to his view of the party system as a whole. There were four major poles—Conservative, Catholic, Liberal, and Socialist—and of these all but the Catholic had real or potential divisions into two or more major parties.[10] The volatility

---

[7] Henry Bernhard, 'Das Kabinett Stresemann', *Deutsche Stimmen*, 35/24, 20 Dec. 1923. Stresemann wrote this account of his administration but published it under the name of his private secretary: Bernhard (ed.), *Vermächtnis*, i. 85. The concept of the *Volksgemeinschaft* came into common use during the First World War to maintain morale on the home front and to express an alternative form of patriotism, stretching from the SPD to the Centre and Liberal parties, against the exclusive claims of the German Patriotic Party. The term again became popular during the Ruhr crisis. As, in the later 1920s, the Weimar Republic became torn by sectional disputes, *Volksgemeinschaft* became instead a propaganda tool of the NSDAP. Gunther Mai, '"Verteidigungskrieg" und "Volksgemeinschaft". Staatliche Selbstbehauptung, nationale Solidarität und soziale Befreiung in Deutschland in der Zeit des Ersten Weltkrieges (1900–1925)', in Wolfgang Michalka (ed.), *Der Erste Weltkrieg* (Munich: Piper, 1994), 585–602. (I am grateful to Jeremy Noakes for this reference.)

[8] Speech to the party conference, 3 Dec. 1920: BAK, R 45 II/26.

[9] 'Zum Parteitag in Nürnberg', *Deutsche Stimmen*, 32/50, 14 Dec. 1920.

[10] The Catholic Centre Party was also split from January 1920, with the Bavarian wing organizing separately as the BVP, but this remained a regional division. A few extreme

of the electorate, seen in the swing away from the government coalition in June 1920, meant that—apart from the Catholic pole— the distribution of the vote between the parties within each pole and even across them was unstable. Stresemann remained firmly of the view that the future of the DVP lay with the Centre Party in the middle of the spectrum. He feared that otherwise the coalition of 1919—SPD, Centre, and DDP—might be revived, perhaps as a minority government or even with the USPD as a majority. In that event the DVP would once again be isolated with the DNVP on the right, a position he always sought to avoid.

In Stresemann's view, there was no prospect of constructing an alternative majority on the right, since the Centre and DDP refused to consider coalition with the DNVP.[11] He did not believe, as his critics argued, that the DVP should try to force the Centre and the DDP to the right by themselves refusing to join a coalition without the DNVP. That, he objected, would give the DNVP a 'blank cheque' to decide the DVP's future.[12] It might also be counter-productive, driving the Centre and DDP to recreate the coalition with the SPD.[13] He preferred to accept the terms which the Centre and DDP imposed: exclusion of the DNVP and a willingness to see the coalition extended to the SPD. In return the DVP gained influence in government at the cost of losing votes to the DNVP. As Stresemann told the party conference, the DNVP should not complain since it had the easier task.[14]

Stresemann's attitude was also influenced by wider considerations. The future of the Republic remained precarious, threatened by developments abroad and enemies at home. As a consequence of the DVP's success in the elections, Stresemann became chairman of the Reichstag committee on foreign affairs where he acquired a detailed knowledge of the limited options for a German foreign minister.[15] In an atmosphere of continued political violence and with talk of replacing the Republic with a dictator-

right-wing Catholics also joined the DNVP. Rudolf Morsey, *Die Deutsche Zentrumspartei 1917–1923* (Düsseldorf: Droste, 1966), 280–5.

[11] Speech to the party conference, 3 Dec. 1920: BAK, R 45 II/26.

[12] Speech to the Zentralvorstand, 5 Oct. 1920: Kolb and Richter (eds.), *Nationalliberalismus*, 362.

[13] 'Politische Umschau', *Deutsche Stimmen*, 32/37, 12 Sept. 1920. Also a report by Eduard Dingeldey on the meeting of the Zentralvorstand, 5 Oct. 1920: Kolb and Richter (eds.), *Nationalliberalismus*, 374–5.

[14] Speech to the party conference, 3 Dec. 1920: BAK, R 45 II/26.

[15] He had taken the lead in proposing such a committee to the Reichstag in October 1916 (see above pp. 82–3), at that time unsuccessfully, and had been a member of the committee since its foundation in 1919.

ship of the right or the left, he also became an increasingly committed defender of the existing parliamentary institutions. As he told the party conference in December 1920, no other basis existed apart from the Weimar Constitution. National recovery and domestic peace both required that the constitutional issue should be allowed to rest. It was the purpose of the DVP to combine 'what was healthy in the old Germany with what we have learned from the new era'.[16] During these years he made his peace with the Republic, becoming not only a *Vernunftrepublikaner* but increasingly identifying himself with it. As his attachment to the Republic grew, so did his reputation, with the result that by November 1922 he was widely expected to be offered the chancellorship. And as his career became linked to the success of the Republic, the DVP became more closely bound to the coalition of the centre on which the Republic depended.

Minority Government

The formation of the new government in June 1920 was preceded by unsuccessful attempts by the SPD to persuade the USPD to join the existing government and then by the DVP leader in the Reichstag, Heinze, who was invited by Ebert to form a government, to persuade the SPD to agree to a coalition.[17] The only alternative remaining was the minority government of Centre, DVP, and DDP which was formed under a Centre Party chancellor, Konstantin Fehrenbach, on 25 June. The SPD agreed to vote for it in the Reichstag to allow it to continue at least until a conference with the Allies, which was about to meet to discuss reparations, had taken place.

There were two difficulties in the coalition negotiations. The DDP demanded that its partners should recognize the constitution and oppose monarchist agitation, a move clearly aimed at the DVP after its ambiguous role in the Kapp putsch. The DVP reacted by refusing to alter its

[16] Speech to the party conference, 3 Dec. 1920: BAK, R 45 II/26.
[17] Heinze was later criticized for not having first asked the Centre and DDP to form a coalition including the DNVP. The critics argued that, even though it was known that the Centre and DDP would refuse, it would have protected the DVP against DNVP criticism that they had not tried to bring about a bourgeois majority government. Stresemann admitted that there might have been party advantage in such a tactic, but said that at the time their purpose had been to see a government formed. Speech to the Zentralvorstand, 5 Oct. 1920: Kolb and Richter (eds.), *Nationalliberalismus*, 362.

programme, but agreed to declare that it accepted the constitution and would defend it.[18]

The composition of the government created further problems. Stresemann was passed over, perhaps because Ebert and the SPD still distrusted him, perhaps because there was no suitable post given the claims of the other coalition parties to keep the offices they had held in the previous government.[19] Heinze became minister of justice and vice-chancellor, and negotiations centred on what further posts should be offered the DVP. The party had demanded during the election that the major economic ministries should be filled by 'experts'. Stresemann was now embarrassed to discover that some of the industrialists, such as Vögler, were unwilling to leave their directorships for the doubtful pleasures of office. The DVP also wanted to displace the existing minister of finance Joseph Wirth, who belonged to the left wing of the Centre Party and was seen as Erzberger's heir.[20] After lengthy negotiations, in which the need to secure the SPD's toleration of the new government played an important part, the DVP was forced to accept Wirth and had to be content with the less important ministries of Economics and the Treasury. These were filled by Ernst Scholz (previously lord mayor of the Berlin district of Charlottenburg) and Hans von Raumer (a prominent representative of the electro-technical

[18] Peter Wulf (ed.), *Das Kabinett Fehrenbach* (Boppard: Harald Boldt, 1970), pp. xvi–xvii.

[19] Ibid., p. xix; Wolfgang Stresemann, *Mein Vater*, 189; Otto Gessler, *Reichswehrpolitik in der Weimarer Zeit* (Stuttgart: Deutsche Verlags-Anstalt, 1958), 150. Stresemann's name appears as chancellor, foreign minister, or minister of the interior on a typed list with handwritten annotations (but not in his hand), headed 'Proposals for appointment' (Nl. 115, H 139270). The document carries a handwritten date 'June 1920', but this may well have been added later by Bernhard, who was not at that time his secretary. It has been suggested that the list represents Stresemann's own ideas in June 1920: Hirsch, *Stresemann*, 125–6, and Baechler, *Stresemann*, 269. However, the document has curious features. Names are proposed for only five ministries: chancellor, foreign minister, and ministers of the interior, defence, and finance. In addition Rudolf Nadolny is proposed as state secretary in the Foreign Ministry, 'after he has conducted negotiations with Russia in Warsaw'. The list also gives the names of commanding officers for an army 'to be raised', each to take charge of a sector of Germany's frontier with Poland, and a detailed list of diplomatic appointments. At the top of the document is a shorthand note (possibly by Stresemann): 'Has Ebert refused the state of war'. These features suggest strongly that the proposal dates rather from July or August 1920 when the DVP wanted the government to be reconstructed and when it was feared that the Red Army would continue its victorious march through Poland into East Prussia. The list may represent Stresemann's ideas for a government of national emergency to deal with the crisis, or it may have come from another source.

[20] There are two recent studies of Wirth: Heinrich Küppers, *Joseph Wirth. Parlamentarier, Minister und Kanzler der Weimarer Republik* (Stuttgart: Franz Steiner, 1997), and Ulrike Hörster-Philipps, *Joseph Wirth 1879–1956. Eine politische Biographie* (Paderborn: Ferdinand Schöningh, 1998), 82–3. For the domestic politics of the Wirth governments Ernst Laubach, *Die Politik der Kabinette Wirth 1921/22* (Lübeck: Matthiesen, 1968) remains informative.

industry).[21] Stresemann replaced Heinze as leader of the party in the Reichstag.

A more serious threat to the coalition came from Allied attempts to enforce reparations payments. Two basic strategies were open to the German government. It could either agree to Allied terms in the hope that these would be revised if they proved impossible to fulfil, or it could refuse and take the risk of French occupation of the Ruhr to enforce payment. German hopes that they might be able to escape this dilemma by offering the French bilateral agreements came to nothing. Hugo Stinnes, the greatest of the Ruhr mine-owners and a member of the DVP in the Reichstag, canvassed schemes for German and French firms to cooperate in rebuilding the devastated areas of north-east France and for a Franco-German customs union in return for revision of the treaty.[22] French industrialists might be attracted by such ideas, but it was unrealistic to expect French governments to agree to a form of cooperation which, as Stinnes intended, would enable the Germans to recover the ascendancy.

The gap between what the Germans considered feasible and what the Allies would accept became obvious at the conference which met at Spa in July. The main issue was the amount of coal due as part of reparations. Stinnes, who was attending as part of the German delegation, declared that the amount fixed under the treaty of 2.4 million tonnes per month was unrealistic and accused the Allies of suffering from 'victors' mania'. This outburst earned him the jubilant support of nationalist groups at home but did not impress the Allies. In the end, against the opposition of Stinnes and some others, the German delegation was forced to accept a figure of 2 million tonnes rather than the 1 million they had offered. Stinnes argued that it would have been better to refuse even at the cost of the occupation of the Ruhr, since that would happen anyway when the Germans were unable to supply the coal and if the occupation took place in the winter its effects would be even more catastrophic. However others including Walther Rathenau, the head of the electronics-based Allgemeine Elektrizitätswerke (AEG), felt that the occupation was to be avoided at all costs, since it would allow the French to take the full amount of coal and the ensuing crisis might lead to the break-up of Germany.

[21] Wulf (ed.), *Kabinett Fehrenbach*, pp. xix–xx.

[22] Peter Wulf, *Hugo Stinnes. Wirtschaft und Politik 1918–1924* (Stuttgart: Klett Cotta, 1979), 201–4; Gerald D. Feldman, *The Great Disorder: Politics, Economics, and Society in the German Inflation 1914–1924* (New York: Oxford University Press, 1997), 312–14; id., *Hugo Stinnes. Biographie eines Industriellen 1870–1924* (Munich: C. H. Beck, 1998), 621–3.

The government had to have the approval of the Reichstag for its decision. Stinnes's opposition and the publicity he had received posed a problem for Stresemann. He had himself urged the DVP ministers to reject the terms, but he did not want the coalition to fall.[23] He showed great skill in defusing the anger of Stinnes and his supporters while at the same time side-stepping their main demands. These were that the DVP should refuse to take responsibility for the Spa agreement and, while remaining in the coalition, should demand that it be reconstructed. In particular, Stinnes thought that Fehrenbach and Wirth should be replaced.[24]

Stresemann immediately summoned a meeting of those members of the Reichstag and Prussian Landtag parties and the standing committee who were in Berlin. After hearing reports from Heinze, Stinnes, and Scholz on the proceedings at Spa, Stresemann made a strong appeal for the party to remain in the government. He warned of the advance of Russian troops through Poland towards East Prussia, saying that Germany could not afford to be without a government. He also pointed out that the consequences of their leaving the government would probably be the return of the previous coalition.[25] At the same time he suggested that they should demand additional representation in the cabinet and that Wirth should be removed if a suitable successor could be found. At a full meeting of the party's representatives the following week, Stresemann was given a free hand to negotiate for a stronger DVP presence in the coalition without being tied to any particular demands.[26] Speaking for the DVP in the Reichstag, Stresemann ostentatiously defended Stinnes and criticized the government's tactics at the Spa conference, but went on to argue that an occupation of the Ruhr had to be prevented at all costs and reaffirmed the DVP's support for the coalition.[27]

Stinnes and his supporters soon realized that they had been outmanoeuvred and looked for ways to strengthen their hold on the party. The

---

[23] Transcript of Stresemann's telegrams to Heinze, 9 and 10 July 1920: (Nl. 141).

[24] Entry for 20 July 1920 in a diary of major events and meetings kept by Stresemann's private secretary at that time, Friedrich Rauch (Nl. 141).

[25] Minutes of the meeting, 21 July 1920: Kolb and Richter (eds.), *Nationalliberalismus*, 320.

[26] Minutes of the meeting of the *Reichstagsfraktion*, the *Vorstand* of the Prussian *Landtagsfraktion*, and the GA, 26–7 July 1920: ibid. 322–42. The DVP was not able to force a reconstruction of the government. A proposal to secure the appointment of a leading member of the DVP, perhaps Stresemann himself, as vice-chancellor was dropped after it had been prematurely disclosed in the press: Rauch diary entries, 28 and 29 July 1920 (Nl. 141), and minutes of the GA, 13 Sept. 1920; Kolb and Richter (eds.), *Nationalliberalismus*, 345; and see n. 19 above.

[27] Reichstag speech, 28 July 1920: Zwoch (ed.), *Reichstagsreden*, 81–114.

competition for control between Stresemann and Stinnes was a complex process.[28] Each had original ideas and they were equally determined. Stinnes was single-minded in furthering the interests of his industrial empire but intelligent and flexible in his tactics. He had been a moving spirit in reaching agreement with trade union leaders in December 1918 to pre-empt the new republican government. Similarly when, with Germany's defeat, it was no longer possible to think of annexing the Lorraine iron ore fields, Stinnes became an advocate of cooperation with the French mining industry since as the stronger partner the Germans stood to benefit most.

Stresemann respected Stinnes's intelligence and agreed with him on important issues, including the conciliation of trade unions and Franco-German economic cooperation. However, they had different priorities. For Stinnes the interests of Ruhr industry came first. For Stresemann preventing the Reich falling apart and maintaining constitutional government were more important. Stinnes regarded the DVP as the political arm of Ruhr industry. But he was only able to carry the party with him when his views were more widely shared. The threat to Stresemann came not from the Ruhr group as such but from their ability to articulate the more general unease within the DVP at taking responsibility for implementing the Versailles treaty.

An analysis of party membership shows the degree to which different interests were represented. The left-wing slogan that the DVP was the 'industrialists' party' was generally accurate, but the jibe that it was the 'Stinnes party' was exaggerated. Among active party members, the national executive, and the party in the Reichstag, industry, commerce, and banking formed easily the largest group with between a third and half of the total. In the Reichstag party, representatives of large and medium-sized industry alone always made up at least 30 per cent of the total, rising to 39 per cent after the 1924 elections and an astonishing 51 per cent after 1928.[29]

However, the business world was divided. Ruhr industry itself did not always unite behind Stinnes, and even when it did its views were not necessarily shared by manufacturers and bankers. There were also other

<hr />

[28] Gerald D. Feldman, 'Hugo Stinnes, Gustav Stresemann, and the Politics of the DVP in the early Weimar Republic', in Pyta and Richter (eds.), *Gestaltungskraft des Politischen*, 421–42. Wulf, *Stinnes*, 132–55.

[29] Döhn, *Politik und Interesse*, 77–90, 315, 348. For a comprehensive analysis of party membership at every level, see Richter, *Deutsche Volkspartei*, 177–93.

significant groups in the party, notably the *Beamten*, including professors and teachers who numbered between a quarter and a third of the total active membership. Together with other professional groups and the party officials, they provided a natural counterweight to the industrial lobbies.

The Ruhr group felt that it was entitled to special consideration because of its financial support for the party. The costs of the initial election campaign in 1919 left the DVP with sizeable debts and these and the costs of building up the party organization and financing the 1920 election campaign were met in large part by substantial contributions from the Ruhr.[30] The importance of this connection was symbolized by the appointment of Vögler as one of the two party treasurers (although he subsequently resigned pleading pressure of work) and by Stinnes himself becoming a member of the Reichstag. Stresemann would have preferred that leading industrialists, particularly Stinnes, had stayed out of the Reichstag because they were an electoral liability. But Stinnes was not to be put off and used financial pressure to improve his position and that of a colleague, Reinhold Quaatz, on the national list of DVP candidates, thus ensuring their election.[31]

Stresemann was particularly sensitive to any challenge from the Ruhr because of his pre-war conflicts with them. He was determined not to become the passive victim of their opposition, like Bassermann, who had feared that if he counter-attacked the party would split. Stresemann did not believe that the Ruhr would defect to the DNVP, since only the DVP offered it direct influence in government. He therefore reacted sharply when Quaatz complained at a meeting of the Reichstag party about the lack of representation of heavy industry on party committees and ham-fistedly threatened that the Ruhr would look elsewhere to protect its interests. Stresemann pointed out that the party also represented manu-facturing industry and that in practice leading industrialists had found themselves too busy to attend the Reichstag. Taking the offensive, he added that the party had carried the unpopularity of its association with heavy industry, that it was only through the DVP that the interests of the Ruhr were represented in government, and that he could not believe that 'such clear-minded people as our leading industrialists' would want to undermine their effectiveness by joining the DNVP. Quaatz protested that he had been misunderstood, but he had to beat a humiliating retreat.

---

[30] Döhn, *Politik und Interesse*, 349–77. For a detailed analysis of DVP finances, see Richter, *Deutsche Volkspartei*, 194–213.

[31] Hartenstein, *Die Anfänge*, 214–23; Feldman, 'Hugo Stinnes, Gustav Stresemann', 423–7.

Stresemann capitalized on the situation by sending Stinnes and Vögler an account of the incident, saying with light irony that he could not believe that they had encouraged Quaatz. He received a diplomatic answer from Stinnes, dissociating himself from Quaatz but maintaining that business-men did have a special claim to be represented on important committees.[32]

In the autumn of 1920 a committee set up by the previous government reported in favour of nationalization of the coal mines. On such an issue there was no difference of principle between the DVP and the Ruhr group and Stresemann cooperated closely with them. The DVP's two ministers, Raumer and Scholz, skilfully postponed a decision until, in 1921, the project was abandoned partly on the grounds that state control would lay the mines open to seizure as a guarantee for reparations.[33] Stresemann was even criticized by some mine-owners for publicly associating the party with Stinnes's unorthodox ideas, which were designed to head off nationalization by offering a proportion of the share capital to public bodies and employees, a suggestion that was too radical for some of the Ruhr firms.[34]

At the same time, Stresemann watched suspiciously for evidence that the Ruhr group was trying to take over the party. In November 1920, in connection with an attempt by one of the Reichstag members from the Ruhr, Carl Cremer, to force a change in the party press service in favour of a group controlled by him, Stresemann noted that the influence of heavy industry had become intolerable. He referred to attempts to take over constituency associations, to set up economic organizations which could throttle the party financially and a concerted effort to pack the party's central decision-making bodies, driving out the intellectuals and bankers.[35]

Stresemann defended his policy of remaining in the coalition success-fully at meetings of the Reichstag party and the national executive and to

[32] Stresemann's account of the meeting of 4 Aug. and copies of his letters to Stinnes and Vögler, all dated 5 Aug. 1920, and Stinnes's reply, 7 Aug. 1920 (Nl. 214): Feldman, 'Hugo Stinnes, Gustav Stresemann', 429-30.

[33] Wulf, *Stinnes*, 229-39; Feldman, *The Great Disorder*, 289-92; Feldman, *Stinnes*, 634-55.

[34] Stresemann's account of the incident and a draft letter of explanation, dated 13 Nov. 1920 (Nl. 141). The main difference was between Stinnes's strategy of 'vertical integration', i.e. the amalgamation of the producers and users of coal and steel into vast enterprises including some where the municipal authorities had majority control, for instance the Rheinisch-Westfälische-Elektrizitätswerke, and the pure mining interests who feared Stinnes's form of 'socialization'. In addition, some of Stinnes's associates persuaded him to make concessions on share ownership to workers and trade unions. Feldman, *Stinnes*, 634-55.

[35] Rauch diary entry for 3 Nov. 1920 (Nl. 141).

the party conference which met at the beginning of December.[36] His central argument remained that if the DVP left the government, its place would be taken by the SPD. This was all the more convincing as the USPD had split, losing a third of its members to the KPD while the remainder drew closer to the SPD. This reduced the threat to the SPD from its left, making it easier for it to consider joining a coalition but also—because its left wing was strengthened—hardening its opposition to joining a coalition with the DVP. Stresemann feared in September that the SPD would try to win back the Centre and DDP to recreate the coalition of 1919, excluding the DVP. To forestall such a manoeuvre, he reiterated his willingness for the SPD to join the existing coalition.[37] In face of demands from constituency organizations that they should leave the government, he told his colleagues to keep cool.[38]

The main problem for Stresemann arose from the determination of the Allies to enforce reparations. On 29 January 1921 the German government was informed that the Allies had set the total sum due at 226 billion gold marks to be paid over forty-two years, plus 12 per cent of the value of German exports. The note came as a shock, since it cut across the preparatory discussions of officials at which Germany was represented. It was also a disappointment since at the end of 1920 there had been hopes that the French, needing German coal and lacking a market for their iron ore, were willing to negotiate.[39]

Stresemann was well informed about these developments. As chairman of the Reichstag foreign affairs committee he heard the confidential reports by the foreign minister Walter Simons. Through Stinnes and Vögler, he knew of the thinking of Ruhr industry. He also cultivated contacts with the British and French embassies. From Lord Kilmarnock, the British chargé d'affaires, he heard an openly critical view of Allied policy. Kilmarnock described French policy as 'foolish' and told Stresemann that the Foreign Office disapproved of Lloyd George giving in to the French. Kilmarnock wanted to see a 'reorientation of Europe against Bolshevism' which he said was threatening British interests in

[36] Diary entries for 30 Sept. to 5 Oct. 1920 (Nl. 141); speech to the Zentralvorstand meeting, 5 Oct. 1920: Kolb and Richter (eds.), *Nationalliberalismus*, 359–67; speech to the party conference in Nuremberg, 3 Dec. 1920: BAK, R 45 II/26.

[37] 'Politische Umschau', *Deutsche Stimmen*, 32/37, 12 Sept. 1920; 32/39, 26 Sept. 1920, and 32/42, 17 Oct. 1920; record of a meeting of the coalition parties, 2 Sept. 1920 and of a conversation with Schiffer, 20 Sept. 1920 (Nl. 141).

[38] Speech to the GA, 13 Sept. 1920: Kolb and Richter (eds.), *Nationalliberalismus*, 345.

[39] Wulf, *Stinnes*, 241–66; Krüger, *Aussenpolitik*, 116–22.

Stresemann and his family

1. Stresemann's father, Ernst (1833–1905). *Politisches Archiv, Auswärtiges Amt, Berlin.*

2. Stresemann's mother, Mathilde (1843–1895). *Politisches Archiv, Auswärtiges Amt, Berlin.*

3. Stresemann as a boy. *Politisches Archiv, Auswärtiges Amt, Berlin.*

4. Stresemann's class at the Andreas *Realgymnasium*. Stresemann is at the end of the front row on the right. *Politisches Archiv, Auswärtiges Amt, Berlin.*

5. Stresemann in the uniform of his *Burschenschaft. Politisches Archiv, Auswärtiges Amt, Berlin.*

6. Käte Stresemann (1885–1970) with elder son, Wolfgang (1904–98). *Politisches Archiv, Auswärtiges Amt, Berlin*

7. Stresemann and his sons, Wolfgang and
Joachim (1908–99). *Politisches Archiv,
Auswärtiges Amt, Berlin.*

8. Stresemann and Käte, on their silver wedding anniversary,
20 October 1928. *Politisches Archiv, Auswärtiges Amt, Berlin.*

Stresemann's Career

Dr. Guſtav Streſemann
Syndikus des Verbandes Sächſiſcher Induſtrieller

9. Syndic of the Association of Saxon Industrialists. *Politisches Archiv, Auswärtiges Amt, Berlin.*

10. At the Café Scheurer during a break from the Locarno negotiations, October 1925. On the left of the group is Carl von Schubert, Stresemann's secretary of state. *E. Meerkämper, Davos; Stresemann family collection.*

11. After signing the treaty of Locarno, London, 1 December 1925.
Front row from right: Baldwin, Luther, Lady Chamberlain and daughter,
Briand, Émile Vandervelde (Belgian foreign minister); on the stairs from
the right: Skrzyński, Stresemann, Vittorio Scialoja (Italy's representative at
the League), and Beneš; behind them Churchill and Chamberlain.
Politisches Archiv, Auswärtiges Amt, Berlin.

12. With the Soviet delegation after signing the treaty of Berlin, 24 April
1926. From the left: Schubert and Friedrich Gaus, and on Stresemann's left
the Soviet ambassador Nicolai Krestinski. *Scherl/Süddeutscher Verlag—
Bilderdienst.*

13. On the train to Paris for the signing of the Kellogg–Briand
Pact, August 1928. *Erich Salomon, Bildarchiv Preußischer
Kulturbesitz, Berlin.*

14. In discussion with journalists in the Reichstag, 1929.
Erich Salomon, Ullstein Bilderdienst.

15. During the Reichstag debate, 24 June 1929. *Ullstein Bilderdienst.*

16. Speech to the League of Nations, 9 September 1929. *Ullstein Bilderdienst.*

17. German People's Party poster for the Reichstag elections, May 1928. *Scherl/Süddeutscher Verlag—Bilderdienst.*

18. Stresemann at the Hague Conference, August 1929. *F. Siegler, The Hague; Stresemann family collection.*

India.[40] The French ambassador, Charles Laurent, was also pessimistic. He described France's financial situation as 'deplorable' (worse than at any time since before Cardinal Richelieu) while the reparations expert, Professor Haguenin, called the Versailles treaty 'impossible' and 'ruinous' for France.[41]

Stresemann did not expect these attitudes to change Allied policy in the short term. The collapse of the Soviet invasion of Poland in September 1920 removed the immediate fear of Bolshevism spreading across Europe and with it the hope of a reversal of Allied policy.[42] But he managed to sound confident that in the longer term economic interdependence would bring a fresh start. In a speech to the Reichstag on 28 April 1921, he contrasted the attitude of French industrialists who were willing to co-operate with that of the politicians who, having promised that Germany would pay, were now trapped in a self-defeating policy. He also referred to others who were looking only for a pretext to take the Rhine.[43] Stresemann warned that if such plans were carried out the result would be the destruction of France as well as Germany. They shared 'a common destiny'. He urged that the international economy had to be made to work again and that Germany could help France only if it was itself allowed to recover. He did not expect these views to prevail immediately over the bitterness resulting from the war and he warned that any German government faced a very difficult future for many years. Nevertheless, looking ahead, he declared his confidence 'in the possibility of an international understanding. It will come because it must come.'[44] These remarks take on a special significance from the fact that at the time Stresemann expected the government to fall and there was already a serious possibility that he would become chancellor or foreign minister.

Stresemann's problem was that in 1921 there was as yet no sign of an understanding being reached and the DVP would not willingly remain in

[40] Draft letter from Stresemann, dated Feb. 1921, describing the conversation which took place on 24 Feb. (Nl. 237). In July 1920 Stresemann had already visited Kilmarnock with the German industrialist Arnold Rechberg, to propose an Anglo-French-German alliance against the advancing Soviet army: Rauch diary entries, 24 July, 31 July 1920 (Nl. 141); Baechler, *Stresemann*, 278.

[41] Draft letter from Stresemann, dated Feb. 1921, describing the conversations which took place between 21 Feb. and 24 Feb. (Nl. 237).

[42] Record of a conversation between Stresemann and Simons, 21 Sept. 1920 (Nl. 141).

[43] Haguenin had told him that this was the policy of Marshal Foch: draft letter, dated Feb. 1921 (Nl. 237).

[44] Rheinbaben (ed.), *Reden und Schriften*, i. 349–69. Stresemann had already expressed similar ideas in a previous speech to the Reichstag on 5 Mar. 1921: ibid. 328–49.

a coalition which submitted to Allied terms. When the Allied proposals were received at the end of January, he tried to find a way out of the dilemma by persuading both the DNVP and the SPD to join the government in a united front to oppose the Allies. This was in a sense logical since all parties rejected the terms. However, it was also doomed since the SPD was not willing to join a government with the DVP let alone the DNVP and the DNVP was also unenthusiastic.[45] As pressure from the Allies intensified in the spring, Stresemann made increasingly desperate efforts to find a solution.

The opposition from within the DVP was led by Stinnes. In a meeting of the standing committee he attacked the foreign minister, Simons, for the way he had handled the German counter-proposals on reparations which had been discussed with the Allies at a conference in London at the beginning of March. Stinnes accused Simons of keeping the rest of the government in the dark about the advice he had received from industrialists and then of going beyond what the government had agreed in talking to the Allies. He made it clear that he thought Simons should resign. The DVP ministers, von Raumer and Scholz, confirmed Stinnes's account and Stresemann was also critical, referring to Simons's 'completely inexplicable behaviour'.[46] However, as after the Spa conference in July, Stresemann again saved the situation. He ignored Stinnes's demand for Simons's resignation and in his public commentary in the *Deutsche Stimmen*, he played down the clash between the two which had spread to the foreign affairs committee of the Reichstag. With his usual skill, Stresemann contrived to praise both Simons and Stinnes and argued that the important thing was to prepare properly for future conferences.[47]

The question of whether the DVP should remain in the coalition was raised by Stresemann at the standing committee in connection with the situation in Prussia. Elections to the Landtag in February had produced a

[45] Reichsgeschäftsstelle der Deutschen Volkspartei (ed.), *Die Bemühungen der Deutschen Volkspartei um die Bildung einer nationalen Einheitsfront* (Berlin [1921]); copy in BAK, ZSg.1, 42/1. Memorandum by Stresemann of conversations with Fehrenbach and Koch, 21 Feb., and of a meeting with leaders of the coalition parties 22 Feb. (Nl. 237); minutes of a meeting of the GA, 8 Mar. 1921: Kolb and Richter (eds.), *Nationalliberalismus*, 406–7. Stresemann was not alone in his idea of a broad national coalition from the SPD to the DNVP. Erich Koch, a leading member of the DDP and a minister in the Fehrenbach government, shared the hope, though he was sceptical about how long such a coalition would last: Koch-Weser's diary, 4 and 7 Mar. 1921: BAK, Nl. Koch-Weser, 27, 28.

[46] Minutes of the meeting of the GA, 8 Mar. 1921: Kolb and Richter (eds.), *Nationalliberalismus*, 404–16.

[47] 'Politische Umschau', *Deutsche Stimmen*, 33/13, 27 Mar. 1921.

shift to the right increasing the DVP's representation from twenty-one to fifty-eight. Although the previous coalition still retained a narrow majority of six, it seemed possible that the DVP might be able to gain entry to the Prussian government provided it did not desert its coalition partners in the Reich. Under these circumstances the committee offered no dissent to Stresemann's view that the existing Reich coalition should be maintained.[48]

This success for Stresemann was, however, short-lived. The SPD remained unwilling to join a coalition with the DVP, and eventually a minority government was formed in Prussia at the end of April under Adam Stegerwald, who came from the trade union wing of the Centre Party. More humiliating for the DVP, he left them out of his government in the hope of persuading the SPD to join. At the same time the fortunes of the Reich government went from bad to worse. In March the Allies rejected the German counter-proposals and occupied three Ruhr towns. In a desperate bid to prevent the situation deteriorating further, Simons appealed to the United States to arbitrate and subsequently made new proposals which went a long way to meeting Allied demands.

These concessions were too much for the DVP. On the same day, 22 April, Stinnes told the Reichstag party that they should leave the government. Stresemann opposed him, but the party insisted over the next few days that both the chancellor and foreign minister should resign.[49] The attitude of the DVP started a wave of speculation about a possible reconstruction of the government until it eventually decided to resign on 4 May. For the first time, Stresemann himself became a serious candidate for the chancellorship.

A Stresemann Government?

Stresemann's own part in these events is not entirely clear since the evidence is incomplete and the account he gave of it afterwards was

[48] Minutes of the meeting of the GA, 8 Mar. 1921: Kolb and Richter (eds.), *Nationalliberalismus*, 404–14.

[49] Memorandum by Stresemann, marked 'Strictly confidential!', giving a summary of events in note form (Nl. 212 and another copy in Nl. 234). The memorandum was clearly dictated on or soon after 1 May where it ends, although the dating 'May 1921' and 'beginning of May 1921' may have been added later by Bernhard. Stresemann also made entries for each day in a small diary, which appears to have been overlooked by historians. The diary gives the date of the meeting of the Reichstag party as 22 Apr. while the memorandum gives 23 Apr. (Nl. 362).

intended to justify his actions. Two facts stand out. He wanted the DVP to
remain part of a reconstructed government and he grasped the opportunity to make it a government of his own. In this he had the support of the
DVP, including that of Stinnes and his circle, but only provided he reverse
the foreign policy of Simons to one of resistance to Allied demands.
Stresemann could only lead such a government however, if a majority in
the Reichstag could be found to support it. At the end of April it was
already known that the Allies were preparing their final terms on reparations. If these produced a united front among at least the coalition parties
for rejection, Stresemann could hope to form a government. His first
efforts together with the Stinnes group in the last week of April were
directed towards this end. Vögler canvassed the idea of a Stresemann
government among members of the Centre Party, where he found some
support. Stresemann himself sounded out the DNVP on the choice of
foreign minister.[50] This indicates that he was thinking in terms of forming
a government of the existing coalition parties but tolerated by the DNVP
rather than the SPD to reject the Allied terms.

Stresemann knew the risks of committing himself to a policy of rejection.
On 5 May the Allies presented their final terms, threatening to occupy the
whole of the Ruhr if the Germans did not accept within a week. The new
terms could in fact be seen as not very far from the last German offer, but
that had itself been wholly unacceptable to Stinnes and the DVP. There was
also a risk to the future of Upper Silesia. Following an indecisive plebiscite
in March, Poland tried to pre-empt an Allied decision on the future of the
province by occupying the areas it claimed at the beginning of May with an
army of Polish settlers. The risks in domestic politics were, from Stresemann's point of view, equally serious. If a Reichstag majority decided to
accept the Allied ultimatum and the DVP persisted in opposition, then it
would be excluded from power, which would pass back to the SPD, Centre,
and DDP. The attitude of the Centre Party was decisive since on it
depended whether there would be a majority for acceptance or rejection.

Despite the talk of national resistance, Stresemann's tactics shifted with
receipt of the ultimatum. He realized that it might have to be accepted,

---

[50] Stresemann's memorandum (Nl. 212 and 234) and diary for 26 and 29 Apr. (Nl. 362). He
suggested either Graf Brockdorff-Rantzau, who as the first foreign minister of the Weimar
Republic had become famous for his speech condemning the Versailles treaty, or his predecessor,
Paul von Hintze. With Stresemann as chancellor and either of these appointments as foreign
minister, the government would clearly have signalled its intention to reject the ultimatum and
challenge the Allies to occupy the Ruhr.

both because of the risks of rejection and because the Centre Party's position was uncertain. According to Koch, Stresemann had already told him on 5 May that the ultimatum would have to be accepted, though when Schiffer, who was also hoping to lead a new government, said that the DDP would not accept it Stresemann became more guarded.[51] Instead of outright rejection of the Allied note, Stresemann probably already thought in terms of conditional acceptance as a way of heading off the occupation of the Ruhr and winning the support of a majority in the Reichstag. If the Centre Party decided in favour of acceptance, he would have to look for a majority of the parties of the old coalition supported as before by the SPD not the DNVP.[52] He also hoped that as the party of industry the DVP would be able to secure concessions from the Allies if it led the government. He later emphasized that it was only when the Centre decided to accept the ultimatum on 8 May that he had tried to find a compromise, but he admitted that he had anticipated their decision for several days.[53] He kept quiet about his alternative proposal until the Centre had made up its mind, in order not to be blamed for having undermined a possible majority for rejection.

When on 8 May the Centre Party decided to accept the ultimatum, Stresemann was ready with the proposal that the former coalition partners should make their acceptance conditional on receiving certain guarantees, particularly about the future of Upper Silesia. He secured the assent of the other parties and put his plan into action.[54] On 9 May he asked Kilmarnock to obtain clarification of certain points and for an assurance that Germany would keep the greater part of the industrial districts of Upper Silesia. Kilmarnock at once communicated the questions to the Foreign Office, which sent a favourable reply with respect to the

[51] Koch's diary 5–7 May 1921: BAK, Nl. Koch-Weser, 27.

[52] There are two draft cabinets in Stresemann's papers, neither dated and neither in his hand, but probably drawn up either after the Centre Party decided on 8 May in favour of acceptance of the ultimatum or in anticipation of this decision (Nl. 234). One of these includes Noske as minister of defence and the former SPD chancellor, Gustav Bauer, as minister of the interior. Görlitz (*Stresemann*, 123) asserts that Stresemann gained the support of the SPD for his plan, but the idea was almost certainly to include Noske and Bauer as individual 'personalities' without requiring the SPD to commit itself. Schiffer had argued along the same lines within the DDP for a cabinet of 'strong men' independent of their parties, specifically mentioning Bauer and Noske. Koch's diary, 29 Apr. 1921: BAK, Nl Koch-Weser, 27. See also Wulf, *Stinnes*, 262.

[53] 'Nach der Entscheidung', *Deutsche Stimmen* 33/20, 15 May 1921.

[54] Stresemann's speech to the Zentralvorstand, 11 June 1921: Kolb and Richter (eds.), *Nationalliberalismus*, 420–7. In a draft statement entitled 'Ultimatum, deutsche Volkspartei und Regierungsbildung', Stresemann noted, however, that the Centre Party did not commit itself to his plan and was prepared to accept the ultimatum unconditionally (Nl. 235).

ultimatum but a more qualified one on Upper Silesia the following evening.[55]

Stresemann, however, had miscalculated his ability to carry his party with him. The Stinnes group had no intention of agreeing to conditional acceptance of the ultimatum and on this occasion they had the support of the Reichstag party. Without waiting for the reply from London, it voted to reject the ultimatum after a meeting which lasted from 6 p.m. on 9 May to 1 a.m. the following morning. The coalition was thereby in Stresemann's words 'blown up', ending his chance of becoming chancellor.[56] Even if Stresemann had already known the terms of the British reply it seems unlikely that they would have affected the outcome, though according to the British ambassador Lord D'Abernon they made a great impression on him.[57] In public he put a good face on the party's decision, saying that it had been right to put national interests above considerations of domestic politics.[58] In private he saw things differently. In a note on 13 May he recorded, 'Wild days behind me. My candidacy as Reich chancellor... fails on the No of the German People's Party to the ultimatum.' The note ended 'Party division or entry into the government', which suggests that he was already thinking of threatening to split the party if it remained unwilling to contemplate a return to government.[59]

Stresemann's behaviour during these weeks was inconsistent.[60] He was at first willing to form a government with at least the toleration of the

[55] Viscount D'Abernon, *An Ambassador of Peace*, i: *From Spa (1920) to Rapallo (1922)* (London: Hodder & Stoughton, 1929), 169; *Documents on British Foreign Policy (DBFP)*, 1st Ser. xvi, no. 612. D'Abernon says he received the reply on the morning of 10 May but it was only sent at 9.30 p.m. that evening so he presumably saw it first on 11 May.

[56] Diary entry for 9 May 1921 (Nl. 362). In the same entry he refers to a vote of 10 in favour to 30 against. In his speech to the party conference in Stuttgart on 1 Dec. 1921, he referred to 'the overwhelming majority' against the ultimatum: BAK, R 45 II/27. According to Koch the voting was 59 to 5 (diary 9 May 1921; ibid., Nl. Koch-Weser, 27). A possible explanation for the discrepancy is that, according to Görlitz (*Stresemann*, 124), two votes were taken. In the first Stresemann voted with the minority, but then, seeing that he would not win, he joined the majority on the second vote. This appears to be based on information from Katharina von Kardorff-Oheimb, who voted with the minority. See also the account in her memoirs, *Politik und Lebensbeichte* (Tübingen: Hopfer [?1962]), 108–20.

[57] D'Abernon, *Ambassador of Peace*, i. 168–9.

[58] Speech to the party conference, 1 Dec. 1921: BAK, R 45 II/27.

[59] Bernhard (ed.), *Vermächtnis*, i. 20–1. Bernhard describes his source both as a memorandum and as a diary entry. The passage does not appear in the small diary in Nl. 362, which suggests that Stresemann kept a second diary, possibly a calendar of appointments, which has not survived. In later years he kept more than one diary for different purposes (Nl. 361).

[60] There is an interesting discussion of Stresemann's motives in Baechler, *Stresemann*, 288–9. See also Turner, *Stresemann*, 84–7; Wulf, *Stinnes*, 261–4; Feldman, 'Hugo Stinnes, Gustav Stresemann', 430–1. See Plate 21.

DNVP to oppose Allied demands, as Stinnes and a majority of the DVP Reichstag party wanted. When Fehrenbach resigned and the ultimatum was received, Stresemann changed his position to conditional acceptance of the ultimatum and seeking the toleration of the SPD. What remained consistent, however, was his desire to keep the DVP in government and his fear that power would otherwise return to the coalition of SPD, Centre, and DDP. He tried to finesse the problems created on the one hand by Allied pressure and on the other by Stinnes's implacable hostility to the government. Despite his efforts to find a compromise, he was unable to prevent the DVP bolting back to opposition.

'Objective Opposition'

Stresemann regarded the new government which was formed by the Centre Party under chancellor Wirth with the SPD, and after some hesitation the DDP, as a setback.[61] However, he did not give up hope of returning to government and for the next eighteen months he manoeuvred to bring this about, claiming that the DVP conducted 'purely objective opposition'.[62] He refused to join forces with the DNVP and doggedly persisted in building bridges to the SPD. The goal of recovering 'the latchkey to power' proved elusive but Stresemann was tenacious in pursuing it.[63]

He faced a difficult situation. He did not want to force new elections, which he still thought would benefit only the SPD because of the divided state of the USPD. He therefore agreed to give the DVP's support to the new government in the initial vote of confidence, since otherwise the DDP refused to join it and that might have sparked another crisis leading to elections.[64] On the other hand, the new chancellor was a bête noire to the DVP and it was difficult to persuade them to join a government under him. Wirth belonged to the left wing of the Centre Party and, Stresemann suspected, would have liked to turn his coalition into a majority with the help of the USPD. Stresemann therefore sought to counter Wirth's influence by cooperating with those groups within the

[61] 'Nach der Entscheidung', *Deutsche Stimmen*, 33/20, 15 May 1921.

[62] 'Zur politischen Lage', *Deutsche Stimmen*, 34/8, 19 Feb. 1922.

[63] Speech to the party conference, 1 Dec. 1921: BAK, R 45 II/27.

[64] 'Reichsregierung und Preußenregierung', 7 June 1921: *Deutsche Stimmen*, 33/24, 12 June 1921.

Centre and DDP which wanted to see the DVP brought back into the coalition.[65]

The political situation also offered some opportunities for bargaining. New taxes were required to meet the terms of the Allied ultimatum and the government needed the consent of the DVP to be sure of a majority. In addition, the government required a loan from industry to meet its immediate needs since its own credit was exhausted. This offered the DVP a role in helping this loan to be raised (or preventing it). The situation in Prussia might also be turned to advantage. The SPD was keen to return to the Prussian government. However, the Prussian Centre and DDP were not willing to allow the SPD to join unless the DVP did as well. This meant that the SPD would be forced to drop its refusal to enter a coalition with the DVP and that might open the way to the formation of a 'great coalition' from the SPD to the DVP at Reich level as well.

Stresemann's hopes of joining the coalition were jeopardized by the assassination of Erzberger at the end of August. The work of right-wing fanatics, it threatened to polarize left against right again as the Kapp putsch had done. Stresemann was quick to condemn the murder and to try to limit the political damage it caused.[66] He renewed the DVP's commitment to defend the constitution and he supported the emergency decree powers taken by President Ebert against anti-republican organizations while insisting that these powers should be applied to the left as well as the right.[67] In articles and speeches he warned of the danger of civil war and appealed for reason: 'Germany must follow the way, between dictatorship and Bolshevism, of constitutional, organic development on the basis of the present structure.'[68]

Opinion in the DVP about joining the coalition was divided. On the left of the Reichstag party was a small group which thought that the party

[65] 'Politische Umschau', *Deutsche Stimmen*, 33/25, 19 June 1921, and 33/27, 3 July 1921; memorandum of a meeting with Wirth, 3 Sept. 1921 (Nl. 231).

[66] 'Politische Umschau', *Deutsche Stimmen*, 33/36, 4 Sept. 1921, repr. as 'Erzberger' in Rheinbaben (ed.), *Reden und Schriften*, i. 378–88. He had earlier condemned the assassination of a Bavarian USPD politician, Gareis: 'Zur Geschichte der Deutschen Volkspartei', *Deutsche Stimmen*, 33/29, 17 July 1921.

[67] Memorandum of a meeting with Ebert, 31 Aug. 1921 (Nl. 231); Turner, *Stresemann*, 91.

[68] 'Vor wichtigen Entscheidungen', *Vossische Zeitung*, 28 Aug. 1921; 'Politische Umschau', *Deutsche Stimmen*, 33/37, 11 Sept. 1921, and 33/38, 18 Sept. 1921; 'Rechtsblock oder Politik der Mitte', *NLC*, 48/194, 16 Sept. 1921; speech to a party conference in south Westphalia, *NLC* 48/197, 21 Sept. 1921. After a second speech the same evening Stresemann was apparently himself the target of a bullet fired through a window from outside the hall, which lodged in a chair on the platform (ibid.).

should have accepted the ultimatum in May and remained in the government. It included the former ministers Heinze and Raumer and the ambitious and independent-minded, Siegfried von Kardorff.[69] They were critical of Stresemann for the way in which he had adjusted his views in public to those of the majority in May 1921, although he had personally been in favour of entering the government. At the other extreme was the Ruhr group, but this was itself divided between those, like Vögler, who were opposed to any coalition with the SPD, and Stinnes, who was not opposed in principle since he recognized the advantage of having a DVP presence in government but wanted himself to be the judge of when it should occur.[70]

The main body of opinion within the party which had swung behind the Ruhr group in May became less opposed to entering the government once the ultimatum had been accepted. In September the SPD decided to lift its ban on coalition with the DVP and the DVP Reichstag party in turn endorsed the goal of a broad coalition.[71] Wirth immediately opened discussions with the DVP.[72]

The main sticking point was the SPD's insistence that new taxes should include a property tax. The bourgeois parties argued that the proposed loan from industry, which the DVP was expected to support, already represented a considerable burden and could, if necessary, be supplemented by a second instalment of a levy on property. Another difficulty was the position of Wirth. The DDP and DVP would have liked him to stand down but the Centre and SPD were determined to keep him. Nevertheless, Stresemann gave a favourable report on the discussions to the standing committee and won general support for entering the coalition, though strong reservations were expressed about Wirth.[73]

The situation took a new turn as a result of the decision by the League Council on the division of Upper Silesia, which was officially communicated on 20 October though it had been anticipated in Berlin ten days

[69] Raumer to Kardorff, 29 July, 26 Nov. 1921: BAK, Nl. Siegfried von Kardorff, 12; Heinze to Kardorff, 4 Jan., 26 July, 6 Dec. 1921: ibid. 10; Raumer to Stresemann, 18 Sept., 14 Dec. 1921: Nl. 230, 229.

[70] Feldman, 'Hugo Stinnes, Gustav Stresemann', 431–4.

[71] Hagen Schulze, *Otto Braun oder Preußens demokratische Sendung* (Frankfurt: Ullstein, 1977), 343–5; 'Politische Umschau', *Deutsche Stimmen*, 33/40, 2 Oct. 1921.

[72] Minutes of the discussions between representatives of the coalition parties and the DVP, 28 Sept., 3 Oct. 1921: Ingrid Schulze-Bidlingmaier (ed.), *Die Kabinette Wirth I und II*, 2 vols. (Boppard: Harald Boldt, 1973), nos. 102, 106.

[73] Minutes of the GA meeting, 3 Oct. 1921: Kolb and Richter (eds.), *Nationalliberalismus*, 431–5.

earlier. The greater part of the region, including important industrial areas, was given to Poland despite the plebiscite which showed a German majority overall and in the urban areas, though a Polish preponderance in the countryside. Within Germany the decision was seen as a further humiliation, and Wirth was expected to resign.

Stresemann faced a similar dilemma to that which had confronted him in May. Wirth's resignation would be welcome to the DVP, but the idea of accepting the decision on Upper Silesia, as any new government would have to do, was anathema. The Reichstag party met on 19 October and according to Stresemann's diary three members of the right wing—Cremer, Quaatz, and Curtius—spoke against entering a great coalition, and Stinnes spoke against entering at that time. Stresemann was angered by these attitudes and threatened to resign.[74] The Reichstag party met again the following day in a calmer mood.[75] According to a letter from his secretary, Stresemann was thinking in terms of two main possibilities, both involving Wirth's resignation. He would be replaced either by a moderate Social Democrat (such as Gustav Bauer or the Reichstag president Paul Löbe) or by a minority coalition of Centre, DDP, and DVP under the Centre Party chairman Wilhelm Marx. The main problem for a great coalition was that the SPD wanted to keep Wirth, which was unacceptable to the DVP, though they might be prepared to let him stay as finance minister. Stresemann thought that the DVP's position was a strong one, as without their votes Wirth would have to rely on the USPD which would in turn alienate the Centre and DDP.[76]

The previous negotiations for the DVP to join the coalition were resumed on 17 October.[77] Stresemann did not make Wirth's resignation a formal condition for the DVP's entry into the government to prevent it becoming a matter of prestige for the Centre Party to keep him.[78] The SPD refused to be rushed into admitting the DVP until agreement had been reached on the issue of taxation. That in turn depended on what

---

[74] Diary for 19 Oct. 1921 (Nl. 362). The threat of resignation almost certainly referred to his position as chairman of the Reichstag party. In a letter to a party official in Hamburg, he accused some members of being not just against a coalition under Wirth but against a great coalition as such. He added that the next few days would show whether the DVP would pursue an independent policy or 'sink to a branch of the DNVP', in which case he would resign as chairman of the Reichstag party. Stresemann to Rose, 22 Oct. 1921 (Nl. 225).

[75] Diary for 20 Oct. (Nl. 362).

[76] Rauch to Arming, 20 Oct. 1921 (Nl. 225).

[77] Schulze-Bidlingmaier (ed.), *Die Kabinette Wirth*, nos. 114–16.

[78] 'Politische Umschau', 20 Oct. 1921, *Deutsche Stimmen*, 33/43, 23 Oct. 1921; Stresemann to Rose, 22 Oct. 1921 (Nl. 225).

industry would be prepared to offer as a loan, which was unclear because of obstruction from groups in the Ruhr.[79] The delay saved Stresemann the embarrassment of having to admit openly that the DVP would not be willing to serve under Wirth in any case. Wirth was finally forced to resign on 22 October by the DDP and the Centre Party as a protest against the League's decision on Upper Silesia.

Stresemann was, however, still hamstrung by the DVP's refusal to take part in a government which accepted the decision on Upper Silesia. The Reichstag party had already decided to reject the decision on 21 October and this was confirmed unanimously the following day.[80] Ebert, who favoured a great coalition, asked the DVP and DDP in the first instance to find an agreed position. Stresemann drafted a statement for both parties on 23 October refusing to appoint a German commissioner to negotiate detailed arrangements for the division of Upper Silesia as the Allies required.[81] The following day Stresemann secured the consent of the Reichstag party to negotiations with the other parties for a 'note about Upper Silesia'.[82] In talks involving all four parties (SPD, Centre, DVP, and DDP) Stresemann agreed, subject to the approval of the Reichstag party, to the terms of a formal protest over Upper Silesia but without a commitment to refuse to cooperate with the Allies in carrying out the division. There was also agreement to shelve the issue of new taxes until the government was formed, which represented an important concession by the SPD. No decision was taken on the person to be chancellor.

This did not go far enough for the Reichstag party. In a further meeting which followed at 10 p.m. and lasted to midnight it 'refused entry into the government'.[83] It is not clear how far Stresemann tried to win his colleagues over. There were clearly formidable difficulties. What would the coalition do when the Allies rejected the protest? There was in reality no alternative to submission and the DVP would have to take responsibility in a way it had evaded both over the Versailles treaty and the ultimatum. There was also the further problem that neither the SPD nor the DVP had been able to find a generally acceptable alternative to Wirth as

[79] Feldman, *The Great Disorder*, 358–76.

[80] Stresemann's diary, 21, 22 Oct. 1921 (Nl. 362). Stresemann did not record his own attitude, though he did note on 21 Oct. that he had clashed with a member of the right wing, Johann Becker.

[81] Copy with draft in Stresemann's hand, dated 23 Oct. 1921 (Nl. 225).

[82] Stresemann's diary, 24 Oct. 1921 (Nl. 362).

[83] Ibid.

chancellor, who now formed a new government.[84] In addition, the Ruhr members were opposed to joining the coalition as they did not want to be committed to taxation or even the loan. In these circumstances the prospects of the DVP joining the government were bleak indeed.

The DVP attempted to justify its refusal by arguing that the other parties, particularly the SPD, were not prepared to carry their opposition over Upper Silesia beyond a protest.[85] The other parties were naturally infuriated: the SPD accused the DVP of seeking party advantage at the expense of the national interest and Marx, who had worked to bring the DVP into the coalition, spoke bitterly of 'the darkest hour in the history of the DVP'.[86] Stresemann was credited in some quarters with having opposed the decision.[87] That his preference would have been to join the coalition is supported by a later note: 'Over Upper Silesia, same situation as at the ultimatum.'[88] In public, however, he declared that he had known it would be futile to join a coalition that would not last beyond the Allies' rejection of the German protest and that the decision had been unanimous.[89] Probably he saw that it would be impossible to carry the party with him and acquiesced in the hope that once the international situation improved the DVP would be able to reopen the question of returning to the government.

He achieved an important success immediately when he intervened in the negotiations for a reconstruction of the Prussian government and persuaded the DVP Landtag party to enter a great coalition under an SPD minister president, Otto Braun.[90] What he called his 'energetic intervention' in favour of a great coalition won a majority of 28 to 14 in the Reichstag party but was opposed by nearly half the Landtag party, which resented his interference.[91] The situation reminded him of the divisions in the National Liberal Party, and he decided to confront the

[84] The DDP formally withdrew from the coalition, but it allowed one of its members, Otto Gessler, to remain as defence minister.

[85] Stresemann to Ebert, 25 Oct. 1921 (Nl. 225) and NLC, 48/224, 25 Oct. 1921.

[86] NLC 48/225, 26 Oct. 1921; Ulrich von Hehl, Wilhelm Marx 1863–1946. Eine politische Biographie (Mainz: Matthias Grünewald, 1987), 199. Wirth still nursed bitter memories of the incident twenty years later: Küppers, Wirth, 130–1.

[87] Laubach, Kabinette Wirth, 104. His ambition to be a coalition-maker was satirized in Kladderadatsch, 74/43, 23 Oct. 1921; see Plate 22.

[88] Entry for 21 Nov. 1921, quoted by Bernhard from a diary which has not survived (see above, n. 59); Bernhard (ed.), Vermächtnis, i. 21.

[89] Speech to the party conference, 1 Dec. 1921: BAK, R 45 II/27.

[90] Schulze, Braun, 349.

[91] Diary for 5 Nov. 1921 (Nl. 362); Schulze, Braun, 349.

opposition directly at the party conference in December.[92] He admitted that the idea of forming a great coalition posed 'a severe test' since reason and emotion pulled in different directions.[93] But in a passionate appeal to the conference, he urged the party to accept his leadership, to shape events, and not allow themselves to be excluded from power like the pre-war National Liberals.[94] He fiercely criticized the Western powers for their short-sighted policy which he saw as impoverishing the whole of Europe, but urged the party to accept its patriotic duty to enter the government as soon as Germany was offered terms it could fulfil.

Stresemann swept all before him at the conference. Only one voice was raised in criticism and that came from the minority who believed it had been a mistake not to enter the coalition in May or October. The opponents of the great coalition remained silent. There was no one among them who could match Stresemann's eloquence or give alternative leadership. He was justified in claiming to the editor of the *Kölnische Zeitung* that during the previous year he had won over the great majority of the party to the idea of a great coalition even if in the interests of party unity he had sometimes had to follow a roundabout route.[95]

Stresemann clearly hoped for an invitation to join the government in the immediate future. He discussed cabinet posts with colleagues and indicated his willingness to become vice-chancellor, minister of the interior, or foreign minister.[96] He faced more opposition in the Reichstag party where on 15 December his left- and right-wing opponents combined against him, but after 'excited argument into the morning hours' he won a vote of confidence with only Heinze holding out against him.[97]

[92] Diary for 21 Nov.: Bernhard (ed.), *Vermächtnis*, i. 21.

[93] 'Politische Umschau', *Deutsche Stimmen*, 33/48, 27 Nov. 1921.

[94] Speech to the party conference in Stuttgart, 1 Dec. 1921: BAK, R 45 II/27.

[95] Stresemann to Ernst Posse, 4 Jan. 1922 (misdated 1921) (Nl. 238).

[96] Raumer to Stresemann, 14 Dec. 1921 (Nl. 229); Stresemann to Becker, 18 Dec. 1921 (Nl. 227), printed in Harttung (ed.), *Schriften*, 231–2. Stresemann also canvassed Schiffer's opinion at about this time, saying he would prefer to become foreign minister but his party wanted him to have the Ministry of the Interior. Schiffer replied with some condescension that since he lacked expertise in the business of any ministry it did not much matter which he took, but that as the minister of the interior also acted as government spokesman he would be well qualified for that task. Undated typescript note, BAK, Nl. Schiffer 1, part 1, fo. 115.

[97] Diary, 15 Dec. 1921 (Nl. 362). Stresemann was helped by the fact that, for reasons of his own, Stinnes was no longer opposed to the DVP entering the government: Rauch to Major Kilburger, 16 Dec. 1921 (Nl. 227). There had been rumours of an attempt to force Stresemann to stand down as chairman. Stresemann to Dingeldey, 15 Dec. 1921, and to Rose, 21 Dec. 1921 (Nl. 227), and 'Was geht in der Fraktion der Deutschen Volkpartei vor?', *Leipziger Neueste Nachrichten*, 6 Dec. 1921 (Nl. 229).

Stresemann was probably hoping that an improvement in the international situation—the Allies agreed to reduce the payments due from Germany in 1922 at a conference in Cannes in January—would create a favourable climate for the DVP to enter the government. On 18 January he discussed coalition with Wirth and on 26 January a compromise was reached on the tax issue, with the SPD accepting the proposal for a compulsory loan rather than a property tax.[98] On the 31st the executive committee of the Reichstag party gave its approval for a great coalition with Stresemann as minister of the interior and vice-chancellor and Becker as minister for reconstruction. These hopes were soon dashed, however, when Wirth asked to see him the same day and told him that he had decided to appoint Walther Rathenau foreign minister.[99]

The DVP objected to Rathenau's appointment on the grounds that such an important post should not be filled in advance of the reconstruction of the government.[100] However, there was more to their opposition. Rathenau was disliked by some DVP industrialists as an exponent, like Wirth, of the policy of 'fulfilment' of the Versailles treaty—albeit in the hope that this would lead to its revision—and as an unreliable intellectual whose economic theories bordered dangerously on socialism. Stinnes saw in Rathenau a rival to his own schemes for solving the reparations problem and dismissed his ideas in the Reichstag foreign affairs committee as 'utopias'.[101] Behind such attitudes there was a strong element of anti-Semitism.[102] The DVP had found it difficult to stomach the idea of serving in a coalition with the SPD under the left-wing Catholic, Wirth.

[98] Diary for 18 and 26 Jan. 1922 (Nl. 362); Laubach, *Kabinette Wirth*, 157–9. The government had been forced to abandon the idea of a loan from industry after Stinnes succeeded in making the privatization of the railways a condition, which was unacceptable to the SPD. Feldman, *The Great Disorder*, 358–76.

[99] Diary for 31 Jan. (Nl. 362).

[100] Records of a meeting between Wirth and DVP representatives, 6 Feb. 1922, and of the inter-party committee, 10 Feb. 1922: Schulze-Bidlingmaier (ed.), *Die Kabinette Wirth*, nos. 202, 205.

[101] Feldman, *Stinnes*, 687–738, quotation p. 735. Stinnes criticized Rathenau for concluding the Wiesbaden agreement with France in Oct. 1921 to allow reparations to be paid in goods rather than currency. Stinnes proposed privatization of the railways (from which he stood to gain) to provide security for an international loan to pay reparations, and an international consortium for the reconstruction of Russia. Stresemann was careful to dissociate the DVP from the idea of privatization of the railways in his speech to the party conference, but in notes for another speech he praised Stinnes as 'the coming man'. Speech to the party conference in Stuttgart, 1 Dec. 1921: BAK, R 45 II/27; notes for a speech, marked Stuttgart 1 Dec. 1921, and possibly intended for his address to the Zentralvorstand the day before, which he cancelled because of illness (Nl. 226).

[102] In the case of Stinnes this was not consistent: Feldman, 'Hugo Stinnes, Gustav Stresemann', 428; Wolfgang Stresemann, *Mein Vater*, 210–12.

The thought of Rathenau as foreign minister as well was too much for it.[103]

Stresemann was affronted by Wirth's appointment of Rathenau at the very moment when he was negotiating to join the coalition.[104] He still had to overcome opposition within the full Reichstag party and Rathenau's appointment ruined his chances.[105] In retaliation, he threatened to renege on the tax compromise, saying that Wirth had deliberately flouted the conditions which the DVP had set for its agreement.[106]

The DVP registered its protest by voting against the government on a confidence motion in the Reichstag, which it survived only with the help of the USPD. But Stresemann made it clear that the DVP still wanted a great coalition and discussions continued on the issue of a loan from property, which was finally settled at the beginning of March with the guarantees demanded by the DVP.[107] Foreign policy brought the government and the DVP together for the first time when Wirth and Rathenau rejected a demand from the Allied Reparations Commission for additional taxation and for the commission to supervise German fiscal policy. In the Reichstag Stresemann welcomed the government's firm 'No' and defended it against the DNVP, which still wanted to tar it with the brush of 'fulfilment'. Stresemann repeated his view of the interdependence of the world economy. Rathenau, who spoke next, took up this theme, declaring in words which could equally well have come from Stresemann that 'the collapse of Germany means the collapse of Europe'.[108]

The Genoa conference, called by Lloyd George in April 1922, to discuss the problems of European reconstruction with both the Germans and the Soviet Union appeared to be a hopeful start in a new

---

[103] Stresemann's secretary wrote that 'even the extreme left of the party would find it impossible to swallow Wirth and Rathenau together in charge of foreign policy': Rauch to Kilburger, 16 Dec. 1921 (Nl. 227).

[104] 'Politische Umschau', *Deutsche Stimmen*, 34/6, 5 Feb. 1922.

[105] Although the executive committee of the Reichstag party had given its approval for the negotiations, according to Jakob Rießer the Reichstag party itself was still 'not yet decided and in no way united' about joining the coalition. Rather, it had agreed to try to prevent Rathenau's appointment if this could be achieved without joining the coalition: Rießer to his son Hans, 22 Jan. 1922: BAK, Kleine Erwerbungen, no. 549, 1–2; Morsey, *Deutsche Zentrumspartei*, 445.

[106] Minutes of the inter-party committee, 10 Feb. 1922: Schulze-Bidlingmaier (ed.), *Die Kabinette Wirth*, no. 205 and p. 551, quoting *Die Zeit*, 2/53, 1 Feb. 1922.

[107] 'Zur politischen Lage', *Deutsche Stimmen*, 34/8, 19 Feb. 1922; 'Politische Umschau', *Deutsche Stimmen*, 34/10, 5 Mar. 1922; Laubach, *Kabinette Wirth*, 155–9.

[108] Stresemann's and Rathenau's speeches to the Reichstag, 29 Mar., and a further statement by Stresemann, 30 Mar. 1922: *Verhandlungen des Reichstags*, vol. 354, pp. 6643–57, 6706–7.

direction.[109] Stresemann was guardedly optimistic, writing that the future depended on a growing realization that all would share a common fate and that 'The weakness of Russia and Germany is in this respect their strength.' At the same time he cautioned that economic considerations might not dictate events in the short term, as 'the only decisive military and therefore political power in Europe rests with France'.[110]

He was taken by surprise when Germany and the Soviet Union combined to sign the treaty of Rapallo on 16 April, which came as a shock to the other powers and broke up the conference. Acting on information from members of the German delegation, he accepted that it had been right to conclude the treaty in order to prevent the Western powers reaching an agreement with the Soviet Union giving it a claim to reparations from Germany.[111] In the *Deutsche Stimmen* he welcomed the treaty as a further step away from 'fulfilment' to making it clear that Germany could not pay the reparations demanded.[112] However, to a critic he admitted that the prospects of trade with the Soviet Union were not immediately significant and that it was regrettable that it had to be signed with a Bolshevik government.[113]

Stresemann shared the growing confidence in Berlin in the summer of 1922 that a solution would be found to the reparations problem with American aid.[114] He wrote to a business associate, 'I am not pessimistic about the future and believe we will come out of the worst. Until then we must, of course, tack from side to side [*lavieren*] and treat the whole reparations question in a dilatory fashion.'[115] He explained that American

---

[109] Carole Fink, Axel Frohn, and Jürgen Heideking (eds.), *Genoa, Rapallo and European Reconstruction in 1922* (Cambridge: Cambridge University Press, 1991).

[110] 'Politische Umschau', *Deutsche Stimmen*, 34/16, 16 Apr. 1922.

[111] Raumer to Stresemann by telegram, 18 Apr. and by letter, 21 Apr. Stresemann's reply, 29 Apr. Hermann Bücher to Stresemann, 20 Apr. 1922 and Stresemann's reply, 29 Apr. 1922 (Nl. 243). Under article 116 of the Versailles treaty, the Allies reserved the right of Russia to reparations.

[112] 'Politische Umschau', *Deutsche Stimmen*, 34/20, 14 May 1922.

[113] Stresemann to Schoen, 10 May 1922 (Nl. 243).

[114] On the question of American participation in a loan see Werner Link, *Die amerikanische Stabilisierungspolitik in Deutschland 1921–32* (Düsseldorf: Droste, 1970), 122–35, Berg, *Stresemann und die Vereinigten Staaten*, 110–11.

[115] Stresemann to Litwin, 2 June 1922 (Nl. 116). On Stresemann's connections with Litwin see H. W. Gatzke, 'Stresemann und Litwin', *Vierteljahrshefte für Zeitgeschichte*, 5 (1957), 76–90. Litwin was a major donor to the DVP and in 1921 Stresemann became deputy chairman on the board of his firm, Deutsche Evaporator A. G., though he resigned from this position together with all his directorships when he became chancellor in August 1923. Litwin was arrested for breaching foreign currency regulations in July 1923, but released a few days later, and the case against him was struck out. Responding to allegations that he had been involved in covering up

banks were prepared to offer a loan which would enable reparations to be paid provided they were set at a reasonable level (about 30 billion gold marks), the Rhineland occupation was given up, and Germany was given back the right to negotiate her own trade treaties.[116] He admitted, however, that the French government was not for the time being willing to accept such a scheme. In this connection, he criticized Stinnes for opposing the stabilization of the mark since his attitude was having a bad effect on opinion abroad and also on Germans whose savings had been devalued.

The Assassination of Walther Rathenau

The political balance was again shaken by the assassination of Walther Rathenau on 24 June by two former members of the *Freikorps*. The trade unions and working-class parties organized mass demonstrations in defence of the Republic, and the USPD offered to discuss entering the government which would have given it an overall majority.[117] Wirth responded by declaring in the Reichstag that 'this enemy is on the right'.[118]

These developments filled Stresemann with apprehension. He was appalled by the murder of Rathenau, for whom he had a high regard. It convinced him that political assassination could no longer be treated as an isolated incident but was the work of organized groups. He also feared that it would upset the progress that had been made towards a consolidation of the Republic around the political centre. He compared the shock to that of the Kapp putsch and the murder of Erzberger and warned that

Litwin's crimes, Stresemann took the matter to court in 1927 and won. Gatzke suggests that Stresemann had committed himself too far to Litwin and may indeed have received funds for an account in his own name as well as direct contributions to the DVP. Litwin occasionally boasted of his connection with Stresemann, and Stresemann was clearly not anxious that the extent of Litwin's donations to the party should become known, offering him 80,000 marks in 1928 in repayment of a loan to the *Deutsche Stimmen*, but there is no evidence that his dealings with Litwin were corrupt. There is a reference to Litwin's use of the connection in the diary of the political editor of the *Berliner Tageblatt*, Ernst Feder: Cécile Lowenthal-Hensel and Arnold Paucker (eds.), *Ernst Feder. Heute sprach ich mit … Tagebücher eines Berliner Publizisten 1926–1932* (Stuttgart: Deutsche Verlags-Anstalt, 1971), 127.

[116] Under the Versailles treaty (articles 264–70) Germany was forced to give the Allies most favoured nation status and was subject to other restrictions for five years.

[117] David W. Morgan, *The Socialist Left and the German Revolution* (Ithaca: Cornell University Press, 1975), 419–25.

[118] Hörster-Philipps, *Wirth*, 266–8.

once again Germany faced the danger of civil war.[119] He wrote to a colleague, 'Politics often seems to me like the labour of Sisyphus. Whenever one has pushed the stone up so far that one can believe in a general restoration of peace and calm, some fanatic or other plunges us into a new misfortune.'[120]

He reacted instinctively to counter the danger of polarization by identifying the DVP more closely with the Republic. He published a warm appreciation of Rathenau, praising his patriotism and his unusual gifts both as a person and a diplomat.[121] He pointedly contrasted Rathenau's wide intellectual and cultural interests, inherited from his Jewish background, with what Stresemann described as 'a period of crass materialism' in the German business community since 1871. He also drew an implicit parallel between some of Rathenau's attitudes and his own. He recalled that Rathenau had been ambivalent in his attitude toward the Wilhelmine regime, had supported territorial expansion during the war, and had latterly become an advocate of a great coalition. He condemned the murder as a crime for which no punishment could be too harsh and called for the DNVP to break with its extreme right wing which had been at the forefront of the agitation against Rathenau and other republican figures.

Stresemann developed his ideas in a key speech to the Reichstag in the debate which followed on new legislation to protect the Republic against terrorism.[122] The measure required a two-thirds majority since it suspended certain constitutional rights. It could pass only with support from the DVP. Stresemann offered his party's cooperation but appealed to the republican parties to recognize the good faith of all those who worked loyally with the existing state whatever their personal convictions. He pointed to Rathenau himself as an example of someone who had served the Republic despite his monarchist sympathies. Germany would never find peace so long as it tore itself apart in conflicts about the past, he declared. Equally he appealed to the extreme right to stop blaming republican governments for all the misery that had befallen the German people. Those who claimed to understand that international politics was

[119] 'Politische Umschau', *Deutsche Stimmen*, 34/27, 2 July 1922; Reichstag speech, 5 July 1922: Zwoch (ed.), *Reichstagsreden*, 117. Stresemann suspected shortly afterwards that he too was to be the target of an assassination attempt: diary for 13 July (Nl. 362), Stresemann to Polizeipräsidium, 14 July 1922 (Nl. 248).

[120] Stresemann to Landgerichtspräsident Becker, 10 July 1922 (Nl. 248).

[121] 'Politische Umschau', *Deutsche Stimmen*, 34/27, 2 July 1922.

[122] Reichstag speech, 5 July 1922: Zwoch (ed.), *Reichstagsreden*, 115–33.

about power should be able to appreciate the limits on what a German government could achieve.

This appeal for understanding was followed by a statement by the Reich Committee of the DVP that national recovery was possible only on the basis of the republican Constitution.[123] Stresemann returned to the theme in the Reichstag, arguing that given the French government's determination to force Germany to the point of collapse, there was an overriding imperative to let the constitutional issue rest. This meant that even the idea of changing the form of state by legal means should be given up.[124] Despite Stresemann's pleas the DVP was split: thirty-six voted for the law, twenty-three abstained or were absent, and three voted against.[125] This was sufficient, however, for the two-thirds majority.

Stresemann's defence of the Constitution corresponded to his belief in the middle way but it was also a shrewd parliamentary tactic. The middle-class parties in the coalition, the Centre and DDP, were unhappy at the prospect of a one-sided extension of the coalition to the USPD. They therefore issued a parallel invitation to the DVP to discuss joining the coalition on the basis of a common defence of the Constitution. Stresemann welcomed this invitation and his speeches paved the way for cooperation. Nothing came of the discussions, however: the SPD vetoed inclusion of the DVP to maintain its rapprochement with the USPD and the Centre and DDP vetoed inclusion of the USPD without the DVP. The only positive outcome for Stresemann was the formation of a Reichstag group with the Centre and DDP, calling itself the 'alliance of the constitutional centre'. This countered the formation of a similar arrangement between the SPD and USPD and preserved the DVP's claim to enter the coalition in the future.[126]

Stresemann considered this halfway house much better than the alternatives which had threatened if he had opposed the law for the protection

---

[123] Declaration of the Reichsausschuß, 7 July 1922: Kolb and Richter (eds.), *Nationalliberalismus*, 445–6. The Reichsausschuß, which was added to the party organization in 1921, was composed of the central party leadership and representatives of provincial party organizations. Its main task was to draw up the order of candidates on the party list for Reichstag elections. It was also able, as in this instance, to take urgent decisions on behalf of the Zentralvorstand. Stresemann made use of it, as again in this instance, to strengthen his hand on issues where he faced opposition in the Reichstag party. Ibid. 36*–40*; diary for 9–10 July 1922 (Nl. 362).

[124] Reichstag speech, 18 July 1922: *Verhandlungen des Reichstags*, vol. 356, pp. 8708–12.

[125] Ibid. 8787–9. In a meeting of the Reichstag party the previous evening there had been a majority of 20 to 10 in favour of the law; diary for 17 July (Nl. 362).

[126] *Archiv der Deutschen Volkspartei*, 15 Aug. 1922, 118–27; Turner, *Stresemann*, 100–1; Baechler, *Stresemann*, 296–302.

of the Republic. That might have led the coalition to accept the USPD alone and possibly to the law being passed in an extreme version (with the support of the KPD), aimed explicitly against monarchists. Instead, the DVP had been able to influence the draft so that it was neutral as between anti-republican activity from the right or the left.[127] An even more worrying prospect had been that the law might fail to pass, leading to the fall of the government and new elections. Stresemann saw no good coming from an election, since it would be fought on the issue of Republic versus monarchy and against the background of hardship caused by rapid inflation.[128] In these circumstances he feared the revival of a republican majority as in 1919.

Despite these sound tactical arguments and despite the care with which he chose his words to avoid giving offence to those with monarchist sympathies, he had to face opposition from about a third of the Reichstag party. To a supporter he wrote that his position had been 'exceptionally difficult', complaining that many of their friends swore by Bismarck in speeches but had no conception of the realpolitik which Bismarck had practised.[129] The extent of the opposition is surprising given that the DVP had already declared its willingness for loyal cooperation in 1919 and Stresemann had moved this position only slightly by referring specifically to the 'republican constitution' in the statement from the Reich committee and renouncing working even by legal methods to restore the monarchy in his second speech to the Reichstag.[130] More important was the fact that he committed the DVP to the defence of the Republic in a highly charged atmosphere where the legislation depended on the DVP and there was a fear that it would be used against the right. This was a severe test of the sincerity of the DVP's repeated protestations of loyalty, and meant drawing a clear line between the DVP and the DNVP on the issue. The legislation was also unpopular in parts of the Reich, particularly Bavaria, where it threatened to produce a conflict with the Reich government.[131]

[127] Gotthard Jasper, *Der Schutz der Republik* (Tübingen: Mohr, 1963), 87–9.

[128] 'Politische Umschau', *Deutsche Stimmen*, 34/31, 30 July 1922. Also Stresemann to the Crown Prince, 21 July 1922, and other replies to critics of his policy (Nl. 248).

[129] Stresemann to Professor Bückelmann, 21 July 1922 (Nl. 248).

[130] Baechler, *Stresemann*, 298–9.

[131] Stresemann to the Bavarian minister president Graf Lerchenfeld, 11 July 1922 (Nl. 248). Stresemann himself went to Munich for what became a seven-hour debate in the DVP constituency association, in which he spoke three times and which concluded with a unanimous vote of confidence. He was also consulted by the Bavarian legation in Berlin, and noted his satisfaction when the conflict eased. Diary for 5, 9, 10 Aug. 1922 (Nl. 362).

Stresemann showed both courage and tactical acumen. He was probably fortunate to have the support of Stinnes, who wrote that 'The Rathenau murderers have in my opinion shot the monarchy. Stresemann...shares this opinion.'[132] Characteristically he also tried to convince the Crown Prince that he had adopted the right tactics.[133] It is unlikely that Stresemann retained any illusions about the prospects of restoring the monarchy, but he aimed as usual to achieve the widest possible measure of support for the course he believed to be right.[134] His goal was the rebuilding of Germany on the basis of the Republic. He believed that required reconciliation between left and right and that the DVP could make a vital contribution to the process.

Towards the Great Coalition

The cause of the great coalition now found an unexpected ally in chancellor Wirth. Previously sceptical of the DVP, he had become convinced that the rapidly deteriorating economic position made their inclusion necessary. The backing of the 'party of industry' would help to restore German credit abroad, and their presence would add weight to a programme for increased production and exports which was essential to halt the downward spiral of the mark.[135] The situation was all the more serious as the French government under Raymond Poincaré, who had replaced Briand in January, refused any further concessions by the Allies to the Germans.[136] Wirth told Stresemann at the end of July that he hoped to form a great coalition when the Reichstag reconvened after the summer recess. As he then anticipated, the SPD and USPD agreed to unite at their party conferences in September which gave his administration a substantial majority without the DVP.[137] This did not deflect him, however, from his view that the DVP should also be included.

[132] Stinnes to Vögler, 9 July 1922: Feldman, *Stinnes*, 768.
[133] Stresemann to the Crown Prince, 21 July 1922 (Nl. 248).
[134] Feldman argues that, unlike Stinnes, Stresemann 'retained an attachment to the idea of restoring the monarchy': 'Hugo Stinnes, Gustav Stresemann', 432. It is more likely in my view that he was intent on carrying monarchists with him while leading in the opposite direction.
[135] Laubach, *Kabinette Wirth*, 286–7, 294–5; Hörster-Philipps, *Wirth*, 276–7.
[136] According to the leading French authority, Poincaré was initially favourable to an agreement with Germany for deliveries in kind, but he became convinced that German evasion and Allied division left him no alternative to occupation of the Ruhr. Stanislas Jeannesson, *Poincaré, la France et la Ruhr (1922–1924)* (Strasbourg: Presses Universitaires de Strasbourg, 1998), 73–147.
[137] Stresemann to Stinnes, 3 Aug. 1922 (Nl. 249).

At this point a new obstacle arose in the form of a proposal that the Reich president should be directly elected, as was provided for in the Constitution. Ebert had been elected to the office by the National Assembly on a provisional basis until the boundaries of the Republic were settled. With the division of Upper Silesia settled, he was understandably keen to have his mandate confirmed. At the beginning of October, the coalition parties agreed to support an election and the date was fixed for 3 December.[138] Stresemann opposed the plan and he was able to persuade first the Centre and the DDP and then the reunited SPD to accept an extension of Ebert's term by Reichstag resolution to 30 June 1925 instead.

Stresemann's opposition arose from his fear that an election would divide the nation once again into republican and monarchist camps and would encourage the movement for secession in Bavaria, where feeling against the 'red' Berlin Republic ran high.[139] The danger would be all the greater if the winter produced, as expected, a crisis over reparations. He hoped for a settlement along the lines being pursued by Stinnes, who had negotiated a direct agreement with French industrialists for a joint cartel which would manage the supply and distribution of materials for reconstruction to be credited to the reparations account.[140] Stresemann defended this agreement and hoped that it would produce political consequences in a relaxation of the French government's attitude on reparations, but equally he knew that if that failed then there was a serious risk of Poincaré proceeding to occupy the Ruhr.[141] This in turn could create the conditions for revolution from the left or the right. In the Reichstag, he warned that a presidential election campaign might upset the chances of a reparations settlement and result in the collapse of the Reich.[142]

The proposal for a presidential election also threatened to undermine Stresemann's attempts to lead the DVP back into government. An election in which Ebert was the republican candidate would reopen the division between the DVP and the coalition parties particularly if—as he feared—

---

[138] Schulze-Bidlingmaier (ed.), *Kabinette Wirth*, nos. 295, 297, 381.

[139] Record of a meeting between Wirth and party leaders, 16 Oct. 1922: ibid., no. 387.

[140] The so-called Stinnes–Lubersac agreement, signed by Stinnes on 4 Sept. 1922: Wulf, *Stinnes*, 324–43; Feldman, *The Great Disorder*, 460–3.

[141] Speech to the Zentralvorstand meeting, 24 Sept. 1922: Kolb and Richter (eds.), *Nationalliberalismus*, 447–8.

[142] Reichstag speech, 20 Oct. 1922: *Verhandlungen des Reichstags*, vol. 357, pp. 8828–30. Also 'Politische Umschau', *Deutsche Stimmen*, 34/41, 20 Oct. 1922 and 34/42, 5 Nov. 1922.

Hindenburg were to stand as the DNVP's candidate.[143] In 1919 Stresemann had welcomed the possibility of Hindenburg standing as a way of
rallying opinion against the Republic. The reversal of his position by 1922
was a measure of how far he had travelled. He was pleased to have diverted
the demand for an election and saw it as a success for the parties of the
'constitutional centre'.[144] Ebert, however, felt cheated of a victory which
he was set to win. Although Stresemann made a point of defending him in
the Reichstag against criticism from the DNVP and praised his achievement in leading Germany back from revolution to constitutional government, Ebert is reported to have resented his intervention.[145]

   With the question of the election disposed of, Wirth grasped the nettle
of bringing the DVP into the coalition.[146] Despite the support of Ebert
and although the party leaders agreed on a common programme, the
proposal failed on the resistance of the SPD Reichstag party.[147] It was at
this stage that Stresemann met the SPD leaders over lunch to discuss the
party's opposition.[148] Forced by Wirth to decide, the SPD finally rejected
the DVP by a large majority on 14 November and Wirth thereupon
resigned.[149]

   Stresemann became once again a candidate for office either as chancellor or foreign minister. With the SPD having ruled out a great coalition
and the Centre Party making it clear that it wanted relief from the
thankless task of providing chancellors, it would have been natural for
Ebert to think in terms of a minority government of the bourgeois parties
under a DVP chancellor. Stresemann expected to be asked and claimed
that the SPD leaders agreed that this was the right course.[150] Ebert,

---

[143] Stresemann commented that the reasons which had led Hindenburg to withdraw his
candidacy after the Kapp putsch might be considered to apply even more strongly now: *Deutsche
Stimmen*, 34/41, 20 Oct. 1922.

[144] 'Politische Umschau', *Deutsche Stimmen*, 34/42, 5 Nov. 1922.

[145] Reichstag speech, 20 Oct. 1922: *Verhandlungen des Reichstags*, vol. 257, p. 8830. Bernhard
(ed.), *Vermächtnis*, i. 22.

[146] Minutes of the cabinet meeting, 23 Oct. 1922: Schulze-Bidlingmaier (ed.), *Kabinette Wirth*,
no. 391.

[147] Laubach, *Kabinette Wirth*, 307–11.

[148] On 6 Nov. he had lunch with the SPD leaders, Rudolf Hilferding, Hermann Müller, Otto
Wels, and Rudolf Breitscheid at the home of the liberal journalist, Georg Bernhard, and on 14
Nov. he met them again, except for Hilferding: diary, 6 and 14 Nov. 1922 (Nl. 362).

[149] Heinrich August Winkler, *Arbeiter und Arbeiterbewegung in der Weimarer Republik*, i: *Von der
Revolution zur Stabilisierung 1918–1924* (Berlin: J. H. W. Dietz, 1985), 499–501; Schulze, *Braun*,
407–8.

[150] Stresemann to Dingeldey, 4 Dec. 1922 (Nl. 253); diary for 13 and 15 Nov. 1922 (Nl. 362);
Wolfgang Stresemann, *Mein Vater*, 216–17. Morsey, *Zentrumspartei*, 489–90.

however, turned to a non-political figure, Wilhelm Cuno, the leader of the Hamburg–America shipping line who had served as a reparations expert. The reason for this surprising choice may have been partly Ebert's reservations about Stresemann but also the hope that, as a non-party figure, Cuno would be more acceptable to the SPD.[151]

In fact the SPD refused to join a Cuno government and he was also unable to reconcile the conflicting demands for office of the bourgeois parties. Instead, he formed an administration of individuals who were not, at least officially, party representatives. His cabinet was nevertheless composed of politicians from the DVP, Centre, and DDP and non-political 'experts'. In this form it was accepted by the Reichstag, with only the KPD voting against.[152]

Stresemann's reaction to the Cuno government was mixed. It was obviously a disappointment to him—Cuno had in fact agreed to serve under him as economics minister—and he did not think that the new chancellor was the strong man he was reputed to be.[153] On the other hand he was content that the DVP again had two ministers in the government (Johann Becker and Heinze), albeit not as official representatives.

The Cuno government was also a setback for Stresemann's hopes of a great coalition. It was the first government to enjoy the support of the DNVP and as such represented a shift to the right. The DNVP leader Hergt enjoyed this victory and renewed his call for the DVP to join a 'bourgeois block' against the SPD.[154] Potentially even more dangerous was the encouragement given by the DNVP to opponents of parliamentary democracy itself. The political parties were blamed for their inability to form a government and for their obstruction of Cuno. With the rise in living costs caused by the rapid surge in inflation, support for right-radical movements appeared to be on the increase. Hitler started to find an echo in mass rallies in Munich, and Mussolini's 'march on Rome' in October 1922 provided a tempting model for the unsophisticated.

Stresemann saw the dangers and spoke out clearly against them. He warned the DNVP that dictatorship would lead to civil war and the

[151] According to the defence minister Otto Gessler, a member of the DDP, Ebert told him that 'he knew no one who deserved general mistrust as much as Stresemann': Gessler, *Reichswehrpolitik*, 329.

[152] Karl-Heinz Harbeck (ed.), *Das Kabinett Cuno* (Boppard: Harald Boldt, 1968), p. xx.

[153] Stresemann to Dingeldey, 4 Dec. 1922 (Nl. 253).

[154] Stresemann as usual replied that this would lead to their exclusion from government: 'Politische Umschau', *Deutsche Stimmen*, 34/45, 20 Dec. 1922.

disintegration of the Reich.[155] He continued to plead for a parliamentary solution to Germany's problems based on reason and moderation. The public bar talk of a Hitler- or Mussolini-style dictatorship would, he predicted, lead to Communists and the radical right beating each other's heads in. How much better it would be to try to cure the teething troubles of German parliamentarism.[156] In defence of the political parties, he pointed out that Cuno had not been their choice and he could not resist adding that the last chancellor to be appointed without consultation with the parties, Bethmann Hollweg's successor Michaelis, had not been a great success. In the Reichstag Stresemann referred sympathetically to the dilemma faced by the SPD in choosing between government and opposition, drawing a parallel with the pressures which divided the DVP.[157] It was clearly a gesture intended to hold the way open for a great coalition in the future.

The Making of a Republican Statesman

By the end of 1922 Stresemann spoke with new authority and conviction. He had come to terms with the Republic and its institutions. Indeed he had taken a prominent role in defending them against their enemies. This was the result in part of a process of pragmatic accommodation. He saw that the Republic could be brought to serve his own political goals instead of socialist revolution. He had taken the view already in 1919 that the basic structure of the party system had not changed and that the DVP could be influential in alliance with the Centre and the DDP and, wherever possible, the SPD—a revival of the wartime cooperation for reform on the inter-party committee. By 1922 his intensely emotional reaction against the Republic at the time of the revolution had faded. In March 1920 the DVP had adopted an equivocal attitude towards the Kapp putsch and he had been prepared to use it to force elections on the legal government. By the end of 1922 the idea of another revolution was anathema to him. As his resentment ebbed away, it was replaced by horror at right-wing fanaticism and respect for his murdered adversary Erzberger and admiration for Rathenau. This made it possible for him to transfer not only his reason and political skills to the defence of the

[155] 'Politische Umschau', *Deutsche Stimmen*, 34/42, 5 Nov. 1922.
[156] Ibid., 34/44, 5 Dec. 1922.
[157] Reichstag speech, 25 Nov. 1922: Rheinbaben (ed.), *Reden und Schriften*, ii. 22–3.

Republic—becoming a classic example of a *Vernunftrepublikaner*—but also something more, a level of emotional identification which has been less well understood but which fits well with his earlier career.

The Republic, as he saw it by the end of 1922, conformed fairly closely to his concept of a constitutional democracy. It was not a monarchy and, in theory, Stresemann was still a monarchist. But one may wonder how deeply Stresemann felt about the Hohenzollerns. He adopted a tone of exaggerated respect towards the Crown Prince, was flattered by his attentions, and maintained a fitful correspondence with him. There was in this relationship an element of historical romance as well as a large dose of political insurance against his enemies in the DNVP. But the court was not Stresemann's natural home. He did not come from the governing class and he had criticized it before 1918 for its arrested political development and social exclusiveness. The positions he took in 1922 against dictatorship and civil war and in favour of conciliation through parliamentary democracy were all positions he had taken from the start of his political career. In an important sense, he had returned to his roots. This made his defence of the Republic authentic, not merely expedient. It engaged his emotions as well as his intellect. He would never identify with the revolution of November 1918 but the wound had healed.

There is a further dimension to this complex process. By the end of 1922 Stresemann's attention was fixed not on past battles but on the imminent threat to the unity and survival of Germany. He still hoped that American and British influence might dissuade Poincaré from occupying the Ruhr, but he was clear that the decision lay with France. He also understood that the real nightmare for France was German recovery to become again the stronger power, and that this rather than reparations lay at the root of French policy.[158] In December 1922 he referred to an idea that had been canvassed in the United States for 'some kind of international agreement for the preservation of the status quo on the Franco-German frontier' and he suggested that this political initiative might have more influence on French opinion than the much-discussed proposal for an international loan.[159] Stresemann's argument showed his sensitivity to

[158] 'Politische Umschau', *Deutsche Stimmen*, 34/45, 20 Dec. 1922.
[159] Ibid. The idea of a non-aggression pact for the Rhine frontier was suggested by the Cuno government to the American secretary of state Charles Hughes, on 15 Dec. through the German ambassador Otto Wiedfeldt. Stresemann obviously knew of this development, which was first made public by Cuno in a speech on 31 Dec.: Harbeck (ed.), *Kabinett Cuno*, no. 32; Krüger, *Aussenpolitik*, 190–9.

French fears and his awareness that an economic solution alone would not be adequate. The idea of a Rhineland pact contained the seed of the Locarno treaty.

Stresemann was not yet in power but he knew that if Cuno failed he was likely to be called on. Already he spoke with the authority of someone who was the natural choice of the coalition parties for the chancellorship. He was also close enough to the centre of events to understand the nature of the responsibility he would assume. The interests of both Reich and Republic were now joined to his career, if not yet in his hands. From the 'compromised' politician who had been spurned by the Republic in 1919, he had become one of its remaining assets. This completed the conversion from opposition to commitment which was to make him in the years following the leading statesman of the Republic.

6

'All but political suicide'

Ruhr Occupation and Chancellor, 1923

The Ruhr Occupied

The long-threatened occupation of the Ruhr by French and Belgian troops began on 11 January 1923 after last-minute attempts by the German and British governments to find a compromise had failed. Britain and the United States opposed the occupation but adopted a policy of non-intervention. Cuno condemned the action as a violation of the Versailles treaty and announced a policy of passive resistance in the Ruhr.[1]

Stresemann saw his task as helping to rally opinion at home against the French, as he had during the war, but also increasingly—and unlike his wartime stance—to assist in finding a negotiated solution. He loyally supported the Cuno government and checked his speeches in advance with the Foreign Minister.[2] The government used him as an unofficial channel for airing ideas which it wished to make public without being committed to them.[3] The crisis confirmed Stresemann in his view that Germany could only recover—and indeed only survive—by agreement of the moderate parties of the parliamentary centre and, if possible, a great coalition including the SPD. The battle of the Ruhr could hardly be

---

[1] Harbeck (ed.), *Kabinett Cuno*, pp. xxix–xxxii. See Map 1.

[2] Stresemann to Otto Spangenberg, 23 Apr. 1923 (Nl. 258): 'Politische Umschau', *Deutsche Stimmen*, 35/10, 20 May 1923.

[3] Stresemann to Walther Randhahn, 17 May 1923 (Nl. 258).

fought against the Social Democrats, he pointed out.[4] Equally he believed in the need to reach what he called an 'understanding' with France to end the conflict.

Stresemann's twin policies—consensus at home and conciliation abroad—made him a natural target for the extreme right, who became more active as a result of the Ruhr occupation. Hitler and his para-military SA (Sturmabteilung), and their allies among Bavarian monarchists, the DNVP, Reichswehr officers, and some Ruhr industrialists—saw in the crisis the opportunity to overthrow the Republic and prepare for war against France. Stresemann denounced what he called 'the right-wing politicians of catastrophe' who preferred disaster to a settlement and regarded negotiations as treason. Such people were in his view as dangerous as the Communists.[5] He wrote to a DVP colleague that the racists concentrated their attacks on him because they saw in him the obstacle to a 'great right' and an exponent of 'understanding'. These groups regarded the politics of the centre as 'a putrid parliamentary swamp' and their ideal was 'a German Mussolini'. In his view, they had acquired importance only as a result of the financial support of DNVP industrialists such as Hugenberg.[6]

Against this opposition Stresemann set the ideal of a nation united by the Ruhr conflict behind the Republic. He acknowledged the vital role of working-class resistance in the Ruhr and saw that it might give the Republic new legitimacy as a true union of nationalism and democracy, corresponding to his ideal of the 1848 revolution.[7] In a meeting of the national executive, he welcomed the government's decision that the anniversary of the Weimar Constitution should be officially observed as a day of commemoration for the Ruhr and Rhine.[8]

A major threat to national unity was the inflation that spiralled out of control in June because of the cost of supporting passive resistance in the Ruhr. Stresemann was concerned about the obvious injustices to which this gave rise with loss of savings for some, tax and debt evasion, and speculative gains for others. He had supported the government's original commitment to stabilizing the mark, saying that any other policy would

[4] Stresemann to his Reichstag colleague Adolf Kempkes, 27 July 1923 (Nl. 260).
[5] Unsigned article in *Die Zeit*, 3/125, 2 June 1923: Bernhard (ed.), *Vermächtnis*, i. 66–7.
[6] Stresemann to Spangenberg, 23 Apr. 1923 (Nl. 258).
[7] 'Politische Umschau', *Deutsche Stimmen*, 35/3, 5 Feb. 1923; 'Deutsche Ostern', *Die Zeit*, 3/76, 1 Apr. 1923; 'Frankfurter Paulskirche und Gegenwart', *Die Zeit*, 3/114, 19 May 1923.
[8] Report of the Zentralvorstand meeting, 7 July 1923: Kolb and Richter (eds.), *Nationalliberalismus*, 469.

be criminal.[9] He also supported a tax on capital and measures to combat speculative gains.[10] On these issues, his attitude was shared by the SPD and this helped to prepare the way for a great coalition.

Stresemann was also concerned about the effect of hyperinflation on middle-class groups and the danger that they would be driven to support the political extremes. He criticized the way in which the law benefited the speculator by taking no account of inflation, enabling debtors to repay loans at a fraction of the real cost.[11] He attributed Hitler's success to the way he exploited such grievances, blaming everything on the Jews. This was effective with 'the unthinking masses' because of the effects of Jewish immigration from east Galicia. Stresemann dissociated himself from Hitler's anti-Semitism, but he also hit out at 'Germans and non-Germans' who exploited inflation and in particular he attacked east Galician Jews who got rich from property dealing. He described them as 'vultures with an instinct for knowing where something was rotting'. Following the examples of Russia, Poland, and Austria, they now thought Germany was in a state of terminal decay (*Verrecken*) and they had descended on Berlin and were cheating mortgage lenders of the value of their loans.[12] This angry outburst shows both Stresemann's anxiety about the growth of support for racist groups and once again that he was not immune from expressing anti-Semitic sentiments himself.[13]

Stresemann's commitment to the middle ground of politics was well established by 1923 and had deep roots. What of the other side of his policy, the idea of 'understanding' with France? He had argued since 1921 that the facts of economic interdependence made an understanding necessary and at some point inevitable. He hoped that France could be persuaded to reduce the burden of reparations both because it needed the cooperation of German industry to produce them, and as a result of pressure from its Anglo-American allies to adopt what they saw as a realistic total. In practice, however, in 1921–2 he saw little scope for

[9] Reichstag speech, 25 Nov. 1922: Rheinbaben (ed.), *Reden und Schriften*, ii. 28.
[10] Speech to the Zentralvorstand meeting, 7 July 1923: Kolb and Richter (eds.), *Nationalliberalismus*, 470–3. 'Politische Umschau', *Deutsche Stimmen*, 35/15, 5 Aug. 1923.
[11] 'Vom Rechte, das mit uns geboren', *Deutsche Stimmen*, 35/3, 5 Feb. 1923.
[12] Stresemann appears to be referring here to the practice of house-owners themselves issuing mortgages on parts of their property (or other property belonging to them) to other occupants. This practice made them mortgage creditors and therefore at risk of losing this asset. I am grateful to Professor Peter-Christian Witt, Kassel, for suggesting this explanation. In his tax declaration for 1917 Stresemann had himself declared mortgages among his assets: see above, p. 63, n. 149.
[13] Wright, 'Liberalism and Anti-Semitism', 117.

agreement and was inclined to interpret French policy as driven more by fears for its long-term security than its economic interests. He was also constrained by the DVP, which was unwilling to be associated with the policy of 'fulfilment'—which was precisely a policy to create understanding—followed by Wirth and Rathenau. Stresemann's only contribution was to support Stinnes's schemes for cooperation with French industry, but these never went far enough to satisfy the French government.

The occupation of the Ruhr dramatically raised the stakes for both sides. In public Stresemann put a brave face on events, predicting that France would not be able to subdue the 10 million Germans who lived there, that the costs would ruin French public finances, and that by its attempt to dominate Europe France would become diplomatically isolated.[14] In private he was less sanguine, writing that if Poincaré succeeded in getting coal from the Ruhr he would have won and the consequences would be 'difficult to foresee' and, in another letter, that they were engaged in a 'life and death' struggle with France and that it was also possible that Poland would attack in the east and they would be faced with defending Germany against partition.[15]

For Stresemann, the preservation of a united Germany was the main objective. He strongly suspected that one of the aims of French policy was to detach the Rhineland, a war aim they had failed to achieve at the peace settlement because of American and British opposition. Even before the occupation, Stresemann had commented on Poincaré's refusal to negotiate over reparations that 'France does not want the Rhinegold, France wants the Rhine'.[16] In a speech to the Reichstag in March he said that of the three possible objects of French policy—reparations, control of the German economy and separation of the Rhine and Ruhr—the last seemed to be gaining support.[17]

What could Germany oppose to French tactics? It did not have the military means to defend itself. Passive resistance, in other words the

---

[14] 'Zur Lage', NLC 50/3, 8 Jan. 1923: 'Politische Umschau', Deutsche Stimmen, 35/3, 5 Feb. 1923.

[15] Stresemann to the editor of the Königsberger Allgemeine Zeitung, Alexander Wyneken, 16 Jan. and to Major Raabe, 17 Jan. 1923 (Nl. 256). See also Stresemann's diary entry for 15 Jan. 1923, commenting on a conversation with the Austrian envoy, Riedl: 'Danger in the East! Memel: Franco-Lithuanian game. [A reference to the Lithuanian annexation of Memel.] Poland against Germany = Russia against Poland. Germany battleground!': Stresemann material, Berlin.

[16] 'Die außenpolitische Lage bei Jahresbeginn', Deutsche Stimmen, 35/1, 5 Jan. 1923.

[17] 7 Mar. 1923: Zwoch (ed.), Reichstagsreden, 136–7. Cf. Jeannesson, Poincaré, la France et la Ruhr, 151–279.

refusal of German officials and the labour force to work for the French authorities, depended on receiving financial support from the German government and this could not be maintained once the reserves were exhausted. The German economy could in any case not survive for long without what Stresemann called its 'heart', the Ruhr coalfield which was sealed off from the rest of the country by the French.[18] There was no reason to suppose that Britain or the United States would come to the rescue: the most they would offer was moral support until the French were ready to negotiate. The French too had their problems: they had failed to win over the people of the Ruhr and the occupation was a financial burden. Nevertheless an agreement with the French which maintained German sovereignty over the Rhine and Ruhr would clearly be in the national interest. Stresemann had learned from 1918 that will power alone would not bring victory. He saw a parallel in Prussia's situation during the Napoleonic Wars when, after being forced to sign the humiliating peace of Tilsit in 1807, Stein had been willing to conclude an alliance with Napoleon.[19] He therefore supported the government's attempts to reach a settlement, saying that 'No sane person in Germany has opposed, or will oppose, an understanding with France', though he added that France had destroyed any basis for agreement.[20]

The case for negotiations was also pressed by Stinnes, who, in contrast to his earlier views, now argued that France could hold out for longer than Germany.[21] The difficulty was to know what Germany could offer that would satisfy France. In March Stresemann argued in the Reichstag that the government had already offered all it could: reparations to the limit of its capacity, cooperation between the mining industries of the two countries, and an international guarantee of the Rhine frontier.[22] In April he went further, suggesting that they should consider whether state frontiers should be allowed to divide natural economic units such as iron and coal. The idea of 'a far greater economic community', which might also include

---

[18] Speech in Dortmund, 21 Feb. 1923: Bernhard (ed.), *Vermächtnis*, i. 38.

[19] In Oct. 1922 he wrote to a colleague that he had been confirmed in his view of the need for rapprochement with France by reading Lehmann's biography of Stein. Stresemann to Senator Bömers, 3 Oct. 1922 (Nl. 252); Max Lehmann, *Freiherr vom Stein*, 3 vols. (Leipzig: Hirzel, 1902–5).

[20] Reichstag speech, 7 Mar. 1923: Zwoch (ed.), *Reichstagsreden*, 136.

[21] Stresemann's note of a conversation with Stinnes, 19 Mar. 1923 (Nl. 257): Feldman, *Stinnes*, 867–8. In his diary for 19 Mar. Stresemann noted, 'St[innes] very depressed': Stresemann material, Berlin.

[22] Reichstag speech, 7 Mar. 1923: Zwoch (ed.), *Reichstagsreden*, 145–6.

the new states of central Europe, could open the way 'to heal the wounds of the war'.[23]

At the time such ambitious ideas, which were also canvassed by others including Stinnes, had little hope of breaking the deadlock.[24] Of more immediate significance, Stresemann committed himself in the same speech to the proposal that industry, finance, and agriculture should provide guarantees for the payment of reparations.[25] His support for the idea led to criticism and the accusation that the DVP had now adopted a policy of 'fulfilment'. At a meeting of the national executive he replied that those who had benefited from inflation, while others had lost everything, had the self-evident duty to make a sacrifice for the fatherland.[26] In public, he argued that political imperatives must take priority over the economy.[27] France would no doubt be prepared to reduce its demands for reparations in return for keeping the Rhineland, but no decent German would contemplate such an arrangement. Instead, they must go to the limits of what they could pay, even if this meant putting their very economic substance at risk.

Stresemann had difficulty explaining why this should satisfy a French government which also put political interests first and feared Germany's potential to launch a new war in the future.[28] He could only repeat Cuno's offer to guarantee the Rhine frontier and stress that Germany needed a long period of peace to rebuild. But he added a warning. In an obvious reference to the Soviet Union, he said that a dismembered Germany would seek allies where it could find them. He offered France good neighbourly relations and the benefits of reparations, industrial cooperation, and progress towards a customs union; if, however, it tried to hold on to the Rhine and Ruhr he predicted that it would put its future security and existence at risk.

[23] Reichstag speech, 17 Apr. 1923: *Verhandlungen des Reichstags*, vol. 359, pp. 10572–80.

[24] Feldman, *Stinnes*, 855. Keynes also proposed a 'Free Trade Union' of Germany and central Europe, and hoped that France, other west European powers, and Britain would join: Keynes, *The Economic Consequences of the Peace*, 168–70.

[25] This became part of an official proposal from the government on 7 June 1923: Krüger, *Aussenpolitik*, 203–5.

[26] Report of the Zentralvorstand meeting, 7 July 1923: Kolb and Richter (eds.), *Nationalliberalismus*, 469–71.

[27] 'Politik und Wirtschaft', *Die Zeit*, 3/110, 15 May 1923. (Baechler, *Stresemann*, 303, misdates this article to 1921.)

[28] 'Politik und Wirtschaft', ibid.

Stresemann's skilful presentation of Germany's case increased his reputation at home and abroad.[29] His diary for these months suggests the way he was coming to be seen as the chancellor-in-waiting by politicians, ministers, officials, journalists, and foreign diplomats.[30] He took an active part in the social and club life of Berlin, moving among the worlds of politics, government, business, and the theatre.[31] He held discussions with Ebert, Cuno, and the foreign minister von Rosenberg;[32] he was invited by D'Abernon,[33] and the papal nuncio, Pacelli,[34] and had several discussions with the Austrian envoy Riedl;[35] one evening the Stresemanns invited twenty-six guests, including the Czech, Austrian, and Dutch envoys, and Stresemann noted that it 'Went very well';[36] they were guests in their turn, for instance at the fashionable salon of the director of the Hamburg–

[29] He was frequently interviewed and quoted in the foreign press, for example in the London *Daily News* (*NLC* 50/56, 3 July 1923); see also Turner, *Stresemann*, 106. D'Abernon had noted in his diary on 24 Dec. 1922 that with the deaths of Erzberger and Rathenau there 'is no-one left of the class of these two except Stresemann': *Ambassador of Peace*, ii. 144–5.

[30] Diary for 1923: Stresemann material, Berlin. Stresemann also kept a second diary from the time he became chancellor (Nl. 361). Some of the entries were published in Bernhard (ed.), *Vermächtnis*, vol. i.

[31] The diary incidentally affords a glimpse into an under-studied subject, the social dimension of Berlin's political world. Stresemann was a regular user of three clubs: the DVP's Reichsklub, which with its leather armchairs and portraits of Bismarck and Hindenburg exuded the atmosphere of traditional National Liberalism; the Club von Berlin, whose members were mainly industrialists, businessmen, and bankers but also included civil servants and professional people; and the Deutscher Bühnen-Klub (Theatre Club), which brought together actors and theatre-lovers for social and cultural evenings. Prominent in the Bühnen-Klub was the Social Democrat director of the Staatstheater, Leopold Jessner, and other politician members included Wirth, Scheidemann, and Löbe. Stresemann addressed it twice on his favourite theme of Goethe. An anonymous publication, *Gestalten Rings um Hindenburg. Führende Köpfe der Republik und die Berliner Gesellschaft von Heute*, 2nd edn. (Dresden: Reissner, 1929), 131–8, gives a brief, gossipy account of Berlin club life; there is a collection of photographs of the DVP Reichsklub among correspondence between Stresemann and his nephew Franz Miethke (Stresemann material Berlin); Max I. Wolff, *Club von Berlin 1864–1924* (Berlin: privately printed, 1926) is an informative club history—I am grateful to Jean Stresemann for obtaining a copy for me. Despite the enormous literature on Weimar theatre, I have been unable to find a history of the Bühnen-Klub, but for Jessner, see Ruth Freydank, *Theater in Berlin. Von den Anfängen bis 1945* (Berlin: Argon, 1988), 374–83. (I am grateful to Eckhart Hellmuth for this and other theatre references.)

[32] With Ebert on 25 Jan. and 27 June, and dinner on 29 June; with von Rosenberg on 4 Mar. and 16 Apr., with Cuno on 29 Jan. (together with the Ruhr industrialist Fritz Thyssen and Karl Helfferich), 26 Mar., 13 and 16 Apr., 2 and 4 June, 11 and 28 May, 28 July and 7 Aug., and with both Rosenberg and Cuno on 23 Apr., 1 and 26 May, and 21 June.

[33] 19 Jan.

[34] 3 Jan.

[35] 16 Jan., 8 Mar., 11 Apr., 30 June. Riedl was an early advocate of a Rhineland pact as a way of breaking the deadlock. Ernst Jäckh, 'Beiträge zum Locarno- und Kellogg-Vertrag', in id., *Politik als Wissenschaft. Zehn Jahre Deutsche Hochschule für Politik* (Berlin: Hermann Reckendorf, 1931), 1–12.

[36] 8 Jan.

America shipping company, Arndt von Holtzendorff, where Stresemann noted 'Very nice company', which included General von Seeckt, Reich defence minister Gessler, Schacht, and Cuno and his wife,[37] and, on another occasion, at the home of his sociable DVP colleague, Katharina von Oheimb, where the guests included Ebert, the Bavarian envoy in Berlin Konrad von Preger, and party colleagues;[38] another invitation came from the then head of the British and American department at the Auswärtiges Amt, Carl von Schubert, where Stresemann noted 'Large, international company'.[39] He also had regular contacts with leading members of the SPD, in addition to Ebert. He spent an evening together with Hans von Raumer, a DVP industrialist of independent views and former minister, and Rudolf Hilferding, an ex-USPD Marxist theoretician and expert on the currency question, foreshadowing his subsequent appointment of them to the Economics and Finance ministries respectively;[40] he later met them again, together with the leader of the SPD in the Reichstag, Hermann Müller, and the party chairman, Otto Wels.[41] He also had discussions with Erich Koch about a fusion of the DVP with the right wing of the DDP.[42] Among German journalists, Stresemann recorded meetings with Georg Bernhard, the editor of the prestigious, left-liberal *Vossische Zeitung*,[43] and with the newspaper proprietor Franz Ullstein, owner among other titles of the *Berliner Tageblatt*, and one of his journalists, Max Reiner.[44] He also had discussions with the influential Prussian official responsible for maintaining public order, Robert Weismann.[45] Stresemann was clearly aware that he was considered a future chancellor of a great coalition and he was preparing himself for the task.

The Cuno government meanwhile appeared increasingly helpless as the French refused to negotiate and it became clear that passive resistance

[37] 30 Jan., also 7 Apr.
[38] 24 June.
[39] 15 Mar.
[40] 21 Mar. He also met Hilferding in the Club von Berlin on 14 Apr., an interesting place to choose. Stresemann apparently did not mind taking the Marxist theoretician of finance capital to the club of bankers and businessmen.
[41] 9 May. He also noted a conversation with Müller alone on 15 Apr.
[42] 25 Mar.
[43] 14 Jan., 10 Mar. On Bernhard's attitudes and his support for Stresemann, see Michael Klein, *Georg Bernhard. Die politische Haltung des Chefredakteurs der Vossischen Zeitung 1918–1930* (Frankfurt: Peter Lang, 1999), 191–7.
[44] 6 Apr.
[45] 25 Jan., 4 June.

could not be sustained much longer. Stresemann criticized the government, as he had during the war, for its lack of political skill and for failing to maintain public support and influence opinion abroad.[46] No doubt he felt he could give better leadership himself. Nevertheless he did not try to bring it down. If it fell, the French might see this as a sign that Germany was prepared to capitulate and the new government would be attacked by the right for betrayal. He therefore intervened to find a compromise when, at the end of May, the government nearly broke up following a typically abrasive reaction from the Association of German Industry over the terms of a guarantee for reparations.[47] His growing authority was captured in a front-page cartoon in the satirical journal *Simplicissimus*, where he was portrayed as a guardian angel, guiding the figure of Germany as it walked a tightrope over a ravine, with the caption: 'He looks to the right, he looks to the left—he will save me!'[48]

In letters to Käte, who was away from Berlin, Stresemann expressed the tensions he felt: 'The Cuno cabinet no longer enjoys any respect. Cuno wants to resign, but to assume his legacy is all but political suicide. At the same time, there is no other candidate apart from me. I had a very sleepless night.' Shortly afterwards he wrote again:

It is not yet clear, how long Cuno will stay, but all speak of me as the last great reserve, which Germany might have, and many urge me to step into the breach now. How little I long for that, you know... But I cannot shirk it, if it comes. At the same time, I am very doubtful about whether I can meet the hopes which have been placed in me—the situation is too much of a mess, the power of the chancellor too little and I still have to gain experience in international negotiations. I am staking my whole political reputation, which I have built up over twenty years, and maybe my life. What oppresses me most is the thought that I am being put at the wheel of the ship, while outside some people are saying that I am bursting with ambition and cannot wait for the day when I move into the Wilhelmstrasse.[49]

---

[46] 'Passiver Widerstand, aber aktive Politik', *Die Zeit*, 3/147, 28 June 1923: Bernhard (ed.), *Vermächtnis*, i. 69–71.

[47] Harbeck (ed.), *Kabinett Cuno*, p. xli, nos. 168–9. An unsigned article by Stresemann, 'Warum Krise', *Die Zeit*, 3/121, 29 May 1923 (Bernhard (ed.), *Vermächtnis*, i. 65–6); 'Politische Umschau', *Deutsche Stimmen*, 35/11, 5 June 1923. Wulf, *Stinnes*, 383–7; Feldman, *Stinnes*, 872–5.

[48] *Simplicissimus*, 28/7, 14 May 1923: Bernhard (ed.), *Vermächtnis*, vol. i, facing p. 240. See Plate 23.

[49] Stresemann to Käte, 28 May and, probably, 3 June 1923: Wolfgang Stresemann, *Mein Vater*, 224–5.

Although he made no move to unseat Cuno, Stresemann maintained his position as the alternative chancellor. He continued to work for cooperation with the SPD and resisted DNVP attempts to detach the DVP from the great coalition in Prussia.[50] At a meeting of the national executive in July he made the concept of the 'community of the nation' the centrepiece of his speech, warning that the Ruhr conflict could destroy both German unity—with consequences more serious than the Versailles treaty—and parliamentary government: 'We are dancing on a volcano and we are facing a revolution, if we are unable to achieve conciliation by a wise and decisive policy'.[51]

His efforts were finally rewarded when the Reichstag met in August. Cuno's relations with the SPD had been strained by his appeasement of right-radical groups and his inability to bring inflation under control. On 11 August the SPD decided to withdraw its support from his government and expressed its willingness to join a great coalition.[52] The leaders of the middle parties were put in a delicate position. They had already decided that if Cuno resigned they would try to form a coalition with the SPD. Stresemann had secured a similar decision from the DVP Reichstag party.[53] However, neither Stresemann nor the leaders of the other middle parties wanted to force the resignation of the Cuno cabinet in which they were represented. Stresemann in particular had to be careful not to alienate the right wing of the DVP which did not want to see Cuno overthrown.[54] On 9 August he delivered a powerful speech to the Reichstag appealing for unity behind the Constitution as the only way to defeat the French in the Ruhr.[55] On 10 August he noted that Cuno had decided to stay on.[56] However, Cuno had no desire to continue and, once the SPD endorsed the idea of a great coalition, he grasped the opportunity to resign the following day, 12 August. Stresemann, somewhat surprised by the speed with which events had moved at the end, found himself asked by Ebert to form a government the same evening as

[50] He defended the coalition in an article entitled 'Kritische Bedenken', *Die Zeit*, 3/169, 24 July 1923; Schulze, *Braun*, 430–2.

[51] Report of the Zentralvorstand meeting, 7 July 1923: Kolb and Richter (eds.), *Nationalliberalismus*, 467–74.

[52] Harbeck (ed.), *Kabinett Cuno*, pp. xxiii–xxv.

[53] Stresemann's note of the Reichstag party meeting, 10 Aug. 1923 (Nl. 87): Bernhard (ed.), *Vermächtnis*, i. 77–8.

[54] Minutes of the meetings of the leaders of the middle parties with Cuno, 12 Aug. 1923: Harbeck, *Kabinett Cuno*, nos. 247–8.

[55] *Verhandlungen des Reichstags*, vol. 361, pp. 11771–8.

[56] Bernhard (ed.), *Vermächtnis*, i. 77.

the unanimous choice of the SPD, DDP, Centre, and BVP.[57] Even a hostile critic, General von Seeckt, admitted grudgingly, 'Stresemann was in the air.'[58]

Reich Chancellor

Stresemann's chancellorship lasted just over three months, from 13 August to 23 November 1923. Even within this short period, there were technically two administrations, and, in practice, three. The government resigned first on 5 October over its inability to agree on legislation to extend the eight-hour day. Given the lack of an alternative, Stresemann was able to form a new administration of the same parties, but this broke down on 2 November when the SPD withdrew in protest over the use of force against the extreme left in Saxony without similar measures being employed against the extreme right in Bavaria. Thereafter Stresemann continued at the head of a minority government until 23 November when he lost a vote of confidence in the Reichstag.

Even this bare summary shows that his apprehension about assuming office was justified. The desperate situation made the great coalition possible. Stresemann and the SPD leaders both saw it as the last chance for constitutional government.[59] If it failed then the alternatives were civil war and dictatorship. But the crisis which made the coalition possible also gave it very little scope for success. And its enemies on the right and left, including significant elements within both the DVP and the SPD, were eager to profit from its failure.

The problems facing the new government were impressive by any standard. The French and Belgian occupation showed no sign of weakening despite passive resistance. Rather, the resistance could not be maintained much longer as the mark became worthless. The most urgent problem was the creation of a new currency, but its stability depended on balancing the budget and that meant giving up support for the Ruhr. That would in turn provide the signal for revolt in Bavaria where the government was no longer able or willing to control the anti-republican forces.

---

[57] Stresemann's statement to the press, 12 Aug. 1923: Bernhard (ed.), *Vermächtnis*, i. 88.

[58] Seeckt to his sister, 19 Aug. 1923: Harbeck, *Kabinett Cuno*, 737.

[59] Otto Wels explained the SPD's willingness to join the government in these terms. Karl Dietrich Erdmann and Martin Vogt (eds.), *Die Kabinette Stresemann I und II* (Boppard: Harald Boldt, 1978), no. 14.

With fears that Bavaria's northern neighbours, Saxony and Thuringia, were meanwhile drifting under left-wing governments towards a Communist insurrection, it seemed possible that Germany would break up in chaos. The willingness of the Reichswehr to maintain order would be crucial and its price might well be the installation of an authoritarian regime in Berlin.

It would have been surprising if Stresemann's governments had survived for long against such odds. Yet, despite their short life, they left a solid record of achievement. Passive resistance was given up, a new currency was introduced and proved stable, constitutional government survived, and Poincaré eventually agreed to an international committee to examine Germany's capacity to pay, opening the way to a solution of the Ruhr conflict. The foundations were laid for the relative stability of the Republic in the years that followed. These achievements were partly due to luck, the internal divisions of the opposition, the patriotism of the Ruhr working class, and the effect of Anglo-American pressure on France. But they were also a result of the courage and determination shown by Stresemann's cabinets and the care they took to build as broad a consensus as possible for the unpopular measures they had to take. This was not Stresemann's achievement alone but it reflected his leadership and his commitment to constitutional government.

The Stresemann Cabinets

It took Stresemann only a day to reach agreement with the coalition parties on the composition of the cabinet. This was all the more remarkable since it was the first great coalition and the first government under a DVP chancellor, but it showed the extent to which he had prepared himself in advance for the task. Stresemann became foreign minister as well as chancellor, an arrangement which was supposed to be provisional but became permanent.[60] Given the overriding importance of foreign policy and Stresemann's own interest in the subject, it was inevitable that he would want to take the major decisions himself. In the state secretary at the Auswartiges Amt, 'Ago' von Maltzan, and the head of the English and American department, Carl von Schubert, he had two

---

[60] Minutes of the cabinet, 14 Aug. 1923: Erdmann and Vogt (eds.), *Kabinette Stresemann*, no. 1. According to Wolfgang Stresemann, his father would have liked to appoint a senior diplomat, but there was no obvious candidate: *Mein Vater*, 228–9.

shrewd and experienced advisers, and the same was true of the German chargé d'affaires and later ambassador in Paris, Leopold von Hoesch.[61]

His dual office meant that Stresemann was not able to give the same attention to other areas, in particular the vital question of currency stabilization. This required concessions from both business and labour to achieve cuts in public spending and increases in both revenue and production. Stresemann tried the ingenious solution, which as we have seen he had planned previously, of appointing Hilferding as finance minister and Raumer, as economics minister, to symbolize the great coalition. They had previously cooperated successfully to produce an economic programme to be submitted to the Allied Reparations Commission in November 1922, a programme which could form the basis of a great coalition.[62] Unfortunately, this success was not repeated in government. Hilferding exasperated Stresemann by his inability to reach a decision on currency stabilization—he was, in the caustic phrase of his party colleague Otto Braun, 'too clever to be a minister'.[63] Raumer, for his part, failed to give an alternative lead and bridge the gap to the SPD: indeed he angered them by his defence of industrial interests without thereby disarming suspicion of him within the DVP, where he was regarded as dangerously progressive.[64] When the cabinet was reconstructed in October both Hilferding and Raumer were replaced. Hans Luther, a former lord mayor of Essen, who had no formal party affiliation though he was close to the DVP, moved from the Ministry of Agriculture to become finance minister and carried the process of currency stabilization to a successful conclusion.

The only difficulty in the formation of the first cabinet arose from SPD opposition to Otto Gessler remaining as Minister of Defence. The SPD was sceptical about the loyalty of the Reichswehr and felt that Gessler had been too protective of its autonomy and too willing to follow the lead of its self-willed chief, General von Seeckt. Stresemann shared these doubts: in a letter to the Crown Prince, written three weeks before he became chancellor, he described Gessler's confidence in the army's loyalty to the

[61] Peter Krüger, 'Zur Bedeutung des Auswärtigen Amts für die Außenpolitik Stresemanns', in Michalka and Lee (eds.), *Stresemann*, 400–15.

[62] Stresemann gave this as the reason for their appointment: Henry Bernhard [Gustav Stresemann], 'Das Kabinett Stresemann', *Deutsche Stimmen*, 35/24, 20 Dec. 1923. Richter, *Deutsche Volkspartei*, 274.

[63] Otto Braun, *Von Weimar zu Hitler* (New York: Europa, 1940), 126–7.

[64] Cabinet minutes, 7 Sept. 1923: Erdmann and Vogt (eds.), *Kabinette Stresemann*, no. 47. Also Raumer's post-war recollections in Hirsch, *Stresemann*, 313–15.

Republic as 'unjustified optimism'.[65] Nevertheless Stresemann refused to give way to the SPD as he wanted to avoid a conflict with the Reichswehr at such a critical time.[66] The inclusion of the SPD in his cabinet was in itself regarded as a provocation by right-wing groups. Stresemann, whose natural instincts were to conciliate, was anxious to persuade those in responsible positions of his patriotic credentials and avoid a conflict. Early in his administration he made friendly gestures to both the Reichswehr and the Bavarian government, though in neither case was he successful in achieving a lasting rapprochement.[67]

The SPD secured the appointment of Wilhelm Sollmann to the Ministry of the Interior. As chief editor of the *Rheinische Zeitung*, he had taken a strong stand against separatism. It also acquired two further portfolios: Gustav Radbruch, a professor of law, became minister of justice and Robert Schmidt, who had served in several previous administrations, became minister of reconstruction and vice-chancellor. The strong representation of the SPD left fewer posts for the Centre Party.[68] It had to be content with the reappointment of the long-serving minister of labour, a Catholic priest Heinrich Brauns, a newly created ministry for the occupied territories for the former *Oberpräsident* of the Rhine province Johannes Fuchs, who had been expelled by the French, and the Ministry of Posts. The smallest member of the coalition, the DDP, was represented by Rudolf Oeser from the editorial staff of the *Frankfurter Zeitung* at the Ministry of Transport, in addition to Gessler at Defence.

It was a strong cabinet, composed predominantly of party politicians rather than 'experts' and with three prominent representatives of the occupied territories, Luther, Sollmann, and Fuchs. Stresemann appointed

---

[65] Stresemann to the Crown Prince, 23 July 1923 (Nl. 262): Bernhard (ed.), *Vermächtnis*, i. 215–19.

[66] Wolfgang Stresemann, *Mein Vater*, 227. Otto Braun took the same view in the SPD: Schulze, *Braun*, 433.

[67] On 7 Sept. he spent an evening at the military camp at Döberitz near Berlin. He and Seeckt made speeches, Seeckt offering the support of the Reichswehr if Stresemann followed 'the German path' and, according to Seeckt, Stresemann answered skilfully. F. L. Carsten, *The Reichswehr and Politics 1918 to 1933* (Oxford: Clarendon Press, 1966), 165; Hans Meier-Welcker, *Seeckt* (Frankfurt am Main: Bernard & Graefe, 1967), 370–1. Stresemann recorded the incident in his diary and noted 'Strong impressions' (diary, erroneously entered first under 14 Sept., later cancelled and a briefer note made for 7 Sept.): Stresemann material, Berlin; cf. Bernhard (ed.), *Vermächtnis*, i. 108. Stresemann went to Munich for talks with the Bavarian minister president Eugen von Knilling on 25 August. In his diary he recorded that the atmosphere was 'at first very excited, later very pleasant': Stresemann material, Berlin; cf. Bernhard (ed.), *Vermächtnis*, i. 99.

[68] Morsey, *Zentrumspartei*, 516–18.

his party colleague, Werner von Rheinbaben, as state secretary in the Reich Chancellery, hoping that his previous diplomatic experience would be useful. This appointment proved to be a mistake as Rheinbaben did not share Stresemann's commitment to the great coalition and soon promoted schemes for an alternative cabinet without the SPD.[69] Another party colleague, Arnold Kalle, was appointed press officer, although Stresemann in practice managed relations with the press himself. As his private secretary Stresemann brought with him Henry Bernhard, who had first worked with him in 1911 at the Association of Industrialists. Stresemann carried the major load, working according to Bernhard a sixteen- to eighteen-hour day, at times to the point of exhaustion.[70]

When he became chancellor at the age of 45, Stresemann had no previous experience of public office. He also lacked the legal qualifications and experience of administration normal to the German governing class. In 1917, when he had thought he might be offered a government appointment, he had decided to refuse because he felt his background was unsuitable for dealing with the court and senior civil servants.[71] The Republic changed that, but he still appeared ill at ease at social gatherings. His misgivings can be seen in his comment to Käte that he lacked experience of international conferences, and he appointed Rheinbaben partly because he wanted someone on his staff with a command of foreign languages to receive visitors.[72] Whatever his doubts, however, he had achieved his ambition and his commitment was total. To Lord D'Abernon he quoted Bismarck: 'If you have to jump a ditch you must fling your heart over first.'[73]

---

[69] Werner von Rheinbaben, *Erinnerungen*, 216–28; Wolfgang Stresemann, *Mein Vater*, 229–30. Eschenburg suggested that Stresemann made the appointment deliberately to counter opposition to the great coalition from the right wing of the DVP: interview, 4 Sept. 1998. According to another official, Rheinbaben also lacked the experience to take control of the government machine and coordinate the work of the departments efficiently: Max von Stockhausen, *Sechs Jahre Reichskanzlei. Erinnerungen und Tagebuchnotizen, 1922–1927* (Bonn: Athenäum, 1954), 83.

[70] Bernhard (ed.), *Vermächtnis*, i. 84.

[71] Typescript for Schiffer memoirs, and Stresemann to Schiffer, 9 Aug. 1917: BAK, Nl. Schiffer, 2, part 1, p. 206 and Nl. Schiffer 12; Eugen Schiffer, 'Stresemann', in *Deutsches Biographisches Jahrbuch*, ed. Verband der deutschen Akademien, xi: *Das Jahr 1929* (Stuttgart: Deutsche Verlags-Anstalt, 1932), 300–2.

[72] Cabinet minutes, 14 Aug. 1923: Erdmann and Vogt (eds.), *Kabinette Stresemann*, no. 1.

[73] D'Abernon, *Ambassador of Peace*, ii: *The Years of Crisis June 1922–December 1923*, 237.

The Coalition

It was soon clear that Stresemann would need all his formidable political skills. The problem lay less in cabinet, where he rapidly established his authority as an able and considerate chairman, but in maintaining the support of the coalition parties, of which none was more awkward than the DVP.[74] Its lack of solidarity was shown on the first day when Stresemann presented his government to the Reichstag. Twelve members of the party walked out before the vote of confidence in protest against the number of ministries allocated to the SPD.[75] Stresemann's problems were made worse because his successor as DVP leader in the Reichstag, Ernst Scholz, was unsympathetic to the great coalition and erratic in his loyalty to Stresemann. The scepticism within the DVP was echoed from within the SPD. About a third of each refused to vote for the new government on 14 August so that, although it won easily by 239 to 76, this represented—allowing for abstentions—an overall majority of only nineteen.[76] Measured against Stresemann's appeal for all constitutional groups to rally to the defence of the state, it was not an overwhelming mandate.[77]

The Abandonment of Passive Resistance

The government faced a desperate situation. The financial position according to Hilferding 'exceeded the worst expectations' and was too grave to be made known in full to the Reichstag. In the first half of August expenditure was sixteen times greater than total receipts.[78] The difference was largely attributable to the cost of passive resistance, which was estimated at 40 million gold marks per day.[79] The result was runaway inflation

[74] Luther, Sollmann, and Radbruch spoke highly of Stresemann's qualities as chairman. Hirsch, *Stresemann*, 145–6; Hans Luther, *Politiker ohne Partei. Erinnerungen* (Stuttgart: Deutsche Verlags-Anstalt, 1960), 110; Gustav Radbruch, *Der innere Weg. Aufriß meines Lebens* (Stuttgart: K. F. Koehler, 1951), 169.

[75] Memorandum about the activities of Dr Quaatz, one of the leaders of the group (Nl. 267); Turner, *Stresemann*, 115.

[76] Erdmann and Vogt (eds.), *Kabinette Stresemann*, p. xxvii. The opposition was composed mainly of the KPD and DNVP. The BVP abstained.

[77] *Verhandlungen des Reichstags*, vol. 361, pp. 11839–41.

[78] Minutes of a meeting of ministers with leaders of the coalition parties, 22 Aug. 1923: Erdmann and Vogt (eds.), *Kabinette Stresemann*, no. 14.

[79] Memorandum by Stresemann, 7 Sept. 1923: Bernhard (ed.), *Vermächtnis*, i. 108–14.

with the paper mark falling in value from 262,000 to the gold mark at the beginning of August to 2,454,000 by the end of the month.[80]

The cabinet nevertheless decided not to end passive resistance immediately. Stresemann hoped that they could buy more time by various expedients—raising a loan valued in gold, confiscating the foreign currency balances of private industry, and reducing expenditure—since he believed that the international situation was moving in Germany's favour. On 11 August the British foreign secretary Lord Curzon condemned the occupation of the Ruhr as illegal, potentially disastrous, and doomed to failure.[81] Stresemann hoped to increase the pressure on France by refusing to negotiate with France alone, and instead offering guarantees for reparations to the Allies collectively provided German sovereignty was restored to the Ruhr. However, he admitted to the cabinet that Germany's ability to carry out the policy was itself limited by its desperate domestic situation.[82]

Stresemann attempted to gain international support by renewing the offer for part of the economy to be used as security for reparations and for Germany to join in an international guarantee of the Rhine frontier.[83] With the help of D'Abernon, German policy was tailored to the views of the British Foreign Office.[84] These efforts were in vain. Poincaré saw that passive resistance would collapse soon in any case and had no reason to give up the Ruhr at the moment of victory, in return for guarantees which he would not control. His position remained that there could be no negotiations until passive resistance had been given up and that the Ruhr would be evacuated only as reparations were actually paid.[85]

Stresemann suspected that Poincaré's real intention was to remain in the Ruhr indefinitely and encourage a gradual separation from the Reich.[86] But there was no alternative to accepting that for the time being he was master of the situation. Britain could offer no real help

---

[80] Erdmann and Vogt (eds.), *Kabinette Stresemann*, p. 1218.

[81] *DBFP*, 1st ser. xxi, no. 330. A detailed study of British policy, and its inconsistencies, is provided by Elspeth Y. O'Riordan, *Britain and the Ruhr Crisis* (Basingstoke: Palgrave, 2001).

[82] Cabinet minutes, 23 Aug. 1923: Erdmann and Vogt (eds.), *Kabinette Stresemann*, no. 18.

[83] Speeches on 24 Aug. and 2 Sept. 1923: Bernhard (ed.), *Vermächtnis*, i. 98–101.

[84] Memorandum by Schubert, 29 Aug. 1923: *ADAP*, ser. A, viii, no. 123; D'Abernon to Curzon, 30 Aug. 1923: *DBFP*, 1st ser. xxvi, no. 340.

[85] Jacques Bariéty, *Les Relations franco-allemandes après la première guerre mondiale* (Paris: Éditions Pedone, 1977), 223–36.

[86] On Poincaré's intentions and his hesitant encouragement of separatism in the Rhineland, see Jeannesson, *Poincaré*, 285–8, 329–60.

since France had rejected its mediation. By the end of August Stresemann knew that he would have to settle directly with France after all.[87] He still hoped that the French would agree to some concessions, albeit unofficially, in return for Germany giving up passive resistance. He pressed Hilferding to produce plans for currency stabilization to allow time for his foreign policy to work and to maintain public support.[88] At the same time he started to prepare public opinion for the inevitable decision in meetings with political and business leaders, representatives of the *Länder*, and leaders of the occupied territories.[89]

Poincaré refused to be drawn into negotiations or even face-saving measures for the German government, such as allowing those expelled from the Ruhr to return.[90] When on 19 September the British prime minister Stanley Baldwin met Poincaré in Paris and it was announced that the two governments were in total agreement, Stresemann knew that further delay would be futile.[91] He held another series of meetings with representatives of the occupied territories, the parties, and the *Länder*. With the paper mark now valued at over 43 million to the gold mark there was general agreement that passive resistance had to be abandoned.[92] Stresemann, warning that a 'total collapse of the whole German economy' would otherwise be inevitable, described passive resistance as a weapon which now hurt Germany more than their opponents.[93] The cabinet took the final decision on 25 September and it was announced the next day.[94]

This was a humiliating defeat. Stresemann had been forced to accept what amounted to unconditional surrender. He compared it to signing the treaty of Versailles.[95] The DVP had always previously avoided such responsibility. This time there was no escape. Stresemann had the courage to accept the inevitable and impose it on his party.[96] It marks the moment when he ceased to be merely an outstanding politician with an unusual attachment to consensus politics and showed qualities of statesmanship.

[87] Memorandum by Schubert, 29 Aug. 1923: *ADAP*, ser. A, viii, no. 122.
[88] Cabinet minutes, 30 Aug. 1923: Erdmann and Vogt (eds.), *Kabinette Stresemann*, no. 33.
[89] Minutes of the meetings, 28 Aug., 6 and 15 Sept. 1923: ibid., nos. 27, 43, 59.
[90] Memoranda by Stresemann and Maltzan, 18 and 19 Sept. 1923: *ADAP*, ser. A, viii, nos. 152, 155.
[91] Cabinet minutes, 20 Sept. 1923: Erdmann and Vogt (eds.), *Kabinette Stresemann*, no. 71.
[92] Ibid., nos. 76–80 and p. 1218.
[93] Ibid., no. 79.
[94] Ibid., no. 81.
[95] Ibid., no. 79.
[96] On the unpopularity of the decision with local parties and their fear that the DNVP would gain at their expense, see Jones, *German Liberalism*, 199.

On the Brink of Civil War

The decision to end passive resistance was made easier because it was already breaking down and could not have lasted the winter. The collapse of the currency led to farmers hoarding food, causing shortages in the towns and raiding parties looting the countryside.[97] The Ruhr industrialists were desperate to be allowed to restart production.[98] Paradoxically, Stresemann was also helped by Poincaré. By denying that he had any intention of annexing the Ruhr, he enabled Stresemann to claim that in giving up passive resistance they were not accepting any loss of sovereignty.[99]

Only one alternative proposal emerged from the discussions. Karl Jarres, the lord mayor of Duisburg, argued that since France and Belgium had violated the Versailles treaty, Germany should declare that it would no longer consider itself bound by the treaty in relation to those two states.[100] The idea of repudiating the treaty was taken up by the Bavarian government, the DNVP, and the right wing of the DVP.[101] Stresemann firmly rejected it. He pointed out that it would leave the Ruhr wholly at the mercy of the occupiers and it would also destroy any chance of British intervention. He held out the hope, which he described as 'objectively based' in 'the European distribution of power', that Britain would intervene should France attempt to break Germany up.[102]

Although there was no real alternative, the reaction from the right followed immediately. The Bavarian government declared a state of emergency under article 48 of the Constitution and appointed a leading monarchist, Gustav von Kahr, as commissioner with dictatorial powers. Stresemann and Ebert summoned the cabinet the same night and replied

[97] Otto Braun urged an immediate end to resistance for this reason: minutes of the meeting of the joint Reich and Prussian cabinets, 15 Sept. 1923, in Erdmann and Vogt (eds.), *Kabinette Stresemann*, no. 59.

[98] Stinnes appealed to his DVP colleagues in terms strikingly different from those he had adopted before the Ruhr occupation: 'Have confidence in us in the occupied territory that we will reach a modus vivendi with the French, which is worthy of Germany'. Minutes of the Reichstag party meeting, 25 Sept. 1923 (Nl. 87); Feldman, *Stinnes*, 893.

[99] For instance in the announcement to the German people of the end of passive resistance, 26 Sept. 1923: *Schulthess' Europäischer Geschichtskalender*, NS 39 (1923), ed. Ulrich Thürauf (Munich: Beck, 1927: repr. Nendeln and Liechtenstein: Kraus, 1976), 177–8.

[100] Erdmann and Vogt (eds.), *Kabinette Stresemann*, no. 52.

[101] Ibid., nos. 79, 80; minutes of the DVP Reichstag party, 25 Sept. 1923 (Nl. 87).

[102] Minutes of a meeting with the minister presidents of the *Länder*, 25 Sept. 1923: Erdmann and Vogt (eds.), *Kabinette Stresemann*, no. 79.

with a declaration of emergency for the whole Reich, appointing Gessler (as minister of defence) Reich commissioner.[103]

Despite this show of strength the situation was precarious. Stresemann wanted to avoid a conflict with Bavaria if at all possible. The political costs were too high: if it came to a breach the SPD could not be expected to tolerate Bavarian defiance of the Reich government, whereas the DVP and the right wing of the Centre Party would not support the use of force. In any case Stresemann could not rely on the Reichswehr, neither on its Bavarian units to remain loyal nor on the willingness of the rest to suppress a Bavarian rebellion.[104] He therefore played for time, persuading the cabinet not to demand that Bavaria rescind Kahr's appointment and to allow the Reich and Bavarian states of emergency to run in parallel.[105] This avoided an outright Bavarian refusal to accept the Reich's authority, while in practice leaving Kahr and the commander of the Bavarian forces, General von Lossow—who was formally Gessler's representative in Bavaria under the Reich emergency decree—to work out a modus vivendi. That soon proved unsatisfactory, however, as Lossow's loyalties were to Kahr rather than to the Reich authorities.

By the end of September the cabinet faced a crisis of confidence. With the Reichstag due to reconvene on 2 October the cohesion of the coalition parties, which had never been strong, was dissolving. The tension with Bavaria provided a welcome pretext for the right wing of the DVP and the Centre Party to turn on the SPD. They claimed that only a reconstruction of the coalition to bring in the DNVP would resolve the problem.[106] In

---

[103] In declaring a military state of emergency and appointing Gessler, Ebert and Stresemann may have hoped to make the decision more acceptable to the Bavarian authorities. The alternative would have been to treat the crisis as a civil emergency and appoint Wilhelm Sollmann, the SPD minister of the interior, but that would have provoked the Bavarians and led to friction with the Reichswehr. Heiner Möllers, *Reichswehrminister Otto Geßler. Eine Studie zu 'unpolitischer' Militärpolitik in der Weimarer Republik* (Frankfurt am Main: Peter Lang, 1998), 228–30.

[104] Gessler told the cabinet on 30 Sept. 1923 that military intervention was 'out of the question': Erdmann and Vogt (eds.), *Kabinette Stresemann*, no. 94. Möllers, *Geßler*, 236–7.

[105] Cabinet minutes, 27 Sept. 1923: Erdmann and Vogt (eds.), *Kabinette Stresemann*, no. 83. Stresemann also tried to invoke the authority of the archbishop of Munich, Cardinal von Faulhaber, on his side. After some hesitation, Faulhaber replied on 6 Nov. supporting the idea of greater autonomy for Bavaria, 'but only by constitutional and peaceful methods': Stresemann material, Berlin; Bernhard (ed.), *Vermächtnis*, i. 129–31.

[106] Minutes of the DVP Reichstag party meeting, 25 Sept. 1923 and an account of events between 3 and 6 Oct. 1923, sent by the central party office (Reichsgeschäftsstelle) which was responsible to the chairman of the GA, Adolf Kempkes, to the provincial party organizations (Nl. 87); Richter, *Deutsche Volkspartei*, 280–2; Jones, *German Liberalism*, 200–1. On the Centre Party, see Morsey, *Zentrumspartei*, 521; von Hehl, *Marx*, 238–40.

addition, with passive resistance ended it was urgent for the government to bring forward a programme of economic reform which was bound to cause division between the SPD and the bourgeois parties. The authority of the government was further undermined by the French, who were in no hurry to open negotiations and preferred local agreements with German representatives in the occupied territories. In the Ruhr, separatist movements were reported to be waiting only for a lead from Bavaria to mount a coup of their own. Anti-republican groups elsewhere were also expected to follow the signal from Bavaria, and on 1 October there was an abortive mutiny near Berlin by members of the 'Black' Reichswehr—unofficial units recruited from right wing groups in case of war with France.[107]

In an attempt to keep control of the situation, the cabinet decided to ask the Reichstag to agree to an Enabling Act, which would allow the necessary economic measures to be taken by decree, and then adjourn. This was a way of relieving the coalition parties directly of responsibility and thus holding the coalition together.[108] When this was put to the leaders of the coalition parties on 2 October, however, it became clear that they lacked the will to agree.[109] The SPD was unhappy with the proposal that the Enabling Act should include extension of the eight-hour day since in their eyes this represented one of the main achievements of the Republic. The DVP representative, Scholz, for his part appeared determined to destroy the coalition. He not only insisted on extension of the eight-hour day but proposed that the DNVP should join the coalition and, for good measure, added that the DVP would make its agreement to the Enabling Act conditional on changes in the cabinet. Not surprisingly the SPD attitude hardened.

Further attempts to broker an agreement in cabinet were again rejected by the parties. The SPD ministers were prepared to see the eight-hour day come under the Enabling Act, but the Reichstag party, by a majority, refused. The party was prepared to consider normal legislation on the issue, and the Centre Party and the DDP were willing to accept this alternative, provided the SPD did not oppose the legislation. Stresemann knew there was no hope of persuading the DVP, however, and there was

---

[107] Report on the separatist movement, 28 Sept. and cabinet minutes, 30 Sept and 1 Oct. 1923: Erdmann and Vogt (eds.), *Kabinette Stresemann*, nos. 89, 94, 97. On the mutiny, see Carsten, *Reichswehr*, 168–9.

[108] Cabinet minutes 30 Sept., 1 Oct. 1923: Erdmann and Vogt (eds.), *Kabinette Stresemann*, nos. 94, 97.

[109] Record of the meeting: ibid., no. 99.

no certainty that the SPD would support the legislation. With DNVP obstruction likely in order to force a change of government, the legislation would fail. Unlike Scholz and the DVP right wing, he did not want to drive the SPD out of the coalition, but neither he nor the SPD ministers could find a solution. After three fruitless sessions on 3 October, the cabinet resigned.[110]

A Second Chance

Stresemann's hopes lay in ruins. The great coalition had lasted a shorter time than any previous cabinet and had been brought down largely by his own party. He feared he would be remembered only for the surrender of passive resistance.[111] In his diary he recorded 'deepest depression'.[112] Ebert asked him to form a new government, but it was far from clear how this could be done.

The natural alternative to the great coalition was to replace the SPD with the DNVP and this was what Scholz and the right wing of the DVP wanted. But they had totally miscalculated. Stresemann did not want to lead a centre-right government formed to drive the SPD from office. He had staked his reputation on the great coalition and it would have meant a complete reversal of direction.[113] A few members of the Reichstag party would have been prepared to sacrifice him for the sake of coalition with the DNVP, but the majority drew back from such blatant disloyalty. At a meeting on 3 October, he received unanimous support with the single exception of Stinnes.[114] The DNVP in turn made it clear on 4 October that it had no intention of serving under Stresemann.[115] Its aim was to replace parliamentary government with some form of authoritarian rule, whether through the emergency powers of the president or through an

[110] Cabinet minutes 2–3 Oct. 1923: Erdmann and Vogt (eds.), *Kabinette Stresemann*, nos. 102, 104–6; account of events 3–6 Oct. 1923 and Stresemann to a member of the Zentralvorstand, Ludwig Schultz, 9 Oct. 1923 (Nl. 87).

[111] Wolfgang Stresemann, *Mein Vater*, 243.

[112] Entry for 4 Oct. 1923: Bernhard (ed.), *Vermächtnis*, i. 145.

[113] In an article in the *Kölnische Zeitung* on 29 Apr. 1924 he said that such a reversal would have been 'unprincipled' (*charakterlos*): Bernhard (ed.), *Vermächtnis*, i. 327–8.

[114] Minutes of the meeting of the Reichstag party, 25 Sept 1923, and account of events 3–6 Oct. 1923 (Nl. 87). Stinnes hoped for the establishment of a 'national dictatorship' which would carry through the social and economic reforms wanted by the industrialists, particularly the extension of the eight-hour day. Feldman, *Stinnes*, 883–95; Wulf, *Stinnes*, 452–65.

[115] Günther Arns, *Regierungsbildung und Koalitionspolitik in der Weimarer Republik 1919–1924* (Ph.D., Tübingen, 1971), 166.

outright coup. For their part, the DDP and the majority of the Centre Party were not willing to join an anti-socialist coalition with the DNVP.[116] It was therefore a non-starter.

Faced with apparent deadlock among the Reichstag parties, Stresemann briefly considered forming a 'cabinet of talents'.[117] Encouraged by Rheinbaben, he saw a number of leading industrialists, including Friedrich Minoux, a director of the Stinnes group, and Otto Wiedfeldt, a Krupp director and ambassador to Washington. He also discussed with Seeckt the possibility of his entering the cabinet.[118] No details are known about these conversations but, not surprisingly, nothing came of them. The same people were also being canvassed by the DNVP for a government of 'directors', and they were more likely to be sympathetic to approaches from the DNVP than from Stresemann.[119]

In any case Stresemann's heart was not in it. The only justification for such an 'above party' government would have been that it was the only way to resolve the crisis within the Constitution. Yet to have a Reichstag majority it would have needed, like the Cuno government, the support of the DNVP. But once the DNVP made it clear that it would not support a Stresemann government, the only possibility left would have been for Stresemann to rely on Ebert for presidential decree powers followed by a dissolution of the Reichstag but with no real prospect of achieving a majority in a new election. Stresemann was later reported to have said that, while he could understand Rheinbaben's view that the party deadlock made such measures necessary, he was too much of a parliamentarian himself to follow this path.[120] In retrospect, it is surprising that he even toyed with the idea. He was clearly reluctant to surrender the chancellorship. He may also have thought that it was better to try to find a solution himself than to see power pass to those who made no secret of their desire to do away with parliamentary government.

The crisis was resolved by a suggestion from the leaders of the DDP and Centre Party that they should see whether agreement could be reached after all on the eight-hour day and the great coalition revived.[121]

---

[116] Morsey, Zentrumspartei, 521. Erdmann and Vogt (eds.), Kabinette Stresemann, pp. 484, 489.

[117] Werner von Rheinbaben, Erinnerungen, 223–6; Turner, Stresemann, 121–3.

[118] Erdmann and Vogt (eds.), Kabinette Stresemann, p. 1184.

[119] According to Rheinbaben, Wiedfeldt scornfully rejected Stresemann's approach: Werner von Rheinbaben, Erinnerungen, 225.

[120] Ibid. 226; Wolfgang Stresemann, Mein Vater, 245.

[121] Memorandum of a discussion between Stresemann and the leaders of the coalition parties, 5 Oct. 1923: Erdmann and Vogt (eds.), Kabinette Stresemann, no. 113; Morsey, Zentrumspartei, 523.

With the DVP willing to compromise after the DNVP had rejected a Stresemann-led coalition, and the SPD fearing that if it did not agree to legal modification of the eight-hour day the mine-owners would be strong enough to force it through in any case, there was a willingness on all sides to find a solution. After negotiations which lasted into the small hours of 6 October a formula was found: the issue would be resolved by legislation with SPD support, allowing the eight-hour day to remain the norm but providing for exceptions where the national interest made it imperative.

Stresemann hastily reconstructed his cabinet. Luther became finance minister and a non-party senior official, Joseph Koeth, economics minister.[122] As a concession to the agrarian wing of the DNVP Graf Kanitz, a landowner from their ranks, subsequently became minister of agriculture. The changes weakened the influence of the SPD compared to the first cabinet. Stresemann also replaced Rheinbaben with Adolf Kempkes, who could be relied on to represent Stresemann's views to the DVP and to warn him of trouble from that quarter.[123]

The new cabinet faced the Reichstag the same day, 6 October, with essentially the same programme as before. Stresemann defended the record of the first eight weeks in a frank and powerful speech. He said he had been well aware that the decision to give up passive resistance could cost him the leadership of his party and even his life but that the courage to take responsibility was what Germany lacked. He attacked those who by talking of dictatorship and undermining the institutions of

[122] Stresemann had first considered Wiedfeldt and then Hjalmar Schacht for the post of finance minister. Wiedfeldt posed conditions, and questions were raised about Schacht's conduct in the wartime occupation of Belgium. Although he was held not to have acted dishonourably, the delay caused by the investigation meant that he was passed over. Schacht's suitability was questioned by Franz Schroeder, the state secretary in the Finance Ministry. See the account in a memoir of Stresemann by Werner von Rheinbaben: PA Berlin, Nl. von Rheinbaben, 4. Also Erdmann and Vogt (eds.), *Kabinette Stresemann*, pp. 500–1; Gessler, *Reichswehrpolitik*, 273; Luther, *Politiker ohne Partei*, 118–20.

Stresemann clearly had a high opinion of Schacht's abilities. He had dealings with Schacht in the latter's capacity as a director of the Danatbank. Schacht arranged a credit for *Die Zeit* in July 1923 (Stresemann to Zander, 14 July 1923: Stresemann material, Berlin). Schacht was also the chairman of the board of Litwin's company, Evaporator A.G., of which Stresemann was deputy chairman. More important for a public appointment, Schacht had connections with financial circles abroad. On 23 May 1923 Stresemann recorded in his diary: 'With Dr Schacht about his London journey. Shimmer of hope for understanding'. (Stresemann material, Berlin; Bernhard (ed.), *Vermächtnis*, i. 65). On his London visit, Hjalmar Schacht, *My First Seventy-Six Years*, Eng. edn. (London: Alan Wingate, 1955), 174–6.

[123] Erdmann and Vogt (eds.), *Kabinette Stresemann*, pp. xxxv–xxxvi; Richter, *Deutsche Volkspartei*, 286.

state were endangering the very survival of the Reich.[124] In a subsequent exchange with the DNVP leader Westarp, he defended the policy of coalition with the SPD as the only realistic, constitutional way of proceeding. With the battle for the Rhineland at its height and without military means of defence, he said he could not understand the desire to divide the nation between right and left. The battle could only be fought with the idea of the community of the whole nation and that was the truly national policy.[125]

The cabinet received a vote of confidence on 8 October and scored its first significant victory on 13 October with the passage of the Enabling Act by 316 to 24. The outcome hung in the balance until the last moment.[126] The Constitution required that at least two-thirds of the Reichstag should be present and that two-thirds of those present should support the bill. The DNVP and KPD successfully obstructed its passage on 11 October by leaving the chamber. Stresemann was supported by Ebert, however, who agreed to a dissolution of the Reichstag should the bill fail. He was then able to persuade the Bavarian People's Party to remain in the chamber, albeit to vote against the bill, and thus secure the necessary majorities.[127]

Poincaré Victorious

The first problem facing the new cabinet was the Ruhr. With the end of passive resistance, industry had to resume production as the alternative was bankruptcy, mass unemployment, and starvation. Stresemann pressed Poincaré for negotiations about how the economy could be restarted and deliveries of coal resumed.[128] He hoped to persuade Poincaré that Germany was willing to pay reparations again but was simply not in a position to do so until the Ruhr was working normally. His object was to maintain the authority of the Reich government which would otherwise be undermined by local agreements, such as that negotiated by the Phoenix–Rhine steel group with the French authorities on 10 October.

---

[124] Rheinbaben (ed.), *Reden und Schriften*, ii. 58–87.

[125] Reichstag speech, 8 Oct. 1923: ibid. 87–99.

[126] Stresemann's diary entry for 13 Oct. 1923: Bernhard (ed.), *Vermächtnis*, i. 157.

[127] Erdmann and Vogt (eds.), *Kabinette Stresemann*, pp. xxxvi, 500, 543; Luther, *Politiker ohne Partei*, 121–2. In protest against the compromise on the eight-hour day, twelve DVP deputies, including Stinnes, Quaatz, Sorge, and Vögler, were absent on the first occasion and abstained when the vote was taken: Jones, *German Liberalism*, 203.

[128] Stresemann to Hoesch, 7 and 14 Oct. 1923: *ADAP*, ser. A, viii, nos. 181, 190.

Poincaré flatly rejected Stresemann's pleas. He had no incentive to negotiate with the German government when he could impose his will directly on the Ruhr. He told Hoesch that negotiations would follow the resumption of reparations payments, not precede them.[129] Poincaré may also have hoped that by remaining firm he could help to bring Stresemann down and Germany to the point of collapse, making possible the establishment of a separate Rhine state.[130] French control of the railways and plans for a new currency for the Rhineland showed how the links with the Reich could be broken and naturally intensified suspicion in Berlin.[131]

The German government had no effective means of resistance. An organization was established under Kurt Jahnke, who had made a name for himself as a German agent in the United States in the war.[132] It carried out acts of sabotage and terror against the French occupation authorities and separatist leaders. A parallel Bavarian organization was also established in Heidelberg to operate in the Palatinate where the separatist movement had a following among the rural population.[133] The Bavarian organization was responsible for a particularly brutal massacre of separatists in February 1924. How far Stresemann was complicit in these operations it is impossible to say. There are reports that Jahnke later established an intelligence organization for Stresemann.[134] But according to information from Jahnke himself, at the beginning of October 1923 he was involved in the unofficial Reichswehr plot either to overthrow

[129] Hoesch to Auswärtiges Amt, 10, 13, and 17 Oct. 1923: *ADAP*, ser. A, viii, nos. 186, 188, 193.

[130] Bariéty, *Les Relations franco-allemandes*, 237–41; Jeannesson, *Poincaré*, 307–60.

[131] Cabinet minutes, 20 Oct. 1923: Erdmann and Vogt (eds.), *Kabinette Stresemann*, no. 156.

[132] I am grateful to Dr Gerd Krüger, who has made a study of 'active' German resistance during the Ruhr occupation, for this information. On the proliferation of intelligence organizations in the Weimar Republic, see Gerd Krüger, '"…ich bitte, darüber nichts sagen zu dürfen". Halbstaatliche und private politische Nachrichtendienste in der Weimarer Republik', *zeitgeschichte*, 27/2 (2000), 87–107.

[133] Stephen A. Schuker, 'Bayern und der rheinische Separatismus 1923–1924', *Jahrbuch des Historischen Kollegs 1997*, 75–111.

[134] Charles Drage, *Als Hitler nach Canossa ging* (Berlin: ikoo, 1982), 101, based on information from Walther Stennes, who had been recruited by Jahnke to work for the 'active resistance' against the French occupation. After the abortive 'Stennes revolt' of the SA in Berlin against Hitler's policy of using legal tactics against the Republic, Stennes emigrated to China, where he recounted his reminiscences to Drage. The reference does not occur in the original English version, *The Amiable Prussian* (London: Anthony Blond, 1958), 66. There is also a reference to Stresemann being a client of Jahnke's intelligence organization in Claire Nix (ed.), *Heinrich Brüning: Briefe und Gespräche 1934–1945* (Stuttgart: Deutsche Verlags-Anstalt, 1974), 447 n. 4. I owe these references to Dr Gerd Krüger.

Stresemann or to force on him a change of policy.[135] It is certain, however, that the Reich Chancellery and the Ministry for the Occupied Territories financed the purchase of weapons for the Bavarian group.[136] And Stresemann condoned the massacre in February 1924, blaming the French occupation authorities for having stirred up national passions to the point where such horrific acts were committed.[137]

A more serious danger than the generally unrepresentative separatist groups was that the French might succeed by stages in creating a separate Rhineland state. Industrialists and established local leaders, such as Konrad Adenauer, the lord mayor of Cologne, were understandably anxious to achieve at least a modus vivendi with the occupier and the Reich government, unable to guarantee its continued support, was in a weak position to prevent them.

Stresemann had no alternative but to allow negotiations in October between the Ruhr industrialists and the French and Belgian authorities.[138] That, however, was not enough for the mine-owners. To start production they demanded in addition a credit of 150 to 200 million gold marks and that the Reich should resume financial responsibility for reparations deliveries and the coal tax claimed by the French. Otherwise they threatened that the works would have to close, the labour force would be driven to despair, and the end result would be that the French would take over the Ruhr.[139] To assume obligations of this size, however, would undermine all hope of introducing a stable currency and defeat the whole purpose for which passive resistance had been given up. The cabinet therefore refused.[140] As Stresemann explained to Stinnes, 'We are now fighting for the bare existence of the German people and we must subordinate every other consideration to this one.'[141]

---

[135] See above, p. 222. Unsigned memorandum, dated 'beginning of December 1926'; *ADAP*, ser. B, i/ii, no. 224. This memorandum comes from Stresemann's papers (Nl. 302) and may have been dictated by him; if so, it would show that by 1926 Jahnke was reporting to him.

[136] Schuker, 'Bayern', 96–8.

[137] Speech in Elberfeld, 17 Feb. 1924: Bernhard (ed.), *Vermächtnis*, i. 298–9; Reichstag speech, 22 Feb. 1924: *Verhandlungen des Reichstags*, vol. 361, p. 12433; Schuker, 'Bayern', 104.

[138] Cabinet minutes, 11 Oct. 1923: Erdmann and Vogt (eds.), *Kabinette Stresemann*, no. 128. The occupying powers had established a civilian body called the Mission Interalliée de Contrôle des Usines et des Mines, abbreviated to MICUM, and it was with this body that the mine-owners negotiated.

[139] Minutes of a meeting of ministers with the Ruhr industrialists, 9 Oct. 1923: ibid., no. 121.

[140] Cabinet minutes, 10 and 11 Oct. 1923: ibid., nos. 125, 128.

[141] Stresemann to Stinnes, 12 Oct. 1923: ibid., no. 131. The industrialists had done nothing to make themselves popular with the cabinet. In addition to their opposition to the great coalition,

As this decision showed, when they were forced to choose the government put the interests of the Reich as a whole above those of the occupied territories. On 15 October it agreed to the foundation of a new bank, the Rentenbank, secured by a mortgage of agricultural land and industrial assets.[142] The new currency, the Rentenmark, was to be issued on 15 November when relief measures to the Ruhr would have to cease to prevent new inflation. The new currency was intended only as an interim measure until the Reich was in a position to return to the gold standard. A special Currency Commissioner was appointed to oversee the introduction of the Rentenmark and to maintain its value by a strict control of credit. With Stresemann's support, and quite possibly at his instigation, Schacht was appointed to the post.[143] To ensure success Luther converted taxes to gold values and the cabinet embarked on a ruthless programme of cutting public expenditure, which included a 25 per cent reduction in the number of state employees and a reduction in the salaries of the remainder to some 60 per cent of their pre-war level.[144] These measures enabled the Rentenmark to maintain parity with the gold mark and to establish an exchange rate with the paper mark of one to a million million.

Within the constraints of this overriding priority, Stresemann was anxious to cushion the blow to the occupied territories as far as possible. He eagerly accepted an ingenious solution put forward by Stinnes to the immediate problem of starting production. This was for the Reich to accept the obligation to fund reparations deliveries but only to make payment once its finances permitted. Industry would raise foreign loans to cover the cost in the interim.[145] In a special cabinet to discuss the Ruhr on 20 October, Stresemann urged this solution as the only alternative to the separation of the occupied territories and a 'catastrophic famine'.[146]

they had committed the blunder of raising with the French authorities the question of extending the eight-hour day. Feldman, *Stinnes*, 894–7.

[142] Cabinet minutes, 15 Oct. 1923: Erdmann and Vogt (eds.), *Kabinette Stresemann*, no. 136. The idea came from Karl Helfferich, formerly secretary to the treasury, who had joined the DNVP and became its leading expert on financial questions. John G. Williamson, *Karl Helfferich 1872–1924: Economist, Financier, Politician* (Princeton: Princeton University Press, 1971), 383–94.

[143] Feldman, *The Great Disorder*, 792–3. Feldman suggests that Stresemann's support was in part to satisfy the DDP, to which Schacht belonged. Stresemann may also have been influenced by Schacht's commitment to a return to a gold-based currency, and hoped that his appointment would favourably impress financial circles abroad. Schacht to Stresemann, 6 Oct. 1923: Erdmann and Vogt (eds.), *Kabinette Stresemann*, no. 118; Feldman, *The Great Disorder*, 751.

[144] Erdmann and Vogt (eds.), *Kabinette Stresemann*, pp. lxxxiv–lxxxv.

[145] Minutes of a meeting of ministers with the committee of Ruhr industrialists, 19 Oct. 1923: ibid., no. 149.

[146] Ibid., no. 156.

There was no dissent since no immediate expenditure was involved. The cabinet was, however, split about whether it would be possible to hold on to the occupied territories. Luther disclosed that, in order to balance the budget, he was planning to exclude both the occupied territories and reparations payments. Braun, attending as minister president of Prussia, which included the Ruhr and much of the Rhineland, also argued that they would have to put the survival of the unoccupied territory first so that there would be something left for the Rhine and Ruhr to rejoin later. The two Rhinelanders, Sollmann and Fuchs, however, vigorously contested these views, saying that so long as the occupied territories were part of Germany they had a right at least to equal treatment with the rest—for instance, to receive unemployment benefit. Stresemann, mediating, said he hoped that the situation would be eased by getting coal production started but that if a break had to come, it should be on an amicable basis with the understanding that it would not be permanent—'We will come again.'[147]

The only other strategy open to Germany was to encourage international pressure on France—as Stresemann told the cabinet, 'We must above all attract the attention of the world to our terrible position.'[148] To open a new line for negotiations, Germany notified the inter-Allied Reparations Commission on 24 October that it was unable to resume payments and invited the commission under article 234 of the Versailles treaty to examine its capacity to pay.[149]

For this strategy to succeed Stresemann was careful to avoid giving the Allies any pretext to refuse. He resisted Luther's attempts to stop paying the occupation costs of Allied troops in the Rhineland pending the outcome of Germany's appeal to the commission.[150] He also counselled against an open break with France. He refused to recognize the French administration of the railways of the Rhine and Ruhr regions, describing that as 'establishing the basis of a French Rhine state'.[151] But he also rejected calls for a dramatic gesture, saying that to break off relations with

---

[147] In private he was deeply pessimistic. Having heard his views, Rießer wrote to his son of the probability of a French takeover of the Rhine and Ruhr and of the 'greatest difficulties' which threatened from Bavaria, Saxony, and Thuringia and of the danger of revolt against rising fuel and food prices in the winter. Jakob to Hans Rießer, 19 Oct. 1923: BAK, Kleine Erwerbungen, no. 549, 2.

[148] Cabinet minutes, 24 Oct. 1923: Erdmann and Vogt (eds.), *Kabinette Stresemann*, no. 173.

[149] *ADAP*, ser. A, viii, no. 195.

[150] Cabinet minutes, 15 Oct. 1923: Erdmann and Vogt (eds.), *Kabinette Stresemann*, no. 136.

[151] Cabinet minutes, 20 Oct. 1923: ibid., no. 156.

France would be 'a serious mistake'.[152] His tactics were to isolate Poincaré by showing restraint despite the political costs.

The Return of the Crown Prince

Surprisingly, Stresemann was willing to risk the displeasure of the Allies by agreeing to Crown Prince Wilhelm's desire to return to Germany in the autumn of 1923. This episode, like Stresemann's relations with the Crown Prince in general, throws an interesting light on his character.

Wilhelm had fled to Holland with the Kaiser in November 1918. He had been placed on the list of those wanted by the Allies for war crimes, but since no attempt had been made to enforce this demand, it was not in itself an obstacle to his return. There had been concern that his return might be regarded as provocative by the Allies and affect the decision over Upper Silesia in 1921. But the main objection had been the fear that his return would cause domestic unrest.

Stresemann visited Wilhelm in September 1920 and advised him to wait. He formed a favourable impression of the prince, revising his earlier views.[153] Wilhelm showed him letters he had written to the High Command during the war urging moderation and told him that he had advised the Kaiser to conclude peace after the battle of the Marne in September 1914. Stresemann later published a sympathetic portrait of the prince, arguing that he had been misjudged and comparing his poor reputation to those of Frederick the Great and Edward VII before they succeeded to their thrones.[154]

No doubt Stresemann was flattered to be courted by a Hohenzollern prince and was inclined to invest him with the qualities which had been lacking in his father.[155] The prince was, he said, living in the real world whereas his father inhabited a dream world.[156] Perhaps Stresemann had

---

[152] Cabinet minutes, 24 Oct. 1923: Erdmann and Vogt (eds.), *Kabinette Stresemann*, no. 173.

[153] Memorandum on Stresemann's visit by his private secretary, Rauch, 23 Sept. 1920 (Nl. 141). Stresemann noted in his diary for 24 Sept., 'Deep impression of his human personality' (Nl. 142). Cf. above, p. 114.

[154] 'Väter und Söhne', *Deutsche Stimmen*, 34/8, 19 Feb. 1922: Rheinbaben (ed.), *Reden und Schriften*, ii. 379–89.

[155] According to Wheeler-Bennett, Stresemann liked being referred to by the prince's children as 'Uncle Gustav': John W. Wheeler-Bennett, *The Nemesis of Power: The German Army in Politics 1918–1945*, 2nd edn. (London: Macmillan, 1967), 105.

[156] Rauch's memorandum, 23 Sept. 1920 (Nl. 141).

not completely closed his mind to the possibility of an eventual Hohen-zollern restoration; certainly in 1920 the Crown Prince still entertained such hopes for his son.[157] More immediately, Stresemann saw that the Crown Prince could be a useful ally in right-wing circles if he owed his return to Stresemann.

When Wilhelm renewed his efforts to be allowed home in July 1923, even threatening the Cuno government with an appeal to the constitu-tional court, Stresemann promised his support and sent him a detailed memorandum on the political situation.[158] When Stresemann became chancellor, Wilhelm naturally pressed him for a decision, even warning at the end of September that if he had not heard within a week he would return in any case.[159]

Stresemann took the matter to cabinet, explaining that Wilhelm had agreed to live on his estate in Silesia—instead of in Potsdam—and to abstain from political activity.[160] Stresemann pointed out that if they refused, there was a danger that he would return anyway and perhaps to Bavaria where he had been invited. Having secured the consent of Braun for the Prussian government in advance of the meeting, Stresemann had no difficulty getting his way in cabinet.

He then set about soothing the ruffled feathers of the Allies. He explained the decision to Lord D'Abernon with his usual skill, claiming

---

[157] Rauch's memorandum, 23 Sept. 1920 (Nl. 141). In his memoirs, Brüning claimed to have favoured this idea as chancellor in 1930–2 as a way of forestalling Hitler, although at the time of writing the memoirs (1934–5) he may have exaggerated his attachment to a restoration of the monarchy to impress conservative and military circles: Heinrich Brüning, *Memoiren 1918–1934* (Stuttgart: Deutsche Verlags-Anstalt, 1970), 453–4, 512–13, 519–21; Wheeler-Bennett, *Nemesis of Power*, 230–1; William L. Patch Jr., *Heinrich Brüning and the Dissolution of the Weimar Republic* (Cambridge: Cambridge University Press, 1998), 1–13. There is one report, which originated with Brüning, that Stresemann was starting to think on similar lines before he died. In conversa-tion about what was to happen when Hindenburg's term as president came to an end in 1932, Stresemann is reported to have suggested that Hindenburg should be replaced by Crown Prince William as regent (*Reichsverweser*). The story comes from the memoirs of an official in the Ministry of Economics, Hans Staudinger, reporting a conversation with Hilferding about a conversation between Hilferding and Brüning. Hagen Schulze (ed.), 'Hans Staudinger, "Wirtschaftspolitik im Weimarer Staat. Lebenserinnerungen eines politischen Beamten im Reich und im Preussen, 1889 bis 1934"', *Archiv für Sozialgeschichte*, supplement 10 (1982), 90–1; Patch, *Brüning*, 7. It is very doubtful, however, that Stresemann ever considered such a proposal seriously; see below, p. 457, n. 46.

[158] Harbeck (ed.), *Kabinett Cuno*, no. 206; Stresemann to the Crown Prince, 23 July 1923 (Nl. 262): Bernhard (ed.), *Vermächtnis*, i. 215–19.

[159] Crown Prince to Stresemann, 29 Sept. 1923: Bernhard (ed.), *Vermächtnis*, i. 219–20.

[160] Cabinet minutes, 23 Oct. 1923: Erdmann and Vogt (eds.) *Kabinette Stresemann*, no. 167; Stresemann to the Crown Prince, reporting the cabinet's agreement, 24 Oct. 1923: *ADAP*, ser. A, viii, no. 202.

that the SPD ministers had agreed because the Republic would be safer if there were two pretenders to the throne rather than one—implying that it was a way of dividing the right between Bavarian monarchists loyal to the Wittelsbachs and the Prussians loyal to the Hohenzollerns.[161] This wry comment was effective with D'Abernon, and after an initially angry reaction from Lord Curzon, Britain decided to take no action. Finding itself isolated, France agreed to let the matter pass with a protest.[162]

Stresemann's motives were probably a mixture of genuine sympathy for the prince and political calculation. He would no doubt have preferred him to stay in Holland, but as he told D'Abernon it was better that he should return with republican permission rather than without it. Stresemann also hoped that there would be long-term advantage in deserving the prince's gratitude. Like most of Stresemann's attempts to win the support of people on the right this proved to be at best a temporary success.[163] With all his political skill, he was curiously naive in thinking that opponents could be won over by appealing to their patriotism.

Dancing on a Volcano

At the end of October Stresemann was also engaged in increasingly desperate efforts to prevent civil war breaking out over Saxony and Bavaria. Relations between Gessler, who still held executive powers under the state of emergency, and the Saxon government were extremely tense. The Saxon minister president Erich Zeigner, a convinced left-wing Social Democrat who had formed a government with KPD support in April 1923, had attacked the Reichswehr for complicity with anti-republican paramilitary groups, quoting statements by Gessler and Seeckt, and announced the formation of proletarian defence organizations. The tension rose when the KPD entered the Saxon government on 10 October and that of neighbouring Thuringia a few days later. The KPD leaders started to prepare for the arming of so-called proletariat 'hundreds', anticipating that there would be Reichswehr intervention which would provoke a

---

[161] D'Abernon, *Ambassador of Peace*, ii. 267, 269, 277–8.

[162] *ADAP*, ser. A, viii, no. 246, ix, no. 14; *DBFP*, 1st ser. xxi, nos. 640–1, 644–5, 650–1, 653, 655, 657–8, 660–1.

[163] While Stresemann was alive the Crown Prince kept in the background. In 1932–3, however, he openly associated with the anti-republican right and endorsed Hitler's candidacy in the elections for Reich president in Apr. 1932. Klaus W. Jonas, *The Life of Crown Prince William*, Eng. edn. (London: Routledge & Kegan Paul, 1961), 152–78.

revolutionary situation.[164] At the first meeting of the new Reich cabinet on 6 October, Gessler demanded that the Saxon government must either stop attacking the Reichswehr or be deposed. He threatened otherwise to resign, adding ominously that in that event he could not be responsible for the reaction of the Reichswehr.[165] On 16 October Stresemann discussed the situation with Ebert.[166] Relations with Bavaria also deteriorated rapidly. Here the immediate cause was the refusal of General von Lossow either to carry out an order to ban the Nazi *Völkischer Beobachter* (which had had the temerity to heap abuse on Seeckt as well as Stresemann) or to resign. Attempts to persuade him to go quietly were rebuffed and led only to further recrimination.[167]

Stresemann was caught in the crossfire between the Reichswehr and the SPD. Gessler and the Reichswehr pressed for action against Saxony. The SPD ministers, though embarrassed by the Saxon government, naturally played down the danger from that quarter and insisted that in any case Saxony and Bavaria had to be treated equally.[168] There was therefore a stalemate in cabinet. Meanwhile there was a risk that the various paramilitary forces assembled in Bavaria might march on Saxony as the first step to Berlin.

Stresemann tried to manage the crisis by showing as much consideration as he could for the SPD ministers while in practice following the policy of the Reichswehr. This was to take control of Saxony and Thuringia but to keep talking to Bavaria. It was not, as he subsequently admitted, an even-handed policy. He justified the bias by saying that no understanding was possible with the KPD directed from Moscow, whereas the patriotic associations in Bavaria were fundamentally well meaning though

---

[164] Whether there was a danger of revolution spreading from Saxony is still disputed among historians of the SPD. Winkler describes the danger, at this time, as 'really present'. Rudolph, however, argues that the purpose of the 'proletariat hundreds' was defensive. Winkler, *Von der Revolution*, 652; Karsten Rudolph, *Die sächsische Sozialdemokratie vom Kaiserreich zur Republik (1871–1923)*, (Weimar: Böhlau, 1995), 379–92. See also Michael Rudloff (ed.), *Erich Zeigner—Bildungsbürger und Sozialdemokrat* (Leipzig: Friedrich Ebert Stiftung [1999]).

[165] Erdmann and Vogt (eds.), *Kabinette Stresemann*, no. 115.

[166] Diary entry: Stresemann material, Berlin, Bernhard (ed.), *Vermächtnis*, i. 166.

[167] Stresemann to the Bavarian minister president, Eugen von Knilling, 20 Oct. 1923: Ernst Deuerlein (ed.), *Der Hitler-Putsch. Bayerische Dokumente zum 8./9. November 1923* (Stuttgart: Deutsche Verlags-Anstalt, 1962), no. 55.

[168] Sollmann to Kempkes, 22 Oct. 1923: Erdmann and Vogt (eds.), *Kabinette Stresemann*, no. 166.

misguided. He also claimed to have foreseen that the alliance of Pan-German and Conservative rebels in Bavaria would fall apart.[169]

The main reason, however, was the attitude of the Reichswehr which meant that in practice he had no alternative. They would not march on Bavaria and, if a putsch spread from Bavaria to other parts of the Reich, it was not certain that the Reichswehr would remain loyal. It was also important not to give Seeckt and those who favoured authoritarian government a pretext to force their views on Ebert.

Stresemann opposed the immediate deposition of the Saxon government at the beginning of October, but he supported the reinforcement of the Reichswehr in Saxony and Thuringia to maintain order and to seal the border with Bavaria. He warned the cabinet that otherwise the situation could lead to 'civil war and therefore the collapse of the Reich'.[170] At the same time Ebert, acting in agreement with Seeckt, decided to dismiss Lossow in order to restore the authority of the Reich—and of Seeckt himself—in Bavaria.[171] When the Bavarian government responded by taking charge of the Bavarian seventh division of the Reichswehr itself and cancelling Lossow's dismissal, Stresemann once again sought to conciliate by arranging for a meeting with the heads of government of all the *Länder* to find a solution.[172]

In a long session on 24 October Stresemann scored a personal triumph.[173] He explained that the authority of both the Reich and the Reichswehr was being undermined and bitterly criticized Kahr for claiming to represent a patriotic Germany against an unpatriotic Reich government. This, he said, had destroyed their whole campaign to isolate Poincaré by presenting the world with a Germany united in defence of the Ruhr. Instead, the world saw Germany breaking up. He suggested that the only reproach which could be made against the government, and against him personally, was that they had tried too hard to reach agreement—'I

---

[169] 'Das Kabinett Stresemann', *Deutsche Stimmen*, 36/3, 5 Feb. 1924, 46–7. The differences between the rebel groups and the danger of driving them together by taking a tough line had been a consistent theme of the advice from the Reich government representative in Bavaria, Edgar von Haniel: Erdmann and Vogt (eds.), *Kabinette Stresemann*, nos. 84, 87, 93, 98, 129, 135, 138, 143, 161, 201.

[170] Cabinet minutes, 6, 17 and 19 Oct. 1923: Erdmann and Vogt (eds.), *Kabinette Stresemann*, nos. 117, 144, 151; quotation, p. 614.

[171] Cabinet minutes, 19 Oct. 1923: ibid. no. 151.

[172] Memorandum by Stresemann of a conversation with the Bavarian envoy Konrad von Preger, 21 Oct. 1923: Bernhard (ed.), *Vermächtnis*, i. 173–4.

[173] Erdmann and Vogt (eds.), *Kabinette Stresemann*, no. 174.

incline by nature much more to conciliation than to conflict.' The *Länder* representatives, apart from Bavaria, unanimously endorsed the position of the Reich and recommended negotiations to end the crisis.

Stresemann had to leave the same evening for urgent talks with representatives of the occupied territories.[174] Here he faced a more difficult task. The group of some fifty leading politicians, officials, and businessmen, who had asked for the meeting, was obviously deeply concerned about the future. They faced mass unemployment, food shortages, repudiation of the paper mark, and a rising tide of separatism.[175] Stresemann was not in a position to reassure them beyond the next few weeks.[176] In particular he could not promise that the occupied territories would receive the Rentenmark, and without it they would be forced to introduce a currency of their own or face total breakdown.

In these circumstances the local representatives had to be allowed to negotiate with the French and Belgian authorities. Stresemann envisaged a political committee which would negotiate along the same lines as the mine-owners while keeping in close contact with the Reich government. Discussions among the local leaders had already produced two main ideas about how they should proceed.[177] Stresemann's DVP colleague Paul Moldenhauer favoured an ad hoc solution under which the occupied territories would be given full powers by the Reich to take the necessary measures. Adenauer, the lord mayor of Cologne, opposed this idea on the grounds that it would in fact reduce the occupied territories to the status of a French colony. He proposed instead that the occupied territories should form a new *Land*, separating themselves from Prussia but remaining if possible within the Reich. He hoped that this change would induce the French to allow an improvement in the conditions of the occupied territories to the benefit of the whole Reich.

---

[174] Minutes of the meeting, 25 Oct. 1923: Erdmann and Vogt (eds.), *Kabinette Stresemann*, no. 179. The meeting was held in the town of Hagen, which lay just outside the occupied zone.

[175] In the days immediately before the meeting separatists, supported by the Belgians, had seized public buildings in Aachen and proclaimed a 'Rhine Republic', and their example had been followed in the French zone in Bonn, Koblenz, Trier, Wiesbaden, and elsewhere. Further south, Social Democrats in the Palatinate had declared their secession from Bavaria in reaction to the Kahr regime and put themselves under French protection. Bariéty, *Les Relations franco-allemandes*, 250–5, Jeannesson, *Poincaré*, 329–44. Erdmann and Vogt (eds.), *Kabinette Stresemann*, nos. 169, 171, 202.

[176] Luther had at the last moment agreed that regular payments, such as government salaries and unemployment benefit, as well as some subsidies, would be continued as long as possible. Luther to Stresemann, 24 Oct. 1923: Erdmann and Vogt (eds.), *Kabinette Stresemann*, no. 175.

[177] Karl Dietrich Erdmann, *Adenauer in der Rheinlandpolitik nach dem Ersten Weltkrieg* (Stuttgart: E. Klett, 1966), 87–106.

Stresemann knew of the division of opinion before the meeting. He started by saying that as chancellor he absolutely refused to discuss the separation of parts of the Reich.[178] The government had not given up the Rhineland and it could not therefore regard the Rhineland as 'some part of Germany which was able by its own decision to separate itself from the Reich'. He then explained the 'cheerless' financial position and the details of the assistance the Reich could still provide. He also described the government's attempts to isolate Poincaré and the first signs of success—for instance, support from the South African prime minister, General Smuts, at a conference of member states of the British empire in London. He explained why the government had not broken off diplomatic relations with France, reminding his audience that the over-hasty German decision for war in 1914 had united the world against her. He appealed for unity, warning that internal conflicts like that with Bavaria could destroy them—'Ajax fell through Ajax's strength.' He then delivered a sharp blow to the Adenauer plan, saying that it was 'utopian' to imagine that 'the creation of a Rhine state [*Rheinstaat*] will solve the Rhine question'. Military occupation and reparations would both continue. He suggested instead that since the government was not able to negotiate with the French, the Rhinelanders should elect representatives to undertake this task and prevent power falling into the hands of the separatists.

Stresemann has been criticized for playing a double game—on the one hand grandly declaring that he would not even discuss separation, on the other making it clear that the Reich could not continue its support much longer and that the leaders of the occupied territories must draw their own conclusions. In other words his aim was to avoid taking the responsibility for the inevitable separation and pass it on to the unfortunate Rhinelanders.[179]

This criticism is misplaced. The position of Stresemann and the cabinet was that the separation of the Rhineland was being forced on them. For the government to have authorized discussions about separation would have played into Poincaré's hands. Nevertheless, Stresemann knew that as a practical necessity the leaders of the occupied territories must be allowed to talk to their de facto rulers and establish a new basis for the economy of

---

[178] Minutes of the meeting, 25 Oct. 1923: Erdmann and Vogt (eds.), *Kabinette Stresemann*, no. 179, pp. 769–82.

[179] Hans-Peter Schwarz, *Konrad Adenauer*, i: *From the German Empire to the Federal Republic, 1876–1952*, Eng. edn. (Oxford: Berghahn, 1995), 179–83.

the region. His position involved an element of contradiction, but it was understood by his audience and explicitly acknowledged by Adenauer.[180]

The difference between them was not on this ground but on whether an ad hoc committee or the Adenauer plan offered the best hope of keeping the Rhineland. Stresemann wanted each stage of the separation to be seen to be forced by the French. He may also have objected to breaking up Prussia, as did its minister president, Otto Braun, who accompanied him.[181] Adenauer, on the other hand, had been thinking of a separate *Land*, remaining within the Reich but with strong economic links to France, as a solution to the Franco-German problem since 1919.

Stresemann's view prevailed at the meeting since Adenauer's support was confined to the Centre Party. A committee was elected without a clear mandate, except that it was not authorized to discuss a separate status for the Rhineland at least for the time being.[182] On the other hand persistent questioning by Adenauer and others had revealed that support from the Reich would probably cease on 15 November.[183] In these circumstances, the chances of their remaining within the Reich were slim. Stresemann had bought a little time, no more.

Intervention in Saxony: The End of the Great Coalition

Stresemann returned to Berlin to face a new crisis. Kahr had brusquely rejected the idea of negotiations with the Reich.[184] The situation was made more difficult by the attitude of Seeckt. He wanted to assert his authority by securing the removal of Lossow, but he refused to contemplate armed intervention in Bavaria. His solution was for a new Reich government to be formed, possibly under his leadership, of individual 'personalities' who would be able to end the Bavarian rebellion peacefully. Constitutional forms could be preserved by Ebert allowing this 'directorate' to rule by decree powers under article 48. Seeckt warned Ebert on 23 October that the 'national groups who looked to him would hold on only for a few more days'. The following day he told Stresemann that 'things

---

[180] Minutes of the meeting, 25 Oct. 1923: Erdmann and Vogt (eds.), *Kabinette Stresemann*, no. 179, pp. 782–6.

[181] Schulze, *Braun*, 439–46.

[182] Minutes of the meeting, 25 Oct. 1923: Erdmann and Vogt (eds.), *Kabinette Stresemann*, no. 179, pp. 814–21, 828–32, 835–6.

[183] Ibid., pp. 788–97.

[184] Cabinet minutes, 26 Oct. 1923: ibid. no. 184.

could not go on like this' and, making it clear that he thought Stresemann should resign, he 'offered' to take over the government himself.[185]

Stresemann tried to keep control of the situation by working closely with Ebert and Gessler. On 26 October the cabinet agreed to demand that the Bavarian government dismiss Lossow with the threat that otherwise the Reich would stop paying the salaries of the Bavarian division of the Reichswehr.[186] The next day, Gessler announced that he intended to depose the Saxon government using his powers as Reich commissioner. Stresemann supported Gessler saying that he could not recognize a government containing Communists as constitutional. He revealed a more important reason, however, when he added that it would strengthen the Reich's position towards Bavaria and thus 'allow a conflict with unforeseeable consequences to be avoided'.

The SPD ministers were taken by surprise. Sollmann warned that one-sided action against Saxony could lead to the break-up of the coalition. They proposed that an attempt should first be made to persuade the minister president of Saxony Erich Zeigner to resign. At Ebert's suggestion, it was agreed that Stresemann should write to Zeigner demanding his resignation and the formation of a new government without the KPD, making it clear that otherwise the Reich would appoint a commissioner.[187]

It is obvious that Stresemann and Gessler had decided (probably with Ebert's acquiescence) that the deposition of the Saxon government was necessary, not because of any new threat from Saxony but to buttress the Reich's authority against their real worry, Bavaria.[188] Stresemann was sensitive to criticism of his conciliatory tactics and felt the time had come for 'energetic, clear action'.[189] He had evidently hoped that it

[185] Material collected by General Lieber; entries for 23–4 Oct. 1923: Erdmann and Vogt (eds.), *Kabinette Stresemann*, pp. 1190–1, and Seeckt's draft programme for government, pp. 1203–10; Carsten, *Reichswehr*, 163–73; Meier-Welcker, *Seeckt*, 393–4.

[186] Erdmann and Vogt (eds.), *Kabinette Stresemann*, no. 184.

[187] Cabinet minutes and Stresemann to Zeigner, 27 Oct. 1923: ibid., nos. 186, 188. Rudolph, *Sächsische Sozialdemokratie*, 402–3; Donald B. Pryce, 'The Reich Government versus Saxony, 1923: The Decision to Intervene', *Central European History*, 10 (1977), 112–48; Benjamin Lapp, *Revolution from the Right. Politics, Class, and the Rise of Nazism in Saxony, 1919–1933* (Boston: Humanities Press, 1997), 96–110.

[188] On Ebert's position see Walter Mühlhausen, 'Reichspräsident und Sozialdemokratie. Friedrich Ebert und seine Partei 1919–1925', in Eberhard Kolb (ed.), *Friedrich Ebert als Reichspräsident* (Munich: Oldenbourg, 1997), 296–7.

[189] Cabinet minutes, 27 Oct. 1923: Erdmann and Vogt (eds.), *Kabinette Stresemann*, no. 186, p. 855. The previous day he had reacted indignantly to the suggestion that 'he only negotiated and did not advance matters': ibid., no. 184, p. 850.

would be possible to carry the SPD ministers with him by presenting first new measures against Bavaria and then Gessler's plan for Saxony as the necessary consequence. It was a bold attempt to find a way out of the crisis, but it put at risk the great coalition on which his majority depended.

It quickly became apparent that the plan had miscarried. Zeigner refused to resign and Stresemann, who had meanwhile obtained Ebert's authority to appoint a commissioner, decided to act late on Sunday evening, 28 October.[190] He chose his DVP colleague, Heinze, who had briefly been minister of justice and then head of government in Saxony in October 1918. This proved a bad mistake. Heinze behaved tactlessly, ordering the Saxon ministers to leave their departments, while the Reichswehr made matters worse by marching through Dresden with bands playing to occupy the public buildings. Stresemann, disturbed by the reaction of the SPD ministers to these events, gave Heinze strict instructions not to interfere in the formation of a new government, apart from excluding the KPD.[191] The SPD formed a new government with the DDP on 31 October and the commissioner was immediately withdrawn.

The damage, however, had been done. The SPD ministers clearly regretted that they had gone along with the ultimatum to Zeigner and argued that a commissioner should not have been appointed without a further cabinet meeting.[192] In a meeting of the coalition party leaders on 29 October, Hermann Müller said the SPD could only accept what had happened if Bavaria received the same treatment. Ebert, whom Stresemann had been unable to consult the previous evening about Heinze's appointment—because he had already gone to bed—was also angry, complaining that the action had lost him the trust of the working class.[193] Stresemann frankly admitted that it had been necessary to remove the

[190] Zeigner to Stresemann, 28 Oct. and cabinet minutes 29 Oct. 1923: Erdmann and Vogt (eds.), *Kabinette Stresemann*, nos. 191, 194. It is interesting that Ebert authorized Stresemann rather than Gessler (who was still Reich commissioner). The intention may have been to keep the intervention under civilian control to make it more acceptable to the SPD members of the cabinet. Stresemann had previously expressed his dissatisfaction at the way in which the Reichswehr dealt directly with the Saxon government without consulting him as Reich chancellor. Möllers, *Geßler*, 263–5.

[191] Stresemann's memorandum of a telephone conversation with Heinze, 29 Oct. 1923: Bernhard (ed.), *Vermächtnis*, i. 189–91. Rudolph argues that Stresemann and the SPD leaders hoped that it would be possible to form a minority SPD government in Saxony and maintain the great coalition in the Reich, but the basis for agreement was destroyed by Heinze's arbitrary actions: *Sächsische Sozialdemokratie*, 405–9.

[192] Note by Stresemann of a conversation with the SPD ministers, 28 Oct. 1923: Erdmann and Vogt (eds.), *Kabinette Stresemann*, no. 192.

[193] Stresemann's diary, 28–9 Oct. 1923: Bernhard (ed.), *Vermächtnis*, i. 187.

'stumbling block' in Saxony to prevent a right-wing putsch; otherwise, he said, the Reichswehr would all have gone over to the Bavarian side.[194] On the same day he recorded in his diary a statement of Seeckt's that 'the Reichswehr will no longer stand with the cabinet and behind the Reich chancellor'.[195]

The argument continued over two cabinet meetings the same day, with Sollmann furious at the incoming news of the provocative use of force in Dresden, which he described as 'the crassest militarism'. Stresemann tried to calm the atmosphere. He pointed out that at last the international situation seemed to be improving—Poincaré had accepted an expert committee to investigate Germany's capacity to pay—and said it would be 'fatal' to destroy this process by bringing the government down and tearing the Reich apart.[196] The SPD Reichstag party met on 31 October and decided it would remain in the coalition only if a number of conditions were satisfied, including lifting the state of emergency and treating Bavaria as in breach of the constitution.[197]

Stresemann's attitude towards the SPD hardened when these demands were made public. He told the cabinet that they could not afford to give the impression that they were operating 'under Marxist pressure' and that in any case it was impossible to end the state of emergency when the guns might go off on the Bavarian–Thuringian frontier the next day. Gessler went further and suggested that if the SPD left the cabinet it would be easier to reach agreement with Bavaria—'Lossow would immediately disappear.'[198]

This view found more support in a meeting without the SPD ministers present on 2 November. Brauns, Luther, Oeser, and Koeth all joined Gessler in thinking that the situation would be improved by the departure of the SPD ministers.[199] Stresemann did not resist, although he pointed out that without the SPD the government could be brought down in the Reichstag. He said he would be willing to continue only if Ebert granted him a decree to dissolve the Reichstag and force new elections (as a way of deterring a vote of no confidence). Once again contemplating looking to

---

[194] Erdmann and Vogt (eds.), *Kabinette Stresemann*, no. 193.

[195] Nl. 361. I am grateful to Dr Gutzler for deciphering this shorthand entry.

[196] Cabinet minutes, Erdmann and Vogt (eds.), *Kabinette Stresemann*, nos. 194–5. The quotation is from the second meeting.

[197] Winkler, *Von der Revolution*, 660–2.

[198] Cabinet minutes, 1 Nov. 1923: Erdmann and Vogt (eds.), *Kabinette Stresemann*, no. 212.

[199] Gessler had been unnerved to discover that Hindenburg, whom he had hoped to use as a mediator, in fact took the Bavarian side. Minutes of the meeting, 2 Nov. 1923: ibid., no. 214.

the right for support instead of the SPD, he said he would not be willing to form an administration with an 'aggressive German-National [DNVP] character', though individuals from the right could be appointed and he would try to win over the more reasonable of the patriotic associations.[200]

A painful meeting of the full cabinet followed where Sollmann went on to the offensive and accused the other ministers of being prepared to give up the Rhineland, being unwilling to defend Saxony and Thuringia against fascism and for failing to condemn the 'mediaeval expulsion of Jews' which Kahr had ordered in Munich.[201] Stresemann countered that they were all of one mind on the question of Jewish expulsions. Brauns was so angered by Sollmann's remarks that he walked out. The SPD ministers resigned later the same day.[202]

There are good reasons in retrospect for thinking that the deposition of the Saxon government was a mistake. The danger of Communist revolution had already passed when the call for a general strike was rejected by a conference of working-class parties and trade unions at Chemnitz on 21 October.[203] An uprising in Hamburg on 23 October was a local incident and collapsed after two days. There had been problems for the Reich government in Saxony. There had been persistent complaints from employers' organizations—including the Association of Saxon Industrialists—of violence and intimidation.[204] There had also been incidents between the Reichswehr and demonstrators and provocative speeches by KPD ministers.[205] But none of these justified the deposition of the government—an action of doubtful legality—and above all one which carried the immense political risk of breaking up the Reich coalition.[206] There

---

[200] He referred to the veterans' organization, the Stahlhelm, and the Jungdeutscher Orden, a group dedicated to keeping alive the experience of the front and at the time one of the most numerous of the patriotic leagues. The Stahlhelm had indicated its support, but soon changed its mind when it realized that Stresemann was not going to lead a 'national dictatorship'. Volker Berghahn, *Der Stahlhelm. Bund der Frontsoldaten 1918–1935* (Düsseldorf: Droste, 1966), 43–4.

[201] On Stresemann's attitude to the Jewish expulsions, Wright, 'Liberalism and Anti-Semitism', 117–18.

[202] Cabinet minutes, 2 Nov. 1923, and a joint letter of resignation from the three SPD ministers: Erdmann and Vogt (eds.), *Kabinette Stresemann*, nos. 215, 216.

[203] Winkler, *Von der Revolution*, 652–4; Rudolph, *Sächsische Sozialdemokratie*, 396–401.

[204] e.g. a letter from Stresemann's DVP colleague Franz Brüninghaus, 22 Sept. 1923: Erdmann and Vogt (eds.), *Kabinette Stresemann*, no. 75.

[205] Cabinet minutes, 17 Oct. 1923: ibid., no. 144. On 27 Oct., in the town of Freiberg, troops fired into a crowd of demonstrators who refused to disperse, killing twenty-three. Winkler, *Von der Revolution*, 655.

[206] In cabinet, Radbruch as minister of justice raised constitutional objections. Otto Meissner, the senior official in the office of the Reich president, on the other hand, claimed that article 48

was much to be said for Sollmann's alternative of isolating the KPD by restraint, taking the same attitude as towards Bavaria. Indeed, Stresemann had originally hoped that he could encourage Zeigner to form a great coalition though, by October, he had lost patience, describing Zeigner as 'not fully accountable for his actions'.[207] Nevertheless, according to some sources, Zeigner was on the point of breaking off the coalition with the KPD and resigning when Stresemann's ultimatum arrived and led him to react in the opposite way.[208]

The idea that removing the festering sore of Saxony would make Bavaria more inclined to peace also proved, as Stresemann later acknowledged, 'quite mistaken'.[209] On the contrary, the Bavarian government decided to stall, anticipating correctly that the Reich coalition would break up.[210] At the beginning of November the Reichswehr units on the Thuringian frontier were reinforced to deter the irregular troops on the Bavarian side. But this could have been done without deposing the Saxon government or, as now happened, forcing the SPD–KPD coalition in Thuringia to resign as well.[211] Nor did Stresemann reap any reward in loyalty from the Reichswehr. The reverse was the case. Now that the government had lost its majority, Seeckt and those who thought like him saw their opportunity to get rid of it altogether.

There remains, however, one important consideration on the other side which illustrates the extreme difficulty of Stresemann's position. The mood in the Reichswehr was so inflamed against the SPD–KPD coalitions in Saxony and Thuringia, and predisposed to side with Bavaria, that intervention was seen as necessary to steady its loyalty to the state. This was the position of Gessler. The same attitude was to be found among the bourgeois parties in the coalition. Several ministers saw the intervention—and the departure of the SPD—as necessary to reassure their supporters.[212] If Stresemann had not gone along with them he would have

could be used in this way to protect public safety. Cabinet minutes, 27 Oct., and legal opinion: Erdmann and Vogt (eds.), *Kabinette Stresemann*, nos. 186, 187.

[207] Stresemann to Wels, 27 Aug. 1923: cabinet minutes, 17 Oct. 1923: ibid., nos. 26, 144. Rudolph, *Sächsische Sozialdemokratie*, 373–4.

[208] Minutes of the meeting with party leaders, 29 Oct. 1923: Erdmann and Vogt (eds.), *Kabinette Stresemann*, no. 193.

[209] 'Das Kabinett Stresemann', *Deutsche Stimmen*, 36/3, 5 Feb. 1924, 41.

[210] Bavarian cabinet minutes, 30 Oct., 3 Nov. 1923: Deuerlein, *Der Hitler-Putsch*, nos. 71, 78.

[211] Winkler, *Von der Revolution*, 671. Protest from the Thuringian cabinet to Stresemann, 8 Nov. 1923: Erdmann and Vogt (eds.), *Kabinette Stresemann*, no. 230.

[212] Gessler, Kanitz, and Brauns, for instance; cabinet minutes, 27 Oct. 1923: Erdmann and Vogt (eds.), *Kabinette Stresemann*, no. 186.

had to face Gessler's resignation and quite possibly a split with the DVP and sections of the Centre Party rather than with the SPD.[213]

'I will not give in': Reichswehr Intrigue and Hitler Putsch

Stresemann now faced a concerted attempt by Seeckt and his friends to force him to resign. Seeckt wanted to remain within the letter of the constitution and he therefore adopted the technique of making it known that Stresemann no longer enjoyed the confidence of the Reichswehr. He tried to persuade Ebert that a change of chancellor was necessary and on 4 November, claiming that he had Ebert's authority, he wrote to Wiedfeldt asking him to be ready to lead 'a small cabinet with the character of a directorate and full emergency powers'.[214]

Perhaps having heard of the intrigue, Stresemann authorized a member of his staff, Heinrich Ehlers, to sound out Seeckt's views the same afternoon.[215] Seeckt repeated the view which he had already expressed to Stresemann previously that the chancellor had lost the confidence of 'national groups' and the Reichswehr and should resign. This time, however, he was more specific. According to Ehlers he said, 'It was his firm conviction that he ... would not be in a position either to master the legal and illegal, right-wing organizations, or to keep control of the right-wing

[213] The DDP, despite Gessler being one of its ministers, took a different view. It wanted a stronger stand against Bavaria and the party chairman Koch criticized the way the SPD had been 'driven out' of the coalition: Erdmann and Vogt (eds.), *Kabinette Stresemann*, nos. 193, 214, 228.

[214] Seeckt had a stormy audience with Ebert on 3 Nov. because he refused Ebert's demand for military action against Bavaria after a report that the seventh division was planning to march on Berlin, a report which later proved false. At this meeting Seeckt seems to have expressed his usual lack of confidence in Stresemann. The following day one of Seeckt's officers recorded that Ebert agreed that a Stresemann cabinet was 'no longer possible' and had authorized Seeckt to approach Wiedfeldt. Lieber material; entries for 3–4 Nov. 1923, Seeckt to Wiedfeldt, 4 Nov. 1923: Erdmann and Vogt (eds.) *Kabinette Stresemann*, pp. 1192–3, 1197, 1215–16. The difficulty of Ebert's situation is illustrated by a warning sent by General Groener on 1 Nov. that, in the event of conflict breaking out between the Communists and the patriotic leagues, Bavaria would become a dictatorship under Kahr, north Germany would be taken by the patriotic leagues, and there would be bloody conflicts in Saxony, Thuringia, and elsewhere. Groener predicted that in these circumstances the Reichswehr would 'simply be crushed' between the millstones and would not survive as a force available to the government. Given the cooperation between Groener and Ebert in November 1918 to maintain the provisional government against a feared Bolshevik revolution, Ebert was likely to take Groener's advice seriously. This helps to explain why he was apparently willing to acquiesce in Seeckt's proposed directorate. Heinz Hürten (ed.), *Das Krisenjahr 1923. Militär und Innenpolitik 1922–1924* (Düsseldorf: Droste, 1980), p. xxii.

[215] Ehlers's account of the incident, 10 Nov. 1923: BAK, Kleine Erwerbung, no. 511.

circles of the Reichswehr, if the chancellor remained.' When Ehlers reported the conversation late that evening, Stresemann appeared deeply shocked and said, 'So that means the removal of the chancellor by the Reichswehr.' Later, according to one report at 2.30 a.m., he telephoned Ebert to inform him of what Seeckt had said.[216] According to Stresemann, he offered Ebert his resignation, but Ebert begged him to continue.[217] The following morning Stresemann saw Seeckt with Gessler present and when the general repeated his view that Stresemann had lost the confidence of the troops, Stresemann—according to Gessler's later recollection—immediately asked, 'Are you giving notice that the Reichswehr will no longer obey the government?' Seeckt gave no answer and Gessler said, 'Reich chancellor only I can do that', and with that they left.[218]

What lay behind these extraordinary scenes? The most likely explanation is that Stresemann had seen through Seeckt's tactics and had decided to force him into the open. He faced Seeckt with the choice of either declaring that the Reichswehr would no longer obey the constitutional government or withdrawing his threat. Seeckt's adjutant thought that Stresemann had staged the incident to discredit Seeckt with Ebert.[219] Seeckt's refusal to answer enabled Stresemann to interpret the conversation in the way he wanted. When the matter was raised by his opponents in the DVP Reichstag party the following day, Stresemann said that Seeckt had merely been expressing his own opinion that it might be possible to stop the radical right without bloodshed with a different cabinet. Gessler had confirmed that this was Seeckt's political view and had nothing to do with the Reichswehr as such and Seeckt had agreed.[220]

Stresemann needed all his tactical skill. The DNVP backed Seeckt and again refused to join a Stresemann cabinet. Its chairman, Hergt, told Scholz that Stresemann might at most lead a transitional government

[216] Stresemann had been free to see Ehlers only after midnight because of other callers, including Major Kurt von Schleicher, who also told him he had lost the confidence of the troops; Lieber material, entry for 5 Nov. 1923: Erdmann and Vogt (eds.), *Kabinette Stresemann*, pp. 1197–8. Meier-Welcker, *Seeckt*, 401–3.

[217] Minutes of the DVP Reichstag party meeting, 6 Nov. 1923 (Nl. 87); extract in Bernhard (ed.), *Vermächtnis*, i. 198–201.

[218] Gessler, *Reichswehrpolitik*, 299. According to Gessler, Seeckt first told Ebert that Stresemann had lost the confidence of the Reichswehr and Ebert sent them to tell Stresemann: ibid. Stresemann, in his account of the incident to the DVP Reichstag party, said that he had asked to see Seeckt: Bernhard (ed.), *Vermächtnis*, i. 200.

[219] Diary entry for 5 Nov. 1923 of Oberstleutnant von Selchow: Erdmann and Vogt (eds.), *Kabinette Stresemann*, p. 1198.

[220] Minutes of the meeting, 6 Nov. 1923 (Nl. 87).

until Wiedfeldt took over and Stresemann could then perhaps replace Wiedfeldt as ambassador in Washington.[221] Stresemann had no intention of falling in with these plans. On 5 November he gave the cabinet a reassuring account of internal security, saying that the Reichswehr was present on the Thuringian frontier in adequate strength to repel any attack from Bavaria. He added that the radical right had no clear political goals: some were against Seeckt, some against Ludendorff; others wanted a directorate of Kahr, Wiedfeldt, and Minoux. He said it was his view, no doubt shared by the rest of the cabinet, that while they were ready at any time to make way for people who enjoyed in greater measure the confidence of the nation, it was impossible for them to resign 'in such a labile and unclear situation as the present'. The other ministers agreed.[222]

A further blow was delivered by the DVP, which again began to waver in its support. As usual its right wing wanted to bring in the DNVP. Scholz reported on his negotiations to the Reichstag party on 5 November and proposed that they should 'hold fast to Stresemann' but ask him to issue an official invitation to the DNVP, which Scholz thought—despite the discouraging results of his unofficial soundings—the DNVP would accept.[223] Most of those who spoke were critical of the government and supported an approach to the DNVP.

Stresemann came in to the meeting and delivered a terse and bitter rebuke to his colleagues. He started with the familiar argument that the DNVP would not bring a Reichstag majority because the Centre and DDP would not join them.[224] Stresemann said firmly: 'I will not approach Hergt', and continued, according to the telegram style of the minutes:

This week will decide whether the national leagues [i.e. the Nazis and their Conservative allies] dare to fight. Civil war means the loss of the Rhine and Ruhr and Franco-Rhenish fraternization. Therefore the first requirement is order at home. The government has sufficient troops around Coburg [on the Thuringian frontier], and the Reichswehr has said it will reply even to friendly overtures by shooting. If the Reichswehr fails, these groups will win. Then,

[221] Scholz's report of the discussion to the DVP Reichstag party meeting, 5 Nov. 1923 (Nl. 87). The meeting with Hergt and Westarp took place on 4 Nov. with Stresemann's knowledge and with Kempkes present to keep him informed.

[222] Erdmann and Vogt (eds.), *Kabinette Stresemann*, no. 222.

[223] Minutes of the meeting (Nl. 87).

[224] Carl Petersen, the chairman of the DDP Reichstag party, made clear the party's opposition to the DNVP in a formal letter to Stresemann on 7 Nov. 1923: Erdmann and Vogt (eds.), *Kabinette Stresemann*, no. 228. The Centre Party was more divided but a majority favoured continuing with the existing coalition: Hehl, *Marx*, 242–3; Morsey, *Zentrumspartei*, 547–9.

perhaps German-National dictatorship. I am sick of the dog's life—intrigues from within the DVP—...If the armed bands should enter Berlin—I am not going to Stuttgart, then they will have to shoot me at the place at which I have a right to sit.[225] Leave off fighting over the composition of the cabinet...

After Stresemann had spoken, no one except Stinnes dared to challenge him and the meeting quickly ended.

The following day, without Stresemann present, his critics took up the challenge again. Alfred Gildemeister, a lawyer from Bremen, said they must go their own way: 'We are not a Stresemann party.' Julius Curtius, another lawyer from Baden who later became a close colleague of Stresemann's, also accused Stresemann of behaving like a dictator and said he must be made to give up the party leadership. Heinze complained about the way Stresemann had hampered him as commissioner in Saxony and helped the SPD to form a new government. Voices were also raised in Stresemann's defence and Siegfried von Kardorff said they should not stab him in the back. The discussion took a new turn when Maretzky revealed that Seeckt had asked Stresemann to resign and this sensational news was confirmed by Kurt von Lersner, an ex-diplomat. Two representatives from the Ruhr, Quaatz and Hugo, joined the chorus for negotiations with the DNVP and Karl Hepp, president of the Farmers' Association (Reichslandbund), added that agriculture was wholly against Stresemann.

At this point Scholz reported that he had spoken on the telephone to Stresemann, who had denied that Seeckt had said he no longer had the confidence of the Reichswehr. This confused the opposition. Stresemann then appeared himself, fresh from discussions with Hergt, to say that the DNVP leader refused to join the coalition and had told Stresemann to recruit individuals for an 'unpolitical cabinet' and then 'depart without resentment', although for the moment they had no successor to replace him, since Wiedfeldt had declined. Stresemann then gave his version of what had passed between him and Seeckt. Scholz explained that a series of members present thought that an official approach should be made to the DNVP and Stresemann promptly left.

It is not surprising that in retrospect Stresemann wrote that, of all the difficulties, those with his own party were the most crippling because they were the most deeply depressing.[226] It would have been understandable if he had given up and resigned. In resisting the pressure from so many sides,

---

[225] A reference of the flight of the government during the Kapp putsch.
[226] 'Das Kabinett Stresemann', *Deutsche Stimmen*, 36/5, 5 Mar. 1924, 80.

he showed remarkable courage and tenacity. Without his commitment, the Republic might not have survived the next few weeks, or even days. Had he resigned, Ebert would have been under intense pressure to accept some form of 'national dictatorship' with incalculable consequences.

When the news of the Hitler putsch reached Berlin shortly before midnight on 8 November, Stresemann called a cabinet meeting with Ebert presiding and Seeckt in attendance.[227] The situation looked grim. Kahr and Lossow were reported to have joined the rebels and, as Stresemann wrote later, 'civil war seemed unavoidable'. It was possible that the rebellion would spread to parts of Prussia and, according to Stresemann, the DNVP newspapers were working all night waiting to announce the victory of the revolution.[228] The key question was how the Reichswehr would react. When asked by Ebert, Seeckt is reported to have replied 'The Reichswehr will obey me, Mr President', and when asked by the Prussian minister of the interior Carl Severing, what the position would be if the Bavarian division marched on Berlin, Seeckt would say only 'The Reichswehr will not fire on the Reichswehr.'[229] Stresemann gave a similar account to his family, describing how Seeckt had maintained his reserve until the news arrived that Lossow had been appointed minister of defence by the rebels. The thought of Lossow as his superior was too much for Seeckt, who rose and said 'President, gentlemen, *now* we must act.'[230]

However mixed their feelings, Ebert and the cabinet decided to entrust Seeckt with full executive power under article 48 'to take all measures necessary for the security of the Reich'.[231] In view of Seeckt's evident ambivalence this was a bold move. It was a gamble on his desire to remain within the Constitution and also his anger at Lossow's refusal to obey orders. A declaration was issued, signed by Ebert, condemning the putsch as high treason and promising that it would be ruthlessly suppressed.[232] Nevertheless when Stresemann returned to the private rooms of the Reich

[227] No minutes were kept: Erdmann and Vogt (eds.), *Kabinette Stresemann*, p. 997.
[228] 'Das Kabinett Stresemann', *Deutsche Stimmen*, 36/3, 5 Feb. 1924, 45–6.
[229] Stockhausen, *Sechs Jahre Reichskanzlei*, 89; Carl Severing, *Mein Lebensweg*, 2 vols. (Cologne: Greven, 1950), i. 446–7.
[230] Wolfgang Stresemann, *Mein Vater*, 275.
[231] Meissner wrote out the decree—cancelling some passages—and it was immediately signed by Ebert, Stresemann, and Gessler, itself an indication of the pressure under which they were working. BAB Büro des Reichspräsidenten, 67.
[232] H. Michaelis and E. Schraepler (eds.), *Ursachen und Folgen. Vom deutschen Zusammenbruch 1918 und 1945 bis zur staatlichen Neuordnung Deutschlands in der Gegenwart* (Berlin: Dokumenten Verlag Dr Herbert Wendler, 1958–64), vol. v, no. 1175b.

Chancellery in the early hours of the morning he would say only, 'We do not know what today will bring; I will not give in.'[233]

In fact the situation cleared rapidly on 9 November. News arrived first that Kahr, Lossow, and the Bavarian state police chief, Hans von Seisser, had repudiated their initial support for the putsch. In the afternoon came the further news that the attempt by Hitler and Ludendorff to retrieve the situation by marching with their paramilitary formations into Munich had been swiftly ended by the Bavarian state police.[234]

The failure of the putsch brought Stresemann only temporary relief. Seeckt continued to conspire against him, pressing Ebert again on 9 November for a change of cabinet and the following day renewing his call to Wiedfeldt—again claiming Ebert's authority—to take over as chancellor and foreign minister. When Wiedfeldt again refused, the Reichswehr leaders 'racked their brains' unsuccessfully to find an alternative candidate.[235]

The DVP also renewed its debate on 9 November.[236] Stresemann's supporters argued that the party should close ranks behind the chancellor. However, a resolution in favour of negotiations with the DNVP was passed by a majority of 31 to 15, while an amendment that the negotiations should be conducted only through Stresemann was narrowly rejected (by 22 votes to 20 with two abstentions). The voting was confused by Scholz as chairman ruling that the amendment was superfluous since it was 'self-evident' that Stresemann would remain as chancellor in a reconstructed cabinet. Nevertheless, it was clear that the party was deeply divided.[237]

The opposition to Stresemann promptly wasted their advantage by leaking the results to the press; this incensed Scholz, who issued a statement of his own. He said that the great majority wanted negotiations with the DNVP but also that Stresemann should remain chancellor and, commenting on a renewed demand by the DNVP for Stresemann's resignation, he added that this made agreement impossible. His view was endorsed by an overwhelming majority on 10 November and Gildemeister, who had been responsible for the press leak, could raise only three

---

[233] Wolfgang Stresemann, *Mein Vater*, 276.

[234] Erdmann and Vogt (eds.), *Kabinette Stresemann*, nos. 232, 235. Harold J. Gordon, *Hitler and the Beer Hall Putsch* (Princeton: Princeton University Press, 1972), 313–65.

[235] Lieber material, entries for 9–10 and 17–18 Nov. 1923: Erdmann and Vogt (eds.), *Kabinette Stresemann*, pp. 1199–200; Meier-Welcker, *Seeckt*, 408–11.

[236] Minutes of the Reichstag party meetings, 9 and 10 Nov. 1923 (Nl. 87).

[237] Turner, *Stresemann*, 139–40.

votes for keeping open the possibility of talks with the DNVP. Stresemann who, despite his initial reluctance, had agreed to talks being held had probably anticipated that this would be the result.[238]

He was not content to let the matter rest there. On 11 November he spoke at a provincial party conference in Halle which, he noted in his diary, was 'deeply refreshing'.[239] He described the events in Bavaria as 'grotesque' but in reality 'very tragic' because they revealed Germany's internal divisions. He poured scorn on the call for a 'national dictatorship' as a mere 'empty slogan' which solved nothing: 'Putting Adolf Hitler in charge of Germany's political fortunes in a beer cellar will not help the German people!'[240]

Stresemann then proceeded to a showdown with his opponents in the Reichstag party. The national executive was summoned to a meeting on 18 November.[241] Before this large body of constituency representatives, party officials and members of the various *Landtage* as well as the Reichstag party, Stresemann demanded a clear decision between him and the opposition.[242] The audience gave him a standing ovation and passed a vote of confidence in him and his policy of maintaining the existing coalition by 206 votes to 11. Scholz felt it necessary to declare that no member of the Reichstag party would be willing to sacrifice Stresemann to get agreement with the DNVP, which was patently untrue.

Lersner and Gildemeister later protested at the way Stresemann had referred to the opposition at the meeting. Stresemann replied that the attempt to bring down their own Reich chancellor by quoting Seeckt against him at a party meeting and, in Lersner's case, going to see president Ebert with the same story was 'an intrigue more discreditable than anything seen previously in the history of German parliamentary parties'.[243]

---

[238] Turner considers that Stresemann allowed negotiations because he did not realize that the opposition was prepared to oust him to get agreement with the DNVP, but Kempkes would have kept Stresemann fully informed. Turner, *Stresemann*, 139.

[239] Diary entry, 11 Nov. 1923: Bernhard (ed.), *Vermächtnis*, i. 207.

[240] Part of the speech is printed ibid. 207–11.

[241] He had already decided on this course earlier, writing to a colleague that 'The air must be cleared for once and we must have it out with those who are conducting nothing other than German-National policy': Stresemann to Rudolf von Campe, the chairman of the DVP in the Prussian Landtag, 8 Nov. 1923 (Nl. 87).

[242] Report of the Zentralvorstand meeting, 18 Nov. 1923: Kolb and Richter (eds.), *Nationalliberalismus*, 476–87.

[243] Stresemann to Lersner, 1 Dec., and, including the quotation, to Gildemeister, 10 Dec. 1923 (Nl. 88): Bernhard (ed.), *Vermächtnis*, i. 233.

An Independent Rhineland?

With the defeat of the Hitler putsch, the problems of the occupied territories again became the most pressing issue. Negotiations were formally between the mine-owners and the French and Belgian authorities. Stresemann tried to resist concessions which would imply recognizing the legitimacy of the occupation, but in practice he was forced to give way because of the overriding need to get the Ruhr back to work. He therefore agreed to refund the mine-owners the coal tax imposed by the occupiers. However, when the French demanded that payment be used to defray their occupation costs rather than credited as reparations, the cabinet refused and negotiations broke down.[244] Eventually a face-saving compromise was found, under which the final decision on the allocation of payments would be made by the Reparations Commission.[245] The French were by this time themselves keen to reach an agreement before the international committee of experts investigated Germany's capacity to pay, and the treaty was signed on 23 November, the day that Stresemann's government fell.

The question of what was to happen when the Rentenmark was introduced on 15 November proved more difficult. It was discussed at a series of cabinet meetings and with representatives of the occupied territories. The question aroused bitter feelings which divided the cabinet, and no final decision had been reached by the time the government fell. As a result policy was allowed to drift. This worked to Germany's advantage, as a settlement was deferred to the following year when the international situation had moved in her favour. Stresemann had originally hoped for just such an outcome, but the delay owed more to chance, confusion, and the inability to agree than to deliberate policy.

On 7 November Luther told the cabinet that all payments to the occupied territories would have to cease if the new currency was to succeed, and on 9 November the cabinet agreed that the Rhineland should be allowed to establish its own bank and issue its own currency.[246] The decision to stop payments was, however, immediately reversed on 11 November through the intervention of Karl Jarres, the lord mayor of Duisburg in the occupied zone, who had agreed to become minister

---

[244] Minutes of a meeting of ministers and the mine-owners' committee and Stresemann to the committee, 13 Nov. 1923: Erdmann and Vogt (eds.), *Kabinette Stresemann*, nos. 246, 250.

[245] Stresemann to the mine-owners' committee, 21 Nov. 1923: ibid., no. 275.

[246] Ibid., nos. 227, 233.

of the interior (in succession to Sollmann). He managed to persuade Luther to tide the occupied territories over for a further ten days to enable them to organize emergency currency of their own.[247]

The following day the cabinet discussed how to empower the occupied territories to make their own arrangements.[248] Stresemann was in favour of delegating authority from the Reich, but Brauns objected that this could provide the basis for a new state. On the other hand the Rhinelanders Fuchs, Jarres, and Luther argued strongly that an independent state was much more likely to arise if the Reich refused delegated powers.

The issues led to bitter exchanges at inconclusive meetings with the *Länder* governments, to which the occupied territories belonged, and with representatives of the occupied territories themselves.[249] The cabinet had to abandon the idea of delegated powers because of the united opposition of the *Länder*, who saw that as an invasion of their rights. The representatives of the occupied territories, for their part, naturally resisted an end to financial support. On 13 November Adenauer clashed with Stresemann over the lack of clarity that existed about the extent of the powers which the occupied territories were to be allowed.[250] He then had a sharp exchange with Luther, saying he did not believe that the Reich could no longer afford financial support and that it would not matter if the Rentenmark followed the paper mark into oblivion—'the Rhineland must be worth one, two, or even three new currencies'. Woundingly, he accused Luther of planning to surrender the Rhineland in order to be free of reparations. At the final meeting, Stresemann defended the government's record, saying they had done everything possible to reach agreement with France and had never considered buying Germany free from reparations by surrendering territory.[251] 'French policy', he said, 'is based on a great fear of Germany. Germany has continually tried to achieve an international settlement of the reparations and Rhineland questions.' The only hope for the future lay in British and American pressure on France. Further meetings were planned, but did not take place before the government fell.

---

[247] Jarres's account, Erdmann and Vogt (eds.), *Kabinette Stresemann*, pp. 1034–5; Luther, *Politiker ohne Partei*, 179–81.

[248] Erdmann and Vogt (eds.), *Kabinette Stresemann*, no. 242.

[249] Minutes of the meetings on 13 and 17 Nov. 1923: ibid., nos. 245, 247, 249, 266–7.

[250] Ibid., no. 249. Stresemann collapsed during the meeting and had to be helped out, suffering from what Adenauer later described as a heart attack: Paul Weymar, *Konrad Adenauer*, Eng. edn. (New York: E. P. Dutton, 1957), 53.

[251] Minutes of the meeting on 17 Nov. 1923: Erdmann and Vogt (eds.), *Kabinette Stresemann*, no. 267.

'In the open battlefield': The Defeat of the Government

With the departure of the SPD from the coalition on 2 November, Stresemann had lost his majority. This need not have been fatal to the government. Unless the opposition parties united to pass a vote of no confidence, there was no constitutional requirement for the government to resign. Stresemann at first hoped to reach a modus vivendi with the SPD, especially since the alternative to his government might be the anti-socialist 'directorate' wanted by the DNVP.[252]

The SPD was not, however, prepared to smooth Stresemann's way. Against Ebert's advice, it insisted on a meeting of the Reichstag which Stresemann had hoped to avoid.[253] Again against Ebert's wishes, the SPD decided on 20 November to put down a motion of no confidence, criticizing the government for its unequal treatment of Saxony and Thuringia compared to Bavaria.[254] The previous day Stresemann had taken the view that the cabinet was not obliged to seek a positive vote of confidence, and that it was quite possible for the government to survive votes of no confidence from each of the opposition parties as they would not combine to vote together. By the next cabinet meeting on 22 November, however, he had decided that if the SPD brought in a no confidence motion he would ask for a positive vote of confidence. This was a high-risk policy, as the opposition parties were much more likely to unite against a vote of confidence.

Why did Stresemann change his mind? The main reason was probably the realization that unless he could win the SPD's toleration, the government would be too weak for it to be worth continuing.[255] The issue of the eight-hour day had yet to be resolved, and out of office the SPD would regard itself as released from the obligation to vote for the solution previously agreed. The consensus in cabinet was also against continuing without a new mandate from the Reichstag, and it supported Stresemann's decision unanimously.[256]

---

[252] Schubert reported Stresemann's view of the situation to D'Abernon on 2 Nov. 1923: *ADAP*, ser. A, viii, no. 225.

[253] Cabinet minutes, 12 Nov. 1923: Erdmann and Vogt (eds.), *Kabinette Stresemann*, no. 242.

[254] Winkler, *Von der Revolution*, 677. According to Stresemann, Ebert had promised 'to exert all his influence' to prevent such a motion; cabinet minutes, 19 Nov. 1923: Erdmann and Vogt (eds.), *Kabinette Stresemann*, no. 268.

[255] Subsequently he gave this as the main reason to foreign journalists: Bernhard (ed.), *Vermächtnis*, i. 245.

[256] Cabinet minutes 19 and 22 Nov. 1923: Erdmann and Vogt (eds.), *Kabinette Stresemann*, nos. 268, 278.

There were also wider considerations. Stresemann had come to power as the architect of the great coalition. He had then remained in power as the defender of constitutional government against military dictatorship, even if dressed up as a civilian directorate. But with the collapse of the putsch, the alternatives were no longer so stark. Ebert was free to consider other options. Ebert and Stresemann had drawn closer during the crises of the previous weeks and Ebert tried to prevent the SPD bringing the government down. But he seems to have been unwilling to grant Stresemann a decree dissolving the Reichstag for Stresemann to use as a threat against the opposition parties.[257]

Ebert's attitude, like that of the cabinet, probably conveyed to Stresemann the sense that, although they were loyal, they no longer regarded him as indispensable. If so, it would have been a mistake for him to try to cling to power. The alternative of challenging the Reichstag to provide a vote of confidence also had a certain attraction. Stresemann was a parliamentarian par excellence; he thrived on debate. The gesture of rejecting survival 'by the backstairs of rejected votes of no confidence' and instead being the first government to fall 'in the open battlefield' appealed to his theatrical instincts.[258] He could also claim that he had a serious constitutional purpose. By demanding a vote of confidence, he forced the Reichstag to take responsibility for bringing down a cabinet rather than leaving it, as on every previous occasion since 1919, to negotiations behind closed doors between the parties and the president.

Stresemann's speech to the Reichstag on 22 November was a brilliant performance—perhaps the best he ever made—and it won the admiration even of his critics.[259] Facing constant interruptions from the KPD in the first half of his speech, he held his own with a combative style relieved by

---

[257] Documentation on Ebert's attitude is sparse, as many of his presidential papers were removed by his widow and son and subsequently lost; Meissner to Wirth, 16 Oct. 1926 (BAB, Büro des Reichspräsidenten, 0/3/9); Mühlhausen, 'Reichspräsident und Sozialdemokratie', 260. On the question of Stresemann's request for a decree of dissolution, most accounts agree that Stresemann asked Ebert probably shortly after the cabinet meeting on 19 Nov. Wolfgang Stresemann's version sounds authentic: Ebert refused on the grounds that it would be improper to use the presidential power to preserve a particular government, though he later indicated that he would have been prepared to use the power to support a new Enabling Act (as he had previously for Stresemann and did again for Stresemann's successor, Marx, in December 1923). *Mein Vater*, 280; see also Stockhausen, *6 Jahre Reichskanzlei*, 93–5; D'Abernon, *Ambassador of Peace*, ii. 274; Bernhard (ed.), *Vermächtnis*, i. 244.

[258] The first remark was recorded by Bernhard, the second was used by Stresemann to foreign journalists: Bernhard (ed.), *Vermächtnis*, i. 244–5.

[259] Zwoch (ed.), *Reichstagsreden*, 155–206. Seeckt wrote to his wife that 'he [Stresemann] is said to have spoken splendidly today': Erdmann and Vogt (eds.), *Kabinette Stresemann*, p. 1201. During

touches of humour. His main theme was that French policy, in the hands of Poincaré, had left the government no alternative to the decisions it had taken. He welcomed indications of American interest in restoring the world economy, emphasizing that the whole world was interdependent. In this connection he criticized the idea of a 'United States of Europe'— put forward by the SPD chairman Wels—as too narrow. He looked forward to a change in the international situation, though he did not claim the credit for it, except in so far as his government had made no secret of the desperate situation. He suggested that the idea of using German industry and agriculture as a guarantee for reparations might yet be taken up by an international committee of experts as a solution to the reparations problem. Nevertheless, he saw the future as 'comfortless', with the people driven to the extremes by what he called later 'the whiplashes' of French imperialism.

Stresemann defended the government's record against the criticisms from the SPD and the DNVP—the state of emergency, the intervention in Saxony, and the harsh measures necessary for currency stabilization—and he predicted that further hard and even brutal measures would be required. Most of the difficult decisions, he claimed, had been taken by the great coalition and the SPD therefore shared responsibility for them. He even contrived to praise the leadership of the Reichswehr and stress the importance of maintaining its authority and not allowing any doubt to arise about its loyalty to the Constitution. He ignored, however, Wels's most effective criticism, that he had allowed the SPD to be driven out of his cabinet rather than act against Bavaria, because he could not answer it without admitting the degree to which policy towards Bavaria had been shaped by the Reichswehr.

Stresemann then turned to Hergt's argument that as 'the inventor and fanatical advocate of the idea of the great coalition', he must stand and fall with it. This prompted him into a renewed and eloquent defence of the need for national unity, as they faced up to the consequences of the lost war. 'Not restoration and not counter-revolution, but evolution and co-operation must be the guiding principles.' Power politics alone could not provide a lasting solution: 'There is scarcely anywhere else a country which is so divided by political, economic and social differences. Only

the debate von Graefe of the racist German Racial Freedom Party (Deutschvölkische Freiheit-spartei; DVFP) conceded that Stresemann had a 'wonderful gift for public speaking', and Johann Leicht, the chairman of the BVP, paid tribute to his 'mastery' of parliamentary debate: *Verhandlungen des Reichstags*, vol. 361, pp. 12203, 12254.

by bridging over these differences can a lasting recovery be achieved.' He also restated his belief in the great coalition as the parliamentary expression of national unity and as the only way in the long run to prevent the Reich falling apart. He accepted that there was some truth in Hergt's view that the German people were not sufficiently mature for parliamentary democracy, though he added with gentle irony that he could think of others apart from 'the people' of whom this might be said.

Stresemann then gave a historical context to their present difficulties, blaming the 'teething troubles' of the parliamentary system on the failure to develop a suitable tradition in the nineteenth century, in contrast to the English model whose unwritten conventions had been established over centuries. He looked back to Stein and Hardenberg, who had tried to forge a popular sense of political responsibility in the aftermath of Prussia's defeat by Napoleon. He saw parallels of 'almost photographic accuracy' between that time and their own—both concerned with setting up a new state after a lost war. He quoted in support the way Stein had been attacked as a 'Jacobin', and his taxation reforms described as turning Prussia into 'a modern Jewish state'.[260] The failure to establish a parliamentary system then had been the first blow to the whole process. Later, after being overwhelmed by Bismarck, German parliaments had for too long been content to rest on the government's lap. It was therefore only natural that after war and revolution their new system should suffer from the opening of the floodgates to a people who were politically without much education.

For that very reason, however, he argued that it was premature to condemn German democracy as incapable of improvement. At least they should not abandon it until they had something better to put in its place. Either Bolshevism or fascism—although the latter under Mussolini's gifted leadership might suit Italy—would tear Germany apart. Germany was too sick to survive another civil war. A truly responsible and national policy was one which avoided that danger even at the cost of compromise and flexibility. Whatever criticism there might be of political parties, at least they allowed different interests to be balanced, whereas the economic groups on which Hergt wanted government to depend were purely self-interested. He concluded by pointing out, despite his underlying confidence in democracy, that they were facing not so much a cabinet crisis as a

---

[260] For this incident see R. M. Berdahl, *The Politics of the Prussian Nobility: The Development of a Conservative Ideology 1770–1848* (Princeton: Princeton University Press, 1990), 135–6. (I am grateful to Dr Brendan Simms for this reference.)

crisis of parliament, since no group of parties in the Reichstag was capable of forming a majority government.

The final section of Stresemann's speech was a statement of his political faith. His interpretation of German nineteenth-century history would not satisfy historians today. The view he expressed that Germany had followed a separate and unfortunate path compared to Britain is clearly oversimplified. The German political system in the nineteenth century had its own rationale in terms of the kind of society it represented, and its progress cannot simply be measured against the 'model' of the British or other systems.[261] Nevertheless, he was right to point out the relative weakness of the Reichstag under the German empire compared to the British parliament and the consequences of this difference for German political culture.

Stresemann's views were to become widely accepted among democratic politicians and liberal academics in the Federal Republic after 1949. It is a measure of his originality, however, that in the Weimar Republic his was a comparatively lonely voice. Defeat, revolution, and inflation had sharply polarizing effects, favouring authoritarian nationalism on the right and social revolution on the left. Stresemann consistently warned against both, and insisted that there was an alternative which could be made to work despite all the difficulties, namely parliamentary government based on moderation, reason, and consensus. It was above all his consistent faith in liberalism against the odds which gave him a distinctive place in Weimar's political culture.

Stresemann's speech to the Reichstag had the air of a political testament because everyone was aware that his chancellorship was in all probability at an end. The following day the DNVP, SPD, and KPD put down motions of no confidence and Stresemann at once asked the government parties to propose a vote of confidence, saying that the cabinet was not willing to continue on the basis of 'parliamentary arithmetic' and wanted 'a clear, unambiguous decision as to whether the government has the confidence of parliament or not'.[262]

[261] David Blackbourn and Geoff Eley, *The Peculiarities of German History: Bourgeois Society and Politics in Nineteenth-Century Germany* (Oxford: Oxford University Press, 1984); David Blackbourn and Richard J. Evans (eds.), *The German Bourgeoisie* (London: Routledge, 1991); Jarausch and Jones (eds.), *In Search of a Liberal Germany*, and, with the broadest historical sweep, Heinrich August Winkler, *Der lange Weg nach Westen*, i: *Deutsche Geschichte vom Ende des Alten Reiches bis zum Untergang der Weimarer Republik*, and ii: *Deutsche Geschichte vom "Dritten Reich" bis zur Wiedervereinigung* (Munich: C. H. Beck, 2000).
[262] *Verhandlungen des Reichstags*, vol. 361, pp. 12240–1.

The vote was lost by 156 to 231 against with seven abstentions, one invalid vote and some sixty absentees.[263] The vote for the government was twelve short of the total strength of the coalition parties, and the vote against some fifty short of the opposition's full potential. The DVP failed to unite behind its leader even on this occasion: six of its members were absent, including Stinnes, Vögler, and Hepp from among Stresemann's opponents. The cabinet resigned the same evening. Stresemann recorded in his diary Ebert's rebuke to the SPD: 'What made you overthrow the chancellor will be forgotten in six weeks, but you will feel the conse- quences of your stupidity for ten years.'[264]

On 31 December 1923 D'Abernon noted in his diary:

> Thus ends a year of crisis. The dangers from without and within have been such as to threaten the whole future of Germany. . . . Looking back, one sees more clearly how near to the precipice this country has been. . . . Political leaders in Germany are not accustomed to receive much public laudation; those who have seen the country through these perils deserve more credit than is likely to be their portion[265]

This still seems a fair verdict on the Stresemann government, which bore the brunt of the crises during its hundred days. It was a period when cabinet and president were forced to take executive action in a series of emergencies.[266] The Reichstag met for only short periods to authorize what had been done.[267] But despite the reliance on executive powers, Stresemann showed himself a true and ultimately successful defender of constitutional government against its enemies.

There were, however, casualties of the crises. In political terms, Stre- semann's patiently constructed great coalition did not survive. The inter- vention in Saxony and Thuringia without corresponding action against Bavaria was too much for the SPD to stomach. Stresemann was never again to lead a great coalition or hold the position of chancellor.

More serious for the future stability of the Republic was the turmoil caused by inflation and currency stabilization.[268] As Stresemann said in

---

[263] *Verhandlungen des Reichstags*, vol. 361, pp. 12292–4.

[264] Diary entry for 23 Nov. 1923 (Nl. 361): Bernhard (ed.), *Vermächtnis*, i. 245.

[265] D'Abernon, *Ambassador of Peace*, ii. 290.

[266] The government passed sixty-nine acts with the force of law: sixteen of these were through normal legislation, fiften were decrees under article 48, and thirty-eight were decrees under the Enabling Act: Erdmann and Vogt (eds.), *Kabinette Stresemann*, p. li.

[267] It met only thirteen times between 12 Aug. and 23 Nov.: ibid.

[268] Feldman, *The Great Disorder*, 837–58.

his final speech to the Reichstag, they were only just beginning to face up to the consequences of the lost war.[269] Inflation had sustained some sections of the economy artificially, allowing investment and employment in export industries by making German goods cheap abroad. But with the Ruhr occupation and hyper-inflation this advantage was lost and the costs became evident: rising unemployment and prices, loss of savings, and chaotic public finances. Currency stabilization was as necessary for the survival of the state as the preservation of law and order. But it inevitably caused great hardship and unpopularity: the value of savings could not be restored; government retrenchment meant unemployment; there had to be real increases in taxation.

Stresemann was aware of the injustice which resulted, just as he had been aware of the consequences of driving the SPD out of the coalition. In both cases he could see no alternative if the state was to be preserved. The harsh realities of power were sometimes at odds with the lofty ideals of the 'community of the whole nation'. As D'Abernon saw, Stresemann and his colleagues deserved every credit for negotiating the precipice, but the political and social cost of their achievement made it, at best, insecure.

[269] Zwoch (ed.), *Reichstagsreden*, 195–6.

7

'A gleam of light on the otherwise dark horizon'

The Dawes Plan and the Road to Locarno, 1924–1925

Between November 1923 when Stresemann resigned with the French still supreme in the Ruhr and October 1925 when the treaties of Locarno were signed, the situation in Europe was transformed. Under American and British pressure France gave up the Ruhr in return for Germany accepting international obligations. The change in the international situation for which Stresemann had hoped in 1923, while almost despairing that it would ever come about, happened with dramatic suddenness in 1924–5.

Appointment as Foreign Minister

The future was far from clear to Stresemann in the aftermath of his defeat in the Reichstag. He remained in office at Ebert's request until a new chancellor had been found, but at home he mused about retiring from politics.[1] This mood was changed by a warm letter from the chairman of the Centre Party, Wilhelm Marx, asking him to remain as foreign minister

[1] Wolfgang Stresemann, *Mein Vater*, 285.

in the next government.[2] This was a highly unusual gesture from another party. Since no government could be formed without the Centre Party, Marx was in effect warning the DNVP and Stresemann's enemies in the DVP that they should not try to form a government without him. Stresemann, suffering at the time from influenza, had the satisfaction of seeing a succession of candidates for the chancellorship each of whom needed his agreement to be foreign minister.[3]

The situation was complicated. The natural alternative to a great coalition remained a majority government of the middle parties with the DNVP. The Centre Party was at first unwilling to supply the chancellor and Marx declined Ebert's invitation to form a government. Stresemann would have liked the DNVP to be asked, so that there could be no complaint subsequently that it had been bypassed.[4] He may also have hoped that if neither the Centre Party nor the DNVP could supply a chancellor, he would be asked again.[5] Ebert, however, was not willing to trust the DNVP with the chancellorship. He tried a succession of other candidates, including—to Stresemann's chagrin—his DVP colleague Kardorff. When none of these was successful, Ebert returned to the Centre Party and asked the leader of the Christian trade unions, Adam Stegerwald, who was known to have support in the DNVP. Stegerwald nearly succeeded, the DNVP dropping its opposition to Stresemann remaining as foreign minister.[6] However, with what Stresemann called 'unbeatable stupidity' the DNVP then demanded that it should also be admitted to the Prussian government, replacing the SPD.[7] This demand was unacceptable to the Prussian Centre Party and DDP and negotiations therefore broke down.

There now appeared to be no alternative to continuing with the existing minority coalition, dependent on the toleration of either the SPD or the DNVP. Marx, who was universally trusted, succumbed to Ebert's renewed appeal that he should serve, and formed a cabinet on 30 November

[2] Marx to Stresemann, 24 Nov. 1923 and Stresemann's reply, 28 Nov. 1923: Bernhard (ed.), *Vermächtnis*, i. 247–8; Hehl, *Marx*, 250–1.

[3] Diary for 24–9 Nov. 1923: Bernhard (ed.), *Vermächtnis*, i. 255; Wolfgang Stresemann, *Mein Vater*, 286–7.

[4] Stresemann to Siegfried von Kardorff, 25 Jan. 1924: Bernhard (ed.), *Vermächtnis*, i. 255–6. Kardorff to Meissner, 13 Dec., and Meissner's reply, 14 Dec. 1923: BAB, 06.01, 41.

[5] Jakob Rießer to his son Hans, 26 Nov. 1923: BAK, Kleine Erwerbungen 549, 2.

[6] Arns, *Regierungsbildung*, 178–82; Günther Abramowski (ed.), *Die Kabinette Marx I und II* (Boppard: Harald Boldt, 1973), pp. vii–viii.

[7] The comment came in Stresemann's anonymous 'Wochenschau', *Die Zeit*, 3/280, 9 Dec. 1923: Bernhard (ed.), *Vermächtnis*, i. 258–9.

consisting mainly of Stresemann's ministers. The new cabinet survived its first major test when, backed by Ebert's threat of dissolution, it secured a two-thirds majority for a new Enabling Act.

Stresemann had to adjust to his new situation. He had groomed himself for the role of chancellor of a great coalition before 1923. Now he found himself remaining as foreign minister but to a different chancellor. However, this position had several advantages. He no longer had responsibility for the whole range of government and he was able to some extent to spare his health, which was already causing concern.[8] As foreign minister he enjoyed considerable independence, and over time acquired an authority which gave him continuity in office, such as he could never have expected as chancellor. A man of his bold temperament was bound to excite opposition even when he advocated consensus. The self-effacing Marx was better suited to the indispensable but humdrum role of mediator between the parties.[9]

Stresemann versus Adenauer

Stresemann's first task was to restore a clear direction to foreign policy after the way it had drifted in the last desperate weeks of his chancellorship. He resumed the search for an agreement on reparations that would free the Ruhr. At first it was far from obvious that he would succeed. The general internal situation improved rapidly with the Rentenmark, but that of the occupied territories remained precarious. The Ruhr factories returned to work but on terms which left Poincaré in control. There was no reason to assume that British and American pressure would be more successful than in the past. Committees of experts were established by the Reparations Commission with the participation of the American businessmen Charles Dawes and Owen Young to investigate Germany's capacity to pay, but the committees remained subordinate to the Reparations Commission and Germany was not allowed to appoint representatives to them. Stresemann

[8] He no longer had to attend all cabinet meetings for instance, allowing senior officials to represent him on occasion.

[9] D'Abernon described Stresemann in Feb. 1924 as 'the sheet-anchor' of the government and his relationship to Marx as follows: 'The present combination is not a bad one—a conciliatory and deeply religious chancellor, obviously filled with the best intentions but without parts brilliant enough to excite animosity; subordinate to him in form rather than substance—a foreign minister who is bold, vocal and perhaps less orthodox, but with clear views and determination': *Ambassador of Peace*, iii: *The Years of Recovery January 1924–October 1926*, 48.

renewed his appeal to Poincaré for direct negotiations, but the difference between their positions meant there was no real basis for discussion.[10] Stresemann was holding out for an agreement on reparations which would allow the Ruhr to return to German control. Poincaré was still in a position to bypass the German government and conclude agreements directly with the Ruhr industrialists.[11] The outlook at the end of December was extremely gloomy. Hoesch suggested from Paris that Germany might have to abandon the policy of 'shaking off the opponent' and accept a 'close interlocking' of German and French interests in the Ruhr.[12]

This conclusion had already been anticipated by Adenauer. Seeing no help forthcoming from the Reich government, he proceeded with his plans for a new *Land* consisting of the occupied territories. He hoped that this *Land* would meet the French need for security, since its economy would be naturally linked to that of France through the mutual interests of the coal and iron fields and its population, being that of a frontier area, would be naturally peace-loving. He explained his proposals both to the committee of Rhineland politicians and businessmen—winning the support of Stinnes—and then to a French intermediary, who undertook to convey them directly to Poincaré.[13]

To secure his position in Berlin, Adenauer contacted the new chancellor on 6 December, taking advantage of the fact that Marx was a fellow Rhinelander and party colleague. Marx gave his approval to Adenauer's initiative, agreeing that if the response from Paris was favourable, negotiations would be taken over by the government. This was an interesting use of the chancellor's discretion. As it happened, at a discussion in cabinet the previous day Stresemann had dismissed the idea that Adenauer's proposals could lead to a solution as 'out of the question' and the cabinet had agreed that the committees in the occupied territories should cease negotiations, which might otherwise cut across Stresemann's attempts to open direct talks with Poincaré.[14] On 14 December Adenauer reported to Marx with

[10] Memorandum of a conversation with the French ambassador Pierre Jacquin de Margerie, 11 Dec., Stresemann to Hoesch, 12 Dec. and 22 Dec., and Hoesch to Auswärtiges Amt, 15, 18, and 25 Dec. 1923: *ADAP*, ser. A, ix, nos. 48, 50, 60, 64, 69, 73.

[11] Schuker argues that Stresemann was not seriously interested in negotiations. The same could be said of Poincaré. The truth is rather that the two sides were still too far apart. Schuker, 'Bayern', 94.

[12] Hoesch to Auswärtiges Amt, 29 Dec. 1923; *ADAP*, ser. A, ix, no. 77. Hoesch at the time had the status of German chargé d'affaires in Paris; he was appointed ambassador on 2 Feb. 1924.

[13] Erdmann, *Adenauer*, 136–86.

[14] Cabinet minutes, 5 Dec. 1923: Abramowski (ed.), *Kabinette Marx*, no. 9.

sufficient optimism for Marx to authorize him to continue the soundings; not suprisingly they decided that Stresemann should not be informed at that stage.[15]

Despite the interest of Adenauer's proposals, particularly in view of the parallel with his European policy as chancellor after 1949, there is no evidence that the French government considered them a satisfactory solution in the winter of 1923–4.[16] Stresemann's objection that Adenauer's private diplomacy weakened the position of the government was justified. His fear that Poincaré intended to remain in control of the Ruhr and establish a separate Rhineland state by stages with the help of people such as Adenauer was also natural, if exaggerated. Poincaré claimed to Hoesch that he was protecting the rights of the Rhinelanders against the Reich government.[17] Even Adenauer feared that he might be being used by the French.

Stresemann's ability to resist both French plans to retain control of the Rhineland and Adenauer's attempts to find a compromise received a sudden boost at the beginning of January. Schacht, who had become president of the Reichsbank at the end of December 1923 with Stresemann's support, secured the agreement of the governor of the Bank of England, Montagu Norman, for a German gold discount bank backed by a British loan.[18] This would both ease German credit restrictions and, even more important—as Norman realized—undermine plans for a separate Rhineland bank backed by French and Belgian capital, which the leaders of the occupied territories wanted to see established. Schacht and Stresemann worked together to defeat Adenauer and Stinnes.[19]

[15] Erdmann, *Adenauer*, 163; Hehl, *Marx*, 272.

[16] Erdmann, *Adenauer*, 162–8; Jeannesson, *Poincaré*, 350–3, 360.

[17] Hoesch to Auswärtiges Amt, 25 Dec. 1923: *ADAP*, ser. A, ix, no. 73.

[18] Feldman, *The Great Disorder*, 821–35. Schacht, *My First Seventy-Six Years*, 188–200. The alternative candidate for the presidency of the Reichsbank was Karl Helfferich. He was supported by the directors and central committee of the Reichsbank and the interest groups represented by the DNVP (who opposed Schacht's policy of credit restriction). However, this raised doubts about his commitment to maintaining the value of the currency and, in addition, his reputation as an anti-republican politician and distrust of him abroad, in the circles on whom Germany depended for new loans, made him unacceptable to Stresemann and the cabinet. Schacht's gold discount bank was eventually founded on 7 Apr. 1924 with British and American loans. The Reichsbank finally returned to a gold-backed Reichsmark with the implementation of the Dawes Plan in Oct. 1924 and Schacht resigned his post as Currency Commissioner. Marx to Schacht, 19 Oct. 1924: Abramowski (ed.), *Kabinette Marx*, no. 337.

[19] Schacht's memorandum of his London visit, 1–3 Jan., and Schacht to Stresemann, 22 Jan. 1924: BAK, Nl. Schacht, 3.

Schacht reported to the cabinet on his successful visit to London on 8 January.[20] The following day at a meeting between ministers and representatives of the Ruhr, Adenauer set out his view that it might be necessary as a last resort to allow the formation of a separate west German *Land*, and Stinnes and Vögler asked for authority to negotiate a reparations settlement with the French which would include a Franco-German industrial partnership and an exchange of shares. Stresemann was not inclined to give the industrialists such authority. At the meeting he countered Adenauer's pessimism, and pointed out that Poincaré's position had been weakened by a fall in the value of the franc. He suggested that any new initiatives should be deferred until after the French elections in the spring, which might see Poincaré removed from office.[21]

Stresemann had to leave the meeting before it finished. Stinnes drew up the minute of the discussion, omitting Stresemann's objections and giving authority for unofficial soundings to continue. When Stresemann saw the minute, he refused to sign it and protested vigorously to Marx.[22] He pointed out that Adenauer had been wrong to say that no help could be expected from Britain. The Bank of England and the chancellor of the exchequer had just agreed to a loan to establish a new German gold discount bank. He warned Marx of the reaction that could be expected from the Prussian government if it discovered that the Reich had secretly approved feelers to rob it of its two best provinces. He added that there was also a danger that the negotiations, once started, would, in fact, lead to the virtual separation of the Rhineland. His opposition put an end to Adenauer's private diplomacy. Stinnes's schemes also came to nothing, as the French were interested in acquiring shares in German mines but not in an exchange of shares, and the idea of a separate Franco-German arrangement was itself overtaken by the Dawes plan.[23]

The difference between Adenauer and Stresemann left a lasting legacy of mutual mistrust. Adenauer suspected quite rightly that Stresemann had

---

[20] Cabinet minutes, 8 Jan. 1924: Abramowski (ed.), *Kabinette Marx*, no. 51.

[21] Minutes of the meeting, 9 Jan. 1924: Abramowski (ed.), *Kabinette Marx*, no. 53; notes made at the meeting, probably by Jarres: Erdmann, *Adenauer*, 351–3.

[22] Stresemann to Marx, 16 Jan. 1924: *ADAP*, ser. A, ix, no. 99.

[23] Erdmann, *Adenauer*, 180–6; Wulf, *Stinnes*, 496–507; Feldman, *Stinnes*, 909–17. Poincaré showed more interest in the ideas of another German industrialist, Arnold Rechberg, who unlike Stinnes advocated a one-way transfer of shares from Germany to France. Hoesch to Auswärtiges Amt, 29 Dec. 1923: *ADAP*, ser. A, ix, no. 77; Eberhard von Vietsch, *Arnold Rechberg und das Problem der politischen West-Orientierung Deutschlands nach dem 1. Weltkrieg* (Koblenz: Bundesarchiv, 1958).

not been open with the Rhinelanders about his failure to persuade Poin-caré to negotiate.[24] Adenauer therefore let it be known that Poincaré had in fact refused to negotiate with the Reich government. This 'Adenauer affair' was discussed in cabinet, and Marx reported that Adenauer claimed to have acted 'in good faith'.[25] Stresemann's suspicions lingered. In May 1925, after attending the celebrations to mark a thousand years of the history of Cologne, he noted in his diary: 'Personally Adenauer is un-doubtedly splendid for Cologne, whether he always acts in the interests of the Reich may well be doubted.'[26] Adenauer also did not forgive easily. As late as August 1928, Poincaré was reported as saying that Adenauer had warned them against Stresemann's 'deceit' and 'bad faith'.[27]

The clash between Stresemann and Adenauer was partly personal in origin. They came from different backgrounds—Berlin Protestant and Rhineland Catholic—and each was used to getting his own way.[28] The clash was also a consequence of their different positions—Stresemann representing the Reich government and Adenauer the occupied territor-ies. In addition, there was a genuine difference of policy between them, though both wanted to keep the Rhineland German. Stresemann's tactic of involving Britain and the United States in a settlement and resisting change in the status of the Rhineland was successful in 1924–5. However, he never completely overcame French fears, and this set limits to Franco-German détente. Adenauer was prepared to go further to satisfy France. In 1923–4 his ideas found favour neither with the German nor the French government, but in very different circumstances after 1949 he made an essential contribution towards a more far-reaching programme of Euro-pean unity.

---

[24] Stresemann warned Hoesch on 21 Dec. 1923 not to press Poincaré too hard in case he received an outright refusal which would encourage the Rhinelanders' desire for local negoti-ations. Schubert explained to D'Abernon on 17 Jan. 1924 that they had to continue the exchanges with Poincaré to prevent the Rhinelanders taking the initiative, which could lead to 'an estrange-ment of the Rhineland from Germany'. Stresemann refused to give details of Poincaré's reaction to representatives of the occupied territories at a meeting on 7 Feb. 1924, saying that Poincaré had made it a condition that these remain secret. *ADAP*, ser. A, ix, 69; Abramowski (ed.), *Kabinette Marx*, nos. 66, 92.

[25] Cabinet minutes, 21 Feb. 1924: Abramowski (ed.), *Kabinette Marx*, no. 117.

[26] Bernhard (ed.), *Vermächtnis*, ii. 300.

[27] Memorandum by the Belgian foreign minister Paul Hyams, 27 Aug. 1928: *Documents diplomatiques belges 1920–1940*, ii (Brussels: Palais des Académies, 1964), no. 184; quoted in Hirsch, *Stresemann*, 249.

[28] The difference should not, however, be exaggerated. Schwarz points out that Adenauer's family was loyal to the Bismarck Reich and that his father had fought in the wars of unification: Schwarz, *Adenauer*, 35–58. On Stresemann's side, his suspicion of political Catholicism as a young

Revision of the Treaty of Versailles

Stresemann's immediate goal in January 1924 was defensive—to rescue the Ruhr from French control. In his eyes it was the French who were trying to revise the treaty and his aim was to prevent their succeeding. He stood by the offers previously made of reparations secured by German assets and an international guarantee of the Rhine frontier. He was able to present his policy in these terms as serving the interests of European peace and recovery. Nor was this mere rhetoric: there is every reason to suppose that he hoped that a lasting settlement could be achieved in the west with the support of Britain and the United States.

The situation in the south and east was different. Here German aims were clearly to revise the treaty—the Polish frontier, *Anschluß* or union with Austria, and perhaps the recovery of colonies—and these aims could not so readily be presented as in the best interests of Europe as a whole. Nor could they be actively pursued until the western frontier was stabilized. Stresemann saw his task as to keep alive German hopes of revision without prejudicing the prior task of a settlement in the west.

His foreign policy therefore acquired a double character: open and statesmanlike in the west, less open elsewhere. To the complications of managing international opinion were added the complications of domestic politics. Stresemann had to convince German voters that in his search for agreement with the Western powers, he had not abandoned revision. There was more than the usual temptation for a foreign minister to speak with one voice abroad and another at home. Stresemann was aware of the tension and, on one occasion, wrote about his sense of suffering a loss of identity under the strain.[29] He became increasingly preoccupied with the statecraft of Stein or Bismarck, admiring them as masters of the art of the possible, though on occasion he gave way to bouts of nostalgia for the romantic nationalism of 1848.

In his first meeting as chancellor with the Italian ambassador in August 1923, Stresemann spoke with undiplomatic frankness of their common interest in preventing the revival of 'the old Austria' in the form of a federation of Danube states, and said that Germany and Italy should seek

---

man had been modified by the war and he saw the Centre Party as something of a model for the DVP. There remained, however, important differences between Liberalism and Catholicism, particularly over education.

[29] See below, p. 293.

instead to establish a common frontier.[30] This brazen assertion of Germany's claim to *Anschluß* was followed by a greetings telegram to the Austrian chancellor Ignaz Seipel, declaring Germany's intention 'to bring closer the right of the two ethnically related peoples to achieve their unification'.[31] Maintaining the impetus for *Anschluß* was also a motive for trade negotiations, which were started with Austria in February 1924.[32] It was, of course, relatively easy to work for *Anschluß* so long as there was no danger of it occurring. Later Stresemann became more cautious and conscious of the problems it would create, both for domestic politics and foreign policy.[33]

The Polish frontier was if anything even more sensitive—it was resented by all German political parties with the exception of the Communists. The creation of Danzig as a Free City under the League of Nations and the separation of East Prussia from the rest of Germany by the Polish 'corridor' to the sea were regarded by Stresemann as the worst mistakes of the treaty.[34] He also felt strongly about Upper Silesia. The Bismarck Reich had been broken up to benefit Poland in ways which were—unlike the detachment of Alsace-Lorraine in the west—at least questionable in terms of self-determination. Stresemann, as indeed any German foreign minister of the time, was bound to aim for revision.

Although in 1924 the priority was clearly to achieve a settlement in the west, it was not possible to avoid the subject of German policy on the Polish frontier, as Poincaré linked the two. He told Hoesch that even if one accepted that there was no threat to France, it needed to keep troops in the Rhineland as a way of deterring a German attack on France's ally, Poland.[35] The recently appointed president of the Reichsbank, Schacht, had told Poincaré with characteristic indiscretion that 'no German would ever accept the corridor'. Stresemann immediately raised the subject with the French ambassador, de Margerie, telling him that Schacht had not been thinking of war but of an international conference 'which would meet Germany's economic needs'.[36] Stresemann continued:

[30] Memorandum by Stresemann, 17 Aug. 1923: Erdmann and Vogt (eds.), *Kabinette Stresemann*, no. 8.

[31] Stresemann to Seipel, 20 Aug. 1923: *ADAP*, ser. A, viii, no. 109.

[32] Cabinet minutes, 22 Feb. 1924: Abramowski (ed.), *Kabinette Marx*, no. 118.

[33] See below, pp. 326, 400.

[34] Wolfgang Stresemann, *Mein Vater*, 492. See Map 2.

[35] Hoesch to Auswärtiges Amt, 12 Feb. 1924: *ADAP*, ser. A, ix, no. 147.

[36] Memorandum by Stresemann, 12 Feb. 1924: ibid., no. 148. For Schacht's account of his meeting with Poincaré, see Schacht, *My First Seventy-Six Years*, 207–11.

If one wants to avoid war in Europe for a long time, then one must remove the things which are unsettling to a certain extent, and they include the separation of Germany from East Prussia which in my opinion is unpolitical and is seen as oppressive. But it is not at all an immediate question and certainly not a question of war...

Stresemann and his officials considered offering Poland an arbitration treaty as a way of pre-empting French objections, but the difficulty, as the German envoy to Poland Ulrich Rauscher pointed out, was that the Poles were bound to demand German recognition of their frontiers. Germany could not agree to this, yet it would be embarrassing to refuse.[37]

A further problem in Germany's relations with the Western powers was its policy towards the Soviet Union. Germany and the Soviet Union had established diplomatic relations in April 1922 by the treaty of Rapallo, and there was also a programme of secret military cooperation between the Red Army and the Reichswehr. Germany and the Soviet Union also both had frontier disputes with Poland—Poland having annexed territory to its east in 1921 after driving the Red Army back out of Poland—and this gave them an important interest in common.

Germany's relations with the Soviet Union caused suspicion and concern among the Western powers. As the two outcasts from the Paris peace settlement, they had the potential one day to overturn it if they acted together. Immediately the relationship raised problems for the question of Germany's possible entry into the League of Nations. The Soviet Union feared that Germany, as a member of the League, might join the Western powers in a capitalist crusade against it. Germany feared losing the advantages of its relationship with the Soviet Union if it joined, yet membership of the League was also attractive as a means of rapprochement with the West and of reasserting its status as a great power. The problem was considered by the Auswärtiges Amt in 1924, when the newly elected Labour prime minister Ramsay MacDonald showed an interest in encouraging German membership. Schubert indicated the difficulty which Germany anticipated to D'Abernon.[38] State Secretary Maltzan thought that the problem might be overcome by persuading the Soviet Union to join the League as well (which was also MacDonald's aim) but

---

[37] Stresemann to Rauscher, 8 Mar. and Rauscher's reply, 11 Mar. 1924: *ADAP*, ser. A, ix, nos. 189, 197.
[38] Undated memorandum given to D'Abernon on 11 Feb. 1924: ibid., no. 146; also Stresemann to the German ambassador in London, Friedrich Sthamer, 16 Mar. 1924: ibid., no. 211.

the German ambassador to Moscow, Graf Ulrich von Brockdorff-Rantzau, saw no prospect of that happening.[39]

Stresemann never attached primary importance to relations with the Soviet Union. He was suspicious of the expansionist ideology of Communism. He was also sceptical of the value of military cooperation and, together with Ebert and Brockdorff-Rantzau, he had tried as chancellor to get it stopped but the Reichswehr had continued on its own authority.[40] However, Stresemann believed that it was important to maintain the link to the Soviet Union in order to prevent a new Franco-Russian alliance, which would complete Germany's isolation on the Continent, and also because a Soviet link could provide Germany with some leverage with Britain and France as it struggled to regain its standing as a great power. At the lowest point in Germany's fortunes in December 1923, when there were rumours of a rapprochement between France and the Soviet Union, he encouraged Brockdorff-Rantzau not to betray any lack of confidence to his Soviet hosts. In language designed to appeal to the aristocratic ambassador, he wrote: 'Every policy for the future must reckon with Germany. The marked decline in socialism, the powerful increase of all national organizations is a guarantee that in the historically foreseeable future we will regain our strength to be attractive as an ally to our friends and dangerous to our enemies.'[41]

The Dawes Plan

The crucial breakthrough in the west came as a result of the report of the committee of experts under the chairmanship of General Dawes. Stresemann had followed its deliberations with increasing optimism and conducted foreign policy to maximize its chances of success. The committee visited Berlin at the end of January and the German government

[39] Maltzan to the German embassy in Moscow, 24 Mar. 1924, and note of Brockdorff-Rantzau's replies: ibid., no. 229. Brockdorff-Rantzau also wanted Germany and the Soviet Union to concert their tactics towards the League in order to maximize Germany's bargaining power. A comprehensive and perceptive study of Brockdorff-Rantzau is provided by Christiane Scheidemann, *Ulrich Graf Brockdorff-Rantzau (1869–1928). Eine politische Biographie* (Frankfurt am Main: Peter Lang, 1998), here pp. 626–7.

[40] Brockdorff-Rantzau to Stresemann, 27 Feb. 1924, enclosing his memorandum on the secret rearmament programme: *ADAP*, ser. A, ix, no. 170. Manfred Zeidler, *Reichswehr und Rote Armee 1920–1933* (Munich: Oldenbourg Verlag, 1993), 77.

[41] Stresemann to Brockdorff-Rantzau, 1 Dec. 1923: *ADAP*, ser. A, ix, no. 32.

provided all the information it required. Stresemann reported to a meeting with representatives from the occupied territories that the committee had accepted the need to restore the Ruhr to German control and to provide an international loan, secured on German assets like the railways, to fund reparations to France.[42] He continued to oppose Stinnes's alternative plans for a direct settlement with France, telling the cabinet that they amounted to sabotage of government policy and of the work of the committee.[43] For the same reason he opposed a renewal of the agreement between the mine-owners and the French authorities, though he was prepared to sanction temporary extensions to prevent deadlock in the Ruhr.[44] In a speech in Elberfeld on 17 February he referred to the work of the Dawes committee as 'a gleam of light on the otherwise dark horizon'.[45]

The Auswärtiges Amt continued to address the question of French security in the Rhineland, anticipating that this would be raised as another reason for the occupation of the Ruhr if a solution was found on reparations. In conversation with D'Abernon, Schubert indicated that they might be willing to accept D'Abernon's idea of an 'iron curtain' between France and Germany by a prohibition on either using the Rhineland for military operations.[46] When MacDonald discussed neutralized areas with Poincaré, Stresemann instructed the German ambassador in London to say that Germany could not accept a special political status for the Rhineland which might lead to its separation. However, if German sovereignty were respected he believed that a solution could be found which would guarantee peace. Deftly going to the heart of the difference between MacDonald and Poincaré, Stresemann added that 'A clear decision is unavoidable, whether one wants to secure the peace of Europe by the method of power politics by weakening and tearing Germany apart or by the method of introducing legal guarantees. There can be no compromise between these two possibilities.'[47]

[42] Minutes of the meeting, 7 Feb. 1924: Abramowski (ed.), *Kabinette Marx*, no. 92.

[43] Cabinet minutes, 29 Jan. 1924: ibid., no. 79.

[44] Cabinet minutes, 27 Mar., 2 and 9 Apr. 1924, and minutes of meetings with the mine-owners, 9–10 Apr. 1924: ibid., nos. 155, 163, 171–3.

[45] Stresemann was quoting the words of Carl Bergmann, the German representative to the Reparations Commission: Bernhard (ed.), *Vermächtnis*, i. 300.

[46] Memoranda by Schubert, 2 and 5 Feb., 7 Mar. 1924: *ADAP*, ser. A, ix, nos. 131, 135, 184 and undated memorandum, no. 146.

[47] Stresemann to Sthamer, 10 Mar. 1924: ibid., no. 194.

The security issue remained in the background while attention concentrated on the report of the Dawes committee. By the time it was presented to the Reparations Commission on 9 April 1924, Germany had already embarked on an election campaign. The Enabling Act, under which the government had imposed new taxes and a controversial, limited revaluation of private debts (in practice meaning a 90 per cent loss on the original asset), expired on 15 February.[48] The government was not willing to allow these measures, which it considered vital to maintain the stability of the currency, to be undermined by amendments in the Reichstag, but Marx was unable to persuade the SPD and DNVP to accept them as they stood. Marx therefore requested and obtained from Ebert a dissolution of the Reichstag in March with elections to be held on 4 May. In this period the cabinet was in something of a political limbo and Stresemann carried the main responsibility for arguing that Germany should respond positively to the Dawes proposals.

Although the schedule of payments proposed by Dawes was considered 'very high' by Luther (who remained finance minister) and there was considerable doubt as to whether Germany could keep to it, and although it meant submitting to international supervision of the railways, the new central bank, and the budget, Stresemann was in no doubt that the plan should be accepted.[49] He told the *Länder* minister presidents that the report had come about against Poincaré's opposition and that its general approach was the one Germany had repeatedly requested.[50] The participation of the United States, 'the only power which perhaps still has influence over France', was crucial. For this reason alone, a brusque rejection of the report was impossible: if that happened, France would be given a free hand and no country would help Germany again. Stresemann pointed out that the provisional nature of the plan could work to Germany's advantage. The essential precondition of the plan was the restoration of German economic and fiscal unity: 'he had to say that

---

[48] Feldman, *The Great Disorder*, 818.

[49] Cabinet minutes, 11 Apr., and minutes of a meeting of ministers with the minister presidents of the *Länder*, 14 Apr. 1924: Abramowski (ed.), *Kabinette Marx*, nos. 174–5.

[50] The plan proposed annual payments without giving a final total, but its capital value in 1924 has been estimated at 39 to 40 milliard (thousand million) gold marks, compared to the figure of 132 milliard gold marks set by the Reparations Commission in 1921. Payments were to be made from the German budget and mortgage bonds issued on German industry and the railways. Germany was to receive a partial moratorium on payments for four years and a foreign loan of 800 million gold marks. Stephen A. Schuker, *The End of French Predominance in Europe: The Financial Crisis of 1924 and the Adoption of the Dawes Plan* (Chapel Hill: University of North Carolina Press, 1976), 180–6.

after the lost battle of the Ruhr it seemed to him an honourable peace, which brought back under the control of the German Reich the economy and railways of the occupied zone'. The cabinet decided the same day, 14 April, to respond positively.[51]

The Elections of May 1924

Stresemann knew that the elections would be difficult for the DVP. Its gains in June 1920 had been made on a generally anti-republican and anti-Versailles platform. Since then he had led the party into government and coalition with the SPD, to acceptance of defeat in the Ruhr, and now towards something suspiciously like fulfilment of the hated treaty in the Dawes plan. More than that, the DVP shared responsibility for the hardship brought by currency stabilization to substantial numbers of its own voters—middle-class savers, state employees suffering from the cuts, and peasant farmers suffering from a shortage of credit. It was clearly going to require an enormous effort to persuade them that his policy had been right and that the worst was over.

The campaign started badly with an attempt by the opposition within the DVP Reichstag party to commit it to an anti-Socialist alliance with the DNVP. Stresemann had himself become more critical of the SPD after it had voted down his government in November 1923, but he was no more willing to be tied to the DNVP than in the past. He wanted policy to be determined by the bourgeois middle parties with the DNVP allowed to join if it accepted their terms, not the other way round.[52]

Stresemann foiled the opposition by having a resolution which he believed committed the party too strongly to the DNVP, and which had been adopted by the Reichstag party, redrafted by its executive committee to allow it to be interpreted flexibly.[53] The opposition were not content to leave the matter there. The day before the Reichstag was dissolved, they announced the formation of a 'National Liberal Union' to campaign for a change of direction. The group included all Stresemann's main opponents. Although Stinnes was too ill to take part himself, he was angry at Stresemann's rebuff of his attempts at private diplomacy and also at

[51] Cabinet minutes, 14 Apr. 1924: Abramowski (ed.), *Kabinette Marx*, no. 177.
[52] 'Wochenschau', *Die Zeit*, 4/17, 20 Jan. 1924: extract in Bernhard (ed.), *Vermächtnis*, i. 286–7.
[53] Memorandum concerning Dr Quaatz (Nl. 267); Turner, *Stresemann*, 156–7; Jones, *Liberalism*, 213–14; Richter, *Deutsche Volkspartei*, 307–10.

Stresemann's opposition to his standing again for the Reichstag which had led to a bitter exchange of letters. This rift made him a natural ally of the opposition.[54] It was based in the Ruhr, which supplied twenty of its twenty-five founding members, including Vögler and Quaatz, which meant that there would be no lack of funds for the new group. It also had support from elsewhere: its twelve Reichstag deputies included Gildemeister (Bremen), Lersner (Leipzig), Maretzky (Potsdam), Dauch and Piper (Hamburg), the farmers' representatives Döbrich and Hepp, and a Christian trade unionist, Adams.[55] It was obviously a significant challenge.

Stresemann reacted immediately, seeing the parallel with the 'Old Liberal Association' and determined not to allow himself to be bullied as Bassermann had been. On 15 March he secured a resolution from a little-used committee known simply as the party executive—on which the leadership had a dominant influence—declaring that a separate organization would not be tolerated within the party.[56] A full meeting of the national executive on the eve of the pre-election party conference at the end of March confirmed the decision.[57] Confounded by this determined counter-attack, the National Liberal union collapsed. Half its Reichstag members withdrew from the union; others, including Quaatz, defected to the DNVP.[58] Once again Stresemann had used his control over the DVP's national organization to suppress a revolt in the Reichstag party.

Having re-established his authority, Stresemann set about rallying the party for the election. At the party conference in Hanover he gave a vigorous defence of his leadership.[59] Anticipating criticism for inconsistency he argued that they had been right to honour the memory of the 'old Germany' with its army, fleet, and colonies against the spirit of the National Assembly in 1919. Equally, they had been right after the elec-

---

[54] Wulf, *Stinnes*, 522–8; Feldman, 'Hugo Stinnes, Gustav Stresemann', 439–42; Bernhard (ed.), *Vermächtnis*, i. 356–9.

[55] Turner, *Stresemann* 158–9; Richter, *Deutsche Volkspartei*, 310–13.

[56] Bernhard (ed.), *Vermächtnis*, i. 354. The Parteivorstand consisted of the party chairman (Stresemann),the chairman of the Geschäftsführender Ausschuß (Kempkes), the chairmen of the Reichstag and Prussian Landtag *Fraktionen* (Scholz and von Campe) and five members elected from the Zentralvorstand; Kolb and Richter (eds.), *Nationalliberalismus*, 37*.

[57] Report of the Zentralvorstand meeting, 28 Mar. 1924: Kolb and Richter (eds.), *Nationalliberalismus*, 490–1.

[58] Turner, *Stresemann*, 160–1; Jones, *Liberalism*, 215–16; Richter, *Deutsche Volkspartei*, 313–22.

[59] 'Fünfter Parteitag der Deutschen Volkspartei in Hannover am 29. und 30 März 1924', *NLC* Sonderausgabe; BAK, R 45 II/28. Stresemann's speech is repr. in Rheinbaben, *Reden und Schriften*, ii. 164–93.

tions of June 1920 had made them a large party to seek positive cooperation in government. From 1920 to 1924 they had taken allies where they
could find them and in this they had followed the example of Bismarck,
not the political philistines who put 'principle' above everything.

Turning to foreign policy, he again referred to Bismarck: they followed
his realpolitik not illusions and, as a disarmed nation, this meant operating
within narrow constraints. The struggle for the Ruhr had not been in vain,
as France was not comfortable with its victory and international opinion
had moved towards Germany. The work of the committee of experts, for
instance, held the promise of a certain détente. German policy was determined by the priority of saving the occupied territories, just as after its
defeat in 1806 Prussia had refused to barter part of Silesia for a reduction
in the indemnity it had to pay to France. It would be easy for him to strike
popular poses, to shout with Hitler 'With the black-white-red banner over
the Rhine', but it would be irresponsible.

Stresemann also defended currency stabilization, admitting that the
middle class had suffered unacceptable losses, but pointing out that the
real cause had been the inflation, and claiming that the situation was now
improving.[60] He reviewed the record of his administration, saying that he
would not wish on his worst enemies the crises of those months. He
poured scorn on the would-be dictators of Bavaria and claimed that the
great coalition with the SPD had helped to isolate the Communists and
made it possible for the intervention in Saxony and Thuringia to be
carried out without bloodshed.

Looking to the future Stresemann accepted that the SPD could no
longer be regarded as a reliable coalition partner, and he welcomed the
fact that the DNVP was preparing for government—they would soon
discover that it was very different from an election rally. He predicted that
the DVP would be at the centre of the future government.

Stresemann received the customary ovation from the conference. Only
Maretzky from among his opponents dared to argue for a clearly anti-
Socialist course, but Stresemann brushed him aside, jesting that they
could perhaps set up a committee to decide whether they were a party

---

[60] Stresemann's concern for the losers by inflation was genuine, seeing in them the kind of
patriotic middle class of his own background. In cabinet he had spoken against Luther, in favour
of a modest revaluation of private debts, saying that 'The full legal proletarianization by law now
of precisely those groups of the population who had earlier been those who supported the state
was an intolerable idea'. Cabinet minutes, 17 Dec. 1923: Abramowski (ed.), *Kabinette Marx*, no.
30; Feldman, *The Great Disorder*, 817.

of the right or the middle. He then, however, reaffirmed his view that the role of the party was to mediate between right and left, making possible what he called 'that great diagonal without which no statesmanlike policy can be conducted'.

Stresemann's attempts to combine respect for the past with loyalty to the Republic obviously suited the DVP's tactics. But there was another purpose to his rhetoric which became clearer in exchanges during the campaign. He did not want patriotism to be the exclusive preserve of the right. Replying to criticism of his speech in the United States, he told the New York Times that he had demonstrated his loyalty to the Constitution during the Munich putsch. But equally Americans with their own great traditions must allow Germans to respect their past. 'Democracy and national pride are not contradictions but complement each other.'[61]

A similar issue arose in an exchange with Sollmann about the great coalition.[62] Sollmann had described Stresemann as a *Vernunftrepublikaner* and Stresemann did not reject the description, saying only that he thought it had been first used by his colleague Wilhelm Kahl—he obviously forgot the earlier incident with Scheidemann in 1919.[63] Stresemann went on to criticize the SPD for its constant attacks on the Reichswehr, saying that the SPD and the Republic in general had made a great mistake in not identifying themselves with the memory of the war and treating war memorials, for instance, as a matter over which all parties should unite. This criticism was less than fair: the SPD had good reason to distrust the Reichswehr as Stresemann well knew. But he understood the importance of symbolism, and continued to hope that the Republic would acquire greater legitimacy as a focus of national unity.[64] He also thought it lacked glamour, and argued that a new system of honours should be introduced for those who were 'deserving of the fatherland'. Stresemann was never able completely to bridge the divide between empire and republic or right and left, but his comments showed a shrewd understanding of what many, at least of his constituents, felt was lacking in the Republic.

The campaign gave the DNVP an ideal opportunity to attack the government parties for the unpopular results of currency stabilization,

---

[61] Interview, 4 Apr. 1924: Bernhard (ed.), *Vermächtnis*, i. 377–80.
[62] *Kölnische Zeitung*, 29 Apr. 1924: Bernhard (ed.), *Vermächtnis*, i. 326–8.
[63] See above p. 145.
[64] On the Republic's fractured political culture, see Detlev Lehnert and Klaus Megerle (eds.), *Politische Teilkulturen zwischen Integration und Polarisierung* (Opladen: Westdeutscher Verlag, 1990).

and Stresemann in particular for the great coalition and for his new version of 'fulfilment'. Karl Helfferich, their leading foreign policy spokesman, described the Dawes plan as a 'second Versailles'.[65] At a lower level, a DNVP member of the Reichstag, Freytag-Loringhoven, spread a story that Stresemann's father-in-law was involved in a Czech arms factory and that this had influenced his judgement as foreign minister.[66]

In the elections, the DVP vote fell by a third—from 13.9 per cent to 9.2 per cent—and its representation in the Reichstag from sixty-six to forty-five.[67] There was as usual considerable regional variation in the results. The greatest losses occurred in the rural provinces of the Prussian east and in northern Bavaria. In Pomerania the DVP vote fell by 75 per cent and in Franconia it was virtually wiped out. The party also fared badly in the Berlin region. Losses were below average, however, in the occupied territories and in parts of Saxony and Thuringia, suggesting that Stresemann's policies had won support there. Small percentage gains were even recorded in Baden and Württemberg, both areas where the DVP had found it hard to win back voters from the DDP after 1919. The DDP was the other main loser among the bourgeois parties, holding only twenty-eight of its thirty-nine seats in the Reichstag.

As expected, the DNVP was the clear winner on the right: with 106 seats altogether in the Reichstag, including ten elected on the Farmers' Association (Landbund) list, it became the largest party, with over 20 per cent of the vote. In addition the racist DVFP, which was shortly to merge with the NSDAP, won thirty-two seats. Another worrying development was the growth of rural and middle-class splinter groups, representing regional and sectional interests.[68] On the left, the trend to the extremes was equally marked. The SPD which, after joining with the USPD in 1922, had 171 seats in the Reichstag, was reduced to 100. The KPD was the beneficiary, increasing its seats from seventeen to sixty-two.

Despite the heavy losses, Stresemann was reasonably content with the DVP's performance.[69] He had feared worse, and believed that support was

---

[65] Williamson, *Helfferich*, 397–400.

[66] Stresemann pointed out in the Reichstag that his father-in-law had been dead for twenty years and had never been involved in foreign arms factories: Bernhard (ed.) *Vermächtnis*, i. 324–6.

[67] Milatz, *Wähler*, 99–100, 116–17; Richter, *Deutsche Volkspartei*, 330–3; *Archiv der Deutschen Volkspartei*, 1924/3, 4 May, 98–103; Wolfgang Stresemann, 'Das Ergebnis der Reichstagswahlen', *Deutsche Stimmen*, 36/9, 5 May 1924.

[68] Jones, *Liberalism*, 222.

[69] 'Politische Umschau', *Deutsche Stimmen*, 36/12, 20 June 1924.

already starting to return as the situation improved. He blamed the losses on the inevitable unpopularity of government and weaknesses in party organization and the press. Party finances had suffered in the inflation and as a result of the defection of Ruhr industrialists, although the losses from the Ruhr were to some extent made good by contributions from the chemical industry, where Carl Duisberg became an important source of support.[70]

As a born journalist, Stresemann was keenly aware of the DVP's poor representation in the press. His attempts to improve matters is a subject which deserves more attention than it has yet received.[71] Unlike Britain, Germany had an enormous range of newspapers both in Berlin and the provinces, and each of the major parties had its own mouthpiece. In the first phase of the Republic, while the DVP was an opposition party, it benefited with the DNVP from the support of the right-wing press. But once Stresemann adopted a policy of coalition with the SPD that support fell away. The newspaper-owners, who were supposed to give equal representation to the views of the DVP and the DNVP, increasingly supported the DNVP alone. The situation was particularly bad in Berlin. The only editor in the capital who supported the DVP, Heinrich Rippler of the *Tägliche Rundschau*, was sacked in September 1921 before the newspaper was closed in 1922. Stresemann took the bold step of founding a new daily, *Die Zeit*, in December 1921, with Rippler as its first editor. Keeping it going, however, was a constant financial struggle which he eventually abandoned in June 1925.[72] *Die Zeit* was then taken over by the *Tägliche Rundschau* which had been revived by Rippler in 1924 and which now supported the DVP, but it was soon in financial difficulty and ceased publication in June 1928.

The situation in the provinces was only slightly better. Some prestigious former National Liberal papers, notably the *Kölnische Zeitung*, the *Hannoverscher Kurier*, and the *Königsberger Allgemeine Zeitung* transferred their allegiance to the DVP, although the *Hannoverscher Kurier* opposed Stresemann's coalition policy.[73] The DVP also had looser connections with a number of other regional papers, but a survey in 1926 showed that

---

[70] Jones, *Liberalism*, 219–20; Richter, *Deutsche Volkspartei*, 323–5.

[71] The fullest account remains Starkulla, 'Pressepolitik'. See also Döhn, *Politik und Interesse*, 373–7 and Hans Jürgen Müller, *Auswärtige Pressepolitik und Propaganda zwischen Ruhrkampf und Locarno (1923–1925)* (Frankfurt am Main: Peter Lang, 1991), 45–8.

[72] Starkulla, 'Pressepolitik', 40–54.

[73] Ibid. 12–21.

only 2 per cent of Germany's 3,252 newspapers saw themselves as National Liberal or DVP. The weakness of the DVP's position could be seen by comparison with the Democratic and Nationalist press. With the *Frankfurter Zeitung* and *Berliner Tageblatt*, the DDP had at least the critical support of two of the best-known German newspapers, while Hugenberg's press agency, the Telegraphen-Union, exerted a pervasive influence over the provincial press in favour of the DNVP. In the constituency of North Westphalia alone, Stresemann alleged, Hugenberg had founded five newspapers whose main purpose was to attack the DVP.[74]

Nevertheless, the success of the DNVP in the May elections did not disturb Stresemann unduly because, as he wrote to Jarres, 'Greatness creates responsibility.'[75] The party would no longer be able to avoid decisions and so 'a correction of the election results will automatically take place at the next elections'. Stresemann knew that the major interests supporting the DNVP in industry and agriculture desperately needed credit, which could come only in the form of foreign loans by acceptance of the Dawes plan.[76] It also seemed likely that the Dawes plan would need a two-thirds majority in the Reichstag, since the transfer of the railways to private control, which it entailed, would probably require a constitutional amendment. The DNVP would therefore be forced to choose between allowing it to pass or losing the credits.[77] That decision would divide the party between its pragmatic sections and the radical right ideologues, a process from which the DVP could expect to benefit.

'I hated all night'

The elections were followed by weeks of manoeuvring between the parties over the formation of a new government. During this time Stresemann was made painfully aware that his judgement was not shared by the Reichstag party and that he could not rely on its loyalty. The majority had never been enthusiastic about his policies, expecially the great coalition, and it was only natural that they should now blame him for the loss of

---

[74] 'Politische Umschau', *Deutsche Stimmen*, 36/12, 20 June 1924, 184–5. On the Hugenberg empire, see Heidrun Holzbach, *Das 'System Hugenberg'* (Stuttgart: Deutsche Verlags-Anstalt, 1981), 259–313.

[75] Stresemann to Jarres, 9 May 1924 (Nl. 90): extract in Bernhard (ed.), *Vermächtnis*, i. 406.

[76] Reichstag speech, 28 Feb. 1924, *Verhandlungen des Reichstags*, vol. 361, p. 12525.

[77] Stresemann's memorandum of a conversation with the American ambassador Alanson Houghton, 4 June 1924: *ADAP*, ser. A, x, no. 122.

electoral support. They were determined to bring the DNVP into government and were prepared, if necessary, to force Stresemann to stand down.

Stresemann's failure to inspire affection and trust within the Reichstag party, except among a handful of supporters, was a serious weakness which almost proved fatal to his career. It is interesting to reflect on its causes. There was a natural resentment against his dominant style and his willingness to use the national party organizations against the Reichstag party. He sometimes treated his colleagues with what Count Kessler called on one occasion 'a sovereign display of contempt' and some of them, distinguished men in their own fields, did not like being taken for granted.[78] There was also, as we have seen, the major policy difference over relations with the SPD and the DNVP respectively. He seemed willing to conciliate the SPD but intolerant towards the right wing of his own party. Some thought personal reasons contributed to the differences—Paul Moldenhauer, for example, believed that Käte Stresemann being of Jewish descent made an alliance with the DNVP impossible because of the strength of anti-Semitism in the DNVP.[79]

Another cause of division may have been Stresemann's modest background, making it hard for his mainly upper-middle-class colleagues to feel they knew him, and him not wholly at ease in their company. He once wrote that he no longer felt at home either in the society from which he had come or in the one into which he had climbed: the former had become too narrow and the latter was too full of hypocrisy.[80] His brilliance as a public speaker also contributed: it made him envied and at the same time distrusted as glib and lacking in gravitas. D'Abernon noted that he was regarded as 'arbitrary' and 'not a sound party man'.[81]

The twists and turns of Stresemann's career during and after the First World War also led naturally to accusations of opportunism. Since he was

[78] Kessler diary entry for 25 June 1920. Kessler's comment was prompted by Stresemann remaining at lunch with him until 2.45 although he was due at a party meeting at 2 p.m. When Werner von Rheinbaben remonstrated with him, Stresemann replied 'Far better... to let the members blow off steam first and then... put in an appearance and take matters in hand.' Charles Kessler (ed.), *The Diaries of a Cosmopolitan: Count Harry Kessler 1918–1937*, Eng. edn. (London: Weidenfeld & Nicolson, 1971), 129. On Kessler and his role on the margins of Weimar politics, see Peter Grupp, *Harry Graf Kessler 1868–1937. Eine Biographie*, 2nd edn. (Munich: C. H. Beck, 1996).

[79] BAK, Nl. Moldenhauer, 1, 'Politische Erinnerungen', 30–1.

[80] In his autobiographical short story, 'Die Barre'; Bernhard (ed.), *Vermächtnis*, i. 533; Jonathan Wright, 'Die Maske: Stresemanns politische Persona', in Pohl (ed.), *Stresemann*, 41–63.

[81] Entry for 25 May 1924: D'Abernon, *An Ambassador of Peace*, iii. 65.

often in the position of leading the Reichstag party in a direction it did not want to go, he tended to stress tactical arguments rather than the direction itself. This reinforced the impression of a skilful politician, lacking real convictions. These suspicions were shared by colleagues in other parties. Koch-Weser, chairman of the DDP, referred in May 1924 to the 'fickle Stresemann' and the gentle, elderly chairman of the Centre Party, Fehrenbach, warned Hindenburg as Reich president in December 1925 that Stresemann 'inspired general trust neither in his own party nor among the other coalition parties'.[82] Stresemann also had his defenders both within the Reichstag party and among other parties—for instance, Kahl, Kempkes, Marx, and, by 1924, Ebert. But the general lack of loyalty he inspired made him more vulnerable than he realized.

The question of the terms under which the DNVP would enter the government dominated discussions after the May elections.[83] The cabinet did not resign immediately, Stresemann arguing that they should wait at least until after the French elections on 11 May so as not to disturb the expected swing against Poincaré.[84] In order to strengthen the hand of the coalition parties towards the DNVP Marx proposed—perhaps at Stresemann's suggestion—that they should operate together as a group.[85] Stresemann declined, however, an approach from the DDP for an actual fusion of their two parties which would have had no chance of acceptance by the DVP.[86] As it was, the DVP Reichstag party rejected the idea of the coalition parties forming a group.[87]

The DNVP demanded the government's resignation on 15 May. The cabinet refused, arguing that the negotiations over the Dawes plan were too important to be interrupted and pointing out that with the support of

---

[82] Koch-Weser to Irmgard von Blanquet, 15 May 1924: BAK, Nl. Koch-Weser, 31; minutes of a meeting between Reich President Hindenburg and Fehrenbach, 13 Dec. 1925: BAB, Büro des Reichspräsidenten, 43.

[83] Robert P. Grathwol, *Stresemann and the DNVP* (Lawrence: The Regents Press of Kansas, 1980), 21–9.

[84] Cabinet minutes, 6 May 1924: Abramowski (ed.), *Kabinette Marx*, no. 193.

[85] Hehl, *Marx*, 283.

[86] Report by Anton Erkelenz to the DDP Vorstand, 21 May 1924: Konstanze Wegner and Lothar Albertin, (eds.), *Linksliberalismus in der Weimarer Republik. Die Führungsgremien der Deutschen Demokratischen Partei und der Deutschen Staatspartei 1918–1933* (Düsseldorf: Droste, 1980), 318. Turner argues that this would have been the best opportunity for the parties to fuse, and is inclined to blame Stresemann for not reacting more favourably: Turner, *Stresemann*, 166–7. However, the DDP chairman Koch-Weser also had reservations about union: Gerhard Papke, *Der liberale Politiker Erich Koch-Weser in der Weimarer Republik* (Baden-Baden: Nomos Verlagsgesellschaft, 1989), 159.

[87] Cabinet minutes, 15 May 1924: Abramowski (ed.), *Kabinette Marx*, no. 199.

the SPD there would be a majority in the Reichstag for the plan. They asked the DNVP to clarify its attitude.[88] The following day Stresemann proposed that the cabinet should resign just before the Reichstag met at the end of the month, since there was a general view that the election results made its resignation necessary. The cabinet then drew up a joint position from which to conduct negotiations with the DNVP.[89]

The DNVP did not want to be drawn into a discussion of the Dawes plan, however, since that would expose its differences. Instead it proposed that Tirpitz should become chancellor. The coalition parties refused and Stresemann hastily collected statements from foreign embassies showing that Tirpitz would not be acceptable. The negotiations appeared to be about to break down and Stresemann told the cabinet that he understood that the DNVP had decided not to join the government until the autumn, that is, after the Dawes plan had been accepted.[90]

The negotiations were given new life, however, by the DVP Reichstag party. In an attempt to break the deadlock it decided on 26 May to force the resignation of the cabinet. To meet the demand for a change of either chancellor or foreign minister, Scholz adopted the formula that the DVP 'holds firm to Stresemann so long as he wants to go on'.[91] Stresemann had no option but to accept this thinly veiled invitation to stand down. He accordingly told Marx, whom Ebert had asked to form a new government, that Marx need take no account of his person in the negotiations.[92]

Both the Centre Party and the DDP were prepared to see Stresemann go. He was saved only by the loyalty of Marx, who was determined to keep him, and by the intransigence of the DNVP which now again demanded that it should be allowed to enter the Prussian government at the same time. Marx broke off negotiations and made it clear that he was ready to form a government with only the DDP if necessary.[93] At this point the

---

[88] Cabinet minutes, 15 May 1924: Abramowski (ed.), *Kabinette Marx*, no. 199.

[89] Cabinet minutes, 16 May 1924: ibid., no. 201.

[90] Minutes of two meetings of the cabinet, 24 May 1924: ibid. nos. 206, 207. On 24 May the American, Japanese, Belgian, and British embassies were contacted and declared their opposition to Tirpitz, and Ebert was informed accordingly. Memoranda from the Auswärtiges Amt, 12–13 and 14 May 1924: BAB, 06.01, 41. D'Abernon, *Ambassador of Peace*, iii. 66.

[91] Cabinet minutes, 26 May 1924: Abramowski (ed.), *Kabinette Marx*, no. 209. Koch-Weser quoted Scholz's formulation in a report to the DDP executive: Wegner and Albertin, (eds.), *Linksliberalismus*, 327. Stresemann also noted it in his diary for 30 May (Nl. 361); Bernhard (ed.), *Vermächtnis*, i. 412.

[92] Stresemann to Marx, 2 June 1924: Bernhard (ed.), *Vermächtnis*, i. 413.

[93] Marx's report to the cabinet (in Stresemann's absence), 31 May 1924: Abramowski (ed.), *Kabinette Marx*, no. 212.

DVP gave up what it called its 'honest broker role' and renewed its support for the old coalition.[94] The DNVP encouraged a last round of talks, but these were finally abandoned on 3 June and the second Marx government took office with Stresemann remaining as foreign minister.

Stresemann had survived, but it was a humiliating experience. He told D'Abernon that he now understood what Bismarck had meant when he said 'I hated all night'.[95] He also recorded in his diary Ebert's comment: 'It is a tragedy how a man like Stresemann is treated by his own party.'[96]

The Fight for the Dawes Plan

Stresemann now devoted all his energies to the successful conclusion of the Dawes plan. He was encouraged by Hoesch who, in remarkably outspoken dispatches from Paris, urged a change of policy away from the resistance to the occupation of the Ruhr and the Reichswehr's secret preparations for a future war to creating confidence in Germany abroad and grasping the possibilities of peace.[97] Hoesch was writing under the influence of the French elections, which led to the fall of Poincaré and the formation of a centre-left government with a narrow majority under Édouard Herriot on 15 June. Hoesch advised that 'By freely adopting a policy of understanding, of peace and of international solidarity' there was a real prospect for Germany to regain, if not its old power, at least sovereignty, equal rights, and freedom. But this chance would be squandered if the new French National Assembly did not see the policy of understanding bearing fruit.[98] Stresemann noted on the dispatch that ordinary Germans—'the pub regulars' (*an den Stammtischen*)—did not understand the need to be sensitive to international opinion, but he also agreed with Hoesch's conclusion that French policy could change again if Germany did not respond.

During the summer he did his utmost to mobilize support. In the Reichstag and in meetings with the minister presidents of the *Länder*, party leaders, and the national executive of the DVP and in public

---

[94] Stresemann's diary, 31 May 1924 (Nl. 361): Bernhard (ed.), *Vermächtnis*, i. 412.
[95] D'Abernon's diary for 30 May 1924: D'Abernon, *Ambassador of Peace*, iii. 68.
[96] Diary for 3 June 1924 (Nl. 361); Bernhard (ed.), *Vermächtnis*, i. 413.
[97] Hoesch to Auswärtiges Amt, 15 May, 4 and 6 June 1924: *ADAP*, ser. A, x, nos. 81, 118, 126.
[98] Ibid., no. 126.

speeches and newspaper articles he argued the advantages of the Dawes plan.[99] Convinced of his cause, he was at his most eloquent and persuasive, varying his arguments with his audience.

His central theme was that the Dawes plan gave them the chance to enlist the whole power of American as well as British capital against 'French imperialism'.[100] This made it a 'very great world political event', a real change in the international situation. It was unthinkable that Germany should reject such an opportunity: that would unite the world against them, including the whole power of the United States which saw the Dawes plan as its own work; they would lose the occupied zone, and the German economy would be ruined by a lack of capital for investment. With the plan, foreign loans would flow in and they would have the chance to rebuild. The reparations would be heavy when they reached their normal level, after the partial remission allowed in the first four years, but both the British and Americans understood that the full level of payment might itself have undesirable consequences for international trade and tacitly expected further reductions.[101]

To the objections of a DNVP minister president that they would be taken over by Anglo-American capitalism, Stresemann replied that that had been the decisive factor in winning the war and that once the German economy was strong again it could 'throw away the crutches'. Similarly, to the argument that Europe's problems could only be solved 'by the sword', he replied that if that was so 'and I believe that ultimately these great arguments are always decided by the sword', then he hoped that it would be put off as long as possible as Germany did not have the power of the

---

[99] Reichstag speeches, 6 June, 23 and 28 August: *Verhandlungen des Reichstags*, vol. 381, pp. 166–77, 779–88, 1014–20; meeting with the *Länder* minister presidents, 3 July: Abramowski (ed.), *Kabinette Marx*, no. 243; confidential briefing of party leaders, 16 June: Bernhard (ed.), *Vermächtnis*, i. 433–7 (date from cabinet minutes, 11 June, Abramowski (ed.), *Kabinette Marx*, no. 218); meeting of the DVP Zentralvorstand, 6 July: Kolb and Richter (eds.), *Nationalliberalismus*, no. 56; speeches in Magdeburg, 29 Apr., and Karlsruhe, 15 June: *Die Zeit* 4/102, 1 May, 4/140, 17 June; 'Politische Ostern', *Die Zeit*, 4/94, 20 Apr. and 'Das Gutachten des Sachverständigenkomitees', *Die Zeit*, 4/102, 1 May 1924.

[100] See in particular the statements to the minister presidents of the *Länder* and the DVP Zentralvorstand, 3 and 6 July, where he spoke most freely.

[101] There were two possible damaging consequences of large transfers. In order to make them without inflation Germany would have to achieve equivalent trade surpluses—which might not be welcome to its competitors—and the effect of large transfers on the exchange rate of the currencies of recipient countries might also damage their exports. The Dawes committee thought that the first problem could be managed, on the assumption that there would be a general growth of world trade, and a transfer committee was established to supervise the problem of the actual payments.

sword. If one wanted a more important role, one must first lay the foundations for it.[102]

To the DVP national executive he explained his view of how Germany could once again influence events. Describing the five years since January 1919 as a period of progress at home, he went on:

Only abroad, we have at present neither political power nor influence. You can conduct successful policy only if you have one or the other or the first through the second. I consider all the elaborate games to recover power secretly as total nonsense. You cannot produce heavy artillery or build a thousand planes secretly, that damages our foreign policy without bringing us anything. The only policy which can succeed is that which aims to become a worthwhile ally [*bündnisfähig*] for other nations, so as at the moment of becoming a useful ally to receive from the other side what you would never get with old, buried guns.

He hoped to see in the next five years a consolidation of Germany's international position, which meant putting an end to the conflict over reparations. This was the course of 'sober realpolitik'.[103]

These arguments mark an important stage in the development of Stresemann's policy. The goal of becoming 'a worthwhile ally' was not new—he had formulated it in 1919—but in the intervening years not much progress had been possible.[104] Now Germany had the chance to break out of isolation and resume its place among the European great powers. There it could bring its economic and political weight to bear for revision of the Versailles treaty. At last there appeared to be a viable strategy to follow instead of simply reacting to the policies of other powers. The only alternatives, Seeckt's secret preparations for war and the associated policy of close relations with the Soviet Union, had no realistic chance of success while the Western powers were militarily and economically dominant.

Nevertheless, Stresemann had a difficult task answering the criticism that revision of the treaty would not come about peacefully. He talked as though Germany's dependence on the Western powers would be a temporary stage until it could again emerge as a free and sovereign power. He was also ambivalent—whether as a debating tactic or because it reflected his own real views—as to whether military force would be required at some stage in the future. He conceded to his opponents that 'ultimately' force would decide, but he immediately countered that as a disarmed state

---

[102] Abramowski (ed.), *Kabinette Marx*, pp. 828–9.
[103] Kolb and Richter (eds.), *Nationalliberalismus*, 512–13.   [104] See above p. 147.

Germany had no alternative but to pursue other methods and he clearly hoped that results could be achieved by negotiations.

The conflict between Stresemann and Seeckt immediately arose in cabinet over an allied demand to resume inspection of German compliance with the disarmament provisions of the treaty, a process which had been interrupted by the Ruhr conflict.[105] Seeckt, fearing disclosure of his illegal methods of recruiting and training, wanted the cabinet to refuse and came close to threatening resignation.[106] Stresemann, however, with Marx's support, persuaded the cabinet that the issue should not be allowed to jeopardize negotiations for the Dawes plan and Seeckt grudgingly gave way.

The London Conference, July–August 1924

Apart from mobilizing support at home, Stresemann also did his best to influence opinion abroad.[107] To the foreign journalists in Berlin, he set out the German view of what was needed for 'a peaceful cooperation of the nations, and especially a peaceful modus vivendi, a peaceful understanding between France and Germany'.[108] The main problem was that while the Dawes plan provided that Germany would resume control of the economy and therefore the administration of the Ruhr, it said nothing

---

[105] Cabinet minutes, 25 June 1924: Abramowski (ed.), *Kabinette Marx*, no. 234.

[106] Seeckt's argument was that, under the treaty, control was supposed to pass to the League of Nations once Germany had disarmed. The Allies, however, quite rightly did not accept that Germany had yet complied with the treaty. Michael Salewski, *Entwaffnung und Militärkontrolle in Deutschland 1919–1927* (Munich: Oldenbourg, 1966), 241–70.

[107] On his campaign to win American support, see Berg, *Stresemann und die Vereinigten Staaten*, 202–17.

[108] Speech to foreign journalists, 30 June 1924: Bernhard (ed.), *Vermächtnis*, i. 441–8, quotation p. 447. Stresemann both understood the importance of cultivating foreign journalists and enjoyed their company. In 1925 he started the practice of briefing them every Friday afternoon over tea. According to Edgar Stern-Rubarth, who attended in his capacity as the chief editor of the German government press agency, Wolffs Telegraphisches Büro, Stresemann soon dominated the sessions by his wit, intelligence, and instinctive understanding of the world of journalism: 'he used this forum to spread his ideas, to justify his methods, and win the allegiance of the world'. Edgar Stern-Rubarth, *Three Men Tried... Austen Chamberlain, Stresemann, Briand and their Fight for a New Europe* (London: Duckworth, 1939), 79–80. For an appreciation by a foreign journalist, see the memoirs of Louis P. Lochner, who worked in Berlin for Associated Press from 1924 and was chief of the Berlin bureau from 1928 to 1941: *Always the Unexpected: A Book of Reminiscences* (New York: Macmillan, 1956), 128–36. Other informal channels included leading members of the SPD: Hermann Müller gave the German view at an international trade union conference in Amsterdam, and Rudolf Breitscheid acted as an intermediary between the German delegation and Herriot at the London conference in July. Cabinet minutes, 9 July 1924: Abramowski (ed.), *Kabinette Marx*, no. 248, and see below p. 430, n. 152.

about the military occupation, regarding that as beyond its terms of reference. Yet without the withdrawal of French and Belgian troops Stresemann stood little chance of securing Reichstag approval.

Not surprisingly this soon became a sticking point. Herriot did not have a secure majority and wanted to be able to demonstrate continuity with Poincaré's policy.[109] He offered an amnesty for those imprisoned or expelled from the Ruhr, but indicated that further concessions would have to wait until the Dawes legislation had been passed and reparations were being paid.[110] At the end of June his position hardened. He told Hoesch that the Dawes legislation would have to be passed before an Allied conference met in London on 16 July to consider the implementation of the plan.[111] In addition, Herriot wanted to retain a role for the Reparations Commission in enforcing the Dawes plan, and the French right to reimpose unilateral sanctions.[112]

Stresemann remained hopeful that with British and American help—particularly since the bankers would have an interest in German economic recovery to safeguard their loans—French opposition could be overcome. He persuaded the cabinet to stick to the position that the Reichstag would pass the legislation only once the consequences for the Ruhr were clear and that these must include military evacuation by a definite date. Through Hoesch he threatened resignation, since there was no prospect of the DVP, let alone the DNVP, voting for the Dawes plan without an agreement on evacuation.[113]

The outcome remained in doubt until the end of the London conference.[114] The conference met in two stages. In the second half of July the Allies met on their own. MacDonald acted both as chairman and as an effective advocate of the German cause, seeing that no issue was settled in a way to which Germany would object.[115] He raised the issue of military evacuation with Herriot although it was not part of the official agenda.

---

[109] Bariéty, *Les Relations franco-allemandes*, 321–501.

[110] Stresemann's memorandum of a meeting with de Margerie, 20 June, and Hoesch to Auswärtiges Amt, 21 June 1924: *ADAP*, ser. A, x, nos. 145, 147. Bariéty, *Les Relations franco-allemandes*, 366–7.

[111] Hoesch to Auswärtiges Amt, 28 June 1924: *ADAP*, ser. A, x, no. 160.

[112] Hoesch to Auswärtiges Amt, 15 July 1924: ibid., no. 205.

[113] Cabinet minutes, 30 June, 9 and 15 July 1924: Abramowski (ed.), *Kabinette Marx*, nos. 241, 248, 252.

[114] Bariéty, *Les Relations franco-allemandes*, 505–716; Schuker, *End of French Predominance*, 295–382.

[115] Bariéty, *Les Relations franco-allemandes*, 586–91; David Marquand, *Ramsay MacDonald* (London: Jonathan Cape, 1977), 342–51.

The bankers made it clear that they would not accept a renewal of unilateral sanctions by the French, and that the procedure of the Reparations Commission would have to be changed accordingly.

When the Germans were invited to join the conference on 2 August, they were already in a strong position.[116] Marx, Stresemann, and Luther led the German delegation. Marx immediately impressed by his sincerity—Stresemann wrote to Käte that Marx was called 'the honest man'.[117] D'Abernon recorded that Stresemann by contrast was less popular as he 'always inspires those who do not know him with the erroneous view that he is unreliable'.[118] Stresemann was somewhat apprehensive at first, but he soon wrote to Käte that he felt quite 'at home' and that he was able to follow the French and English contributions of the other delegates almost completely.[119]

The official agenda did not raise serious problems. The powers of the Reparations Commission had already been whittled away so that a renewal of sanctions would require a 'flagrant default' by Germany and a unanimous decision by the Commission or, if it was divided, arbitration by a tribunal under an American chairman.

The difficult issue was military evacuation. The French delegation knew that they would have to give way, but were divided as to what they should demand in return. Herriot indicated an interest in linking evacuation to German disarmament and a security pact. The finance minister Étienne Clémentel, on the other hand, wanted negotiations for a commercial treaty to replace the provisions of the Versailles treaty which were due to lapse in January 1925. The Germans refused to link evacuation to disarmament on the grounds that they needed a definite date to take back to the Reichstag.[120] On the other hand, they welcomed the idea of a security pact and agreed to negotiations over trade.

Stresemann tried to persuade Herriot at a private meeting that the nationalist movement in Germany had passed its peak and that military evacuation was important to win public support for the Dawes plan.[121]

---

[116] The delegation diary and supporting documents are printed in Abramowski (ed.), *Kabinette Marx*, pp. 1283–1342; see also *ADAP*, ser. A, xi.

[117] Stresemann to 'Katerchen', 6 Aug. 1924: Stresemann family papers, Berlin.

[118] *Ambassador of Peace*, iii. 90.

[119] Wolfgang Stresemann, *Mein Vater*, 311.

[120] Seeckt was also asked his opinion, which was unsurprisingly negative. Abramowski (ed.), *Kabinette Marx*, pp. 1290, 1292.

[121] Stresemann reporting on the meeting of 8 Aug. to Auswärtiges Amt, 9 Aug. 1924: *ADAP*, ser. A, xi, no. 15.

Herriot was conciliatory, but after consulting his cabinet in Paris he told Stresemann that he could agree to evacuate only a year after the implementation of the plan; to offer more would mean that his government would be overthrown. Stresemann replied that a year was 'decidedly too long'.[122] The date the Germans had in mind was 10 January 1925 when the first military occupation zone of the Rhineland, the Cologne zone occupied by the British, was due to be evacuated. The Germans feared that if the French had not withdrawn from the Ruhr by that date they might occupy the Cologne zone as they would need it to supply their troops in the Ruhr.[123] Stresemann tried to persuade Herriot that a trade treaty would depend on earlier evacuation. When that made no impression, he astutely raised the question of when the evacuation would begin, pointing out that this was as important for public opinion as when it ended. Herriot first promised to produce a plan for evacuation in stages, but when one element in his coalition threatened to withdraw he said he could not commit himself.[124]

A crisis followed, with the conference apparently deadlocked. Eventually, after MacDonald and the American ambassador in London, Frank Kellogg, had warned them that Herriot could go no further, the German delegation decided to accept the terms after extracting three further concessions.[125] Herriot agreed that the year should run from the date of the end of the conference rather than from the implementation of the plan in October; he also offered to order the evacuation of the area round Dortmund immediately and the Allies jointly agreed that the three cities—Düsseldorf, Duisburg, and Ruhrort—which had been occupied as sanctions in 1921—should be evacuated with the rest of the Ruhr. With the consent of the full cabinet in Berlin, the delegation signed the agreements subject to ratification on 16 August.

The London conference was a major success for Germany. Under the Dawes plan parts of the economy were put under international control under the general supervision of an American 'agent general', Parker Gilbert, but the advantages of the plan—return of the Ruhr and the vital foreign credits—were of far greater importance. The conference marked

---

[122] Stresemann's report on the meeting of 11 Aug. to Auswärtiges Amt, 12 Aug. 1924: *ADAP*, ser.. A, xi, no. 27.

[123] Minutes of a meeting between the German delegation and MacDonald, 12 Aug. 1924: Abramowski (ed.), *Kabinette Marx*, pp. 1308–9.

[124] Minutes of a meeting of the delegations, 13 Aug. 1924: ibid., pp. 1317–27.

[125] Minutes of meetings, 14 Aug. 1924: ibid., pp. 1329–37.

the moment when Germany again met the Allies on equal terms and began to be treated more as a partner than an ex-enemy. The Germans also won their key demand, a definite date for military evacuation, and in the end they were not required to make any concession in return. The French pursued neither the question of a commercial treaty nor that of a security pact, although the Germans were willing for negotiations on both issues. With better organization the French delegation could have achieved more.[126] Nevertheless once the French government decided that the Ruhr occupation had to be given up, it was inevitable that it would have to accept British and American ideas of how the reparations issue was to be settled. That meant abandoning coercion for cooperation with Germany exactly as Stresemann had hoped. He was now able to think in terms of how Germany's new status could be put to use to achieve further revision of the treaty in cooperation with its ex-enemies.

The Drama of Ratification

The first task was to secure the necessary majorities for the Dawes legislation in the Reichstag by 30 August, the date agreed at the conference. The attitude of the DNVP was crucial. Without at least some of its votes, there would not be the two-thirds majority necessary for the bill to change the status of the railways. Stresemann had taken care to see that their foreign affairs spokesman, the historian Otto Hoetzsch, was kept informed during the London conference.[127] Hoetzsch told ministers that the DNVP would oppose the terms because of the delay in evacuation, but he indicated that they might allow the railway bill to pass.[128] The cabinet hoped that the attraction of Dawes loans to the industrial and agricultural wings of the party would be sufficient to win it over.[129] Marx increased the pressure on the DNVP by gaining Ebert's consent to a dissolution of the Reichstag if the legislation was defeated and making this known on 27 August, the day of the vote on the second reading. Nevertheless the DNVP voted against, and the railway bill failed to win a two-thirds

---

[126] Bariéty, *Les Relations franco-allemandes*, 594–601, 635–42; Schuker, *End of French Predominance*, 295–300, 325–34.

[127] Bariéty, *Les Relations franco-allemandes*, 674.

[128] Minutes of a meeting between ministers and party leaders, 15 Aug. 1924: Abramowski (ed.), *Kabinette Marx*, no. 277.

[129] Cabinet minutes, 21 Aug. 1924: ibid., no. 285. The Reich Association of German Industry voted overwhelmingly for acceptance and the Reich Farmers' Association moved from rejection

majority. What would happen in the final and decisive vote on 29 August remained in doubt until the last moment.

Stresemann spoke twice during the debate. He described the London conference in MacDonald's words as the beginning of 'international cooperation on an equal basis' and warned that rejection would revive the spirit of Poincaré.[130] Among those who heard him in the public gallery was Theodor Eschenburg, then a first-year student in Berlin. He wrote in 1929 that Stresemann's speeches had made a deep impression on him. They were, he said, not just 'fine talking or, as they were often described, deception of the public' but the products of 'the most honest conviction, passion and an unbending will'.[131]

Stresemann also became involved in intensive lobbying of the DNVP. The American ambassador, Houghton, was persuaded to tell the DNVP leaders that there was no prospect of loans without acceptance of the plan.[132] On 23 August Stresemann was approached by two of his DVP colleagues, Curtius and Zapf, with a different kind of inducement. According to their information, the DNVP would be willing to promise enough votes for the legislation to pass in return for a declaration by the DVP that it would force a reconstruction of the cabinet in October to include the DNVP. Curtius and Zapf assured Stresemann that the Reichstag party would take no measures without his agreement—in contrast to its conduct in May. Stresemann expressed agreement with the proposal in principle, but said that he could not act behind the chancellor's back and would have first to discuss the proposal with Marx. Curtius and Zapf agreed, saying that the DNVP did not intend to bring about a change of chancellor or foreign minister—again in contrast to their attitude in May.[133]

to acceptance because agriculture needed the credits: Werner Liebe, *Die Deutschnationale Volkspartei 1918-1924* (Düsseldorf: Droste, 1956), 81-3.

[130] Reichstag speeches 23 and 28 Aug. 1924: *Verhandlungen des Reichstags*, vol. 381, pp. 779-88; 1014-20.

[131] Theodor Eschenburg, 'Stresemann und die Studenten', *Nord und Süd*, 52 (1929), 998-1003, here p. 999; extract repr. in Harttung (ed.), *Schriften*, 404-8. Eschenburg consulted Stresemann for his doctoral dissertation on Bülow's policy, and Stresemann wrote the preface for the published version. They continued to meet to discuss politics in the years 1927-9, establishing a friendship across the generation gap. Eschenburg later published a perceptive short appreciation, 'Stresemann', in Eschenburg, *Die improvisierte Demokratie*, 143-226; see also Eschenburg, *Also hören Sie mal zu*, 187-9, 196-209, 219-31.

[132] Berg, *Stresemann und die Vereinigten Staaten*, 216.

[133] Stresemann's memorandum of the conversation, 24 Aug. 1924 (Nl. 269). Richter argues that Stresemann dismissed the proposal: *Deutsche Volkspartei*, 343-4. The wording of Stresemann's memorandum is complicated but, in my view, Stresemann reiterated his objection to an

What happened next is uncertain. If Stresemann spoke to Marx on the subject there is no record of the conversation. Marx did apparently allow Jarres to conduct similar talks which did not bind him or the cabinet.[134] Both in the Reichstag and later in cabinet Marx made it clear that the government as such had not taken part in negotiations of this kind and was not committed by them.[135] However, whether with Marx's tacit consent or without it, Stresemann decided to act after the DNVP voted against the legislation in the second reading on 27 August. On 28 August, with Stresemann's approval, the DVP offered to support bringing the DNVP into the government provided it helped to pass the legislation, and the Centre Party made a similar offer.[136] Marx did not hold the incident against Stresemann, though in retrospect he described him as the prisoner of a party which was prone to intrigue.[137]

In the final vote on 29 August the DNVP split down the middle, 48 voting for the railway bill and 52 against, and the Dawes legislation was saved. Whether this result could have been achieved without any concessions to the DNVP, as Marx seemed to think, it is impossible to say. The vote had a significance beyond the Dawes plan, vital though that was. The split in the DNVP was exactly what Stresemann had been working for. If the division could be made permanent, it would take the pressure from the DVP and strengthen the chances of consolidating the Republic around the pragmatic parties of the middle ground.

Disillusionment with Politics?

Immediately after the vote in the Reichstag, Stresemann took the night train to join his family for the summer holiday on the island of Norderney in the North Sea. Relaxing here for a few days, he composed an autobiographical short story called 'The Bar', a reference to the sandbank which

immediate entry of the DNVP into government and rejected unilateral action by the DVP to bring the cabinet down, but he did not rule out an agreement with the DNVP to secure the votes for the Dawes legislation in return for a reconstruction of the cabinet in October, provided that the chancellor was informed of the proposal and, presumably, consented.

[134] Cabinet minutes, 6 Oct. 1924: Abramowski (ed.), *Kabinette Marx*, no. 317.
[135] Cabinet minutes, 1 Oct. 1924: ibid., no. 309; Hehl, *Marx*, 309.
[136] Richter, *Deutsche Volkspartei*, 344; Grathwol, *Stresemann and the DNVP*, 50. It is not clear either whether the Centre Party leaders acted with Marx's approval; Karsten Ruppert, *Im Dienst am Staat von Weimar. Das Zentrum als regierende Partei in der Weimarer Demokratie 1923–1930* (Düsseldorf, Droste, 1992), 77–9.   [137] Hehl, *Marx*, 320.

protected Norderney from the full force of the sea.[138] In the story a young friend visits and points out that the sandbank gives Norderney a subdued character, unlike the outer islands where the waves were wild and free. Stresemann was reminded of the constraints of his career as a successful politician, compared to the spontaneity and idealism of his youth. The idealism, he wrote, had been worn away by the need to compromise until he no longer felt that he was the same person. The effect of rising above his social origins and the shock of rejection by his first love had both contributed to a sense of disorientation. He took a perverse pleasure in the harsh reality of life and developed an urge to compromise:

His face became often only a mask adapted to his surroundings. Some called him unprincipled but those who looked more deeply detected an element of cynicism which arose from seeing that the ideas of public life served . . . mainly as a cover for the interests of individuals.

He dreamed of escaping to a private existence of reading and writing and dreaming, but he was held back by all the ties of his career; as he gazed at the sandbank, it seemed to laugh at him.

One should not read too much into an escapist sketch written on holiday by a middle-aged politician (Stresemann was now 46), who had just survived a punishing year. Nevertheless the tone of disillusionment which runs through the story is interesting, particularly since he had just won a great victory. Part of the explanation may be a reaction to the negotiations with the DNVP and the undertaking given with his authority to bring them into the government. This was bound to be seen as unprincipled, given his previous support for a great coalition. The reference in the story to ideas serving as a cover for interests was particularly appropriate to the DNVP. According to Wolfgang Stresemann, his father often said that he would much rather work with the SPD than the DNVP.[139] 'The Bar' was a way of expressing his frustration at the compromises required of a successful politician.

Stresemann already felt reservations about the commitment to the DNVP. He wrote from Norderney to the leader of the DVP in the Prussian Landtag, von Campe, saying that the question of bringing the DNVP into government was still a long way from solution.[140] He

---

[138] Nl. 314: Bernhard (ed.), *Vermächtnis*, i. 549–53.   [139] *Mein Vater*, 324.

[140] Campe had suggested that a change in the Prussian coalition should be used as a bargaining counter with the DNVP to create a 'bourgeois bloc' in the Reich. Campe to Stresemann, 5

argued that the commitment given by the DVP had been based on the 'self-evident assumption' that those who voted for the Dawes plan would control the party. However, since the vote one DNVP constituency association after another had come out in favour of the 'no' voters and the party leaders, Hergt and Westarp, were allowing themselves to be fêted as 'no' voters. This, he suggested, would undermine support for the 'so-called bourgeois bloc' in the DDP and the left wing of the Centre Party. He added that he had always been opposed to a 'bourgeois bloc' and they should find a better term, one that made it clear that what they were planning was 'a new tactical, parliamentary position not a change of conviction'.

Membership of the League of Nations?

Stresemann cut short his holiday on 11 September and returned to Berlin, abandoning a previously planned visit to the spa town of Bad Wildungen to consult a specialist about a kidney complaint.[141] A furore had arisen over the question of how to notify the Allies of a declaration about war guilt which the government had promised the DNVP it would make at the London conference. In fact Marx had written MacDonald a letter about the matter after the conference. In reply MacDonald warned that it would be counter-productive to make a declaration, and mentioned that he hoped to bring about Germany's admission to the League of Nations.[142] The DNVP again pressed for a declaration in the ratification debate, and the cabinet agreed and issued an appropriate statement promising to notify other governments.[143]

The reaction from abroad was so hostile, however, that State Secretary Maltzan—in the absence of Marx and Stresemann on holiday—delayed notification, fearing that it might upset the return of the Ruhr to German control.[144] The situation became more delicate when on 4 September MacDonald spoke strongly in favour of Germany's admission to the

---

Sept. (Nl. 90) and Stresemann's reply, 8 Sept. 1924 (Nl. 15); extract in Harttung (ed.), *Schriften*, 234–6.

[141] Bernhard (ed.), *Vermächtnis*, i. 561; Wolfgang Stresemann, *Mein Vater*, 321.

[142] Marx to MacDonald, 16 Aug., and MacDonald's reply, 28 Aug. 1924: Abramowski (ed.), *Kabinette Marx*, pp. 1340–2.

[143] Ibid., no. 290.

[144] Undated memorandum of the Auswärtiges Amt [10 Sept. 1924], ibid., no. 298.

League, referring to the 'menacing, vacant chair in our midst'. The SPD pressed for a positive response and there was newspaper speculation about a rift between Marx and Stresemann both over the war guilt question and the League.[145] Stresemann was accused of intriguing with the DNVP to bring the government down.[146]

Immediately on his return, Stresemann tried to repair the damage by giving journalists a detailed account of what had occurred.[147] He made it clear that the negotiations with the DNVP over war guilt had been endorsed by the whole cabinet. As for the League, he pointed out that the question had not been raised by the British government in London and that Germany had not yet received an invitation. It could agree only if it was treated as a great power and given a permanent seat on the League council. Not for the last time, Stresemann trusted too much in the power of his eloquence. Instead of calming the storm, his frankness fuelled a new round of speculation about differences in the cabinet. On 14 September he noted in his diary 'Very depressed at the effect of the press conference. More reserve.'[148]

There were in fact no important differences between Marx and Stresemann over the conduct of foreign policy. The notification of the declaration on war guilt was postponed and the cabinet, meeting with Ebert, agreed to Stresemann's proposal that they should express their willingness to join the League provided a number of conditions were satisfied.[149] Stresemann saw advantages in membership in giving Germany a voice over questions that fell under the League, such as the rights of minorities, and the Saar (which had been placed under League trusteeship for fifteen years after which a plebiscite would be held to determine its future), and the great political questions of security and disarmament. He also saw some disadvantages: the impression that they were voluntarily recognizing the Versailles treaty and the possibility of Germany being involved, against its interests, in collective action by the League against the Soviet Union.

---

[145] Christoph M. Kimmich, *Germany and the League of Nations* (Chicago: The University of Chicago Press, 1976), 54-5.

[146] Stresemann's report to the cabinet, 15 Sept. 1924: Abramowski (ed.), *Kabinette Marx*, no. 301.

[147] Bernhard (ed.), *Vermächtnis*, i. 563-9.

[148] Ibid. 570.

[149] Technically this was a meeting of the Council of Ministers (Ministerrat) because it was chaired by Ebert as head of state, exercising the right of the Reich president to be directly involved in a decision which could affect Germany's position in international law. Minutes of

The cabinet decided to circulate the members of the League council with a memorandum setting out Germany's conditions for joining the organization. These were a permanent seat on the council, exemption from the obligation under article 16 of the League covenant to take part in sanctions in view of Germany's disarmed status (in fact to protect its position towards the Soviet Union), not being required to accept war guilt again, and being given the right to become a colonial power in the form of the mandate system (by which other powers had been allocated the former German colonies). These conditions effectively buried the issue of Germany's admission since the other powers made it clear that Germany could not be exempted from the obligations of the covenant.[150]

Bringing the DNVP into Government

By the end of September 1924 Stresemann had come round to the view that the DNVP should be brought into government.[151] It probably suited him quite well that the question of German entry into the League was deferred in the interim since it would be unpopular with the DNVP. The main reason for Stresemann's new attitude was the desire to protect the coalition, and in particular the DVP, from the kind of attack which the DNVP was able to mount in opposition. The future agenda of foreign policy—how to satisfy the French need for security and achieve the evacuation of the Rhineland, entry into the League, disarmament—would offer the DNVP constant opportunities for criticism. Stresemann believed that they would be less trouble as part of the government.[152] He also saw their inclusion as a way of influencing the struggle for power within the DNVP, following its division in the Dawes vote. He told the cabinet that the party was serious about clearing out its radical wing and that if this led to a split, it would be for the good.[153]

Marx disagreed with Stresemann. He distrusted the DNVP and thought that allowing them into the government would adversely affect

the meeting, 29 Sept. 1924. Abramowski (ed.), *Kabinette Marx*, nos. 304a and 304b. For a detailed account of German policy, see Joachim Wintzer, 'Deutschland und der Völkerbund 1918–1926', unpublished Ph.D., Heidelberg, 1998.

[150] Kimmich, *Germany and the League*, 57–61.

[151] Cabinet minutes, 1 Oct. 1924: Abramowski (ed.), *Kabinette Marx*, no. 309.

[152] Minutes of a meeting of ministers with the coalition parties, 10 Oct., and cabinet minutes, 15 Oct. 1924: ibid., nos. 324, 329.

[153] Cabinet minutes, 6 Oct. 1924, and 15 and 16 Oct. 1924: ibid., nos. 317, 329, 334.

relations with France and Britain.[154] When the DVP formally demanded that the DNVP be brought in, Marx countered by opening negotiations with both the SPD and the DNVP. These negotiations quickly failed because of the mutual hostility between the two parties and Marx then agreed to negotiations with the DNVP alone, which accepted the government's programme. However, the DDP rejected an extension of the coalition to the DNVP. Although negotiations continued, Marx and the Centre Party were unhappy at the prospect of coalition with only the DVP and the DNVP. It would represent a marked shift to the right and would also have only a narrow majority. The DNVP did not help matters by demanding more ministerial posts than Marx offered and proposing for office two of its members who had voted against the Dawes legislation. Negotiations broke down and on 20 October the cabinet decided to ask for a dissolution in the hope that elections would break the deadlock. Ebert agreed, and elections were set for 7 December.

Stresemann would have preferred to avoid new elections. At first sight, this is surprising. The government parties seemed to have a good chance of capitalizing on the Dawes success and recovering ground they had lost in the May elections. In particular, the DVP appeared to be in a position to profit from the disarray of the DNVP. Stresemann sensed dangers, however. He feared that elections would divide the country once again between republican and anti-republican blocs and that the DNVP would reunite on an opposition platform.[155] Although he did not say so, he was probably also worried at the prospect of a shift to the left, with the SPD recovering its vote from the KPD and drawing the DDP and the Centre Party into coalition. That would face the DVP with the awkward dilemma of the great coalition or, at worst, a return to opposition as in 1919.

Stresemann therefore pitched his campaign in a moderate and statesmanlike key. He presented the DVP as the party which wanted to overcome the divisions of the past and consolidate the state around the Dawes plan.[156] He was conciliatory towards the DNVP, arguing that having been brought to accept realities it should be allowed a share in government. The reason for the political stability of Britain, he argued, was that every

[154] Hehl, *Marx*, 312–16.

[155] Cabinet minutes, 15 Oct. 1924: Abramowski (ed.), *Kabinette Marx*, no. 329.

[156] 'Politische Umschau', *Deutsche Stimmen*, 36/20, 20 Oct. 1924; 'Warum Erweiterung nach rechts', *Die Zeit*, 4/248, 21 Oct. 1924; speech to the party conference, 14 Nov. 1924: BAK, R 45 II/29, published as *Nationale Realpolitik. Rede des Reichsaußenministers Dr. Stresemann auf dem 6. Parteitag der Deutschen Volkspartei in Dortmund am 14. November 1924* (Berlin: Staatspolitischer Verlag, 1924).

party had experience of government. If the Republic excluded the DNVP from office, it would be making the same mistake as the empire had made towards the SPD. He criticized the SPD and DDP for trying to revive a left bloc of republicans, saying that this would be just as divisive as the right bloc of monarchists. Instead he offered the alternative of all consti-tutional bourgeois parties uniting behind a foreign policy of 'national realpolitik'.

'National realpolitik' was an attempt to build a bridge to the DNVP. Stresemann defined it rather awkwardly as a policy—free of the illusions of both right and left—'which is conscious of the limitations on our power, which seeks understanding and peace because we need both, but which does not try to bring about peace by creating an atmosphere but sees the concept of understanding as a mutual process of conciliation achieved by conscious, tough effort'.[157] In seeking to distance himself from the SPD, Stresemann also argued that given the financial stringency which the Dawes plan would make necessary, the SPD would probably prefer to remain in opposition.

The SPD and DDP naturally attacked Stresemann as an opportunist who had betrayed his ideal of the great coalition. Stresemann was sensitive on this score, saying with some exaggeration that he felt like a St Sebastian shot through with political arrows. He claimed that the great coalition had been brought down by the SPD. With more justification he argued that, rather than the DVP moving to the right, the DNVP had been brought to accept the Dawes plan. He admitted that the DVP had made a tactical shift in accordance with 'parliamentary possibilities', but he rejected the charge that he was unprincipled. Instead he presented himself as continu-ously ahead of his time: opposing the revolution in 1919, for the great coalition in 1921, and in favour of the Dawes plan as soon as it was announced. He argued that bringing the DNVP into government would be an act of statesmanship. No party, he said, had more reason than they to dislike the DNVP: 'But one cannot make foreign policy or domestic policy with sentimentality. Here too it is a question of adopting realpoli-tik, it is a question of what the policy of state requires.'[158]

There is no reason to doubt that Stresemann's motives were to create a broad front behind his foreign policy and consolidate the Republic by giving the DNVP a stake in it. He had not relapsed into the anti-republicanism of 1919.[159] As he pointed out, the DNVP had become the

---

[157] Speech to the party conference, 14 Nov. 1924: BAK, R 45 II/29.   [158] Ibid.
[159] Turner, *Stresemann*, 175.

strongest bourgeois party, representing the greater part of the Protestant rural areas, important business interests, part of the working class, and 'above all' a large part of the intelligentsia and the urban middle class. It had far outgrown the old Conservative Party.[160] In recognizing this fact, Stresemann was also revising his earlier assumption that the Conservative Party would suffer a decline in support because of its hostility to democracy. If the groups it represented could be brought to pragmatic acceptance of the Republic that would clearly represent an important gain. Given the ideological barriers that had to be overcome and the social and economic problems caused by inflation, it would not be easy to win over such groups. The only way was to offer, as Stresemann suggested, a policy of 'calm, rational development' in which the DNVP could share.[161]

With the benefit of hindsight, a better strategy might have been to go all out to defeat the DNVP in elections held immediately after the Dawes vote.[162] Stresemann himself wrote that it would have been possible to inflict a crushing defeat on them then, but that the potential for renewed opposition would have remained.[163] Characteristically he hoped for a more permanent gain from a policy of conciliation. But by the time the elections were held in December, the DNVP had been able to patch up a united front to present to the electorate without resolving its internal divisions over participation in government.[164]

Stresemann spent three exhausting weeks campaigning across the length and breadth of Germany. The results were disappointing. The DVP improved its share of the vote by only 0.9 per cent, gaining six seats to bring its total in the Reichstag to fifty-one. There were again large regional variations: in the Palatinate the DVP vote rose from 16.3 per cent in May to 23.6 per cent but in the Berlin region it again declined to a miserable 4.9 per cent.[165] The other government parties also made small gains. The SPD as expected did well, displacing the DNVP as the largest party with 131 seats. The surprise of the election, however, was that the

---

[160] 'Dr. Stresemann über die Regierungserweiterung nach rechts', *Die Zeit*, 4/309, 28 Dec. 1924.

[161] Speech to the party conference, 14 Nov. 1924: BAK, R 45 II/29.

[162] Eyck (at the time an active member of the DDP) argues that the elections should have been held even before the Dawes vote, but that would have endangered the legislation. Erich Eyck, *A History of the Weimar Republic*, Eng. Edn., 2 vols. (Cambridge, Mass.: Harvard University Press, 1962), i. 313–14; Turner, *Stresemann*, 170.

[163] 'Politische Umschau', *Deutsche Stimmen*, 36/20, 20 Oct. 1924.

[164] Liebe, *Deutschnationale Volkspartei*, 97–8.

[165] Milatz, *Wähler*, 100; Richter, *Deutsche Volkspartei*, 356–8.

DNVP managed to increase its representation slightly to 111 (including eight elected on the Landbund list). The clear losers were the extremes: the KPD from sixty-two to forty-five and the NSDAP more drastically from thirty-two to fourteen. In addition, as in May, some 2 million voters or 8 per cent of the electorate supported middle-class and regional splinter groups.

The election did not clarify the question of how a new government was to be formed. The two main majority combinations, the great coalition or a coalition from the DDP to the DNVP, remained blocked by the DVP and the DDP respectively.[166] The DVP decided to push for a government with the DNVP and the Centre Party, believing that the DDP would join subsequently. Stresemann told the cabinet that they needed the DNVP to share responsibility for foreign policy and the effects of revaluation.[167] The DVP also thought it would be easier to work with the DNVP than the SPD over fiscal policy and the new tariffs, which would become possible in January 1925 when Germany regained its freedom under the Versailles treaty to negotiate trade treaties with other states.[168] Stresemann made it clear that the DVP was not prepared to continue with the existing coalition and Marx submitted the resignation of the cabinet on 15 December.

There followed a series of fruitless attempts to break the deadlock. Stresemann was asked by Ebert to form a government but he had to give up when the Centre Party refused to join a coalition with the DVP and DNVP. Marx then tried again, but he was unable to break the deadlock or to recruit individual 'personalities' who would be acceptable to the DNVP. The DNVP insisted that the Prussian government should be reconstructed first and the DVP supported this demand by itself withdrawing from the great coalition in Prussia.

At Stresemann's suggestion Ebert turned to Luther, who eventually succeeded in putting together an 'above party' cabinet in which the DNVP, DVP, Centre Party, and BVP were all represented without being formally bound to support it.[169] Martin Schiele, the newly elected chair-

---

[166] Technically there existed a narrow right-wing majority even without the DDP (consisting of the DNVP, DVP, Centre, BVP, and Landbund). A majority of the Centre Reichstag Party was willing to contemplate such a coalition, but Marx resisted and the party then reversed its stance. Ruppert, *Im Dienst*, 79–85; Richter, *Deutsche Volkspartei*, 359.

[167] Cabinet minutes, 10 Dec. 1924: Abramowski (ed.), *Kabinette Marx*, no. 368.

[168] Minutes of a meeting between Marx and DVP representatives, 18 Dec. 1924: ibid., no. 374.

[169] Karl-Heinz Minuth (ed.), *Die Kabinette Luther I und II* (Boppard: Harald Boldt Verlag, 1977), pp. xix–xxiv; Luther, *Politiker ohne Partei*, 315–18.

man of the DNVP Reichstag party, a leader of the party's agrarian wing and a moderate, became minister of the interior. Stresemann and Brauns continued in office representing the DVP and the Centre Party. Luther also gained the reluctant consent of the DDP for Gessler to remain as minister of defence. Other portfolios were distributed among senior officials who were known to support the parties represented in the cabinet. Stresemann had succeed in engineering the shift to the right—D'Abernon noted that he was regarded as 'the politician behind the throne'—but it was an extremely fragile construction.[170] The government obtained a vote of approval from the Reichstag on 22 January only thanks to the abstention of the DDP, while the support of the DNVP remained conditional and precarious.[171]

The Proposal for a Security Pact

It was in these circumstances that Stresemann took the initiative which led ultimately to the Locarno pact.[172] His hand was forced by fear that the international situation was again changing to Germany's disadvantage. The twin problems of French security and the control of German disarmament had led to decisions at the League which Stresemann saw as a setback, because they were made without German participation. In September 1924 the League council prepared to take over responsibility for inspecting German disarmament from the Allied Military Control Commission and accepted a plan which would have allowed a permanent staff to be maintained in the demilitarized zones of the Rhineland. In October, at MacDonald's suggestion, the League Assembly adopted the so-called Geneva Protocol which strengthened the provisions of the covenant for arbitration of disputes and sanctions against aggression. It also provided for demilitarized zones under permanent control. Stresemann feared that such control might allow the French to remain in the Rhineland and revive the idea of a neutral Rhineland state.[173]

---

[170] *Ambassador of Peace*, iii. 127.

[171] In the debate Breitscheid for the SPD and Koch-Weser for the DDP made fun of Stresemann for switching coalitions, and Breitscheid predicted that Stresemann would end by adopting the DNVP's foreign policy rather than the DNVP adopting his. *Verhandlungen des Reichstags*, vol. 384, pp. 98–108, 139–46. The government's declaration of policy was approved by 247 to 160 with thirty-nine abstentions: ibid. 231–4.

[172] Krüger, *Aussenpolitik*, 269–79.

[173] Minutes of a meeting of Luther, Stresemann, and Schiele, 17 Mar. 1925: Minuth (ed.), *Kabinette Luther*, no. 50; Kimmich, *Germany and the League*, 61–2.

When the Conservatives returned to power in Britain in November 1924, it became evident that Britain would not ratify the Geneva Protocol. The new foreign secretary, Austen Chamberlain, was known to be pro-French, however, and he was prepared to offer France a mutual defence pact in place of the Geneva Protocol.[174] In addition, it became known in December that the Allies did not intend to evacuate the first of the Rhineland zones on the prescribed date, 10 January, on the grounds that Germany had failed to comply with the disarmament clauses of the treaty. These developments convinced Stresemann that Germany was becoming once more merely 'the object of the policy of the others'.[175]

The obvious means to counter the danger of renewed isolation was for Germany to bring forward proposals of its own for European security. The subject had been considered in the Auswärtiges Amt since the end of 1922 and both Cuno and Stresemann had offered German support for an international guarantee of the Rhine frontier.[176] The problem of how to include Poland in a security system without giving up German claims to frontier revision had also been considered.[177] When D'Abernon, who was himself opposed to an Anglo-French pact, suggested to Schubert on 29 December that Germany would do well to revive its earlier proposals, Schubert was ready to respond.[178] As head of the department concerned with Britain and the United States, he had been closely involved in the earlier discussions and had recently succeeded Maltzan as secretary of state. With Stresemann he believed that the priority of German foreign policy lay in its relations with the Western powers. Writing of the German memorandum which followed in January 1925, D'Abernon described Schubert as 'the principal author... or , at any rate, the principal thinker behind it'.[179]

The German memorandum which, on D'Abernon's suggestion, was communicated first through him to the British government on 20 January and then in a slightly different form to the French on 9 February, was

[174] Anne Orde, *Great Britain and International Security 1920–1926* (London: Royal Historical Society, 1978), 68–98.

[175] Cabinet minutes, 20 Oct. 1924: Abramowski (ed.), *Kabinette Marx*, no. 376.

[176] See above, pp. 200–1, 218.

[177] Peter Krüger, 'Der Deutsch-Polnische Schiedsvertrag im Rahmen der deutschen Sicherheitsinitiative von 1925', *Historische Zeitschrift*, 230 (1980), 580–6.

[178] Memorandum by Schubert, 29 Dec. 1924: *ADAP*, ser. A, xi, no. 259; Angela Kaiser, *Lord D'Abernon und die englische Deutschlandpolitik 1920–1926* (Frankfurt: Peter Lang, 1989), 333–43.

[179] D'Abernon to Chamberlain, 20 Mar. 1925: *DBFP*, 1st ser. xxvii, no. 263.

carefully constructed to be as attractive as possible to each recipient.[180] First, it suggested along the lines of the Cuno note a general guarantee of the states concerned in the Rhineland not to go to war with each other, with the United States acting as trustee, and backed by a comprehensive arbitration treaty. To anticipate the objection that Poland would be put at risk, it stated that Germany would be willing to sign 'arbitration treaties providing for the peaceful settlement of juridical and political conflicts with all other states as well'. Reflecting Schubert's view that a general guarantee of the Rhineland states would not be specific enought to satisfy France, the memorandum proposed 'a pact expressly guaranteeing the present territorial status on the Rhine'. The memorandum also declared Germany's willingness to consider other possible solutions and concluded that, given 'a desire for guarantees for peaceful evolution in all the states concerned, a secure treaty foundation for them cannot be difficult to find'.

The memorandum was a remarkable document. D'Abernon was impressed with its 'vast importance'.[181] It had an immediate tactical purpose. As Stresemann explained to Hoesch, the danger of an Anglo-French pact 'made it necessary for us to take the initiative'.[182] Nevertheless it was a bold move. As Stresemann pointed out in the same letter, it contained a voluntary renunciation of claims to Alsace-Lorraine. On the eastern frontiers, Hoesch was authorized to tell Herriot that Germany could not accept the same 'solemn recognition' of them as in the west, but the reference to arbitration treaties had been made with Poland in mind and such treaties 'offer in practice a thoroughly secure guarantee for the preservation of peace'. On the face of it, Germany was committing itself to what Stresemann later called in the Reichstag 'a peace offensive on the

---

[180] Memorandum by Schubert, 20 Jan. 1925; undated memorandum by Stresemann; Stresemann to Hoesch, 5 Feb. 1925: *ADAP*, ser. A, xii, nos. 37, 64, 67. D'Abernon to Chamberlain, 20 Jan. 1925: *DBFP*, 1st ser. xxvii, no. 189.

[181] *Ambassador of Peace*, iii. 127. D'Abernon was also of course indicating the importance of his own role in the event. His importance has been questioned by Gaynor Johnson, '"Das Kind" Revisited: Lord D'Abernon and German Security Policy, 1922–1925', *Contemporary European History*, 9 (2000), 209–24. Johnson argues convincingly that D'Abernon's main contribution was to have given the impression in Berlin that the British government would consider the German proposals favourably, at a time when Chamberlain was in fact giving priority to closer relations with France. In my view, however, she goes too far in seeing D'Abernon as manipulated by Schubert in a situation where Germany alone was pursuing a clear strategy and was not prepared to compromise its relations with the Soviet Union in the interests of détente with the West.

[182] Stresemann to Hoesch, 5 Feb. 1925: *ADAP*, ser. A, xii, no. 67.

grand scale' in order to establish its credentials to be treated as a partner by the other great powers in the solution of European problems.[183]

The memorandum was also a bold move in domestic politics. It was drawn up in great secrecy while Germany was between governments. Luther was informed of its contents and gave his approval on his appointment as chancellor, immediately before the memorandum was given to D'Abernon.[184] Both the British and French governments were asked to keep it strictly confidential. Stresemann hoped to win their support before it became public to maximize the chance of overcoming the opposition both in Germany and in the other countries concerned.[185] In Germany the situation was particularly delicate since the DNVP, which Stresemann had finally succeeded in bringing into the government, was likely to be hostile.

Chamberlain's initial reaction to the German memorandum was unfavourable. He suspected that it was a manoeuvre to divide Britain from France and he wanted to pursue the Anglo-French pact first.[186] Stresemann was disappointed, feeling that the historic importance of the German proposals had not been recognized—and also that he had been misled by D'Abernon—and he threatened to drop them.[187] However, opposition within the British cabinet to the idea of an Anglo-French pact led Chamberlain to consider more sympathetically the proposal for a multilateral pact including Germany. Chamberlain's change of front forced the French cabinet to take it seriously as well and by the middle of March it had become the focus of diplomatic activity.

Germany was asked to clarify its attitude to its eastern frontiers and to entry to the League of Nations.[188] Chamberlain was baffled by the fine distinctions in the German position on the Polish frontier. Germany was not willing to recognize the frontier, even in the form of a non-aggression pact with respect to it. This was the difference it drew between the Rhine frontier and the east. It was willing to sign an arbitration treaty with

---

[183] Reichstag speech, 22 July 1925: Zwoch (ed.), *Reichstagsreden*, 217.

[184] Note by Schubert, initialled by Stresemann, 19 Jan. 1925: *ADAP*, ser. A, xii, no. 37, n. 2.

[185] Stresemann to Hoesch, 5 Feb. 1925: ibid., no. 67; Stresemann's briefing of German journalists, 7 Mar. 1925: Bernhard (ed.), *Vermächtnis*, ii. 64–5.

[186] Orde, *Great Britain*, 85–9.

[187] D'Abernon, *Ambassador of Peace*, iii. 132–4; Kaiser, *Lord D'Abernon*, 348–9; also the graphic account by a well-informed journalist, Vallentin, *Stresemann*, 171–2.

[188] Crowe to D'Abernon, 9 Mar., and D'Abernon's reply, 13 Mar. 1925: *DBFP*, 1st ser. xxvii, nos. 230, 231. Memorandum by Luther of a discussion with D'Abernon, 10 Mar. 1925: Minuth (ed.), *Kabinette Luther*, no. 43. Memorandum by Stresemann of a meeting with de Margerie, 16 Mar. 1925: *ADAP*, ser. A, xii, no. 169.

Poland which it claimed would in practice eliminate the danger of war, although the form of treaty which the Germans envisaged did not include binding arbitration on frontier issues but only a conciliation procedure.[189] As Schubert had explained to D'Abernon this left open the theoretical possibility of war if either side rejected the results of the conciliation procedure.[190] Chamberlain understandably wanted to know whether the Germans were renouncing the use of force to bring about frontier revision in the east or not, and was inclined to blame the hapless German ambassador in London, Friedrich Sthamer, when he could not get a clear answer.[191] Between them, Schubert and D'Abernon managed to parry the question and send a soothing reply.[192]

D'Abernon, according to his own account, took advantage of a visit by Augustus John to Berlin and arranged for him to paint a portrait of Stresemann. It gave D'Abernon the opportunity to explain to Stresemann 'the larger possibilities' to which the pact might lead, without Stresemann's customary interruptions since John forced him to remain still and silent. Whether Stresemann needed re-convincing or not, by the end of March Schubert and D'Abernon could congratulate themselves that 'the child', as they called the pact proposals, had survived an awkward birth.[193]

Stresemann had already been forced by Chamberlain's public reference to the German proposals to defend them at a press conference on 7 March.[194] He admitted that the proposals meant the voluntary renunciation of Alsace-Lorraine, 'but I believe no one could have any doubt that the German people—either now or in the future—would not follow a government which undertook a war of aggression against France with the goal of reconquering Alsace-Lorraine'. He then made the point, which he

---

[189] Poland too had objections to submitting its frontiers to arbitration since it did not wish to suggest that there could be any question about their status; memorandum by Stresemann of a meeting with de Margerie, 16 Mar. 1925: *ADAP*, ser. A, xii, no. 169.

[190] Schubert to D'Abernon, 22 Jan. 1925: ibid., no. 37, n. 5. Krüger argues forcefully that the arbitration treaty was intended by Schubert to be an instrument of purely peaceful revision: 'Der Deutsch-Polnische Schiedsvertrag', 577-612.

[191] Chamberlain to D'Abernon, 25 and 26 Mar. 1925, following an incident in the House of Commons where Sthamer asked to see Chamberlain to correct a statement Chamberlain had just made on the German position: *DBFP*, 1st ser. xxvii, nos. 269, 273.

[192] Memoranda by Schubert, 26-8 Mar. 1925: *ADAP*, ser. A, xii, nos. 201-2, 206, 212-13; Schubert to Sthamer, 30 Mar. 1925: ibid., no. 215; D'Abernon to Chamberlain, 28 Mar. 1925: *DBFP*, 1st ser. xxvii, no. 274.

[193] D'Abernon, *Ambassador of Peace*, iii, 15-16, 152-3; Kaiser, *Lord D'Abernon*, 358-62. See frontispiece.

[194] Bernhard (ed.), *Vermächtnis*, ii. 64-73.

always regarded as central and which showed the lasting effect of the Ruhr occupation on him, that the pact would also guarantee Germany against France: 'The essence of European politics in this connection is the question to whom does the Rhineland belong; in this way it would be decided that the Rhineland belongs to Germany.'

On the eastern frontiers, Stresemann explained the position on the arbitration treaties thus: 'What we cannot do is to accept an official guarantee of the frontiers in the east because we must reserve the possibility of solving these matters by peaceful methods.' He suggested that they could make use of article 19 of the League covenant which referred to altering treaties 'which have become inapplicable', and he added that a considerable body of European opinion was beginning to wonder whether the arrangements in the east had not already become 'inapplicable'.

Stresemann developed similar arguments to the foreign affairs committee of the Reichstag and in print.[195] He was above all concerned to show that the security pact was in Germany's national interest. To Maltzan, who had become German ambassador in Washington, he wrote robustly, 'Our policy over the security pact offer was undoubtedly right, secures the Rhineland from the consequences of a French policy of persecution, has burst the entente apart and opens new possibilities for the East.'[196]

Despite his efforts Stresemann was unable to overcome the reservations of the DNVP. Schiele warned on 17 March that his party felt that the memorandum had gone 'very far' and they missed guarantees for what Germany would gain in return.[197] The DNVP made a clumsy attempt to divide Luther from Stresemann, implying that he had acted independently of the chancellor as well as the cabinet. Luther immediately rejected the criticism and forced the DNVP to make a partial retraction.[198] At a further meeting Stresemann was pressed to give details of what he saw as the gains for his policy. He replied as usual that it would safeguard Germany against France. Beyond that he was able to suggest only that it would facilitate the evacuation of the Cologne zone and the Ruhr in August and perhaps shorten the occupation of the remaining zones, that it would help to change the climate of opinion towards frontier revision in

---

[195] Speech to the Reichstag foreign affairs committee, 11 Mar. (Nl. 277); article in *Kölnische Zeitung*, 13 Mar. 1925: Bernhard (ed.), *Vermächtnis*, ii. 74–81.

[196] Stresemann to Maltzan, 7 Apr. 1925: *ADAP*, ser. A, xii, no. 238.

[197] Minutes of a meeting between Luther, Stresemann, and Schiele, 17 Mar. 1925: Minuth (ed.), *Kabinette Luther*, no. 50.

[198] Minutes of a meeting with DNVP leaders, 22 Mar. 1925: ibid., no. 55; Grathwol, *Stresemann and the DNVP*, 70–5.

the east, and that German entry into the League would give it new influence. This was not enough to satisfy Hergt, who objected that Germany would be voluntarily accepting parts of the treaty of Versailles for the first time and seriously weakening its position on the eastern frontiers.[199]

The Election of Hindenburg as Reich President

On 28 February Ebert died suddenly. This was a blow to Stresemann, who had come to respect Ebert, recognizing in him someone like himself from a modest social background, who supported the great coalition and worked to bridge the gap between republicans and anti-republicans.[200] Shortly before Ebert's death, a court ruled that his attempt to mediate in a strike of Berlin munition workers in January 1918 was, in a legal sense, 'treason'. On Stresemann's suggestion the cabinet presented Ebert the following day with a statement of support, saying they were convinced that he had always acted in the best interests of the fatherland.[201]

Given the critical stage of the security pact negotiations Stresemann was above all anxious that Ebert should be succeeded by someone who would continue to support his foreign policy.[202] When it appeared likely that Gessler would be nominated as the candidate of the bourgeois parties Stresemann intervened to block him, arguing that Gessler's election would cause problems with France because he was considered too close to Seeckt. Stresemann had to impose his authority on the DVP Reichstag party, which had decided in favour of Gessler. Stresemann persuaded the Reich committee, which had been summoned to decide on the DVP's choice of candidate, to nominate Jarres instead.[203]

[199] Minutes of a meeting with DNVP leaders, 2 Apr. 1925: Minuth (ed.), *Kabinette Luther*, no. 62.

[200] His appreciation of Ebert was first published in *Die Zeit*, 5/80, 1 Mar. 1925. repr. in Bernhard (ed.), *Vermächtnis*, ii. 37–43. In a subsequent article he wrote of the snobbish scorn at Ebert's origins and added, 'It is a fine feeling to be the heir of a great family tradition, but the great forces that moved world history have often come from those who were the first of their family not the last': *Deutsche Stimmen*, 37/5, 5 Mar. 1925.

[201] Note of the discussion in cabinet, 23 Dec. 1924: Abramowski (ed.), *Kabinette Marx*, no. 379.

[202] Under article 45 of the Constitution, the Reich president represented the Reich in international law, concluded treaties, and appointed ambassadors. In practice these rights were exercised on the advice of the cabinet, but they gave the president the right to be informed and to take part in major decisions. For instance, the president chaired meetings of the cabinet when matters such as joining the League of Nations or acceptance of the Locarno treaties were discussed. See above, p. 295, n.149.

[203] Turner, *Stresemann*, 191–201; Bernhard (ed.), *Vermächtnis*, ii. 43–61. There is an excellent account of these events in Richter, *Deutsche Volkspartei*, 366–89. Jarres had earlier been the

Stresemann's action caused deep resentment in the Reichstag party and even more in the DDP.[204] His objections to Gessler dated back to his chancellorship when Gessler had stood very close to Seeckt. Since then, Gessler had faithfully defended Seeckt's obstructive tactics over disarmament.[205] Stresemann probably feared that he would continue to support Seeckt in opposition to his foreign policy. Stresemann also had doubts of a more personal kind. He mentioned at home that Gessler seemed curiously distracted during cabinet meetings and passed the time reading French novels.[206]

However reasonable Stresemann's fears, his tactics rebounded on him. Gessler might have been able to unite voters from all the bourgeois parties and win on the first round. Jarres, however, faced alternative candidates from the Centre and DDP, as well as from the SPD and the radical extremes. He polled the most votes —38 per cent—but it was not enough to prevent the election going to a second round. The SPD, DDP, and Centre Party then united behind Marx, which prompted the DNVP to approach Hindenburg. Whatever objections Stresemann had felt towards Gessler were multiplied several times at the thought of Hindenburg as Reich president. He was also concerned at the reaction to the news abroad, particularly in the United States on whom, he noted in his diary, 'our fate depends'.[207]

Stresemann hoped that Hindenburg would withdraw in favour of Jarres. Instead Jarres withdrew and Hindenburg confirmed his candidacy. Stresemann now faced a dilemma. If he opposed Hindenburg it would

preferred choice of an independent committee set up to find a common candidate for the bourgeois parties, but under pressure from the DDP and Centre it was willing to choose Gessler.

[204] Koch-Weser accused him of destroying a united front 'from personal enmity' towards Gessler, and Theodor Heuss also thought that Stresemann's arguments were bogus. Koch-Weser's diary notes, c.15 Mar. 1925: BAK, Nl. Koch-Weser, 32; Heuss, *Erinnerungen*, 247–98. Gessler's account of the incident, written after the Second World War, was notably free of bitterness: *Reichswehrpolitik*, 334–8. Möllers suggests that a more important factor than Stresemann's opposition was the desire of the Centre Party and the DVP—as represented by their constituency parties—to nominate a candidate of their own: *Geßler*, 296–304.

[205] Cabinet minutes 20 and 25 June, 17 July, 26 Aug., 23 Sept. 1924: Abramowski (ed.), *Kabinette Marx*, nos. 229, 234, 253, 256, 286, 304a; Salewski, *Entwaffnung und Militärkontrolle*, 241–70.

[206] Gessler was also considered to be under the influence of the headstrong personality of Katharina von Oheimb, a former member of the DVP Reichstag party who ran a political salon in Berlin and resigned from the DVP in protest when it withdrew its support from Gessler. Wolfgang Stresemann, *Mein Vater*, 345; Kardorff-Oheimb, *Politik*, 152–4.

[207] Diary entry for 15 Apr. 1925: Bernhard (ed.), *Vermächtnis*, ii. 48; Stresemann to the German embassy in Washington, 9 Apr. 1925 and similar telegrams to the embassies in Paris, London, and elsewhere: *ADAP*, ser. A, xii, no. 244.

destroy the coalition with the DNVP and it might in any case be counter-productive to warn voters against Hindenburg because of the fear he aroused abroad. With Luther he discussed trying to persuade both Hindenburg and Marx to stand down in favour of a third candidate, but Marx refused.[208] Stresemann was now 'frankly and honestly in despair' according to Kessler, but comforted himself with the hope that Hindenburg would not be elected.[209] Stresemann himself referred to 'the almost impossible situation'.[210]

Hindenburg was elected on 26 April, defeating Marx by some 900,000 votes. Stresemann fell ill with a painful angina on election night, but when he had recovered he was encouraged by Hindenburg's first public appearance as president.[211] He saw him as belonging more to the period of unification, of William I, rather than to that of the Kaiser, and he felt sure that he would try to be a constitutional president. He began to fit Hindenburg into his strategy of bringing the right as well as the left to unite behind his policy and he thought that Hindenburg could be more useful in this respect than Marx would have been.[212]

Stresemann's first interview with Hindenburg also went well. Hindenburg seemed to understand the importance of the security pact and he did not utter 'the ominous catchword: "Renunciation of Alsace-Lorraine"'. He was reserved about the League of Nations but relieved to discover that there was no alliance with the Soviet Union. Stresemann summarized his impression of the president as someone who made no secret of his

[208] Stresemann's diary entry, 15 Apr. 1925: Bernhard (ed.), *Vermächtnis*, ii. 48. Memorandum of a conversation between Luther and the president of the *Reichsgericht*, Walter Simons, 14 Apr. 1925: Minuth (ed.), *Kabinette Luther*, no. 69. Hehl, *Marx*, 343.

[209] Kessler's diary, 19 Apr. 1925: *Diaries of a Cosmopolitan*, 263-4.

[210] Stresemann's diary, 19 Apr. 1925: Bernhard (ed.), *Vermächtnis*, ii. 50. In public Stresemann endorsed Hindenburg, but added that the DVP did not regard the election as being about the form of the state or foreign policy. With much greater emphasis than he felt, he declared his 'unconditional confidence' that Hindenburg would not allow himself to be made use of by those of narrow or extreme views but would serve the whole people and respect the Constitution. 'Deutsche Volkspartei und Reichspräsidentenwahl', *Die Zeit* 5/160, 19 Apr. 1925: repr. in Bernhard (ed.), *Vermächtnis*, ii. 50-2.

[211] There is a conflict of evidence as to which way Stresemann himself voted. His secretary Bernhard remembered Stresemann telling him the next day that he had voted for Marx but, according to Wolfgang Stresemann, his father had intended to vote for Marx but was so irritated by the attacks of the left-wing press on Hindenburg that he voted for him after all. Hirsch, *Stresemann*, 191; Wolfgang Stresemann, *Mein Vater*, 348.

[212] Diary for 12 May 1925: Bernhard (ed.), *Vermächtnis*, ii. 59. He also noted with satisfaction that Seeckt, 'who hitherto had a unique position beside the government', was displeased as he would no longer have the same authority as he had in relation to a civilian Reich president; transcript of the diary (Nl. 272). (This passage was omitted from the extract in the *Vermächtnis*.)

Conservative background—the arch-Conservative *Kreuzzeitung* was the
only newspaper on the table—but who intended to work honestly with the
government. He added presciently, 'The main thing is that irresponsible
people do not gain influence over him.'[213] After his next interview he was
less confident. He found it difficult to discuss the complications of foreign
policy with Hindenburg, who was inflexible and one-sided. He also
suspected that the president had already been got at by people who were
critical of the Auswärtiges Amt.[214] At home he said that he missed his
conversations with Ebert.[215]

Stresemann was generally considered to have mishandled the presidential election. With the wisdom of hindsight it is clear that he overreacted
to the danger of Gessler, who was in fact to support him in cabinet over
Locarno.[216] He also ignored the danger that Hindenburg might be nominated in a second round, and in the end Hindenburg's influence proved
disastrous for the Weimar Republic. Stresemann could not foresee
the future and his actions were influenced by the memory of October–
November 1923 when Seeckt and Gessler had worked together to undermine the great coalition and came close to cooperating even to force his
resignation. That experience did not as it happened prove a good guide to
the future, but it helps to explain his behaviour at the time.

The Security Pact and the Soviet Union

The most awkward problem raised by the security pact was how to make it
acceptable to the Soviet Union. It was clear that Germany would be
expected to join the League as part of a settlement with the Western
powers and the Soviet Union regarded the League as a capitalist organization directed against itself. As German policy became increasingly
oriented to the west in 1924, the Soviet Union responded by emphasizing
the common German–Soviet interest in revising the Polish frontiers

---

[213] Diary for 19 May 1925 (Nl. 272): Bernhard (ed.), *Vermächtnis*, ii. 60.

[214] Diary for 9 June 1925: ibid., 60.

[215] Wolfgang Stresemann, *Mein Vater*, 350.

[216] Stresemann noted in his diary on 19 July 1925: 'Curiously help came in the cabinet
discussions from the side I would least have expected, namely from defence minister Dr Gessler,
who in total opposition to His Excellency Seeckt took the position that whether the security pact
was a political necessity was a question for the Auswärtiges Amt to decide and further...asked
Schiele what could be the basis of a security pact if not the status quo' (Nl. 272): Bernhard (ed.),
Vermächtnis, ii. 152. Möllers, *Geßler*, 188–201.

'according to ethnographic principles'.[217] The idea of cooperation against Poland was something which the Auswärtiges Amt wanted to keep alive. Maltzan authorized Brockdorff-Rantzau to reply to Soviet approaches by expressing their common interest in 'driving Poland back to its ethnographic frontiers' and this was confirmed by Schubert at the end of December.[218]

The Soviet foreign minister Georgi Chicherin, delighted that the Germans had swallowed the bait, thereupon proposed a treaty whereby each side would agree not to join political or economic groups directed against the other, a proposal which would have given the Soviet Union a veto over German entry into the League.[219] This faced the Auswärtiges Amt with a choice between the security pact proposals, which were being formulated at the same time, and the Soviet proposals. The situation was not made easier by Brockdorff-Rantzau's opposition to any downgrading of Germany's relations with the Soviet Union. Schubert decided to play for time, complaining later that Stresemann would not take an interest in the matter and that Ebert alone supported him.[220] Stresemann's refusal to take a decision may have reflected his own uncertainty about the future of the security pact after Chamberlain's initially cool reaction. The result was that the Soviet proposals were treated in a dilatory fashion while the security pact negotiations went ahead.

Nevertheless the problem of how to respond to the Soviet Union remained, with the president of the Council of People's Commissars, Alexej Rykov, even suggesting a military alliance.[221] At a meeting with Luther and Stresemann to discuss the security pact on 17 March, Schubert said, 'The Russian problem is very difficult in this whole context', and described the instructions being drawn up for Brockdorff-Rantzau as intended to make 'the whole matter more plausible to the Russians'.[222]

---

[217] Walsdorff, *Westorientierung und Ostpolitik*, 59–63.

[218] Maltzan to the German embassy in Moscow, 13 Dec. 1924, and Schubert to the same, 29 Dec. 1924: *ADAP*, ser. A, xi, nos. 230, 258; Walsdorff, *Westorientierung und Ostpolitik*, 65–70; Scheidemann, *Brockdorff-Rantzau*, 643–9.

[219] Brockdorff-Rantzau to Stresemann, 29 Dec. 1924: *ADAP*, ser. A, xi, no. 261; Walsdorff, *Westorientierung und Ostpolitik*, 68–70.

[220] Schubert's later comment on his memorandum of a conversation with Ebert, 12 Feb. 1925: Krüger collection, Marburg, Nl. Schubert Staatssekretär Akten, O Ru 1; Krüger, 'Der Deutsch-Polnische Schiedsvertrag', 594.

[221] Brockdorff-Rantzau to Auswärtiges Amt, 24 Feb. 1925: *ADAP*, ser. A, xii, no. 115; Walsdorff, *Westorientierung und Ostpolitik*, 74.

[222] Minuth (ed.), *Kabinette Luther*, no. 49.

The dispatch to Brockdorff-Rantzau, which was signed by Stresemann, clearly revealed the tensions between the security pact and policy towards the Soviet Union.[223] Stresemann argued that the pact did not involve any form of recognition of Germany's eastern frontiers. The arbitration treaties had been offered 'purely to provide the French government with a facade' to enable it to drop its demand that Poland be included in the pact. On the League of Nations, he pointed out that with a permanent seat on the council Germany would be in a position to veto sanctions against the Soviet Union. Even if, to avoid isolation, Germany did not exercise its veto, it would not have to take part in sanctions. He then addressed the delicate issue of whether membership of the League would prevent Germany taking part in a joint attack on Poland with the Soviet Union. He admitted that it would, but argued that since in practice Germany was not strong enough to face the opposition of the Entente in any case, entry into the League would not affect the real position.[224] Stresemann's conclusion, in which he suggested that Brockdorff-Rantzau should try to persuade the Russians of the advantages to them of German membership of the League, showed that despite his at times convoluted language the western policy was to have priority. Rantzau's angry marginal comments and his subsequent opposition to the Locarno policy also showed that he was in no doubt about its significance.[225]

[223] Stresemann to Brockdorff-Rantzau, 19 Mar. 1925: *ADAP*, ser. A, xii, no. 182.

[224] The relevant passage reads: 'If for example I imagine the case, that events occur, which make driving Poland back into its ethnographic frontiers directly possible then it could very well be that active intervention by Germany would be severely restricted by its membership of the League. This is unquestionably a consideration of great importance. All the same its importance is reduced by the consideration that, if we were not a member of the League, we would have to reckon with the certain opposition of the Entente powers, at least of France, Belgium and Czechoslovakia. There would really only be a difference then if Germany and Russia were strong enough and determined to oppose any coalition with armed force. As a member of the League we could do this only by a flagrant breach of the covenant and therefore only by offending the public opinion of the whole world. Nevertheless, I believe I am at one with Your Excellency in thinking that an open or secret German–Russian military alliance, as is here presupposed, cannot belong to our political goals for the foreseeable future': ibid., pp. 463–4.

[225] Brockdorff-Rantzau believed like Stresemann that Germany should use its economy as the lever for revision of the treaty of Versailles. He was therefore an opponent, like Stresemann, of Seeckt's reliance on military power and disliked the cooperation between the Reichswehr and the Red Army. Unlike Stresemann, however, Rantzau favoured a neutral course between east and west, and when Stresemann gave the west priority, he reacted by arguing for alignment with the Soviet Union. Scheidemann, *Brockdorff-Rantzau*, 656–9, 712–19.

Revision of the Polish Frontier

The weakest point in Stresemann's argument for the security pact was whether there was any real prospect of peaceful revision of the German frontiers in the east. Rauscher, the German envoy in Poland, did not believe that there was, nor did he believe that a guarantee pact would prevent a military solution if one became possible. He therefore advocated at this stage the cynical policy of guaranteeing the Polish frontier to satisfy the Western powers, in the knowledge that if circumstances changed the guarantee would be simply 'a piece of paper'.[226]

Stresemann and Schubert did not agree with this analysis and Rauscher himself later became an advocate of détente with Poland.[227] Stresemann hoped that the climate of opinion could be changed so that the frontier would become increasingly regarded as unjust and unviable. He was encouraged when Chamberlain and Baldwin both acknowledged Germany's right to work for revision and *The Times* published an article recommending that Poland make a voluntary gesture to win the friendship of its mighty neighbour.[228]

Stresemann circulated German embassies with a background paper, emphasizing that frontier revision was not an immediate matter and that it would only cause mistrust if it was connected to the security pact, but at the same time stressing the importance of winning over public opinion for the future. German aims were not 'a new partition of Poland' but the restoration of Danzig, the northern half of the corridor which cut off East Prussia, and Upper Silesia. The former Prussian province of Posen would not be reclaimed because its population was overwhelmingly Polish. Poland would be compensated with a free port in Danzig and rights of transit, similar to those Germany had been given in the corridor.

---

[226] Rauscher to Auswärtiges Amt, 13 Feb. 1925: *ADAP*, ser. A, xii, no. 92; Krüger, 'Der Deutsch-Polnische Schiedsvertrag', 596.

[227] Krüger, 'Der Deutsch-Polnische Schiedsvertrag', 596; Kurt Doß, *Zwischen Weimar und Warschau. Ulrich Rauscher. Deutscher Gesandter in Polen 1922–1930. Eine politische Biographie* (Düsseldorf: Droste, 1984), 79–137.

[228] 'Initiative der deutschen Aussenpolitik', anonymous article by Stresemann, *Hamburger Fremdenblatt*, 10 Apr. 1925: Bernhard (ed.), *Vermächtnis*, ii. 91–2. Stresemann was referring to a leader in *The Times* (4 Mar. 1925) about the German proposals for a security pact, which argued that for the sake of friendly relations with Germany Poland would be well advised to seek a 'reasonable compromise in the matter of frontiers'. Stresemann suggested that the article must have been cleared in advance with the Foreign Office.

A further scheme for giving Poland accesss to Memel, perhaps with another 'corridor' through Lithuania, was also mentioned.[229]

The document was notably vague about how revision might occur. It did not expect Poland to be willing to make concessions without pressure. The main source from which this might come was seen as the Soviet Union: 'A solution of the corridor question without cooperation between Germany and Russia is hardly conceivable.' But it also referred to the possibility of Anglo-American pressure in return for loans to stabilize the Polish currency.

Quite how pressure from the Soviet Union and peaceful revision could be combined was not made clear. In an anonymous article Stresemann argued that:

Things in the east are not in their final form. At the moment when Russia decides whether it will remain in its existing frontiers or whether it will open up the questions of the border states and Poland: at that moment a new era of European history will begin. Here too one does not have to think of a new world war or of a decision by force. But one could well imagine that all these questions will be discussed at a great international conference, which will create a new just order, namely in relation to real self-determination of the nations.[230]

Presumably Stresemann thought in terms of a Soviet attack or threat of attack on Poland leading to League intervention, with Germany able to mediate from a neutral position and Poland being forced to concede revision of its frontiers in a new peace settlement. But in 1925 this was no more than a vague aspiration.

Conflict over the Security Pact

The negotiations over the security pact were in suspense in April and May while the French considered their reply to the German proposals. Stresemann waited with mounting impatience. He had to defend his policy in the Reichstag on 18 May before the French reaction was known. He gave a tour d'horizon of German foreign relations and was careful to pay equal attention to east and west, arguing that 'The task of

---

[229] Runderlaß, 30 June 1925: *ADAP*, ser. A, xiii, no. 177. Christoph M. Kimmich, *The Free City: Danzig and German Foreign Policy, 1919–1934* (New Haven: Yale University Press, 1968), 73–5. See Map 2.

[230] *Hamburger Fremdenblatt*, 10 Apr. 1925: Bernhard (ed.), *Vermächtnis*, ii. 88–95, quotation p. 93.

German policy will always consist in balancing its interests towards the west and the east.'[231] In his diary he recorded with relief that his speech had been generally well received and that the DNVP had offered only muted criticism, a benefit as he had hoped of their being represented in the government.[232]

The calm continued during the first half of June, but Stresemann sensed that storms lay ahead. On 11 June he noted:

It is after all a question of giving a new order to Europe and everyone is trying to gain an advantage on the other. The reply on the security pact is finally due this week and then it will be a case of 'Clear the decks for action!' We will see whether the cabinet survives the shock or whether the right wing of the German Nationals [DNVP] takes flight. It will also be the real test of Hindenburg's capacity to take the strain...[233]

The French reply, which was delivered on 16 June and signed by Briand, who had become foreign minister in April, justified Stresemann's apprehension. As expected, it made German entry into the League a condition of any agreement. More worrying, it insisted that the arbitration treaties should provide for compulsory decisions in political as well as juridical matters and that other powers should have the right to guarantee the treaties. This meant that compulsory arbitration would apply to the German–Polish frontier and France would act as a guarantor of a German–Polish arbitration treaty. Neither was acceptable to Germany. The first would imply a weakening of its commitment to revision, and Germany was still smarting from the decision of the League over the division of Upper Silesia in 1921. The second would allow France to be the judge of whether Germany or Poland was to blame if a conflict broke out and no German would accept that France—already in alliance with Poland—would act independently in such a situation.[234]

The cabinet met on 24 June in a mood predominantly hostile to the security pact and critical of Stresemann.[235] He introduced the discussion, defending the original initiative and explaining that the French note was a 'brilliant' attempt to turn it to their advantage by extending the pact on the same terms from the west to the east. Although this was unacceptable,

---

[231] *Verhandlungen des Reichstags*, vol. 385, pp. 1868–82.
[232] Diary for 18 May 1925 (Nl. 272).
[233] (Nl. 272): Bernhard (ed.), *Vermächtnis*, ii. 103.
[234] Stresemann's speech to the foreign affairs committee of the Reichstag, 1 July 1925: ibid. 114–18.
[235] Minuth (ed.), *Kabinette Luther*, no. 110.

he suggested that Germany should take its time in replying and allow the Ruhr to be evacuated first.

He then broadened the discussion to relations with the Soviet Union, explaining Soviet fears that Germany would commit itself to the West. The Russians wanted an alliance and were thinking of a secret treaty. Stresemann reported that he had refused these suggestions but that he would be willing to offer a preamble to a commercial treaty, promising to maintain friendly relations. However, Brockdorff-Rantzau did not think that would be enough. Stresemann went on:

Here was revealed again the very fundamental question of German foreign policy, whether it was possible for Germany to orient itself simultaneously towards the west and the east. In his opinion, given Germany's position, it was possible only to try to reach a compromise between the two approaches. An exclusive orientation towards the east was in his opinion completely out of the question.

Stresemann's argument was cleverly constructed to confront the cabinet with the real choices and to show that, despite the French note, the security pact—maintaining Germany's relations with the Western powers—was the right policy. The discussion showed, however, how far his thinking was still ahead of that of his colleagues. The main onslaught came from General Seeckt, who was attending the cabinet in an expert capacity together with officials from other departments. He said he had been unable to find any advantage for Germany in the proposed pact, which simply relieved French fears by guaranteeing the western frontiers. Stresemann claimed that these could still be changed by agreement but 'history taught the reverse, that frontiers are never drawn by treaties but by armed force'. Stresemann had said that they could not think of recovering Alsace-Lorraine, but 'he must say that Germany should think only of this'. Seeckt added that Britain was not to be relied on, that an understanding with Russia was 'necessary in all circumstances', and that acceptance of the League sanctions clause (article 16) was impossible. Entry into the League would also, he predicted, prevent union with Austria. He was prepared to allow Stresemann to continue the negotiations but he was convinced that they would fail, and he would warmly welcome their failure. He was supported by Schiele for the DNVP, who argued that they were caught in a net of their own making.

Stresemann replied patiently that entry into the League did not mean giving up revision of the treaty. He cut through Seeckt's pretensions with characteristic skill: 'He agreed in general with the remarks of General von Seeckt but not his conclusions. The role which he intended for Germany we could only play when we were materially and militarily a power. This would not be the case for a long time ahead.' Stresemann then returned to the question of how they should proceed, indicating that he would not be prepared to continue negotiations without the support of the cabinet. At this point he received support from Luther and Gessler. Determined that the cabinet should be clearly committed to the policy, Stresemann proposed that the discussion should be continued the following day.

It immediately became apparent that the DNVP was not prepared to be bound by Stresemann's policy. This was no surprise. He had authorized the security pact without at first informing them. He had acted within the Constitution, which allowed individual ministers to conduct policy within their area of responsibility provided they stayed within the guidelines set by the chancellor.[236] But he had deliberately kept the DNVP in the dark because he anticipated their opposition. They now faced the unappealing alternatives of either accepting the policy or withdrawing from the government and thus losing influence over fiscal and tariff matters.

The DNVP resorted to the tactic of blaming Stresemann and disclaiming responsibility. Schiele tried to argue that the cabinet had first considered the matter on 24 June, ignoring an earlier briefing by Stresemann on 21 March.[237] Stresemann insisted that the cabinet agree to a communiqué giving a fuller statement of the background and endorsing the security pact memorandum, which it did after protracted discussion on 25 June.[238] This did not, however, settle the matter. Despite assurances from Schiele that the DNVP would cooperate in the agreed policy, sections of the Nationalist press told a different story. There were suggestions that the DNVP was only remaining in the government to sabotage its foreign policy, and demands for Stresemann's resignation.[239]

In contrast to previous crises, Stresemann enjoyed the full support of the DVP Reichstag party, which was determined that the DNVP should accept its full share of responsibility. At a meeting on 30 June the DVP

[236] Article 56 of the Weimar Constitution.

[237] There are no minutes of this meeting, but a summary record by Schubert: Minuth (ed.), *Kabinette Luther*, no. 54.

[238] Ibid., no. 111. Also Stresemann's memorandum about these events dictated on 5 July 1925 (Nl. 275), which forms the basis of the following account: Bernhard (ed.), *Vermächtnis*, ii. 128–43.

[239] Grathwol, *Stresemann and the DNVP*, 90–1.

leaders decided to initiate a Reichstag debate 'to clarify the political position', in other words to force the DNVP to declare itself.

The strains between the coalition parties became open at a meeting of the foreign affairs committee of the Reichstag on 1 July. The DNVP chairman, Westarp, made it clear that he did not consider the cabinet responsible for the memorandum, saw no advantage in it, and that the DNVP would reserve its position about whether negotiations should proceed.[240] This statement was immediately pounced on by the opposition, which demanded to know where the government stood. Since Luther remained silent, Stresemann spoke again, saying that Luther had been fully consulted and had seen the Auswärtiges Amt files before the memorandum had been sent and that the full cabinet had been briefed in March.[241]

There followed an extraordinary and rather comic scene between Luther and Stresemann. In trying to hold his cabinet together Luther had led the DNVP leaders to believe that he had not been properly briefed by Stresemann; this explained his silence at the foreign affairs committee. He may indeed not have understood the real significance of the memorandum when Stresemann first submitted it to him in January. Luther proposed to call a special cabinet to present his version of events. On the evening of 1 July he showed Stresemann a memorandum in which he disclaimed responsibility for the initial stages of the policy. Stresemann asked Luther directly whether he would like him to resign, offering to go on a long sea cruise. Luther seemed in two minds, saying that he could not manage without Stresemann but then suggesting that Stresemann's cruise would take him to London. Stresemann was at a loss to know what Luther meant, but the chancellor then indicated that he was suggesting that Stresemann should become Germany's ambassador to Britain. Stresemann immediately replied that he would remain in politics as party leader and Luther at once withdrew saying that Stresemann's resignation would leave him in an impossible position, dependent on the DNVP.[242]

That evening Stresemann discussed the situation with Schubert and the chief legal expert of the Auswärtiges Amt, Friedrich Gaus, who had also

---

[240] Memorandum of the discussion, 1 July 1925: *ADAP*, ser. A, xiii, no. 179.

[241] Bernhard (ed.), *Vermächtnis*, ii. 126–8.

[242] In his post-war memoirs Luther confirmed that he was trying to keep both the DNVP and Stresemann in his cabinet and denied that he ever 'seriously considered, even for a moment, parting with Stresemann'. *Politiker ohne Partei*, 358–64; Hans Luther, 'Luther und Stresemann in Locarno', *Politische Studien*, 8/84 (Apr. 1957), 9.

been involved in drafting the security pact memorandum. Both were incensed at Luther's conduct. The next morning Stresemann telephoned the state secretary at the Reich Chancellery, Franz Kempner, and told him that he would neither receive a letter from the chancellor nor exchange statements at cabinet: 'I am sick of allowing the responsibility to be loaded on me alone...if he [the chancellor] insists on this letter, then I will answer him from the floor of the Reichstag...'. Luther gave way, agreeing that instead they should each prepare a memorandum giving their own version of events and, following a further threat of resignation by Stresemann, he also agreed to omit the statement implying that he had been inadequately informed.

Stresemann had won, but his relations with the chancellor were strained. The cabinet persuaded Stresemann to withdraw the DVP's threat to force a debate on foreign policy but only after Schiele had given an assurance that the DNVP would not demand Stresemann's resignation.[243] Stresemann remained wary. The following day he learned that Westarp had told a meeting of the DNVP party in the Prussian Landtag that Stresemann's position was too strong to be challenged but that they would continue to look for an opportunity to overthrow him or, if that failed, to leave the government.[244] Later he heard that the DNVP had even put out feelers to the SPD asking whether they might cooperate in finding a successor for Stresemann.[245]

In this uneasy atmosphere the cabinet turned to discussing the draft German reply to Briand's note. This basically restated the German position on the points in dispute. Schiele performed what Stresemann described as 'mental gymnastics' in his attempt to dissociate the proposed note from the original memorandum and thus maintain the DNVP thesis that it had not been responsible for what had happened previously.[246] Stresemann had no difficulty in getting the support of the cabinet. He made use of the argument that the continued flow of American loans depended on a positive German attitude to the security pact, the argument that would carry most weight with the DNVP.[247] There was some discussion of the wording of the arbitration treaties and Gaus explained that this

---

[243] Cabinet minutes, 2 July 1925: Minuth (ed.), *Kabinette Luther*, no. 116.

[244] Diary for 3 July 1925 (Nl. 272): Bernhard (ed.), *Vermächtnis*, ii. 143.

[245] Diary for 17 July 1925: ibid. 151.

[246] Diary for 19 July 1925 (Nl. 272): ibid. 152; cabinet minutes, 15 July 1925: Minuth (ed.), *Kabinette Luther*, no. 123.

[247] He quoted the views of Benjamin Strong, governor of the Federal Reserve Bank of New York, and Montagu Norman, governor of the Bank of England, who were in Berlin.

had deliberately been left 'somewhat unclear' to protect their aim of having a less binding formula in the east than the west.

Stresemann then discussed the note with representatives of the coalition parties, the foreign affairs committee of the Reichstag, and the minister presidents of the *Länder*, in each case securing their approval before the note was delivered on 20 July.[248] Subsequently the policy was debated in the Reichstag. Stresemann made a short but effective speech contrasting the security pact proposals with Poincaré's plans to detach the Rhineland in 1923. He drew a parallel between their present efforts and the London conference. Just as that had been an attempt to solve the reparations question, so the security pact was 'the attempt at a solution of the political issues of peace in Europe'.[249] Despite the taunts of the SPD and the NSDAP, the DNVP joined the other coalition parties in approving the note, giving the government a comfortable majority.[250]

Stresemann had succeeded in manoeuvring the DNVP into supporting his policy, but he did not deceive himself that the situation was stable. To Käte he wrote that the situation had calmed down, though a fortnight earlier his fall had seemed certain. He attributed his survival to the support of the DVP, which had faced the DNVP with the prospect of 'seeing the cabinet blown up if they overthrew me. As soon as one opposes these people energetically they draw back.' Nevertheless, he added, 'I see the whole thing as only a truce, battle will start again in the autumn.'[251]

Towards Locarno

On 24 August the Allies proposed that negotiations should be continued at a meeting of foreign ministers, preceded by a preliminary meeting of legal advisers.[252] The lawyers met at the beginning of September and narrowed the differences between the Allied and German conceptions of

[248] Minuth (ed.), *Kabinette Luther*, i. 437; minutes of the meeting with the *Länder* minister presidents, 17 July 1925: ibid., no. 127; Stresemann's speech to the Reichstag foreign affairs committee, 17 July 1925: Bernhard (ed.), *Vermächtnis*, ii. 146–51. The note is printed in Ministerium für Auswärtige Angelegenheiten der Deutschen Demokratischen Republik (ed.), *Locarno-Konferenz 1925* (Berlin: Rütten & Loening, 1962), no. 16.

[249] 22 July 1925: Zwoch (ed.), *Reichstagsreden*, 207–17, quotation, p. 217.

[250] *Verhandlungen des Reichstags*, vol. 387, pp. 3387–3466.

[251] Stresemann to 'Katerchen', 22 July 1925: Stresemann family papers, Berlin. See also diary for 2 Aug. 1925 (Nl. 272): Bernhard (ed.), *Vermächtnis*, ii. 162–3.

[252] Memorandum by Stresemann of a meeting with de Margerie, 24 Aug. 1925: *ADAP*, ser. A, xiv, no. 25.

the pact. Gaus secured the important concession that the arbitration treaties would follow the German model, distinguishing between justiciable disputes and others which would be subject only to an unbinding conciliation procedure.[253] He was not, however, able to move the French from their insistence that they should act as the guarantors of the eastern treaties.

The cabinet now had to decide whether to attend the foreign ministers' conference to which it was invited on 15 September. The DNVP reacted by drawing up a list of what Stresemann called 'unfulfillable demands'.[254] The danger of DNVP defection was now greater because the Reichstag had passed the new tariff on 12 August, thus fulfilling one of the DNVP's reasons for joining the government. The DNVP's tactics became clear when Schiele did his utmost to prevent Luther accompanying Stresemann to the conference, explaining that if the conference led to domestic difficulties the authority of the chancellor would not then be impaired but at most that of the foreign minister. In other words, Stresemann should be sent to the conference with what he called 'pretty much all the problems of the present world' and if the conference failed he could be dispensed with.[255] Schiele's tactics, however, rebounded on him. Luther was offended at the suggestion that he should avoid taking responsibility and made it clear in the most uncompromising terms that he intended to go.

At a meeting of the full cabinet on 23 September, Schiele bowed to Luther's decision, and agreement was also reached on the wording of a statement on war guilt demanded by the DNVP.[256] Schubert warned that

[253] This made very little difference in law to the question of frontier revision. Gaus thought that the definition of 'justiciable' disputes under article 13 of the League covenant might include frontiers, and in any case on joining the League Germany would be bound by the covenant to pursue only peaceful revision. The purpose of retaining the distinction in the arbitration treaties was political: to maintain an apparent rather than a real difference between the guarantees it was offering in the west and the east, to underline its claim to revision in the east. The difference was even more artificial in that the Germans also wanted to keep open the possibility of peaceful revision in the west. This was partly to satisfy DNVP objections to the 'renunciation of Alsace-Lorraine', but also in the hope of recovering the small territory of Eupen-Malmédy which had been allocated to Belgium by the treaty (in compensation for Germany's violation of Belgian neutrality in 1914). Germany hoped to regain Eupen-Malmédy in return for a financial settlement of Belgian claims arising from the wartime occupation. Gaus's report to the cabinet, 18 Sept. 1925: Ministerium (ed.), *Locarno Konferenz*, no. 20; Krüger, 'Der Deutsch-Polnische Schiedsvertrag', 602-7; Enssle, *Stresemann's Territorial Revisionism*, 80-114.

[254] Diary for 22 Sept. 1925 (Nl. 272): Bernhard (ed.), *Vermächtnis*, ii. 179; Grathwol, *Stresemann and the DNVP*, 108-20.

[255] Diary for 23 Sept. 1925: Bernhard (ed.), *Vermächtnis*, ii. 179-80; minutes of meetings between Luther, Stresemann, Brauns, and Schiele with officials 22-3 Sept. 1925: Minuth (ed.), *Kabinette Luther*, nos. 158-9.

[256] Minuth (ed.), *Kabinette Luther*, no. 160.

this statement might disrupt the conference, but Stresemann argued that the risk was worth taking if it helped to unite the German people behind the delegation. The cabinet approved Stresemann's list of objectives for the conference, which included reducing Allied controls in the Rhineland and the length of the occupation, and gaining acceptance of the principle that Germany could decide for itself how far as a member of the League it would take part in sanctions under article 16. These decisions were then rehearsed at further meetings with Hindenburg, with the minister presidents of the *Länder*, and the foreign affairs committee of the Reichstag, and after a final cabinet on 2 October had approved the guidelines for the delegation, Luther and Stresemann left for Locarno.[257]

Soviet Threat of Embarrassment

On 1 October, the day before his departure for Locarno, Stresemann received the Soviet foreign minister, Chicherin, who had announced his visit shortly before. Stresemann's hopes of appeasing the Russians by a preamble to a commercial treaty, affirming the spirit of Rapallo, had come to nothing. Chicherin had dismissed the idea as 'fine phrases' and the negotiations for the commercial treaty also proved difficult, with the Russians insisting on a series of exceptions to most favoured nation status.[258] Chicherin returned to the proposal of a treaty which would give the Soviet Union a veto over German entry into the League and he backed this proposal with threats that the Soviet Union might otherwise be forced to improve its relations with France and Poland.

Stresemann attached importance to maintaining Germany's relations with the Soviet Union, but he was convinced that the security pact should have priority. He also distrusted the Soviet Union because of the activities of the Communist International. He was outraged at the attempted assassination of the king of Bulgaria and other leading figures in April 1925, and he reacted sharply again in June when two German students were put on trial in the Soviet Union for alleged terrorism in an obvious act of retaliation for the trial in Germany of a Soviet citizen on the same charge.[259] In July he noted: 'Many people are very concerned about our

[257] Minuth (ed.), *Kabinette Luther*, nos. 161, 162, 170.
[258] Walsdorff, *Westorientierung und Ostpolitik*, 109–38.
[259] Stresemann to Houghton, 4 June 1925 (Nl. 276): Bernhard (ed.), *Vermächtnis*, ii. 257–64; memorandum of a conversation with the Bulgarian ambassador, 23 Apr. 1925 (Nl. 272): ibid.

future relationship to Russia. I do not count on much from cooperation, at least not so long as Bolshevism is in power there.'[260] To the foreign affairs committee of the Reichstag he said that the Soviet Union would have to observe the norms customary 'between civilized states'.[261] Nevertheless, he wanted to avoid a breakdown in relations which would weaken Germany's position towards Poland and strengthen the domestic opposition to him from the right, which—ironically—favoured a pro-Soviet course from hatred of Versailles and the Allies. He therefore pressed Brockdorff-Rantzau to find a solution which would allow relations to return to normal and persuaded the cabinet to approve an albeit limited commercial treaty before the Locarno conference.[262]

When Chicherin announced his intention of visiting Berlin via Warsaw at the end of September, Stresemann had no real cause for concern. When they met, however, Chicherin took the offensive, saying he could not understand the security pact policy in view of Brockdorff-Rantzau's remarks the previous December that they should cooperate 'to drive Poland back to its ethnographic frontiers' which could only mean 'military cooperation...to smash the present day Poland'.[263] Stresemann was caught off guard and reacted with astonishment, telephoning Schubert even though it was after midnight. Schubert disputed Chicherin's account, saying that the initiative had come from the Soviet side. The following day, after consulting the records, Stresemann had to concede that Brockdorff-Rantzau had been authorized to speak in these terms, but he added rather awkwardly that it had not been 'the central point' of the discussion and it had not meant the offer of an alliance.[264]

It is hard to understand why Schubert and Stresemann failed to foresee that Chicherin would deploy this argument. The most likely explanation is that they had simply forgotten that the phrase 'driving Poland back to

297–8. On the abortive coup in Bulgaria, see R. J. Crampton, *A Short History of Modern Bulgaria* (Cambridge: Cambridge University Press, 1987), 101–2.

[260] Diary for 19 July 1925 (Nl. 272): Bernhard (ed.), *Vermächtnis*, ii. 154.

[261] Stresemann's speech, 17 July 1925: ibid. 150.

[262] Memorandum of a conversation with Brockdorff-Rantzau, 21 June 1925: *ADAP*, ser. A, xiii, no. 139; cabinet minutes, 1 Oct. 1925: Minuth (ed.), *Kabinette Luther*, no. 167.

[263] Stresemann's memorandum of the discussion on 1 Oct., misdated 30 Sept. 1925: *ADAP*, ser. A, xiv, no. 109. K. D. Erdmann, 'Das Problem der Ost-oder Westorientierung in der Locarno Politik Stresemanns', *Geschichte in Wissenschaft und Unterricht*, 6 (1955), 153–62. The version in Bernhard (ed.), *Vermächtnis*, ii. 523–7 is heavily censored.

[264] Stresemann's memorandum of the discussion on 2 Oct. 1925: *ADAP*, ser. A, xiv, no. 110.

its ethnographic frontiers' had been used to the Russians before the security pact negotiations got under way. Chicherin's remarks—he also referred to the military cooperation between the two countries—carried the clear threat that the Soviet Union was in a position to embarrass Germany by revealing the nature of the discussions. In fact Chicherin seems only to have intended to extract from Stresemann further assurances that Germany would not guarantee Poland's frontiers in any way and would insist on exemption from article 16 of the League covenant. When Stresemann complied, Chicherin seemed content, and the threat of a calculated indiscretion by the Soviet side remained in abeyance.[265]

Stresemann's Goals Before Locarno

In preparation for the conference, Stresemann set out his goals in two unsigned articles which enabled him, in the manner of Bismarck, to explain his policy more openly than he could in an official capacity, though informed opinion would recognize him as the author.[266] In the first he discussed criticism of Germany joining the League.[267] He referred to the Soviet fear that in the League Britain would be able to use Germany as its 'Continental sword', but he pointed out that Germany lacked the means for such a role and that French opposition made German rearmament impossible. He rejected the alternative of a Russian alliance to throw off the shackles of Versailles, arguing that Russia was more interested in Asia than Europe, France was in any case militarily stronger, and a Russian army would be the bearer of communism, 'a world religion' which 'can only exist if it is able to expand'. Once it was in the League, Germany could be the spokesman for the German populations under League administration in Danzig and the Saar, and more generally for the 10–12 million Germans living as minorities in other states. Whether inside or outside the League, German policy would have to consist in preserving peace, in economic development, and in educating the German people for a recovery which could only come gradually, not with the seven-league boots of the world of fantasy.

---

[265] Walsdorff, *Westorientierung und Ostpolitik*, 137–8.
[266] Müller, *Auswärtige Pressepolitik*, 258.
[267] Dr Hans Schumann [Stresemann], 'Sicherheitspakt, Völkerbund und Ostfragen', *Deutsche Stimmen*, 37/15, 5 Aug. 1925.

Stresemann followed up with a second article in the *Hamburger Fremdenblatt* in September.[268] In this he again asked what were the alternatives to his policy:

One could imagine a German foreign policy which is based on forgetting nothing and having only one goal: to recover Germany's old position. Even if Germany were a military power, one would have to be clear in conducting such a policy that one would thereby bring back to life an alliance of the whole world against Germany.

Stresemann illustrated what he meant by listing the disputes between Germany and its neighbours resulting from the 'diabolical nature' of the treaty of Versailles: France (Alsace-Lorraine), Belgium (Eupen-Malmédy), Denmark (the frontier), Poland (Danzig, the corridor, Upper Silesia), Czechoslovakia (German Bohemia and the prohibition on union with Austria), Lithuania (Memel).[269] He added to this list the suppression of German minorities in Yugoslavia, Rumania, and Italy (the South Tyrol), and finally the confiscation of German colonies.

The fact of German disarmament, which he said was disputed by 'only a few fools', prescribed 'the limits, type and method of German foreign policy'. However, policy did not have to be inactive, aimless, or simply a policy of renunciation of revision. The first task was to protect Germany against French aggression by finding allies. Further, Germany should become the stronghold of German minorities and strive for a revision of the eastern frontiers, 'whose impossible nature is today recognized on all sides'. Another goal was the recovery of colonies. Finally it should be the champion of self-determination which, in relation to Austria, had been treated with 'unparalleled cynicism' by the Allies. Progress in these areas did not depend on the military capacity which Germany lacked. It did require, however, the cooperation and understanding of the powers whose influence was decisive and that required the recognition of the inviolability of the western frontier and the security pact.

At the conclusion of the article, Stresemann looked beyond the solution of the problems of European security to the development of 'economic understanding between the great industrial nations of Europe...and

---

[268] 'Zwischen London und Comersee. Deutschlands Paktpolitik', *Hamburger Fremdenblatt*, 255, 14 Sept. 1925, repr. in *NLC* 52/174, 19 Sept. 1925: Bernhard (ed.), *Vermächtnis*, ii. 170–5.

[269] Germany ceded the Baltic port of Memel to the Allies by the treaty of Versailles (article 99). It was occupied by Lithuania in 1923, and this was recognized by the Allies in the Memel Convention of 8 May 1924.

beyond that something like the structure of a European community in comparison to the present system which has created a Europe reminiscent of the old Germany with its dozens of states and customs barriers'.[270]

Stresemann's letter to the Crown Prince of 7 September 1925, which some historians see as evidence of the hypocrisy of his Locarno policy, belongs to the same period of efforts to convince, in this case, a sceptical observer.[271] The letter replied to some specific points raised by Wilhelm and was clearly written in the hope that it would influence his DNVP friends, and particularly those around Hindenburg.[272] The argument followed the usual pattern, but was adapted to Wilhelm and his circle. Stresemann wrote that the major tasks 'for the immediate, foreseeable future' were first the solution of reparations and securing the peace which was the precondition for Germany to regain its strength; second, the protection of German minorities; third, the correction of the eastern frontiers. 'In the background' lay union with Austria, though Stresemann listed disadvantages which would weigh with Wilhelm—strengthening Catholic influence, Bavaria and Austria combining against Prussia, the dominance of clerical and socialist parties in Austria. To achieve these aims they needed to concentrate on them and they needed peace—hence the security pact. They were required to renounce war for Alsace-Lorraine, but this renunciation was only 'theoretical' in that no possibility of war with France existed. Stresemann underlined the importance of a settlement in the west since Germany would probably already be unable to pay the reparations due under the Dawes plan in 1927. They were entitled to ask for a new investigation of Germany's capacity to pay, but they had to bear in mind that their opponents carried at least as heavy a burden in interest payments on their war debts.

The remainder of the letter discussed the balance of German policy between east and west. Wilhelm had repeated the standard objection that by joining the League Germany would lose its freedom of action. Strese-

---

[270] Stresemann had met the champion of the pan-European movement, Count Coudenhove-Kalerghi, on 11 June 1925 and noted in his diary, 'Whatever one may think about him, he is certainly a man of exceptional knowledge and great energy. I am convinced that he will yet play a great role' (Nl. 272): Bernhard (ed.), *Vermächtnis*, ii. 307. On the movements for European integration during the Weimar Republic, see Reinhard Frommelt, *Paneuropa oder Mitteleuropa. Einigungsbestrebungen im Kalkül deutscher Wirtschaft und Politik 1925–1933* (Stuttgart: Deutsche Verlags-Anstalt, 1977).

[271] Nl. 29: printed in Harttung (ed.), *Schriften*, 336–40.

[272] Crown Prince Wilhelm to Stresemann, 28 Aug. 1925 (Nl. 28). Henry Bernhard, 'Gustav Stresemann. Tatsachen und Legenden', *Aus Politik und Zeitgeschichte*, B 41/59 (7 Oct. 1959), 530.

mann replied with his usual answer that lacking military power, Germany was not in a position to choose an alliance with either Britain or Russia. He added a warning against

the utopia of flirting with Bolshevism. When the Russians are in Berlin, the red flag will at once fly over the palace and in Russia, where they want world revolution, they will be quite content to have bolshevized Europe as far as the Elbe and they will leave the rest of Germany to be devoured by the French.

Nevertheless, he said he believed in the Soviet Union's 'evolutionary development', that Germany was ready to reach an agreement with it 'on a different basis', and that Germany was not 'selling itself to the West' by joining the League—all of which he offered to explain more fully in conversation.

Stresemann then returned to the original priorities—reparations and peace—and said that for these:

The most important thing ... is the liberation of German territory from foreign occupation. We must first get the strangler from our neck. Therefore German policy, as Metternich said of Austria—it must be after 1809—must in this respect consist first in showing finesse [*finassieren*] and avoiding fundamental decisions.

The language of this letter has caused controversy ever since it was first published in the *Vermächtnis* in 1932.[273] It can be read as showing that Stresemann had a hidden agenda for a future when Germany was once again a military power.[274] On the other hand it can be read simply as a cogent defence of the policy of peaceful revision in terms which a typical DNVP supporter could understand.[275]

There is no doubt that the letter was intended to influence opinion at a critical stage when the cabinet and Hindenburg were soon to be asked to agree to German participation at the conference. Its central aim was to warn against the only alternative offered by Stresemann's opponents, namely closer relations with the Soviet Union. This was the policy of

[273] Bernhard (ed.), *Vermächtnis*, ii. 553–5, with a few omissions of minor importance. The publication coincided with elections in France, and politicians including Poincaré and André Tardieu argued that the letter showed that Stresemann's policy of European understanding had been hypocritical. Bernhard replied to these accusations in *NLC* 59/90, 10 May 1932, and in a further article: *NLC* 59/101, 26 May 1932.

[274] The best statement of this case remains Thimme, *Stresemann*, 89–106.

[275] R. Grathwol, 'Gustav Stresemann: Reflections on his Foreign Policy', *Journal of Modern History*, 45 (1973), 52–70.

Seeckt, Brockdorff-Rantazu, and those who thought like them in the Crown Prince's circle.[276] On this point Stresemann was emphatic, indeed prophetic in his vision of Germany under Soviet domination as far as the Elbe. Against this clear warning, the maintenance of an eventual option on a Soviet alliance for some remote future loses its importance.

Stresemann defended his policy of admission to the League in language the Crown Prince would appreciate—the French occupation of the Rhineland being described as 'the strangler' at 'our neck'. He also presented his policy as one of realpolitik, comparing Germany's situation to that of Metternich when Austria had been defeated by Napoleon and there was no viable Russian alliance to which to turn. This required now, as then, a policy of 'finesse'. To drive the point home, he sent Wilhelm a copy of a short work describing the mission of another Prussian Prince Wilhelm to Napoleon in 1808 to plead for a relaxation of the treaty of Tilsit, which had also imposed a French army of occupation and an indemnity.[277] Wilhelm was to offer Napoleon a formal alliance with Prussia and also, if necessary, the Crown Prince in marriage to the eldest daughter of Joseph Bonaparte and himself as a hostage. The message of Stresemann's letter was clear: however unpalatable entry into the League might be, it paled into insignificance compared to the sacrifices which Wilhelm's ancestors had been prepared to make to save Prussia from Napoleon.

Although the purpose of the letter is clear, some questions remain. Stresemann's technique, as so often in argument, was to try to convince his opponent that they were on the same side. That was what made him so effective. It may, however, also raise legitimate doubts as to which side he was really on or whether even, in his own words, his face was 'only a mask adapted to his surroundings'.[278] To the Crown Prince he compared his policy to the ruthless competition between the European states of the age

---

[276] Wilhelm was in touch with Seeckt over his letter to Stresemann: Grathwol, 'Stresemann', 55. Brockdorff-Rantzau's twin brother had been a dinner guest of Wilhelm's, together with Stresemann, on 24 July 1925 (Nl. 272): Bernhard (ed.), *Vermächtnis*, ii. 308–9; cf. Edgar Stern-Rubarth, *Graf Brockdorff-Rantzau. Wanderer zwischen zwei Welten* (Berlin: Reimar Hobbing, 1929), 11. After the DNVP left the coalition in October, Stresemann noted with satisfaction that Wilhelm had been very critical of their behaviour: diary for 16 Dec. 1925: Bernhard (ed.), *Vermächtnis*, ii. 381–2.

[277] This work, which was written at Stresemann's request by Prince Otto von Bismarck, the grandson of the chancellor and a member of the Auswärtiges Amt, was published as *Prinz Wilhelm und Napoleon. Neue Bilder aus Preussens Notzeit* (Dresden: Carl Reissner, 1929). Stresemann to Herbert Eulenberg, 8 Aug. 1928: Bernhard (ed.), *Vermächtnis*, iii. 496–8. Jonathan Wright, 'Stresemann and Locarno', *Contemporary European History*, 4/2 (1995), 128–9.

[278] See above, p. 293.

of Napoleon. In the *Hamburger Fremdenblatt* a week later he looked forward to economic integration of the major industrial nations in a 'European community'. Which represented his real view of the future?

He probably expected elements of both to be present. He was too subtle a politician to commit himself to a single blueprint. He quoted Bismarck's scornful remark that consistency in a politician meant he had only one idea.[279] This did not mean that Stresemann simply kept his options open. On another occasion he quoted Bismarck again, saying that of all states Prussia, in the centre of Europe, could least afford an aimless course.[280]

Stresemann was convinced that a settlement with the West lay in Germany's interests. That would be followed by a long period of peaceful revision, of progressive dismantling of the sanctions of the Versailles treaty and the re-emergence of Germany as a great power. In 1925 he had not given up hope of territorial revision—the Polish frontier, possibly Austria and colonies. He was open to new ideas such as European economic integration and aware of how the German economy had been transformed by unification. At the same time he did not expect international relations to lose their competitive character. He had lived through a violent age and he knew enough of the history of the European state system to insulate him from such idealism.

For the moment the security pact was the right policy and he wanted to carry the DNVP with him. How far he would remain committed to the policy depended on how successful it would be and, as always, what the alternatives were. He already set a high value on peace to enable Germany to recover from the war and, as he was to emphasize increasingly, because of Germany's vulnerable position in the centre of Europe. Peace inevitably constrained revision to what could be achieved with the support of other powers. In 1925 Stresemann was optimistic about the possibilities and he had grounds for optimism. Compared to 1923 Germany's position was much stronger. But he knew his domestic opponents were waiting for peaceful revision to fail. If he succeeded, it would help to ensure consensus at home and stabilize the Republic. Equally, if he failed, the divisions over foreign policy dating from the war could be expected to return with new violence.

---

[279] 'Politische Gedanken zum Bismarck-Gedenktage', *Deutsche Stimmen*, 37/7, 5 Apr. 1925, 128–9.

[280] Stresemann's speech to the Arbeitsgemeinschaft deutscher Landsmannschaften in Gross-Berlin, 14 Dec. 1925: *ADAP*, ser. B, i/i, pp. 752–3.

8

Locarno and the League,
1925–1926

'The development of a politician to a statesman takes place in a life,
in which one learns not only to express what one personally sees as
desirable, but in which one learns to overcome oneself when it is a
question of fitting the individual self into the greater whole and into
belief in the future.'[1]

The conference which opened at Locarno on 5 October 1925 set the scene
for the European détente which followed and which lasted, despite increasingly severe strains, until Stresemann's death in October 1929. The
conference set the scene in three ways: in what it agreed, in the differences
that remained, and in the will to reach agreement despite the differences.
It also shaped the future of German domestic politics, triggering the
resignation of the DNVP and forcing the government to rely on the
SPD and DDP for support of its foreign policy.

Behind the will to reach agreement lay external pressures on each of the
main contenders, France and Germany. There was first the powerful
incentive for both of American loans and the knowledge that an agreee-
ment on European security was regarded as vital by American bankers.
There was also the opportunity to involve Britain in Europe on the only
terms it would accept, namely a guarantee of the Rhine frontier to both
sides. This was less than the French had expected since 1919 but was

[1] Stresemann's speech to the Bund der Auslandsdeutschen: *NLC* 52/168, 12 Sept. 1925.

preferable, in Briand's view, to no agreement with Britain.[2] For the Germans it marked an important gain: a formal British commitment to defend the Rhine frontier, unlike the situation in 1923 when Stresemann had faced Poincaré with only moral support from Britain. In return, Germany renounced the recovery of Alsace-Lorraine and agreed to join the League.

The heart of the Locarno agreement was Franco-German rapprochement through the Rhineland pact. This in turn raised three areas of contention. The first was France's relations with its east European allies, Poland and Czechoslovakia, and the terms under which they could be associated with the security pact. The second was Germany's relations with the Soviet Union and the way in which these would be affected by its membership of the League. The third was the German claim that the security pact should lead to the elimination of the discriminatory clauses of the treaty of Versailles ahead of time, in particular by the evacuation of the Rhineland but also by bringing forward from 1935 the plebiscite in the Saar, recognition of the German right to colonies, and progress towards general disarmament. These three areas formed the major subjects of debate at Locarno and provided the major sources of tension in the détente that followed.

The Locarno Conference

The German delegation reached Locarno on 3 October, leaving behind an autumn landscape north of the Alps and emerging from the St Gotthard tunnel into high summer on the shores of Lake Maggiore.[3] Stresemann had received an uncomfortable reminder of the dangers of his position when the German envoy to Switzerland, Adolf Müller, joined the train and warned him of an assassination plot by the Ehrhardt Brigade which had been responsible for the murders of Erzberger and Rathenau.[4]

The conference met in the cramped surroundings of the town hall where the rectangular table was scarcely big enough to accommodate

[2] Edward D. Keeton, *Briand's Locarno Policy: French Economics, Politics and Diplomacy, 1925–1929* (New York: Garland, 1987), 126–37.

[3] Paul Schmidt, *Statist auf diplomatischer Bühne 1923–45* (Bonn: Athenäum, 1953), 75.

[4] Diary for 2–3 Oct. 1925: Bernhard (ed.), *Vermächtnis*, ii. 186–7 (transcript in Nl. 30). On Adolf Müller's varied career, see Karl Heinrich Pohl, *Adolf Müller. Geheimagent und Gesandter in Kaiserreich und Weimarer Republik* (Cologne: Bund, 1995).

the chief delegates, with the result that the interpreters had to sit behind and could not always hear what they had to translate.[5] At Luther's
request, to emphasize the equality of the delegations there was no
formal chairman, although in practice Chamberlain acted as informal
chairman.[6]

In this atmosphere the conference got off to a good start, assisted by
Briand, whose humorous asides suggested a willingness to overcome the
difficulties. The two difficult areas, the French guarantee of the eastern
arbitration treaties and the conditions for German League membership—
dubbed by Briand the two 'neuralgic' points—were reserved for later
discussion.[7] When the Germans proposed a change in the draft pact to
allow it to be cancelled by a single state rather than two, on the grounds
that Germany stood alone whereas the Allies formed a group, Briand
countered that if he had thought that this division would continue, he
would not have come to Locarno. He also paid tribute to 'the courageous
deed' of the German memorandum. Chamberlain echoed Briand's view
that if Europe remained divided into two camps the pact would have
failed. Stresemann noted in his diary that the atmosphere had been 'polite
and with a certain, growing warmth'.[8]

The following day the discussion focused on the question of the French
guarantee of the eastern arbitration treaties.[9] Stresemann asked how
France could be both a guarantor of the pact and an ally of one party to
the pact. Briand replied that France had obligations to its allies which it
could not ignore. He offered to be flexible about how the guarantee was
achieved but said he would not sign a pact without it. Stresemann replied
that Germany had already accepted two different kinds of security to meet
French concerns—the arbitration treaties and entry into the League. He
also asked how the proposed guarantee could be compatible with the
League sanctions procedure under article 16. Briand replied that article
16 lacked precision and the French guarantee was necessary to fill the gap.
Chamberlain supported Briand, indicating that Britain would take a dif-

[5] Schmidt, *Statist*, 76–7.

[6] Stresemann thought Luther was too concerned with appearances; diary for 5 Oct. 1925:
Bernhard (ed.), *Vermächtnis*, ii. 187.

[7] German record of the meeting, 5 Oct. 1925: Minuth (ed.), *Kabinette Luther*, no. 172. Each
delegation kept its own records. The British version is printed as an appendix to *DBFP*, 1st ser.
xxvii.

[8] Diary for 5 Oct. 1925: Bernhard (ed.), *Vermächtnis*, ii. 187–8.

[9] German record, 6 Oct. 1925: Minuth (ed.), *Kabinette Luther*, no. 173. Stresemann's diary for 6
Oct.: Bernhard (ed.), *Vermächtnis*, ii. 188–90.

ferent attitude to its obligations under article 16 if the issue in dispute were in South America rather than the Rhine frontier. No decision was reached at the meeting and the matter was subsequently referred to the lawyers.

Eventually the British legal expert Sir Cecil Hurst found a way round the difficulty. This was for France to give guarantees to Poland and Czechoslovakia in a separate agreement, while the security pact would reserve the right of France (and Germany) to resort to force, not only if the terms of the pact regarding the Rhineland were violated, but also under the provisions of the League covenant.[10] Reference was made both to action under article 16 (which required a unanimous decision of the council, excluding states involved in the dispute) and to article 15, paragraph 7, which reserved the right of members of the League to take action even if the council was unable to agree. One restriction was added to this latter case, namely that such action could only be taken 'against a State which was the first to attack'.[11]

The upshot of this neat legal footwork was that France guaranteed Poland and Czechoslovakia in separate treaties, which were concluded at Locarno and mentioned in the final protocol of the conference.[12] The Germans thus tacitly acknowledged their existence without raising any objection. On the other hand, the Germans did not themselves have to sign a treaty which included the French guarantees. Honour was therefore satisfied all round. In practice, the agreements meant that if Germany attacked Poland, France was explicitly empowered and obliged to go to Poland's aid. If, however, war broke out between Germany and Poland and it was not clear that Germany had attacked first, then in the event of France invading Germany, Germany could appeal to Britain for support as a guarantor of the Rhine frontier.

Before this compromise had been reached, the conference passed to the next major controversial question, the conditions for German entry into the League.[13] Stresemann took the lead, arguing that since Germany was incapable of defending itself, it could not be expected to assume the full obligations of article 16 and cooperate in sanctions against an aggressor.

[10] Notes of a conversation between members of the British delegation, 7 Oct. 1925: *DBFP*, 1st ser. xxvii, appendix 7.

[11] Record of the meeting, 13 Oct. 1925: Minuth (ed.), *Kabinette Luther*, no. 186.

[12] C. A. Macartney (ed.), *Survey of International Affairs 1925*, 2 vols. (London: Oxford University Press, 1928), ii. 439–42, 451–2.

[13] Record of the meeting, 8 Oct. 1925: Minuth (ed.), *Kabinette Luther*, no. 179. Stresemann's diary for 8 Oct.: Bernhard (ed.), *Vermächtnis*, ii. 191–2.

He asserted that this applied not only to military action but also to allowing foreign troops to cross its territory and to economic sanctions, since each of these could lead to war. He asked for an interpretation of article 16 which would allow Germany to decide how far it could take part in sanctions.

With typical boldness, he introduced the example of a Soviet attack on Poland, saying that a German boycott would immediately lead to a Soviet declaration of war on Germany and if, as in 1920, the Red Army reached the German frontier, Germany would be defenceless with its fortresses razed to the ground and Bolshevism sweeping on to the Elbe. Briand replied forcefully that the League was the pivot of all their proceedings and if this foundation were undermined all their arrangements would fail. It was not possible, he said, for Germany 'to stand with one foot in the League of Nations and with the other, or at least the tip of the toe, in another camp'. Chamberlain too pointed out that Germany could not expect the advantages of League membership while refusing the obligations.

After further exchanges between Briand and Luther, Stresemann spoke again at length. He pointed out that if they had wanted simply to avoid their obligations they could have relied on the right of veto in the council. He insisted that if the Soviet Union was the aggressor Germany would give its full moral support to the League. But in the event of war Germany would need all its forces to control unrest at home. He rejected the idea that Germany was asking for a privileged position, pointing out that they had not wanted to be disarmed. He was asking only for an interpretation of how the covenant was to apply to a disarmed nation. He suggested that they should use the precedent of the Geneval protocol which had included provision for states to cooperate in sanctions in so far as their military and geographical position allowed.

This discussion made a deep impression on the delegates. Chamberlain told Stresemann that he had never attended a more interesting debate and the French interpreter Hesnard told him that he had gone to the limits of what was politically acceptable but had done so in a manner which had won the recognition of Briand.[14] A British official, Miles Lampson, wrote the following day:

I claim to be as phlegmatic and unemotional as most of my countrymen: but I admit having been thrilled to the bone once or twice by the eloquence and

---

[14] Diary for 8 Oct. 1925: Bernhard (ed.), *Vermächtnis*, ii. 192.

obvious sincerity of both Briand and Stresemann. Yesterday, over the question of Germany's entry into the League, they were both at their best and I have never before had the good fortune to hear a discussion conducted on so high a plane. It was really wonderful...'[15]

Stresemann's gifts in debate had once again proved their worth. By speaking openly about a Soviet–Polish war he showed he was not afraid to discuss the example that was in the back of all their minds. By playing on the dangers of Bolshevism, he established common ground with both Chamberlain and Briand. However, the arguments he used were less than the whole truth. He could not say that Germany wanted to maintain the link with the Soviet Union as a means of pressure against Poland and that in the event of a Polish–Soviet war Germany hoped to be able to revise its frontier with Poland. There was clearly a gap between his claim at Locarno that Germany would give the League its full moral support and his argument to Chicherin that the purpose of their stand on article 16 was to keep Germany out of sanctions against the Soviet Union. His 'obvious sincerity' was less than total and France and Britain remained suspicious of German relations with the Soviet Union.

An irony in the German position was revealed by Gaus. Having heard Briand and Chamberlain argue that article 16 did not impose precise obligations, he decided that it might be better for Germany to accept the article after all. Stresemann sharply reminded him that in that case they had misled German public opinion over the previous year.[16] This incident, trivial in itself, shows that the real determinant of Stresemann's policy was less the actual obligations of article 16 than the political importance of achieving exemption. He needed a formula to satisfy the Soviet Union and his domestic critics that Germany would retain its independence—Hindenburg for instance regarded article 16 as 'a noose around the neck'.[17]

The breakthrough on this question came during an excursion on the lake in a launch called *Orange Blossom*, ostensibly to celebrate Mrs Chamberlain's birthday. Stresemann later explained that the reality was far from the idyll this conjured up and which was seized on by the press, hungry for news. The delegates had in fact spent five hours in the ship's cabin locked in debate between the lawyers, which had left him more exhausted than

[15] Lampson to Tyrrell, 9 Oct. 1925: *DBFP*, 1st ser. xxvii, no. 529.
[16] Walsdorff, *Westorientierung und Ostpolitik*, 141.
[17] Hermann Pünder to Kempner, 12 Oct. 1925: Minuth (ed.), *Kabinette Luther*, no. 183.

ever before.[18] The result was satisfactory from the German point of view—a note from the other powers giving their interpretation of article 16 as requiring cooperation from a member state 'to an extent which is compatible with its military situation and takes its geographical situation into account'.[19] The Germans interpreted this as applying also to economic sanctions and the other delegates raised no objection. The Germans also pressed for a new initiative for general disarmament and appropriate sentiments were included in the final protocol.[20]

This left as the only major business of the formal agenda the arbitration treaties between Germany and both Poland and Czechoslovakia. Edouard Beneš and Aleksander Skrzyński, the Czech and Polish foreign ministers, had not had an easy time at the conference. Excluded from the main proceedings until the last two days, they were forced, as Stresemann later commented with satisfaction, to 'sit in a side room, until we allowed them in'.[21] Their negotiating position depended on France, and once Briand had accepted the compromise over the French guarantee they had no option but to agree. Polish attempts to include recognition of the frontiers or a general renunciation of force in the arbitration treaties were refused by Gaus at a meeting which, according to Stresemann, became so heated that Gaus asked to be released from further negotiations with the Poles.[22] The final version of the treaties distinguished, as the Germans wanted, between justiciable issues with binding arbitration and others which would be referred to a Permanent Conciliation Commission whose decisions were not binding, although an unresolved dispute could then be brought before the League to be dealt with under article 15.[23]

The Germans had achieved their main objective, to make a distinction between the Rhine frontier where they had renounced the use of force and accepted the guarantees of Britain and Italy and the eastern frontiers where they had refused to renounce force or accept the French guarantee. The preambles to the treaties with Poland and Czechoslovakia did contain statements that the signatories were 'resolved to maintain peace' and

---

[18] Speech to the Arbeitsgemeinschaft deutscher Landsmannschaften, 14 Dec. 1925: *ADAP*, ser. B, i/i, p. 737.

[19] German record, 12 Oct. 1925: Minuth (ed.), *Kabinette Luther*, no. 182; Macartney (ed.), *Survey 1925*, ii. 451.

[20] Macartney (ed.), *Survey 1925*, ii. 439–40.

[21] Speech to the Arbeitsgemeinschaft deutscher Landsmannschaften, 14 Dec. 1925: *ADAP*, ser. B, i/i, p. 752.

[22] Ibid., p. 740.

[23] Macartney (ed.), *Survey 1925*, ii. 446–50.

recognized 'that the rights of a state cannot be modified save with its consent' but these were meaningless. Stresemann later dismissed them as 'pure platitudes' since in law consent could include the situation of a defeated country signing a peace treaty.[24]

The political distinction drawn between the western and eastern frontiers was of great importance. It meant that some European frontiers were more firmly recognized and guaranteed than others. For this reason Mussolini would have liked to see Italy's frontier with Austria included in the pact, but the Germans were not prepared to extend the pact in this way and nor was Chamberlain.[25] Stresemann argued that Germany could not be expected to guarantee a frontier between two independent states—it was a matter for Italy and Austria.[26] He also had no desire to be drawn into recognition of the Italian acquisition of South Tyrol, which would annoy Austria and give the DNVP a new argument against Locarno. But Italian concern and Polish dismay showed the way in which the agreements were seen as a success for German revisionism.[27]

The German delegation had one further objective, to achieve concessions—especially in the Rhineland occupation—as a consequence of the Locarno pact. At a meeting in Chamberlain's rooms, Stresemann presented a detailed list of demands, including evacuation of the Cologne zone, relaxation of the occupation regime, bringing forward the evacuation of the remaining zones and the Saar plebiscite, amendment of the League's procedures for supervising German disarmament to eliminate any permanent organization in the Rhineland, and the lifting of restrictions on German air traffic in the occupied zone.[28] By presenting the whole list he carried out the cabinet's instructions. His main argument was that since French security would now be guaranteed by the Locarno pact, there could be no justification for the occupation of the Rhineland.

---

[24] Speech to the Arbeitsgemeinschaft deutscher Landsmannschaften, 14 Dec. 1925: *ADAP*, ser. B, i/i, p. 741. Briand said of the preamble, 'One might as well say that the majority is normally larger than the minority' (ibid.).

[25] Alan Cassels, 'Locarno: Early Test of Fascist Intentions', in Gaynor Johnson (ed.), *Locarno Revisited: European Diplomacy, 1920–1929* (forthcoming); Sally Marks, 'Mussolini and Locarno: Fascist Foreign Policy in Microcosm', *Journal of Contemporary History*, 14 (1979), 423–39.

[26] Chamberlain to Tyrrell, 8 Oct. 1925: *DBFP*, 1st ser. xxvii, no. 522; Stresemann to the German embassy in Rome, 23 May 1925: *ADAP*, ser. A, xiii, no. 55.

[27] Anna M. Cienciala and Titus Komarnicki, *From Versailles to Locarno. Keys to Polish Foreign Policy 1919–1925* (Lawrence: University Press of Kansas, 1984), 270–3.

[28] Summary by Schubert, 12 Oct. 1925: *ADAP*, ser. A, xiv, no. 138. There is a full account of the discussion in *DBFP*, 1st ser. xxvii, appendix 11.

Briand was taken aback by Stresemann's boldness, which he subsequently described as 'bordering on recklessness'. He responded that
Stresemann's list almost extended to the treaty of Versailles itself and
would require another conference.[29] Briand and Chamberlain refused to
accept any kind of bargain as a condition of the pact, but they held out the
prospect that the détente, which would follow, would allow many of the
changes the Germans wanted. A compromise was reached over evacuation
of the Cologne zone, which was still held up by the inability of the
German and Allied military experts to agree on whether Germany had
satisfied its disarmament obligations. Germany would explain its view to
the competent Allied body—the ambassadors' conference—and that
body would reply, asking for German cooperation in settling the
remaining matters in dispute and giving a date for evacuation.[30] Stresemann tried to press for further concessions, but Briand and Chamberlain
lost patience and made it clear that they resented what they saw as the
German tactic of raising last-minute conditions. Chamberlain subsequently complained to his senior official, 'It shows once again how difficult it is to help a German...'.[31]

The German delegation had clearly achieved all that was possible at
Locarno and it was sufficiently confident of the results to initial the
agreements, against the advice of the rest of the cabinet in Berlin.[32]
The atmosphere of cordiality which had been strained to breaking point
the night before returned for the final ceremony on 16 October. Stresemann told Briand that Luther—on being presented with a telegram from a
prominent member of the DNVP warning him not to sign the agreement
had said, 'Tell him to "kiss my a——" [in English] I mean to sign.'[33] At
Briand's request, Stresemann made only a passing reference to the improvements which Germany hoped would follow from the pact in his
closing statement, allowing Briand to respond by promising that France

[29] Stresemann's diary for 13 Oct. 1925: Bernhard (ed.) *Vermächtnis*, ii. 194: *DBFP*, 1st ser. xxvii,
appendix 11.

[30] German record, 15 Oct. 1925 and memorandum by Luther: Minuth (ed.), *Kabinette Luther*,
nos. 195a, 195b. *DBFP*, 1st ser. xxvii, appendix 14.

[31] Chamberlain to Tyrrell, 16 Oct. 1925: *DBFP*, 1st ser. xxvii, no. 547.

[32] Minutes of a meeting of ministers, 16 Oct. 1925 and Luther to Hindenburg, 16 Oct. 1925:
Minuth (ed.), *Kabinette Luther*, nos. 197, 200.

[33] Diary entry by Neville Chamberlain, 22 Oct. 1925, recording a discussion with Austen the
night before: University of Birmingham, Chamberlain papers, NC 2/21. I am grateful to Dr
Richard Grayson for providing me with references from this source. Stresemann told his family
that in fact Luther had hesitated for a long time before deciding to sign because he feared the
reaction of the DNVP. Wolfgang Stresemann, *Mein Vater*, 389; Luther, *Politiker ohne Partei*, 390.

would 'do everything in her power' to bring about 'a feeling of appease-ment and détente between our two countries'.[34]

Stresemann had been impressed by Briand. Briand's unorthodox polit-ical career from socialist to annexationist wartime premier to pragmatic architect of détente resembled his own in important respects. Both also came from modest backgrounds, unlike Austen Chamberlain, whose rela-tions with Stresemann were based on mutual respect but lacked warmth.[35] Stresemann was also unable to resist Briand's mischievous sense of humour. The German interpreter, Schmidt, recorded that at one point Briand interrupted Luther who was giving a solemn account of Germany's difficulties, saying 'If you go on, we will all start to cry' and when Luther looked annoyed he made such a 'comic, frightened expression' that Stre-semann burst out laughing.[36]

At another level, Stresemann was attracted by Briand's analysis of their respective political difficulties, telling the DVP's national executive that it had been 'very witty and imaginative'.[37] Briand described the German opposition as believing 'in a curious, mystical way' that one day, somehow, the international situation would change in Germany's favour without any need for concessions, and compared it to his problems with people like Poincaré, who imagined that France was in an immensely strong position and criticized him for giving it away. Stresemann even suggested that what they had been offered at Locarno went further than a German government, had it been victorious in the war, would have been prepared to concede.

'These donkeys': The DNVP Returns to Opposition

The next task was to rally public opinion behind the Locarno treaties. Stresemann wrote later that he had anticipated great difficulties, but not

[34] Diary for 18 Oct. 1925: Bernhard (ed.), *Vermächtnis*, ii. 201; German record, 16 Oct. 1925: Minuth (ed.), *Kabinette Luther*, no. 199.

[35] Stresemann found Chamberlain rather haughty, and he noted in December that Cham-berlain's attitude to Germany regaining a colony was 'very unpleasant and painful'. Diary for beginning of December 1925: Bernhard (ed.), *Vermächtnis*, ii. 251. Chamberlain, according to his half-brother Neville, found Luther sympathetic: 'Stresemann on the other hand has not a sympa-thetic personality. But A[usten] expressed great admiration for his courage both physical, for he is in constant danger of assassination and moral. But he is trusted by no one & generally unpopular in Germany.' Diary for 22 Oct. 1925: University of Birmingham, Chamberlain papers, NC 2/21.

[36] Schmidt, *Statist*, 80.

[37] Minutes of the Zentralvorstand meeting, 22 Nov. 1925: Kolb and Richter (eds.), *Nationalli-beralismus*, no. 61.

the bitter divisions which followed.[38] The first cabinet with Hindenburg went well.[39] Stresemann and Luther reported on what had been achieved and the other ministers, including Schiele, were impressed; even Hindenburg expressed his satisfaction.

This unusual harmony did not last. The following day the DNVP Reichstag party forbade Schiele to agree to anything in cabinet until the party had expressed an opinion. Luther tried to save the situation by making it clear to Westarp, in Stresemann's presence, that the DNVP could not expect to destroy the Locarno treaties and remain in the government.[40] However, Westarp and the other moderate DNVP leaders were trapped by the determination of the party's provincial organizations to oppose the treaties and avoid another fiasco like the split over the Dawes plan. On 23 October a meeting of the DNVP's executive committee and provincial party chairmen decided to reject the treaties. On 25 October the DNVP Reichstag party decided that it had no alternative but to withdraw from the coalition and the DNVP ministers resigned, Schiele declaring in an emotional farewell speech that they had been swept away by a storm tide.[41]

The bolt by the DNVP back into opposition transformed the political landscape. It weakened the government's position abroad, since with the largest nationalist party in opposition France and Britain would no longer have the same confidence in the stability of the Locarno treaties and might therefore be more wary about withdrawing from the Rhineland.[42] It also created a very difficult situation at home. The government had lost its majority and had to look to the SPD and DDP to provide the votes for the Locarno treaties. Yet the SPD had no obligation to support a Luther government, whose tariff and fiscal policies it opposed. Its price for supporting the treaties might be a reconstruction of the government or new elections.[43] Stresemann's strategy of creating a broad national front behind his foreign policy had collapsed. He commented sourly in his

---

[38] Diary for the beginning of December 1925: Bernhard (ed.), *Vermächtnis*, ii. 246–7.

[39] Minutes of the meeting, 19 Oct. 1925: Minuth (ed.), *Kabinette Luther*, no. 201.

[40] Diary for 27 Oct. 1925: Bernhard (ed.), *Vermächtnis*, ii. 205–7.

[41] Grathwol, *Stresemann and the DNVP*, 140–2. Cabinet minutes, 26 Oct. 1925: Minuth (ed.), *Kabinette Luther*, no. 208. Diary for 27 Oct. 1925: Bernhard (ed.), *Vermächtnis*, ii. 206–7.

[42] Luther's report to the coalition party leaders, 3 Nov. 1925: Minuth (ed.), *Kabinette Luther*, no. 216.

[43] Meeting of coalition party leaders, 3 Nov. 1925: ibid. Heinrich August Winkler, *Der Schein der Normalität. Arbeiter und Arbeiterbewegung in der Weimarer Republik 1924 bis 1930*, 2nd edn. (Berlin: J. H. W. Dietz, 1988), 255–9.

diary: 'In any event the situation has become as impossible as it has ever been through the inconceivable folly of the German Nationals.'[44]

The cabinet decided to remain in office with the aim of securing the ratification of the treaties but leaving open the question of its future thereafter.[45] The remaining coalition parties—Centre, DVP, and BVP—agreed that the DNVP should not be allowed to rejoin the government in the foreseeable future.[46] This was necessary to overcome SPD suspicion that it might be used to provide a majority for the Locarno treaties only for the DNVP subsequently to be allowed back into the government. But feelings also ran high against the DNVP among the coalition parties. The Centre party swung back in favour of a great coalition. The DVP preferred to continue with a minority coalition of the middle parties, looking to the SPD for support in foreign policy and the DNVP for domestic policy, but whether this was practicable remained doubtful. Stresemann was emphatic that the DNVP could not be allowed back into the government even if the Allies failed to make concessions over the Rhineland and the government decided against ratification of the treaties. 'The DNVP', he said, had 'robbed us of the possibility of presenting our demands abroad supported by an overwhelming majority of the German people.'[47]

The government was forced to defend the Locarno treaties against a strident campaign in the DNVP press, largely controlled by Stresemann's long-standing enemy, Hugenberg.[48] In retrospect Stresemann thought that they had allowed themselves to be manoeuvred by the opposition into adopting the wrong tactics. They had played down the success of the treaties and, to maintain pressure on the Allies, put the emphasis on the concessions to be expected in the Rhineland. When the Allies agreed to a date for the evacuation of the Cologne zone, the government again felt it had to treat this as a disappointment to maintain the pressure for further concessions. In fact they had achieved far more than they expected and their restraint played into the hands of the DNVP.[49]

[44] Diary for 28 Oct. 1925: Bernhard (ed.), *Vermächtnis*, ii. 209.

[45] Minutes of two cabinet meetings, 26 Oct. 1925: Minuth (ed.), *Kabinette Luther*, nos. 208, 209.

[46] Minutes of a meeting of ministers with party representatives, 3 Nov. 1925: ibid., no. 216.

[47] Ibid.

[48] Stresemann told the DVP Zentralvorstand that there were 369 DNVP newspapers compared to only forty-five for the DVP, and commented on the spiteful tone of those influenced by Hugenberg. Minutes of the meeting, 22 Nov. 1925: Kolb and Richter (eds.), *Nationalliberalismus*, 619.

[49] Diary for the beginning of Dec. 1925: Bernhard (ed.), *Vermächtnis*, ii. 246–8.

Stresemann played a major part in the campaign in speeches, press briefings, and a broadcast.[50] He patiently explained the significance of the Locarno treaties, claiming that they represented the end of the era of dictated terms and ultimatums and the end of Poincaré's ambitions in the Rhineland. On the other hand, he said, Germans had to understand the French need for security, and he quoted Bismarck on the importance of respecting 'the imponderables', in this case the importance of responding to the international desire for a guarantee of European peace. He held out the goal of 'a peaceful Germany at the centre of a peaceful Europe'.[51] He also explained the economic motives for Locarno, pointing out that both Germany and France needed American loans and that a peaceful Europe was an essential prerequisite. France was also interested in economic cooperation: 'We are needed for a great European economic new course.'[52]

On two occasions Stresemann went further and spoke more freely, without journalists present, about Germany's revisionist goals. The first of these was at a meeting of the DVP national executive just before the debate on ratification of the treaties in the Reichstag.[53] Stresemann's relations with his party had never been better; his anger at the resignation of the DNVP—'these donkeys'—was generally shared. Departing from the form of what he called his usual 'academic, ministerial speech' he paid tribute to Briand's imaginative grasp of their common problems and his willingness to break with the policies of Poincaré.

Later in the speech he summarized what had been achieved as security for the Rhineland and the end of the entente between Germany's opponents. He argued that the latter—'this spirit of Locarno'—was what mattered most. The best way to overcome the treaty of Versailles was to undermine it by persuasion. Applying this precept to Poland, he said that if Poland's economic problems led to a proposal for international aid then Germany could raise the question of frontier revision under article 19 of the covenant and it would be 'of decisive importance for us that at this moment Germany should have the best and friendliest relations with those world powers who will decide this question'. No such opportunity

---

[50] Speech in Karlsruhe, 23 Oct. 1925, published as 'Das Werk von Locarno', *Deutsche Stimmen*, 37/21, 5 Nov. 1925; press conference in Dresden, 31 Oct. 1925: Bernhard (ed.), *Vermächtnis*, ii. 211–19; broadcast, 3 Nov. 1925: Rheinbaben (ed.), *Reden und Schriften*, ii, 211–23.

[51] 'Das Werk von Locarno', *Deutsche Stimmen*, 37/21, 5 Nov. 1925, 432.

[52] Press conference in Dresden, 31 Oct. 1925: Bernhard (ed.), *Vermächtnis*, ii. 218–19.

[53] Minutes of the Zentralvorstand meeting, 22 Nov. 1925: Kolb and Richter (eds.), *Nationalliberalismus*, no. 61. The ratification debate took place from 25 to 27 November.

would have existed without Locarno. Here was a clear indication of how Stresemann hoped that peaceful revision might work in practice.

Stresemann's other major off-the-record speech about Locarno was to an association in Berlin representing Germans from frontier regions which had been lost or divided by the treaty of Versailles.[54] He took care to cultivate such groups both from a concern to maintain the minorities as an instrument of revision and, also, in order to be able to demonstrate their support for his policy against attacks from the DNVP.[55] Shortly after the meeting, he saw representatives from the lost territories in the east to discuss their problems.[56]

In his speech Stresemann adopted the style and language of his audience. He could do this the more readily because of his own nationalist background and sympathies. He presented a similar argument to that he had given to the national executive of the DVP, but he emphasized the goal of Germany's recovery as a great power and made no reference to 'the spirit of Locarno'. He went to the limits, and in some of his remarks beyond the limits, of what was legitimate to defend Locarno to an archnationalist audience.

He described German policy as torn between the 'absolute need of a Germany thirsting for recovery to establish good relations with other states and the anguished protest of the national soul against what German ethnic groups had to suffer in Europe'. He then discussed the means available to Germany—its lack of the 'main means', armed force, and its lack of 'a united national will' except during the Ruhr crisis—here he delivered his usual rebuke to those who questioned the patriotism of others just because they disagreed with the policy. The one great weapon for Germany, he argued, was its economic position, in particular its importance as a market for other countries and its position as a great debtor nation.

---

[54] Speech to the Arbeitsgemeinschaft deutscher Landsmannschaften in Gross-Berlin, 14 Dec. 1925: *ADAP*, ser. B, i/i, pp. 727–53 (Nl. 33). I have been unable to find details of this particular group, but it was probably a regional branch of the main umbrella organization, the Deutscher Schutzbund für das Grenz-und Auslandsdeutschtum: Dieter Fricke (ed.), *Lexikon zur Parteiengeschichte* (Leipzig: VEB Bibliographisches Institut, 1984), 290–310.

[55] On the support of minorities, see Kimmich, *The Free City*; Norbert Krekeler, *Revisionsanspruch und geheime Ostpolitik der Weimarer Republik* (Stuttgart: Deutsche Verlags-Anstalt, 1973). On the domestic political aspect, see Bastiaan Schot, *Nation oder Staat? Deutschland und der Minderheitenschutz* (Marburg: J. G. Herder Institut, 1988). Stresemann had earlier addressed a parallel organization, the Bund der Auslandsdeutschen, which represented Germans overseas: NLC 52/168, 12 Sept. 1925; cf. Heuss, *Erinnerungen*, 248, 306–10.

[56] Minutes of the meeting, 28 Dec.1925: *ADAP*, ser. B, ii/i, no. 19.

'Nations', he said, 'are always egoists' and relations with other states depended on 'parallel interests'. Britain, France, and the United States had an interest in preventing the collapse of the German economy because of the effect that would have on the international economy. This 'led us to consider whether it might not be possible to solve political questions by economic means' and in this way 'to change the direction of things since Versailles'. He pointed out that they might need a revision of the Dawes plan by 1927 and therefore they had to have the kind of relationship with the Western powers which would prevent a reimposition of sanctions. He also suggested that the French might be interested in realizing some of the assets which acted as guarantees for the plan, in return for earlier evacuation of the Rhineland. In general he underlined the advantages of being a debtor: provided your debts were big enough, creditors would have an interest in your recovery. He joked that the healthiest man in Dresden before the war had been up to his neck in debt: whenever he coughed each of his creditors sent him to a specialist, thinking that so long as he was alive at least he would pay the interest! That had been the reason for American support of Britain and France during the war and the same alignment of interests was now becoming true for Germany.

Turning to Locarno, Stresemann said that the economic understanding of the Dawes plan had to be followed by a political one. He admitted that he saw no way of getting back Alsace-Lorraine, but he claimed that Locarno made it easier for the Germans in Alsace to press for cultural autonomy since they could no longer be accused of disloyalty. On Eupen-Malmédy he suggested that they might be able to buy it back. His main emphasis, however, was on revision of the Polish frontier. He gave a cynical account of the arbitration treaty and of the French guarantee to Poland designed to show that neither limited Germany's freedom of action. He suggested—wrongly—that the French guarantee could only come into effect with the unanimous backing of the League council, and cast doubt on whether the League would ever be able to agree on who had been the aggressor.[57] He said Germany 'had never behaved more stupidly' than in its haste to declare war in 1914 and he contrasted Bethmann-Hollweg's admission of the wrong done to Belgium with Frederick the Great's assertion at the beginning of the Silesian wars that he had the right to march through Saxony. He went on: 'That is what one means by

---

[57] In fact, as we have seen, the French retained the right to act, under article 15, if the council was divided. See above, p.333.

politics and I believe that other nations let the guns go off somewhere or other and then declare that they are hurrying to the help of the victim. That is how most wars start.'

The parallel with Hitler's tactics in 1939 is striking. Yet it would be wrong to conclude that Stresemann was contemplating war with Poland. His purpose was rather to rebut the DNVP's argument that Germany had surrendered rights at Locarno. He immediately explained that he was only concerned to show that the automatic right of France to intervene on the side of Poland had been limited by Locarno. He went on:

I am not thinking of war in relation to the eastern question either, where the right of self-determination has been violated in an unheard of way. But what I imagine is that if conditions once arise which appear to threaten peace or the economic consolidation of Europe through developments in the east, and if the question arises as to whether the whole instability of Europe is not caused by the impossible way the frontiers are drawn in the east, that then it may also be possible for Germany to succeed with its demands, if it has previously established ties of political friendship and an economic community of interests with all the world powers who have to decide the issue. In my opinion, this is the only practical policy.

This was his real strategy, and in contrast to the unscrupulous methods of aggressive war, which he had appeared to commend, it meant building up a relationship of good faith with the Western powers. He referred to the importance of 'securing the peace towards France' while warning that they should not expect results too quickly—they should not behave like a child writing a Christmas list of all the presents he wanted in the next fifteen years. He pointed out that it was French insecurity which was the chief obstacle to territorial revision. He conceded that Locarno also had disadvantages—it had aroused Italian fears for the Brenner frontier leading to fascist oppression of the Germans in South Tyrol. On the other hand they had also scored some successes—the Poles had agreed to halt the expulsion of ethnic Germans who had opted for German nationality.[58] He hinted that the Poles faced serious problems, caught

[58] Under article 91 of the Versailles treaty, Germans living in Poland had the right to opt for German nationality within two years of the treaty coming into force, and the right to move to Germany without loss of property within the following year. The Polish measures were directed against those who had not left within the specified time. The Polish suspension of the evictions due in Nov. 1925 came after pressure from Chamberlain at Locarno. Stresemann disappointed the Poles by refusing to respond with a statement welcoming this gesture. Harald von Riekhoff, *German–Polish Relations, 1918–1933* (Baltimore: Johns Hopkins University Press, 1971), 52–71;

between financial crisis and growing French indifference. This might be the moment he said, echoing a phrase of Bismarck's, for Germany to seize the opportunity and grasp 'the tip of the mantle' of God's progress through history.[59] 'But for that', he reminded them again, 'it is necessary, if one does not have military power oneself, to create friendships or alliances or economic ties.'

The speech was a consummate blend of statesmanlike argument and nationalist rhetoric. Judging by the stenographer's record, which notes frequent expressions of approval and laughter from the audience and 'stormy, long-lasting applause' at the end, it served its purpose. It also reflected the tension between the two sides of Stresemann's policy: a historic understanding with France in order to open the way to revision in the east. The difference in his feelings towards each side was clearly reflected in praise for Briand and Chamberlain and his pleasure at the way Beneš and Skrzyński had been humiliated at Locarno. Poland he said was now regarded by France as 'the moor' who 'has done his duty' and could be dispensed with.[60] However, while keeping alive expectations for peaceful revision in the east, Stresemann still had only the vaguest idea of how it might come about. His strongest argument remained that there was no viable alternative to the policy he proposed.

The attempts to influence public opinion had no effect on the DNVP's opposition to the Locarno treaties. There was some dissent, but it was not sufficient to threaten party unity. Stresemann tried to encourage the dissent, writing to one of the moderate leaders, Walter von Keudell, on the day of the Reichstag vote that he regretted the breach. He compared Locarno to an armistice and said simply: 'I see in Locarno the preservation of the Rhineland and the possibility of recovering German land in the east.' In an obvious hint to Keudell, he added that he regretted the absence of the old Free Conservative Party which had acted as a moderating influence, even though as leader of the DVP he would have cause to fear such a party.[61]

Christian Raitz von Frentz, *A Lesson Forgotten. Minority Protection under the League of Nations: The Case of the German Minority in Poland, 1920–1934* (New York: Lit, 1999), 145–50.

[59] Not, as has been suggested, to 'pull off her [Poland's] top clothes': Cienciala and Komarnicki, *From Versailles to Locarno*, 274. The full Bismarck quotation is in Lothar Gall, *Bismarck: The White Revolutionary*, Eng. edn., vol. i (London: Allen & Unwin, 1986), 28.

[60] The reference to the moor occurs originally in Friedrich Schiller's, *Die Verschwörung des Fiesco zu Genua*, Act III, scene iv, but passed into the language to describe someone who has served his purpose. I am grateful to Professor Lesley Noakes for her help on this point.

[61] Stresemann to von Keudell, 27 Nov. 1925 (Nl. 274): Bernhard (ed.), *Vermächtnis*, ii. 246; also diary for 29 Oct. 1925 (Nl. 272). There were also feelers from members of the Reich Farmers'

No split occurred, and the DNVP even declared that it would not recognize the Locarno treaties since in their view the treaties should have been subject to a two-thirds majority in the Reichstag. Stresemann noted that if a two-thirds majority had been required the DNVP might have split, but that in any case by their statement the DNVP had excluded themselves from office.[62]

The government was helped towards ratification by the Allies, who agreed to return much of the Rhineland administration to German control, to reduce the size of the occupying armies, and to evacuate the Cologne zone on 1 December. The cabinet thereupon asked the Reichstag to approve the treaties and to give authority for Germany to enter the League.[63] There was some opposition from Hindenburg, who had been swayed by the DNVP and a last-minute intervention by Brockdorff-Rantzau.[64] Luther, however, performed what Stresemann called 'the great service' of standing up to Hindenburg and he grudgingly gave way.[65] The SPD supported ratification in return for Luther making it clear that the government would resign once the treaties had been signed, and the treaties were approved by a large majority in the Reichstag on 27 November.

Luther and Stresemann went to London for the signing ceremony on 1 December. Stresemann responded to a speech by Briand by saying that they had the right to speak of 'a European idea' following the losses they had suffered in the war, above all the loss of a generation with all its potential, meaning that they could only recover by cooperation in peace.[66] There followed a round of dinners which Stresemann found resembled each other too closely, a reception at Buckingham palace, and a visit to the House of Commons which he enjoyed most.[67] There was also one business meeting where the Germans pressed Briand on the question of troop

Association enquiring whether they could join the coalition and take over the Ministry of Agriculture provided they broke with the DNVP. Stresemann replied encouragingly: ibid. 380. Michael Stürmer, *Koalition und Opposition in der Weimarer Republik 1924–1928* (Düsseldorf: Droste, 1967), 133–4; Richter, *Deutsche Volkspartei*, 408.

[62] Diary for the beginning of Dec. 1925: Bernhard (ed.), *Vermächtnis*, ii. 248.

[63] Minutes of meetings of the Ministerrat (cabinet with Hindenburg presiding), 16–17 Nov. 1925: Minuth (ed.), *Kabinette Luther*, nos. 223–4, 226.

[64] Brockdorff-Rantzau's memorandum for Hindenburg, 7 Nov. 1925, in which he argued that Locarno would deprive Germany of the 'ace' of Rapallo, namely the threat of closer relations with the Soviet Union, going even as far as military cooperation: *ADAP*, ser. A, xiv, no. 222.

[65] Diary for the beginning of Dec. 1925 (Nl. 272).

[66] Bernhard (ed.), *Vermächtnis*, ii. 252–4.

[67] Diary for the beginning of Dec. 1925; ibid. 248–52.

levels in the Rhineland and Chamberlain made it clear, 'to avoid misunderstanding in the future', that Britain would never give up a colonial mandate to Germany.[68] At the final dinner, however, Chamberlain gave Stresemann an interesting account of the background to Locarno, saying that the German security pact memorandum had arrived at a critical time enabling him to accomplish in one step what he had intended to do in two—namely first a pact with France and Belgium and then a multilateral pact including Germany.[69] Soon after he returned to Berlin, an assassination plot against Stresemann was reported to the police and the culprits arrested.[70]

The Second Luther Cabinet

The cabinet resigned on 5 December. The two main alternatives without the DNVP were either another attempt at a great coalition or a minority government of the middle parties. The Centre and DDP were strongly in favour of a great coalition. The SPD, however, was not attracted by the prospect of government, partly because a sharp rise in unemployment made them afraid of losing support to the KPD, partly because of disillusionment with the Stresemann coalition of 1923.[71] The tactics of the DVP leaders were to express support for a great coalition provided that a common programme could be agreed, but in practice their main aim was to avoid being blamed if the negotiations failed, so that the other parties would agree to form another minority government.[72]

Stresemann was sceptical of the prospects of a great coalition. He told the cabinet that a great coalition would be possible if 'truly statesmanlike figures' such as Otto Braun and Carl Severing were included, but not with people such as (his former ministers) Schmidt and Sollmann. Alternatively, he suggested that SPD goodwill towards a minority government

---

[68] *DBFP*, ser. 1a, 1, no. 122; Luther's record of the meeting, dated 4 Dec. 1925: Minuth (ed.), *Kabinette Luther*, no. 239. A. J. Crozier, 'The Colonial Question During the Locarno Conference and After: An Essay on Anglo-German Relations 1924–1927', *International History Review*, 4/1 (1982), 51–2.

[69] Diary for the beginning of Dec. 1925: Bernhard (ed.), *Vermächtnis*, ii. 251–2; note dated 6 Dec. 1925 (Nl. 272).

[70] Bernhard (ed.), *Vermächtnis*, ii. 321.

[71] Winkler, *Der Schein der Normalität*, 255–64.

[72] Scholz was open with Hindenburg about his tactics; minutes of their discussions on 7 and 11 Dec. 1925: BAB, Büro des Reichspräsidenten, 43.

might be forthcoming if it was given extensive representation in the German delegation to the League.[73] When the first attempt to form a great coalition failed, Stresemann came out strongly in favour of Luther being asked to form a new government, saying 'I do not believe in the great coalition and I do not think it is right to form one if the parties have to be forced into it.'[74]

The DVP's tactics were successful and Luther formed a new government with the DVP, Centre, DDP, and BVP on 19 January 1926. Stresemann was content with the result. He did not expect the SPD to want to force new elections until the economic position improved.[75] The DNVP would remain under pressure to accept Locarno if it wanted to rejoin the government. On a personal level, despite their differences, Stresemann appreciated the way Luther had stood up to Hindenburg and the DNVP.[76]

Luther was immediately warned by the DNVP that if he went ahead with entry into the League, they would put down a motion of no confidence.[77] At Stresemann's suggestion, Luther took the offensive, proposing that the government should itself ask for a vote of confidence, and he obtained Hindenburg's authority for a dissolution if he lost.[78] After a speech by Luther which Stresemann regarded as marking a break with the DNVP and a skilful appeal to the SPD, the government won by the narrow margin of 160 to 150, thanks to the abstention of the SPD.[79]

Despite the difficulties of domestic politics, Stresemann could look to the future with some confidence for the first time. Locarno had already borne fruit in improvements in the Rhineland and there was every prospect of further gains. It would become increasingly difficult for the Allies

---

[73] Cabinet minutes, 5 Dec. 1925: Minuth (ed.), *Kabinette Luther*, no. 243.

[74] Minutes of a meeting of party leaders with Hindenburg, 1 Jan. 1926: BAB, Büro des Reichspräsidenten, 43. Also Kempner to Luther, 4 Jan. 1926: Minuth (ed.), *Kabinette Luther*, no. 259.

[75] Stresemann's note of a conversation with D'Abernon, 22 Dec. 1925: Bernhard (ed.), *Vermächtnis*, ii. 382; D'Abernon's report, *DBFP*, ser. 1A, 1, no. 158.

[76] Stresemann remained the stumbling-block for the DNVP. During the negotiations for the new government Schiele told an official in the Reich Chancellery, Hermann Pünder, that the DNVP would tolerate a minority government under Luther only if Stresemann was dropped from the Foreign Ministry. Note of Pünder for Luther, 14 Dec. 1925: Minuth (ed.), *Kabinette Luther*, no. 252; Grathwol, *Stresemann and the DNVP*, 157.

[77] Memorandum by Luther of a conversation with the DNVP leaders, 28 Jan. 1926: Minuth (ed.), *Kabinette Luther*, no. 273.

[78] Diary for 28 Jan. 1926: Bernhard (ed.), *Vermächtnis*, ii. 386–7. Cabinet minutes, 28 Jan. 1926: Minuth (ed.), *Kabinette Luther*, no. 274.

[79] Diary for 28 Jan. 1926: Bernhard (ed.), *Vermächtnis*, ii. 386–7.

to defend the occupation of the remaining zones as they invoked 'the spirit of Locarno' and welcomed Germany into the League. Germany's financial position was also much improved with a continued flow of foreign loans.[80] The economic situation was still serious with high unemployment and particular problem areas, especially in agriculture. Nevertheless, the cabinet was able to discuss measures of relief to be funded from a budget surplus, an extraordinary transformation from the time of Stresemann's chancellorship.

The return of Germany's right to negotiate trade treaties with the Allies in January 1925 also marked an important step towards normality. Agreements were reached with the United States and Britain and negotiations started with France, Italy, and Poland. These negotiations were never straightforward, the chief problem being to balance Germany's interest in opening foreign markets to its industrial exports against the problems created for German farmers by cheap agricultural imports, especially from the Mediterranean and central Europe. Stresemann consistently favoured low tariffs and the expansion of foreign trade against the protectionist lobbies of agriculture and heavy industry. Contrary to a widely held view he also opposed in cabinet, though unsuccessfully, a trade war with Poland from fear of the consequences for the German community in Upper Silesia.[81]

Despite its improved position Germany still depended on the support of the Western powers to achieve its aims. The United States remained unwilling to intervene openly in European affairs; Briand, though apparently conciliatory, was constrained by domestic opposition, and Chamberlain disliked what he saw as German ingratitude when each concession seemed to produce only more demands. Stresemann had to tread a narrow path, asserting those interests which were necessary to maintain domestic support, while not destroying the détente on which his hopes for the future were based.

[80] The president of the Reichsbank, Schacht, reported on 5 Dec. 1925 that the total volume of foreign debt had stabilized, with long-term loans replacing short-term ones: Minuth (ed.), *Kabinette Luther*, no. 244.

[81] Krüger, *Aussenpolitik*, 254–9, 284–91, and Matthias Schulz, *Deutschland, der Völkerbund und die Frage der europäischen Wirtschaftsordnung 1925–1933* (Hamburg: Dr R. Krämer, 1997). See also H.-J. Schröder, 'Zur politischen Bedeutung der deutschen Handelspolitik nach dem ersten Weltkrieg', in G. D. Feldman (ed.), *The German Inflation Reconsidered* (Berlin: Walter de Gruyter, 1982), 236–50; Karl Heinrich Pohl, 'Deutsche "Wirtschaftsaussenpolitik" 1925/26. Zu einigen Aspekten der Stresemannschen Europa-Politik', in Michalka and Lee (eds.), *Stresemann*, 426–40.

Deadlock Over Entry to the League

The first step was to negotiate admission to the League. Stresemann was disturbed by a report that the occupying armies in the remaining zones were not to be reduced significantly after the Cologne zone had been evacuated on 31 January 1926. He immediately raised the matter with the French and British governments, warning that it might prevent Germany entering the League.[82] In his letter to D'Abernon, he pointed out the inconsistency of maintaining large armies of occupation with Locarno: 'Either Locarno means peace on the western frontier or it does not have this meaning.'[83] Briand authorized Stresemann to make a reassuring statement to the Reichstag and the crisis passed.[84] At the same time the French Foreign Ministry indicated its interest in a complete end to the occupation in return for a financial settlement.[85]

A much more serious problem arose when the Germans learned that Briand intended to press for Poland to be given a permanent seat on the League council together with Germany and that he had Chamberlain's support for this scheme. Stresemann decided to apply for membership immediately in order to forestall any change in the League's organization before Germany became a member. Despite the objections of Hindenburg, he secured the cabinet's agreement.[86] After the rumours of French intentions had been confirmed, the cabinet also agreed unanimously that a Polish seat on the council would be unacceptable.[87] To avoid the embarrassment of being drawn into discussing their objections to individual countries—Spain, Brazil, and Belgium were also pressing their claims—the cabinet decided to take the position that Germany had been invited to become a member of the League on the understanding that it would take its place as one of the five great powers to have a permanent seat on the council. Any departure from this basis before Germany joined would create a new situation.

In his instructions to the German embassies in Paris and London, however, Stresemann added that the idea of giving Poland—'a state

---

[82] Stresemann to Hoesch and D'Abernon, 13 Jan. 1926: *ADAP*, ser. B, i/i, nos. 36, 37.

[83] Chamberlain admitted the force of this argument; Chamberlain to Crewe, 30 Apr. 1926: *DBFP*, ser. 1A, i, no. 487.

[84] *Verhandlungen des Reichstags*, vol. 388, pp. 52227–8.

[85] Hoesch reporting discussions with Philippe Berthelot, the senior official at the French Foreign Ministry, 15 and 28 Jan. 1926: *ADAP*, ser. B, i/i, nos. 41, 67.

[86] Cabinet minutes, 8 Feb. 1926: Minuth (ed.), *Kabinette Luther*, no. 284.

[87] Cabinet minutes, 11 Feb. 1926: ibid., no. 288.

which was so young and inwardly so unstable'—this status would never have arisen without Germany's entry into the League and was clearly intended to create a counterweight to Germany.[88] This would be seen as proof that no real relationship of trust existed between the Locarno powers, especially as Germany had been given no warning of the proposal.

German hostility to Poland was expressed even more clearly in a dispatch to the German envoy in Sweden, a power which was regarded as friendly to Germany and which occupied one of the non-permanent seats on the League council and was therefore in a position to veto any change to the council's composition. This referred to an 'artificial' attempt to give Poland the character of a great power, a state which had 'unresolved conflicts with both its great neighbours' and which would be encouraged by this elevation 'in its dangerous ambitions and militarist tendencies'.[89] This indicated the underlying reason for German opposition, the fear, as a German official noted, that a permanent seat for Poland on the council would constitute an 'almost insuperable obstacle for our frontier wishes' as the other great powers, having given Poland equal status, were hardly going to bring the necessary pressure to bear for frontier revision.[90]

Briand and Chamberlain replied to German objections not very convincingly that they had no intention of detracting from the importance of Germany's admission to the League but that it was inevitable that any change would force the consideration of other long-standing claims.[91] Briand admitted that he had promised to support Poland's bid for a council seat for a long time and claimed that it would have the advantage of freeing France from acting on the council as Poland's protector and thereby being involved in permanent friction with Germany. Chamberlain supported Briand and, once Sweden had declared its intention of vetoing any additional permanent members of the council apart from Germany, Chamberlain condemned German tactics as 'doubly foolish' and liable to 'arouse unnecessary hostility'.[92]

The Germans resented being cast in the role of troublemakers but they agreed to meet the other Locarno powers to discuss a solution immedi-

[88] Stresemann to Sthamer with a copy to Hoesch, 12 Feb. 1926: *ADAP*, ser. B, i/i, no. 95.

[89] Stresemann to the German legation in Stockholm, 6 Feb. 1926: ibid., no. 83.

[90] Memorandum by Herbert von Dirksen, then a senior official in the eastern department, 9 Feb. 1926: ibid., no. 90.

[91] Sthamer, 15 Feb., and Hoesch, 17 Feb. 1926 to Auswärtiges Amt: ibid., nos. 101, 106.

[92] Chamberlain to D'Abernon, 19 Feb. 1926: *DBFP*, ser. 1A, i, no. 282, n. 2; *ADAP*, ser. B, i/i, no. 114.

ately before the special session of the League at Geneva, called to approve Germany's admission on 8 March.[93] Each side rehearsed its arguments without making much impression on the other.[94] Briand said that Germany had made it very clear that it intended to take up the question of minorities in the League, and he could think of no better way for Germany and Poland to resolve their differences than for both of them to be represented in the council—France could not be put into the position of always having to appear in the council carrying the Polish documents.[95] Stresemann countered that under League rules Poland could in any case attend council meetings when issues concerning it were being discussed. He suggested that a solution might be for a committee to examine the whole question of enlargement of the council, while Germany would declare after its admission that it was not opposed in principle to enlargement.

This proposal did not find favour, and over the following week the German delegation came under increasing pressure to agree to a compromise.[96] The most dangerous proposal from the German point of view was that they should agree that the additional permanent seat for Germany should be balanced by the creation of an additional non-permanent seat. Britain and France would press for Poland to be given this seat but the decision would be for the League as a whole. This cleverly raised the issue to the constitutional level of maintaining the balance between permanent and non-permanent members of the council. The Germans were forced on to the defensive, claiming that in fact the proposal was intended to benefit a particular state and that public opinion in Germany made it impossible for them to accept.[97] A crisis followed, with both Briand and Chamberlain threatening to resign and Chamberlain declaring that Locarno would be destroyed.[98]

Eventually an elaborate scheme was agreed under which both Sweden and Czechoslovakia would resign their non-permanent seats with Sweden

[93] Memorandum by Stresemann, 24 Feb., and by Schubert, 25 Feb. 1926 of conversations with D'Abernon: *ADAP*, ser. B, i/i, nos. 118, 119.

[94] Memorandum of the meeting, 7 Mar. 1926: ibid., no. 145; Chamberlain's summary in *DBFP*, ser. 1A, i, no. 327.

[95] At a later meeting, on 13 Mar. 1926, Briand quipped that it would be better if Poland did not exist but they could not ignore the fact that it did. *ADAP*, ser. B, i/i, no. 159.

[96] Kimmich, *Germany and the League of Nations*, 81–4.

[97] Memoranda of the meetings on 12 Mar. 1926: *ADAP*, ser. B, i/i, nos. 153, 154.

[98] Ibid., no. 153 and memorandum of a meeting on 13 Mar. 1926: ibid., no. 158; Chamberlain's reports in *DBFP*, ser. 1A, i, nos. 336–7, 341, 343–4.

to be replaced by another neutral power, such as Holland, and Czecho-slovakia by Poland.[99] Just as the situation appeared to have been saved, however, Brazil declared that it would insist on vetoing Germany's admission to the council unless it was also given a permanent seat. There was therefore no alternative but to defer Germany's admission to the next regular meeting of the League assembly in September. Meanwhile Stresemann's idea of a committee to discuss the whole issue of council membership was accepted and Germany was invited to serve on it.

The German delegation returned to Berlin without having achieved its objective but also without having given its opponents much to criticize. Stresemann defended their actions in an effective speech to the Reichstag, striking a balance between the fact that they had given nothing away and the importance of maintaining the Locarno policy. He pointed out that the crisis of the League had been caused precisely because with Germany's entry it was no longer 'an instrument of the victor powers'. Germany should continue with the goal of cooperation as 'a great power with equal rights'. To have broken off the negotiations and returned to Berlin, as they had been urged to do, would have earned them a cheap triumph, but their task was to change the climate of opinion abroad in Germany's favour and there was no alternative to continuing on the same course.[100]

The Treaty of Berlin

The question of how to redefine German relations with the Soviet Union in the light of Locarno and the commitment to join the League posed another challenge. The Soviet Union had been reluctantly forced to accept Germany's western policy, but it continued to press for a new treaty to limit the damage.[101] Its main demand was for an agreement that each side would remain neutral if either was involved in conflict with a third power, and that Germany would prevent League sanctions being imposed against the Soviet Union. When Stresemann and Schubert objected that Germany could not conclude a treaty which contradicted its obligations to the League, the Soviet ambassador Nikolai Krestinski suggested that these clauses be kept secret. Neither side pursued the idea as Stresemann was opposed to secret clauses and the Soviet government also preferred an

[99] Memoranda of discussions on 14 Mar. 1926: *ADAP*, ser. B, i/i, nos. 160–2.
[100] Reichstag speech, 22 Mar. 1926: Zwoch (ed.), *Reichstagsreden*, 218–47; quotation, p. 237.
[101] Walsdorff, *Westorientierung und Ostpolitik*, 157–63.

open treaty.[102] The problem was therefore how to find formulas which were acceptable to the Russians and consistent with the League covenant.

The German government's motives for the agreement were mixed. There was the desire to maintain pressure on Poland—Stresemann reacted sharply to a suggestion that the Soviet Union might reach an accommodation with Poland giving some sort of recognition to the Polish–Soviet frontier.[103] There was also the lurking fear of a Franco-Soviet rapprochement if Germany rejected Soviet advances. More immediate benefits were anticipated in domestic politics. A treaty with the Soviet Union would help to answer the criticism of those such as Hindenburg, Brockdorff-Rantzau, and the DNVP, who regarded the Locarno policy as one-sided.[104] There were even rumours of a Reichswehr plot to make Gessler chancellor and reverse foreign policy to a pro-Soviet course.[105] A treaty with the Soviet Union would also be popular with business circles which, according to Schubert, were 'hypnotized' by the prospects of trade with Russia to counteract the recession at home.[106] On the other hand, Stresemann and Luther were not persuaded by a ham-handed Soviet attempt to get them to agree to a major expansion of the joint arms factories in the Soviet Union, regarding this as 'irreconcilable with the whole line of our policy'.[107]

After protracted negotiations a text was agreed for a short treaty and an exchange of notes.[108] The Germans managed to insist that an unqualified guarantee of neutrality in the event of war between the Soviet Union and a third power would be inconsistent with the League covenant. The Soviet

[102] Memorandum by Schubert, 11 Dec. 1925: *ADAP*, ser. B, ii/i, no. 5.

[103] Stresemann to Brockdorff-Rantzau, 27 Mar. 1926; ibid., no. 93. Brockdorff-Rantzau reminded Chicherin that the negotiations had begun in Dec. 1924 'on the basis of the common German-Russian interest in pushing Poland back to its ethnographic frontiers'. Brockdorff-Rantzau to Auswärtiges Amt, 15 Mar. 1926: ibid., no. 84.

[104] Stresemann gave this as a reason to the cabinet; minutes of the meeting of 24 Feb. 1926: Minuth (ed.), *Kabinette Luther*, no. 299. Brockdorff-Rantzau resigned in protest against Locarno, but was persuaded to stay on as ambassador by Hindenburg with the right of reporting directly to Hindenburg, though Stresemann insisted that he be sent copies of the reports. Memorandum by Stresemann, 15 Dec. 1925, and by Brockdorff-Rantzau, 23 Jan. 1926: *ADAP*, ser. B, ii/i, nos. 8, 45.

[105] Memorandum by Henry Bernhard, 6 Feb., and by Stresemann, 28 Feb. 1926: *ADAP*, ser. B, ii/i, no. 58 and ibid. i/i, no. 127, n.4.

[106] Schubert to Hoesch, 20 Jan. 1926: ibid. ii/i, no. 41.

[107] Schubert to Brockdorff-Rantzau, 3 Apr. 1926, enclosing a memorandum of a meeting in the Soviet embassy where Luther and Stresemann had been pressed by a Soviet military representative to expand the programme in connection with the proposed treaty. Ibid., no. 102; Carsten, *Reichswehr*, 235; Zeidler, *Reichswehr und Rote Armee*, 135–9.

[108] Walsdorff, *Westorientierung und Ostpolitik*, 167–81.

side resisted the inclusion of the qualifying phrase on war—'without provocation from its side'—but finally accepted 'despite peaceful behaviour' instead. Germany also agreed not to join an economic boycott of the Soviet Union. In an accompanying note Germany restated the interpretation it had been given of article 16 by the Locarno powers which in effect gave Germany the freedom not to participate in sanctions so long as it was disarmed.

The treaty was ready for signature shortly after the failure of the negotiations over Germany's entry into the League in March. This was embarrassing to the German government as it had intended the treaty to follow admission to the League and it would now be seen as retaliation for Germany's rebuff at Geneva. Nevertheless, having warned Britain, France, and the United States of his intention, Stresemann signed the treaty of Berlin, together with Krestinski, on 24 April 1926.

Its significance, at least in the short term, was limited. Gessler told the cabinet that it was of little practical importance 'as in military terms there would be nothing behind Russia for years ahead'. Stresemann agreed, saying that the purpose was 'more negative', to prevent Russia assuming a hostile attitude.[109] In domestic politics however, it was a triumph, with Stresemann enjoying the unique experience of unanimous support in the Reichstag with the exception of three Trotskyite members.[110] The DNVP foreign affairs spokesman, Otto Hoetzsch, visited the Auswärtiges Amt to offer his congratulations, comparing the achievement to Bismarck's 'Reinsurance Treaty' of 1887.[111] The liberal *Vossische Zeitung* compared Stresemann's triumph somewhat ambiguously to that of the tyrant of Samos, Polycrates.[112]

Reaction abroad was naturally more critical. Chamberlain at first thought that Germany had been 'a fool... but that is her business', but he later accepted that the treaty was legally consistent with the covenant and took the view that it would be politically unwise to protest as 'It might merely serve to drive Germany further into the other camp.'[113] At the

---

[109] Cabinet minutes, 24 Feb. 1926: Minuth (ed.), *Kabinette Luther*, no. 299.

[110] Stresemann joked to the press that he 'dreaded the jealousy of the gods' at receiving such approval. Bernhard (ed.), *Vermächtnis*, ii. 511.

[111] Note by Stresemann, 20 Apr. 1926: ibid. 537.

[112] Ibid. 536. Polycrates supported the Persian king in his expedition against Egypt although he had himself previously formed an alliance with Egypt: M. C. Howatson (ed.), *The Oxford Companion to Classical Literature*, 2nd edn. (Oxford: Oxford University Press, 1989), 453. I am grateful to Peter Parsons for this reference.

[113] Chamberlain to D'Abernon, 25 Apr. 1926, and Chamberlain to H. M. representatives in Prague, Paris, Brussels, Rome, and Warsaw, 3 May 1926: *DBFP*, ser. 1A, i, nos. 464, 492.

same time he told D'Abernon that he hoped Stresemann would give clear proof of his 'good faith' in his public statements about the treaty.[114] Briand was more disturbed and Hoesch reported that his opponents would claim that the treaty showed the bankruptcy of Locarno and would also increase his problems with Poland.[115] Neither France nor its allies, however, persisted with their objections once it became clear that Britain would not support them.[116]

Stresemann responded to the requests of his Locarno partners for public reassurance in a broadcast about the treaty.[117] He coolly described it as 'rather something to be taken for granted than a sensation' claiming that 'Locarno and the treaty of Berlin are not contradictions, but belong together. Both together give Europe the guarantee of peaceful development.' At the same time he reminded his critics abroad that Germany had a right to pursue an independent policy 'not under the tutelage of any power or group of powers, whether in the east or the west'. German policy was to extend the system of peaceful agreements to all of Europe and Germany was 'by virtue of its geographic position the natural great mediator and bridge between east and west'. Stresemann claimed that the treaty had already succeeded in modifying Soviet hostility to the League. Germany knew that it could not conduct power politics but it was following in its own way 'a quite definite goal' to secure peace and protect its vital interests.

How far did this claim correspond to reality? The officials of the Auswärtiges Amt naturally spoke to each other in more practical terms. But the twin ideas that Germany must pursue its goals peacefully and that it should maintain a balance between West and East was common ground among them. Different diplomats favoured closer relations with the West, like Hoesch, or the East, like Brockdorff-Rantzau.[118] But most agreed that a balance had to be struck to preserve a 'free hand' for Germany.

When Hoesch criticized the proposed treaty with the Soviet Union, arguing that a de facto offer of neutrality would provoke the Locarno powers and that Russian tactics were to disrupt the trust that was building up between Germany and the West, Schubert replied with a classic

---

[114] *DBFP*, ser. IA, i., no. 492, copy to Berlin.

[115] Hoesch to Auswärtiges Amt, 11 Apr. 1926: *ADAP*, ser. B, ii/i, no. 124.

[116] Walsdorff, *Westorientierung und Ostpolitik*, 168.

[117] 1 May 1926; text in Rheinbaben (ed.), *Reden und Schriften*, ii. 250–60.

[118] The range of views held by officials concerned with the Soviet Union is described by Ingmar Sütterlin, *Die 'Russische Abteilung' des Auswärtigen Amtes in der Weimarer Republik* (Berlin: Duncker & Humblot, 1994).

exposition of the policy of balance.[119] He pointed out that Locarno had acquired 'a much greater political importance' than its original 'defensive purpose' and now offered 'possibilities of the most highly active kind'. Russian fears that Germany had committed itself further to the West than it realized were therefore not wholly unjustified. Schubert went on:

Basically, therefore, we are facing once again the old problem of our foreign policy, to harmonize our interests in the East with those in the West, a problem which is unavoidably forced on us by our central geographical position and is made only all the more sensitive by our lack of power. Whilst our pre-war policy failed because we did not decide in time for one side, because we did not want to bind ourselves, the problem has at present become easier for us, in that the possibility of binding ourselves does not exist. Neither the East nor the West is able or wants to attract us to a real alliance, which could induce us to give up our policy of keeping a free hand. It is all the more necessary for us, precisely because we want to remain free, to take care that the scales are not loaded to one side. While you are of the opinion that binding agreements with Russia mean a one-sided weight in favour of the Eastern side of the scales, I believe that the Western side will be so privileged by Locarno and the League of Nations, that the East can justifiably expect a compensation.

This perfectly expressed the dominant view in the Auswärtiges Amt. Germany had leant heavily to the West with Locarno and important new prospects of revision were opening up as a result. But good relations with the Soviet Union also served German interests and the treaty of Berlin was the necessary concession to keep the Russians in tow. Schubert was not above hinting to Chicherin that the time for the kind of far-reaching treaty the Soviet Union wanted 'would only have been reached in some years'.[120] Whether Schubert or Stresemann seriously considered a close relationship with the Soviet Union in the future is very doubtful. Stresemann hoped rather that Germany would one day be able to use its position as a mediator between East and West to press its claims against Poland. But the essential point was that Germany should strike the right balance between its interests in West and East and maintain its independence.

---

[119] Hoesch to Schubert, 31 Dec. 1925, and Schubert's reply, 20 Jan. 1926: *ADAP*, ser. B, ii/i, nos. 25, 41. Schubert made use of a text prepared for him by Dirksen. This is of some importance, since Schubert was a leading exponent of a Western course, whereas Dirksen was inclined to favour an Eastern policy. On this occasion Schubert seems to have found Dirksen's arguments useful to defend the proposed treaty to Hoesch. On Schubert's differences with Dirksen, see Krüger, *Aussenpolitik*, 317.

[120] Memorandum by Schubert of a meeting with Chicherin, 19 Dec. 1925: *ADAP*, ser. B, ii/i, no. 12.

Although an elegant concept, this two-sided policy was not in practice of much benefit to Germany. The Soviet Union was in no position to threaten Poland and was more concerned with its own security. It engaged in complex diplomacy with the Baltic states and Poland, culminating in a multilateral regional pact renouncing war in February 1929.[121] In the West the treaty of Berlin aroused suspicion, setting a limit to the Locarno détente. It may have prompted Chamberlain to urge Briand to make concessions to Germany—on one occasion he reminded Briand that they were engaged in a struggle for 'the soul of Germany' to prevent it turning to the Soviet Union.[122] But in France it increased the opposition to Locarno, reducing Briand's room for manoeuvre.

The other areas of cooperation with the Soviet Union were also of limited value. The secret military programmes were popular with the Reichswehr, but the Auswärtiges Amt regarded them more as a means of maintaining the relationship with the Soviet Union than as of value in themselves. Similarly, trade remained at very modest levels until significant growth occurred during the depression.[123]

The treaty was mainly of symbolic importance. It asserted Germany's independence in a way that seemed appropriate to its interests, geography, and status as a great power. It held out the prospect that Germany might one day mediate conflicts between West and East in a way which would enable it to satisfy its own desire for frontier revision and contribute to lasting peace on a new basis. As Stresemann put it in his broadcast on the treaty 'we want to go our own way in the policy of securing peace'.[124]

Peaceful Revision

It was one thing to assert independence; it was another to make it work as an instrument of revision. Just how limited the options were became increasingly apparent in the case of Poland. German policy was to maintain

---

[121] Walsdorff, *Westorientierung und Ostpolitik*, 190–200.

[122] Chamberlain's record of a conversation with Briand, 18 May 1927: *DBFP*, ser. 1A, iii, no. 201 (pp. 309–10).

[123] Zeidler, *Reichswehr und Rote Armee*, 131–2, 272. Figures for German–Soviet trade in Hartmut Pogge von Strandmann, 'Grossindustrie und Rapallopolitik. Deutsch–Sowjetische Handelsbeziehungen in der Weimarer Republik', *Historische Zeitschrift*, 222 (1976), 337; see also Werner Beitel and Jürgen Nötzold, *Deutsch-sowjetische Wirtschaftsbeziehungen in der Zeit der Weimarer Republik* (Baden-Baden: Nomos, 1979).

[124] Rheinbaben (ed.), *Reden und Schriften*, ii. 259.

the claim for revision of the frontier, support the German minority on whom this claim depended, and hope that Poland would be sufficiently weakened, in the first instance by economic failure, to be willing to cede territory. The Polish government reacted by taking measures against the German minority.[125] In June 1925 a trade war broke out when the Polish right to export coal from Upper Silesia to Germany free of duty lapsed.[126]

The strain on the Polish economy briefly raised German hopes that it might be possible to secure frontier revision as part of an international operation to restore Polish finances.[127] The idea was vigorously canvassed by Schacht and feelers were put out in London by the German embassy. However, Rauscher and Schubert counselled caution since it was unlikely that Poland would agree to frontier revision short of total collapse, and in any case Germany was not in a position to persuade its Locarno partners to make the substantial changes which the Germans wanted.[128] Given that Germany had only just succeeded in preventing Poland from acquiring a permanent seat on the League council and that Chamberlain had been offended by the treaty of Berlin, the idea that Germany might be able to persuade Britain, let alone France, to support extensive frontier revision was obviously far-fetched. Stresemann adopted the advice of his officials and authorized new instructions to London warning that 'exceptional caution' was required.[129]

The convoluted argument of this dispatch showed the difficulty of reconciling goals with means. It described the solution of the Polish frontier question as 'not only the most important task of our policy, but also perhaps the most important task of European policy altogether'. Only a peaceful solution 'comes into consideration for us'. But there would have to be a total collapse 'of the whole Polish body politic' before it would

---

[125] In addition to expulsions of those who had opted for German citizenship and the confiscation of their property (see above, p. 345), there was further confiscation of German property under the terms of an agrarian reform law, and the German minority also complained of discrimination in education and employment. The petitions from the German minority to the League are discussed in Frentz, *A Lesson Forgotten*, 170–244.

[126] Krüger, *Aussenpolitik*, 290–1; memorandum by Schubert of a conversation with Skrzyński, now Polish prime minister, 4 Dec. 1925: *ADAP*, ser. B, ii/i, no. 2.

[127] Kimmich, *The Free City*, 156–9.

[128] Krüger, *Aussenpolitik*, 307–11; Schubert to Rauscher, 6 Jan. 1926; memorandum by Dirksen of a discussion between Schubert and Schacht, 17 Apr. 1926: *ADAP*, ser. B, ii/i, nos. 31, 148.

[129] Stresemann to Sthamer, 19 Apr. 1926: *ADAP*, ser. B, ii/i, no. 150; Krüger, *Aussenpolitik*, 308. Schubert's influence is clear from a summary in his hand of the same date: PA, St.S.Po, vol. 1 (R29328). I owe this reference to Professor Krüger. For the land Germany wished to recover, see Map 2.

agree to peaceful revision and Germany's 'general political position, especially in relation to the Western powers is for the time being still too weak' for it to succeed with its demands in an international body. Germany could accept only an 'unlimited recovery of sovereignty in the territories in question', which were defined as the corridor, Danzig, Upper Silesia, and parts of central Silesia. It was therefore essential to resist 'interim solutions' which did not conform to these goals. It was also important to prevent a lasting solution to Poland's economic problems before Germany was in a position to benefit from them. Poland could hardly be restored without German support since even during the current trade war more than half Poland's foreign trade went to Germany. They should not refuse to take part in an international loan to Poland as that would look like sabotage, but the aim should be to ensure that the loan offered Poland only temporary relief.

Without the means for peaceful revision, German officials fell back on the argument that in the longer term Poland's economic dependence on Germany and Germany's improved international standing would bring success. This was always unrealistic and its unrealism became increasingly apparent. Marshal Piłsudski's coup d'état in May 1926 restored political stability to Poland, and in October 1927 it received an international loan from the United States and Britain.[130]

The difficulty of peaceful revision was even more obvious in relation to other longer-term goals. When Stresemann met the Austrian chancellor and foreign minister Rudolf Ramek in March 1926 they agreed that *Anschluß* was not part of the current agenda (*aktuell*) and that active propaganda for it would be counter-productive.[131] Stresemann also told Ramek that he saw no possibility of altering the German–Czech frontier 'in the foreseeable future' though he was not prepared to guarantee it. Stresemann did not regard the Sudeten Germans as an instrument of revision, unlike the German minority in Poland. When the Sudeten parties overcame their reservations and entered the Czech government in October 1926—a development favoured by Beneš as helping to consolidate the new state—Stresemann welcomed the decision.[132]

[130] Neil Pease, *Poland, the United States, and the Stabilization of Europe, 1919–1933* (New York: Oxford University Press, 1986), 81–104.

[131] Memorandum of the discussions on 27–8 Mar., dated 29 Mar., 1926: *ADAP*, ser. B, iii, no. 105.

[132] Note by Stresemann on a dispatch from the German envoy to Prague, 15 Oct. 1926: ibid., no. 202. F. Gregory Campbell, *Confrontation in Central Europe: Weimar Germany and Czechoslovakia* (Chicago: University of Chicago Press, 1975), 168–71.

Another German minority for whom the German government felt some responsibility was that in South Tyrol. In October 1925 Mussolini intensified a campaign to 'Italianize' the region. Stresemann thought that, having failed to get the Italian frontier guaranteed at Locarno, Mussolini was deliberately stirring up a conflict with Germany to demonstrate a German threat.[133] When Mussolini made an inflammatory speech, Stresemann gave a firm reply in the Reichstag ridiculing the idea of a German threat to Italy and warning that mistreatment of minorities could be raised at the League.[134] Mussolini soon dropped the matter, but Stresemann continued to regard him as a danger, telling Ramek that Mussolini was 'a lasting source of unrest, who constantly whipped the Italians up into megalomania and could thus find himself forced into some kind of action sometime'.[135]

In the absence of any real opportunity for territorial revision, German policy concentrated on providing help to the minorities. Most of this effort was directed towards Poland as the primary target for revision.[136] Assistance was urgently needed to maintain a German population in some areas. It was estimated that about 70 per cent of the pre-war German community in the Prussian provinces of Posen and Eastern Pomerania had left for Germany by 1925. It was therefore essential to support Danzig, which was overwhelmingly German, and the remaining Germans, mainly farmers, in the corridor. A secret programme of subsidies was sponsored by the Auswärtiges Amt, and Stresemann gained cabinet approval for a grant of 30 million marks in 1926.[137] The Auswärtiges Amt also sponsored various types of propaganda to draw attention to the plight of Germans in Poland and what they considered 'the quite insane frontiers'.[138]

The financial aid also served the important purpose in domestic politics of maintaining support from the minority organizations for Stresemann's policy. He also hoped to gain influence over the DNVP by this method. On the proposal of the Auswärtiges Amt Hans-Erdmann von Lindeiner-

---

[133] Stresemann's discussions with Ramek, 27–8 Mar. 1926: *ADAP*, ser. B, iii, no. 105.

[134] Reichstag speech, 9 Feb. 1926: Rheinbaben (ed.), *Reden und Schriften*, ii. 233–50. Stanley Suval, *The Anschluss Question in the Weimar Era* (Baltimore: Johns Hopkins University Press, 1974), 134–9.

[135] *ADAP*, ser. B, iii, no. 105, p. 207.

[136] Kimmich, *The Free City*, 77–101; Krekeler, *Revisionsanspruch*, passim.

[137] Stresemann to Kempner, 23 Mar. 1926: *ADAP*, ser. B, i/i, no. 178; Krekeler, *Revisionsanspruch*, 90–3.

[138] A phrase used by Schubert to D'Abernon, 27 Feb. 1926: *ADAP*, ser. B, ii/i, no. 71.

Wildau, who had dissociated himself from Hugenberg and joined the pragmatic wing of the DNVP, was appointed in March 1926 as the managing director of the main front organization which channelled loans to the German minority. It would be surprising if there had been no ulterior motive behind this appointment.[139]

Stresemann was also energetic in trying to aid other German minorities and not too choosy about whom he employed for the purpose. A former rebel from the Kapp putsch Major Pabst was paid to report on events in the South Tyrol and channel funds to the German community.[140] Stresemann also looked beyond Europe: in 1926 he persuaded the cabinet to agree to a loan to help the Mannesmann firm retain its iron ore mines in Morocco.[141] He also pressed the finance minister for a loan to help German settlers return to Tanganyika, painting a rosy picture of the economic prospects and stressing the importance of building up local resistance to possible British plans to unite Tanganyika with its other East African possessions.[142]

Acting as the champion of the rights of German minorities in other countries had implications for the way Germany treated its own minorities. The Auswärtiges Amt was aware of the parallel and tried to encourage other departments and the *Länder* to take appropriate measures. A memorandum, circulated by Stresemann in January 1925, pointed out that there were some 9 million Germans living elsewhere in Europe, not counting Switzerland and Luxembourg.[143] Of these, it claimed that those in states bordering Germany and Austria were subject to campaigns to destroy or absorb them. Germany could not help them by force and could offer only limited financial support. Propaganda was therefore all the more important. A German campaign could make use of the minority

---

[139] Schot, *Nation oder Staat?*, 175–81. The full title of the organization was the Ossa Vermittlungs-und Handelsgesellschaft m.b.H. Heinrich Köhler who was minister of finance from January 1927 to June 1928 comments in his memoirs on Stresemann's use of secret Auswärtiges Amt funds to buy the support of nationalist politicians in opposition parties, i.e. the DNVP. Josef Becker (ed.), *Heinrich Köhler, Lebenserinnerungen des Politikers und Staatsmannes 1878–1949* (Stuttgart: W. Kohlhammer, 1964), 210.

[140] Pabst to Stresemann, undated [1925] (Nl. 274): Thimme, *Stresemann*, 101–2.

[141] Cabinet minutes, 5 Feb. 1926: Minuth (ed.), *Kabinette Luther*, no. 278.

[142] Stresemann to Reinhold, 6 May 1926: *ADAP*, ser. B, i/i, no. 201. Hartmut Pogge von Strandmann, 'Imperialism and Revisionism in Interwar Germany', in Wolfgang J. Mommsen and Jürgen Osterhammel (eds.), *Imperialism and After* (London: Allen & Unwin, 1986), 90–119; Adolf Rüger, 'The Colonial Aims of the Weimar Republic' in Hellmuth Stoecker (ed.), *German Imperialism in Africa*, Eng. edn., (London: C. Hurst, 1986), 313–16.

[143] Circular dated 13 Jan. 1925: *ADAP*, ser. A, xii, no. 20.

protection legislation which the new states of eastern Europe had been forced to accept as part of the peace settlement. It could also play on the desire of the Anglo-Saxon powers to promote peaceful conditions in Europe. There was a further consideration:

The creation of a state, whose political frontiers include all of the German people, who live within the borders of the areas of central Europe settled by Germans and want union with the Reich, is the distant goal of German hopes, the step-by-step revision of the politically and economically most untenable frontier provisions of the dictated peace (Polish corridor, Upper Silesia) is the first goal of German foreign policy.

However, given the mixture of nationalities in central Europe, the achievement of either goal would involve the incorporation of foreign minorities in Germany. This would obviously be more acceptable to other states if Germany was known to guarantee minority rights.

The memorandum is a perfect example of the gap between German aspirations and the means to achieve them. Even the idea of giving Germany's minorities cultural autonomy proved complicated. It took over a year to arrange a meeting with the *Länder* and then doubts were expressed about the wisdom of the proposal.[144] The Prussian representatives feared that the Poles would not reciprocate and would exploit the new rights for the Polish minority in East Prussia as part of their campaign to undermine the German hold on the province. Stresemann conceded that German minorities abroad were unlikely to receive equal treatment but argued that the important thing was to put their opponents in the wrong, so that Germany could conduct a 'moral offensive'.

Despite the obvious problems of peaceful revision, the Auswärtiges Amt showed no willingness at this stage to reconsider the goal of frontier revision in relation to Poland. No one argued that the German minority should be encouraged to leave Poland or accept assimilation.[145] That would have been considered a breach of trust. There was, rather, an almost frantic desire to argue that only revision of frontiers, which were regarded as both unjust and unworkable, could bring peace to the region.

---

[144] Memorandum of the meeting on 10 Feb., dated 16 Feb. 1926: *ADAP*, ser. B, i/i, no. 102.

[145] Bastiaan Schot, 'Die Bedeutung Locarnos für die Minderheitenfragen', in Ralph Schattkowsky (ed.), *Locarno und Osteuropa. Fragen eines europäischen Sicherheitssystems in den 20er Jahren* (Marburg: Hitzeroth, 1994), 163–81; Carole Fink, 'Stresemann's Minority Policies, 1924–29', *Journal of Contemporary History*, 14 (1979), 403–22.

Coalition Politics

The second Luther government was brought down by a sudden crisis over a decision to extend the use of the flag flown by the merchant marine to consular and trade offices abroad. This recondite matter acquired political significance because the merchant marine had been allowed by the Weimar Constitution to retain the imperial colours though with an inset of the republican colours in one corner. Luther and Stresemann both favoured the change to avoid different flags being used abroad.[146] It was also welcomed by Hindenburg, who issued the appropriate decree. This provoked an unexpected storm in the Reichstag, which culminated in a resolution expressing disapproval of Luther being passed on 12 May 1926. Luther immediately resigned and refused even to remain in office with the rest of the cabinet, pending the formation of a new government. Stresemann considered whether he should also resign since he had been jointly responsible for the decision but, according to his son, remembering how Luther had earlier been prepared to sacrifice him to the DNVP, he decided against the gesture.[147]

Luther's fall reopened the question of the future of the coalition.[148] Immediately there was no alternative to a renewal of a minority government. Extension to the DNVP was still blocked by their opposition to the League, while extension to the SPD was blocked by a referendum for the expropriation of the former royal houses over which the SPD had joined forces with the KPD. However, both issues would be decided in the near future and both the DNVP and the SPD would then become eligible coalition partners. Advocates of extending the coalition in either direction therefore wanted to see the immediate crisis resolved in a way which kept open their preferred solution. The Centre Party leadership hoped to return to a great coalition, while Scholz hoped to bring back the DNVP.

Stresemann's position was more complicated. He had not wanted the crisis, telling the cabinet that 'a new right-wing government was all we needed' and adding that it would be 'quite catastrophic for foreign policy'.[149] On the other hand, he made no move towards a great coalition

[146] Luther to Stresemann, 20 Apr. 1926: Minuth (ed.), *Kabinette Luther*, no. 339. Stresemann's statement to the press: Bernhard (ed.), *Vermächtnis*, ii. 389–92.

[147] Wolfgang Stresemann, *Mein Vater*, 414–15.

[148] Stürmer, *Koalition und Opposition*, 151–5.

[149] Cabinet minutes, 10 May 1926: Minuth (ed.), *Kabinette Luther*, no. 361.

either. He probably hoped that if the DVP adopted the same tactics as it had the previous December, expressing willingness for a great coalition in the expectation that it would not happen, another minority government of the middle would be the result.

The situation took an alarming turn from Stresemann's point of view on 14 May when the Centre Party asked Adenauer to see if he could get agreement for a minority government leading to a great coalition.[150] Stresemann did not want Adenauer as chancellor. He still felt the antagonism left from their clash during the Ruhr crisis. He recognized in Adenauer a man with a will as strong as his own and he sensed that Adenauer would not allow him the free hand in foreign policy which he had come to expect after nearly three years in office. Adenauer was, indeed, critical of the substance and style of Stresemann's policy, referring to its 'vacillating and see-saw character' when Germany as a disarmed nation should be avoiding any kind of commitment.[151]

Stresemann was determined to stop Adenauer, telling his son that he would have been unwilling to serve in an Adenauer cabinet.[152] In fact, Adenauer's equal determination to agree to the chancellorship only if the parties committed themselves to a great coalition made it easy for the DVP to refuse. Scholz told Adenauer on 15 May that the position of the SPD on expropriation of the royal houses and the flag decree made a great coalition impossible. Encouraged by Adenauer to be frank, he then made clear his opposition to a great coalition under any circumstances and said that 'the swing to the right must come', predicting that the DNVP would soon make this possible by accepting Stresemann's foreign policy.[153]

Scholz's indiscretion proved embarrassing to Stresemann. Adenauer reported Scholz's view to the Centre Party Reichstag delegation, which was taken aback since they had been led to understand that the DVP was not opposed to a great coalition.[154] The same day Stresemann proposed to the rump cabinet that Marx should be nominated for the chancellorship

---

[150] Adenauer's account, written shortly after the event, is printed in Weymar, *Adenauer*, 77–86.

[151] Schwarz points out that this does not suggest that Adenauer anticipated his pro-Western policy of the 1950s. Adenauer even suggested that Germany should not have signed the Dawes plan. Schwarz, *Adenauer*, i. 203–4; Weymar, *Adenauer*, 79.

[152] Wolfgang Stresemann, *Mein Vater*, 416.

[153] Weymar, *Adenauer*, 81–3.

[154] Minutes of the meeting, 15 May 1926: Rudolf Morsey (ed.), *Protokolle der Reichstagsfraktion und des Fraktionsvorstands der Deutschen Zentrumspartei 1926–1933* (Mainz: Matthias Grünewald, 1969), 38–40.

Stresemann in Liberal Caricature

Mit Friedenszweig und Kriegsfackel. „Ihr naht Euch wieder, schwankende Gestalten!"

19. Stresemann as the leader of the National Liberal Party. The caption reads: 'With the branch of peace and the torch of war. "You draw near again, wavering figures!"' (a quotation from Goethe's *Faust*). Holtz, *Ulk*, satirical supplement to the *Berliner Tageblatt*, 40, 5 October 1917. *From Gustav Stresemann's collection (Nl. 305), by kind permission of the Politisches Archiv, Auswärtiges Amt, Berlin.*

Lumpenſammler Streſemann *Zeichnung von Paul Halke*

DEMOKRATISCHE PARTE

Der Demokrat:

Fort mit dem Zeug! Mag er mit Fleiß
den Abfall ruhig ſieben!

Der Streſemann fiſcht, wie man weiß,
ſeit jeher gern im Trüben.

20. Stresemann as a tramp collecting recruits for the German People's Party
from the rubbish dump of the Democratic Party. The caption reads: 'The
Democrat: "Away with the stuff! Let him sift the rubbish in peace! One knows
that Stresemann has always liked to fish in troubled waters."' Paul Halke, *Ulk*,
Berliner Tageblatt, 49/20 (14 May 1920). *From Gustav Stresemann's collection
(Nl. 305), by kind permission of the Politisches Archiv, Auswärtiges Amt, Berlin*

— „Keine Bange, meine Herrschaften! Wenn ich auch noch so laut mein ‚Nein' brüllte — ich bin deshalb doch kein wirklicher Löwe, sondern nur der Reichstagsabgeordnete Gustav Stresemann!" Stinnes aus dem Publikrm: „Gut gebrüllt, Löwe!"

21. Stresemann playing the lion in *A Midsummer Night's Dream*, roars 'No', while at the same time reassuring his audience that he is 'not a real lion but only the Reichstag deputy, Gustav Stresemann'. Stinnes calls out from the audience 'Well roared lion'. The reference is to Stresemann's efforts in May 1921 to resolve the contradiction between keeping the DVP in government and rejecting the Allied ultimatum on reparations. H. Abeking, *Berliner Tageblatt*, 27 May 1921. *From Gustav Stresemann's collection (Nl. 305), by kind permission of the Politisches Archiv, Auswärtiges Amt, Berlin.*

22. Stresemann, the acrobat of unity, trying to build a coalition composed of the DVP, the DDP, the Centre, the SPD, the DNVP and the USPD. The figure of *Kladderadatsch* warns: 'Gustav, Gustav, don't overdo it.' Lindloff, *Kladderadatsch*, 23 October 1921.

Die drei Nobelpreiskönige

. . . und es zogen drei Könige aus, das Friedenskindlein zu suchen . . .

24. The three Nobel prize kings, Stresemann, Briand, and Chamberlain. The caption reads: '. . . and three kings set out to seek the little child of peace'. Werner Hahmann, *Kladderadatsch*, 26 December 1926. *From Gustav Stresemann's collection (Nl. 305), by kind permission of the Politisches Archiv, Auswärtiges Amt, Berlin.*

Nr. 34. — 82. Jahrg.
Berlin, 25. August 1929.

Preis 60 Pfg.

Kladderadatsch

JOHNSON

Gustav Delorges

„ . . . Der Leu mit Gebrüll
Richtet sich auf, da wird's still!

Und der Ritter im schnellen Lauf,
Steigt hinab in den furchtbaren Zwinger."

Aus Schillers „Handschuh"

25. In the manner of the knight, Delorges, from Schiller's ballad '*Der Handschuh*' ('*The Glove*'), Stresemann cheerfully enters an arena where a fight is about to break out between the British lion and French tiger. The reference is to Stresemann's ultimately successful attempts to save the Hague Conference from failure over the conflict between Britain and France about the proportion of reparations each was to receive under the Young Plan. Johnson, *Kladderadatsch*, 82/34, 25 August 1929. *From Gustav Stresemann's collection (Nl. 305), by kind permission of the Politisches Archiv, Auswärtiges Amt, Berlin.*

Arminius: „Stecken wir unsere Schwerter ein, meine Herren; ich sehe, meine Methode ist veraltet! Stresemann schafft die
Befreiung schneller und besser auf friedlichem Wege!"

26. The nationalist hero Arminius (leader of a revolt against the
Romans) tells Hugenberg and his Stahlhelm and Nazi allies: 'Sheathe
your swords, gentlemen; I see that my method is obsolete! Stresemann
will achieve liberation faster and better by peaceful means!'. Wilke in
the *Berliner Tageblatt*, 432, 13 September 1929. *From Gustav Stresemann's
collection (Nl. 305), by kind permission of the Politisches
Archiv, Auswärtiges Amt, Berlin.*

and denied that the DVP was opposed to a great coalition.[155] The contradictory attitudes of the DVP suggested it was playing 'a double game' to eliminate Adenauer, although in fact Scholz had simply expressed his own views, as he was prone to do. Suspicion against Stresemann in the Centre Party deepened when it became known that he had sent a message to a senior SPD politician, Rudolf Breitscheid, saying that Adenauer would be unsuitable as chancellor since he was a right-wing opponent of Locarno. Scholz tried to repair the damage by telephoning Centre Party leaders to say that Adenauer must have misunderstood him, leading Marx to comment drily that it was 'curious how often such decisive conversations with Dr Scholz turned out later to have been "misunderstandings"'.[156]

Marx accepted Hindenburg's commission to form a government and negotiations were held between the Centre Party and the DVP to clarify the position. A formal agreement was reached, under which a minority government would be formed with the understanding that this should be replaced as soon as possible by a majority formed exclusively from those parties 'which recognize that existing international agreements are legally valid and offer a guarantee that the present foreign policy will continue'.[157] This sounded like an endorsement of the great coalition but it left open the possibility that the DNVP would be eligible if it dropped its opposition to the government's foreign policy. Marx assumed the chancellorship on 17 May and the rest of the cabinet remained unchanged.[158]

Stresemann could afford to be satisfied with the result. The threat of Adenauer had been averted and he had extricated his party from the damage produced by Scholz's démarche. He liked working with Marx, who gave him a free hand. The agreement reached with the Centre Party also protected him against the DNVP. All this showed the strength of the position he had built as foreign minister and his ability to manage the cross-currents of coalition politics. The only cost was that he had added to his reputation for deviousness and for being unable to tolerate a strong

[155] Hehl, *Marx*, 377. Confronted by Marx with Scholz's statement to Adenauer, Stresemann declared that 'this must certainly be incorrect', and after telephoning Scholz reported that Adenauer must have misunderstood him. Weymar, *Adenauer*, 86.

[156] Hehl, *Marx*, 377.

[157] Morsey, *Protokolle*, 41–2.

[158] The positions which Marx had held under Luther as minister of justice and minister for the occupied territories were left vacant with the intention of filling them when a majority government was formed. Günter Abramowski (ed.), *Die Kabinette Marx III und IV* (Boppard: Harald Boldt, 1988), p. xix.

chancellor.[159] So long as his policies were successful this did not matter, but he would carry the responsibility if they failed.

A Time for Optimism

In the summer and autumn of 1926 the prospects both at home and abroad looked better than at any time since 1919. The Republic was becoming accepted even by its enemies as a fact of life. In September 1926 Paul Silverberg, the deputy chairman of the Association of German Industry, spoke out in favour of a great coalition.[160] In October Seeckt was forced to resign as chief of the army command after it became known that he had allowed the eldest son of the Crown Prince to take part in manoeuvres.[161] Although Stresemann was suspected of having engineered Seeckt's dismissal, he was not directly involved though he no doubt welcomed the removal of an old adversary.[162] The new Reichswehr leadership under General Heye made it clear that they wanted to cooperate with the government and in future would only rearm in ways for which the government was prepared to take responsibility.[163] The DNVP also again changed tack and made a concerted bid to rejoin the government.

Stresemann's increasing confidence about the future can be seen in a speech he gave to the students' association in Berlin. University students were a predominantly middle-class and right-wing group, who had reacted violently against the Republic. Stresemann nevertheless enjoyed addressing student audiences, seeing them as an influential group in shaping public opinion and trusting to his powers of persuasion.[164]

---

[159] Gessler told Adenauer that Stresemann feared that 'I was too strong a man for him to deal with': Weymar, *Adenauer*, 85. Breitscheid was also reported as saying, 'Stresemann brought down Adenauer's candidacy because Adenauer was too strong for him; he needs a chancellor, beside whom he can in reality exercise the chancellorship': Morsey, *Protokolle*, 40.

[160] Heinrich August Winkler, *Weimar 1918–1933*, 2nd. edn. (Munich: C. H. Beck, 1994), 316–17.

[161] Carsten, *Reichswehr*, 245–50.

[162] Marx did, however, threaten Hindenburg with the resignation of the entire cabinet if Seeckt was not dismissed. Hehl, *Marx*, 388; Möllers, *Geßler*, 318–24.

[163] Cabinet minutes, 29 Nov. 1926: Abramowski (ed.), *Kabinette Marx III*, no. 130.

[164] Eschenburg gives a vivid description of his address in May 1927 to a student group in Heidelberg, who hated him and had come to demonstrate their opposition but ended by loudly applauding him. Shortly before he died, Stresemann said he would like to tour the German universities campaigning against Hugenberg's referendum against the Young plan. Eschenburg, 'Stresemann und die Studenten', 1000–1; id., *Also hören Sie mal zu*, 187–9.

His main theme was that students should become involved in the Republic.[165] He praised the contribution of student movements to national unification and criticized the philistinism of the empire with its snobbery and class division. He stressed the importance of the alienation that had grown up between the universities and the SPD with the result that, at the end of the war, the SPD had lacked educated leaders and the bourgeois academic world had turned against the Republic. He praised Ebert for having restored Germany to constitutional paths and warned that any departure from that basis would mean civil war. He suggested that, given all it had been through, the German people had not done badly and he declared himself optimistic about the future. He defended his own achievements from the near collapse of 1923 to the more stable conditions which were now developing, and he appealed for their support in taking the process further. He described his policy as one of national recovery by peaceful understanding and promoting foreign investment, with the ultimate purpose that Germany should again be independent and free. He dismissed the idea of Germany being able to fight a new war as utopian and added, interestingly, that even a successful war—which would be impossible—would not bring stability: 'It is our task to work with all our strength for the preservation of peace in Europe and to see that during this era of peace Germany gets the chance to heal the wounds which it suffered in war.'[166]

As the benefits of his policies started to become apparent, Stresemann was determined that the DNVP should not be allowed to recover the political initiative. In January 1926 he shrugged off a newspaper attack by Hugenberg, who described him as a 'disaster for the German middle class', and claimed that only Stresemann prevented a union of the DNVP and DVP to form the strongest party in the country. Stresemann replied in an unsigned article, distributed by the DVP press agency, that Hugenberg was driven by hatred, having lost influence in the DNVP and in industry. The DVP and DNVP, Stresemann said, were going in different directions: the DVP had joined the new Germany whereas the DNVP was a colourful amalgam of different fads—Pomeranian royalists, the Christian Social Party, racists, and middle-class interest groups—which lacked leadership and bowed to mass pressure.[167]

---

[165] 6 July 1926; Rheinbaben (ed.), *Reden und Schriften*, ii. 262–302.

[166] Ibid. 297.

[167] *Deutscher Zeitungs-Dienst*, 12 Jan. 1926; Bernhard (ed.), *Vermächtnis*, ii. 398–401. In Apr. 1926 Stresemann persuaded Luther that the Reich government should acquire the prestigious

The idea of a closer association with the DNVP was not, however, to be disposed of so easily. Marx was expected to take an initiative to bring about a great coalition with the SPD. Negotiations were held at the beginning of July, although they failed on the question of the expropriation of the royal houses.[168] The DNVP responded by telling Hindenburg that it would be prepared to join a new government and would accept Stresemann as foreign minister.[169] The right wing of the DVP, which was also opposed to a great coalition, welcomed the overtures from the DNVP.

Stresemann therefore found himself having to counter a threat from his own ranks. When Jarres published a declaration together with a DNVP colleague in the Prussian Staatsrat (the upper house of the Prussian parliament) in favour of a formal partnership between the DVP and DNVP, Stresemann reacted sharply.[170] He told Jarres that an alliance with the DNVP would lead to the formation of a German Liberal Party which would take the greater part of the DVP's vote and form a permanent left coalition with the SPD and the Centre. In an anonymous article for the press, he argued that it was understandable that the DNVP wanted an alliance as it offered an escape from the isolation into which its policies had brought it. That was no reason, however, why the DVP, which had lost a third of its vote in the previous elections as a result of demagogic attacks by the DNVP, should now help it out of the mess of its own making.[171]

Stresemann was equally annoyed when the so-called 'patriotic associations' in Saxony—consisting principally of the ex-servicemen's Stahlhelm—made support for the DVP conditional on the party forming an electoral pact with the DNVP and binding itself never to form a coalition

---

Deutsche Allgemeine Zeitung to prevent it falling into Hugenberg's hands. The money came jointly from the discretionary funds of the chancellor and foreign minister and the cabinet was not informed. The *Deutsche Allgemeine Zeitung* continued to take a right-wing stand on domestic politics, but it modified its previous opposition to Stresemann's foreign policy. In November the fact of the government's acquisition became public, forcing the sale of the newspaper to a Ruhr consortium, but it remained independent of Hugenberg and continued to benefit from an indirect government subsidy. Kurt Koszyk, *Geschichte der deutschen Presse*, iii: *Deutsche Presse 1914–1945* (Berlin: Colloquim, 1972), 143–53; Starkulla, 'Pressepolitik', 54–71.

[168] Stürmer, *Koalition und Opposition*, 160–1; Winkler, *Der Schein der Normalität*, 285–9.

[169] Note by Stresemann on information from Meissner, 3 July 1926: Bernhard (ed.), *Vermächtnis*, ii. 407.

[170] Stresemann to Jarres, 30 July 1926: ibid. 412–16. The full correspondence is in Nl. 95 and BAK, Nl. Jarres, 37.

[171] *Deutscher Zeitungsdienst*, 13 July 1926; Bernhard (ed.), *Vermächtnis*, ii. 416–19.

with the SPD. Stresemann wrote to his colleague Dingeldey that he would 'under no circumstances remain in a party which allowed itself to be degraded in this way'.[172] He protested in similar terms to the DVP general secretary in Dresden, Johannes Dieckmann—who felt that the party could not afford to break with the 'patriotic associations'—saying that he would not accept directives from the Stahlhelm or 'anti-Semitic propagandists': 'I have not committed myself to the Deutsche Volkspartei just to sell it to others . . . at the moment when its policy is proved right.'[173]

As usual, Stresemann was able to win the support of the DVP national executive, which met immediately before the party conference in October.[174] He warned that a merger of the DVP and DNVP would produce a party composed of such contradictory elements that it would be a broken instrument from the moment of its foundation and unable to keep its voters. He reminded his audience that when the free trader National Liberals joined the Left Liberals in 1880, the so-called united party had lost 40 per cent of its vote in the following elections. He added that as a Liberal he would not be willing to serve in a party which contained some of the groups still to be found in the DNVP. Instead he reaffirmed the position adopted by the party in January 1924 of independence towards both right and left.

The tone of the discussion at the national executive was conciliatory and, unlike 1924, there was no attempt to challenge Stresemann's authority. However, it was clear that a significant section of the party regarded a right-wing majority government as a natural and desirable development. Others apart from Jarres were no longer prepared to accept Stresemann's argument that the Centre Party would not join a coalition with the DNVP, believing rather that if the DVP took the lead the Centre Party would follow.

[172] Stresemann to Dingeldey, 9 Aug. 1926 (Nl. 96): Harttung (ed.), *Schriften*, 237–8.

[173] Stresemann to Dieckmann, 25 Aug. 1926 and further correspondence (Nl. 96); ibid. 238–40. The situation in Saxony tended, as before the war, to a polarization between the SPD and the middle-class parties, as, unlike Prussia, Saxony had no Catholic Centre presence to modify the competition. The polarization grew worse as a result of the events of 1923. Stresemann argued that, particularly in such a situation, a great coalition was the right policy, but the Saxon DVP was under heavy pressure from its voters to join a united anti-socialist front of the bourgeois parties. Stresemann to Kaiser, 27 Oct. 1926 (Nl. 97): Bernhard (ed.), *Vermächtnis*, iii. 86–90; Richter, *Deutsche Volkspartei*, 434–8; Lapp, *Revolution from the Right*, 143–50.

[174] Minutes of the *Zentralvorstand*, 1 Oct. 1926: Kolb and Richter (eds.), *Nationalliberalismus*, no. 64.

Dingeldey, in reply to Stresemann's letter, added a further consideration.[175] He argued that in the long term the problem was to create the basis for a bourgeois majority so that the parliamentary system could operate properly with a regular transfer of power between two roughly equal blocks: 'Otherwise the system of parliamentary government will fail because it has taken a form in Germany which is incompatible with the true sense of parliamentary government.'

Stresemann has been criticized for not ousting his opponents in the way he had dealt with the National Liberal Union in 1924.[176] But the opposition now was more broadly based and more thoughtful. Stresemann had himself favoured bringing the DNVP into power after the elections of May 1924. Their behaviour subsequently had made him understandably wary of repeating the experiment. But the argument put forward by Dingeldey that the parliamentary system would benefit from an alternation in power of like-minded groups of parties on the right and the left rather than minority governments, surviving by different majorities on different issues, was not to be dismissed lightly. The real question was whether the DNVP was capable of developing into a pragmatic and constitutional party and providing the consistent support which Stresemann needed for his foreign policy. The right wing of the DVP believed that it was. Stresemann remained sceptical, accusing the DNVP leadership of a lack of moral courage, of coming 'like Nicodemus in the night' to admit that they now accepted his foreign policy while continuing to misrepresent it in public and failing to get rid of their racist wing. Each side had a serious point.[177]

There was a particular reason for Stresemann's caution. Dramatic new developments in Franco-German relations seemed possible and he did not want these upset by the DNVP, whose new-found pragmatism was still untested. The majority for his foreign policy had been consistently provided by the SPD. His preference was for a continuation of minority government with SPD support, but if that was no longer feasible then a return to the great coalition. Only if that too was ruled out by the radical wing of the SPD was he prepared to contemplate another coalition with the DNVP, and then only if it provided formal assurances that it would accept his policy.

[175] Dingeldey to Stresemann, 16 Aug. 1926 (Nl. 96).

[176] Turner, Stresemann, 225–6.

[177] Speech to the Zentralvorstand, 1 Oct. 1926: Kolb and Richter (eds.), Nationalliberalismus, 702–3.

Entry into the League and Thoiry

The problems which had prevented Germany's admission to the League in March were overcome during the summer, although Germany had to agree to Poland becoming a non-permanent member of the council with the right to be re-elected at the end of its three year term.[178] Germany was formally admitted on 10 September amid scenes of great enthusiasm. State Secretary Pünder reported to the cabinet that their first appearance at Geneva had been 'a total success for Germany', which had become the centre of attention to such an extent that some of the other chief delegates, such as Chamberlain, were rather put out.[179]

In his speech to the assembly, Stresemann said that the fact that Germany could take its place alongside its former enemies showed that the League had the potential to give mankind a new direction.[180] The earth-shattering events of a terrible war had led humanity to reflect on the purpose of nations. He spoke of how to combine the distinctive culture of each nation with international understanding and of the importance of international trade. He claimed that the work of peaceful cooperation, exemplified by Locarno, now enjoyed the support of the great majority of the German people. He praised the attempts being made to strengthen international law and stressed the need for progress towards general disarmament. It was a tactful and restrained performance with a more muted delivery than his usual style since, in view of the importance of the occasion, he decided to read the text rather than speaking freely from notes. It was left to Briand in reply to electrify the assembly with a magical tour de force containing the famous peroration, 'Away with the rifles, machine guns, cannon! Clear the way for conciliation, arbitration, peace.'[181]

How to put these sentiments into practice was the subject of wide-ranging discussions between the two men a week later in the congenial surroundings of a small restaurant in the village of Thoiry.[182] The meeting had been under consideration since Locarno, but it had been put off by the fall of the first Luther government, then by the impasse over Germany's admission to the League, and finally by a financial crisis in

---

[178] Kimmich, *Germany and the League*, 85–91.

[179] Cabinet minutes, 20 Sept. 1926: Abramowski (ed.), *Kabinette Marx III*, no. 83.

[180] *League of Nations Official Journal*, Special Supplement no. 44: *Records of the Seventh Ordinary Session of the Assembly* (Geneva, 1926), 51–2.

[181] Ibid. 52–5. The scene is described in Wolfgang Stresemann, *Mein Vater*, 423–31.

[182] The background is explained by Jacques Bariéty, 'Finances et relations internationales à propos du "plan de Thoiry" (septembre 1926)', *Relations internationales*, 21 (Spring 1980), 51–70.

France.[183] As a consequence of that crisis Poincaré returned to power as minister president and finance minister, while Briand remained as foreign minister.

Two main ideas lay behind the meeting. First there was Briand's concept of a 'general settlement' involving the evacuation of the Rhineland, return of the Saar, and the end of military control. This was a bold proposal for a French foreign minister. On the other hand, France would be obliged under the terms of the Versailles treaty to make each of these concessions in any case over the next ten years and there was therefore much to be said for adopting them positively rather than being forced to give way in an atmosphere of mounting hostility. As Briand told Stresemann, partial solutions were useless as they 'always harboured new dangers' and, he claimed, he had found support in the foreign affairs committee of the chamber of deputies for the idea of a general settlement.[184] The advantages for Stresemann were obvious: as he instructed Hoesch to tell Briand, a great gesture like the evacuation of the Rhineland 'would correspondingly strengthen the spirit of Locarno'.[185]

It would have been unrealistic, however, to have expected the French to give up the Rhineland and the Saar unilaterally. What made it appear feasible was the second idea, that Germany could provide the key to stabilizing the franc, whose value had fallen sharply. The scheme, which was advanced first by Berthelot and gained increasing support in French official circles as the financial crisis worsened during the summer, was to obtain advance payment of reparations by the sale of part of the bonds which Germany had deposited as security under the Dawes plan.[186] German consent was required for the sale and could be presented as the German contribution to détente, making it a mutual process and therefore politically acceptable.

Stresemann was well briefed on what to expect at the meeting.[187] His own view could be described as one of cautious optimism. In July he wrote

---

[183] Memorandum by Stresemann, 4 Feb. 1926, Hoesch to Auswärtiges Amt, 22 May 1926, memorandum by Schubert, 2 July 1926: *ADAP*, ser. B, i/i, nos. 80, 225, 264.

[184] Stresemann's memorandum about the Thoiry meeting, 20 Sept. 1926: ibid. i/ii, no. 94.

[185] Stresemann to Hoesch, 4 Feb. 1926: ibid., i/i, no. 78.

[186] Hoesch to Auswärtiges Amt, 1 Dec. 1925, 26 Jan. 1926; Hoesch to Schubert, 28 Jan. 1926; memorandum by Stresemann, 12 July 1926: ibid., nos. 2, 61, 67, 276.

[187] Briand's intermediary was Professor Hesnard, the head of the press department at the French embassy in Berlin. He visited Stresemann while Stresemann was on holiday in Aug. 1926 and was also on hand in Geneva. Memorandum by Stresemann, 5 Aug. 1926, by Schubert, 11 Sept. 1926, and by Stresemann, 20 Sept. 1926: ibid. i/ii, nos. 11, 82, 94.

two anonymous newspaper articles in which he argued that economic and political cooperation with France was essential to restore stability to Europe and to consolidate the progress made since Locarno.[188] He praised the progress made towards a common organization of the steel industries of France, Germany, Belgium, and Luxembourg.[189] He also praised Briand as the French statesman who had consistently identified French and European interests with cooperation with Germany.

Stresemann was disappointed when Poincaré returned to power and vetoed proposals for Belgium to restore Eupen-Malmédy to Germany in return for financial compensation.[190] There had been unofficial soundings which had appeared to find a receptive hearing in Brussels, which like France was suffering from currency depreciation. When Briand argued that Locarno prohibited frontier changes Stresemann reacted angrily, saying that he considered this view 'completely wrong and endangering the whole work [of Locarno]'.[191] Eupen-Malmédy was important to the Germans precisely in order to demonstrate that peaceful revision of frontiers was possible. As Schubert pointed out to Hindenburg, it was sensitive for both sides because it created 'a breach in the frontier system of the Versailles treaty'.[192]

Despite this disappointment Stresemann remained hopeful. Before leaving for Geneva he obtained the cabinet's permission to discuss the sale of Dawes bonds in return for political concessions, despite the objections that were immediately raised by the ministers of finance and

[188] Articles for the *Hamburger Fremdenblatt*, and for the *Hannoverscher Courier*, 23 July 1926: Bernhard (ed.), *Vermächtnis*, ii. 454–61.

[189] A reference to the international steel cartel agreed in July 1926 between the industries of the participating countries to manage the problem of over-production by a system of quotas, which went into force on 30 Sep. 1926. In fact it reinforced protectionism rather than interdependence; the German producers, finding their quota too restrictive, announced their withdrawal in May 1929 and the cartel collapsed in 1931. The steel cartel had parallels in other industries, for example aluminium, dyes, and nitrogen. For a balanced assessment of their political significance and further literature, see Clemens August Wurm, 'Internationale Kartelle und die deutsch–französischen Beziehungen 1924–1930: Politik, Wirtschaft, Sicherheit', in Stephen A. Schuker (ed.), *Deutschland und Frankreich. Vom Konflikt zur Aussöhnung* (Munich: Oldenbourg, 2000), 97–115. On the opposition within Ruhr heavy industry to Stresemann's foreign policy, see Karl Heinrich Pohl, *Weimars Wirtschaft und die Außenpolitik der Republik 1924–1926. Vom Dawes-Plan zum Internationalen Eisenpakt* (Düsseldorf: Droste, 1979).

[190] Briand too expressed reservations about the idea: Enssle, *Stresemann's Territorial Revisionism*, 115–58.

[191] Memorandum by Stresemann of a conversation with the French chargé d'affaires, 22 Aug. 1926: *ADAP*, ser. B, i/ii, no. 55.

[192] Memorandum by Schubert, 3 Aug. 1926: ibid., no. 1.

economics.[193] From Geneva he wrote to his younger son Joachim: 'My great discussion with Briand, on which very much depends, is to be on Friday, please keep your fingers crossed.'[194]

The meeting went as well as Stresemann had dared to hope.[195] Briand offered to discuss the evacuation of the Rhineland and the return of the Saar in return for German financial assistance. Stresemann stressed the objections to a sale of the railway bonds, since as he admitted Germany hoped in time to achieve a revision of the Dawes plan and advance payments would weaken their case. However, he thought that an agreement would be possible if evacuation of the Rhineland were completed within a year. Briand nodded approval and asked how much financial assistance would be available. Stresemann suggested 300 million gold marks for the Saar mines (which had been ceded to France under the Versailles treaty) and a sale of bonds worth 1.5 billion, of which France would be entitled to 52 per cent under the normal division of reparations among the Allies, giving a total for France of about 1 billion in all. This seemed to satisfy Briand, though both agreed that the details would have to be referred to experts. In further discussion, Briand agreed to waive the requirement for a plebiscite in the Saar and promised that the International Military Control Commission would be withdrawn as soon as the remaining issues over disarmament had been resolved. He also agreed that France would lift its veto on the return of Eupen-Malmédy as part of the whole settlement.

In discussion of other matters, Briand complained that the activities of the Stahlhelm made it difficult for him to persuade his military chiefs to give up controls over Germany. Stresemann attempted to reassure him, describing the Stahlhelm as simply a nostalgic relic of the old army and of no military significance, but an organization which, with its uniforms and bands, filled a psychological gap in the Republic. Stresemann asked about the position of Poincaré, pointing out that Germany had no interest in strengthening him by helping to stabilize the franc. Briand responded that

[193] Cabinet minutes, 2 Sept. 1926: Abramowski (ed.), *Kabinette Marx III*, no. 75.

[194] Stresemann family papers, Berlin.

[195] Stresemann wrote two accounts of the meeting on 17 and 20 Sept. 1926: *ADAP*, ser. B, i/ii, nos. 88, 94. Hesnard, who acted as interpreter, left a different account of it, which gives the impression that Briand simply listened to proposals from Stresemann. However, Bariéty has shown from Hesnard's diary that Briand made him alter his account at the beginning of November, after Briand had encountered opposition in the French cabinet. It appears therefore that Stresemann's accounts are to be preferred. Bariéty, 'Finances et relations internationales', 69; Baechler, *Stresemann*, 688–9.

an understanding with Germany would be seen as a success for his (Briand's) foreign policy and that he did not expect Poincaré's government to last. Briand in turn warned Stresemann about the Reichswehr, saying he had the impression that it was up to all sorts of things of which Stresemann had no knowledge. Stresemann countered that soldiers were always concerned about national defence but that he did not take the matter too seriously because Seeckt was a realist. They also discussed possible economic cooperation in the Soviet Union.

Stresemann was pleased with the outcome, writing to Joachim that 'the atmosphere was good and we reached a complete understanding. Briand said of our conversation, in the language which is only natural to the French, that our souls were as white as the snow on Mt Blanc.' Stresemann added, however, that 'we both have to overcome glaciers: Poincaré in Paris and H[inden]burg in Berlin. On the other hand the whole cabinet is on my side. But as always I have to expect more tough battles in Berlin. Naturally the Hugenberg press is to the fore. But things will work out.'[196] Pünder gave a glowing account of the talks to the cabinet, leading Marx to comment presciently that the news seemed too good to be true.[197] Stresemann gave a further report on his return from Geneva and despite the doubts of the minister of economics, his DVP colleague Curtius, about the feasibility of the bonds scheme, the cabinet unanimously approved taking the negotiations further.[198]

Before leaving Geneva, Stresemann had been the guest of the German colony there at a 'beer evening' and made a short speech in which he struck a different tone from the one he had used to the League assembly.[199] Responding to the atmosphere of a group which had spent the war years as a besieged German minority in a French canton, he spoke in self-congratulatory terms of the achievements of the German people in

---

[196] Stresemann added that the meeting had lasted for over five hours; it had been very hot and they had consumed four bottles of wine (press speculation ranged from three to seven). Stresemann to Joachim, 21 Sept. 1926: Stresemann family papers, Berlin.

[197] Cabinet minutes, 20 Sept. 1926: Abramowski (ed.), *Kabinette Marx III*, no. 83.

[198] Cabinet minutes, 24 Sept. 1926: ibid., no. 84.

[199] Stresemann's speech on 21 Sept. 1926 from the shorthand notes of a German journalist, Max Beer, the representative of a pro-DVP newspaper, the *Kölnische Zeitung*: ADAP, ser. B, i/ii, pp. 665–9. Beer wrote of Stresemann in a memoir about the League: 'He presented the world with a living, a struggling but also a friendly Germany; and when he enthusiastically quoted Goethe everyone felt that he was thinking of Bismarck, and felt the courage and ambition to become the Bismarck of a defeated nation... He was Germany at the moment at which she cast aside the confusion of defeat and invested herself with the pride of a great nation.' Max Beer, *The League on Trial: A Journey to Geneva*, Eng. edn. (London: Allen & Unwin, 1933), 381.

holding out over four years of war against the rest of the world and, after seven years' humiliation, being restored as a great power to the League of Nations, despite their having rejected war guilt and asserted the right to have colonies. He interpreted the applause that had welcomed Germany to the League as offering moral satisfaction for the previous accusations. German critics of the policy of joining the League should judge by the results. Already German representatives from Danzig and Memel had said what an encouragement it was for them to see Germany in the League to protect their interests. To those who said that the route adopted was neither sufficiently fast nor consistent, he replied:

One should not always worry about the methods so long as one is moving forward. For in the end success decides which methods are right... That is also ultimately the sense of German foreign policy. Do not doubt one thing, there is only one goal for German foreign policy: Germany's freedom and Germany's greatness.

He continued to give an outline of what this meant for current policy: 'Our path is a more limited one than in earlier periods. Today it is a question of German sovereignty on German soil and beyond that by a skilful and carefully considered policy to find a way, working with other nations, to re-establish the right of self-determination where it is violated.' The Ruhr and Cologne zone had already been evacuated. Germany had now raised the question of whether the remaining occupation could be reconciled with German membership of the League and the question of the Saar which would be returned 'in a very short time', and of 'other areas of Europe' which should be allowed to find their way back to Germany.[200] They would have in return to accept certain financial burdens, but these would be worthwhile for the sake of 'the political honour and freedom of the nation'.

These remarks can be interpreted in different ways—as an example of Stresemann explaining his policy to a nationalist audience or as revealing his true motives to exploit the League as a means to restore Germany to a dominant position in Europe. In fact, the contrast is somewhat artificial. There is no reason to believe that Stresemann was insincere in his speech to the League or in his talks with Briand. He genuinely believed in peaceful revision and a close understanding with France on which revision

---

[200] The phrase 'other areas of Europe' was probably a reference to Eupen-Malmédy since the sentence concludes 'so that in a short time a Rhineland will again exist as its used to be'. *ADAP*, ser. B, i/ii, p. 668.

depended. But he also saw himself as a patriotic German in the tradition of Stein and Bismarck, promoting German interests as Briand promoted French interests, and he wanted Germans to see him that way. There was no alternative to peaceful revision: that was therefore his duty and theirs. What would happen thereafter would be a matter for future generations. He never tried to predict that future in detail, though there are several indications that he thought in terms of closer European economic cooperation and none that he thought of a new German military empire in Europe.

Nevertheless the speech to the German colony was a bad mistake, perhaps induced by beer and fatigue at the end of a long evening after an exhausting schedule.[201] It received a predictably hostile reaction in the foreign press and strengthened the opposition to Thoiry in Paris. Stresemann hastily summoned a press conference the next morning to put the record straight, but the damage was done.[202]

It soon became apparent that the Thoiry plan was in difficulty. Briand faced opposition in the cabinet and distanced himself from the plan, presenting it as Stresemann's idea.[203] The sale of Dawes bonds in any case depended on the willingness of American investors to buy them, and that came up against political obstacles. The American government was not willing to see funds made available to France, until France ratified an agreement for repayment of war debts which had been signed by the two governments on 29 April 1926.[204] The French government, however, did not dare to present this proposal to the National Assembly where opposition based on the feeling that France had already paid her debts in blood—French war dead—ran high.[205]

There were also doubts about the feasibility of the bond sales in London and, in the Foreign Office, concern that Thoiry might develop into a Franco-German partnership from which Britain was excluded.[206] The idea of Thoiry thus inevitably became entangled with the wider issue of reparations and war debts. The solution for which the Europeans

---

[201] The meeting with the German colony started at 11 p.m. after Stresemann had already attended a dinner and two other receptions. Engagements diary: *ADAP*, ser. B, i/ii, p. 664.

[202] Bernhard (ed.), *Vermächtnis*, iii. 30–2; Baechler, *Stresemann*, 690–1.

[203] Baechler, *Stresemann*, 688–9; Keeton, *Briand's Locarno Policy*, 218–24.

[204] Stresemann's report to the cabinet, 13 Oct. 1926: Abramowski (ed.), *Kabinette Marx III*, no. 89.

[205] Keeton, *Briand's Locarno Policy*, 167–8, 179–81.

[206] Reports from the German embassy in London, 22 and 29 Sept. 1926, memorandum by D'Abernon for Stresemann, 6 Oct. 1926: *ADAP*, ser. B, i/ii, nos. 100, 120, 131.

hoped, that reparations and war debts could be reduced together, was never going to be popular with American taxpayers, and the American administration was not prepared to tackle it until after the presidential election at the end of 1928.[207] Meanwhile, to everyone's surprise, Poincaré succeeded in stabilizing the franc without outside help, thus removing the immediate incentive for the Thoiry scheme. By November 1926, Stresemann knew that the high hopes he had entertained in September would have to be deferred.

Nevertheless, he tried hard to save the policy. In government, in the Reichstag, at the DVP party conference, his theme was always the same: great issues were at stake and the key was an understanding with France. To the party conference, meeting in Cologne on 2 October, he contrasted those like the DNVP who had learned nothing from the past—whose prayer was 'Give us each day our daily illusion'—with those who were fighting for a policy of 'rational understanding' at home and abroad.[208] He described the League as a 'great political reality' which was helping to give international relations a new form, providing for regular meetings and personal contacts. He held up Franco-German understanding as 'the core of any European understanding and pacification'. He added that he had faith in Briand's will to work to this end. Defending himself against the charge of being an eternal optimist, he said it was quite wrong to believe that policy could be based only on suspicion:

The old system of cabinet policy: trust no one and betray everyone; this was also ultimately very unsuccessful . . . and should be left to the past. For me one thing is certain, that the new Germany and its recovery . . . can only be based on peace. That is the only basis for a restoration of our strength. But how will this peace be possible if . . . it is not founded on an understanding between Germany and France!

Stresemann stressed the importance of the growth of economic cooperation between France and Germany, but he was careful to add that the cooperation was aimed neither at Britain, which was welcome to join the process, nor at the United States. He made the same point in a confidential briefing of the Reichstag foreign affairs committee, saying it had been a mistake for the French to discuss European economic cooperation in

---

[207] Memorandum by Schubert of a meeting with the American ambassador Jacob Schurman, 23 Dec. 1926: *ADAP*, ser. B, i/ii, no. 277.

[208] Verbatim report of Stresemann's speech, *NLC*, Sonderausgabe, 'Siebenter Reichsparteitag am 2. und 3. Oktober 1926 in Köln'.

anti-American terms since Europe needed the United States as the great creditor nation. Nevertheless he thought it was right for there to be integration of Europe's major industries to limit American dominance.[209]

Stresemann reported to the cabinet on 13 October that the Thoiry scheme faced opposition in both France and the United States.[210] He hoped that it would be possible to win over the Americans by persuading them that it would be better to allow the political issues—the Rhine occupation, the Saar, Eupen-Malmédy—to be settled in advance of a final reparations plan so that they would not complicate the financial negotiations in the way that the Ruhr evacuation had complicated reaching agreement on the Dawes plan.[211] But by November it became increasingly clear that the French were no longer interested. Briand tried to shift the responsibility by suggesting that it was up to the Germans to make proposals.[212]

Stresemann was keen to find some basis on which the idea of Franco-German cooperation could be kept alive. Hoesch explained that even those circles in France which supported an understanding with Germany wanted Germany tied to France in a way which prevented it changing direction again, once it was free of the occupation.[213] People were critical of Thoiry because it provided no such assurance. Hoesch warned that Germany should be careful not to discredit Briand, whose position had become dangerously isolated. Stresemann replied that he saw no possibility at that time of accepting new obligations, as the French were suggesting, for example over the east, the Rhineland, or disarmament, but he went on:

Agreements which aim at a reorientation of Franco-German policy on a common basis of parity would have a different character. Perhaps there are possibilities here in particular questions for further rapprochement, for example in joint economic activity, in building up Franco-German trade relations, in

[209] Report to the foreign affairs committee, 7 Oct. 1926 (Nl. 44); extracts in Bernhard (ed.), *Vermächtnis*, iii. 37–41, and Harttung (ed.), *Schriften*, 366–70.

[210] Abramowski (ed.), *Kabinette Marx III*, no. 89.

[211] Memorandum by Schubert of a meeting with Parker Gilbert, 9 Oct. 1926, and of a meeting with the American chargé d'affaires, 11 Oct. 1926; Stresemann to London, Washington and other embassies, 15 Oct. 1926: *ADAP*, ser. B, i/ii, nos. 130, 139, 148.

[212] Hoesch to Auswärtiges Amt, 22 Oct. 1926; memorandum by Pünder of a meeting with Hesnard, 25 Oct. 1926; memorandum by Stresemann of a meeting with de Margerie, 1 Nov. 1926: ibid. nos. 156-7, 176.

[213] Hoesch to Stresemann, 30 Oct. 1926: ibid. no. 173.

developing economic and financial policy towards Russia and, indeed, with respect to the liquidation of the Dawes plan.[214]

The basic problem facing both sides was the size and power of Germany compared to France. How could Germany persuade France that an 'understanding' would be more than a temporary truce? Economic integration might have provided a long-term solution but it did not develop rapidly enough in the 1920s to give France the assurance it needed. French politicians were understandably nervous of giving up their means of coercion through the Rhineland occupation, when the future of German policy was uncertain. Briand appeared willing to go further than most, but even he was not consistent. Indeed, it has been suggested that his policy did not differ very much from Poincaré's and that he used Thoiry to gain Stresemann's confidence without giving much away in return.[215] Stresemann was frustrated by the standstill and wavered between feeling that he must be patient and protect Briand's position and, on the other hand, irritation and the desire to mount a diplomatic offensive for the evacuation of the Rhineland as of right in view of Locarno and German disarmament.[216]

He decided to concentrate on securing the withdrawal of the Allied Military Control Commission. Since the principle of withdrawal was not contested by the Allies, this was the issue on which progress was most likely. Stresemann warned the British and French governments that if a solution were not found at the December meeting of the League council, he would no longer be able to carry public opinion with him.[217] After protracted negotiations and a threat by Briand to resign to overcome the opposition in Paris, agreement was reached to withdraw the Commission on 31 January 1927.[218]

Stresemann also won acceptance for the view that the responsibility for supervising German disarmament, which now passed to the League,

[214] Stresemann to Hoesch, 3 Nov. 1926; *ADAP*, ser. B, i/ii no. 177.

[215] Keeton, *Briand's Locarno Policy*, 174–5, 219–24.

[216] In his speech to the DVP national executive on 1 October 1926 he admitted that the incessant demands of public opinion sometimes made him want to achieve something too fast, but in his statement to the cabinet on 2 Dec. he said that if there was no progress on Thoiry by February he would be forced to demand unconditional evacuation of the Rhineland. Kolb and Richter (eds.), *Nationalliberalismus*, 662–3; Abramowski (ed.), *Kabinette Marx III*, no. 136.

[217] Stresemann to Hoesch, 3 Nov. 1926; memorandum by Stresemann of a meeting with the British ambassador Sir Ronald Lindsay, 24 Nov. 1926: *ADAP*, ser. B, i/ii, nos. 177, 209.

[218] German records of the meetings in Geneva from 5 to 12 Dec. 1926: ibid., nos. 237, 249, 251, 254, 258, 260.

would be carried out by an ad hoc investigation, if an alleged violation was raised in the council, and not by establishing a new machinery of permanent inspection in Germany. Rather to his surprise, Chamberlain and Briand suggested that it might be possible to evacuate the remaining Rhineland zones earlier than under the Versailles treaty if the Germans agreed to a civilian commission, which would include Germans, to ensure the observance of Locarno by both Germany and France.[219] Stresemann made fun of the idea saying that the proposed body would be a huge sinecure and its annual report would be difficult to draw up, since it could hardly say that large armies had not been observed moving in either direction. Nevertheless he was encouraged that early evacuation of the Rhineland had been raised and took it as sign that Briand's position had strengthened. This suggested that it was right to persevere with the policy of détente. The reputation of each of the foreign ministers was also bound up with the success of that policy, a point underlined by the award of Nobel peace prizes to Stresemann, Briand, and Chamberlain, which was announced while they were in Geneva.

'A crisis of the parliamentary system'

While Stresemann was in Geneva a full-scale cabinet crisis had developed in Berlin. The background was the impatience of the DNVP to re-enter the government. In November the DNVP adopted the tactic of voting for an SPD–KPD resolution to raise unemployment relief to demonstrate its ability to cause problems.[220] Marx countered by reaching an agreement with the SPD to allow appropriate policies to be discussed with it in advance so that its views could be taken into account. Stresemann pointed out that this was a shift towards the left and he wanted it made clear that the move was a result of the tactics adopted by the DNVP. He also thought that it would be difficult for the SPD to deliver its support, since it was under pressure from the KPD. He described the situation as 'a crisis of the parliamentary system'.[221]

[219] Memorandum by Schubert of the discussion, 6 Dec. 1926; Stresemann to Auswärtiges Amt, 8 Dec. 1926: *ADAP*, ser. B, i/ii, nos. 237, 244.

[220] Abramowski (ed.), *Kabinette Marx III*, pp. xxxiv–xxxv; cabinet minutes, 10 Nov. 1926: ibid., no. 113; Hehl, *Marx*, 389–93.

[221] Cabinet minutes, 11 Nov. 1926: Abramowski (ed.) *Kabinette Marx III*, no. 114.

The move to accommodate the SPD was unwelcome to the right wing of the DVP. The issue came to a head over the SPD's desire to re-establish the eight-hour day which had remained suspended since the Ruhr crisis. This gave Scholz another opportunity to create a breach with the SPD. Although the DVP Reichstag party decided by a majority of 21 to 16 to support a compromise on the issue, Scholz made a speech attacking the idea of coalition with the SPD and stressing the extent of agreement between the DVP and the DNVP.[222]

The SPD reacted by cancelling their agreement with Marx and threatening to bring in a motion of no confidence.[223] The situation was particularly embarrassing to Stresemann because at the same time the SPD press took up the revelations about German rearmament in the Soviet Union which had just appeared in the *Manchester Guardian*. Since Stresemann was then in Geneva negotiating for the end of the Allied Control Commission, the timing could hardly have been worse. He urged Marx to use his influence with the SPD to postpone a Reichstag debate, saying it would be 'a monumental act of folly' to force a crisis in the middle of the negotiations.[224] The SPD leaders gave way and indicated that they would be willing to drop the debate, provided the government opened negotiations for a coalition.[225] Stresemann supported Marx in getting the cabinet's agreement to these terms, and ministers were also able to persuade Scholz and the DVP, though Stresemann noted that the party was 'somewhat grumpy'.[226]

The situation then changed again as the SPD leaders encountered stronger resistance than they had expected from the Reichstag party, and on 15 December they added two conditions: a debate would have to be held after all though the party chairman, Hermann Müller, promised that they would be very cautious in what they said about the Reichswehr and

---

[222] Minutes of meetings of ministers with leaders of the coalition parties, 30 Nov. and 1 Dec. 1926; cabinet minutes, 8 Dec. 1926: Abramowski (ed.), *Kabinette Marx III.*, nos. 132-3, 141; Stürmer, *Koalition und Opposition*, 162–72.

[223] Winkler, *Der Schein der Normalität*, 295–300.

[224] Stresemann to Auswärtiges Amt for the Reich chancellor and Reich president, 8 Dec. 1926: *ADAP*, ser. B, i/ii, no. 240.

[225] Cabinet minutes, 13 Dec. and 15 Dec. 1926: Abramowski (ed.), *Kabinette Marx III*, nos. 152, 156.

[226] Minutes of a meeting of ministers with representatives of the coalition parties, 15 Dec. 1926: ibid., no. 157; Stresemann's note about the crisis, with the date 'beginning of 1927' added possibly by Bernhard; typescript in Nl. 48. A version with omissions is printed in Bernhard (ed.), *Vermächtnis*, iii. 91.

would not cause problems for Stresemann's foreign policy, and the cabinet would have to resign before negotiations for the great coalition could begin.[227] The last condition was unacceptable to the cabinet, but Marx was also unwilling to accept the advice of Scholz and turn instead to the DNVP.[228]

The SPD made good its threat and on 16 December Scheidemann launched a fierce attack on the Reichswehr, including its contacts with the Red Army, in a speech which showed no concern for the undertaking Müller had given Stresemann the previous day. The Right regarded the speech as treasonable and the DNVP walked out. Stresemann persuaded Scholz and part of the DVP to remain, together with Marx and other ministers, in order to prevent Scheidemann's accusations assuming even greater importance.[229] The following day the SPD's motion of no confidence was carried with the votes of the DNVP, and Marx resigned.[230] Germany entered its third Christmas in succession with only a caretaker government.

Stresemann and Secret Rearmament

In an attempt to head off the SPD's attack Stresemann had been involved, together with Marx and Gessler, in negotiations with the SPD leaders. Gessler tried to shift the blame for the rearmament programme in the Soviet Union to the Auswärtiges Amt, saying it was a continuation of Wirth's Rapallo policy and that the Auswärtiges Amt had been in the know all along.[231] Stresemann disputed this version of events, claiming that the involvement of the Auswärtiges Amt ceased after 1923 when he had agreed with Ebert that the Reichswehr's activities in Russia should stop.[232]

---

[227] Minutes of a meeting between Marx, Stresemann, Gessler, and SPD leaders, 15 Dec. 1926 and cabinet minutes, 16 Dec. 1926: Abramowski (ed.), *Kabinette Marx III*, nos. 158–9. Winkler, *Der Schein der Normalität*, 301. Stresemann's note: Nl. 48.

[228] Minutes of a meeting of ministers with representatives of the coalition parties, 16 Dec. 1926: Abramowski (ed.), *Kabinette Marx III*, no. 160.

[229] Stresemann's note (Nl. 48): Bernhard (ed.), *Vermächtnis*, iii. 92.

[230] Cabinet minutes, 17 Dec. 1926: Abramowski (ed.), *Kabinette Marx III*, no. 161.

[231] Stresemann's note (Nl. 48) and cabinet minutes 15 Dec. 1926: Abramowski (ed.), *Kabinette Marx III*, no. 156.

[232] Stresemann's note, Nl. 48; see above, p. 270.

The truth is more complicated. Stresemann had no objection to secret rearmament in principle. Like most Germans, including many in the SPD, he did not regard the Versailles treaty as morally binding. He also believed, like all governments, in the utility of military force. What Stresemann objected to was that the Reichswehr's independent policy threatened to undermine his foreign policy without promising much in return.[233] He therefore agreed with Brockdorff-Rantzau that the Reichswehr's activities should be brought under control but he never challenged Gessler or Seeckt directly. Perhaps he did not feel strong enough, or perhaps he was held back by an innate respect for the Reichswehr and a fear of damaging its morale.

The threat of Soviet blackmail however, caused concern before Locarno, and the general risk that the rearmament programme would become public was a constant worry.[234] Stresemann was obviously acutely concerned in December 1926 that the revelations would undermine the credibility of his foreign policy and his own reputation. To his surprise there was hardly any reaction from the Allies, who were already well aware of the Reichswehr's activity.

Perhaps because of this lack of reaction, when General Heye asked for political authorization for continued cooperation with the Red Army in the training of pilots, a tank school, and gas warfare, Stresemann agreed.[235] The programme continued on a limited scale throughout his time as foreign minister and was sanctioned even by the SPD chairman, Hermann Müller, when he became chancellor of a great coalition in 1928.

Stresemann's toleration of the secret rearmament measures does not show—as he feared it might seem—that the French general staff was right to regard Locarno as simply 'a screen for German rearmament'.[236] He was prepared, however, to connive at the programme to maintain the Reichswehr's knowledge of modern techniques of warfare. The cooperation with

---

[233] See above, p. 285.

[234] See above, p. 324. The cabinet discussed the danger of publicity arising from the financial problems of the Junkers aircraft factory in the Soviet Union and in relation to the question of allowing an exchange of a Soviet agent: Abramowski (ed.), *Kabinette Marx III*, nos. 38, 50, 63, 68, 152. Also Stresemann to Marx, 22 July 1926: *ADAP*, ser. B, ii/ii, no. 63. Möllers, *Geßler*, 174–80.

[235] Note by Dirksen, 9 Feb. 1927: *ADAP*, ser. B, iv, no. 117; Carsten, *Reichswehr and Politics*, 275–80; Zeidler, *Reichswehr und Rote Armee*, 147–53.

[236] Memorandum of a meeting in the Reich Chancellery to discuss legal action against a journalist who had revealed details of the programme, 18 Dec. 1926: *ADAP*, ser. B, i/ii, no. 270.

the Red Army also served a function for his foreign policy, helping to preserve the link with the Soviet Union despite Soviet dislike for the priority he gave to relations with the West.

'Responsible realpolitik'

In his New Year's message to the DVP for 1927, Stresemann struck a note of qualified optimism. The party had taken responsibility for government in a difficult time at the cost of its own popularity. Despite the serious problems that remained, particularly the level of unemployment, their efforts had not been in vain. The 'psychological crisis of the state' had been overcome and, as conditions stabilized, people would turn increasingly to 'the ideas of responsible realpolitik'.

There was much to justify this optimism and Stresemann could afford to take credit for the transition in Germany's fortunes from the nadir of 1923. However, the outline of future problems was also becoming clear. Peaceful revision had not shown itself successful with regard to the Polish frontier, the Saar, or even Eupen-Malmédy. Locarno confirmed the status quo of 1919 but it was not clear how Germany could move beyond it. Once a measure of stability had been achieved, there was no pressing reason for the Allies to go further. And as the failure of Thoiry demonstrated, Germany, like France and Britain, was dependent on American capital and the goodwill of the American government. In the long term there might be European economic integration which would change the terms of the debate, but in the short and medium term Germany would have to rely on patience and persuasion to make even limited gains. The electoral dividends of 'responsible realpolitik' would be correspondingly constrained.

In domestic politics too the overthrow of the Marx government by a combination of the SPD and DNVP demonstrated that, although the Republic was no longer an issue, it was still unable to provide effective parliamentary government. In a speech during a similar crisis the previous year, Stresemann had blamed the absence of consensus between the parties and the lack of a tradition of responsible opposition, contrasting Germany with Britain and Canada.[237] Because of the radicalism of left and right, he believed that Germany could be governed only from the middle

[237] Speech in Berlin, 10 Dec. 1925: Bernhard (ed.), *Vermächtnis*, ii. 377–80.

and he was determined to keep the DVP in the middle. He reaffirmed his conviction that if the DVP ceased to be 'an independent liberal party' in the middle of the spectrum and tied itself to the DNVP it would lose its raison d'être.[238] As the repeated government crises showed, however, the middle could only govern with the toleration of either the SPD or the DNVP. Given the problems of cooperating with either, it was not clear how the 'crisis of the parliamentary system' could be overcome.

[238] 'Betrachtungen zur Krise', *Deutsche Stimmen*, 39/4, 20 Feb. 1927, 111.

9

Peaceful Revision in the Balance, 1927–1928

'So there arises a double task for international politics and especially
for German policy: the securing of a free Germany with equal rights
and the inclusion of such a Germany together with all other states in
a stable international structure.'[1]

The last years of Stresemann's life were dominated by disappointment and
frustration. Peaceful revision, which had been so successful in the previous
three years, came to a standstill in 1927–28. Hopes of a general settlement
with France faded as Briand became increasingly evasive. In any case, a
solution depended on the United States since the issues of Rhineland
evacuation, a final reparations settlement, and war debts became linked,
and no progress could be expected until after the American presidential
elections at the end of 1928.

Stresemann had to settle for patience and limited gains. In public he
showed self-restraint, which he was aware he had sometimes lacked in the
past, in an attempt to strengthen Briand's position in France. The delay in
evacuation of the Rhineland, however, cost him support at home. The
problem was not so much the predictable opposition of the radical right
but rather that even Stresemann's natural supporters became increasingly
critical of his policy.

[1] 'Neue Wege zur Völkerverständigung', Stresemann's speech to the University of Heidelberg,
5 May 1928.

The development of domestic politics was, at least on the surface, more encouraging. The DNVP entered the government in January 1927 having formally accepted the policies of Locarno and League membership. The coalition broke up again in February 1928 over the issue of education, when the DVP refused some of the concessions to denominational schools wanted by the Centre and the DNVP. Stresemann had been prepared to compromise, but the failure of the coalition was not unwelcome to him. Elections were due in both France and Germany in 1928 in any case. He was encouraged by Briand to think that if the parties supporting rapprochement were successful in both countries it would be possible to proceed with the evacuation of the Rhineland. This suggested that a switch in coalition from the DNVP to the SPD would be well received in France. Since the DNVP had again become critical of his foreign policy, Stresemann also had no reason to want to keep them in the government.

The elections held in Germany in May resulted in gains for the SPD and losses for the DNVP, pointing to an SPD-led great coalition. Stresemann was instrumental in bringing this about from the sanatorium of Bühlerhöhe, where he was receiving treatment after collapsing during the election campaign. The new government appeared to mark a further stage in the consolidation of the Republic and a promising basis for renewed détente.

The success was, however, marred by other developments. The elections held in April in France had strengthened Poincaré's position, though Briand remained as foreign minister. How far their policies towards Germany differed is, in any case, a matter of debate, but Stresemann's hope that Briand would be in a position to conduct a more independent policy came to nothing. At home, Stresemann's initiative in bringing about the great coalition was resented by Scholz and a substantial section of the DVP Reichstag party. They disliked being in coalition with the SPD, particularly as economic and social issues became more central as economic problems mounted. They saw the coalition as a sacrifice made necessary by Stresemann's foreign policy, and that was also seen increasingly as an electoral burden rather than an asset.

Stresemann's health, which had never been strong, deteriorated rapidly after 1927.[2] He was forced to live as a semi-invalid, spending part of the winter in Mediterranean resorts and long periods during the summer at German spa towns and the sanatorium at Bühlerhöhe. However, he

---

[2] The nature of his illness is uncertain. He had a goitre—enlarged thyroid gland—and was commonly thought to have Graves' (known in Germany as Basedow's) disease. One of his consultants, Gerhard Stroomann, however, disputed the diagnosis, arguing that Stresemann did

continued to direct foreign policy and missed only one important meeting of the League, in September 1928.

In periods when foreign policy was becalmed, or during enforced absences through illness, Stresemann turned to history and literature for relaxation. He had a long-standing interest in the period of the Napoleonic Wars and spoke on various occasions on the theme of Goethe and Napoleon.[3] He was an active member, and from 1928 an honorary member of the Deutscher Bühnen-Klub (German theatre club).[4] In 1927 he lectured there on the thesis that when Goethe referred to his 'main occupation' he was not referring to Faust but to another work subsequently lost.[5] In 1927 he also published a long review of a new play about the Napoleonic Wars, because he disagreed with the way it portrayed the Prussian king, Frederick William III, and General von Blücher.[6] His criticism showed a detailed knowledge of the sources and an imaginative understanding of the characters and the tensions between them. These interests undoubtedly represented a genuine 'hinterland' for Stresemann, offering him relief from politics and a chance to contribute insights from his own experience, though in his literary and historical studies he never aspired to be more than a gifted amateur.[7] On one occasion he wrote that he often deeply regretted not having stuck to his original intention on leaving school, 'to dedicate himself to the study of literature and history'.[8]

not suffer from the heart condition typical of advanced stages of the disease. Stresemann's symptoms were repeated kidney infections, breathlessness, and chest pain. His doctors agreed that these symptoms were caused in part by extensive arteriosclerosis. Gerhard Stroomann, *Aus meinem roten Notizbuch*, 2nd. edn. (Frankfurt am Main: Societäts–Verlag, 1960), 133–7; Hermann Zondek, *Auf festem Fusse* (Stuttgart: Deutsche Verlags-Anstalt, 1973), 130–1. I have benefited from the advice of my father and of my son Ben in interpreting the medical opinions.

[3] 'Goethe und Napoleon', lecture to the Goethe Gesellschaft, Berlin, 9 Dec. 1921: Rheinbaben (ed.), *Reden und Schriften*, ii. 350–67; Harttung (ed.), *Schriften*, 51–6; 'Goethe und die Freiheitskriege', lecture in Heidelberg, Aug. 1926: Bernhard (ed.), *Vermächtnis*, ii. 352–62.

[4] Stresemann was made an honorary member during his illness in May 1928; see the special issue in his honour of the *Deutscher Bühnen-Klub*, 2/4–5 (May/June 1928) (Nl. 344).

[5] 'Rätsel um Goethe', 24 Apr. 1927: Bernhard (ed.), *Vermächtnis*, ii. 363–76.

[6] 'Neidhart von Gneisenau', *Deutsche Stimmen*, 39/1, 5 Jan. 1927; 'Der König, Gneisenau und Blücher', *Deutsche Stimmen*, 39/8, 20 Apr. 1927.

[7] It has been pointed out that his lectures on Goethe drew on other sources. Stresemann did, however, acknowledge the debt in both cases. Hans W. Gatzke, 'Gustav Stresemann: A Bibliographical Article', *Journal of Modern History*, 36, (1964), 10–11; cf. Rheinbaben (ed.), *Reden und Schriften*, ii. 351; Bernhard (ed.), *Vermächtnis*, ii. 365.

[8] Stresemann to the poet, Rudolf Presber, 12 July 1928 (Nl. 290).

Another indication of his desire to be associated with a community outside politics was his decision to join the Freemasons. He applied in 1923, writing that he had long hoped to be associated with like-minded people 'who seek to preserve in our time, which is racked by materialism, haste and restlessness, the realm of humanity, inner reflection and the intellect'.[9] There are few details of his activities as a mason. He allowed his portrait to be painted by a fellow member from impressions gained while he was addressing a meeting in his masonic robes.[10] Even as a mason, however, he found himself involved in politics. He objected in 1924 to a speaker who made a racist attack on the government over the Dawes plan.[11] And in 1927, when Ludendorff published an attack on the masons, Stresemann advised against a reasoned reply, saying that it gave the impression of weakness and would never convince people like Ludendorff, 'who are mentally disturbed, so that one does not know whether they are able to think normally'. In future he suggested that any reply should take the form of a vigorous counter-attack, saying that 'the criticism of fools does not concern us'.[12]

According to his son, Stresemann hoped to find in the Freemasons the kind of community which he had come to miss in the Protestant Church.[13] The liberal Protestants, about whom he had been enthusiastic as a sixth-former, always remained a small minority within the Church, though as it happened the grand master of his lodge was a clergyman. In the early 1920s Stresemann continued to take an interest in church elections in his Berlin parish, but later he became less active.[14] He declined to attend the Protestant cathedral in Berlin after being subjected in 1925 to an anti-republican tirade by a former court preacher and DNVP member of the Reichstag, Bruno Doering, at a service to which Stresemann had been officially invited to commemorate the foundation of the Bismarck Reich.[15] It was left to his DVP friend and colleague Wilhelm Kahl, who was also a prominent layman, to

---

[9] Stresemann to Pfarrer Karl Habicht, 10 May 1923 (Nl. 364): facsimile in Bernhard (ed.), *Vermächtnis*, i. 548.

[10] Portrait by Franz Lünstroth; Stresemann to Dr Schiften, 2 July 1926 (Nl. 108).

[11] Stresemann to Habicht, 26 June 1924 (Nl. 364): Bernhard (ed.), *Vermächtnis*, i. 548–9.

[12] Stresemann to Habicht, 1 Sept. 1927 (Nl. 364).

[13] Wolfgang Stresemann, *Mein Vater*, 30–1.

[14] Ibid.; also diary for 23–4 Jan. 1921 (Nl. 362).

[15] Stresemann to the Dom-Kirchen-Kollegium, 17 Feb. 1925: Bernhard (ed.), *Vermächtnis*, ii. 316; Jonathan R.C. Wright, '*Über den Parteien*'. *Die politische Haltung der evangelischen Kirchenführer 1918–1933* (Göttingen: Vandenhoeck & Ruprecht, 1977), 93–4.

argue within the Protestant Church for an accommodation with the Republic.[16]

Stresemann's ideas on foreign policy continued to develop after 1926, partly stimulated by his interest in history. Peace became more clearly his central priority. Whereas he had argued earlier that Germany, as a disarmed power, had no alternative to a policy of peaceful revision, he now argued that a new war would be a disaster for Europe and especially for Germany. His new thinking had implications for his hopes of frontier revision, which became deferred to an increasingly remote future, though he never abandoned what he saw as Germany's just claims. He also came out more clearly against the alternative policy, still canvassed by his opponents, of a Russian alliance, arguing in January 1927 that the policy had already been defunct before 1914. In a number of important speeches he tried to persuade his audiences that peace and détente with the West were the essential elements of Germany's national interest. At the same time he tried to persuade audiences abroad that despite having had to make a difficult adjustment since the war, Germany could be trusted to maintain the peace and that keeping wartime sanctions in place was both unnecessary and counter-productive.

Coalition with the DNVP

The search for a new government resumed in January 1927 after the Christmas break.[17] The circumstances in which the Marx government had been brought down—an SPD vote of no confidence and attack on the Reichswehr—ruled out a great coalition. The remaining options were a right-wing majority government extending from the Centre Party to the DNVP or the re-establishment of the minority government of the middle parties. Hindenburg strongly favoured a right-wing majority government and the DNVP made it clear that it would not tolerate a renewal of the minority coalition.[18]

The Centre Party, which was as usual crucial to the outcome, was divided. Its trade union wing, led by Wirth, was opposed to joining a

---

[16] Wright, 'Über den Parteien', 87–9.

[17] Abramowski (ed.), Kabinette Marx IV, pp. xlv–xlix.

[18] Meissner's notes of the negotiations between Hindenburg and party leaders, 17 Dec. 1926–28 Jan. 1927: BAB, Büro des Reichspräsidenten, 44; Walther Hubatsch, Hindenburg und der Staat (Göttingen: Musterschmidt, 1966), 256–66.

'bourgeois bloc'. Others were prepared to work for coalition with the DNVP, seeing the potential for cooperation over the issue of denominational schools. In the interests of party unity, however, the Centre Party leaders wanted to be able to demonstrate first that a minority government supported by the SPD was not feasible.[19]

The tactics of the DVP were exactly the reverse. Scholz and a majority of the Reichstag party wanted to see a right-wing coalition, preferably with participation of the DNVP but, failing that, with a looser connection to the DNVP. They therefore ruled out a great coalition and also a minority government with a formal association with the SPD. Scholz would also have liked to rule out a minority government with no ties to the SPD, but Stresemann prevented him. However, the DVP insisted that negotiations be held for a right-wing coalition before it would take a position on a new minority government.[20]

Stresemann's priority in these complex manoeuvres was to protect his foreign policy. He accepted that a great coalition had been ruled out by the SPD's behaviour. Of the alternatives he probably preferred a minority government supported by the SPD. The difficulty was to know whether it was feasible, especially as Hindenburg was determined to keep Gessler as minister of defence, after the SPD's attacks on the Reichswehr, and Gessler was a bête noire to the SPD. On the other hand, the prospects for a majority coalition with the DNVP were also unclear so long as the Centre Party was undecided. If neither of these alternatives proved possible, the only way out would be a dissolution of the Reichstag. Stresemann wanted to avoid elections held in the aftermath of the SPD's attacks on the Reichswehr, fearing that they would be damaging to his foreign policy. In these circumstances, he aligned himself increasingly with his party in pushing the Centre towards coalition with the DNVP, while keeping a new minority government of the middle as a fallback solution.[21]

Eventually, Marx was able to form a government of the Centre, DNVP, DVP, and BVP on 29 January. Stresemann was involved in the negoti-

---

[19] Hehl, *Marx*, 394–401; Ruppert, *Im Dienst*, 239–48.

[20] Memoranda by Pünder of negotiations between Marx and Scholz, 17–20 Jan. 1927: Abramowski (ed.), *Kabinette Marx IV*, nos. 168, 171, 172; Stresemann's note, dated 'beginning of January 1927', and memorandum of a telephone conversation with Marx, 19 Jan. 1927: Bernhard (ed.), *Vermächtnis*, iii. 91–3, 99–101; typescript in Nl. 48 and 49.

[21] Stresemann's note, dated 'beginning of January 1927', and memorandum of a telephone conversation with Marx, 19 Jan. 1927: Bernhard (ed.), *Vermächtnis*, iii. 99–101. Also Stresemann to Marx, 14 Jan. 1927: Abramowski (ed.), *Kabinette Marx IV*, no. 167.

ations with the DNVP.[22] His aim was to pin down the DNVP to preclude a repetition of the events of 1925. In a letter to Marx on 14 January he set out his conditions: the DNVP would have to accept unconditionally the policy of Locarno and the League; in addition the DNVP would have to be willing to accept the concessions which might be necessary to achieve evacuation of the Rhineland—the sale of Dawes bonds and the establishment of a commission to verify that the Locarno pact was being observed; alternative foreign policies such as looking to Italy or a military alliance with the Soviet Union must be ruled out; DNVP ministers would have to be people whose previous conduct offered a guarantee that they would defend the Republic and support Stresemann's foreign policy unconditionally.[23]

Marx used Stresemann's letter in the negotiations and the coalition programme committed the parties to continuing the Locarno and League policies. This did not prevent the DNVP proposing as ministers their former party chairman, Hergt, and a member of the radical right wing of the party, Walther Graef. Stresemann threatened resignation and Marx threatened to break off negotiations with the DNVP.[24] The DNVP then agreed to substitute von Keudell for Graef and the crisis passed.[25]

Although the new government was not Stresemann's preferred outcome, he had reason to be satisfied. Marx, with whom he saw eye to eye, remained chancellor. They had kept in contact throughout the negotiations, even while their parties pulled in different directions. Marx had hinted to Stresemann early in the process that he might be available for a new coalition and Stresemann helped to bring it about.[26] Marx asked

[22] Pünder to Marx, 28 Dec. 1926, and Pünder's memorandum on the negotiations from 23 to 31 Jan. 1927: Abramowski (ed.), *Kabinette Marx IV*, nos. 164, 177; memorandum of a meeting between Stresemann, Auswärtiges Amt officials, and DNVP representatives, 25 Jan. 1927: *ADAP*, ser. B, iv, no. 64.

[23] Stresemann to Marx, 14 Jan. 1927: Abramowski (ed.), *Kabinette Marx IV*, no. 167.

[24] Stresemann to Marx, 30 Jan. 1927 (Nl. 49): Bernhard (ed.), *Vermächtnis*, iii. 103.

[25] Lindeiner-Wildau, for whom Stresemann had secured the position of director of Ossa (the organization which channelled subsidies to the German minority in Poland), was also a candidate, but when Graef was forced to stand down, the right wing of the DNVP insisted that Lindeiner-Wildau should also give way. Stresemann recorded an attempt by another moderate member, Gottfried Treviranus, to persuade Marx to insist on Lindeiner-Wildau. Diary for 2 Feb. 1927: ibid. 104. In his post-war memoirs, Treviranus gives a different version, arguing that he asked Marx to make his own choice from the DNVP candidates. Gottfried R. Treviranus, *Das Ende von Weimar* (Düsseldorf: Econ 1968), 97–9.

[26] Stresemann's note, dated 'beginning of January 1927', that Marx had made the 'curious declaration that he was uncommitted': Bernhard (ed.), *Vermächtnis*, iii. 92. (This comment does not appear in the typescript version of the note in Nl. 48: presumably Bernhard was working from an original which has not survived.)

Stresemann to draft the foreign policy section of the new government's statement to the Reichstag.[27] It must have given Stresemann wry satisfaction to hear Hermann Müller, replying for the SPD, taunt the DNVP with Hugenberg's past attacks on Stresemann, and declare that now Stresemann led both parties.[28]

The Priority of Peace

It was fortunate that DNVP criticism was muted by their participation in government since it soon became clear that no major advance in foreign policy could be expected. In a speech in January Stresemann still expressed the hope that '1927 ought to be the year of the evacuation of the Rhineland', but at the March meeting of the League council Briand told him that the opposition in France was too strong.[29] Stresemann faced the difficult task of maintaining the pressure on France without weakening Briand's position. In an attempt to influence French opinion he authorized secret financial support for the newspapers controlled by Joseph Caillaux, who had briefly occupied the post of finance minister in 1926 and whom Stresemann believed to have been responsible for the Thoiry proposals.[30] At the same time he had to face increased scepticism at home about the prospects for peaceful revision. Particularly wounding was the scarcely concealed criticism of some of his colleagues that he had been too trusting of Briand and now had to face the consequences. A joke about the difference between 'Thoiry and practice' hurt because it contained at least a grain of truth.[31]

Stresemann accepted that no immediate progress could be made on Rhineland evacuation. He even admitted to Marx that he might have been at fault in forcing the issue and making Briand's position difficult.[32] He decided instead to concentrate on the reduction in the number of occu-

---

[27] Stresemann's note, dated 20–21 Jan. 1927 (Nl. 49): Bernhard (ed.), *Vermächtnis*, iii. 102.

[28] *Verhandlungen des Reichstags*, vol. 391, p. 8798.

[29] Stresemann's speech to the Reichszentrale für Heimatdienst (a government information service), 28 Jan. 1927: *ADAP*, ser. B, iv, p. 604; Stresemann's memorandum of his meeting with Briand, 6 Mar. 1927: ibid., no. 219.

[30] Jacques Bariéty, 'L'Appareil de presse de Joseph Caillaux et l'argent allemand (1920–1932)', *Revue Historique*, 247 (1972), 375–406; Pohl, *Adolf Müller*, 312–18; Stresemann's speech to the DVP Zentralvorstand, 19 Mar. 1927: Kolb and Richter (eds.), *Nationalliberalismus*, 720–1.

[31] Paul Moldenhauer, 'Politische Erinnerungen', p. 179: BAK, Nl. Moldenhauer, 2; Vallentin, *Stresemann*, 267–9.

[32] Stresemann to Marx, 14 Jan. 1927: Abramowski (ed.), *Kabinette Marx IV*, no. 167.

pying troops which had been promised at Locarno. When Briand prevaricated, Stresemann complained that this made his position impossible and threatened to resign.[33] With the support of Chamberlain, who admitted that he had a 'bad conscience' in the matter, reminding Briand that, 'we were battling with Soviet Russia for the soul of Germany', agreement was reached to reduce the occupation forces to 60,000 men.[34] Another significant success was the conclusion of a comprehensive trade treaty with France in August 1927, following protracted negotiations which involved German concessions over imports of French wine and agricultural produce in return for French concessions on German industrial goods.[35]

Two crises, not of Germany's making, led to an important development of Stresemann's policy during 1927. On 26 May the Conservative government in Britain decided to break off diplomatic relations with the Soviet Union in protest at Soviet propaganda against the British empire and the use of the premises of the Russian trade delegation in London for subversion and espionage.[36] This immediately raised the awkward possibility that, should Britain want to impose League sanctions on the Soviet Union, Germany would no longer be able to maintain its delicate balance between the League and Russia.

The second dispute was between Lithuania and Poland over the territory of Vilna, which Poland had occupied in 1920. German interests were again divided. Germany did not want to see Poland strengthened by a successful war against Lithuania (which might leave East Prussia surrounded by Poland). The Soviet Union also had no desire to see a further extension of Polish territory to the east. On the other hand, Germany was concerned about the treatment of the German population of Memel by the Lithuanians. The Allies had accepted the Lithuanian occupation of the territory by the Memel Convention of 1924 which guaranteed Memel

---

[33] Stresemann to Hoesch, 23 Apr. 1927; Stresemann's memorandum of a meeting with Sir Ronald Lindsay, 28 Apr. 1927: *ADAP*, ser. B, v, nos. 98, 107.

[34] Stresemann's memorandum of a meeting with Chamberlain, 6 Mar. 1927: *ADAP*, ser. B, iv, no. 220; Chamberlain to Lindsay, 15 Mar. 1927, Chamberlain's record of a meeting with Briand, 18 May 1927: *DBFP*, ser. Ia, iii, nos. 46, 201 (p. 310); Briand to Stresemann, 5 Sept. 1927: *ADAP*, ser. B, vi, no. 172. Richard S. Grayson, *Austen Chamberlain and the Commitment to Europe: British Foreign Policy 1924–29* (London: Frank Cass, 1997), 120–2.

[35] Krüger, *Aussenpolitik*, 368–72.

[36] In fact very little incriminating evidence was found in the Soviet premises, but the right-wing 'diehards' in the cabinet had been pressing for a break in relations since 1924. Chamberlain had previously resisted this pressure, partly because of the effect it would have on Germany. Gabriel Gorodetsky, *The Precarious Truce: Anglo-Soviet Relations 1924–27* (Cambridge: Cambridge University Press, 1977), 211–31.

a degree of autonomy. However, these rights had been violated in various ways after a coup d'état in Lithuania in December 1926.[37]

Stresemann's policy in both disputes was to work for a peaceful outcome.[38] He did not expect the Anglo-Russian crisis to lead to war, though he told the cabinet that there was always the possibility that Chamberlain might be pushed even further by the right wing of the Conservative Party and he was also concerned about the 'intense activity' of British agents who were operating from Germany against the Soviet Union.[39] He dismissed the idea that Germany might take sides in the dispute, pointing out that the Soviet Union was too weak to be an ally and Britain was not in a position to bring about revision of the Polish frontier.

At the meeting of the League council two weeks later Chamberlain assured Stresemann that Britain had no intention of taking further action and that he was conscious of the problems which an Anglo-Soviet rift would cause Germany.[40] Stresemann defended Germany's policy of extending credit, and maintaining trade links with the Soviet Union, as the best way to encourage the development of a political and economic system 'with which one could live'. Briand raised the danger of a Russo-Polish war arising out of the recent assassination of the Soviet envoy in Warsaw, and Stresemann had the satisfaction of being asked by Chamberlain to use Germany's special position to urge moderation on the Russians.

Stresemann had already spoken with Chicherin, attempting to dispel his fears of a Polish invasion backed by Britain and France, and his further fear that Germany would allow French troops to march through Germany to go to the aid of the Poles. Stresemann insisted that none of the powers concerned—Britain, France, and Poland—was intent on war and that Germany's waiver from article 16 provided a legal barrier to France

---

[37] Krüger, *Aussenpolitik*, 396–401; Arnold J. Toynbee (ed.), *Survey of International Affairs 1927* (London: Oxford University Press, 1929), 235–47. Schubert to the German delegation in Kowno, 17 Aug. 1927: *ADAP*, ser. B, vi, no. 122.

[38] In a list of points, probably for discussion during the meeting of the League council in June 1927, Stresemann noted 'Alteration status quo a matter of indifference whether peacefully or by war.' This clearly, however, does not refer to his own intentions but rather to the changes of the status quo that had already occurred between Poland and Lithuania. Stresemann headed the notes 'Continuation of the previous foreign policy for peace' and a subsequent point on the same note reads: 'We are for peaceful development but no political hegemony with East Prussia surrounded.' Undated note, sheet numbered H150121, Nl. 283. I am grateful to Dr Gutzler for deciphering part of the heading, which is in shorthand.

[39] Cabinet minutes, 30 May 1927: Abramowski (ed.), *Kabinette Marx IV*, no. 242.

[40] Stresemann's memorandum of the meeting on 14 June, dated 15 June 1927: *ADAP*, ser. B, v, no. 236; the British record is in *DBFP*, ser. IA, iii, no. 240.

sending troops across Germany. He admitted that in practice, if a European war broke out, France might still demand the right to send forces through Germany. In that case he said his own view was that the Reichswehr would not be strong enough to fight and Germany would respond with passive resistance.[41]

Stresemann also urged restraint during the Polish–Lithuanian crisis. In January he warned the officials of the government information service that the dispute could 'start the avalanche' of a major war.[42] By November the crisis looked increasingly serious. Together with the Soviet Union he put pressure on the Lithuanian premier, Voldemaras, to accept a compromise. He made it clear to Litvinov that, if war broke out, Germany would not be in a position to take part and he rejected Litvinov's suggestion that Germany should threaten to occupy the corridor if Poland attacked Lithuania.[43] Stresemann's aim was to reach 'a reasonable modus vivendi' which preserved Lithuanian independence, and this was achieved at negotiations during the League council meeting in December.[44]

Stresemann's commitment to peace became increasingly strong during these years. He used various arguments. War, he told the cabinet in November 1927, would bring 'the very greatest dangers for the whole position of Europe in the world'.[45] Europe needed time to recover from the damage which the last war had done to its economic and social cohesion.[46] In particular, Germany would be the loser from a new war. She did not have the military means to defend herself, even from attack by Poland, let alone against the great powers.[47] Germany's central position

---

[41] Stresemann's memorandum of the meeting in Baden-Baden, 7 June 1927: *ADAP*, ser. B, v, no. 209.

[42] Speech to the Reichszentrale für Heimatdienst, 28 Jan. 1927: *ADAP*, ser. B, iv, p. 586.

[43] Memorandum by Schubert of the meeting, 25 Nov. 1927: ibid. vii, no. 140.

[44] Stresemann to Hoesch, 3 Nov. 1927; ibid., no. 68; memoranda of the negotiations in Geneva, 4–10 Dec. 1927: ibid., Nos.174–5, 179, 181, 197. John Hiden, *The Baltic States and German Ostpolitik* (Cambridge: Cambridge University Press, 1987).

[45] Cabinet minutes, 30 Nov. 1927: Abramowski (ed.), *Kabinette Marx IV*, no. 358.

[46] e.g. Stresemann's speech to the Reichszentrale für Heimatdienst, 28 Jan. 1927: *ADAP*, ser. B, iv, pp. 584–5.

[47] Memorandum by the Auswärtiges Amt official Forster, dated 22 Dec. 1927, on the forthcoming war game to practise defending East Prussia against Polish attack. Even though it was being assumed that Germany's relations with France were so good that there was no danger of French intervention, he reported that the view of the army command was nevertheless that the position would be 'just hopeless'. Schubert reinforced this conclusion by adding, 'Apparently they also assume that Britain has been the victim of a seaquake, America has been ruined partly by typhoons and partly by speculative investment failures, while Czechoslovakia has been completely preoccupied with the conclusion of a Concordat.' *ADAP*, ser. B, vii, no. 226. On

would also make it the natural battleground in any major European conflict. As Stresemann told the foreign affairs committee of the Reichstag in 1929, 'We could not base our policy on what would be the position in future wars, because in almost every contingency we are obliged to present the battlefield.'[48] For all these reasons, he was serious when he told the Reichstag in June 1927, 'We seek peace and nothing other than peace in Europe and in the world.'[49]

The Consequences for Peaceful Revision

The peace which Germany sought was still, however, a peace which kept open the possibility of territorial revision. Although Stresemann knew that such revision could only be a long-term goal, Germany was not prepared to accept an 'eastern Locarno' as Poland wanted or to give up its interest in Austria. German policy was to keep matters open and allow the situation to ripen.[50] Where Austria was concerned Stresemann privately doubted whether union was desirable.[51] Nevertheless German policy was to promote common policies between the two states in as many areas as possible and to prevent Germany being excluded, as Czechoslovakia wanted, from a south-east European economic association.[52]

   In order to forestall Polish and French initiatives to give greater security to existing frontiers, Germany developed peace initiatives of its own. At the meeting of the League assembly in 1927, Stresemann announced Germany's adherence, as the first of the great powers, to the 'optional' clause of the statute of the Permanent Court at the Hague.[53] The optional

---

operational planning, see Gaines Post, *The Civil–Military Fabric of Weimar Foreign Policy* (Princeton: Princeton University Press, 1973), 203–38.

[48] Report by the Bavarian representative in Berlin, Ritter von Preger, dated 26 Jan., of the meeting on 25 Jan. 1929; BH, MA 103543.

[49] Reichstag speech, 23 June 1927: Zwoch (ed.), *Reichstagsreden*, 252.

[50] Stresemann's speech to the Reichszentrale für Heimatdienst, 28 Jan. 1927: *ADAP*, ser. B, iv, p. 601.

[51] Asked about his attitude by Schubert, Stresemann described union with Austria as 'a sacrifice that might perhaps have to be made sometime', adding that while the policies of the two states should be coordinated in as many areas as possible, it would be best if Austria remained independent. Memorandum by Schubert, 16 July 1927: *ADAP*, ser. B, vi, no. 39.

[52] Krüger, *Aussenpolitik*, 402–6.

[53] Stresemann's speech, 9 Sept. 1927; *League of Nations Official Journal*, Special Supplement no. 54, 79–82; Bernhard (ed.), *Vermächtnis*, iii. 180–7.

clause committed Germany to accepting arbitration on justiciable issues, in line with the Locarno treaties. On the other hand, the decision also served a tactical purpose—to head off a Polish proposal for a general non-aggression pact, which was finally watered down by the great powers to a mere declaration.[54]

Following the same policy, Germany produced proposals for the security committee established by the League to work in parallel with preparations for a disarmament conference. The committee was the result of French pressure to make progress on disarmament conditional on improved arrangements for security. The Auswärtiges Amt feared that the result would be proposals 'to perpetuate the present political situation in Europe' by a system of alliances and sanctions.[55] Gaus and Schubert therefore devised an alternative approach for a general system of arbitration for political as well as justiciable disputes, which was accepted by Stresemann and the cabinet (with minor modifications to satisfy the DNVP members) and presented to the security committee.[56] Despite its tactical purpose, this was a far-reaching proposal which, in the words of Gaus, would have meant a 'further limitation of our free-dom of action', restricting the use of force to defence against an aggressor who refused to accept the decision of an arbitrator, and binding Germany to accept arbitration on its eastern frontiers. The German proposal was well received by the security committee though in the end no new procedures resulted. The proposal is, however, a striking demonstration of where thinking seriously about peaceful revision could lead.

The Politics of Foreign Policy

Stresemann could rely on his senior officials for advice, but the major decisions were his responsibility and he had to mobilize support at home and abroad. He reported on the quarterly meetings of the League council to the cabinet and the foreign affairs committees of the Reichstag and the Reichsrat (representing the *Länder*). He also gave regular press confer-ences and made speeches to the Reichstag, DVP meetings, and other groups. His main themes were unchanging—the lack of any alternative

[54] Kimmich, *Germany and the League of Nations*, 99–100.
[55] Schubert to Stresemann with enclosed memoranda, 31 Dec. 1927: *ADAP*, ser. B, vii, no. 246.
[56] Cabinet minutes, 25 Jan. 1928: Abramowski (ed.), *Kabinette Marx IV*, no. 403; Krüger, *Aussenpolitik*, 376–96.

to the policy of peaceful revision and the need for patience—but there were some interesting variations to different audiences.

He set out the main lines of his policy in a major speech (without journalists present) on Germany's position in the world to the officials of the government information service on 28 January 1927.[57] He started by describing the larger context of the instability of the period through which they were living, illustrating his theme with a variety of examples. He claimed that the system inaugurated by the peace treaties was not secure because of the dislocation of the international economy. Britain was suffering from rising and long-term unemployment and imperial unrest. France was suffering from problems with the value of the franc and a decline in its birth rate, hence its opposition to a German union with Austria which would give Germany a population of 70 million to 40 million French. Both Britain and France had war debts to the United States, much larger than any likely receipts from reparations. French public opinion made it very difficult for the government to agree to pay these debts, creating a serious rift with the United States. In another context, the use of colonial troops in the war had created demands for colonial autonomy which signalled the ultimate destabilization of the European empires. Europe as a whole had lost its strength as a capital market, and increasingly its lead in technology, to the United States. Europe had also been weakened by tearing itself apart in war, and the formation of small independent states after the war.

He went on to talk about the conflict between democracy and dictatorship exemplified by the tensions in Greece, Spain, Italy, and Poland. He compared the times through which they were living with the upheavals of the twenty-six years from the French Revolution to the Congress of Vienna, another time of social, political and economic ferment, which he said had moved from liberalism to democracy, socialism, and anarchy, followed by a reversion to authoritarian rule, which had subsequently itself been overthrown. Their own period, by contrast, had begun with war, which had then led to revolution but a deeper and more profound revolution of the spirit than even the French Revolution, and no one could guarantee that this process of social, political, and economic turmoil, and turmoil in the relations between nations, would be concluded in their era.

It was an impressive opening, showing Stresemann's grasp of the complexity of the forces that made up international relations. He had often

---

[57] *ADAP*, Serie B, iv, pp. 581–606.

argued since 1919 that the international system was unstable and he had derived encouragement from this fact, since instability would provide opportunities for revision of the peace settlement. There were still elements of that approach in his thinking. He argued that the weakness of the new 'pygmy states' of eastern Europe was an 'indirect asset' for German foreign policy. But there was also a new caution. Such instability, for instance the Polish–Lithuanian dispute, might spark a new war. The crux of the problem for German foreign policy was how to manage this instability and carry its just demands to a successful conclusion in cooperation with its former enemies.

He suggested that there were basically two views about the right way to proceed. The first was that Germany should stay out of organizations which included former enemy states and wait until a strong Russia could support her, or the old conflict between Italy and France was renewed, allowing Germany to change the situation 'by common action of a political kind'. The second view, his own, was that the effect of the world war had been such that 'any military experiment would be fatal for Germany as a whole' and that for as long as anyone could foresee their aim should be peace with their former enemies on a basis of equality while trying 'by new methods of policy' to obtain revision of the peace treaties.

Stresemann dismissed the idea of reviving the alliance with Russia, which had once helped Prussia to defeat Napoleon. He pointed out that panslavism had already made such a strategy obsolete before 1914, that Soviet Russia was a weakened power, and that, in any case, it would only fight to achieve a Bolshevik Germany. If, on the other hand, the bourgeoisie were to return to power in Russia they would renew the Franco-Russian alliance. He was even more dismissive of relying on Italy, a state that had fought against them in the war and whose foreign policy did not follow any consistent principles.

So far as the future was concerned, he offered only a gradual process of revision by persuasion. 'No kind of military conflict with Poland will ever be started by Germany', and peaceful change would be possible only with the tolerance or support of the west European powers. It would take time for opinion to change and they would have to be content 'for years ahead' with a gradual 'loosening of these chains' and a process of European understanding and domestic consolidation.

The sixtieth anniversary of the foundation of the National Liberal Party in March 1927 provided Stresemann with a different kind of audience, a meeting of the DVP national executive and a party conference.[58] These were the first national meetings to be held since the previous October, when Stresemann had still been full of enthusiasm following his discussion with Briand at Thoiry. His mood by March 1927 was more subdued and defensive. He told the national executive, whose discussions were held in private, that he could not be expected to bring back a new success every three months from the meetings of the League council. He admitted that the situation had grown 'very much worse' since the autumn as Poincaré had stabilized the franc and restored his authority. Briand, he said, was now suffering from amnesia about Thoiry and as a result instead of 'an understanding man to man', Germany would have to launch a diplomatic offensive for the evacuation of the Rhineland. However, the time for that would have to be carefully chosen as 'the European atmosphere is laden with all kinds of explosive'.

Stresemann then attacked the view of his opponents that Germany should exploit the breach between Britain and the Soviet Union by siding with Russia:

Things in the east could under certain circumstances face us with new situations, not in the sense of Russia going to war, for Soviet Russia cannot fight any war. Soviet Russia is in general extraordinarily overrated among us; it can neither help us much in economic terms nor can it offer us much militarily and those who believe that we would find a way out of everything if we joined Soviet Russia are I believe the craziest of foreign policy makers ... Therefore we will do everything to avoid complications and we will absolutely not allow our contacts to the West, to Britain, to be broken off.[59]

Stresemann added that in times of uncertainty Germany could exercise an important moral influence through the League. This should not be underestimated, remembering what it had been like to have the whole world against them during the war.

In the discussion he was asked by the ex-governor of German East Africa, Heinrich Schnee, why he had not raised the colonial issue at

[58] Minutes of the Zentralvorstand, 19 Mar. 1927: Kolb and Richter (eds.), *Nationalliberalismus*, no. 66; record of the 'Sechzig-Jahr-Feier der National-liberalen Partei in Hannover am 19./ 20.3.1927': BAK, R 45 II/23.

[59] Stresemann gave a similar assessment to the Reichstag foreign affairs committee on 18 Mar. 1927. According to the report of the Bavarian envoy in Berlin, Dr Quarck, Stresemann warned against 'playing with the idea of a policy firmly oriented to the East'. He pointed out that revision of the Dawes plan could happen only with the Western powers: 'Therefore we had a great interest in seeing that no world conflict broke out in the meantime.' Quarck to Bayerisches Staatsministerium des Aeussern, 18 Mar. 1927: BH, MA 103542.

Geneva.[60] Stresemann replied that colonies were desirable as a reflection of Germany's importance but he doubted whether in economic terms it would be the right time to reacquire them, especially given the unrest among colonial peoples who had themselves taken part in the war and seen their white masters fight each other. He added that they should take matters in order and not try to raise everything at once:

I am of the opinion that everything must now be done first to achieve the evacuation of the Rhineland...when we have achieved that, then we must consider whether the eastern question is more important than the colonial question, and that further to be considered is whether and when it would be desirable and successful to tackle the Austrian question. For if in my speeches and statements and my appearances in Geneva I let it be known that I wanted *all* that, then they would say to Briand: 'There, we have it! If we evacuate the Rhine, then they attack Poland, then they want Austria and then they want to have colonies!' and then Poincaré would declare: 'That is German imperialism against which you poor French must defend yourselves.' Therefore I have concentrated on one thing and I believe that we must do things one after the other.

These remarks illustrate the difficulty Stresemann felt in keeping the support even of his own party. To counter its disappointment at the setback to his policy, he restated his commitment to the goals of revision while making it clear that Germany could reach them only gradually. In fact he was already growing doubtful about the wisdom of union with Austria or the utility of colonies, though he concluded his speech by assuring his audience that the day he could visit Bagamojo and Dar es Salaam and see the German flag there again 'would be the happiest of my life'.

Stresemann was as usual astute in judging how far he could carry his audience with him. However, the gap between his views and those of his critics remained a problem. Provided he could persuade them that his methods were right, in time they might follow him in growing more sceptical about some of the goals. But the process would require a long period of adjustment. Meanwhile there was the danger that, in his desire to please, he would help to keep alive expectations which he had no means of satisfying.

[60] Schnee was a member of the Reichstag for the DVP, 1924–32, and subsequently for the NSDAP. He campaigned for the return of German colonies, publishing a defence of Germany's record as a colonial power in English: Heinrich Schnee, *German Colonization Past and Future: The Truth about the German Colonies* (London: Allen & Unwin, 1926).

In June 1927 Stresemann made a major speech to the Reichstag, reporting on the recent meeting of the League council.[61] Disappointed by Briand's attempts to distance himself from Thoiry and his obstructive tactics over the Rhineland, Stresemann decided to take the initiative in questioning the direction of French policy.[62] He spoke positively of the achievements of the League, for instance a solution had been proposed to a conflict between Yugoslavia and Albania, an example of Germany playing its part as 'a nation with equal rights in the European concert'. He also reported that the recommendations of a world conference of economic experts in Geneva had been well received by the council, and governments had been asked to examine ways of lowering tariffs.[63] He was also able to report that Lithuania had agreed to restore the constitutional rights of Memel.

However, turning to the question of troop reductions in the Rhineland, he said that the failure to keep the promise made at Locarno had now become a question of trust between Germany and her Locarno partners. He then attacked a recent speech by Poincaré which had questioned German sincerity. Stresemann responded that the real issue was whether Poincaré wanted rapprochement: 'What is the goal of M. Poincaré, Ruhr policy or Locarno policy? One or the other is possible but not one and the other.' Proclaiming Germany's peaceful intentions, Stresemann expressed severe disappointment that the prospects for a general settlement with France were at a standstill: 'Gallia quo vadis?', he asked. Germany, and all nations who wanted peace, had a right to know the answer.

This was an effective appeal which earned Stresemann a storm of applause in the Reichstag and attracted widespread attention abroad. He was careful to protect Briand by name, but Briand could be in no doubt of his concern. At the same time the speech illustrated again his political problems. He could only retain support at home by attacking the dual nature of French policy. Yet French obstruction, whether from Poincaré or Briand, showed up the fragile basis on which his policy rested and could easily be used by his critics to demonstrate its failure.

[61] Reichstag speech, 23 June 1927: Zwoch (ed.), *Reichstagsreden*, 248–69.

[62] Stresemann to the Paris embassy, 18 Mar. 1927; Stresemann's memorandum of a meeting with Briand, 14 June 1927: *ADAP*, ser. B, v, no. 3, n. 1 and no. 227.

[63] Stresemann acted as rapporteur on the work of the conference to the council: *League of Nations Official Journal*, 8/7 (July 1927), 782–4. He had hoped to obtain a commitment from the council to trade liberalization, but in fact had to agree to a weaker form of words because of opposition from the other major powers, including Britain. Schulz, *Wirtschaftsordnung*, 110–15.

A few days later Stresemann went to Oslo to receive the Nobel prize. He decided to use the occasion to create understanding for the difficult adjustment which Germany had made since the war and to offer reassurance about the state of public opinion.[64] He pointed out that the German empire had been full of contrasts: authoritarian, setting a high value on service to the state, unsuccessful in resisting socialism—as the middle class had failed to offer an attractive alternative—and yet a country with a progressive social welfare system. It was a land of barracks, universal military service, and popular support for the armed forces, but also of technology, chemistry, and the most modern research. Most of those who now held positions of responsibility in Germany had spent the greater part of their lives under the empire and they still felt respect for its achievements. But the war had brought about its complete collapse and attitudes were changing, though the process would take generations to complete. The idea of peace was easier for victorious powers to accept since it served their interests. For the defeated it meant accepting what was left to them. To fall to the depths after half a century of climbing to the top was very painful: 'The psychology of a people that has experienced that is not so simple to understand or easy to change as many believe.'

More serious than the loss of territory, colonies, and national property, in Stresemann's view, were the social consequences of defeat—the way inflation had impoverished sections of the middle class, the uprooting of those who had expected careers as officers or civil servants, and the political homelessness of all those who had been loyal to the monarchy. The Ruhr occupation had added a further shock. Since then there had been a recovery and growing international understanding but this had been uneven and, at that very time, was suffering a crisis of confidence.

The development of German public opinion had therefore also not followed a consistent course. Nevertheless, the overwhelming majority was united in the will for peace and understanding. The extremes of left and right had been defeated. The working class was firmly attached to the new state and that was a great gain. The process of consolidation had also advanced steadily among those who had initially rejected the Republic and that progress was symbolized by Hindenburg, a representative figure of the old Germany serving the Republic as Reich president.

---

[64] His speech, given on 29 June 1927, was published under the title 'Der Weg des neuen Deutschland': Bernhard (ed.), *Vermächtnis*, iii. 460–73; Harttung (ed.), *Schriften*, 373–83.

Changing loyalties, however, was not something that happened overnight and those who found it most difficult might offer the most genuine and lasting support. Criticism from abroad of veterans' organizations or memorial ceremonies was misplaced. As everywhere else, the war had been an overwhelming experience for German soldiers and it was natural that it should be remembered. These memories did not prevent a desire for peace in the future as the support for Locarno showed. Locarno meant peace on a frontier which had been the cause of centuries of warfare and it could and should also be the basis for a wider peace, as far as the influence of the Locarno powers reached. Those who fought for this policy, however, could not succeed in the long run if 'for years ahead foreign bayonets were to stand on [their] soil'.

Stresemann's speech combined reassurance with warning, not least to Briand who sat beside him. Germany had made enormous progress in coming to terms with its new situation, but there were real difficulties of adjustment and Locarno needed to regain its impetus if these difficulties were to be finally overcome.

This was a fair and imaginative account of German opinion as Stresemann saw it. As an attempt to gain greater understanding for his policy abroad, however, it was problematic. A critic might feel that given the remaining uncertainties about the direction of German public opinion, it would be wise to maintain effective sanctions. The problem was explained by Berthelot, who was asked by Poincaré whether he believed in German sincerity. Berthelot replied that he did believe that Germany was following Stresemann's policy with conviction at present but that was no guarantee for the future, given the many elements who were either hostile to it, doubtful, or harboured ulterior motives.[65]

The Receding Prospect of Frontier Revision

Stresemann was encouraged by the meetings of the League council in December 1927. Briand was much more optimistic, and suggested that if the elections due in 1928 in both countries produced, as expected, favourable results for the parties of détente, then it should be possible to reach

---

[65] Hoesch to Schubert, 21 Oct. 1927: *ADAP*, ser. B, vii, no. 39.

agreement on Rhineland evacuation by the meeting of the League assembly in September.[66.]

Briand also raised the question of extending the Locarno guarantees to the east to provide the political basis for progress in disarmament. When Stresemann replied that Germany could agree to a new treaty with Poland only if the frontier issue was resolved, Briand encouraged him to raise it directly with the Polish premier, Marshal Piłsudski. Briand expressed enthusiasm for the idea that Poland could be compensated for revision by being given a free port in Danzig and possibly also in Memel.[67] Stresemann had the same conversation with Chamberlain, emphasizing that no German could accept the separation of East Prussia or the loss of Danzig. Chamberlain also appeared receptive, saying that at Versailles they had followed the ethnographic map without considering the effect of separating East Prussia from the rest of Germany and he too urged Stresemann to discuss the matter with Piłsudski.[68] Echoing Briand, Chamberlain said that if a solution could be found on the eastern frontiers they would 'really have established peace in Europe'. Stresemann had already had one meeting with Piłsudski, which had gone well, but he had not liked to raise the question of frontier revision then.[69]

Revision of the Polish frontier was the crucial test of Stresemann's policy in the long term. As the comments of Briand and Chamberlain showed, it was also already regarded as the greatest threat to the future peace of Europe. During 1927 Stresemann realized how limited the prospects of revision were. He had previously thought in terms of Germany benefiting from Soviet military action against Poland and this remained a theoretical possibility for the future. But his appreciation of the dangers of a European war had grown. As we have seen, during 1927 he used his influence in the Polish–Lithuanian dispute for peace. The idea that Poland would collapse from chronic economic failure also looked

[66] Stresemann's memorandum of a meeting with Briand, 4 Dec., memorandum by State Secretary Weismann, 9 Dec. 1927: *ADAP*, ser. B, vii., nos. 173, 193. Stresemann's report to the cabinet, 20 Dec. 1927: Abramowski (ed.), *Kabinette Marx IV,* no. 381.

[67] Stresemann's memorandum of his meeting with Briand, 11 Dec. 1927: *ADAP*, ser. B, vii, no. 200. On Briand's attitude to Poland, see Georges-Henri Soutou, 'L'Alliance franco-polonaise (1925–1933) ou comment s'en débarrasser?', *Revue d'histoire diplomatique*, 95 (1981), 294–348.

[68] Stresemann's memorandum of his meeting with Chamberlain, 12 Dec. 1927: *ADAP*, ser. B, vii, no. 202. Chamberlain's record, 12 Dec. 1927: *DBFP*, ser. IA, iv, no. 91.

[69] Stresemann's memorandum of his meeting with Piłsudski, 9 Dec. 1927: *ADAP*, ser. B, vii, no. 192.

increasingly unrealistic. Stresemann argued in cabinet, against the opposition of the agrarian lobby, for Germany to resume trade negotiations with
Poland.[70] He used the negotiations as a bargaining lever with the Polish
government to secure the right of Germans to set up businesses in Poland
and to protect the German minority from expulsion. But a trade treaty
would contribute to the stability of the Polish state and could only be an
instrument of territorial revision if the Polish economy were to become
totally dependent on Germany. In December 1927, in reply to questions
from the Reichstag foreign affairs committee, Stresemann noted: 'The
fact is the position of Poland is somewhat stronger. There is no doubt that
Poland has become interesting and people no longer take bets as they used
to on how long the Polish state would exist.'[71]

Given the lack of means to apply sufficient pressure on Poland, Stresemann could only hope for the climate of international opinion to turn in
Germany's favour. He was gratified by the encouragement he received
from Briand and Chamberlain and intrigued by the idea of offering
Poland compensation in Memel. He noted statements from Polish
sources suggesting that they might be interested in such a scheme.[72]
However, there were obvious objections.[73] It was not certain that Poland
would agree and, in any case, Lithuania was unlikely to give up Memel
willingly, having only recently gained international recognition for its
control of the territory. There was also the impact on Germany's relations
with the Soviet Union to be considered. It was opposed to any further
expansion of Poland eastwards and would also oppose a solution to the
Polish–German frontier dispute without a corresponding revision of the
Polish–Soviet frontier. The spectre of German revision in the east might
also alarm public opinion in the west, blocking evacuation of the Rhineland and a reparations settlement.

---

[70] Cabinet minutes, 14 July, 27 Oct., 18 Nov., 22 Nov. 1927, 15 and 27 Mar., 4 Apr. 1928:
Abramowski (ed.), *Kabinette Marx IV*, nos. 277, 328, 340, 347, 447, 454, 456. When Stresemann
was outvoted on the person to lead the German delegation and Andreas Hermes, a Centre Party
politician who represented the interests of German farmers, was chosen, Stresemann protested to
Marx, and threatened to resign if the negotiations were treated in a dilatory fashion. Stresemann
to Marx, 24 Nov. 1927: *ADAP*, ser. B, viii, no. 136. Schulz, *Wirtschaftsordnung*, 136–40, 152–5,
168–70.

[71] Reply, dated 19 Dec., to points made by the committee on his report of 17 Dec. 1927 (Nl.
62): Bernhard (ed.), *Vermächtnis*, iii. 243–6.

[72] Note dated 15 Dec. 1927 (Nl. 62): ibid. 246.

[73] P. S. Wandycz, 'Le Pologne face à la politique locarnienne de Briand', *Revue d'histoire
diplomatique*, 95 (1981), 248.

Faced with these complications it is not surprising that Stresemann decided to wait. Addressing a group of prominent East Prussian citizens in Königsberg, he spoke of his hope of resolving the corridor issue peacefully with French and British support.[74] He said that opinion was beginning to change, but when the issue would be ripe for solution no one could say. Preconditions were first the evacuation of the Rhineland and then the removal of French fears of union with Austria and of a German attack on Poland. Then France might accept revision in return for financial compensation. This was in effect to postpone the issue for a very long time, if not sine die.

Stresemann's tactics were questioned at the foreign affairs committee of the Reichstag. A Centre Party member from Upper Silesia, Carl Ulitzka, criticized the 'minor key' to which German aims for eastern revision had been transposed and also the way in which the issue was now presented as the corridor alone with no mention of Posen or Upper Silesia.[75] Stresemann evaded a direct reply by offering to discuss the matter privately, but it was obvious that there was more hope of gaining international support for the return of the corridor as a danger to peace than with respect to the other areas.[76] At a later meeting Stresemann rejected the idea of allowing Poland a free hand in Lithuania in return for getting the corridor back, saying that they could not allow Poland to establish itself between East Prussia and the Soviet Union. Koch-Weser objected that this would be better than having Poland between East Prussia and the rest of Germany and pointed out that, while Stresemann ruled out war, he was also unable to suggest a peaceful way of recovering the corridor. Koch-Weser added in his diary that there was a feeling, shared by SPD members of the committee, that Stresemann was becoming too full of the common endeavours for peace at Geneva, and that they would rather hear of successes for Germany.[77] There was in fact no alternative to Stresemann's patient diplomacy, but he was increasingly vulnerable to the charge, even from among his natural supporters, that peaceful revision was an illusion.

---

[74] Memorandum by Dirksen of Stresemann's speech, 17 Dec. 1927: *ADAP*, ser. B, vii, no. 212.

[75] Preger's report of the meeting on 21–22 Oct., dated 22 Oct. 1927: BH, MA 103528.

[76] Baechler notes that during 1927 Stresemann appeared to drop Upper Silesia from the list of objectives: Baechler, *Stresemann*, 865–8. There was, however, also a tactical motive, namely to avoid giving the Polish authorities the pretext to take new measures against the Germans of Upper Silesia. See Auswärtiges Amt (Köpke) to the Büro des Reichspräsidenten, 12 May 1928: *ADAP*, ser. B, ix, no. 16.

[77] Koch-Weser diary for 4 Feb. 1928: BAK, Nl. Koch-Weser, 37.

Evacuation of the Rhineland and Revision of the Dawes Plan

It soon became apparent that Stresemann's immediate objective, the evacuation of the Rhineland, also did not admit of an easy solution. He was keen to advance matters, both to bolster his credit at home and to prevent the issue becoming tied to the question of reparations and war debts.[78] That would involve delay until a new American president had been elected. Revision of the Dawes plan was also an awkward issue for Germany. If she raised the question of reducing the level of payments, it would annoy the Americans, damage the confidence of foreign investors, and enable Poincaré to claim that the Rhineland occupation must continue as security for reparations.[79]

Stresemann therefore pressed the issue of evacuation. In the Reichstag, at the end of January 1928, he described evacuation as a psychological precondition for the further development of Franco-German relations. He referred to the continued occupation as an 'anomaly' and said that French demands for security contained 'an element of hypocrisy'. In a pointed reference to Briand's dramatic call at the League in September 1926 to do away with machine guns and artillery, he pointed out that they were still in place in the Rhineland.[80] Replying immediately in the Senate, Briand did not rule out early evacuation but insisted that France needed guarantees of security and reparations. He expressed his trust in Stresemann but added that neither of them would be there for ever and, given the views expressed in the Reichstag by the DNVP, France had to be prepared for a change in circumstances. He suggested that if Germany wanted early evacuation of the Rhineland, Stresemann should make specific proposals as had been agreed at Thoiry.[81]

The last comment gave Stresemann the opportunity to challenge Briand directly when they met at the League council in March.[82] Stresemann said that he was 'astonished' at Briand's account of Thoiry and he recorded with satisfaction that Briand was 'obviously uncomfortable'

---

[78] Circular to German embassies, 30 Jan. 1928: *ADAP*, ser. B, viii, no. 52.

[79] Ibid., and Schubert's memorandum of a meeting with Parker Gilbert, 28 Feb. 1928: ibid., no. 123.

[80] Reichstag speech, 30 Jan. 1928 and a further intervention, 1 Feb. 1928: *Verhandlungen des Reichstags*, vol. 394, pp. 12494, 12556–60.

[81] *Journal officiel de la République Française: Débats parlementaires* (Paris: Éditions des Débats parlementaires, 1928): Senate séance du jeudi 2 février 1928, 64–72.

[82] Stresemann's memorandum of his meeting with Briand, 5 Mar. 1928: *ADAP*, ser. B, viii, no. 143.

particularly as the interpreter, Hesnard, who had been the only other witness at Thoiry, gave him no support. Stresemann warned Briand that if he was hoping for a financial arrangement like Thoiry, he would have to act fast as it would require American consent before the presidential elections. If they waited until after the elections, it would be too late for financial compensation since the second zone of occupation was due to be evacuated in any case in 1930. Briand could only reiterate that he would be willing to talk once the French elections were over.

In fact the elections strengthened Poincaré. In any case, Briand had no clear idea of what should be the terms of an agreement on evacuation. Berthelot, his senior official, had proposed the combination which Stresemann feared—evacuation as part of a general settlement, together with reparations and war debts.[83] This was also the view of Poincaré, who regarded the occupation as a lever for securing a satisfactory settlement with both Germany and the United States. The American agent general for the Dawes plan, Parker Gilbert, was also working for a joint solution to reparations and war debts in 1929.[84] Stresemann had no alternative but to bow to the inevitable, although the decision about how to proceed was not taken until the summer.

Stresemann welcomed Gilbert's view, expressed in his annual report on the operation of the Dawes plan in October 1927, that it was time to prepare for a final reparations settlement.[85] Most experts believed that Germany would not be able to sustain the level of payments required under the Dawes plan for long after they reached their maximum level in 1929. That meant that a final settlement could be expected to bring some relief. Since the German government did not want to raise the matter itself, Gilbert's report was especially useful.

Stresemann was also concerned that Gilbert's criticism of the conduct of German public finances, contained in the same report, should not lead to conflict, as he wanted to keep Gilbert's support for future negotiations. He therefore used his influence in cabinet to moderate the reaction of the finance minister, Heinrich Köhler.[86]

---

[83] Hoesch's report of a meeting with Berthelot, 1 Feb. 1928: *ADAP*, ser. B, viii, no. 60.

[84] Schubert's memorandum of a meeting with Parker Gilbert, 28 Feb. 1928: ibid., no. 123. There is a lucid account of these developments in Jon Jacobson, *Locarno Diplomacy: Germany and the West 1925–1929* (Princeton: Princeton University Press, 1972), 156–67.

[85] Circular to German embassies, 30 Jan. 1928: *ADAP*, ser. B, viii, no. 52.

[86] Cabinet minutes, 7 Oct. 1927; Pünder's note on the cabinet meeting, 27 Oct. 1927; cabinet minutes, 2 Nov. 1927: Abramowski (ed.), *Kabinette Marx IV*, nos. 313, 329, 331. Memorandum of a meeting between Stresemann and Gilbert, 6 Oct. 1927: *ADAP*, ser. B, viii, no. 11. Köhler

Stresemann in any case shared Gilbert's concern about the level of German borrowing. They were both critical of municipal loans for public projects which were not directly related to production. In a letter to Jarres, lord mayor of Duisburg, Stresemann warned of the effect these projects had on opinion abroad: 14–20 million marks for the Berlin opera house, Adenauer boasting of having installed the largest organ in the world in his new exhibition hall, Frankfurt incurring a deficit of 2.5 million marks on a music exhibition, Dresden requiring Reich subsidies for a hygiene museum. How, he asked Jarres, was he to answer foreigners who said such projects gave the impression that 'Germany had not lost the war but won it'?[87]

The underlying problems of the German economy, despite its rapid growth since 1924, were obvious. Reparations were being financed by foreign loans, not a trade surplus. Stresemann attached enormous import-ance to the growth of trade. Alone among the great powers, Germany consistently supported measures of trade liberalization at the League.[88] In his annual reports to the Reichstag, Stresemann regularly recorded the progress of trade treaties.[89] He argued, as he had since before the war, that autarky was not possible for Germany given its dependence on imported raw materials, and that it would have to open its home market to foreign competition in order to have access to markets abroad.[90] Protectionism, such as the DNVP minister of agriculture, Schiele, proposed in relation to Poland would mean, he wrote, 'the death of economic policy'.[91] Foreign trade, however, could only provide a solution in the longer term as world trade recovered from the consequences of the war. Immediately, Germany needed to maintain the supply of foreign loans and achieve a revision of the Dawes plan, which he described as 'the great question which...faces us'.[92]

disliked Gilbert intensely and resented Stresemann's mediation. Becker (ed.), *Heinrich Köhler*, 241–51.

[87] Stresemann to Jarres, 24 Nov. 1927 (Nl. 61): Bernhard (ed.), *Vermächtnis*, iii. 263–4.

[88] Schulz, *Wirtschaftsordnung*, 45–173.

[89] e.g. in his speech on 30 Jan. 1928, where he reported on the successful conclusion of treaties with France, Japan, and Yugoslavia and the problems in trade with the Soviet Union, and stressed the importance of the negotiations with Poland: *Verhandlungen des Reichstags*, vol. 394, 12491–3.

[90] e.g. in speeches to a conference of businessmen in Lower Saxony at the beginning of May 1927 and to the chambers of industry and commerce in the Reichstag on 17 Apr. 1928: Bernhard (ed.), *Vermächtnis*, iii. 255–6, 289–92.

[91] Draft letter of Stresemann to Marx, 24 Nov. 1927: *ADAP*, ser. B, vii, no. 136.

[92] Report by Quarck on Stresemann's speech to the Reichstag foreign affairs committee, 18 Mar. 1927: BH, MA 103542.

The Kellogg–Briand Pact

A welcome opportunity to align Germany more closely with the United States was provided by the Kellogg–Briand pact, or, as it was properly called, the General Treaty for the Renunciation of War.[93] This originated in an initiative by Briand to raise the profile of France's relations with the United States on the tenth anniversary of America's entry into the war, by proposing a mutual pact to outlaw war. The American secretary of state Frank Kellogg parried this attempt to involve the United States in a particular responsibility towards France by proposing that the pact should be multilateral. Briand thereupon introduced various qualifications into his original draft to protect the French right to go to war in Europe to uphold the Versailles treaty and its alliance system. Kellogg did not accept the need for these modifications, and in April 1928 invited the views of the German, British, Italian, and Japanese governments on the original proposals, while the French canvassed support for their modified draft.

It was obvious that German interests lay in siding with the United States and that Briand's original plan had backfired. A general obligation to renounce war as an instrument of national policy was consistent with peaceful revision and with Germany's proposals to the security committee of the League. The pact might also help to give new life to the preparations for a disarmament conference, another German aim. In so far as it weakened France's alternative security system through its alliances, that was a further advantage.[94]

Stresemann pointed out to the cabinet that Germany would need American support in the future, if only in the matter of reparations, and it could not afford to be seen as forming a common European front against the United States.[95] The cabinet gave Stresemann authority to act swiftly before Germany was drawn into discussions with France, and Stresemann accepted Kellogg's proposals the same day, making Germany the first power to do so. Justifying this decision to Hoesch—who was concerned about the effect it would have on Briand's reputation—Stresemann pointed out that Briand had made his original proposal to the United States without showing 'any consideration for us either in

[93] Arnold J. Toynbee (ed.), *Survey of International Affairs 1928* (London: Oxford University Press, 1929), 1–47.

[94] Stresemann's circular to German embassies, 12 Jan. 1928; Schubert to Hoesch, 19 Jan. 1928: *ADAP*, ser. B, viii, nos. 18, 32. Stresemann's report to the cabinet, 19 Apr. 1928: Abramowski, *Kabinette Marx IV*, no. 463.

[95] Cabinet minutes, 27 Apr. 1928: Abramowski (ed.), *Kabinette Marx IV*, no. 466.

substance or in form'.[96] That was undoubtedly true and the episode illustrated how far the relationship between the two men had changed since Thoiry. Stresemann no longer expected much of Briand, and Franco-German relations were cooler and more competitive.

Stresemann was not, however, distancing himself from peaceful revision. On the contrary, his policy depended more than ever on identifying Germany with peaceful methods to make the French occupation of the Rhine and its alliance system appear the true barriers to peace. On 5 May 1928 he restated his commitment to peace in an important speech at the university of Heidelberg where he was receiving an honorary degree together with the American ambassador Jacob Schurman, a former student and benefactor of the university.[97] The occasion attracted considerable press interest and, among the foreign press, particularly from the United States.[98]

Stresemann used the speech to explain his view of international relations and of Germany's place in an evolving new world order. He argued that relations between states had not yet been put on a basis of equal rights and nor had adequate forms of an international whole, into which individual states could be incorporated, been discovered: 'So there arises a double task for international politics and especially for German policy: the securing of a free Germany with equal rights and the inclusion of such a Germany together with all other states in a stable international structure.'

Drawing on his work as a student, Stresemann reminded his audience that the forms of inter-state relations had changed in the course of history, as the social basis of the state had changed, and never more rapidly than in their own time. Attitudes to war and peace had been transformed from the professional caste armies of Frederick the Great, to the conflict of ideologies which started with the French Revolution and ended with the dynastic interests of the Holy Alliance, and from there to the Bismarckian system of applying power politics with moderation to construct a peaceful

---

[96] Stresemann to Hoesch, 21 Apr. 1928: *ADAP*, ser. B, viii, no. 248.

[97] Stresemann's speech was published unter the title 'Neue Wege zur Völkerverständigung': *Rede bei dem Akt der Ehrenpromotionen des Reichsministers Dr. Stresemann und des Botschafters der Vereinigten Staaten Dr. Schurman in der Aula der Universität Heidelberg 5. Mai 1928* (Heidelberg: Carl Winters Universitätsbuchhandlung, 1928), 22–36. It was also issued in English. I have attempted to sketch the development of Stresemann's ideas: Jonathan Wright, 'Gustav Stresemann's Concept of International Relations', in Adolf M. Birke, Magnus Brechtken, and Alaric Searle (eds.), *An Anglo-German Dialogue* (Munich: K. G. Saur, 2000), 143–60, and Jonathan Wright, 'Stresemann: A Mind Map', in Johnson (ed.), *Locarno Revisited* (forthcoming).

[98] Universitätsarchiv Heidelberg: B–1523/1a and 2a.

international order. The post-Bismarck generation had not understood how to maintain his system and had been overcome by a mood of fatalism and mistrust. The world war had hugely increased the mistrust, but it had also led to the recognition that if Europe was not to 'tear itself apart' it was essential to escape from 'the system of international anarchy... of alliances and counter-alliances'. The post-war world had therefore seen a curious dual system of 'ruthless application of the principle of national power and dogged attempts to create a system of international understanding based on equal rights'.

Stresemann paid tribute to the American proposals for the renunciation of war, suggesting that without the support of such a mighty power the idea would not have been taken seriously. He said Germany had entered the League in the belief that its own interests were best served by resolving conflicts through understanding and law. However, he criticized the lack of equality which was still to be seen in the fact that one League power maintained a military occupation on the territory of another. He also criticized the lack of progress towards disarmament.

Stresemann then returned to the theme of peace. He said he believed that there was a great majority for peace in Europe and that it was the task of statesmen to remind people that 'a new conflagration would deliver our continent to utter ruin as a result of the horrifying escalation of the technology of destruction'. But he added that foreign policy could no longer be conducted as in the past without popular support. He therefore appealed to his academic audience to give leadership and to students 'not to be carried away by old slogans'. He went on: 'The preservation of peace and the attempts to secure it are not weakness, are not timidity, they are the realistic [*realpolitische*] recognition of our own national interest.'

It was an impressive performance, showing Stresemann's ability to place his immediate theme in a larger historical context, and to combine an argument for peace and international understanding with a reminder of Germany's claim to equal rights as yet unsatisfied. In the context of his audience, like his speech to students in Berlin in 1926, it takes on a particular significance. He was concerned about the high level of support for extreme nationalist and anti-republican groups in the universities, including the NSDAP, which achieved one of its first successes in the student union elections in the winter term of 1928–9. The invitation to Stresemann was itself an unusual gesture for a university to make towards the Republic, the action of a group of liberal professors, including,

ironically, Alfred Weber, who had been instrumental in excluding Stresemann from the DDP in 1919.[99]

The Formation of the Great Coalition

The decision to endorse the Kellogg–Briand pact was one of the last acts
of the Marx government. The issue over which the coalition broke up was
the proposal for a Reich School Law. The Weimar Constitution had
allowed for different types of school, but left the balance between them
to be decided by subsequent legislation, and the matter had never been
resolved. One of the motives for the Centre Party and DNVP in forming
the coalition in 1927 had been to pass a Reich School Law which reflected
the interests of the Catholic and Protestant Churches in denominational
schools. The DVP, true to its National Liberal tradition, was suspicious
of clerical influence in education. The sticking point between the coalition
parties became whether the system of inter-denominational schools,
which was long established in Baden and Hessen and in the Prussian province of Hessen-Nassau, should be allowed to continue there
permanently or whether they should be forced to conform to the new
law.[100]

Stresemann and his fellow DVP minister Curtius made it clear to the
cabinet, when the measure was first discussed, that the DVP would not
accept a change in the status of inter-denominational schools where they
were already established as the norm.[101] When the bill reached the
Reichstag education committee in January 1928, a DVP amendment to
that effect was passed with the support of the opposition parties. When
attempts to find a compromise failed the coalition broke up, although the
government remained in office to conclude necessary business, such as the
budget, before elections were held on 20 May 1928.[102]

Stresemann did not take a leading part in these events. He was involved
in negotiations with Marx and other Centre Party politicians to try to find

---

[99] Christian Jansen, *Professoren und Politik. Politisches Denken und Handeln der Heidelberger
Hochschullehrer 1914–1935* (Göttingen: Vandenhoeck & Ruprecht, 1992), 194–9. In the student
association (Asta) elections in Heidelberg in 1929, the NSDAP won 23 per cent of the vote.

[100] Günther Grünthal, *Reichsschulgesetz und Zentrumspartei in der Weimarer Republik* (Düsseldorf: Droste, 1968), 207–37.

[101] Cabinet minutes, 13 July 1927: Abramowski (ed.), *Kabinette Marx IV*, no. 276.

[102] Minutes of a meeting of coalition party leaders, and cabinet minutes, 15 Feb. 1928: ibid.,
nos. 421–2.

a solution before leaving for the Riviera on 6 February on the instructions of his doctors.[103] Before leaving, he advised Marx to let the matter rest to allow feelings on both sides to cool.[104] He had himself been annoyed when the chairman of the Centre Party in the Reichstag, Theodor von Guérard, threatened that the party would not be willing to see Stresemann remain as foreign minister if the DVP undermined the Reich School Law.[105] When Stresemann learned that the coalition had broken up, he blamed 'hotheads' in the Centre Party for forcing the issue because they wanted a 'Kulturkampf slogan' for the elections (which were due in December 1928 in any case) to hide the differences between the trade union and professional wings of the party.[106]

Nevertheless, Stresemann was not unhappy with the outcome. He had made no secret of the importance he attached to liberal values and deliberately invoked the memory of the first party leader, Bennigsen, and nineteenth-century conflicts over education at DVP meetings.[107] The issue was a useful way of distancing the DVP from the DNVP, which had again started to attack his foreign policy.[108] There was common ground over education between the DVP, DDP, and SPD which could help the formation of a new coalition after the elections.[109] Stresemann's chief concern, however, was as usual to maintain the cooperation of

[103] Abramowski (ed.), *Kabinette Marx IV*, no. 417, n. 1.

[104] Stresemann to the state secretary in the Prussian Staatsministerium, Robert Weismann, 18 Feb. 1928 (Nl. 64): Bernhard (ed.), *Vermächtnis*, iii. 274–5 (where the letter is misdated 15 Feb.).

[105] Memorandum by Stresemann, 15 Dec. 1927 (Nl. 62); edited version in Bernhard (ed.), *Vermächtnis*, iii. 272–3.

[106] Stresemann to Weismann and to the president of the Reichstag and SPD politician Paul Löbe, 18 Feb 1928 (Nl.64, 288); extracts in Bernhard (ed.), *Vermächtnis*, iii. 274–6. Stresemann's analysis has been partly endorsed by recent studies: Hehl, *Marx*, 434–7; Grünthal, *Reichsschulgesetz*, 237–44. Ruppert, however, points out that education was a critical issue between the Liberal and Catholic camps, on which neither side could afford to give way, and when agreement became impossible both sought to make electoral capital from it: *Im Dienst*, 297–9.

[107] Speech to the Zentralvorstand and to the party conference on the sixtieth anniversary of the National Liberal Party, 19–20 Mar. 1927: Kolb and Richter (eds.), *Nationalliberalismus*, 715–17; BAK, R 45 II/23. Also his references to a Reich Concordat in a speech to the DVP Kulturtagung on 3 Apr. 1927; extract in Bernhard (ed.), *Vermächtnis*, iii. 267–8. Stresemann had to defend this speech in cabinet: Abramowski (ed.), *Kabinette Marx IV*, no. 218.

[108] In the final Reichstag debate of the session, held on 29–31 Mar. 1928, Westarp described the policy as a 'fiasco'. *Verhandlungen des Reichstags*, vol. 395, pp. 13884–5; Stresemann's reply, ibid. 13897–9.

[109] From the Riviera, Stresemann encouraged Curtius to make contact with Otto Braun, who was being spoken of as a possible future chancellor. He was pleased to hear from Curtius that both Braun and Severing expected a great coalition to be formed and had said that, if the Centre Party proved difficult over education, they would rather join with the DVP. Stresemann to Curtius, 23 Feb. 1928, and note by Stresemann, dated Mar. 1928 (Nl. 65,66). Schulze, *Braun*, 537–8.

the middle parties 'as the core of every future government' and he therefore wanted to avoid a running battle with the Centre Party.[110]

His weakened health forced Stresemann to take a less active part in the election than usual despite the disappointment this caused to constituency parties, who looked to him to give the lead.[111] The party's reliance on its leader was epitomized by a poster with his portrait and the slogan: 'What do the others matter to you, you vote like Gustav Stresemann'.[112] He decided to stand in two Bavarian constituencies (as well as on the Reich list) in the hope that the DVP might pick up a seat in a region where it had previously been unrepresented. When he spoke in the Bürgerbräu-Keller in Munich on 25 April the meeting was disrupted by an organized Nazi campaign of heckling, singing, and shouting.[113]

Stresemann had decided to reply to Hitler's criticism of his foreign policy. He said he had read one of Hitler's speeches to discover the 'sharpest arguments' of the opposition but had found it a 'firework rocket' without knowledge of the real conditions. He pointed out that Locarno had achieved one of Hitler's goals, the security of the Rhineland, and that Hitler's argument that things could not get any worse hardly fitted the facts if one remembered the situation in 1923.[114] Despite their activism, the Nazis still seemed more of a nuisance than a real threat in 1928. The suggestion by Nazi hecklers at a DVP meeting in Berlin that Hitler would be Stresemann's successor caused general laughter and Stresemann expressed ironic delight at the news.[115]

Stresemann was unable to complete the election campaign. He collapsed with kidney failure on 7 May, three days before his fiftieth birthday, and had to withdraw entirely.[116]

The elections were a victory for the SPD, which increased its Reichstag representation from 131 to 153, and a defeat for the DNVP, whose Reichstag numbers fell from 103 to seventy-three as part of its electorate

---

[110] Stresemann to Pünder, 20 Feb. 1928 (Nl. 64); extract in Bernhard (ed.), *Vermächtnis*, iii. 276–7.

[111] He explained to a DVP journalist that he found speeches a strain under normal conditions, leaving him both mentally and physically exhausted: Stresemann to Walther Jänecke, 20 Apr. 1928; Bernhard (ed.), *Vermächtnis*, iii. 292–3.

[112] Plate 17.

[113] Bernhard (ed.), *Vermächtnis*, iii. 293–5. Also the police report, dated 31 May 1928, with interviews of those prosecuted; BH, Polizeidirektion München, 10179. (I am grateful to Dr Albrecht Tyrell for this reference.)

[114] Stresemann's notes for the speech, 25 Apr. 1928 (Nl. 66).

[115] Josef Buchhorn to Stresemann, 10 May, and Stresemann's reply, 6 June 1928 (Nl. 326).

[116] Wolfgang Stresemann, *Mein Vater*, 508–10.

defected to regional and sectional splinter parties.[117] All the other major parties suffered small losses except the KPD, which gained nine seats, bringing its total to fifty-four. The DVP share of the vote fell from 10.1 to 8.7 per cent and its representation from fifty-one to forty-five. Stresemann was disappointed, especially as he failed to win a seat in Bavaria, although against the trend the DVP's vote there rose slightly.[118] He blamed the apathy of the middle-class electorate—referring to the figure of 10 million non-voters—and his own illness, for the DVP's poor showing.[119]

Nevertheless the overall result was satisfactory. It pointed to a great coalition under an SPD chancellor, the result which Stresemann had anticipated and which he hoped would help rapprochement with France. Although still an invalid, he was determined to see a great coalition formed.

As usual the problem was the contradictory positions of the parties, particularly of the SPD and the DVP at each end of the coalition spectrum. The situation was more difficult because the elections had strengthened the right wing of the DVP, especially the Ruhr group.[120] The Reichstag party agreed to work for a great coalition, but with Scholz leading the negotiations a successful outcome was never likely. The party set a number of conditions, including the formation of a great coalition in Prussia where the DVP wanted to be readmitted to the government.

Stresemann followed events from his sickbed. The stumbling-block quickly became Otto Braun's refusal to give way to the DVP in Prussia. His coalition of SPD, Centre, and DDP had just won a majority and he saw no reason to oblige the DVP, which had itself left the Prussian coalition in 1925 to please the DNVP. Stresemann made the effort to see Braun and urged on him the importance of forming a stable national government, but Braun was willing to offer only the prospect of the DVP joining the Prussian government later, suggesting that negotiations could

[117] On the impact of these parties, which also gained votes from the DVP, see Jones, *Liberalism*, 297–305; Richter, *Deutsche Volkspartei*, 481–4.

[118] Milatz, *Wähler*, 100.

[119] Stresemann to the DDP Reichstag member and ex-minister, Peter Reinhold, and to his DVP colleague Heinrich Havemann, 2 June 1928 (Nl. 100).

[120] Turner, *Stresemann*, 241. The change in the composition of the Reichstag party was, however, probably less important than the prospect of a new great coalition in arousing the opposition of the right wing. Eberhard Kolb, 'Führungskrise in der DVP. Gustav Stresemann im Kampf um die "Große Koalition" 1928/29', in Wolther von Kieseritzky and Klaus-Peter Sick (eds.), *Demokratie in Deutschland. Chancen und Gefährdungen im 19. und 20. Jahrhundert* (Munich: C. H. Beck, 1999), 205.

be held in the autumn.[121] This was not enough to satisfy Scholz or the majority of DVP Reichstag and Prussian Landtag members. They distrusted Braun and were intent on forcing the issue while they had the bargaining power of making or breaking the great coalition at Reich level.[122]

The situation was therefore already critical when Stresemann left Berlin on 20 June to rest and recover at the sanatorium of Bühlerhöhe near Baden-Baden. Before leaving he sent a message by his son Wolfgang to the SPD leaders, suggesting that instead of the fruitless attempts to reach a common programme by negotiations between the parties, a government should be formed by the party leaders who would present a programme to the Reichstag.[123] This was a neat way of presenting the Reichstag party with a fait accompli. The SPD did not react immediately, but the idea had been put into circulation.

The SPD party chairman Hermann Müller, who had been invited by Hindenburg to try to form a great coalition, reported on 22 June that the attempt had failed.[124] He proposed instead to try to form a 'Weimar coalition' (so called because it had been the coalition of 1919) of the SPD, Centre, and DDP, which would have a slender majority if it could also attract the BVP. He hoped that Stresemann would agree to remain in such a coalition as an 'expert' foreign minister. Alternatively, Müller suggested that the SPD might form a minority government. Hindenburg agreed that Müller should make the attempt at a Weimar coalition. At this point, Hindenburg's state secretary, Meissner, introduced Stresemann's idea of 'personalities' from the great coalition parties forming a government to which their parties would not be formally committed but which could develop into a real great coalition when the Prussian government was reconstructed in the autumn.[125] Müller agreed that if the Weimar coalition proved impossible, such a proposal would be well worth trying.

---

[121] Stresemann to Weismann, 14 June 1928 (Nl. 294); Braun, *Von Weimar zu Hitler*, 248–50, Schulze, *Braun*, 544.

[122] Minutes of the meetings of the Reichstag party, 16 and 22 June 1928: BAK, R 45 II/67. Kolb, 'Führungskrise in der DVP', 206–7.

[123] Wolfgang Stresemann, *Mein Vater*, 513.

[124] Memoranda by Meissner, 9 and 22 June 1928: BAB, Büro des Reichspräsidenten, 6. Müller had been chosen as the SPD's candidate for the chancellorship after Braun declined. Schulze, *Braun*, 540–1.

[125] It seems likely that Meissner had been briefed by Stresemann. The state secretary in the Reich Chancellery, Pünder, also knew of the proposal, and in reply to a request for information from Stresemann on 22 June sent him a telegram on 23 June saying he considered a cabinet of personalities 'perfectly possible'. BAK, Nl. Pünder 35; Morsey (ed.), *Protokolle*, 218.

The following day Müller telephoned Stresemann and asked him whether he would be willing to serve as an 'expert' foreign minister in a Weimar coalition government. Stresemann had been expecting this question and immediately refused. He said it would be impossible for him, given his position as party leader, and that a Weimar coalition would be too narrow a basis from which to conduct foreign policy. Müller had expected Stresemann's refusal and then asked about his attitude to a 'cabinet of personalities', warning him that the SPD and Centre Party had reservations about the idea.

Stresemann encouraged Müller to pursue the idea, saying that he remained of the view that 'cooperation from the Social Democrats to the Volkspartei [DVP] is necessary and possible' and that it would be in the spirit of the Constitution to form a government that way since the Constitution referred to the responsibility of ministers but not to that of parties. He made his final agreement subject to the composition of the new cabinet, saying that he attached great importance to the retention of Curtius as economics minister. Stresemann offered to confirm the gist of their conversation by telegram and the following day he secured Curtius's approval for the publication of the telegram.[126] On Monday, 26 June the press carried the news of the 'shot from Bühlerhöhe'.

Stresemann's dramatic intervention achieved its aim. There was a problem with the Centre Party, which wanted Wirth to be named vice-chancellor, as well as transport minister, to keep Stresemann in check.[127] Stresemann helped to stop the proposal, which was in any case opposed by Hindenburg, telling Hindenburg's officials that vice-chancellor was a position unknown to the Constitution and a recipe for confusion.[128] The Centre Party thereupon consented to be represented in the cabinet only by Guérard as an 'observer' at the Ministry of Transport. Nevertheless Müller was able to form a government, and on 5 July the Reichstag passed a motion approving the government programme by 261 to 134

[126] Stresemann's telegram to Müller, 23 June 1928: Friedrich Ebert Stiftung, Bonn, Nl. Hermann Müller, 2; Bernhard (ed.), *Vermächtnis*, iii. 298–9; Stresemann's letter to the DVP Reichstag party, 27 June 1929 (Nl. 101); extract in Bernhard (ed.), *Vermächtnis*, iii. 299–301. Stresemann's telegram to Curtius, 24 June 1928: ibid. 299. Julius Curtius, *Sechs Jahre Minister der deutschen Republik* (Heidelberg: Carl Winter, 1948), 69–70. Koch-Weser claims that he suggested this way of proceeding to Stresemann. Diary for 4 July 1928: BAK, Nl. Koch-Weser, 37. Kolb, 'Führungskrise in der DVP', 208–9.

[127] Hehl, *Marx*, 456.

[128] Memorandum by Stresemann, 28 June 1928 (Nl. 68); edited version in Bernhard (ed.), *Vermächtnis*, iii. 301–3.

votes with the DVP voting in favour, apart from four absentees from the right wing of the party.[129]

Stresemann's tactics had been successful once again but serious problems remained. The coalition parties, particularly the DVP, were only loosely committed to the government, and much depended on whether Braun could be persuaded to allow the DVP into the Prussian government in the autumn. Beyond that the SPD and DVP were divided over economic policy, and compromise became more difficult as the recession grew worse. More immediately Stresemann had to face the reaction of the DVP Reichstag party to being propelled into a great coalition.

'The tyranny of the Reichstag party'

Stresemann's high-handed tactics were deeply resented by Scholz. There had been tensions between them before but this time the conflict was open and their pride was at stake. Each had different views of the direction the party should take. There was also a matter of principle to be resolved, the respective authorities of party leader and chairman of the Reichstag party.

The immediate cause of the dispute was Stresemann's telegram to Müller which, according to the memoirs of Paul Moldenhauer, 'exploded like a bomb' in the Reichstag party.[130] Scholz was furious and at once told the Reichstag party executive that he intended to resign.[131] He was particularly angry because when it had looked as though negotiations for a great coalition would fail, Hindenburg had asked through Meissner whether Scholz would be willing to try to form a government. Scholz did not refuse, although he suggested that Müller should be allowed to continue his efforts for the time being. The same day, without reference to Scholz, Stresemann told Müller that he and Curtius would be willing to

[129] *Verhandlungen des Reichstags*, vol. 423, p. 119. Stresemann, still in Bühlerhöhe, would have preferred the government to ask for a vote of confidence because it would have made a better impression abroad, but Curtius warned that the DVP might not be prepared to vote for it. Stresemann to Schubert, 30 June 1928: Bernhard (ed.), *Vermächtnis*, iii. 304; cabinet minutes 29 June, 3 July 1928: Martin Vogt (ed.), *Das Kabinett Müller II* (Boppard: Harald Boldt, 1970), nos. 2, 5.

[130] Paul Moldenhauer, 'Politische Erinnerungen', p. 209: BAK, Nl. Moldenhauer, 2.

[131] Minutes of the meeting, 26 June 1928: BAK, R 45 II/66; report on the meeting from Albrecht Morath to Stresemann, 29 June 1928 (Nl. 101). Kolb, 'Führungskrise in der DVP', 211–17.

join a Müller cabinet and then published his telegram, again without discussing the matter with Scholz.

Curtius was fortunately able to put a different interpretation on events. He had understood from Meissner that Scholz approved of the idea of a cabinet of 'personalities' and had so informed Stresemann before the telephone call with Müller. Both of them therefore acted under the impression that they had Scholz's backing.

Scholz later admitted that he had given Meissner to understand that he would accept a cabinet of 'personalities'. The difference between him and Stresemann was that he wanted to keep the DVP's participation in such a cabinet 'as weak as . . . possible', restricted to Stresemann himself as foreign minister. He also objected to the tactics Stresemann had adopted as undermining his position and that of the Reichstag party.[132] Stresemann pointed out that he would have been in an impossible position as party leader if he had belonged to a government which his party felt free to attack 'with guns blazing'. As for the tactics, Stresemann pointed out that Scholz had not kept him informed about the failure of the negotiations between the parties and, in any case, Stresemann rejected the view that Reichstag parties could decide whether their members accepted office, calling it a surrender of liberalism to 'formal democracy'.[133]

The real issues are clear from this exchange. Scholz had been happy to see Stresemann excluded from the negotiations and had hoped that the DVP would be committed to the government only by the token representation of Stresemann as foreign minister. Stresemann saw through his plan and successfully torpedoed it. The news from Meissner that Scholz agreed to a 'cabinet of personalities' was an unexpected bonus but he would have acted in the same way without it. Stresemann wanted the party to be committed to the coalition, and having Curtius as economics minister substantially increased the DVP's stake.

Scholz and the right wing of the DVP were naturally angry, but they knew that if Stresemann summoned the national executive or a party conference the great majority would support him.[134] To prevent an escalation of the dispute, the Reichstag party executive drafted a series of resolutions which were accepted by the full Reichstag party on 27 June

[132] Scholz to Stresemann, 2 July 1928 (Nl. 101).

[133] Stresemann to Scholz, 19 July 1928 (Nl. 102); also Stresemann to the Reichstag party, 27 June 1928 (Nl. 101): Bernhard (ed.), *Vermächtnis*, iii. 299–301, 312–16.

[134] Moldenhauer pointed out in his memoirs that this gave Stresemann the whip hand. 'Politische Erinnerungen', p. 210: BAK, Nl. Moldenhauer, 2.

and made public.[135] To soothe Scholz's battered ego these resolutions expressed the Reichstag party's gratitude and continuing confidence in him and declared that 'the proper leadership of the party requires constant contact of all those involved in political decisions with each other and with the leader of the Reichstag party and expects all members of the Reichstag party to behave in this way'.

It was now Stresemann's turn to be offended. He assumed, as did the press, that the resolution was directed at him and he demanded that, if that was not the case, it should be made clear.[136] The harrassed party secretary Adolf Kempkes tried to persuade him that the resolution had been aimed at nobody in particular and that further public statements would only cause more trouble. Stresemann was not satisfied, saying that the resolution had made him look ridiculous and that since the insult had been made public it must be publicly withdrawn. He added that he had no intention of submitting to the 'tyranny of the Reichstag party'.[137]

Stresemann planned to confront the opposition at a meeting of the national executive in the autumn. In preparation, he wrote a memorandum for the Reichstag party which he sent to the party's elder statesman and a personal friend, Wilhelm Kahl, for comment.[138] He criticized the Reichstag party for assuming it could represent the party as a whole and for thinking it had the right to determine who joined the government. He also let his personal resentment show, saying that the party's treatment of him made their declarations of support during the election campaign appear 'one hundred per cent hypocrisy'. He disclaimed any desire to cling to office, saying that his health had been so badly affected that he did not know whether he would ever fully recover or even if had much longer to live. He added that he had committed himself financially to the party to the point where if his creditors insisted on repayment, he would not be able to cover his debts and from that point of view the opportunity to take other employment would be welcome. What kept him in office was the

---

[135] Minutes of the Reichstag party executive meetings, 26–7 June, and of the full Reichstag party, 27 June 1928: BAK, R 45 II/66, 67. Confidential account of events for party members, executive bodies and officials: 'Vertrauliche Mitteilungen', 5 (4 July 1928); BAB, 60 Vo 1.

[136] Telegram to the Reichstag party, 28 June 1928 (Nl. 101): Bernhard (ed.), *Vermächtnis*, iii. 303.

[137] Kempkes to Stresemann, 29 June 1928, and Stresemann's reply, 2 July 1928 (Nl. 101): Bernhard (ed.), *Vermächtnis*, iii. 307–8.

[138] Draft of Stresemann to the Reichstag party, 30 June 1928 (Nl. 101) and covering letter to Kahl, dated 2 July; edited version, incorporating the amendments suggested by Kahl, in Bernhard (ed.), *Vermächtnis*, iii. 308–12.

knowledge that the present situation was 'far from good' and the feeling that it would be an act of cowardice to resign. Kahl replied gently that although there were matters that needed to be resolved he did not believe that there was a 'real personal edge' to the conflict and Stresemann should on no account resign as that would be 'a misfortune and catastrophe' out of all proportion to the cause, 'namely the narrow-mindedness and tactlessness of some party politicians'.[139]

Stresemann thought better of the memorandum and it was never sent. In a letter to Scholz he adopted a different tone, making clear the differences between them but avoiding recrimination.[140] He said he wanted a proper discussion at a party conference in the autumn, not the standard ovation. He knew that opposition to his views existed and he wanted to see it expressed. Indeed he referred to a 'crisis' of the party, adding darkly that a crisis could lead to recovery but it could also have other consequences. Scholz, he said, apparently expected an influx of support from the right and therefore rejected the democratic left. Stresemann went on:

The ideal I have in mind is a great bourgeois Liberal Party which includes the reasonable elements of the Democrats and the left wing of the German National Party and thus acquires a decisive position in the Reichstag. I believe we are facing a realignment of parties and programmes in Germany. We should therefore not hush up the existing differences but resolve them openly.

Stresemann indicated that he would not be willing to remain as party chairman if his views did not find support. He compared the situation to the party conference in 1921 where he had faced similar opposition from some of the same people. The issue, he said, could lead to his resignation and withdrawal from party politics.

The lines of division were drawn but the battle was postponed for the time being. Stresemann's interest in a possible realignment of the parties had been stimulated by news of the struggle for power in the DNVP which followed its election defeat and led in October to Hugenberg becoming party chairman.[141] Stresemann hoped that the moderate elements would secede, enabling him to realize his longstanding project of

---

[139] Kahl to Stresemann, 10 July 1928 (Nl. 101).

[140] Stresemann to Scholz, 19 July 1928 (Nl. 102): Bernhard (ed.), *Vermächtnis*, iii. 312–16.

[141] Rudolf Schneider to Stresemann, 6 July 1928, and Stresemann's reply, 11 July 1928 (Nl. 101). In October, he also learnt from a colleague of Lindeiner-Wildau's assessment of the internal divisions of the DNVP over its future leadership: Werner von Rheinbaben to Stresemann, 8 Oct. 1928 (Nl. 72). John A. Leopold, *Alfred Hugenberg: The Radical Nationalist Campaign against the Weimar Republic* (New Haven: Yale University Press, 1977), 45–54.

extending the DVP to both the DDP (which had been willing to discuss a merger in 1924) and the DNVP, making it the main Protestant party. He was therefore more than ever determined to maintain the independence of the DVP and to resist pressure to move it to the right.

Foreign Minister of the Great Coalition

Stresemann remained convalescing in Bühlerhöhe until the second half of July, when he moved on to the spa town of Karlsbad (Karlovy Vary) in Czechoslovakia and from there in August to Oberhof in Thuringia. The conduct of foreign policy passed to Schubert, who also represented Stresemann in cabinet.

The most important issue remained how to achieve evacuation of the Rhineland and give the Locarno policy a much-needed boost in popularity. In July Schubert suggested a way of proceeding.[142] This was in essence to put the question of evacuation to the French and British during the League meetings in September in terms of 'Do you want to carry on with the Locarno policy actively or not?'. Germany should refuse to be drawn into offers of compensation for early evacuation because of the difficulties of the issues of reparations and war debts. However, following conversations with Parker Gilbert, Schubert suggested that if Germany was asked for financial compensation it might reply, 'Good, let's talk about the possibility of getting the settlement of the Dawes plan under way.' Schubert was therefore suggesting a way for Germany to press for Rhineland evacuation without incurring the odium of raising the issue of reparations and war debts, though he knew his initiative was likely to lead on to a discussion of the financial issues.[143]

Stresemann immediately accepted Schubert's proposal for a démarche on Rhineland evacuation without commenting on the further consequences.[144] He authorized Schubert to inform the British, French, and Belgian governments immediately of German intentions, saying that they must not repeat the Thoiry experience of Briand claiming that he had never received the German proposals.

---

[142] Schubert to Stresemann, 24 July 1928: *ADAP*, ser. B, ix, no. 173.

[143] Schubert's memorandum of a meeting with Parker Gilbert, 27 July 1928: ibid., no. 184; Krüger, *Aussenpolitik*, 428–43. Baechler suggests that Schubert had still not fully thought out the connection to reparations and war debts since he did not explain it to Hoesch. Baechler, *Stresemann*, 775–7.

[144] Stresemann to Schubert, 26 July 1928: *ADAP*, ser. B, ix, no. 183.

Stresemann planned a gradual return to work at Oberhof during August, but he allowed himself to be drawn into lengthy debates with party officials about the way the Müller government had been formed.[145] In consequence, he suffered a slight stroke with resulting dysphasia—experiencing difficulty in speaking and writing. He at once returned to Berlin and saw the leading specialist, Professor Zondek, whom he had first consulted the previous January. Zondek could only recommend further rest. Stresemann was deeply disappointed as he was keen to travel to Paris for the signing of the Kellogg–Briand pact on 27 August. He said this was less to please the French than as a gesture to the American secretary of state, who was visiting Europe for the occasion.[146] In fact, it would give him the opportunity to renew discussions with Briand and have a first meeting with Poincaré.

The stroke threatened to put paid to these plans. Müller later recalled how Stresemann sat in the chancellor's room with tears in his eyes, knowing that his power of speech—his most effective instrument as a politician—was failing him.[147] With dogged determination he relearnt words and phrases from Bernhard and was able to be present at the cabinet meeting on 22 August, though Schubert did most of the talking.[148] Stresemann's doctors reluctantly consented to his trip to Paris, under medical supervision, but Stresemann agreed that Müller would represent Germany at the League in September.

Stresemann was the first German foreign minister to visit Paris since Bismarck had celebrated victory in the Franco-Prussian war in Versailles in 1871. The Paris crowds gave him a warm welcome, a sign of his growing international reputation.[149] His main purpose was to discover how Briand and Poincaré viewed the prospects for Rhineland evacuation. Briand sounded encouraging, saying it was time to end the 'head in the sand policy' and go for a 'complete solution'.[150] However, he still appeared to expect some financial quid pro quo, though when Stresemann said it was too late for the kind of financial compensation they had discussed at Thoiry, Briand refused to be precise.

[145] Wolfgang Stresemann, *Mein Vater*, 521.

[146] Cabinet minutes, 22 Aug. 1928: Vogt (ed.), *Kabinett Müller*, no. 18.

[147] Müller to Theodor Wolff, 27 June 1930, enclosing the text of an article on Stresemann for the *Berliner Tageblatt*: Friedrich Ebert Stiftung, Bonn, Nl. Müller, 7.

[148] Wolfgang Stresemann, *Mein Vater*, 522. Cabinet minutes, 22 Aug. 1928: Vogt (ed.), *Kabinett Müller*, no. 18.

[149] Hoesch to Auswärtiges Amt, 28 Aug. 1928: *ADAP*, ser. B, ix, no. 266.

[150] Memorandum by Stresemann, dated 27 Aug. 1928, of his meeting with Briand on 26 Aug.: ibid., no. 262.

Stresemann learned more from Poincaré, whom he saw the following day.[151] Poincaré had let it be known through intermediaries that he was keen to improve Franco-German relations and, indeed, saw himself as the author of the Thoiry proposals.[152] There was a certain amount of sparring, during which Stresemann defended German feelings for Austria but said he knew it would be futile to demand union at the present time and in any case it would bring complications—'In politics one must distinguish between political realities and emotional attachments.'[153] Stresemann explained the attraction of Austria as that of the land of Mozart and Schubert, representing for Germans a part of their soul which they felt they had lost in an increasingly rushed and American style of life. Poincaré picked up this lead and agreed on the importance of European nations maintaining their own identities in face of the 'immense influence' of America.

Stresemann followed up with the main business saying that he was amazed that Poincaré should regard the Rhineland occupation as security for reparations.[154] The German economy was dependent on American loans. The moment that Germany suggested that it was not in a position to honour its reparations obligations, these loans would be withdrawn and Germany would no longer be able to feed its population. That was, he suggested, a far better guarantee than occupation of the Rhineland. Stresemann then tried to discover how Poincaré envisaged a reparations settlement.

Poincaré replied that negotiations would have to wait until the following year because of the American presidential elections, but that the situation was 'both peculiar and interesting' for Franco-German rela-

---

[151] Memorandum by Stresemann, 27 Aug. 1928: *ADAP*, ser. B, ix., no. 263.

[152] Victor Schiff, the foreign editor of the SPD newspaper *Vorwärts*, to Stresemann, 5 June 1928, enclosing an account of his meeting with Poincaré on 20 Apr.; memorandum by Schubert, 23 June 1928, of the account given to him by the SPD's foreign affairs spokesman, Breitscheid, of his conversations with Poincaré and other French leaders: *ADAP*, ser. B, ix, nos. 63, 92. Stresemann later told the German press that he found Poincaré's claim about Thoiry 'a bit much', given that Poincaré's opposition had ruined the plan. Record of the press conference, 14 Nov. 1928: ibid. x, p. 599.

[153] Poincaré raised the question of Austria because the SPD president of the Reichstag Löbe had expressed support for union on various public occasions and this was seen as a quasi-official gesture by the French. Stresemann regarded Löbe's statements as 'as inept as possible' and Müller asked Löbe to be more careful. Stresemann to Schubert, 4 Aug. 1928: ibid. ix, no. 214; cabinet minutes, 22 Aug. 1928: Vogt (ed.), *Kabinett Müller*, no. 18.

[154] Poincaré's view as reported for instance by Hoesch, 12 July 1928: *ADAP*, ser. B, ix, no. 139.

tions. They shared a common interest in reducing reparations and inter-Allied debt repayments. At this moment an urgent note was sent into the room from Professor Zondek, asking them to bring the conversation to a close. Stresemann therefore changed tack and returned to the question of evacuation of the Rhineland. Poincaré said the matter could only be solved together with reparations and war debts and referred to the linkage established in the Thoiry talks. Stresemann warned that a Thoiry-type solution was no longer possible as American investors would not be willing to buy German bonds until they saw the extent of German obligations in a final reparations settlement. According to Stresemann's account, Poincaré appeared unsettled by this remark, saying only that he was inclined to believe that the American market would take the bonds. At this point a second reminder was brought in from Zondek and Poincaré broke off the conversation.

Stresemann was not encouraged. Poincaré appeared to want to involve Germany in a common stand towards the United States, which Gilbert had warned would undermine German credit and annoy the American government.[155] Poincaré's idea for Rhineland evacuation appeared still to be the one he had explained earlier to Hoesch, a phased mobilization of German bonds together with a phased withdrawal from the Rhineland, starting in the summer of 1929 when France had to make a first payment to the United States.[156] Even if this were feasible, it would take years to complete and might offer Germany no advantage over the Versailles treaty, under which evacuation of the second zone was due in 1930 and the final zone in 1935.[157]

Nevertheless Stresemann did not despair. He returned to Baden-Baden to rest and wrote to Käte that Poincaré's ideas were opposed to his 'but perhaps a compromise can still be found'.[158] Meanwhile, looking for some success for the sake of domestic politics, he suggested to Müller that Germany should indicate its interest in early evacuation of the second zone even though the cabinet had previously been concerned that it might weaken the case for complete evacuation.[159]

---

[155] Gilbert told Schubert that he had been shocked to hear from Poincaré that Stresemann had suggested the idea of a common front towards the United States. Memorandum by Schubert, 1 Oct. 1928: *ADAP*, ser. B, x, no. 53.

[156] Hoesch to Auswärtiges Amt, 12 July 1928: ibid. ix, no. 139.

[157] Hoesch had already pointed this out to Poincaré: ibid.

[158] Wolfgang Stresemann, *Mein Vater*, 533–4.

[159] Jacobson, *Locarno Diplomacy*, 192–5; cabinet minutes, 22 Aug. 1928: Vogt (ed.), *Kabinett Müller*, no. 18.

During September and October Stresemann was again forced to assume the role of observer. Müller consulted him in Baden-Baden before going to the League in September. There he pressed the case for evacuation of the Rhineland in the forceful terms Stresemann had already adopted, showing that there was no difference between the SPD chancellor and his foreign minister in the matter. In his speech to the assembly, Müller referred to the 'double face' of international relations with professions of trust contrasting with the maintenance of sanctions.[160] Briand was stung into a sharp reply, accusing the Germans of not having fulfilled their disarmament obligations and referring to the SPD's own revelations about the secret rearmament programme in the Reichstag two years earlier.[161]

When Stresemann heard of the clash he immediately dictated an anonymous article—'from our special reporter in Geneva'—playing the incident down.[162] Briand, he explained, liked to improvise his speeches and had been carried away as a poet had once described 'larks being borne aloft by their song'. Briand had made real concessions since Locarno and taken political risks. They should not allow 'the politics of two great nations' to depend on an improvised speech.

After lengthy talks, the Locarno powers reached agreement at Geneva both for negotiations for Rhineland evacuation and a committee of experts to draw up a plan for a final reparations settlement.[163] This was a successful outcome for the German delegation, which had resisted French demands that Germany should put forward financial proposals. They also resisted for the time being a French proposal for an international commission to monitor the disarmed status of the Rhineland, which was made the subject of further negotiation. Stresemann was delighted with the result, telling Müller that he had not expected so much.[164]

Stresemann returned to Berlin at the beginning of November. He immediately found himself fighting on several different fronts. Poincaré had reached agreement with Churchill, then chancellor of the exchequer, that the final reparations settlement was to cover the total of their war

[160] *League of Nations Official Journal*, Special Supplement no. 64 (Geneva, 1928), 58–9.
[161] Ibid. 79–83.
[162] Bernhard (ed.), *Vermächtnis*, iii. 370–1.
[163] Jacobson, *Locarno Diplomacy*, 195–201.
[164] Müller visited Stresemann on his way back from Geneva. Pünder to Schubert, 19 Sept. 1928: *ADAP*, ser. B, x, no. 38.

debts and a sum for French reconstruction of its northern and eastern regions, which had borne the brunt of the war. They were encouraged by Gilbert, who argued that it would be futile to try to persuade the United States to reduce war debts and, optimistically, that Germany would be able to pay the 2 billion gold marks per annum required.[165] The agreement undermined the idea of an independent committee of experts which in the German view, like the Dawes committee, would have to consider Germany's capacity to pay.

Since Britain and France also agreed that Rhineland evacuation was dependent on a reparations settlement, the consequences looked serious. The central purpose of the Müller coalition had been to continue the foreign policy of 'peaceful understanding'.[166] But the Locarno policy looked vulnerable in face of a new Anglo-French entente and American detachment.[167] There was increasing unrest among the coalition parties and, with the election of Hugenberg as its leader in October, the DNVP committed itself to aggressive opposition.

Stresemann responded to these multiple challenges with a skilful mixture of defiance and accommodation. He was forthright to Gilbert about the way in which Germany's creditors had staked their claims without considering Germany's ability to pay.[168] He said he had been shocked at the figure of over 2 billion gold marks per annum and that he would have to consider whether Germany would do better to stick with the Dawes plan. Gilbert countered that an expensive settlement would be better than waiting for a crisis of the Dawes plan under which annual payments were about to rise to 2.5 billion. Stresemann replied that a crisis could be the first step to recovery, like the Ruhr crisis. He said that foreigners overestimated the strength of the German economy, which was in fact 'dancing on

[165] Jacobson, *Locarno Diplomacy*, 215–18. On Anglo-French negotiations, see Arthur Turner, *The Cost of War: British Policy on French War Debts, 1918–1932* (Brighton: Sussex Academic Press, 1998).

[166] This had been the first point of the government programme presented by Müller to the Reichstag on 3 July 1928: *Verhandlungen des Reichstags*, vol. 423, pp. 38–9.

[167] The Germans had also been concerned at an understanding reached between the British and French during the summer over their tactics for the disarmament conference, under which the French would support the British (against the Americans) on naval disarmament while the British would support the French (against the Germans) over the question of army reserves. Jacobson, *Locarno Diplomacy*, 187–92. Stresemann pointed out to Briand at their meeting in August that Germany had been neither consulted nor informed of this agreement. *ADAP*, Serie B, ix, no. 262.

[168] Stresemann's memorandum, dated 22 Nov. 1928, of his meeting with Gilbert on 13 Nov.: *ADAP*, ser. B, x, no. 147.

a volcano', and if short-term loans were withdrawn a large part of it would collapse. He would like a solution, but he felt himself faced with a variant of the judgement of Paris in which each of the females was 'decidedly ugly'.[169] Gilbert tried to persuade Stresemann that a reparations agreement would so improve German credit that the annuities could be afforded, but Stresemann pointed out that they were supposed to be paid for from an export surplus and there was no surplus.

The following day Stresemann briefed the German press.[170] He discussed the balance of risks of each of the alternatives but gave a more optimistic assessment. He stressed the importance of the American observer, who was to be invited to serve on the committee of experts. He pointed out that the American market would not absorb anything like the scale of reparations bonds for which Poincaré was hoping, and also that there was an American interest in keeping down the level of reparations, in order to safeguard the repayment of its own 'colossal' loans to Germany. He asked the journalists to concentrate on the fact that Germany was living on borrowed money. He said no one could imagine the scale of the crisis they faced and it was time to say openly that they had 'gone to the dogs': 'We are not only militarily disarmed, we are financially disarmed. We have no more resources of our own.'

Stresemann's tactics were to lower expectations of what Germany could afford, in order to counteract the impression given by Gilbert. He could not be so open in public for fear of precipitating the financial crisis. In reply to communications from the French and British governments setting out their views, the cabinet agreed to say that such discussion should wait for the report of the experts and that a solution was possible only within Germany's capacity to pay and without endangering the standard of living of the German people.[171]

Stresemann used the same formula in the Reichstag.[172] He also defended the Locarno policy against the growing tide of criticism. He admitted that the policy had suffered a setback over Rhineland evacuation. But in reply to those who accused him of pursuing a phantom great power

---

[169] The three alternatives were the Anglo-French understanding of what a new reparations settlement would involve, continuing with the Dawes plan in the expectation that it would lead to a crisis, and what Stresemann referred to as 'a theoretical possibility', namely continuing with the Dawes plan without it leading to a crisis.

[170] Record of the meeting, 14 Nov. 1928: *ADAP*, ser. B, x, pp. 597–607.

[171] Cabinet minutes, 17 Nov. 1928: Vogt (ed.), *Kabinett Müller*, no. 68; Stresemann to Hoesch, 22 Nov. 1928: *ADAP*, ser. B, x, no. 150.

[172] Reichstag speech, 19 Nov. 1928: Zwoch (ed.), *Reichstagsreden*, 270–9.

position, under which Germany had become dependent on real great powers, he asked whether the phantom did not lie rather in the minds of those who thought that protests and strong language made a great power. There was, he suggested, no alternative to the policy of 'reasonable, peaceful understanding on the basis of equality' and it was this policy alone which had made it possible for them to put a serious case for the evacuation of the Rhineland.

The December meeting of the League council, held in Lugano rather than Geneva out of consideration for Stresemann's health, gave him the opportunity to discuss the position with Briand and Chamberlain.[173] He tried to impress on them the serious consequences of the delay in evacuation, pointing out that even the Centre Party was becoming critical.[174] Briand responded by reminding him that there was also French public opinion, whose confidence in Locarno had been shaken by the constant agitation of the Hugenberg press.

Stresemann gained one concession. Briand and Chamberlain agreed that negotiations for evacuation could start when the committee of experts met to discuss reparations and that evacuation would not be dependent on a successful outcome of the reparations negotiations.[175] On the other hand Briand made it clear that the general settlement of outstanding issues he had in mind did not include the Saar which, he said, presented difficult legal issues. There was a lengthy discussion of Briand's proposed commission for the Rhineland. Stresemann maintained his opposition to the idea on the grounds that it was unnecessary and that the people of the Rhineland would not accept it. He was adamant that he could not agree to a permanent body that would continue in the Rhineland beyond 1935, but he suggested that it might be possible to set up a conciliation procedure which would operate on a case-by-case basis. In return, Briand suggested that it might be possible to evacuate the second Rhineland zone early. Stresemann responded enthusiastically that if the evacuation question

[173] Memoranda of Stresemann's meetings with Chamberlain, 9 Dec. 1928, and Briand, 12 Dec. 1928: *ADAP*, ser. B, x, nos. 189, 199.

[174] In the Reichstag debate in November the Centre Party politician Ludwig Kaas referred to 'the undeniable failures and the undeniable stagnation of German foreign policy', although he rejected a change of course. At the beginning of December, he succeeded Marx as chairman of the party. *Verhandlungen des Reichstags*, vol. 423, pp. 426–35. Hehl, *Marx*, 455–62.

[175] Memorandum of the meeting between Stresemann, Briand and Chamberlain, 14 Dec. 1928: *ADAP*, ser. B, x, no. 208. Chamberlain did not mention the second point in his account of the meeting. Chamberlain to Lindsay, enclosing a memorandum of the meeting, 13 Dec. 1928: *DBFP*, ser. 1A, v, no. 287.

could be resolved the process of rapprochement would make 'huge progress' and the opposition would be dumbfounded.

At the end of December Stresemann wrote an anonymous article, which he intended to be used by Jules Sauerwein, the foreign correspondent of the Paris newspaper *Le Matin*, in an attempt to influence French opinion.[176] Under the title 'The Crisis of Confidence in the Locarno Policy', he summarized the position by saying that the honeymoon was over, there had been a serious argument in the marriage, and they had to see that it did not end in divorce. He described his unsuccessful efforts to get the evacuation of the Rhineland as a labour of Sisyphus and said his failure had left him no answer to his growing number of critics. The centre of the opposition was the DNVP, which he described as having adopted a fascist organization, since it had voted Hugenberg almost 'dictatorial' powers. He continued:

There are no greater opposites of a real or personal kind than those expressed in the names Hugenberg and Stresemann. The conflict over Germany's political attitude will be fought out more between them than between the concepts of left and right. If the foreign minister succeeds in consolidating the cooperation between the German People's Party and the present coalition, Germany will continue to develop on peaceful lines. If he is defeated by Hugenberg and the middle class goes over to the German Nationals again, it is hard to predict how the situation will develop.

Stresemann addressed directly the fears that Germany would exploit the evacuation of the Rhineland to present 'a great list of demands'— Austria, the Polish corridor, colonies. On Austria, he denied that Ger-

[176] *ADAP*, ser. B, x, pp. 609–14. This document has not previously been properly identified. There are copies of the text in two different files of Stresemann's *Nachlaß*. In one (Nl. 75) the typescript has corrections in Stresemann's hand. Both copies also have an additional note in shorthand, probably by Bernhard. Dr Gutzler kindly deciphered these notes, showing that the text is the draft of an article for Sauerwein from Dec. 1928 (the other copy has Jan. 1929 (Nl. 302)), but that negotiations for its publication in *Le Matin* failed. Sauerwein later described how in January 1929 he visited Stresemann, who explained that he wanted to publish an article in the French and foreign press as 'a last plea' for concessions and also a justification of his past policy to the German people. The article would be attributed to a high-level German source, from which it would be clear that it was in fact by Stresemann. After consulting Poincaré and Briand, Sauerwein did not in the end publish the article. Jules Sauerwein, 'Bei den Großen der Erde. Was ein Journalist erlebte', v, 'Stresemann ii', *General-Anzeiger für Dortmund*, 141 (24 May 1932). See also Henry Bernhard, 'Jules Sauerwein über Stresemann', ii, *NLC* 78 (19 Apr. 1932). Bernhard invited Sauerwein to Berlin on 29 December 1928 (Nl. 75). The exact date of Sauerwein's visit is unclear, but on 24 Jan. 1929 he wrote to Bernhard, saying that he had been unable to pay a second visit and asking whether Stresemann had approved his draft for the article (Nl. 76). Cf. Jules Sauerwein, *30 ans à la une*, 185–7.

many had any intention of raising the question of political union, though they would continue to do everything possible to draw closer in other ways, such as coordinating their legal systems, and they would oppose Beneš's attempts to draw Austria into an economic union with other states. He admitted that their relations with Poland were strained because of the corridor and Upper Silesia. Nevertheless, he said that frontier revision was not a current issue and he pointed out that he was strongly committed to the conclusion of a trade agreement with Poland. On colonies he took his usual line that although they had not given up hope of once again being a colonial power, it was advantageous for Germany in winning markets in many parts of the world to be seen to have no territorial ambitions, especially at a time when subject peoples were starting to demand their independence.

This was an interestingly explicit statement. How far did it correspond to the real goals of German foreign policy? In each of the areas Stresemann mentioned, Austria, Poland, and colonies, the files of the Auswärtiges Amt show that he was giving an accurate account. There were differences of view among officials with Schubert, Hoesch, and Rauscher committed to a future of European cooperation, while others such as Dirksen and Bülow were sceptical. But no one seriously questioned the Locarno policy apart from Brockdorff-Rantzau, who had unsuccessfully tried to prevent it.

Was there an unofficial policy which has left little or no trace in the files but suggests a different answer? Some interesting questions can be raised. Stresemann was careful to keep issues open for the future. Closer links with Austria kept the idea of eventual union alive, despite Stresemann's reservations. Similarly, the unofficial support given to the German minority in Poland kept the issue of frontier revision alive, as it pointed to a danger to European peace of concern to all the Locarno powers. There was also the unofficial activity of Pabst to strengthen the morale of Germans in the South Tyrol against Italianization, an activity which caused a scandal in 1929 when Pabst diverted funds to support the Austrian fascist Heimwehr organization.[177] Even where colonies were

---

[177] Stresemann sent an official, Hans Redlhammer, to explain to the political editor of the *Berliner Tageblatt* that the funds had been intended for the very opposite, the anti-fascist groups in the South Tyrol. However, when asked why someone like Pabst was being used for such a purpose, Redlhammer could offer no explanation. Lowenthal-Hensel and Paucker (eds.), *Ernst Feder. Heute sprach ich mit*, 213. Stresemann may have used his discretionary fund for this purpose, or the money may have come from other funds available for the support of German minorities abroad. His discretionary fund as foreign minister was voted annually by the Reichstag, and rose

concerned, the Auswärtiges Amt continued to be active in seeking financial support for the German settler communities in Africa.[178]

How were such long-term investments to be made profitable? The files of the Auswärtiges Amt give no answer other than through a European concert and, in particular, with the consent of France. But was there a secret alternative mapped out in collusion with the Reichswehr? As we have seen, Stresemann and Marx had given political authority for the rearmament programme in the Soviet Union in 1927 and the policy was continued under the great coalition. In October 1928 the cabinet approved a four-year rearmament budget for the Reichswehr to provide equipment and ammunition for an army of sixteen divisions, instead of the Versailles limit of ten divisions. The rationale of the programme was to enable the Reichswehr to provide frontier defence against Poland. The minister of defence General Groener argued that Germany could hope to mount only a defensive campaign and needed to maintain the benefits of the Locarno détente to be successful.[179] There were other views, however, among the military. In particular, the head of the Truppenamt (the equivalent of the General Staff), Colonel Blomberg, believed that the Reichswehr should also prepare for other situations including an offensive war against Poland in cooperation with the Soviet Union.[180]

How far was Stresemann aware of these divergent views and what attitude did he take? There was contact between his officials and both the Defence Ministry and the Truppenamt. Stresemann also had an independent source of advice, rather remarkably none other than General von

---

from 5 million marks in 1924 and 1925 to 8 million in 1926, but was thereafter cut back until it reached 4.5 million in 1929. It was referred to as a 'secret fund' because the foreign minister did not have to account for how it was spent. Stresemann seems to have spent freely and left a deficit on the fund of 7.75 million marks to his successor Curtius, who was unable to trace how some 5 million marks had been spent. Becker (ed.), *Heinrich Köhler*, 297; Starkulla, 'Pressepolitik', 126–9.

[178] e.g. Schubert on behalf of Stresemann to the state secretary in the Reichskanzlei, 8 Aug. 1928: *ADAP*, ser. B, ix, no. 219.

[179] On Groener, who succeeded Gessler as defence minister in January 1928, see Johannes Hürter, *Wilhelm Groener. Reichswehrminister am Ende der Weimarer Republik 1928–1932* (Munich: Oldenbourg, 1993). Gessler was forced to resign when a film company, Phoebus, went bankrupt and it emerged that Reichswehr funds intended for secret rearmament had been invested in that and other companies by a naval captain, Walter Lohmann, partly to promote patriotic films and partly in the hope of making profits to increase the rearmament budget. Gessler, among others, had guaranteed the investment in Phoebus on behalf of the Reich government. Möllers, *Geßler*, 340–59.

[180] A detailed analysis of the development of military plans is provided by Michael Geyer, *Aufrüstung oder Sicherheit. Die Reichswehr in der Krise der Machtpolitik 1924–1936* (Wiesbaden: Franz Steiner, 1980), 191–217.

Seeckt. Seeckt became an unofficial adviser to the Auswärtiges Amt on disarmament questions in 1927 and had a number of meetings with Stresemann.[181] According to Wolfgang Stresemann they also met privately, and the old hostility between them was partly overcome.[182] Seeckt was probably glad of the position after his enforced resignation as head of the Reichswehr, and Stresemann probably found his expert advice helpful. Stresemann was reported to have said to a colleague, 'One can perhaps go along with the Seeckt of 1929, with that of 1923 and 1924 it was very doubtful.'[183]

Stresemann also had other sources of information. Although little is known of the Auswärtiges Amt intelligence service, there are scattered references in the files. A Dr Jürgens saw Stresemann regularly and briefed him on the activities of the British secret service, in trying to obtain the German cipher and in using Germany as a base for stirring up resistance to the Soviet Union in Georgia and the Ukraine.[184] He also reported the rumours that the Reichswehr planned to establish a dictatorship in 1926.[185]

Stresemann probably had a fair idea of the plans under discussion in the Truppenamt. That is no reason, however, to believe that he took seriously the idea of a German offensive against Poland. The necessary conditions for success did not exist. He would have had to imagine a future not only with Germany rearmed but also the Rhineland evacuated and reparations cancelled, the German economy no longer dependent on American loans, and the Republic consolidated. Even assuming all these favourable conditions, he would have seen obvious objections. What would have been the consequences of attacking Poland for Germany's relations with the Western powers, for European economic cooperation, and for the domestic politics of the Republic? Who would guarantee that a limited war would not turn into a major European war in which, as Stresemann warned,

[181] Meier-Welcker, *Seeckt*, 567–9; Stresemann's appointments for 20 May, 1 June, 6 July 1927 and 1 Apr. 1928: diaries (Nl. 361, 362).

[182] Wolfgang Stresemann, *Mein Vater*, 453.

[183] Ernst Feder, political editor of the *Berliner Tageblatt*, reporting a conversation with Gottfried Kockelkorn, editor of the *NLC*. Lowenthal-Hensel and Paucker (eds.), *Ernst Feder. Heute sprach ich mit*, 229.

[184] Notes by Stresemann, probably from Jan. 1927 (Nl. 49).?Redlhammer to Stresemann, 16 Feb. 1928 (Nl. 64); Stresemann diaries, 2 Oct. 1924 and 1926–8 (Nl. 361, 362). Cf. Stresemann's report to the cabinet, 30 May 1927: Abramowski (ed.), *Kabinette Marx III*, no. 242. Jürgens also reported to Schubert on British knowledge of Germany's rearmament programme in the Soviet Union. Note by Schubert, 26 Nov. 1926: *ADAP*, ser. B,ii/ii, no. 157, n. 8.

[185] Note by Stresemann, 28 Feb. 1926: *ADAP*, ser. B, i/i, no. 127, n. 4.

Germany would be the battlefield? After his experience of defeat in 1918 and of the near disintegration of Germany in 1923, Stresemann was under no illusions about the risks. It is inconceivable that he would have been prepared to take them. He was willing to tolerate the Reichswehr's re-armament so long as it did not damage his foreign policy. But he did not attribute much importance to it, and there was no collusion for war against Poland.

There is a stronger argument against Stresemann, namely that he failed to give the German public a clear lead about the choices that had to be made. He was not prepared to give up German claims to revision of the Versailles treaty in the interests of European security. He did not face up to the fact that in demanding equal rights for Germany he was in effect demanding that France should take second place. His sketchy answer to this problem was the far-sighted one of European economic integration, but despite some interesting initiatives this had not advanced very far by his death and was opposed by important sections of German industry.[186]

The reasons Stresemann was not prepared to abandon what he saw as Germany's just demands are straightforward. He felt strongly that they were just and it would have made it even more difficult to carry public opinion with him. To answer his critics, he had to be able to distinguish his policy of 'understanding' from a policy of 'renunciation'. Given the strength of feeling against the Versailles treaty even within the SPD, it is hard to argue that he was wrong.

Stresemann did however, as we have seen, give a lead on the methods of foreign policy at a time when the priority of peace was not automatically popular. In the autumn of 1928 he addressed the two themes of peace and winning public support in an introductory essay to a volume celebrating the achievements of the first ten years of the Republic.[187] He wrote that after the collapse at the end of the war, the primary task of German foreign policy had been to find new ways to promote its right to peaceful recovery and equality. It had been essential to replace force by an under-standing of the general interest of nations in a peaceful resolution of conflicts:

---

[186] Schulz, *Wirtschaftsordnung*, 67–85. Pohl, 'Deutsche "Wirtschaftsaussenpolitik"', 426–40. How far economic integration would have served to advance German hegemony rather than European stability remains controversial. A perceptive summary of the issues and the literature is provided by Gottfried Niedhart, *Die Aussenpolitik der Weimarer Republik* (Munich: Oldenbourg, 1999), 63–70.

[187] *Zehn Jahre Deutsche Geschichte 1918–1928* (Berlin: Otto Stollberg, [1928]), pp. viii–xii.

Not only because Germany lacked at that moment any basis for a policy of force, but above all because continuing in the old ways of alliances and counter-alliances, economic conflicts between states and open or secret armaments, given the close interdependence of the international economy and, on the other hand, the rapid development of the technology of destruction, would mean that the old Europe with its deep-rooted national conflicts would inevitably tear itself completely to pieces and destroy its economy and civilization. This destruction would be above all Germany's destruction.

He explained that it had been necessary to create a space for reason and trust among nations who were still affected by the emotions of war and victory. But it had also been necessary, and not easy, to win support at home for the new policy. 'For if it is the job of the leader to point out new ways and give shape to new ideas, he can only pursue them successfully abroad in the long term if he has the strong support of public opinion'. Stresemann claimed that there was now the support for a policy of peaceful cooperation and that the overwhelming majority rejected the idea of war, including a war of revenge, as an instrument of national policy.

At the end of 1928 Stresemann's immediate concern, as he made clear in the article for *Le Matin*, was to preserve his achievements against the challenge of Hugenberg. Stresemann took Hugenberg seriously, understanding the power of his press empire and the attraction of the politics of authoritarian nationalism beyond the ranks of the DNVP and the racist right.[188] He wrote to a DVP colleague of Hugenberg's election as DNVP party chairman, 'the beginning is dark but the end may be civil war'.[189]

Nevertheless, there seemed no reason to despair. If a solution could be found to reparations which maintained the flow of loans to Germany, a financial crisis might be avoided. If the Rhineland was evacuated, confidence in the Locarno policy would be renewed. Hugenberg's very extremism might allow a reshaping of Protestant politics. As Stresemann wrote in the same letter 'The clearer our own attitude, the more we will again have the opportunity to become the great middle-class party.'[190]

It looked as though 1929 would be a decisive year. Feeling in better health after his long convalescence in the summer and encouraged by his

[188] Stresemann noticed that Hugenberg's control of Germany's largest film company, Ufa, depended on a relatively small holding of preferential shares which carried multiple voting rights. Stresemann suggested a change in the law to stop the practice, but although the minister of justice Koch-Weser favoured the suggestion it was taken no further. Pünder to Koch-Weser, 6 Oct. 1928: Vogt (ed.), *Kabinett Müller*, no. 37.
[189] Stresemann to Albert Zapf, 23 Oct. 1928 (Nl. 102).
[190] Ibid.

discussions with Briand and Chamberlain at Lugano, Stresemann appeared confident. According to the Austrian envoy in Berlin he was in the best of moods on New Year's eve 1928 and drank beer and champagne until late at night.[191]

[191] Koszyk, *Stresemann*, 339.

10

1929: Stresemann or Hugenberg?

'I can see only that we must work with the left because parts of the right in Germany have gone mad.'[1]

Stresemann committed all his energies during his last months to achieving a solution on reparations, evacuation of the Rhineland, and to keeping the DVP in the coalition. The first two objectives were achieved when the Young plan was accepted at the Hague conference in August, and in the last few days before his death he persuaded the DVP to remain in the coalition. It was a remarkable achievement for a man whose health was broken, showing extraordinary will power. He was driven on by a desire to see his policies reach a conclusion over reparations and the Rhineland and his concern at the threat from Hugenberg, who joined forces with Hitler to campaign against the Young plan. Stresemann realized that their calculations depended on the financial crisis to destabilize the Republic. Up to his death he was continuing to search for the right tactics with which to defeat them.

The Committee of Experts

The first decision was the choice of German representatives for the international committee to draw up proposals for a reparations settlement.

[1] Stresemann's speech to the Reichsausschuß of the DVP, 30 Sept. 1929: Kolb and Richter (eds.), *Nationalliberalismus*, 861.

Although the committee was supposed to be independent, it was clear that its proposals would have to be acceptable to the governments concerned. In Germany there was an additional consideration. The experts had to be people of sufficient standing to command support in the industrial and financial circles whose cooperation would be needed to make any reparations plan work. It was particularly important that they should have sufficient authority to neutralize the anticipated backlash from Hugenberg.

The choice of the Reichsbank president Schacht was inevitable given his acknowledged expertise and international reputation. Briand had tried to warn Stresemann against Schacht and Stresemann knew that he could be difficult. But Stresemann judged, probably correctly, that he would be even more difficult if he was passed over, and that it would appeal to his vanity to be able to demonstrate that financial experts could solve problems that defeated politicians.[2]

As their second expert the cabinet nominated Albert Vögler, who had resigned from the DVP as a member of the 'National Liberal Union' opposition to Stresemann in 1924. As the chairman of the Vereinigte Stahlwerke, Europe's largest steel concern, he represented the industrial interests of the Ruhr. He was also a business associate of Hugenberg.

Two deputies were appointed. They were the banker Carl Melchior and Ludwig Kastl, a senior executive from the Association of German Industry. Stresemann thought that Melchior's cool judgement would help to balance Schacht, whom Stresemann described as having 'an exuberant temperament' like his own.[3] Kastl was recommended by Silverberg, another Ruhr industrialist of moderate views, as someone who could contain Hugenberg's opposition.[4] Stresemann replied that with Vögler and Kastl they had erected 'a rampart of personalities' against the Hugenberg press.[5] The cabinet confirmed the appointments in January and the committee started work in Paris in February under the chairmanship of the American businessman Owen Young.[6]

[2] Memorandum of the meeting between Stresemann, Briand, and Chamberlain, 14 Dec. 1928; Schacht to Stresemann, 11 Dec. 1928: *ADAP*, ser. B, x, nos. 197, 208.

[3] Stresemann to Vögler, 28 Dec. 1928: ibid., no. 240.

[4] Silverberg to Stresemann, 31 Dec. 1928 (Nl. 75).

[5] Stresemann to Silverberg, 4 Jan. 1929 (Nl. 76).

[6] Vogt (ed.), *Kabinett Müller*, no. 99.

The DVP and the Great Coalition

It was important that the Müller government should be put on a more stable basis than the cabinet of 'personalities' with which it had started out, if it was to be capable of taking the decisions that would be necessary when the Young committee reported. Stresemann, however, faced fierce opposition from the right wing of the DVP against accepting a formal commitment to the great coalition. The opposition focused on the failure of the party leadership to secure the entry of the DVP into the Prussian coalition. For some this was a genuine concern but for others it was simply a convenient tactic to secure the DVP's withdrawal from the Müller government and even, in a few cases, to force Stresemann's resignation.[7]

Braun had held out the prospect of negotiations in the autumn but he then adopted delaying tactics, suggesting that the parties should first discuss the issue.[8] This proved a successful ploy: the Centre Party, hitherto the strongest supporter of admitting the DVP, was not prepared to give up one of its cabinet posts and also feared that the DVP might disrupt negotiations for a concordat between Prussia and the Vatican.[9] Braun was able to reply to the pleas of Müller that the problem lay with the Centre Party and the DVP.[10]

Stresemann had planned to confront his critics in the DVP in the autumn of 1928. When the national executive met on 23 November, however, the emphasis seems to have been more on preserving party unity.[11] Scholz proposed Stresemann's re-election as party leader, which was passed by acclamation amid 'ever-renewed storms of applause'. In his speech Stresemann insisted that coalition with the SPD was the right policy to prevent it moving to the left. He also defended his decision to force a break between the DVP and the Stahlhelm, in view of the

---

[7] Richter points out the contradictory goals of those who joined in opposing Stresemann— the representatives of heavy industry who wanted to break up the Reich coalition and the Prussian Landtag party which wanted to regain admission to the Prussian government. Opposition to Stresemann continuing as party chairman came from Saxony and the constituency party of Westphalia South; elsewhere, however, he continued to enjoy strong support. Richter, *Deutsche Volkspartei*, 499–500, 506–7, 530–43.

[8] Schulze, *Braun*, 549–51.

[9] Herbert Hömig, *Das preussische Zentrum in der Weimarer Republik* (Mainz: Matthias Grünewald, 1979), 155–60.

[10] Memorandum by Pünder, 30 Jan. 1929: Vogt (ed.), *Kabinett Müller*, no. 117.

[11] No minutes of the meeting survive. The only record is the report published in the *NLC* Sonderausgabe, 27 Nov. 1928: Kolb and Richter (eds.), *Nationalliberalismus*, no. 70. Kolb, 'Führungskrise in der DVP', 217–18.

increasingly extreme anti-republican position taken up by that organization.[12] In the discussion, the leader of the Prussian DVP, Stendel, made it
clear that they expected the party leadership to renew the pressure for a
reconstruction of the Prussian coalition. He was able to secure a decision—though it was not publicized—that the DVP would enter a formal
great coalition at the national level only if it was admitted to the Prussian government at the same time. The result was therefore a compromise
which left the question of whether the DVP would remain in the coalition
uncertain.

Progress remained blocked until, in February 1929, a crisis erupted
which threatened to bring the Müller government down. The immediate
cause was, paradoxically, Müller's own attempt to solve the problem. He
was anxious at the prospect that he might not be able to obtain a majority
in the Reichstag for the budget.[13] Rising unemployment was creating a
deficit in the social insurance fund. That exacerbated the differences
between the SPD and the DVP. The SPD opposed cuts in benefits and
the DVP opposed increases in employers' contributions. Müller's attempt
to gain approval from the parties for a formal great coalition immediately
triggered a demand from the Centre Party for the three cabinet posts to
which it felt entitled. The DVP, in turn, demanded a reconstruction of the
Prussian government. When no solution could be found, the Centre Party
withdrew its only minister from the government and the government
faced the prospect of defeat in the Reichstag.

Stresemann became involved in the search for a solution. Together with
Kaas and Braun he achieved what he thought was a 'reasonable proposal'.[14] The DVP was to have the Prussian Trade Ministry and Curtius

[12] Stresemann to Kempkes, 23 Sept. 1928, to Scholz, 26 Sept. 1928, and to Oberst Erich von
Gilsa, 14 Oct. 1928. The executive of the Reichstag party decided on 3 Oct. that members of the
Reichstag party should resign from the Stahlhelm. Bernhard (ed.), *Vermächtnis*, iii. 319–22 (Nl.
292). Stresemann was reacting to a declaration by the leader of the Stahlhelm Saxon *Landesverband* expressing hatred for the existing state. He was determined that a clear signal should be sent
by the resignation of DVP members of the Reichstag, but he accepted that party members could
maintain their links with the Stahlhelm and work to return it 'to that above party position, which
is alone its justification'. He also made clear his disapproval of a Stahlhelm proposal for a
referendum for a constitutional amendment to allow the president to appoint a cabinet without
reference to the Reichstag. Speech to the Zentralvorstand, 23 Nov. 1928: Kolb and Richter (eds.),
Nationalliberalismus, 744–5. Berghahn, *Der Stahlhelm*, 113–22; Hans Mommsen, *The Rise and Fall
of Weimar Democracy*, Eng. edn. (Chapel Hill: University of North Carolina Press, 1996), 277–9.
[13] Minutes of a meeting between ministers and party leaders, 27 Nov. 1928: Vogt (ed.),
Kabinett Müller, no. 72.
[14] Minutes of the meeting of the DVP Reichstag party, 21 Feb. 1929: BAK, R 45 II/67; Kolb
and Richter (eds.), *Nationalliberalismus*, 763.

would also join the Prussian government as minister without portfolio while remaining Reich economics minister. The Prussian DVP, however, insisted on the Ministry of Culture (which included education) rather than the less significant Trade Ministry, but that was unacceptable to the Prussian SPD.[15] The negotiations therefore came to nothing and the future of the Müller government remained in doubt.

Stresemann decided to recall the national executive and ask it to release the leadership from the obligation to insist that the DVP be admitted to the Prussian government. He feared that if the Müller government fell the prospects for an agreement on reparations and evacuation of the Rhineland would be put in jeopardy. However, although he avoided saying so he was in effect asking the DVP to allow the Centre party to have three ministers in the Reich without the DVP gaining any quid pro quo in Prussia. Given that sections of the party in any case disliked the coalition, he was taking a big risk.

He prepared carefully for the meeting and, against his normal practice, he read out a text which he also published under the title 'The Crisis of the Parliamentary System'.[16] The speech was intended to be a kind of political testament. At the end he indicated that he might be withdrawing from politics before long and that he would like his words to 'live on' in the DVP. He started with constitutional arguments, saying that they should not deceive themselves—there was a real crisis of the parliamentary system. He blamed first the distortions caused by parties. The responsibility of ministers to parliament did not give parties the right to nominate and withdraw ministers at will. That undermined the authority of the Reich president and also the individual responsibility of ministers. The result would be the end of personalities in politics and of political liberalism itself.

He then applied the constitutional theory to the current situation. He argued that the government could continue without a majority, recalling that the Dawes plan had been accepted by a minority government. However, he added that it would be desirable to have a firmer basis, though he suggested it was doubtful whether the Centre Party, having left the government, would be willing to return. He absolutely ruled out the resignation of the government, saying that it would undermine the

[15] Note by Pünder, 21 Feb. 1929: Vogt (ed.), *Kabinett Müller*, no. 132; Schulze, *Braun*, 552–3.
[16] Minutes of the Zentralvorstand meeting, 26 Feb. 1929: Kolb and Richter (eds.), *Nationalliberalismus*, no. 73; *Deutsche Stimmen*, 41/5, 5 Mar. 1929. Kolb, 'Führungskrise in der DVP', 218–22.

position of the German experts in Paris if, as they had to take a decision affecting future generations, the government collapsed in 'a fit of party rage'. A sense of responsibility towards the state must outweigh considerations of party.

Stresemann dismissed the idea that it would be possible to find an alternative government or that the DNVP might be eligible. That brought him to the question of whether it would be possible to find another partner, in other words going back to the Centre Party, and the problems raised by the obligation to secure the entry of the DVP into the Prussian government. He said that he would like the DVP to be properly represented in Prussia, but that if the negotiations had finally broken down and if the Prussian DVP itself had reservations about entering the government at that time (a reference to the concordat negotiations) then 'the development at Reich level must proceed purely in the interests of the Reich'.

Having presented his audience with the argument which he knew many of them would find difficult to accept, Stresemann then changed direction and launched into a tirade against rising public expenditure, oppressive taxation, the problems of agriculture and small businesses, and the alarming growth in unemployment. He knew these would be popular themes with the party rank and file and he portrayed the DVP as the brake on the irresponsible demands for expenditure of the other parties. He ended his prepared text by referring to the disillusionment of young people with politics. He denied that he was one of those 'fools' who wanted to found a new party but he reaffirmed what he called 'the deepest wish of my life' to see the DVP combine with all those to its left and right who shared its commitment to the state. Despite the talk of dictatorship, he said he believed that they were still a long way from fascism but, returning to his starting point, he warned that they had to find a solution to the problems of parliamentary government and restrain 'the spirit of party' in the interests of the whole.

It was a cleverly constructed and forceful speech but, for the first time, the magic failed to work. The opposition was well prepared and found the support which had been lacking in the past.[17] A whole series of speakers voiced criticisms and doubts. Stresemann was told that it was not enough 'to proclaim lofty goals'—they had to consider how the parliamentary system could be reformed. Several delegates warned of the unpopularity

---

[17] Stresemann's purpose in calling the national executive was known in advance. He had also outlined his views to the Reichstag party the previous day and already met strong opposition there. Richter, *Deutsche Volkspartei*, 530–3.

of current policies: one said they were being held responsible 'for all the stagnation of foreign policy and the failure of economic policy'; voters were leaving them because the party was failing to draw the conclusion from what Stresemann had said about the economy and leave the coalition; they could not afford to go on being the good-natured simpleton ('der gute Michel') who sacrificed himself for the sake of the whole.

It was soon clear that Stresemann's main purpose in calling the national executive had failed: it was unwilling to release the leadership from the obligation to the Prussian DVP and the Prussian DVP was unwilling to relax its conditions for entering a Prussian government. Even a proposal from Scholz to allow the leadership to consider the Reich coalition on its own merits but to make its support conditional on acceptance of the DVP's economic policy fell on deaf ears. Stresemann was forced to intervene repeatedly in the discussion to answer criticism and avoid outright defeat. He showed his usual tactical skill in insisting that the DVP remain in the Reich coalition until the committee of experts reported, but he conceded that then they should decide on the issue of economic policy 'either to remain and use their influence for a reasonable policy or to leave, take up the fight and take the fight to the people'.

In a recess he secured agreement between the different groups for a resolution which reaffirmed the goal that a great coalition in the Reich should be accompanied by a great coalition in Prussia, but postponed the issue until the committee of experts had reported. The resolution was then passed unanimously by the full meeting. Importantly for Stresemann it left open the possibility that in the interim the Centre Party could join the coalition with three ministers and even that a full great coalition could be formed to which each of the parties would be committed.

He had saved the situation and achieved what he wanted but at the price of giving a commitment for the future. He was, however, taken aback at the unprecedented reaction to his speech from the national executive, on whose support he had always previously been able to rely. Once again, as in the previous summer, he felt angry and bitter and talked of resigning once his existing projects as foreign minister were complete.[18]

He poured out his resentment in a long letter to Kahl, written from the peace of a short holiday in San Remo.[19] He said that he could not ignore the fact that there was now a 'far-reaching difference of attitude' between

---

[18] Stresemann to Curtius and to Kempkes, 11 Mar. 1929 (Nl. 77), to Cremer, 19 Mar. 1929 (Nl. 78), to Kockelkorn, 19 Mar. 1929, and to Scholz, 26 Mar. 1929 (Nl. 104).

[19] Stresemann to Kahl, 13 Mar. 1929 (Nl. 104): Harttung (ed.), *Schriften*, 240–5.

himself and the party. The party no longer wanted to, or thought it could, carry the responsibility of government. It preferred to join the opposition, fraternize with the Stahlhelm, and make threatening, if empty, nationalist speeches. It did not like being in government with the Social Democrats whom the right labelled 'traitors' even though the SPD had lost perhaps the highest percentage of dead in the war and had provided the support needed against Poland in the plebiscites in the east and against separatists in the west: 'Everyone approves the great coalition in principle and most go to great efforts to prevent it.' One explanation was that, unlike the old National Liberal Party, the DVP was 'no longer an ideological party but more and more a pure industrialists' party'.

The party had also ceased to support his foreign policy: the policy had been cheered when it appeared to enjoy success but it was now only 'put up with reluctantly'. People forgot that 'The historic achievement of the Locarno policy was to have restored Germany to the society of nations' and their new standing in the United States and elsewhere was a result of this 'very carefully considered policy' which imposed enormous demands of self-control on those who conducted it. Yet in this respect too the party wanted to be free: the Kiel delegation at the meeting of the national executive had passed round an article to the effect that 'We have to follow an unpatriotic policy... because Herr Stresemann wants to remain foreign minister.'

Looking to the future Stresemann said that it was his wish to see the DVP in the Reich and Prussian governments, educating the German people to support the party which had the courage to take responsibility:

I am convinced that over time we would wear down the German National Party which cannot endure a lasting opposition... I regard the entry of the German Nationals into the government with horror because one cannot govern with these professional patriots and those who understand the situation correctly lack the courage to speak out and the others would bring about either the domination of Germany by plutocrats (Hugenberg) or by loud mouths (Frey-tagh-Loringhoven).[20]

As far as his own future was concerned, Stresemann said he would remain in office until the negotiations over reparations and also for a new League procedure for protecting the rights of minorities had been

---

[20] Professor Axel von Freytagh-Loringhoven belonged to the racist wing of the DNVP and clashed on a number of occasions with Stresemann in the Reichstag. Bernhard (ed.), *Vermächtnis*, i. 322–6, ii. 396–8, iii. 326–8.

concluded. If the committee of financial experts produced a favourable report there would still be much to be done to secure its acceptance in Germany. That could mean that he would have to remain a minister longer than the party was prepared to continue to support the government. He was thinking therefore of resigning from his positions within the party to make it free to go its own way.

'These ideas', he confided to Kahl, 'occupy my thoughts almost day in day out and even more at night.' He did not accept the views of those who said his resignation would destroy the party:

I wanted to be the bridge between the old and the new Germany and part of our party has understood this historic mission of our party. Others can only play the old gramophone record and always want to hear the same tune. As Hugenberg is not exceptionally popular it is even possible that some of the people who are today German National will come back to the Volkspartei [DVP] and perhaps we will win a greater number of seats...

However, he was still concerned that his departure might damage the overall position. He had always hoped that the DVP's years in government would make for greater national unity. Others feared that his departure would drive the party completely to the right and bring about that 'great right block' which would he predicted lead to permanent domination by the left: 'The development of Germany will not be to the right but to the left as the number of those dependent on others for their livelihood increases and as the influence of employers becomes increasingly dominant on the right'.

Although upset at his treatment by the national executive, Stresemann was clearly reluctant to sever his ties with his party base. In asking for Kahl's advice he was probably hoping that Kahl would encourage him to stay on. Kahl replied, as expected, saying that the opposition to Stresemann was not representative of the party as a whole: 'The overwhelming majority is today still firmly behind your foreign policy... Looking at the whole picture in the country, the affection and gratitude for the leader is also today *unaltered*.'[21] It followed that there was no reason for Stresemann to resign: that would be a 'misfortune' which would mean 'the end of the party not its revival'. Kahl agreed that the matters in dispute needed to be clarified but he thought that the right moment would be when the budget came to a vote in the Reichstag. If the party refused to support the budget because new taxes were necessary then 'the existing relationship

---

[21] Kahl to Stresemann, n.d. (Nl. 104).

could hardly continue', but he advised postponing fundamental decisions until that time.

Reassured by Kahl and also by other news from Berlin which suggested that the opposition was weakening, Stresemann put aside ideas of resignation.[22] His position was also strengthened by rumours that if the DVP withdrew, the coalition might be able to survive with the support of the Centre Party and the BVP which would give it a narrow majority.[23] After Stresemann's return to Berlin, the coalition parties including the DVP reached agreement on proposals for the budget and also for cooperation with each other and with the government—a great coalition in all but name.[24] The Centre Party then joined the government with three ministers and the DVP Reichstag party acquiesced, though with protests from the right wing.[25] Stresemann tried once again to break the deadlock in Prussia but failed.[26]

Despite this disappointment, the DVP rallied once again behind Stresemann. He summoned a meeting of the Reich committee to demonstrate that the party was again united after the stormy scenes at the national executive. The committee of some seventy leading members and officials met on 30 May and was addressed by Stresemann, Scholz, and the leader of the Prussian party, Stendel. The minutes do not survive but, according to the official report, Stresemann stressed the problems of the economy and the need to make savings and the discussion showed 'unanimous confidence in the party leadership and again, above all, in the policy of Stresemann'.[27] From Stresemann's notes for his speech it seems that he also reported on the progress of the committee of experts and the prospects of achieving a reduction in German reparations payments and that he defended the policy of working with the SPD to achieve cuts in public expenditure.[28]

---

[22] Letters from Cremer, Kockelkorn, and Trücksaess to Stresemann, 23 Mar. 1929 (Nl. 104).

[23] Pünder to Stresemann, 19 Mar. 1929 (Nl. 77); Stresemann to Kockelkorn, 19 Mar. 1929 (Nl. 104).

[24] Cabinet minutes and minutes of a discussion with party leaders, 10 Apr. 1929: Vogt (ed.), *Kabinett Müller*, nos. 168–9.

[25] Minutes of the meeting of the DVP Reichstag party, 10 Apr. 1929: BAK, R 45 II/67 (Vogt (ed.), *Kabinett Müller*, 543). At this meeting, there were only seven votes against the budget proposals—and therefore against the coalition—but Richter estimates that about a third of the DVP Reichstag party was determined to bring down the government as soon as possible. Richter, *Deutsche Volkspartei*, 548.

[26] Stresemann to Kaas, 7 May 1929; Stendel to Stresemann, 20 May 1929 (Nl. 105): Vogt (ed.), *Kabinett Müller*, 543.

[27] NLC, 1 June 1929: Kolb and Richter (eds.), *Nationalliberalismus*, no. 75.

[28] Nl. 105.

Stresemann had clearly succeeded in containing the opposition for the time being. It is worth reflecting on what that reveals about the balance of forces in the DVP in the summer of 1929. There is a natural tendency with the benefit of hindsight to assume that his position was already becoming untenable. The pessimistic tone of his letter to Kahl encourages such a conclusion. But as Kahl pointed out and the events following Stresemann's return to Berlin showed, the opposition was not as powerful as Stresemann had feared. It benefited from the stagnation of foreign policy, the problems of the economy, and the natural unpopularity in a middle-class party of coalition with the SPD. But opposition, centred on the Ruhr, was nothing new. By adjusting his stance to emphasizing the importance of remaining in the coalition to influence economic policy, Stresemann was able to keep the opposition at bay.

Moreover, Stresemann could still rely on the knowledge that if he called a party conference he would receive overwhelming support. No other figure commanded the same following. Paul Moldenhauer, not one of Stresemann's supporters, wrote later about the formation of the great coalition that the only alternative would have been to join the DNVP in opposition but that would have meant sacrificing Stresemann:

Given the whole development that was not possible. The great mass [of the party] outside swore by Stresemann. A storm of indignation would have broken over the Reichstag party and only a small proportion of them were prepared to face it. The party would have split and sunk into complete impotence.

The situation had not changed, he said, at the time of the national executive meeting in February 1929 except that because the members knew that they could not afford to break with Stresemann their 'annoyance was all the greater'.[29]

Stresemann's hints that he was contemplating resignation, fuelling immediate speculation in the press about his intentions, were an effective threat. Scholz wrote to him expressing the concern of party members at press reports that Stresemann was planning to start a new party and suggesting that he should scotch these 'laughable rumours'.[30] Since the opposition in the Reichstag and Prussian Landtag parties was not prepared to force an open break with Stresemann, it had no alternative but to submit to his policy and put the best face on it in the interests of party unity.

[29] 'Politische Erinnerungen', pp. 211, 217: BAK, Nl. Moldenhauer, 2.
[30] Scholz to Stresemann, 20 Mar. 1929 (Nl. 104). Richter, *Deutsche Volkspartei*, 543–4.

Koch-Weser noticed the change in the situation. In February he recorded that the national executive had listened to Stresemann sympathetically as if to 'the singing of a dramatic tenor' but had then ignored his advice. But in July he noted that while the DDP was going downhill, 'The Volkspartei is apparently all the same on the upswing, at least as long as Stresemann is alive', and he wondered whether the time had not come for him and the other leading members of the DDP to join the DVP.[31]

The Political System in Crisis: Reflections and Plans

Stresemann had reasserted his authority in the DVP, but did he have a coherent policy for dealing with what he had called at the national executive 'the crisis of the parliamentary system'? In his speech he had discussed large constitutional issues—the role of political parties and the problem of providing stable government—and immediate political issues—reparations and the looming financial and economic crisis. But apart from maintaining the coalition how did he hope to defeat the challenge from Hugenberg and his allies?

On the constitutional issues there was not very much he could do, except point to the dangers. His goal was to strengthen parliamentary government. The ideal he put forward was anachronistic, that of a nineteenth-century liberal who believed in ideas as the basis of political parties and of parties obedient to outstanding leaders who were imbued with a spirit of service to the state. Nevertheless the criticism which he made of 'the party spirit' in the Weimar Republic and the difficulty it caused for political leadership pointed to a real problem.[32] In a multiparty system effective government depended on parties being willing to form and maintain coalitions despite the compromises of their partisan preferences that such coalitions required. Stresemann correctly identified the lack of a tradition of responsible government among the parties as a hangover from their relative impotence during the empire.

[31] Diary for 27 Feb. and 5 July 1929: BAK, Nl. Koch-Weser, 39.

[32] The problem of how to combine modern party organization with political leadership was at the centre of Max Weber's famous lecture 'Politics as a Vocation': Gerth and Mills (eds.), *From Max Weber*, 111–14. It was also discussed by Alfred Weber, who coined the concept of a 'leadership democracy'. When Eschenburg mentioned this to Stresemann, he retorted 'I cannot stand the fellow but in this respect he is right.' Eschenburg, *Also hören Sie mal zu*, 204. On Alfred Weber's views, which bore a marked similarity to Stresemann's, see Demm, *Ein Liberaler*, 294–306.

Stresemann's desire to make parliamentary government successful set him in opposition to those on the right who thought that the cure for Germany's ills was to strengthen the powers of the president. Stresemann criticized the parties for undermining the authority of the president by claiming in practice the right themselves to make (and withdraw) ministerial appointments. But he thought that the presidential powers were already 'not slight', and that the office had derived additional influence from the personalities of the first two presidents.[33] He had himself fiercely resisted Hindenburg's wishes over the appointment of an ambassador to the Soviet Union, a dispute resolved only when Stresemann threatened to resign.[34] Asked for his attitude by a group of young intellectuals, Stresemann is reported to have replied emphatically: 'What, more power to the president? What nonsense. He has too much power already.'[35]

Nevertheless, Stresemann was aware that if the political parties could not be persuaded to make parliamentary government work, then it might be necessary to fall back—as in 1923—on presidential decree powers. At the meeting of the national executive in February 1929, he said they should demand that the party spirit be limited in the national interest and that parliament accept the overriding need to build 'not only formal but real majorities'. However, if the parties failed in this task, then they (the DVP) should demand that 'responsible personalities find the courage to rule, i.e. to take over the leadership' on the Roman principle of 'Res venit ad triarios'. Later in the discussion he specifically approved the suggestion of an enabling law to allow rule by presidential decree.[36] He clearly, however, saw this as a last resort and the purpose of using such

[33] Speech to the Zentralvorstand, 26 Feb. 1929: Kolb and Richter (eds.), *Nationalliberalismus*, 764–5.

[34] Hindenburg wanted to appoint a conservative diplomat, Rudolf Nadolny, in succession to Brockdorff-Rantzau, and to Stresemann's irritation let this be known before Stresemann had been consulted. Stresemann favoured Rauscher, who was completely unacceptable to Hindenburg. Encouraged by Meissner, Hindenburg argued that the appointment of ambassadors was his prerogative and continued to press the claims of Nadolny, whereupon Stresemann threatened to resign. Hindenburg then agreed to a compromise candidate, Herbert von Dirksen. Memorandum by Stresemann, 18 Nov. 1928; Hindenburg to Stresemann, 22 Nov. 1928: *ADAP*, ser. B, x, nos. 141, 149.

[35] Felix Gilbert, *A European Past: Memoirs 1905–1945* (New York: W. W. Norton, 1988), 79.

[36] Minutes of the Zentralvorstand meeting of 26 Feb. 1929: Kolb and Richter (eds.), *Nationalliberalismus*, 769–70, 793. The Latin quotation is a version of Livy, VIII. 8 meaning 'when things are difficult' and literally referring to the third division of 'veteran soldiers of tested courage', who were capable of surprising an enemy, which did not expect to meet fresh troops once they had overcome the first two divisions. I am grateful to Peter Parsons for explaining this reference to me.

powers would be to manage the crisis until parliamentary government could be restored.

Seeing that such measures might be necessary, Stresemann was (according to Eschenburg) extremely worried that Hindenburg's health might fail and, in any case, about what would happen in 1932 when Hindenburg's term came to an end.[37] He trusted Hindenburg to act within the Constitution. But he saw that Hugenberg would try to unite the anti-republican right to turn the presidential election into a campaign to replace parliamentary government with an authoritarian regime and the real danger that in the conditions of the financial crisis the Republic might be overthrown.[38]

Stresemann also warned against the growth of sectional parties and, within the DVP, the growing influence of the industrialists' lobby. This development was part of the process of fragmentation of the Protestant middle-class parties into different interest-group parties—the Wirtschaftspartei representing artisans and small business, a savers' party protesting against inadequate compensation after the inflation, and regional peasant parties, for instance—all threatening to reduce politics to 'an appendix to the representation of interests'.[39] Stresemann's criticism may seem exaggerated from someone whose career had begun with the representation of the interests of Saxon exporters. But he could justifiably claim that as a politician he had always understood the importance of reaching a compromise which respected different interests.[40] The domination of interest groups was, in turn, alienating young people from democratic politics as they found no vision to attract them. It would also mean that 'personalities' would no longer seek a political career.[41]

The success of Hitler and the NSDAP in attracting disillusioned voters from the Protestant middle-class parties provided dramatic confirmation of Stresemann's fears from 1930 to 1933. The NSDAP effectively appropriated the slogan of the *Volksgemeinschaft* (community of the nation) as a propaganda tool against the apparent weakness and divisions of parlia-

---

[37] Stresemann sent a message via Eschenburg to Carl Petersen, a former leader of the DDP and mayor of Hamburg that, if Hindenburg died, he would be the candidate of the coalition parties. Eschenburg, *Also hören Sie mal zu*, 222, 227.

[38] Ibid. 227.

[39] Stresemann to Scholz, 26 Mar. 1929 (Nl. 104). Jones, *Liberalism*, 251–65.

[40] Stresemann to Scholz, 26 Mar. 1929 (Nl. 104).

[41] He favoured a reform of the electoral system to strengthen voter choice at constituency level and weaken party control over candidate selection through the national list. 'Persönlichkeit, Politik und Organisation', *Hamburger Fremdenblatt*, 363 (31 Dec. 1928) (Nl. 75).

mentary politics, epitomized by the fragmentation of the Protestant electorate.[42] But did Stresemann offer any credible alternative to prevent
erstwhile DVP voters defecting en masse to the Nazis?

He understood the danger. Throughout his political career liberalism
had been divided on economic and social issues. Before the war, he had
tried to hold the National Liberal Party together with a twin appeal to
liberal principles at home—against discrimination and for constitutional
reform—and nationalism and imperialism abroad. His liberalism was no
longer an ideology with mass appeal. Even a sympathetic young intellectual, like Eschenburg, saw it as the creed of a previous generation.[43] What
Stresemann now offered was an appeal to patriotism in the form of
service to the state, a commitment to the Republic which alone offered
the prospect of gradual consolidation at home and recovery abroad. He
offered rational, pragmatic politics and a clear lead against Hugenberg's
alternative in the DNVP. In 1929 he was committed to working within the
coalition for a solution to the issues of foreign policy and the economy,
though he was also prepared to envisage presidential emergency decrees if
necessary. He told the national executive that one could not always offer
people 'lofty goals' but over time he believed that the DVP's 'objective
work' would be rewarded.[44] He found frequent words of praise for the
SPD, describing its discipline as 'the only thing left of the old Prussia' and
the best hope for maintaining control of public expenditure.[45] For the
DNVP he had only contempt, condemning for instance its irresponsible
attempts to gain influence by reviving the issue of monarchism, regardless
of the damage that did to the state on which they all depended.[46]

Stresemann saw the economic crisis coming and did not underestimate
its seriousness. He told the national executive that 'we could be facing a

[42] This was nowhere more evident than in Saxony, a point impressively demonstrated by
Claus-Christian W. Szejnmann, *Nazism in Central Germany: The Brownshirts in 'Red' Saxony*
(New York: Berghahn Books, 1999), 118–21, 181–93.

[43] Eschenburg, 'Stresemann und die Studenten', 1002; Larry Eugene Jones, 'German Liberalism and the Alienation of the Younger Generation in the Weimar Republic', in Jarausch and
Jones (eds.), *In Search of a Liberal Germany*, 287–321.

[44] Minutes of the meeting of 26 Feb. 1929: Kolb and Richter (eds.), *Nationalliberalismus*, 768.

[45] Ibid. 798.

[46] Ibid. This was a reference to divisions over monarchism within the DNVP during the
struggle for the leadership which led to Hugenberg's election. Leopold, *Hugenberg*, 45–54.
Stresemann's comment makes it clear that he was not seriously considering a return of the
monarchy as a possible solution to the problems that would arise when Hindenburg resigned.
His reported suggestion to Brüning that there should be a regency of the Crown Prince may have
been simply a throwaway remark or intended to elicit Brüning's view. See above, p. 232.

catastrophe in Germany which will bury us all'.[47] But he was not fatalistic. He applied all his gifts of political intelligence and determination to finding a way of managing it. Immediately, he looked for relief from the report of the committee of experts on reparations. His new emphasis on the economic crisis and the need to use any saving on reparations to reduce taxation, while maintaining vigilant control over public expenditure, went down well in the party.[48] It gave them a policy on which they could all agree and a reason for remaining in the coalition. On the other hand, that reason would disappear if the coalition was unable to agree on fiscal policy.

Stresemann also had, as we have seen, longer-term plans for a realignment of parties to provide a Protestant alternative to the alliance of Hugenberg with Hitler. He hoped to make the DVP the nucleus of a broad front which would include both the DDP and moderate conservatives alienated by the DNVP's lurch to the right, and he was willing to see the right wing of the DVP break away and join the opposition. The mechanics of realignment were complicated. As Stresemann explained to young intellectuals who supported the goal of liberal unity, it was desirable to attract the new groups from both left and right simultaneously so that neither would be alienated by a one-sided extension. It was also necessary to complete the process well before the next election to give time to overcome local resistance and resolve the vexed question of choosing candidates.[49]

Stresemann had reacted cautiously to approaches from the DDP in the past. In the summer of 1928, however, he and Koch-Weser became honorary co-chairmen, together with Kahl, of an independent group, the Liberal Association, which had been set up in 1924 to promote Liberal unity.[50] In July 1928 he suggested to the organization's chairman, August Weber, that instead of occasional manifestos the association should organize a series of monthly meetings with a meal followed by a lecture and discussion to allow each side to get to know the other better and so work towards 'that union which we all have in mind as the goal'.[51] In 1929

---

[47] Minutes of the meeting of 26 Feb. 1929: Kolb and Richter (eds.), *Nationalliberalismus*, 772.

[48] Ibid. 795. Kockelkorn (editor of the *NLC*) to Stresemann, 23 Mar. 1929 (Nl. 104).

[49] Memorandum of a meeting between Stresemann and leaders of the Front 1929, 26 Apr. 1929 (Nl. 105). The leading figure in the group was Rochus von Rheinbaben, who had edited a selection of Stresemann's speeches and articles in 1926 and published a biography of him in 1928.

[50] There is a detailed description of the history of the Liberale Vereinigung in Jones, *Liberalism*, 267, 271–5, 277–8, 309–14.

[51] Stresemann to Weber, 5 July 1928 (misfiled in Nl. 105 and misdated 5 July 1929 by Richter, *Deutsche Volkspartei*, 564). Weber had been a pre-war colleague in the Saxon National Liberal Party, but had gone over to the DDP in 1918. Jones, *Liberalism*, 310.

Stresemann discussed the prospects for liberal unity with various groups of young intellectuals, including the so-called Front 1929, and with Eschenburg and his friends in Berlin.[52] He urged them to include Artur Mahraun's Jungdeutscher Orden in their plans, saying that despite its mystical philosophy it was loyal to the state and supported his foreign policy. Rheinbaben also tried to establish contact with anti-Hugenberg groups in the DNVP, though Stresemann had heard that to save face they would want to found their own new conservative party as an intermediate stage to joining the 'the great bourgeois centre'.[53] All this activity not surprisingly aroused the suspicion of Scholz and the DVP right wing, and Stresemann was embarrassed when the party newspaper in the Rhineland, the *Kölnische Zeitung*, called on him to place himself at the head of a united party.[54]

In September 1929 more definite plans took shape. In reaction to the alliance of Hugenberg, Hitler and the Stahlhelm for a referendum against the Young plan, Stresemann and Koch-Weser met in the Swiss resort of Vitznau, where Stresemann was recuperating, and agreed to form a 'Patriotic Bloc' (Block der Nationalbewussten).[55] According to Koch-Weser this was intended to be the basis for cooperation on other matters as well such as the next presidential elections and, in time, they assumed it would lead to 'the merger of the middle parties' though that was kept private. Stresemann was the one person who might have been capable of uniting a broad Protestant front behind his leadership. Theodor Wolff pointed out the irony that the Liberal unity which had seemed impossible with him in 1918 now seemed impossible without him.[56] Kahl tried to continue with the process after Stresemann's death but it was abruptly halted by the DVP Reichstag party.[57]

Stresemann was also active in his last months in trying to find ways of curbing the influence of business over the DVP. He had no objection to

---

[52] Jones, *Liberalism*, 326–37; Eschenburg, *Also hören Sie mal zu*, 281–2. There is a detailed account of the groups in Richter, *Deutsche Volkspartei*, 554–65.

[53] Memorandum of a meeting between Stresemann and leaders of the Front 1929, 26 Apr. 1929 (Nl. 105). A separate party was eventually founded in 1930: Erasmus Jonas, *Die Volkskonservativen 1928–1933* (Düsseldorf: Droste, 1965).

[54] Jones, *Liberalism*, 332–3.

[55] Koch-Weser to Stresemann, 11 Sept. 1929 and Stresemann's reply, 17 Sept. 1929 (Nl. 86). Memorandum by Koch-Weser, 29 Nov. 1929: BAK, Nl. Koch-Weser, 101.

[56] 'Erinnerung', 6 Oct. 1929, repr. from the *Berliner Tageblatt* in Bernd Sösemann (ed.), *Theodor Wolff. Der Journalist. Berichte und Leitartikel* (Düsseldorf: Econ, 1993), 266; Bernd Sösemann, *Theodor Wolff. Ein Leben mit der Zeitung* (Munich: Econ, 2000), 235–9.

[57] Jones, *Liberalism*, 346.

the representation of business interests in the DVP, for 'business leaders are of eminent importance in all questions'.[58] Nor did he necessarily disagree with the views of business leaders, as his desire to make budget savings and reduce taxation showed. What worried him was the preponderance of the business lobby within the Reichstag party—he calculated that after the 1928 elections over half the party belonged to it.[59]

There were several undesirable consequences. It was difficult for the DVP to present itself as truly a people's party. Stresemann was particularly worried about the effect on young voters and white-collar employees.[60] It also created conflict within the party when, for instance, the Ruhr group sought to dictate political strategy, opposing the great coalition.

The problem was made worse by the dependence of the DVP on business for finance, since individual constituency parties—like the nineteenth-century parties of 'notables' who financed their own campaigns—had no tradition of fund-raising and were constantly in financial difficulty.[61] In this respect, the SPD and the NSDAP were far more efficient. Stresemann would have liked the party to be self-supporting but he was forced back on to business support. Despite the friction between him and some powerful firms, notably the Stinnes and later the Hugenberg empires, the DVP was relatively successful in raising funds from the Ruhr, the electrical and chemical industries, and the banks. Stresemann was determined, however, that political control should remain in his hands. He understood that while the DVP needed the funds, business lobbies brought few votes with them and themselves needed the DVP's influence in government.[62] He told the story of how Carl Bosch, the head of the I. G.

[58] Speech to the Reich conference of DVP *Angestellten* (white-collar employees), 12 Jan. 1929: *NLC*, supplement, 15 Jan. 1929.

[59] Stresemann to Kahl, 13 Mar. 1929 (Nl. 104). A breakdown of the Reichstag party confirms Stresemann's figures showing twenty-three representatives of large and medium-sized firms from a total of forty-five members of the Reichstag. The second-largest group consisted of twelve *Beamten* who included—apart from government officials—judges, professors, teachers, and clergy. There were six farmers, two from the independent professions, one white-collar employee, and one blue-collar. During the 1924–8 Reichstag there had been twenty businessmen from a total of fifty-one DVP members. Döhn, *Politik und Interesse*, 77–90, 345.

[60] In his New Year's appeal addressed to 'Der deutschen Jugend', *NLC* 55/235, 29 Dec. 1928, Stresemann stressed that the Zentralvorstand had resolved unanimously not to become a representative of interest groups 'but to pursue the ideal of a true people's party'. In his speech to the Reich conference of DVP *Angestellten* on 12 Jan. 1929, he deplored their weak representation in the party and promised to help correct the deficiency at the next election. *NLC*, supplement, 15 Jan 1929.

[61] Richter, *Deutsche Volkspartei*, 194–213.

[62] Henry Ashby Turner, *German Big Business and the Rise of Hitler* (New York and Oxford: Oxford University Press, 1985), 18–31.

Farben chemical group, had made such far-reaching demands over trade, taxation, and social policy before the 1928 elections that he had retorted 'we could also nationalize the companies', and Bosch had immediately climbed down.[63] Nevertheless the perception of the DVP as the industrialists' party was damaging and the party's dependence on business contributions a constant source of friction. Stresemann was sufficiently concerned about the problem to float the idea in May 1928 of state subsidies for party election expenses in proportion to the number of votes won.[64]

Of more immediate significance for the balance of power within the party was a proposed reform of its organization. A committee was established by the national executive in November 1928, following the problems that had arisen in the summer over the formation of the Müller government. The report proposed, as Stresemann wanted, changes which would have strengthened the position of party leader in relation to the Reichstag party and would have also made it easier for the central party bodies to influence candidate selection in the constituencies.[65] Stresemann did not live to see the reforms enacted. They were to have been ratified in October 1929 at a party conference which was postponed, because of his death, to March 1930.

The Young Plan

Stresemann's hopes for the future depended heavily on a successful outcome of the reparations negotiations. The coalition parties had been able to reach agreement on budget proposals in April 1929 only by anticipating a reduction in reparations payments.[66] But success was far from certain.

A major problem became the attitude of Germany's own representatives on the committee of experts, especially Schacht, who assumed the leading role. He made it clear that he expected the experts to be given a free hand

---

[63] Eschenburg, *Also hören Sie mal zu*, 205–6.

[64] Richard Lewinsohn (Morus), *Das Geld in der Politik* (Berlin: S. Fischer, 1930), 119–20; Döhn, *Politik und Interesse*, 371; Richter, *Deutsche Volkspartei*, 210.

[65] Stresemann was kept informed of the progress of the committee by Kempkes, who also communicated Stresemann's views to the committee. Kempkes to Stresemann, 10 and 19 Sept. 1928; Stresemann to Kempkes, 14 Sept. 1928 (Nl. 106); Turner, *Stresemann*, 254–5.

[66] As reported by the minister of finance, Hilferding, to the cabinet on 7 Apr. 1929: Vogt (ed.), *Kabinett Müller*, no. 165.

and it soon became apparent that he intended to pursue political goals on the committee under the guise of economic necessity—the return of colonies as a way of giving Germany raw materials and the return of the Polish corridor to increase food supplies and reverse the economic decline of East Prussia.

Schacht was aware that he was trespassing on Stresemann's territory as foreign minister. He therefore warned Stresemann of his intentions.[67] Stresemann reacted cautiously. He did not want to provoke Schacht's resignation, and the German government had insisted that the experts should be genuinely independent. He may also have been swayed by Schacht's argument that the American experts on the committee were sympathetic to the German case for an enlarged economic base. On the other hand, Stresemann and the cabinet did not want the committee to fail to agree because the German side raised political demands.[68]

Stresemann therefore tried to temper Schacht's enthusiasm and steer it into useful channels.[69] He warned Schacht that Americans tended to underestimate the 'political passions' which the corridor issue aroused in Poland. He set out his own ideas of what would be necessary for a solution, along the lines which he and Schacht had considered previously in 1926: an international aid programme for Poland in which Germany would take a leading role and a comprehensive economic agreement between Germany and Poland extending over many years. He added that he would raise the matter again with his French and British colleagues at Geneva. Stresemann combined this gentle reminder that he was foreign minister with a practical suggestion. If the committee recommended that the recovery of Germany's economic unity and its participation in international colonial projects were of 'the utmost importance for carrying out the plan' that would provide 'an important moral lever' for future policy.

Schacht's reply showed that he had understood.[70] He said that the experts' purpose was to provide 'economic statements' in the report as a basis for foreign policy which 'must naturally be left completely to your judgement and your leadership'. He added that they would be very careful

---

[67] Schacht to Stresemann, 11 Dec. 1928: *ADAP*, ser. B, x, no. 197; Schubert's note of a conversation with Stresemann, 11 Jan. 1929; Schacht to Stresemann, 16 Feb. 1929: ibid. xi, nos. 14, 75.

[68] This was made clear to one of the German experts, Kastl, when he reported on the progress of the negotiations to a group of senior ministers on 1 Mar. 1929: Vogt (ed.), *Kabinett Müller*, no. 139.

[69] Stresemann to Schacht, 24 Feb 1929: *ADAP*, ser. B, xi, no. 86.

[70] Schacht to Stresemann, 26 Feb. 1929: ibid., no. 94.

and that the fears of the Auswärtiges Amt over their handling of the corridor and colonial issues were without foundation: 'We cannot make policy, that must remain the task of the German government.'

Unfortunately, Schacht's actions were at variance with his assurances. He encouraged a retired diplomat, Richard von Kühlmann, to engage in private diplomacy in Paris in pursuit of Germany's colonial demands.[71] When his actions led to an official enquiry from Chamberlain as to Kühlmann's status, and Stresemann replied that he had acted without authority, Schacht was offended and claimed that Stresemann had let the German experts down.[72] Much more serious, on 17 April the German experts presented their proposals to the committee, making the political conditions into a central argument of the terms under which Germany would be able to pay even a much lower sum than the Allies were expecting. The proposals were also put forward in the form of an ultimatum, without consulting the cabinet, and it looked as though the committee's proceedings might come to an abrupt end—indeed this would probably have occurred but for the death of one of the British experts allowing a timely adjournment.[73]

The cabinet was alarmed and met to consider the awkward question of how it could put pressure on its own experts.[74] Stresemann made no secret of his feelings, saying he was 'particularly dismayed' that the government had been presented with a fait accompli. He pointed out that there was a difference between suggesting that political mistakes should be put right and, as the experts had done, making agreement conditional on these demands being met. The other side would claim that the conference had failed because of those demands, with serious consequences both for foreign policy and the coalition. At a subsequent meeting with the cabinet, Schacht and Vögler defended themselves and agreed to continue the negotiations though they did not hold out much prospect of success.[75]

---

[71] Kühlmann had been state secretary of the Auswärtiges Amt in 1917–18.

[72] Stresemann's memorandum of a meeting with the British ambassador Sir Horace Rumbold, 6 Apr., Schacht to Stresemann, 8 Apr., and Stresemann's reply, 10 Apr. 1929: *ADAP*, ser. B, xi, nos. 157, 161, 164.

[73] On these events, see the official history prepared in the Reichsarchiv in reply to Schacht's allegations in his book *The End of Reparations*, Eng. edn. (London: Jonathan Cape, 1931); Martin Vogt (ed.), *Die Entstehung des Youngplans dargestellt vom Reichsarchiv 1931–1933* (Boppard: Harald Boldt, 1970).

[74] Cabinet minutes, 19 Apr. 1929: Vogt (ed.), *Kabinett Müller*, no. 175.

[75] Minutes of the meeting, 21 Apr. 1929: ibid., no. 177.

In fact Schacht changed tactics and started to negotiate on the basis of a compromise proposal put forward by the committee chairman, Owen Young. At the same time he tried to establish an alibi for his new position by blaming German ministers for allegedly having accepted in advance Gilbert's estimate of what Germany would have to pay and therefore undermining the position of the German experts.[76] The situation was not helped by Gilbert appearing to endorse Schacht's version of what had happened.[77] It was unfortunate for Stresemann that the conversation chiefly in question was one between him and Gilbert the previous November. It was true that a sum of 2–2.5 billion marks had been discussed then, but Stresemann had made it clear that he thought the figure too high.[78] The situation was explained to Schacht but he refused to let the matter drop.[79] When he referred to it again in a meeting which had been called to discuss Young's latest proposals on 1 May, Stresemann exploded.[80] He demanded that the chancellor set up an enquiry into the 'appalling accusation' against him which Schacht persisted in making. Schacht at once withdrew saying he accepted that Gilbert, not Stresemann, had been responsible for giving a false view of the German position.

At the same meeting, Schacht grudgingly consented to sign the report of the committee if that was the government's wish. He said he would have to suppress his own convictions and would subsequently retire—he was 'no dictator'. At a full meeting of the cabinet the same evening he again declared his willingness to sign, while making it clear that he thought the proposed payments under the Young plan were 'completely impossible' and that he would prefer to continue with the Dawes plan even though that would result in an immediate crisis.[81]

The senior ministers present were more impressed by the significant savings that the Young proposals offered over the next ten years (compared to the Dawes plan) and had no wish to face a crisis sooner rather than later. Wirth warned that the crisis would be on a scale for which the

[76] Schacht to Müller, 19 Feb. and 27 Apr. 1929; minutes of a meeting between Schacht, ministers, and officials, 29 Apr. 1929: Vogt (ed.), *Kabinett Müller*, nos. 130, 184–5.

[77] Hoesch to Auswärtiges Amt, 29 Apr. 1929: *ADAP*, ser. B, xi, no. 202.

[78] Memorandum of the meeting with Gilbert on 13 Nov., dated 22 Nov. 1928: ibid. x, no. 147. Schacht learned of the conversation from Schubert on 24 Nov. and immediately protested against Stresemann having discussed figures with Gilbert.

[79] Minutes of a meeting between Schacht, ministers, and officials, 29 Apr. 1929; Müller to Schacht, 30 Apr. 1929: Vogt (ed.), *Kabinett Müller*, nos. 185, 188.

[80] Minutes of the meeting between Schacht and senior ministers, 1 May 1929: ibid., no. 190.

[81] Cabinet minutes, 1 May 1929: ibid., no. 191.

methods of parliamentary government would no longer be adequate. After Schacht had left, Stresemann expressed scepticism about experts. He reminded his colleagues that in 1923 Stinnes and Vögler had told Cuno in that very room to leave the economic consequences of the Ruhr occupation to them, only subsequently to bombard Stresemann with demands to reach a settlement with France. He also agreed with Wirth—very few realized 'the horrifying extent' of a financial crisis.

The cabinet agreed to inform the experts of its unanimous view that acceptance of the Young proposals was 'inevitable' given the danger of the alternatives.[82] Partly because of differences between the Allies, the negotiations dragged on for another month. There were two further hitches on the German side. Vögler resigned and was replaced by Kastl, who fortunately shared the government's view of the situation and was determined to sign the report.[83] The last difficulty arose from the Belgian demand for compensation for the inflationary effects of the paper currency issued by the German wartime occupation, a problem made more difficult by the German hope of recovering Eupen-Malmédy as part of a settlement and the personal antagonism between Schacht and the Belgian expert, Émile Francqui. To get round this difficulty Stresemann offered separate negotiations with the Belgian government which were to be concluded before the Young plan was finally approved by the governments concerned.[84] The deadlock was broken and the plan was signed by the experts on 7 June, Schacht surprisingly expressing optimism to Stresemann and describing the plan as 'a very great step forward'.[85]

Protection of Minorities and Frontier Revision

Although reparations and the Rhineland were the key issues of foreign policy in 1929, Stresemann also became heavily involved in the question of League protection of minorities. After an angry exchange with the Polish foreign minister August Zaleski at the council meeting in December 1928, Stresemann introduced a discussion of the principles of minority

[82] Cabinet minutes, 4 May 1929: Vogt (ed.). *Kabinett Müller*, no. 194.

[83] Minutes of a meeting between senior ministers, Kastl, and officials, 20 May 1929: ibid. no. 205.

[84] Cabinet minutes, 31 May 1929: ibid., no. 214; Stresemann's memorandum of a meeting with the Belgian ambassador Robert Everts, 31 May 1929: *ADAP*, ser. B, xi, no. 263.

[85] Pünder to Müller, 9 June 1929: Vogt (ed.), *Kabinett Müller*, no. 222. Stresemann was on his way via Paris to a meeting of the League council in Madrid.

protection and proposals for reform of League procedures at the March meeting and he was only reluctantly persuaded to let the matter rest after modest improvements had been agreed at the subsequent meeting in June. Although not much resulted from the initiative, it throws an interesting light on his policy.

His motives are puzzling.[86] The League's responsibilities in relation to national minorities in the independent states of eastern Europe had been one of the reasons Stresemann put forward for joining in 1924–5. Once Germany became a member, however, he had not tried to make an issue of the protection of German minorities. He did not challenge the principle which the council had tacitly accepted in 1925 that minority protection should be regarded as a temporary measure to assist assimilation. Nor did he protest against a decision, taken in anticipation of German membership, to exclude from the committees which considered petitions from the minorities, states of the same nationality as the minority concerned.

In its first two years as a League member Germany adopted in general a watching brief, accepting the decisions of the committees on most petitions. The priority of German policy was to win the trust of the Western powers and accelerate the end of post-war sanctions. Any attempt to exploit the minorities issue would have cut across this priority by antagonizing Poland and causing suspicion in France and Britain. Meanwhile the minorities were supported by clandestine subsidies and advice on how to present petitions to the League, helping to maintain the German community in Poland in particular as an instrument of future territorial revision, and also helping to keep the support of minority organizations for the government and giving it a measure of control over them.[87]

The challenge is to explain why German tactics changed abruptly in 1928–9 when its priorities—Rhineland evacuation and a reparations settlement—remained unaltered and were more pressing than ever. The change of tactics also seems inconsistent with Stresemann's attempts, through Rauscher, to achieve détente with Poland and conclude both a new trade treaty and a settlement of the issue of the expropriation of German farmers. Stresemann committed his authority in cabinet to the

---

[86] There is a large literature on the subject. Baechler, *Stresemann*, 831–54; Schot, *Nation oder Staat?*; Kimmich, *Germany and the League*, 131–49; Fink, 'Stresemann's Minority Policies'; Marshall M. Lee, 'Gustav Stresemann und die deutsche Völkerbundspolitik 1925–1930', in Michalka and Lee (eds.), *Stresemann*, 350–74.

[87] Krekeler, *Revisionsanspruch*, 43–8; Schot, *Nation oder Staat?*, 177–81.

successful outcome of these negotiations against the obstructive tactics of the German agrarian lobby.[88]

It is natural to look to domestic politics for the answer. By the autumn of 1928 there was growing dissatisfaction with what was seen as the stagnation of the Locarno policy. There was a general sense that Germany had given sufficient evidence of good faith but was still the victim of discrimination—expressed in Müller's reference to the 'double face' of international relations in his speech to the League assembly in September. The comparative neglect of minorities issues by the government aroused criticism not only from the minorities themselves and the opposition parties but also from within the coalition, particularly from the Centre Party on behalf of the Catholic population of Upper Silesia.[89]

The pressure made it increasingly difficult for Stresemann to maintain the policy of restraint. There was probably also a further consideration. Since 1925 he had used the support of the minorities' organizations for his League policy as an answer to nationalist critics, one which proved effective even within the ranks of the DNVP. As we have seen, Stresemann secured the post of director of Ossa, the organization which channelled subsidies to the German minority in Poland, for a prominent DNVP politician, Lindeiner-Wildau. Stresemann may have hoped that Lindeiner-Wildau would succeed Westarp as leader of the party in 1928.[90] Once

---

[88] The protracted bureaucratic battle was eventually decided in favour of the Auswärtiges Amt. Hermes, who had been appointed under the Marx government in Dec. 1927 to conduct the negotiations, despite being a prominent representative of the agricultural lobby (president of the Vereinigung der Deutschen Bauernvereine—the Union of German Peasant Farmers' Associations—1928–33), repeatedly obstructed the process until he was forced to resign in Sept. 1929. Rauscher then took over the trade negotiations as well as those on the expropriation issue. The latter was resolved by a treaty signed on 31 Oct. 1929 and ratified by the Reichstag on 12 Mar. 1930. The trade treaty was signed on 17 Mar. 1930 just before the Müller government fell, but faced opposition both within Germany and Poland and was never ratified. Vogt (ed.), *Kabinett Müller*, pp. xxix–xxx; Doss, *Zwischen Weimar und Warschau*, 116–23; Schulz, *Wirtschaftsordnung*, 190–3, 221–8.

[89] Proceedings of the Reichstag foreign affairs committee, 4 Oct. 1928; Schot, *Nation oder Staat?*, 205–6. Speeches by Kaas and Dr Schreiber in the Reichstag, 19 Nov. 1928; speech by Ulitzka (a member from Upper Silesia), 24 June 1929: *Verhandlungen des Reichstags*, vol. 423, pp. 428, 480; vol. 425, pp. 2826–9.

[90] Stresemann noted that Lindeiner-Wildau had refused to allow his name to go forward as a candidate for party chairman because it would have meant giving up his salary from Ossa. According to Stresemann's information, in 1928 Lindeiner-Wildau had even drawn a double salary of 36,000 marks. If, as seems probable, Stresemann's purpose in securing the position for Lindeiner-Wildau had been to encourage support for his foreign policy within the DNVP, he must have been annoyed that Lindeiner-Wildau should have turned down the chance of becoming leader for the sake of his Ossa salary. Notes, dated 18 Jan. 1929 (Nl. 76).

Hugenberg was elected, Stresemann had a new incentive for keeping the support of the minorities' organizations. By taking up the issue of minority protection, he may have been hoping to divide the opposition and encourage moderate Conservatives to secede from the DNVP.

The background to Germany's new policy was a long-running dispute over the right of parents in Polish Upper Silesia to decide whether their children should go to Polish or German schools.[91] The Polish authorities had been annoyed to find Polish-speaking families opting for German schools for their educational advantages and had taken measures to prevent the practice by imposing a linguistic test. That was resented by the German minority as a violation of their rights, which had been guaranteed by both Germany and Poland in the Geneva convention of 1922. The dispute went to the League council in March 1927, where a compromise was agreed for that school year only. When the Poles renewed the linguistic test in the autumn, Stresemann had the matter referred to the International Court at The Hague, which delivered an ambiguous judgement in February 1928.

At subsequent council meetings the German delegation played down the dispute but the minority organization, the Deutscher Volksbund, became increasingly dissatisfied. In November Stresemann asked his officials what action Germany could take on the minorities issue and they suggested a reform of League procedure for dealing with petitions and possibly the establishment of a permanent League commission for minorities, on the model of the mandates commission, a proposal which various interested organizations had already put forward.[92] A proposal for procedural reform would have the advantage that Germany would be seen to be taking up the issue of minorities without involving itself directly in conflict with Poland.

Stresemann was temporarily diverted from this course when the Polish foreign minister Zaleski launched a violent attack on the Deutscher Volksbund at the council meeting in December. Zaleski was responding to what he saw as an organized campaign to flood the League with petitions from the German minority and thus turn opinion against Poland. In the course of his speech he accused the leader of the Volksbund, Otto Ulitz, of high treason.[93] Stresemann was taken aback. There

---

[91] Baechler, *Stresemann*, 843–6; Raitz von Frentz, *A Lesson Forgotten*, 226–33.

[92] Schot, *Nation oder Staat?*, 207–8.

[93] Minutes of the 53rd session of the council, 10–15 Dec. 1928: *League of Nations Official Journal*, 10/1 (Jan. 1929), 68–70.

had been an agreement that the German and Polish delegations would both simply accept the report of the relevant committee on the latest stage of the school dispute. As Stresemann saw it, 'There was a gentleman's agreement without a Polish gentleman.'[94] Zaleski had warned Schubert that he would have to say something, but Stresemann can scarcely have been prepared for what followed. In attacking the Volksbund, Zaleski also aimed to discredit the German government's tactic of encouraging the minority to submit petitions.

Stresemann had no option but to reply or face the reaction of the minorities and public opinion in Germany. In fact, he let his anger boil over. According to Chamberlain, 'he went absolutely white and it was clear... that his passion was uncontrolled'.[95] He accused Zaleski of being prompted 'by a spirit of hatred' towards the German minority and rejected the suggestion that minorities who asserted their legitimate rights were thereby undermining the authority of the states to which they were subject.[96] Unwisely, he added that 'high treason and love of the old country are very closely akin and there are well-known men held in high esteem who have been guided by that love'—an unmistakable reference to Piłsudsuki who had been imprisoned by both the Russians and the Germans before Poland regained its independence after the war. Stresemann punctuated his speech—and the subsequent translation—by pounding the table with his fist and finished by demanding that the whole question of minorities be discussed at the next meeting of the council.[97] It was left to Briand as chairman to put an end to the unedifying spectacle and, to Stresemann's satisfaction, he appeared to take the German side, saying that there could be no question of the League becoming 'indifferent to the sacred cause of minorities'.[98]

Stresemann's outburst earned him applause at home.[99] He realized, however, that he had made a tactical error, telling his family, 'That was not my best deed.'[100] If Germany were to succeed in obtaining better guarantees of minority rights from the League, it was essential to allay suspicion that the real purpose was to destabilize Poland. By allowing

[94] Stresemann to Auswärtiges Amt, 16 Dec. 1928: *ADAP*, ser. B, x, no. 215.

[95] Chamberlain to Rumbold, 19 Dec. 1928: *DBFP*, ser. 1A, v, no. 299.

[96] *League of Nations Official Journal*, 10/1, 70.

[97] Sauerwein noted that the effect was somewhat comical as Stresemann used his fist at the wrong points in the translation: Sauerwein, *30 ans à la une*, 186.

[98] *League of Nations Official Journal*, 10/1, 70.

[99] See, e.g. the messages of congratulations in Nl. 75.

[100] Wolfgang Stresemann, *Mein Vater*, 547.

himself to be provoked by Zaleski, Stresemann had made the task more difficult.

Before the March 1929 meeting of the council, Stresemann took care to explain his plans to the other powers.[101] He assured them that he intended to conduct the discussion in a way which would strengthen the standing of the League and without referring to particular governments. In his speech to the council he argued that it was the duty of the League to uphold the rights of minorities and that 'a regime of justice' would help to ensure peace.[102] As usual he addressed the objections openly:

It is said, for example, that the rights of minorities may have the effect of supporting a movement which is directed against the integrity of the state and that it may lead to an irredentist agitation. Frankly, I do not think that we have in the present century established a condition of affairs which is eternal, and that idea is very clearly expressed in the covenant of the League of Nations. These, however, are considerations which have nothing to do with the question of minorities . . . It is completely mistaken to say that in supporting the rights and educational liberties of minorities use is being made of a weapon with which to break up states. The peace between nations will be all the more stable as the cry of minorities whose cultural life is threatened is heard less widely in the public opinion of the world.[103]

Stresemann made a number of suggestions for reform of existing League procedures, including the involvement of minorities in the process of considering the petitions and, more controversially, the involvement of states of the same nationality as the minority concerned.

His speech met with a mixed reception. Chamberlain agreed that the purpose of League protection was not cultural assimilation but the creation of conditions which would encourage the loyalty of minorities to their host states.[104] But he criticized Stresemann for having referred to the territorial changes allowed for by the League covenant. Briand, on the other hand, was sceptical. He offered an almost textbook analysis of the problems for an international organization which had to combine 'the

---

[101] Stresemann to German embassies, 15 Feb. 1929: *ADAP*, ser. B, xi, no. 73.

[102] Minutes of the 54th session of the council, 4–9 Mar. 1929: *League of Nations Official Journal*, 10/4 (Apr. 1929), 518–22. Stresemann's speech was also published in German, *Der Schutz der Minderheiten. Rede des Reichsministers des Auswärtigen Dr. Gustav Stresemann in der Sitzung des Völkerbundrats vom 6. März 1929 über die Garantie des Völkerbundes für die Bestimmungen zum Schutz der Minderheiten* (Berlin: Reichsdruckerei [1929]).

[103] *League of Nations Official Journal*, 10/4, 520. (I have made minor changes to the translation from the German text.)

[104] Ibid. 525.

protection of minorities with respect for the sovereignty of nations' and remarked drily that Stresemann's philosophical principles might be exploited by the unscrupulous for political ends.[105]

The whole issue was referred, as Stresemann proposed, to a committee with wide terms of reference, to be chaired by Chamberlain. Despite this success, measured against Polish attempts to restrict the scope of the committee, the reaction in Germany was critical.[106] There was more disappointment when the committee recommended only marginal changes of procedure.[107] Stresemann wanted to defer consideration of the report to the meeting of the League assembly in September, hoping that the recent election of a Labour government under MacDonald—who had endorsed the idea of a permanent minorities commission—would make a difference to the British position.[108] However, Stresemann was not able to attend the first meetings of the council in June and Schubert decided not to press for a deferment in order to preserve the improvements contained in the report. Stresemann was initially dissatisfied with Schubert's explanation—a rare example of friction between them—but he reluctantly accepted the report while making it clear that he reserved the right to raise the matter again.[109]

Stresemann did not let the matter rest. In a German newspaper article entitled 'The Minority Question as a Problem for Peace', he traced the history of the issue to the adoption of the principle of the nation state following the French Revolution and the centuries-old mixture of nationalities in central and eastern Europe.[110] He pointed out that there were German communities in twenty-one of the thirty-one European states and that there were more than 200 German members of parliaments in non-German states. He concluded that 'this historically determined inconsistency between state and nation cannot be removed by the technique of drawing frontiers', though he was quick to add that the Paris peace treaties had been more concerned with weakening the defeated enemy

---

[105] *League of Nations Official Journal*, 10/4, 528.

[106] Fink, 'Stresemann's Minority Policies', 414–15.

[107] Undated memorandum on Schubert's report to Müller on 1 June 1929: *ADAP*, ser. B, xii, no. 12.

[108] Fink, 'Stresemann's Minority Policies', 412.

[109] Minutes of the 55th session of the council, 10–15 June 1929: *League of Nations Official Journal*, 10/7 (July 1929), 1006–7. Schubert's notes on the incident in Krüger collection, Marburg, Nl. Schubert, Staatssekretärsakten, 14.

[110] 'Die Minderheitenfrage als Friedensproblem', *Kölnische Volkszeitung*, 582, 20 Aug. 1929, special supplement.

than respect for the nationality principle. He returned to the subject again in his speech to the League assembly in September, arguing that all members of the League had an interest in making minority guarantees effective in the interests of peace.[111]

Did Stresemann intend, despite his denials, to use the minorities issue as an instrument of territorial revision? A German official in the League organization intepreted it in that way, saying the purpose was to keep the issue alive for a future where Germany would be able to act more freely— 'to keep certain states weak by supporting their minorities' and 'to demonstrate the necessity of returning certain areas to Germany'.[112]

So far as Stresemann is concerned, it is primarily a question of Poland. Apart from Poland, his argument that respect for minority rights would serve the cause of European peace and stability was almost certainly genuine. The case of Poland is more complicated because he had not given up hope of frontier revision in the long term and indeed he believed that peace would never be secure without it.[113] However, in 1929 there was no prospect of frontier revision and his other policies were aimed at improving relations with Poland.

The main explanation for the apparent inconsistency is, as we have seen, the pressure of domestic politics. Specifically the campaign for minority rights provided political cover for reaching agreement with Poland over trade and the expropriation of German farmers. In particular, it served to reassure the German minority that their interests would not be sacrificed and made it possible for Stresemann to claim that he still had their support.[114]

The tactics were no doubt discussed with Rauscher, who spent the Whitsun holiday with Stresemann in Heidelberg in May 1929. The fact that Stresemann invited Rauscher is itself significant. According to Eschenburg, who was there, Stresemann intended to make Rauscher state secretary in succession to Schubert, information confirmed by Wolfgang Stresemann.[115] One motive for the choice of Rauscher was probably to improve relations between the Auswärtiges Amt and the SPD, since

---

[111] *League of Nations Official Journal*, Special Supplement no. 75 (1929), 69–70.

[112] Renthe-Fink to Weizsäcker, 9 Jan. 1929: *ADAP*, ser. B, xi, no. 73, n. 4.

[113] Baechler, *Stresemann*, 852.

[114] For instance in his reply to von Freytagh-Loringhoven in the Reichstag debate on 24 June 1929: *Verhandlungen des Reichstags*, vol. 425, p. 2883.

[115] Eschenburg, *Also hören Sie mal zu*, 224–6. Wolfgang Stresemann to the author, 20 Apr. 1992, and Wolfgang Stresemann, *Wie konnte es geschehen?* (Frankfurt am Main: Ullstein, 1990), 115.

Rauscher belonged to the SPD and had been head of the government press service in 1919–20 before embarking on a diplomatic career.[116] However, Stresemann would hardly have considered promoting his envoy to Poland unless they were agreed on the policy to be followed.

There is no record of their discussions in Heidelberg. However, there is a clue in a letter from Rauscher to Müller in November 1929, defending the agreement he had just reached with the Poles on the expropriation issue.[117] He wrote that the opposition from the German minority to the agreement was motivated in part by the fear that 'a real German–Polish détente could weaken Germany's commitment to stand up for minority interests and cause the German public, especially given good trading conditions, to resign itself to the territorial division created by the Versailles treaty'. He rejected the criticism that the agreement was a stage towards an 'Eastern Locarno', saying it preserved the German community for 'one day, when the corridor question is seriously addressed and becomes truly relevant'. Meanwhile German policy could not afford to be governed by the 'unbridled Polophobia' of the opposition.

In his official report, Rauscher gave his personal assessment of the future of German–Polish relations.[118] The agreement, he said, marked Germany's acceptance of Poland as 'a member of the European family of nations' instead of simply a temporary state heading for collapse. As an agrarian state, he argued, Poland was less vulnerable to crisis than industrial societies and its financial weakness would 'never be such as to threaten its survival as a state'. But this weakness did provide an 'extraordinary opportunity' for German economic penetration. Normalization of German–Polish relations would also weaken Poland's ties to the Western allies and provide the best protection for the German minority—better than action at the League, which had only propaganda value. If Germany seized its opportunities the agreement could become 'an instrument of economic and political expansion'.

---

[116] I owe this suggestion to Professor Krüger, and also the following reference, which offers a striking example of criticism from a leading Social Democrat. In a letter to Müller on 25 Aug. 1928, Otto Braun complained about the limited circle from which the Auswärtiges Amt was recruited, calling them 'monocled apes' and deploring 'Stresemann's weakness in this area and the narrow-minded stupidity of Schubert in all areas'. Friedrich Ebert Stiftung, Bonn, Nl. Müller, 1.

[117] Rauscher to Müller, 17 Nov. 1929: ibid. After Stresemann's death in October Rauscher was clearly looking to Müller for political support.

[118] Rauscher to Auswärtiges Amt, 1 Nov. 1929: *ADAP*, ser. B, xiii, no. 93; Krüger, *Aussenpolitik*, 503–4.

Rauscher's policy could be summarized as détente with Poland, despite the fears of the German minority and the domestic unpopularity of such a course, in the hope that Poland's growing economic dependence on Germany would make possible territorial revision at some time in the future. Given Stresemann's closeness to Rauscher, it is most probable that he shared the same views. Stresemann's initiative on minority rights helped to protect the policy of détente from criticism by the minority itself and the German public. And Rauscher and Stresemann believed that détente was the only policy which might lead ultimately to revision.

A Franco-German Alliance?

Stresemann's main concern in the summer of 1929 was to reach an agreement on the Young plan coupled with Rhineland evacuation. An agreement was crucial to maintaining the confidence of foreign investors and keeping the threat of financial crisis at bay. It was obvious that Hugenberg was pursuing the counter-strategy, hoping that a crisis would provide the opportunity to replace the great coalition with some kind of authoritarian government. Reports confirming these intentions had reached Stresemann already in January 1929.[119] By the summer he was also increasingly concerned by the threat posed by the Nazis and Hugenberg's alliance with Hitler against the Young plan.

Stresemann discussed the prospects with Briand at the June meeting of the League council in Madrid.[120] They agreed that a conference should be held to discuss the Young plan and related issues. Briand was in an expansive mood, talking in Thoiry-like terms of a resolution of all the outstanding issues and 'a kind of liquidation of the war'. He went even further, suggesting that 'the next task' would be to consider how to achieve 'the political and economic consolidation of Europe' to maintain peace and resist American dominance. Stresemann pointed out that Germany was dependent on American capital, but Briand declared airily that financial circles and public opinion at large would support 'the new cooperation' as soon as outstanding issues were settled. To test Briand's resolve, Stresemann raised the issue of the Saar, but even here Briand was conciliatory,

---

[119] Note, dated 18 Jan. 1929, on information from Hans Redlhammer, who was the head of the Auswärtiges Amt section on Germany and through whom internal intelligence sources were channelled. Also note, dated 16 Feb. 1929, on information from Schubert (Nl. 76, 77).

[120] Memorandum of their meeting, 11 June 1929: *ADAP*, ser. B, xii, no. 19.

saying that although a political solution would be very difficult, it might be possible to reach some form of economic agreement.

Stresemann was encouraged by this conversation, although it did not escape the German delegation that Briand's purpose might have been to persuade Stresemann to drop his opposition to the report on minorities procedure, which was about to be considered by the council.[121] However, the Germans also knew that the French had a more serious motive for obtaining early agreement on the Young plan. The French parliament would then be more likely to ratify the agreement on debt repayment to the United States and thus avoid an immediate payment of $400 million which would otherwise fall due. That was confirmed when Stresemann met Poincaré and other members of the French cabinet in Paris on the return journey from Madrid. Poincaré indeed pressed for the conference to meet at the earliest possible date.[122]

Stresemann reported to the cabinet on 21 June at a meeting at which he also presided, as Müller was seriously ill with a perforated gall bladder.[123] The cabinet decided to accept the Young plan as the basis for negotiations at a conference, together with a 'simultaneous total liquidation of the questions still outstanding from the world war'.

The government then had to face a foreign affairs debate in the Reichstag. The timing was awkward as ministers were forced to defend the Young plan without wanting to praise its advantages too loudly in advance of negotiations. Stresemann decided to take the argument to the opposition.[124] Westarp had accused the government of accepting the Young plan merely to save the coalition, by taking advantage of the short-term financial savings which the plan offered. In reply Stresemann attacked the DNVP's alternative of allowing the Dawes plan to continue to a crisis which, he predicted, would mean 'the sacrifice of the whole industrial middle class'. He ridiculed Hugenberg, who had said he would 'rather be a proletarian with the whole nation until the hour of liberation came than a steward and beneficiary of foreign capital against the nation'. Stresemann asked, 'Who will be the proletarian?' and answered that the people who

---

[121] Pünder to the Auswärtiges Amt, 12 June 1929: *ADAP*, ser. B, xii, no. 21.

[122] Stresemann's report to the cabinet, 21 June 1929: Vogt (ed.), *Kabinett Müller*, no. 233.

[123] Ibid.

[124] Reichstag speech, 24 June 1929: Zwoch (ed.), *Reichstagsreden*, 280–94. See Plate 15. This photograph has been dated elsewhere to 8 Oct. 1923: Eschenburg and Frank-Planitz, *Stresemann*, 75; Wolfgang Stresemann, *Mein Vater*, facing p. 288. However, the presence of Curtius, Wirth, Hilferding, and Severing in the government row shows that the date of 24 June 1929, given by the Ullstein picture agency, is correct.

would suffer would not be the powerful but small family firms. He urged his audience to remember the Ruhr crisis where they had all misjudged the severity of the economic consequences, and not to be carried away by facile slogans such as 'through the crisis to freedom'.

Stresemann also included a cautious reference, along the lines of Briand's remarks, to the common interests of Europe in relation to the United States. In a second speech, replying to points made in the debate, he was more specific, saying he believed 'a time will come, when from economic necessity French, German and perhaps other European economies must seek a common way to maintain themselves in face of a competition to which they are not equal'.[125] He added that this would only be successful, however, if the 'poisoning' of their political relations by the remaining issues in dispute from the war was 'completely removed'.

Stresemann made a number of attempts to influence opinion abroad in the spring and summer of 1929. At the end of March, he wrote to D'Abernon protesting against the continued occupation of the Rhineland and saying that it was driving people back to the DNVP and would mean 'the end of the spirit of Locarno'.[126] In July, he asked Sauerwein to visit him at Bühlerhöhe where he was resting in preparation for the conference. According to Sauerwein, Stresemann was now more concerned about Hitler than the DNVP. He told Sauerwein that unlike the 'absolutely conservative nationalist groups' who would never have a very large popular following, Hitler 'preached rebellion not only against the peace treaties but also against the social order. In this way he gathers up not only the patriotic elements but also the discontented . . . These people cause me great anxiety.'

Stresemann told Sauerwein that he hoped to achieve a settlement of reparations and the evacuation of the Rhineland at the forthcoming conference and also 'as soon as possible thereafter' the evacuation of the Saar. When Sauerwein demurred, pointing out that the Saar was a new demand, Stresemann floated ideas for a much more ambitious relationship between France and Germany, which would allow all the difficulties between them to be resolved, saying he dreamed of 'a close military,

---

[125] *Verhandlungen des Reichstags*, vol. 425, p. 2882. Krüger points out that Stresemann and Schubert were prepared to give Briand's ideas for a closer political and economic union of Europe a cautious welcome, though they were concerned about the impact on the United States and unwilling to forgo claims to further revision of the Versailles treaty. Krüger, 'Der abgebrochene Dialog: Die deutschen Reaktionen auf die Europavorstellungen Briands in 1929', in Antoine Fleury (ed.), *Le Plan Briand d'Union fédérale européenne* (Bern: Peter Lang, 1998), 289–306.

[126] Stresemann to D'Abernon, 30 Mar. 1929: *ADAP*, ser. B, xi, no. 144.

economic and political alliance' between the two nations. It would be better to have a moderately rearmed Germany in such an alliance than Germany as a constant source of unrest. Stresemann suggested that there were much more important questions for them to consider than the revision of particular articles of the peace treaties: Russia, the organization of central Europe and the Balkans, and the whole question of Asian politics. He went on: 'You cannot surely expect that Germany will remain for a long time yet, still in the role of a second-class power. Unless you compel it by the constant use of force which is expensive and in the long run very dangerous.' When Sauerwein objected that Germany's other relationships had caused too much mistrust in France for an alliance to be viable, Stresemann reacted passionately, saying there were no grounds for suspicion about German relations with the Soviet Union or other powers. He then added the warning that he did not know how much longer he had to live, and if his successor and the French government failed to maintain the policy of understanding 'peace in Europe will not last long'.

It is difficult to know what to make of this account, which was published by Sauerwein in the German press in 1932.[127] His post-war memoirs also contain a description of the conversation which is similar in several respects but omits any reference to the idea of an alliance.[128] Stresemann's concern about the NSDAP is confirmed from other sources. He obviously had an interest in persuading foreign journalists of the dangers that threatened if concessions were not made in time to a democratic Germany.[129] However he also told Eschenburg of his fears, saying he could not sleep for worry that Hindenburg might die suddenly.[130] He predicted that although Hitler would not win a presidential election he would be sufficiently successful to start a dynamic process which would be hard to

[127] Jules Sauerwein, 'Bei den Großen der Erde. Was ein Journalist erlebte', v, 'Stresemann ii', *General-Anzeiger für Dortmund*, 141 (24 May 1932).

[128] Sauerwein, *30 ans à la une*, 186–7. Only this account has been used previously by historians.

[129] In Apr. 1929 he warned the British journalist Bruce Lockhart, as they watched the SA march down the Wilhelmstrasse from Stresemann's window in the Auswärtiges Amt, that the refusal of the Allies to make concessions had lost him the support of German youth: 'that is my tragedy and your fault'. Bruce R. H. Lockhart, *Retreat from Glory* (New York: Putnam, 1934), 359–63. In his post-war memoirs, Sauerwein gives a particularly graphic account of Stresemann telling him to attend the Nuremberg rally in August to see Hitler for himself and adding: 'What you can give me today in an amicable fashion, he will demand of you in another tone and if you turn a deaf ear, he will take it by force. Remember M. Sauerwein, you must take this chance or go to war again.' Sauerwein, *30 ans à la une*, 187.

[130] Eschenburg, *Also hören Sie mal zu*, 227. Also Wolfgang Stresemann, *Mein Vater*, 578–81.

control. Retrospective accounts must be treated with caution but Eschenburg is a reliable witness. The NSDAP had also already started to make
gains in Landtag elections. It is unlikely that Stresemann had failed to
notice that in his political cradle, Saxony, they won 5 per cent in May 1929
doubling their vote from the 1928 Reichstag elections.[131]

Sauerwein's account of Stresemann's talk of an alliance cannot be confirmed from other sources but it is not inherently implausible. Stresemann
had argued since 1926 that peace depended on Franco-German rapprochement. He and Briand had previously discussed the problems of
piecemeal revision of the Versailles treaty which failed to win over public
opinion on either side. To the Germans, the concessions came too little
and too late. To the French, German lack of gratitude was an argument
against further concessions.

Briand had revived the idea of a settlement of all outstanding differences at their meeting in June. Stresemann could see that evacuation of
the Rhineland and even the return of the Saar would not put Franco-
German relations on a stable basis. If Sauerwein's account can be trusted
he was thinking ahead to how to manage future difficulties, including
making a degree of German rearmament—on which the Reichswehr had
already embarked—acceptable to the French.[132] He said that he would
not dare to speak of the idea of an alliance in the Reichstag or in a public
declaration. On the other hand he knew that Sauerwein would report the
conversation to Briand and the idea might be regarded as an alternative or
complement to the proposal for greater European unity which Briand had
outlined to him in June. The most interesting part of the conversation
is Stresemann's warning that Germany could not be held down by
France indefinitely. There seems no good reason why Sauerwein should
have invented such a statement. There also seems no reason to doubt
that Stresemann remained firmly wedded to the idea of Franco-German

---

[131] Lapp, *Revolution from the Right*, 184–8.

[132] Indeed, Stresemann referred to an interview which Sauerwein had conducted with Seeckt,
in which the General had argued that since France would never agree to disarm there should be a
compromise allowing Germany moderate rearmament. The reference should be read in the light
of the recent failure of the League's commission to prepare for the disarmament conference to
make any progress over disarmament on land. Britain and the United States had given up
demands for land disarmament in return for French support for their views on naval disarmament.
Germany was left isolated on the commission, and on 4 May 1929 withdrew its representative Count Bernstorff in protest. Although Germany continued to argue for general disarmament, within the Auswärtiges Amt the view began to gain ground that if no progress could be
made towards that goal Germany should argue instead for equal rights. Krüger, *Aussenpolitik*,
473–5.

cooperation as the only true basis for European peace. However, the tension remained between his desire for further revision to make Germany once again a first-class power so keeping public support, and Briand's equal need to maintain support by being seen to safeguard French security.

The Hague Conference

The German tactics for the conference which opened at The Hague on 5 August were to delay accepting the Young plan until their political demands had been met.[133] Stresemann was confident that they would obtain the evacuation of both remaining zones of the Rhineland. He also expected to be able to resist Briand's proposal for a new committee to monitor the disarmed status of the area—a proposal which was unpopular in the Rhineland after its experience of the French-dominated commission of occupation.[134] Success over the Saar was much more doubtful and Stresemann aimed only to achieve the opening of negotiations with a commitment to continue them afterwards. Apart from Stresemann the German delegation included three ministers—Hilferding (finance), Curtius (economics), and Wirth (occupied areas)—as well as officials and experts (including Schacht).

The main problem at the conference was the determination of the new British chancellor of the exchequer, Philip Snowden, to renegotiate the division of reparations between the Allies which had been proposed by the Young plan, as it had departed from the percentages agreed in 1920.[135] Snowden saw it as a matter of principle, correcting in his view the pro-French bias of the Conservative administration, and he seemed prepared to break up the conference.[136] Stresemann feared that the real reason was the preference of British Treasury officials for a return to the Dawes plan

[133] Cabinet minutes, 28 June, 2 Aug. 1929: Vogt (ed.), *Kabinett Müller*, nos. 237, 258.

[134] The Centre Party took a public stand against the idea of a new committee in an exchange of letters between Kaas and Wirth, the minister for the occupied territories. Stresemann was offended at the implication that he would not otherwise have remained firm on the issue. Minutes of the meeting of the Centre Party's Reichstag executive, 14 Aug. 1929: Morsey (ed.), *Protokolle*, no. 440; memorandum by Schubert, 15 July 1929: *ADAP*, ser. B, xii, no. 96.

[135] Wheeler-Bennett and Latimer, *Information on the Reparation Settlement*, 106–25; David Carlton, *MacDonald versus Henderson: The Foreign Policy of the Second Labour Government* (London: Macmillan, 1970), 33–56.

[136] Memorandum of a meeting between Stresemann and Snowden, 17 Aug. 1929: *ADAP*, ser. B, xii, no. 180.

and their indifference to German economic collapse, expecting it to benefit British exports.[137]

Snowden's aggressive tactics weakened Briand, whose position was in any case unenviable. Shortly before the conference Poincaré resigned on health grounds and Briand took over the government, maintaining the same coalition. It included representatives of the nationalist right, who regarded Briand with suspicion and limited his freedom of manoeuvre. His tactics were naturally the reverse of Stresemann's: to refuse political concessions until French receipts from the Young plan were guaranteed, including guarantees against German default. France was also isolated from Britain over evacuation of the Rhineland: the British foreign secretary Arthur Henderson made it clear that Britain was determined to evacuate with or without France.[138]

Briand was forced to prevaricate, refusing to give a date for final evacuation and pleading difficulties with his generals and the problem of withdrawing large numbers of troops in winter.[139] Stresemann enjoyed the irony, pointing out that an inability to move troops in winter would hardly reassure France's allies.[140] He understood the difficulty of Briand's position—telling German journalists that if the roles were reversed he was not sure that General Ludendorff would be cooperative—but he resented Briand's refusal to be open with him about his reasons.[141]

The German delegation pressed the French to solve the remaining issues in what Schubert called 'an elegant fashion' to prevent the whole policy of rapprochement being undermined.[142] Stresemann also warned Briand that if they were not able to set in motion an arrangement for the Saar, that could become the focus of discontent once the Rhineland was evacuated.[143] As the conference became increasingly protracted and bad-tempered, Stresemann took two initiatives to break the deadlock. He wrote Briand a personal letter telling him that he needed early evacuation of the Rhineland in order to defeat the opposition to the Young

---

[137] Stresemann's speech to the Reichsausschuß of the DVP, 30 Sept. 1929: Kolb and Richter (eds.), *Nationalliberalismus*, 844–5.

[138] Henderson to Lindsay, 9 Aug. 1929; Phipps to Sargent, 20 Aug. 1929: *DBFP*, ser. 1A, vi, nos. 300, 324.

[139] Memoranda of Stresemann's meetings with Briand, 8, 10, 16, 19, 21 Aug. 1929: *ADAP*, ser. B, xii, nos. 155, 161, 178, 188, 196.

[140] Stresemann's briefing of German journalists, 10 Aug. 1929 (Nl. 84).

[141] Ibid., 17 Aug. 1929 (Nl. 84); Stresemann to Löbe, 19 Sept. 1929 (Nl. 86).

[142] Schubert's memorandum of his meeting with Berthelot, 13 Aug. 1929: *ADAP*, ser. B, xii, no. 171.

[143] Memorandum of Stresemann's meeting with Briand, 16 Aug. 1929: ibid., no. 178.

plan.[144] He described their negotiations as 'a great European event, as the conclusion of the policy of Franco-German understanding which you and I have followed for years'. Stresemann warned that if Briand stuck to the view which he had expressed that afternoon, that evacuation would take over a year to complete, then 'I no longer feel able to continue this policy'.

On 21 August Stresemann addressed the leaders of all the main delegations, pointing out that Germany needed to know by 1 September whether the Young plan was to come into force that day as the experts had recommended.[145] He proposed a temporary arrangement in case they should fail to reach agreement in time, but he appealed to his colleagues 'as a statesman' to recognize that the sums in dispute were relatively small but the political costs of failure in terms of destroying public faith in international cooperation were large.

Stresemann's warnings appeared to have some effect.[146] After a further week of negotiations, including night sessions which brought him to the point of collapse, agreement was reached on both the financial and political issues.[147] The Germans were required to make some financial concessions as their contribution to raising the sum allocated to Britain, but they succeeded in all their political demands.[148] Of the experts present only Schacht opposed the agreement and even he did not at that time consider it important enough to justify resignation.[149]

---

[144] Stresemann to Briand, 19 Aug. 1929: *ADAP*, ser. B, xii, no. 191.

[145] Memorandum of the meeting, 21 Aug. 1929: ibid., no. 198. Cf. Snowden to MacDonald, 22 Aug. 1929: *DBFP*, ser. 1A, vi, no. 328 (enclosure).

[146] Phipps to Lindsay, 23 Aug. 1929; MacDonald to Snowden, 24 Aug. 1929: *DBFP*, ser. 1A, vi, nos. 335, 337. See Plate 25.

[147] Curtius records that during discussions with the French at about 1.30 a.m. one morning Stresemann, who was deathly pale and breathless, suddenly clutched his heart and said, 'I cannot go on any longer.' Hilferding, who was a qualified doctor, helped him back to the hotel and said to Curtius on returning to the meeting, 'Curtius, his time has run out'. Curtius, *Sechs Jahre Minister*, 90. Another member of the delegation recalled Stresemann's doctors saying that they should assume he might die within forty-eight hours: Eckhard Wandel, *Hans Schäffer* (Stuttgart: Deutsche Verlags-Anstalt, 1974), 116.

[148] The most important concession was to raise the amount of the annuity which Germany would have to pay unconditionally, i.e. without being able to ask for a moratorium, from 660 million marks to 700 million. The total amount, including the conditional element, remained unchanged—in the first year at nearly, 1800 million marks. The agreements are printed in Wheeler-Bennett and Latimer, *Information on the Reparation Settlement*, 235–40.

[149] Memorandum of the discussion within the German delegation, 28 Aug. 1929: *ADAP*, ser. B, xii, no. 216. Pünder's report of the further meeting on 29 Aug. 1929 when Curtius, in a pointed rebuke to Schacht, warned against the temptation to seek a cheap triumph at home: Vogt (ed.), *Kabinett Müller*, no. 29. Schacht, *The End of Reparations*, 114.

On the political issues Stresemann won the key prize, an agreement for total evacuation of the Rhineland by the end of June 1930. Nothing survived of Briand's proposed commission other than an agreement to use the existing machinery for arbitration provided for by the Locarno treaties. On the Saar, although not part of the formal business of the conference, the German and French governments exchanged notes agreeing to open negotiations.[150] When, on 31 August, the conference concluded, it seemed that despite all the difficulties it marked a major success for the policy of détente.

Stresemann was content, describing the achievement to the SPD president of the Reichstag Paul Löbe as 'concluding a stage of our foreign policy and making it possible for us to conduct in future a more ambitious policy of understanding free of the constraints of the constant battles over reparations and the occupied territory'.[151] At the same time, while recuperating in Switzerland, he read of the proposed referendum by the joint forces of Hugenberg, Hitler, and the Stahlhelm to convict ministers who signed the Young plan of high treason punishable by imprisonment. He said at first he thought he must have been reading the satirical *Kladderadatsch* rather than the *Neue Zürcher Zeitung*.[152] He predicted to Löbe that the referendum would suffer a heavy defeat. Nevertheless, he said, one had to be very careful as Hugenberg would understand how to win the lasting cooperation of his new allies 'and the goals of this organization are much more far-reaching than people in Germany assume'.

Immediately after the Hague conference Stresemann had returned to Berlin to report to the cabinet.[153] The cabinet approved the decisions taken by the German delegation and also supported Stresemann's proposal for a vigorous campaign against the 'unscrupulous propaganda' of the opposition. Stresemann suggested that when the evacuation of the Rhineland was complete, the German flag should be raised on Schloß Ehrenbreitstein above Koblenz, where during the occupation first the American and then the French flag had flown. He obviously hoped that the liberation of the Rhineland would wrong-foot his critics. As he said to Theodor Wolff, the editor of the *Berliner Tageblatt*, those who condemned his policy would not be in an enviable position.[154]

---

[150] Memorandum by Schubert, 30 Aug. 1929: *ADAP*, ser. B, xii, no. 224.

[151] Stresemann to Löbe, 19 Sept. 1929: ibid. xiii, no. 26.

[152] Stresemann's speech to the Reichsausschuß of the DVP, 30 Sept. 1929: Kolb and Richter (eds.), *Nationalliberalismus*, 855.

[153] Cabinet minutes, 3 Sept. 1929: Vogt (ed.), *Kabinett Müller*, no. 281.

[154] Interview with Theodor Wolff in Geneva, 11 Sept. 1929 (Nl. 86); abridged version in Bernhard (ed.), *Vermächtnis*, iii. 563–6.

Towards European Union?

From Berlin Stresemann went to Geneva for the meeting of the League assembly, where both MacDonald and Briand were also present. The occasion was given special significance by the agreements reached at The Hague. There was a sense that with the forthcoming evacuation of the Rhineland, Germany would be able to participate on a more equal basis as a truly sovereign power. Stresemann's aim, despite the new wave of opposition at home, was to maintain the policy of cooperation, a task he likened at a reception with journalists to the labours of Sisyphus.[155] Briand, with similar motives and facing similar opposition, wanted to move forward with the plans for a European federation which he had first raised with Stresemann in June.

In his speech to the assembly on 5 September Briand proposed an association of the European states with both an economic and a political dimension.[156] He was motivated partly by genuine idealism: a lasting horror of war—he had been the French premier during the battle of Verdun—and the desire to protect Europe from again falling prey to its divisions or to the new threats to its civilization, as he saw them, posed by the Soviet Union and the United States. In practical terms, a European federation would serve this larger purpose in several ways: it would provide a new political framework to make Germany's recovery as a great power more acceptable in France; economic integration would increase Europe's ability to resist American penetration and give it a stronger position in tariff negotiations—Congress had just passed the fiercely protectionist Smoot–Hawley law; an association of European states might also help to maintain the status quo, acting as a surrogate 'eastern Locarno' to block German attempts at frontier revision.[157]

Stresemann was supposed to speak the following day but he was too weak, and it was only on 9 September that he was able to address the assembly.[158] He opened with a review of the international situation,

---

[155] Stresemann's address, 5 Sept. 1929: Bernhard (ed.), *Vermächtnis*, iii. 568–9.

[156] *League of Nations Official Journal*, Special Supplement no. 75 (Geneva, 1929), 51–2.

[157] Franz Knipping, *Deutschland, Frankreich und das Ende der Locarno-Ära 1928–1931* (Munich: Oldenbourg, 1987), 84–9. Jacques Bariéty, 'Aristide Briand: Les Raisons d'un oubli', in Fleury (ed.), *Le Plan Briand*, 1–13.

[158] *League of Nations Official Journal*, Special Supplement no. 75, 67–71; German text in Bernhard (ed.), *Vermächtnis*, iii. 571–80. See Plate 16. Bernhard refers to 'serious heart attacks' preventing his speaking earlier. Count Bernstorff, who was in Geneva as the German representative for the disarmament negotiations, describes finding Stresemann one day leaning against the wall of the hotel 'almost unconscious': *The Memoirs of Count Bernstorff* (London: Heinemann, 1936), 289.

welcoming the evacuation of the Rhineland and drawing attention to the importance of reaching agreement on the Saar. He referred to the proposals under discussion on security and disarmament, making clear the German preference for arbitration as a way of solving disputes rather than new sanctions: 'War cannot be prevented by preparing war against war but only by removing its causes.' He expressed Germany's disappointment at the lack of progress on disarmament on land and demanded that it should be treated with the same urgency as naval disarmament. He also re-affirmed his commitment to an extension of the League's machinery for protecting minorities.

In a departure from his prepared text he then addressed Briand's proposals for Europe in a way which maintained German interests while keeping the way open to cooperation. He rejected the scepticism of those whom he called 'pessimists on principle', quoting the line 'A great idea seems crazy at first'. But he said that they should be clear about their goals and that he was opposed to policies directed against other parts of the world or aiming at economic autarky for Europe. He then warmed to a favourite theme, the excessive fragmentation of the European economy, comparing the situation to pre-unification Italy or Germany before the Zollverein.[59] One could only laugh, he said, at the internal barriers to trade that used to exist in Germany. Yet in their own day fresh divisions had been introduced by the new states established by the Versailles treaty. 'Where', he asked rhetorically, 'is the European currency, the European postage stamp?' Any progress in rationalizing economic conditions would help not only European firms but all who traded with Europe, and he promised German support for efforts towards that objective.

Stresemann concluded his speech by recording his satisfaction at the progress that had been made towards greater international understanding and by warning of the serious problems that remained. Referring to a re-mark of Briand's about the attraction still exercised by war over young people, he suggested that 'the technological wars of the future' would provide little opportunity for acts of heroism, and that the conquest of nature offered sufficient and more fruitful opportunities for such idealism. Their task in the League was the sober one of reducing international conflict. There were still conflicts and the work would not succeed in a

---

[59] The Zollverein was a customs union, which started with a single external tariff for the different parts of Prussia after the Napoleonic Wars and was subsequently extended to other German states.

rush of enthusiasm. It was, rather, the kind of activity described by Schiller which

> In the true building of eternity
> Lays only grain of sand on grain of sand,
> But thus from the mighty debt of time
> Minutes, days, years are struck out!

It was a stirring finale to a speech which had as usual combined Germany's national interests with League principles very effectively. Stresemann spoke as German foreign minister but also as someone who genuinely believed in peace and international cooperation.

Later the same day representatives of the European states met at Briand's invitation to discuss his proposals.[160] Briand expressed regret that Stresemann had restricted his remarks to the economic aspects of European cooperation. Stresemann responded by asking Briand to clarify his political ideas in a memorandum, saying that he must be able to explain at home what form of political cooperation was intended.

That exchange indicated the differences in approach which were to become clear after Stresemann's death. In May 1930 Briand circulated detailed proposals which emphasized the political dimension and included an extension of the Locarno guarantees to all of Europe.[161] In Berlin, where the great coalition had been succeeded by Brüning's minority government, the reaction was predominantly hostile. The proposals were seen by Brüning as obstructing Germany's claim to a 'sufficient, natural living space' and by Bernhard von Bülow, who was about to take over from Schubert as state secretary, as intended 'to impose new fetters on us'. Curtius, as foreign minister, was inclined to reply in a moderate tone but was urged by the cabinet to be more forceful and promised to give Briand's initiative 'a first-class burial'.[162] Given the lack of enthusiasm in Britain and elsewhere as well, the project was soon dead.

There would have been the same conflict of interest between German revisionism and French defence of the status quo if Stresemann had still been foreign minister. Whether his commitment to maintaining

---

[160] Note of the discussion, dictated by Stresemann, dated 9 Sept. 1929: *ADAP,* ser. B, xiii, no. 9.

[161] Knipping, *Ende der Locarno-Ära,* 155–61; Martin Vogt, 'Die deutsche Haltung zum Briand-Plan im Sommer 1930: Hintergründe und politisches Umfeld der Europapolitik des Kabinetts Brüning', in Fleury (ed.), *Le Plan Briand,* 307–29; Schulz, *Wirtschaftsordnung,* 230–48.

[162] Andreas Rödder, *Stresemanns Erbe. Julius Curtius und die deutsche Außenpolitik 1929–1931* (Paderborn: Schöningh, 1996), 113–19.

Franco-German cooperation would have made any difference to the result is a question to which we will return in the final chapter.[163]

Preparing for Hugenberg and Hitler

From Geneva Stresemann went to the Swiss lakeside resort of Vitznau to rest and prepare for the coming battles over ratification of the Young plan. In order to rally the DVP for the campaign he agreed to address the Reich committee on 30 September before a party conference in October.[164]

While he was in Vitznau he received reports that the coalition was in danger of collapsing over the vexed question of the deficit in the unemployment insurance fund. The basic problem was the clash between the SPD opposing cuts in benefits and the DVP refusing an increase in employers' contributions, which had already threatened to produce a crisis while Stresemann and other ministers were at The Hague in August.[165] The cabinet adopted increasingly desperate expedients to find an acceptable compromise but without success. Stresemann advised postponing the matter until it could be taken together with other financial measures connected with the implementation of the Young plan.[166] His hope was that the tax reductions made possible by the Young plan would create a suitable atmosphere for agreement on the unemployment fund. Other ministers, however, felt that the authority of the government had already been weakened by repeated delays and decided to convene the Reichstag to receive draft legislation on 30 September.

If the coalition was to be saved both the SPD and the DVP had to make concessions. The DVP had to accept a 0.5 per cent increase in employers' contributions, which it showed no sign of being willing to do.[167] Stresemann received urgent requests to return to Berlin to break the deadlock. In the words of the Prussian state secretary Weismann, he alone had the 'personal authority... to achieve any kind of willingness to make conces-

---

[163] According to Stern-Rubarth, Stresemann again developed the arguments for a European customs union in what proved to be his last Friday afternoon meeting with the foreign journalists on 27 Sept. 1929, speaking in very similar terms to those he had used at the League. Stern-Rubarth, *Three Men Tried*, 217–19.

[164] Kolb and Richter (eds.), *Nationalliberalismus*, 837.

[165] Minutes of the ministerial meeting, 14 Aug. 1929, and of meetings with party leaders, 15–16 Aug. 1929: Vogt (ed.), *Kabinett Müller*, nos. 266, 268, 271.

[166] His views were reported to a meeting of the cabinet by Pünder on 19 Sept. 1929: ibid., no. 298.

[167] Minutes of a meeting of leaders of the coalition parties, 18 Sept. 1929: ibid., no. 296.

sions from your party'.[168] Against the advice of his doctors he travelled back to Berlin on 25 September.[169]

At a cabinet meeting on 28 September Hilferding outlined the programme of tax cuts which he planned to make in 1930 and succeeding years as a result of savings under the Young plan.[170] Unfortunately, the cabinet was not in a position to make the information public since negotiations over the Young plan were not complete. There remained some subsidiary issues to be settled, including the allocation of the proceeds of German property confiscated by the Allies during the war. Stresemann warned that the German position would be compromised if it was known that the government was planning extensive tax cuts as a result of the reduction in reparations. The cabinet decided therefore simply to continue negotiations with the coalition parties on the unemployment fund without linking it to the tax programme—although, in fact, Hilferding had already briefed some of the parties' representatives confidentially.

On 30 September Stresemann addressed the DVP Reich committee for nearly an hour, allowing his anger and contempt for Hugenberg and his allies free rein.[171] He ridiculed the idea put forward by the Hugenberg camp that by rejecting the 'war guilt lie' Germany could free itself of reparations, pointing out that such 'folly' was hardly consistent with a belief in power politics. He accepted that the Young plan would prove insupportable in the long term—nobody, he said, believed that it would continue for the full fifty-seven years as proposed. But the question was how it compared now with the Dawes plan. Hugenberg had said that it would not matter if there was a major banking crisis; Hugenberg was, said Stresemann, 'not as stupid as he pretended'. The wealthy would be able to buy up family firms dependent on bank loans. Capital would go abroad; there would be a rush into material assets; the currency would come under pressure; savings banks would be stormed; the confidence which had been gradually rebuilt would be lost. No one could say whether Germany would then be offered better terms than the Young plan but given the views of the British Treasury, as represented by the almost Shylock-like

[168] Weismann to Stresemann, 18 Sept. 1929; also Curtius to Stresemann, 20 Sept. 1929 (Nl. 86).
[169] He told the meeting of the Reich committee of the DVP on 30 Sept. that his doctors had told him that he was behaving irresponsibly in attending meetings: Kolb and Richter (eds.), *Nationalliberalismus*, 837.
[170] Cabinet minutes, 28 Sept. 1929: Vogt (ed.), *Das Kabinett Müller*, no. 305.
[171] The text of his speech has only recently come to light. Kolb and Richter (eds.), *Nationalliberalismus*, no. 76.

character of Snowden, it seemed unlikely. Nor should they fall for the line that the crisis would lead to salvation. Stresemann admitted that he had believed that to be true at the time of the Ruhr occupation; he would not make the same mistake again. The Young plan offered Germany relief from at least 7 billion marks in reparations payments over the next few years, as well as the removal of economic controls and evacuation of the Rhineland. Yet Hugenberg, who was developing 'like a political cancer', had discovered a sudden preference for the Dawes plan. The savings from the Young plan offered the prospect of year-on-year tax reductions for five years, up to a quarter of direct taxes—though the government could not yet publicize it—and the attitude of the opposition to such an opportunity showed its total lack of responsibility.

Stresemann then turned to the political goals of the referendum campaign. He laughed off the accusation of treason, saying that the word had become completely devalued: he had been tempted to reply to messages of congratulation from DNVP politicians on the outcome of the Hague conference, thanking them 'with treacherous wishes'. But he accused Hugenberg of adopting the brutal tone of Nazi or Communist propaganda and therefore of being guilty of the violent crimes to which it might lead. Stresemann denied that he was an 'unconditional supporter of the great coalition': he was in favour of strong government and would cooperate with anyone who would follow a sensible policy. But given Hugenberg's attitude there would be no alternative for a long time to the great coalition.

Stresemann warned that Hugenberg's purpose went beyond the Young plan. Indeed business had only dared to attack the plan once it could be sure that it would be adopted. Hugenberg's real purpose was to divide the middle class. He was attracting many people with his talent for organization and money—the Stahlhelm, the association of German officers, the organization for the nobility. Stresemann added that the National Socialists had acquired substantial financial resources from somewhere and declared they would ostracize 'the Stresemann party'.[172] He warned that far from delivering industry from the socialist working class, as they claimed, the NSDAP would strengthen the left by dividing the nation further.

Stresemann then looked to the future. They would soon have to decide, he said, on the great issues of economic policy and whether to remain in the government. Again he blamed Hugenberg, saying that on economic

---

[172] Stresemann's assumption that the NSDAP was receiving large sums from business was widely shared but mistaken; unlike the bourgeois parties they were successful in fund-raising from their own members. Turner, *German Big Business*, 111–24.

issues the DNVP should be on their side and that was what made Hugenberg 'reprehensible' and 'a national plague, the destroyer of middle-class unity'. The coming battles would be 'exceptionally tough, with slander, threats, terror, financial pressure and everything else'. It was up to the DVP to preserve its unity and self-respect. If he possessed the strength he would travel throughout the Reich exposing the truth about the opposition:

Let us beware lest later if the collapse comes all these elements combine into a single organization for the next Reichstag elections, for the next civil war. It is not true that they are still wrestling with the question of what direction they should take; that is rubbish. I can see only that we must work with the left because parts of the right in Germany have gone mad.

Right radicalism, he pointed out, had repeatedly destroyed the process of evolution—the Erzberger murder, the Rathenau murder. Now they were faced with a new wave threatening the progress that had been made: 'Just imagine this bunch ruling Germany!' It was time for the DVP to say: 'This far and no further'.

Stresemann's speech was greeted with storms of applause and the meeting passed a resolution against the Hugenberg referendum unanimously and without discussion. Stresemann, clearly heartened, expressed the hope that their counter-offensive would not only strengthen the party but also perhaps lead to a realignment of the party system.

The meeting of the Reich committee was Stresemann's last great oratorical triumph, made all the more impressive because it was clear to those present that he was gravely ill.[173] He showed an acute understanding of the danger posed by Hugenberg and his allies at a time when they were still underestimated by most democratic politicians. He had always been on the side of parliamentary democracy against dictatorship. He had known Hugenberg for twenty-five years and saw that his tactics were to use the referendum against the Young plan as a way of bringing about an alliance between conservatives, nationalists, and the NSDAP for a joint crusade against the Republic. As so often before, he warned that the result would be civil war.

Having made sure of the support of the national party organization, Stresemann turned to the Reichstag party. As usual it proved more

---

[173] Memorandum by one of the leaders of the Reichstag party, Albert Zapf, who described Stresemann as knowing that he was near death and his speech as 'brilliant': BAK, Nl. Zapf, 8; Kolb and Richter (eds.), *Nationalliberalismus*, 837.

difficult to manage. In meetings between ministers and representatives of the coalition parties on 1 October the DVP spokesman Albert Zapf remained adamant that they could not accept an increase in employers' contributions—a position already taken by the employers' organizations.[174] At the same time he insisted that they did not want to provoke a government crisis and indicated that they might be able to accept higher contributions in two months time when the other financial measures were known. The DVP abstained in the second reading of the bill on the same day, allowing it to proceed to the crucial final vote on 3 October. Although the proposal to raise employers' contributions had in fact been dropped, the right wing of the party continued to oppose the measure, arguing that it was time to restore order to the public finances and that the insurance fund should be made to manage without state subsidies.[175]

A negative vote by the DVP on the third reading threatened to bring down the coalition. Having conferred with Müller, Stresemann— although suffering from a heavy cold—attended a long party meeting on 2 October and warned against rejecting the bill.[176] It was clear that the party was split down the middle and the alternatives were either to allow members to vote as they chose or to abstain en bloc. Stresemann secured a recess during which he consulted Pünder and Müller about the alternatives. They expressed a preference for allowing a free vote, as it would make a better impression on the other middle-class coalition parties who had also threatened defections if the DVP broke ranks.[177] Stresemann did not return to the second session of the meeting which decided against his wishes for abstention but that was sufficient to save the bill and the coalition.

In the evening Curtius called on Stresemann to discuss a meeting the following day at which Curtius was to represent Stresemann in reporting to the *Länder* representatives on the Hague conference.[178] He found Stresemann relaxing in bed in a cheerful and confident mood. He recalled

[174] Reich Association of German Industry to the chancellor, 25 Sept. 1929, and minutes of the meetings on 1 Oct. 1929; Vogt (ed.), *Kabinett Müller*, nos. 302, 308–9.

[175] Turner, *Stresemann*, 259; Richter, *Deutsche Volkspartei*, 575–82.

[176] Minutes of the meeting: BAK, R 45 II/67; Bernhard (ed.), *Vermächtnis*, iii. 582–3; Vogt, 'Letzte Erfolge? Stresemann in den Jahren 1928 und 1929', in Michalka and Lee (eds.), *Stresemann*, 461–2; Turner, *Stresemann*, 260.

[177] Memorandum by Pünder, dated 4 Oct. 1929: Thilo Vogelsang (ed.), *Hermann Pünder. Politik in der Reichskanzlei. Aufzeichnungen aus den Jahren 1929–1932* (Stuttgart: Deutsche VerlagsAnstalt, 1961), 11–13; Richter, *Deutsche Volkspartei*, 581.

[178] Curtius, *Sechs Jahre*, 87–8.

later that Stresemann was looking forward to a period of rest and recovery and then to taking part as foreign minister in the celebrations to mark the evacuation of the Rhineland. Later that evening Stresemann suffered a stroke which left him unconscious and paralysed on the right side. That was followed by a further and fatal stroke early the following morning, 3 October.[179]

[179] Zondek, *Auf festem Fusse*, 141–2.

11

Conclusion

'Only he who changes remains a kindred spirit.'[1]

Stresemann's death came as a shock although he had been seriously ill for over a year and close to death for at least two months. The sense of shock was partly because he had been active until the end. It was also because he was widely seen as irreplaceable. Kessler noted in his diary, 'It is an irreparable loss whose consequences cannot be foreseen.'[2] Stresemann was given a state funeral, which has been described as 'the last great ceremony of the Weimar Republic'.[3] According to some estimates some 200,000 Berliners watched the funeral procession as it followed its course on foot from the Reichstag to two minutes' silence outside the Auswärtiges Amt and from there the considerable distance to the Luisenstadt cemetery, where Stresemann was buried beside the graves of his parents.[4]

The response took even Stresemann's family by surprise.[5] It was as though a broad section of the German public had come to depend on him as a stable element in their political life. As the British ambassador

---

[1] A quotation jotted down by Stresemann and attributed by him to Goethe; note dated 30 Oct. 1927 and marked 'keep safely', probably by Bernhard: Stresemann material, Berlin. Wolfgang Stresemann, *Mein Vater*, 610. In fact, the quotation comes from the concluding poem of Nietzsche's *Jenseits von Gut und Böse*. I am grateful to Dr Roswitha Wollkopf for identifying the reference.

[2] Entry for 3 Oct. 1929: Kessler (ed.), *Diaries*, 367–8.

[3] Eschenburg, *Also hören Sie mal zu*, 228.

[4] Ibid. 229. Reichsgeschäftsstelle der Deutschen Volkspartei (ed.), *An der Bahre von Gustav Stresemann. Ein Gedenkblatt* (Berlin: Staatspolitischer Verlag [1929]).

[5] Wolfgang Stresemann, *Mein Vater*, 20.

Horace Rumbold reported, public opinion 'had developed a kind of vague confidence in him' and 'the suddenness of his death... was unquestionably a very real shock'.[6] The reaction abroad had also taken Germans by surprise, Rumbold thought, bringing 'the sudden realization that the onlooking world had understood more clearly than the Germans themselves the greatness of Stresemann and the merits of his achievement'.

Although they may have been surprised at the extent of his reputation abroad, his German contemporaries were not in fact in doubt about his achievement. He was seen by his admirers from among the great coalition parties as having restored Germany to the ranks of the great powers from the nadir of the Ruhr occupation and as having provided a vital link between right and left which had stabilized the Republic. Müller paid tribute to him in cabinet as a man of compromise who despite the divisions of party politics had performed outstanding service for the general good, and as a man of courage who had brought the Ruhr conflict to an end and pursued his ideals even against his party colleagues.[7] Theodor Wolff similarly praised Stresemann as a creative politican who had used parties as the instrument of his ideas.[8] Stresemann had understood, Wolff wrote, what was required both at home and abroad. His foreign policy had been one of clever realism and at home, despite contradictions in his attitude, he had identified himself ever more closely with the Republic.

Another liberal journalist, Max Reiner, described how in the autumn of 1922 Stresemann had broken the conventions of his political circle and established social contact with leading Social Democrats, preparing the way for the great coalition.[9] The SPD *Vorwärts* also stressed Stresemann's importance in crossing the political divide and described his loss as 'irremediable'.[10] It pointed out that he had been able to make the policy of Franco-German rapprochement acceptable in right-wing circles in a way which would have been impossible for a foreign minister from the SPD.

The view that Stresemann had become central to the stability of the Republic was shared by his critics. The radical pacifist author Carl von Ossietzky wrote that Stresemann's political values were completely

---

[6] Rumbold to Henderson, 10 Oct. 1929: *DBFP*, ser. 1A, vii, no. 22. Martin Gilbert, *Sir Horace Rumbold: Portrait of a Diplomat, 1869–1941* (London: Heinemann, 1973), 326–7.

[7] Cabinet minutes, 3 Oct. 1929: Vogt (ed.), *Kabinett Müller*, no. 310.

[8] 'Erinnerung', 6 Oct. 1929: Sösemann (ed.), *Theodor Wolff*, 262–6.

[9] Max Reiner, 'Stresemanns Aufstieg zu europäischer Größe', *Vossische Zeitung*, 472 (6 Oct. 1929).

[10] 'Stresemann gestorben', *Vorwärts*, 464 (3 Oct. 1929).

undistinguished, typical of the average bourgeois, and had become the prevailing values of the day. Nevertheless, he saw the system as 'badly shaken' by the loss of Stresemann's unique political talent. The sense of helplessness which pervaded the obituary notices showed how far 'the political equilibrium depended on him'.[11] From the other side of the political spectrum, Heinrich von Gleichen, who belonged to the group of 'Young Conservative' intellectuals in the DNVP, also saw Stresemann as essential to the Republic.[12] He described him as a master of the art of parliamentary government who had understood how to exploit the weaknesses of the system to carry through his foreign policy—indeed 'he provided in his person the element which bridged the weaknesses of the system and really preserved it'.

Even the political extremes subscribed with some qualification to the general view. The KPD's *Rote Fahne* described Stresemann's great period as the gradual consolidation of German imperialism after the defeat of the proletariat in 1923, although it predicted that his 'historical mission' had ended with the growing economic crisis and what it called his decision to join the imperialist powers against the Soviet Union.[13] The Nazi *Völkischer Beobachter* also saw Stresemann's influence as having been 'decisive' for the politics of the Republic, in keeping the coalition together and sticking to his 'pacifist illusions' with 'obsessive determination'.[14] Goebbels noted in his diary on Stresemann's death, 'A stone has been removed from the road to German freedom.'[15]

Stresemann clearly enjoyed an immense reputation, unique among the political leaders of the Weimar Republic, by the time of his death. How far was this reputation justified?

Let us consider first what was unusual about him and in the light of his biography how it can be explained. His reputation rested almost entirely on the achievements in the final phase of his career from the time he became chancellor in August 1923 aged 45. Were those achievements, as is often supposed, the result of a sharp break with his earlier career or are there features of the earlier career which help to explain his later and, apparently, surprising development?

[11] 'Abschied von Stresemann', *Weltbühne*, 25/41 (8 Oct. 1929); Harttung (ed.), *Schriften*, 408–12.

[12] *Deutsche Stimmen*, 41/19 (5 Oct. 1929), 600–5.

[13] 'Stresemanns Tod', *Rote Fahne*, 196 (4 Oct. 1929).

[14] 'Nach der Aera Stresemann', *Völkischer Beobachter*, 237 (12 Oct. 1929).

[15] Entry for 3 Oct. 1929: Elke Fröhlich (ed.), *Die Tagebücher von Joseph Goebbels*, i (Munich: K. G. Saur, 1987), 434.

Before the war Stresemann showed energy and ability, built up a highly successful business organization, and made a promising start in politics. But there was nothing that appeared to require particular explanation. Stresemann was a good example of a type of Wilhelmine career: a representative of light industry, on the left wing of the National Liberal Party, a constitutional liberal with an interest in social legislation for white-collar employees, nationalist—even pan-German—in his attitude to foreign policy.

The same was broadly true during the war. His political career progressed rapidly thanks to the patronage of Bassermann, Stresemann's ability as a speaker, and his skill in holding the different wings of the party together. He positioned himself as a liberal on constitutional reform and an annexationist on war aims. On Bassermann's death in 1917, he became leader of the Reichstag party and heir apparent for the party chairmanship. It was an unusual achievement for someone aged 39, especially from a lower-middle-class background, but again seemed to require no particular explanation other than ability and luck. Stresemann's actions during the war were anything but far-sighted. He pressed for unrestricted submarine warfare, the single most disastrous decision of the war, and he took a leading part in bringing down Bethmann Hollweg without any clear idea of what the consequences would be, other than the forlorn hope that the Kaiser could be persuaded to appoint Bülow instead.

It is not surprising that defeat and revolution should have all but destroyed his career. At this low point he did show extraordinary determination in persisting with a political career—the kind of determination which is a mark of all major politicians. He played the part which was thrust upon him of opposition leader: arguing against acceptance of the Versailles treaty and against the Weimar Constitution, making demagogic attacks on the coalition parties, not shrinking even from a thinly disguised anti-Semitism. What was exceptional and original about Stresemann in this phase, however, was that even as he played the role of opposition leader his clearly stated goal was to take his party back to the middle ground of politics and into government. He had no intention of remaining a junior partner of the DNVP in opposition. That was the beginning of his distinctive contribution to the politics of the Weimar Republic, and to explain it we need to look again at his early career.

Stresemann had always believed that the purpose of politics was power: from his first appearance on the political stage he urged the National

Liberals to grasp 'the latchkey to power'.[16] He may be seen as representative of a new type of professional politician in the sense described by Weber: ambitious, looking to new forms of political organization, and impatient of the limited powers of the Reichstag.[17] But his ideas were also shaped by his reading of the history of the National Liberal Party and his belief that its natural role was that of a middle party and preferably a party of government. That role it could only play, however, if it kept its independence from the Conservative Party—a point underlined by its inert dependence on the Conservatives in Saxony before he led it in a new direction.

The war also helped to shape Stresemann's political goals, despite the errors of judgement he made. By 1916–17 he could see the weakness of the imperial government in losing the propaganda war abroad and failing to maintain public support at home. There must be, he told the Reichstag, 'a fault in the political system'.[18] He contrasted that failure with the success of the democracies, particularly of Lloyd George in Britain. He felt he could help to provide what was missing and his campaigns on war aims and for reform both had the purpose of making Germany a more successful state—parliamentarization was necessary for Germany to defeat its enemies. He was also conscious of the administrative failures of the government, particularly in munitions production. When with defeat it became clear that the military and naval leadership—the heart of the old regime—had also been incompetent, his disillusion was complete. As he told a party meeting on 13 October 1918, 'the old system was utterly bankrupt, could no longer be saved and also did not deserve to survive longer'.[19]

During the first eighteen months of the Weimar Republic, his career could not develop in the way he wanted because he was discredited and his political base had fragmented. He was forced into the role of opposition leader of a rump of mainly right-wing National Liberals. But from the beginning it did not satisfy him and he set the DVP the goal of recapturing its old base and becoming a contender for power. In this perspective the period from 1918 to 1923 was not simply a time when he was forced to make a painful adjustment to new conditions but rather an interruption of the natural development of his career. By 1922–3 it had resumed its

---

[16] See above, pp. 34, 181.
[17] 'Politics as a Vocation': Gerth and Mills (eds.), *From Max Weber*, 77–128.
[18] See above, p. 84.   [19] See above, p. 114.

previous path, as he became gradually accepted as a natural and essential partner in Weimar government.

To resume that path he did, of course, have to make a painful adjustment to the Republic and to Germany's changed position in the world and that adjustment took some years to complete. But one reason he was able to make the change was precisely because he continued to believe, as he said in April 1919, that it was the DVP's 'historic task' to become, like the National Liberals, a middle party and the indispensable partner of the state.[20] That view above all defined his leadership and led to conflict with the right wing of the party, which wanted an alliance with the DNVP. Stresemann's determination to recover the middle ground of politics came before he felt much loyalty to the Republic, for at the time of the Kapp putsch that loyalty was still shaky. In the June 1920 elections the DVP recovered, as Stresemann had hoped, much of the old National Liberal vote from the DDP and entered the government. Despite his best efforts it withdrew again in May 1921 and returned only in November 1922. But from that date the DVP was continuously in government to Stresemann's death and beyond to October 1931.

Through his ambition to make the DVP a party of government Stresemann developed by stages from the political bankrupt of 1919 into the Weimar Republic's leading statesman. It was natural that he should become reconciled to the Republic because it represented the only available form of the constitutional democracy in which he believed and for which he had worked during the war. The murder of Rathenau completed his conversion to the defence of the Weimar Constitution against the organized violence of its right-wing enemies. His consistent advocacy of the great coalition as the only alternative to a polarization of politics between right and left, leading ultimately to civil war, made him the unanimous choice of the Republican parties as chancellor during the crisis of 1923. His recognition of the weakness of Germany's international position after the war and of the need to convince Germany's enemies of the facts of economic interdependence, as the only way to secure the revision of the Versailles treaty, also gave him an authoritative voice in foreign policy. From 1923 these twin policies of seeking common ground at home and abroad helped to give shape and coherence to Weimar politics. He played an influential role in the formation of every government. Minority governments of the middle parties were sustained in

[20] See above, pp. 129–30.

power by the SPD for the sake of his foreign policy and even the DNVP was forced fitfully to acquiesce in it as the price of office. Following the success of the SPD in the elections of 1928, he once again, from his sickbed, committed the DVP to a great coalition despite the opposition of a substantial number of its Reichstag members. It is no wonder that at his death he was regarded as the master of the art of parliamentary politics.

Stresemann clearly had distinctive ideas and that is an important part of what made his career unusual. But how was it possible for him to put these ideas into practice? The Marxist historian and former KPD member of the Reichstag, Arthur Rosenberg, wrote later:

It is a remarkable historical drama, that this lonely man who had neither armed force nor a reliable mass organization behind him, was nevertheless able to set his stamp on the development of Germany and essentially remain in power until his death. More than that he was able in foreign policy to achieve for defeated Germany more or less what he considered necessary. Such an achievement certainly does not detract from the importance of Stresemann's personality but it was only possible because the international economic and political situation in those years demanded the kind of solution which Stresemann had in mind.[21]

Let us look more closely at both sides of this explanation. What was the basis of Stresemann's power? How far was his achievement a personal one?

He depended in the first place on his ability to lead the DVP. He had unique authority as its founder, outstanding personality, and only great orator. He dominated the party conferences with speeches which combined wit, argument, and passion with the staple concerns of the rank and file. His position in the party approximated to that of the charismatic parliamentary statesman described by Weber.[22] There is an interesting comparison to be made with Hitler, whose power has also been described as that of a charismatic leader.[23] Their two parties alone in the Weimar Republic were identified in the public mind by their leaders. However, if Hitler's power depended on his success in projecting the social expectations of his followers, Stresemann offered leadership of a different kind.

---

[21] Arthur Rosenberg, *Geschichte der Weimarer Republik* (1st edn. 1935; repr. Frankfurt am Main: Europäische Verlagsanstalt, 1961), 141.

[22] 'Politics as a Vocation': Gerth and Mills (eds.), *From Max Weber*, 79, 107. Weber, writing in 1919, used Gladstone as his example and doubted whether the German party system would be capable of producing such leaders: ibid. 114.

[23] Ian Kershaw, *Hitler 1889–1936: Hubris* (Harmondsworth: Allen Lane, 1998), p. xxvi.

He tried to carry his party with him towards goals they might well not have adopted on their own. That required more than the ability to identify with his audience. He also appealed to their reason and idealism, in developing the National Liberal tradition in the direction he wanted. His hold was never as secure over the Reichstag party, where powerful individuals and interests, notably Ruhr industry, retained their independence. Nevertheless, by playing off the party's national organizations—the party conference, the national executive, and the Reich committee—against the Reichstag party he was able to bully or cajole his opponents into submission. So long as was alive, they dared not force his resignation.

One should also not exaggerate the strength of the opposition. His preference for government was shared by others and not simply those on the left wing of the party. Businessmen wanted influence on issues such as nationalization, reparations, Dawes credits, and trade treaties. Stresemann's argument in the early years of the Republic that there was no majority on the right was persuasive. For that reason he did not expect a collective desertion of even Ruhr industrialists to the DNVP. Instead the DNVP was drawn into government in 1925 and 1927-8.

There was, however, a persistent division between Stresemann and the right wing of the party over what they saw, correctly, as his preference for minority government or a great coalition to a bourgeois coalition with the DNVP. Stresemann tried to draw the DNVP into supporting his foreign policy in 1925 and was prepared to work with them again in 1927, but fundamentally he distrusted the DNVP and feared that bourgeois majority government would drive the SPD to the left. There was frequent tension between him and the leader of the Reichstag party, Scholz, who consistently tried to bring about a bourgeois majority government and prevent a great coalition. After the elections of May 1924 the Reichstag party was even prepared to force Stresemann's resignation as foreign minister to make possible agreement with the DNVP. That was not repeated, but the differences between him and a substantial section of the Reichstag party broke out again over the formation of the great coalition in 1928 and persisted until his death. In resisting the right wing of the DVP, Stresemann was helped by the Centre Party, whose preferences were on the whole similar to his, and paradoxically by the extremism of the DNVP which made them an erratic coalition partner. Nevertheless without Stresemann the DVP would have pursued a different coalition policy, and that is one measure of his importance.

Stresemann's conflicts with the DVP Reichstag party also reflected his concept of leadership. He asserted the right of the leader to decide party policy. In the tradition of nineteenth-century liberalism he defended the ideal of individual responsibility against the party caucus: individuals, he argued in 1929, should decide whether to accept appointment as ministers—they should not allow themselves to be sent into or removed from cabinets at the behest of the party.[24] In asserting this anachronistic doctrine, Stresemann was consciously trying to address the problem of how democratic politics in a multiparty system could be combined with stable government. Stresemann was, as we have seen, in many ways the type of the modern professional politician described by Weber. But he also recognized the dangers of the new form of mass politics. The domination of party caucuses could make government impossible. His own administrations had been brought down in October and November 1923 by the SPD caucus, as had the Marx government in December 1926; DNVP ministers had been forced to withdraw from the coalition in November 1925; in Stresemann's view, the 'hotheads' of the Centre Party had brought the Marx coalition of 1927–8 to a premature end; and the DVP caucus had been a constant thorn in his side, except for the periods of coalition with the DNVP. By the time of the great coalition of 1928–9, Stresemann was determined that the power of the caucus should be brought under control. If democratic government was to continue, the leaders of all democratic parties had to be prepared to take a stand against the narrow partisan interests of their caucuses in the greater interest of the stability of the Republic as a whole.

Stresemann's policy kept the DVP in the middle ground of politics and in government. This maximized its influence when compared with its share of the vote, only around 9 per cent after May 1924. It also, however, required the party to compromise on economic and social issues. But such compromise reflected Stresemann's view of what was in the best interests of the state in a situation which was less than ideal. He believed that given the multiple divisions of German politics and the anti-Republican extremes at both ends, there was a real risk that if the middle parties failed to agree the whole structure would collapse. That danger had been narrowly avoided between 1918 and 1923 and he sensed that it would return with the alliance of Hugenberg with Hitler in 1929. In these

[24] At the meeting of the Zentralvorstand, 26 Feb. 1929: Kolb and Richter (eds.), *Nationalliberalismus*, 764.

circumstances German democracy could not follow the British model where the major parties were all loyal to the state and could alternate in power without bringing the system down. In Germany, parliamentary government could only be maintained by bargaining and compromise at the centre. The aim was to achieve a steady recovery which would in time make the extremes harmless. Stresemann's preference was for the great coalition which corresponded to the ideal of the *Volksgemeinschaft* and isolated the extremes.

Stresemann's warnings about Hugenberg and Hitler proved prophetic. However, his coalition policy also had costs. It meant blurring lines of choice and accountability, taking responsibility for unpopular decisions, and alienating voters. Between 1920 and 1924 the DVP lost almost a third of its vote and there was a further fall in 1928. There was some justification for Stresemann's critics who argued that his policy 'violated the rules of the parliamentary game' and prevented voters getting what they wanted.[25] It is possible that his success in bringing about the great coalition in 1928 would have resulted in a further loss of support even if the economy had not suffered a dramatic collapse.

Stresemann recognized the problem but argued that over time the DVP's 'objective work' would win recognition and the hollowness of the DNVP's opposition would be shown up.[26] To maintain support in the country and in the long run to maintain his authority in the DVP, however, he needed to be able to demonstrate the success of his policies.

Foreign policy provided the key. Despite some setbacks, he could claim an impressive record by 1929. He had helped to rescue Germany from near disintegration in 1923 and set it on the path to recovery. His foreign policy had achieved remarkable results: the Dawes plan and evacuation of the Ruhr, Locarno and entry into the League, a new framework of trade treaties, the Young plan and agreement for evacuation of the Rhineland and negotiations on the Saar, the prospect of further progress towards European economic integration. As he told the DVP's Reich committee on 30 September 1929: 'There is no doubt that today we command a position of respect in the world which no one would have believed it possible to achieve within five years.'[27]

---

[25] The phrase is Paul Moldenhauer's, though in fact he blamed the Centre Party for its reluctance to form coalitions against the SPD. 'Politische Erinnerungen', pp. 66–7: BAK, Nl. Moldenhauer, 1.
[26] See above, p. 457.
[27] Kolb and Richter (eds.), *Nationalliberalismus*, 861.

The record was important in itself. It also gave Stresemann and his party a coherent platform in elections. He was more than simply an agile parliamentarian. His name stood for a consistent policy to which he had held through all the different coalitions, making it a defining feature of Weimar politics in the 'Stresemann era'. Comparisons were frequently drawn both at home and abroad with Bismarck: Rumbold thought Stresemann's task had been 'infinitely the more difficult of the two'.[28] Stresemann's prestige as foreign minister became a second source of power beside his leadership of the DVP. His reputation abroad reinforced his reputation at home, making his appointment as foreign minister in successive coalitions increasingly inevitable.

Foreign policy also served the purpose of domestic consolidation. Peaceful revision of the Versailles treaty provided common ground on which the parties of the great coalition could unite. The SPD would support only a policy of peaceful revision. The DDP and Centre Party could claim to have initiated the policy before Stresemann entered government and, despite doubts about Stresemann's tactics on occasion, they were also generally supportive. The DVP found it more difficult to accept, but Stresemann carried them with him by appealing to their patriotic duty to follow the only viable policy in the national interest. Even the DNVP, though it was never able to shake off its fundamental opposition to a policy of peaceful negotiation, was drawn into government and Stresemann did what he could to encourage support for his policy among its Reichstag party.

Foreign policy thus became for Stresemann the instrument not only to restore Germany as a great power but also to create the domestic consensus on which alone Stresemann believed that power could be based. The consensus was symbolized by Germany's delegations to the League, which included representatives from the SPD to the DVP and, in 1927, also the DNVP.[29] During the war he had seen the connection between parliamentarization and victory. It was an important part of his approach that he continued to think of domestic and foreign policy together. A successful foreign policy required a successful parliamentary democracy and a successful parliamentary democracy required a foreign policy that was both realistic and corresponded to the values of the democracy it served.

---

[28] Rumbold to Henderson, 12 Mar. 1930, enclosing the annual report on Germany for the year 1929. Public Record Office, London. FO 371/14374 14866. (I am grateful to Mr Herbert Behrendt for this reference.)

[29] Memorandum by Stresemann, dated 'Beginning of October 1927': Bernhard (ed.), *Vermächtnis*, iii. 206.

Let us now examine his achievements in foreign policy more closely. On 4 October 1929 Kessler—then in Paris—wrote of the tributes to Stresemann:

It is almost as if an outstanding French statesman had died, the grief is so general and sincere. . . The French feel Stresemann to have been a sort of European Bismarck. A legend is in the making—by his sudden death Stresemann has become an almost mythical personality . . . He is the first to be admitted to Valhalla as a genuine European statesman.[30]

What lay behind the legend? How far did Stresemann deserve the credit for 'his' foreign policy?

Stresemann did not originate the policy of peaceful revision. Rathenau, Wirth—even Erzberger by his willingness to sign the Versailles treaty— led the way. Nor did he pursue it on his own. He had excellent support from his senior officials, above all Schubert, and from diplomats such as Hoesch and Rauscher. He was also generally able to rely on the SPD, Centre, and DDP in the Reichstag and on the loyalty of Marx and Müller as chancellors.

Stresemann also benefited, as Rosenberg suggested, from the change in the international conditions which followed the Ruhr crisis. The failure of French policy, the willingness of the British government to take a lead over Dawes and Locarno, and the encouragement given by the United States in the background transformed the situation in Germany's favour. The flow of American capital, security for the Rhineland, and the gradual lifting of sanctions provided Stresemann with his greatest triumphs but they were only partly of his making. Arguably any German foreign minister who had been prepared to pursue a policy of détente with the West would have benefited from these trends.

Yet, there was also substance to the Stresemann legend. He brought to office his own ideas and a rare political talent. At the end of 1919 he had already seen the importance of European economic interdependence as an argument for revision of the treaty.[31] In April 1921 he predicted in the Reichstag that international understanding 'will come because it must come'.[32] At the time he was still constrained from putting these ideas into practice by the DVP's opposition to the policy of 'fulfilment' followed by Wirth and Rathenau. Stresemann was also influenced by Stinnes who thought that Germany could hold out for better terms and that the French

---

[30] Kessler (ed.), *Diaries*, 368.   [31] See above, p. 147.   [32] See above, p. 175.

would come off worst if they occupied the Ruhr. He later admitted that he had underestimated the scale of the crisis that would follow the occupation.

That crisis, which brought him to power and almost destroyed both the Republic and Germany as a unified state, convinced him of the urgency of rapprochement with the West. Opponents, such as Seeckt, argued that Germany's position was bound to strengthen in time and there was no need to assume obligations in the interim.[33] But Stresemann from his experience as chancellor knew better. Loans and security against a repeat of the Ruhr occupation would not come without winning the confidence of the Western powers and by his policies over the Dawes plan, Locarno, and the League he took the lead in creating that confidence.

Each major policy initiative from the decision to end passive resistance to acceptance of the Young plan required an exhausting process of building consensus at home—in cabinet, the Reichstag and its foreign affairs committee, with president Hindenburg from 1925, with the *Länder* representatives, the DVP, the press, interest groups, and the wider public. To that process was added the preparation of opinion abroad through discussion with foreign ambassadors and instructions to German embassies, and in time international conferences, the quarterly meetings of the League council, and the annual meeting of the assembly. Until his health started to fail in 1928, Stresemann carried the main burden.

He also quickly established his authority within the Auswärtiges Amt, which given his social background and lack of previous experience in government could not have been assumed. On 13 August 1925, his second anniversary in office, he was surprised to receive a delegation of departmental heads, led by Schubert, who thanked him for his 'consistent policy' and for defending the Auswärtiges Amt against criticism.[34] Stresemann had won their respect not least by his boldness in authorizing the German security pact proposals in January 1925 at a time when a new chancellor—Luther—had just been appointed and the DNVP had joined the government for the first time. His initiative led predictably to a reaction which would have destroyed a lesser politician together with the policy. When

---

[33] This view was not confined to those on the right: Eugen Schiffer, for instance, thought that it would be better to remain outside the League so long as Germany was subject to the sanctions of the Versailles treaty. By leaving its place empty and only appearing from time to time, like Banquo's ghost, Germany would be more effective than if it were present in person, humiliated and tolerated. BAK, Nl. Schiffer, 2, part 1, pp. 333–4.

[34] Diary for 13 Aug. 1925: Bernhard (ed.), *Vermächtnis*, ii. 311.

Stresemann died Schubert paid tribute to his 'indefatigable energy and clear eye for the great, decisive questions'.[35]

There is no doubt that Stresemann made an essential contribution to German foreign policy from 1923 to 1929. He provided the leadership in his department, in domestic politics, and abroad. But what were the aims of the policy? Why has it been the cause of so much controversy? There have been three main sources of suspicion about his aims—personal, political, and geographical. Let us consider each in turn.

Stresemann's personality did not immediately inspire trust either at home or abroad. He was too much of an unknown quantity from an unknown background, too dependent on his own gifts for his rise to power, too ambitious and mercurial, too much the professional politician who had learned the art of survival in a highly unstable system. Although he had great personal charm, in public life he was respected but not until the end of his career much liked. D'Abernon drew a comparison with Winston Churchill—'Both brilliant daring and bold'—and, one might add, in both cases their judgement was questioned.[36] Stresemann's capacity to enjoy life—food, drink, theatre, opera, concerts, literature—may also have contributed to doubts about whether he was altogether sound and reliable.[37] D'Abernon later reflected:

His capacity for arousing animosity was quite exceptional. Why, it is difficult to say. Perhaps his mind was too rapid to give an impression of solidity—his enunciation too resonant and the phrases too brilliant to suggest reflection or measure. Of him it may be said, not that he had the qualities of his defects, but that his qualities—cleverness, rapidity and decision—earned him a reputation for defects from which he was entirely free—recklessnesss, and lack of conviction. With the latter weakness he certainly could not be charged, for he adhered steadfastly to beliefs, when they were not only inconvenient, but damaging.[38]

While he was ambassador, however, even D'Abernon was not entirely sure of Stresemann. As late as February 1925 he wrote to Chamberlain about the German proposals for a security pact, 'While I have great confidence in Schubert, I have rather less confidence in the completeness

[35] Cabinet minutes, 3 Oct. 1929: Vogt (ed.), *Kabinett Müller*, no. 310.

[36] D'Abernon, 'Stresemann', in *Ambassador of Peace*, iii. 10.

[37] On his love of food and drink, see ibid. 11; cf. Otto Dibelius, *In the Service of the Lord*, Eng. edn. (London: Faber & Faber, 1964), 132.

[38] D'Abernon, *Ambassador of Peace*, iii. 19–20.

of Stresemann's sincerity.'[39] Chamberlain later reminded D'Abernon of the comment, adding, 'I have always thought that it was by degrees as it were, that Stresemann became a convert to his own policy and accepted its consequences', though he went on: 'In any case it does not detract from the courage and loyalty with which he pursued the policy as it developed in our hands and the skill with which he drew from it all the advantages it offered. What a tragedy it is for us all that he should have died so young.'[40]

In the case of both D'Abernon and Chamberlain the doubts did not last. Chamberlain later dismissed the allegation—following publication in 1932 of Stresemann's letter to the Crown Prince—that Briand had been duped by Stresemann. He wrote: 'The charge is absurd to anyone who like myself collaborated with them both from day to day for the happiest years of their association. It is as unfair to Stresemann as it is unjust to Briand. There was neither knave nor dupe, but a great German and a great Frenchman, who, from amidst the blood-soaked ruins of the past, sought to raise a new temple of peace.'[41]

Suspicions in France went deeper and lasted longer. Poincaré never trusted Stresemann and saw his views confirmed by the letter to the Crown Prince.[42] Stresemann, it is fair to say, also felt reserve about Poincaré, continuing to see in him the rigid opponent of any revision of the Versailles treaty, a view in which he was encouraged by Briand. When asked by a French journalist what he thought of Poincaré, Stresemann replied, 'If I did not know that he might consider it an insult I would say that in his meticulousness, his scrupulousness and his precision he is a typical born German.'[43]

Briand's attitude cannot be established conclusively. His reputation as the architect of Franco-German friendship was tarnished in France by the Second World War and the Vichy regime. Although he died in 1932, he suffered from guilt by association: his chosen biographer, Georges Suarez, became an ardent Vichyite and was executed after the war.[44] In addition to

---

[39] D'Abernon to Chamberlain, 21 Feb. 1925: D'Abernon Papers, British Library, London, Add. MS 48926A.

[40] Chamberlain to D'Abernon, 1 Oct. 1930: ibid., Add. MS 48926B.

[41] Austen Chamberlain, *Down the Years*, 4th edn. (Edinburgh: Edinburgh Press, 1935), 188.

[42] He published his comments on the *Vermächtnis* in the magazine *Illustration* in May 1932 and these were then reported in Germany, for instance in the *General-Anzeiger für Dortmund*, 140 (23 May 1932).

[43] An incident recalled by the chairman of the foreign press association, Erich A. Teuber, in the *Darmstädter Tageblatt* (6 Oct. 1929). PA, Nl. Bernhard, Zeitungsausschnitte, 16.

[44] Bariéty, 'Aristide Briand: Les Raisons d'un oubli', in Fleury (ed.), *Le Plan Briand*, 1–4.

a lack of interest among French historians, there were also problems of source material. Suarez had not had access to Briand's papers for his last volume covering the period 1923 to 1932, and these papers remained unavailable for many years and suffered serious damage.[45] Recent studies have emphasized that Briand, like Stresemann, saw the avoidance of another European war as the overriding priority. Briand had a clear view of the problems of French security, demographically and economically weaker than Germany and unable to rely on the United States or Britain for support. In these circumstances he was prepared to risk cautious rapprochement with Germany, which promoted French economic interests and helped to maintain (unlike the alternative of relying on sanctions) good relations with Britain.[46]

There are no grounds for believing that Briand was duped by Stresemann or vice versa. Neither was so naive as to assume that the other would abandon the interests of his country for the idea of Europe.[47] The question is rather whether, as Suarez suggests, there was a meeting of minds between them although their interests remained separate or, as Sauerwein thought after 1945, they had simply tried to get the better of each other.[48]

Each was certainly sometimes disappointed in the other: Briand at Stresemann's indiscretions over the understandings which Stresemann alleged had been reached at Locarno and Thoiry; Stresemann at the way Briand distanced himself from Thoiry and his procrastination over evacuation of the Rhineland. They also, however, needed each other's cooperation and they understood each other's difficulties. There is no reason to doubt Briand's word that he trusted Stresemann but that since neither of

[45] Georges Suarez, *Briand*, vi: *L'Artisan de la paix, 1923–1932* (Paris: Plon, 1952); Bariéty, 'Aristide Briand: Les Raisons d'un oubli', 4.

[46] Ferdinand Siebert, *Aristide Briand 1862–1932* (Zurich: Eugen Rentsch, 1973); Keeton, *Briand's Locarno Policy*; Bariéty, 'Aristide Briand: Les Raisons d'un oubli', 1–13; Bariéty, 'Aristide Briand et la sécurité de la France en Europe, 1919–32', in Schuker (ed.), *Deutschland und Frankreich*, 117–34.

[47] Briand easily disposed of such criticism at the time in speeches to the foreign affairs committee of the National Assembly on 19 Dec. 1925 and 23 Nov. 1926. Archives nationales Paris: Procès verbaux des séances de la Commission des Affaires Etrangères (1925–1927), C14763, no. 46, pp. 21–2, and no. 62, p. 25.

[48] Suarez, *Briand*, vi. 121; Sauerwein, *30 ans à la une*, 183. Sauerwein's sceptical conclusion was somewhat modified in other comments. He thought that Briand was 'consciente de sa mission européene' but Stresemann was exclusively interested in Germany's recovery although he (Stresemann) believed that this would be possible only through understanding with France. Both of them were also constrained by strong opposition to their policies at home. *30 ans à la une*, 180; Sauerwein, 'Bei den Großen der Erde, Stresemann', *General-Anzeiger für Dortmund*, 140 (23 May 1932).

them would be there for ever French policy had to allow for changed circumstances.[49] Equally there is no reason to doubt his sense of loss at Stresemann's death when he is reported to have said, 'Order a coffin for two. We have two deaths to lament.'[50]

There is more justification for controversy over the goals of Stresemann's foreign policy. There were already sharply contrasting interpretations among his contemporaries, such as Thomas Mann and Claud Cockburn.[51] In recent years there has been a convergence of views among historians but important questions remain. There is general agreement that Stresemann's aim was to revise the Versailles treaty and re-establish Germany as an equal among great powers and that his method was peaceful revision by détente with the Western powers. He believed that by creating common interests— the importance of Germany to the European economy—revision and détente would go together.

The questions which remain are essentially about what would have happened as revision and détente ceased to go together. It has been argued that the conflict between them was already apparent from 1927 and threatened to lead to a breakdown of the Locarno system before Strese-mann died.[52] The root cause of the conflict was simple. The German goal of revision would have made it not merely an equal great power but the greatest power in Europe (apart from the potential of the Soviet Union) and that was incompatible with French security. All the evidence suggests that Stresemann remained committed to peaceful revision, but he could not and would not abandon the goal of equal rights and that meant inevitably that the two halves of his policy were in tension and the result was bound to be problematic. Did he face up to the problem, and was any solution possible?

It has been argued above that Stresemann's policy developed pragmatic-ally. Rapprochement with the West offered the only way out of the Ruhr crisis and the guarantee that it would not happen again. But from that pragmatism Stresemann developed an increasingly strong commitment to European peace. His arguments moved on from mere expedience—Ger-many's lack of military power—at the time of Locarno, to a much clearer

---

[49] See above, p. 412.

[50] François Seydoux, *Beiderseits des Rheins. Erinnerungen eines französischen Diplomaten* (Frank-furt am Main: Societäts Verlag, 1975), 38. On 4 Oct. 1929 the German embassy in Paris reported Briand's concern about who would succeed Stresemann: *ADAP,* ser. B, xiii, no. 41.

[51] See above, p. 2.

[52] The argument is put most forcefully in Knipping, *Ende der Locarno-Ära.*

position in 1926–9 that a new war would destroy Europe and that Germany, as the central battleground, would have most to lose. It is also important to remember that he saw foreign policy and domestic politics together. War would be a disaster for parliamentary democracy as it would intensify the divisions of German politics. What Germany and Europe needed was decades of peace to recover from the last war.

It has also been argued above that as Stresemann's priority became more firmly one of peace, so the revisionist goals which were in conflict with this priority were gradually postponed to an increasingly remote future. That was clearly true of Austria and colonies: Stresemann became increasingly doubtful about whether union with Austria or regaining colonies were even desirable. The Polish frontier is more debatable because Stresemann did consider frontier revision both desirable and in the interests of European peace. However, in practice, as we have seen, he seems to have agreed with Rauscher by 1929 that the problem could be settled only by a long period of economic cooperation with Poland which would make the Polish economy increasingly dependent on Germany.

There were other unsolved problems which were more urgent in 1929: whether the Young plan would be sustainable and, if not, what would follow, the negotiations over the Saar and the still outstanding question of Eupen-Malmédy, the problem of disarmament or, as it was increasingly being seen in Germany, gaining acceptance for German rearmament. Of these, no one could tell in 1929 when the financial crisis would break or whether it would be manageable. Negotiations over the Saar had started and, although it was clear that they would be difficult, Germany was in a strong position since a plebiscite was due in 1935 and the problem was not therefore one which would threaten the peace. A solution to Eupen-Malmédy would require financial compensation to Belgium but the problem again appeared soluble and was not of major importance. Gaining acceptance for German rearmament would clearly be difficult and Stresemann's conversation with Sauerwein in July 1929 suggests that he was already trying to think of ways to make it acceptable to France.

The most probable development of Stresemann's policy would have been for him to continue to try to reach agreement with France and the other Western powers where possible, while explaining to the German public why there was no alternative to patience on other issues. The latter process had already started. In a DVP publication to prepare party members to counter 'the demagogic agitation' against the Young plan, the arguments were clearly stated.[53] It explained that the 'policy of understanding was, is and remains dependent on the recognition of the growing importance of common interests', but in France this recognition was 'paralysed by the fear of a Germany that had recovered its military strength' while in Britain it was 'at the least very muted by the fear of a new economic competition with Germany'. Given that all the new states established by Versailles contained German minorities, any attempt to re-establish the pre–1914 status quo would be

a policy of conflict against the whole world. Even a rearmed Germany, equipped with all the discoveries of the most modern military technology, would have to pay for such a policy with a new world alliance of enemies. The possibilities of German policy are therefore limited. Only if we remain within these limits are we conducting realpolitik ...

It also claimed that Stresemann's policy was 'not a policy of renunciation', that much had already been achieved and that Germany was on 'the surest way to regaining our economic and political freedom, sovereignty at home and abroad'.

There is no evidence that Stresemann was prepared to go further and adopt 'a policy of renunciation', let alone to think in terms of the desirability of strengthening British or American ties to France as a way of managing German power. His agenda was still how to regain equal rights for Germany in a situation where the evacuation of the Rhineland had only just been agreed with difficulty and public opinion in the parties of the great coalition, let alone on the right, would not have accepted less than equal rights. He did on one occasion look beyond the goal of equality to 'the inclusion of such a Germany together with all other states in a stable international structure', but he did not elaborate on what form that might take, apart from pointing out that, unlike the dynastic systems of the past, it would have to command popular support.[54]

His attempts to make German power acceptable to France were limited to encouraging measures of economic integration and looking to other areas of possible cooperation—in joint projects in the Soviet Union and

---

[53] *Archiv der Deutschen Volkspartei*, 1 Oct. 1929, 39–40. The *Archiv* was edited by Gottfried Kockelkorn, who worked closely with Stresemann in the party organization. This number gave a detailed twenty-eight-page summary of the arguments for the Young plan. It obviously had Stresemann's approval and may well have been dictated by him. On Kockelkorn's relationship with Stresemann, see Lowenthal-Hensel and Paucker (eds.), *Ernst Feder. Heute sprach ich mit*, 228–9.

[54] See above, p. 416.

elsewhere. The attempts at economic integration had not progressed very far before they were interrupted by the Depression, and it is still a matter of debate how far they would in fact have led to increasing economic interdependence or become an instrument of German hegemony.[55] Although the axiom of Stresemann's policy of revision remained understanding with France, he did not have a comprehensive answer to the problem of how that could be combined with what he and most Germans saw as their just demands. The most one can say is that he was more likely to have tried to manage the problem by showing finesse rather than changing direction towards the only alternative, preparation for a war which he knew would be disastrous.

It is of course possible to argue that a Germany with equal rights would automatically have become the greatest power in Europe by virtue of its size and resources and that this was indeed Stresemann's long-term hope. As A. J. P. Taylor suggested in a typical paradox, Stresemann believed in peace as 'the safer, the more certain and the more lasting way to German predominance'.[56] Yet that scarcely does justice to Stresemann's view of Germany's place in the world and in particular the interdependence of the international economy and of European security—and therefore Germany's dependence on its great power partners. He was conscious of Germany's strategic vulnerability in the centre of Europe, a Europe whose stability was threatened by other conflicts apart from the Franco-German problem. The Taylor view also ignores Stresemann's fear of the latent power of the Soviet Union, in size and resources far superior to Germany. It also overlooks the continued existence of the French and British empires, which still complicated the calculation of relative power. Finally, it fails to capture the concern, shared by Stresemann, that a divided Europe would be increasingly unequal to the economic competition of the United States. In all these ways the idea that Stresemann aimed at German preponderance in Europe is at best a half-truth. He recognized this fear in others; he knew it had a basis in fact and he had no complete answer to the problem it presented. But it was not the only or even, perhaps, in the long term the most serious problem in the way of the stable and peaceful international order for which he hoped.

It may be objected that this view of Stresemann's goals is a long way from the language in which he sometimes explained his policy,

[55] See above, p. 440.
[56] A. J. P. Taylor, *The Origins of the Second World War* (Harmondsworth: Penguin Books, 1964), 79.

particularly in the letter to the Crown Prince or his speech to the Landsmannschaften.[57] It is indeed the tone and language of these documents
which raise questions about his policy, rather than the arguments. The
primary explanation remains that his arguments were presented in a way
which would convince his immediate audience.

But that is not an entirely satisfying explanation for the crude and
emotive language he used. He was not simply playing a role for political
purposes or, rather, the reason he was able to play it so brilliantly was that
he could identify with the feelings of those to whom he spoke. He too
felt strongly about the rights of Germans in Poland or South Tyrol or
Germany's equal right with Britain or France to be a colonial power.
Moreover he was sensitive to the accusation of being a turncoat, someone
who should have been using his oratorical gifts to rouse the nation to
resistance rather than directing it towards peace. He referred to such
criticism in 1924 saying it would be 'terribly easy to be the most popular
man in the whole of Germany' if he copied Hitler and urged Germans to
attack across the Rhine, but it would be irresponsible.[58]

He clearly felt the tension between the constraints of a responsible
foreign policy and the romantic nationalism of his early career.[59] He
referred in a letter to Kahl to the strains of 'reining in' his 'impetuous
temperament and wild beating heart'.[60] It may be that he needed the
psychological reassurance of being able to explain his policy to a nationalist audience—and to himself—in their terms. This does not show that
his commitment to peace was a sham or a temporary expedient. It does
show the strain of having to explain in the highly charged atmosphere of
defeat and humiliation why Germany had to limit its goals in the interests
of peace.

The last source of controversy about Stresemann's foreign policy is
geographical. How did the Soviet Union fit into his calculations? Is it
conceivable that he might have reversed the policy of peaceful revision
with the Western powers once Germany and the Soviet Union were
strong enough to take joint action against Poland, as Hitler did in 1939?

Stresemann's policy towards the Soviet Union was a source of concern
for both Briand and Chamberlain at Locarno and it cast a long shadow. As

---

[57] See above, pp. 326–9, 343–6.

[58] See above, p. 275.

[59] The tension is best described in the autobiographical short story 'Die Barre'; see
above, pp. 292–3.

[60] Stresemann to Kahl, 13 Mar. 1929 (Nl. 104): Harttung (ed.), *Schriften*, 240–5.

late as 1927 Chamberlain reminded Briand that they were 'battling with Soviet Russia for the soul of Germany'.[61] These fears were not entirely without substance. Stresemann did not want to lose the advantage of joint Soviet–German pressure for a revision of Poland's frontiers and in 1925 he speculated that at some time in the future Soviet recovery might create a situation from which Germany could benefit. He thought, however, of using good relations with both the Western powers and the Soviet Union to enable Germany to mediate and in that way achieve its aims. And in fact in 1927 when the dispute between Lithuania and Poland threatened to escalate, Stresemann did his best to find a solution to prevent the danger of European war developing.

Stresemann was also consistently hostile to the idea of a one-sided alliance with the Soviet Union. He warned against the ideological impulse behind Soviet policy—Bolshevism to the Elbe. He also argued that pan-slavism had already made a German alliance with Russia obsolete before the war and that, should the Russian bourgeoisie ever return to power, they would renew the Franco-Russian alliance against Germany.[62] Given this outlook his policy towards the Soviet Union was bound to come second to good relations with the Western powers. Germany might be able to use her geographical position as 'the natural great mediator and bridge between east and west' but for that she needed the backing of the West as well as the consent of the East.[63]

The Treaty of Berlin maintained the connection at a level which the Soviet Union was just willing to accept and France and Britain were just willing to tolerate. Secret rearmament and trade helped to keep the connection alive and to satisfy the Reichswehr, Hindenburg, and industrial lobbies without, in Stresemann's view, being of much importance. Essentially Willy Brandt was right when he said: 'Stresemann too wanted to pursue a two-sided not a two-faced foreign policy, as Germany's geographical position then required and still requires.'[64] A comparison can be drawn with Germany's success in achieving unification in 1989–90, which depended on having built a position of confidence with both the United States and the Soviet Union.

[61] See above, p. 397.
[62] See above, p. 403.
[63] See above, p. 357.
[64] Speech as foreign minister on the ninetieth anniversary of Stresemann's birth, 10 May 1968: Harttung (ed.), *Schriften*, pp. vii–xvi, quotation p. xv.

The suspicions that have arisen about the aims of Stresemann's foreign policy seem therefore, while in each case natural, not to be borne out by the evidence. He tried to establish a national consensus behind the policy to make it more effective abroad and to consolidate the Republic. That required a degree of flexibility to attract the support of coalition partners as diverse as the SPD and DNVP. But he also succeeded to a remarkable degree in pursuing a consistent course and with increasing conviction as it produced results.

Most of the evidence which casts doubt on Stresemann's sincerity dates from 1924–5, from the battles over Dawes and Locarno, at a time when the success of the policy was still in doubt and Stresemann needed all the support he could muster. Schubert, who worked closely with him, wrote in January 1925 about the hostile reception abroad to bringing the DNVP into the government:

One should have more understanding for the difficulties with which Herr Stresemann in particular has to contend, who has at any rate put his stamp on last year's policy, a policy with which God knows foreign countries can be satisfied. If Herr Stresemann often has to manoeuvre, that is in the nature of the situation and is no evidence that he is not sincerely endeavouring to continue the German policy which was started last year.[65]

This seems in retrospect a fair verdict and one which was only strengthened by the evidence of the years that followed. It is important to devote equal attention to his arguments in these years when, despite setbacks, he became increasingly definite about his commitment to peace and the limits that set to revision. At the end, he did not have an adequate answer to the problem of how to reconcile France to the growth of German power, but nor did he develop an alternative policy to that of 'understanding'.

Stresemann's death was followed over the next three years by the collapse of everything for which he had worked. The immediate cause was the growing severity of the economic depression which dramatically increased the support for the NSDAP—and less dramatically for the KPD—making it difficult, and after the elections of July 1932 impossible, to maintain parliamentary government.[66] The increase in support for the

---

[65] Schubert, marked 'personal', to Albert Dufour-Feronce, an official in the German embassy in London, 19 Jan. 1925: PA, Büro Staatssekretär, Akten betreffend Privatbriefe, 1, R 29304.

[66] The debate about the causes of the Depression, and whether the origins of the crisis in Germany date from the period of relative stabilization from 1924 to 1929, is not relevant here.

NSDAP led German governments to adopt an increasingly nationalist stance, alarming French opinion and damaging foreign investment. The policy of Franco-German understanding, with which Stresemann was identified, was undermined.

It is natural, if ahistorical, to ask whether, if Stresemann had lived longer, he could have done anything to prevent the political crisis developing in the same way to Hitler's appointment as chancellor in January 1933. The fact that Stresemann's career was cut short when he was only 51, and also that he was two years younger than Adenauer, who remained chancellor of the Federal Republic until 1963, make the question more natural.[67] It is, of course, impossible to answer, not least because, as Thomas Mann suggested, the development of Stresemann's views may have been affected by his illness, giving him a heightened sense of the dangers that threatened his policy and the Republic.[68] Nevertheless, it is instructive to sketch the future as Stresemann saw it and to consider in what ways he might have been able to influence events.

The first priority was to defeat the referendum against the Young plan and that was accomplished without difficulty. The referendum collected just enough signatures—10.2 per cent of the electorate—for its proposed legislation to be submitted to the Reichstag and a plebiscite. In the Reichstag it was easily defeated, and the DNVP split—as Stresemann had often hoped it would—over the clause to punish ministers with imprisonment for treason. In the plebiscite on 22 December 1929 only 13.81 per cent of the electorate voted for the proposal, not much above the aggregate of the DNVP and NSDAP vote in the 1928 Reichstag elections.[69] There did not seem to be any immediate threat to the Republic.

Stresemann's second priority was to keep the DVP in the coalition. Initially, that too seemed unproblematic. Curtius replaced him as foreign minister and continued the main lines of his policy.[70] The DVP retained two ministers, Moldenhauer joining the cabinet first as economics minister before replacing Hilferding as finance minister in December. The

---

For a useful summary see Niall Ferguson, 'The German Inter-War Economy: Political Choice versus Economic Determinism', in Mary Fulbrook (ed.), *German History since 1800* (London: Arnold, 1997), 258–78.

[67] As first pointed out by Erich Eyck, *A History of the Weimar Republic* , ii, 213.

[68] See above, p. 2.

[69] Milatz, *Wähler*, 124–5, 151.

[70] Rödder, *Curtius*.

difficulty of holding the two wings of the coalition together, however, increased as the Depression worsened, and the New York stock market crash at the end of October shook the confidence of investors. The promise of tax cuts, which had held the coalition together, receded ever further into the distance; the government was forced into a desperate search for loans against the vociferous and eventually public opposition of Schacht as president of the Reichsbank; and the problem of financing the unemployment insurance fund returned to divide the coalition. Müller succeeded in getting plans for a financial reform programme through the Reichstag on 14 December only by combining it with a vote of confidence and even so the DVP split with fourteen of its members voting against the motion.[71]

Two developments sealed the fate of the coalition. The ratification of the Young plan by the Reichstag on 12 March, securing the quid pro quo of French evacuation of the Rhineland by the end of June, released the DVP from its sense of obligation to remain in the coalition until that goal had been achieved. At the same time the public knowledge that Hindenburg was prepared to grant emergency decree powers to a bourgeois coalition under the Centre Party chairman Heinrich Brüning offered the DVP an attractive way to rid itself of coalition with the SPD.

Under the leadership of Scholz, who now combined the offices of party chairman and leader of the Reichstag party, the DVP took an uncompromising stance on the issue of unemployment insurance in the budget for 1930. The other bourgeois parties, led by Brüning, produced a formula to accommodate the DVP but that was unacceptable to the SPD. Without agreement among the coalition parties and denied the use of emergency powers by Hindenburg, Müller resigned on 27 March 1930.[72]

Would Stresemann have been able to save the coalition? Despite his success in managing similar crises it seems unlikely. He would not have wanted to see it fall. His instincts were always against a polarization of the electorate and the situation was particularly dangerous given the Depression. Brüning's minority government offered no real security as it depended on toleration by the SPD to pass legislation or to prevent its emergency decrees being annulled in the Reichstag. However, it would have been very difficult even for Stresemann to persuade the DVP Reichstag party. He had agreed in 1929 that once the Young plan had been ratified it would be time for the DVP to put the fulfilment of its economic programme first and decide whether it should remain in the government. That enabled Scholz to claim that in breaking up the great coalition they had followed 'directly in the tracks of our Gustav Stresemann'.[73] Stresemann might have appealed to the Reich committee or a party conference against the Reichstag party, but he risked splitting the party in two. He might indeed have decided that this was the time to split the DVP and form a new party with the DDP and the pragmatic sections of the DNVP. But that was also a high-risk policy. The Brüning coalition would probably have seemed the safer option.

There is a stronger case for thinking that had he remained foreign minister in the Brüning government, it would have made a significant difference. He would have had more authority than Curtius and carried more respect in France. With Rauscher as his state secretary, there would have been a greater emphasis on maintaining Franco-German cooperation and détente with Poland.[74] There would still have been serious differences—at root the clash between French fears and German expectations of a more equal role. The atmosphere was made worse by the celebrations of the evacuation of the Rhineland, especially since Curtius refused to make a public gesture of gratitude to France.[75] Mutual suspicion prevented agreement on each of the major issues—early return of the Saar, Briand's plan for European union, revision of the Young plan, and disarmament or German rearmament. There were, however, also incentives to cooperate, above all Germany's need for foreign loans and the availability of surplus capital in France.

French governments made a number of proposals, from joint companies to exploit the Saar mines to plans for German firms to participate in major construction projects in France, and both short- and long-term loans.[76] The German government was not prepared to regain the Saar by making concessions which would limit German control beyond the plebiscite date of 1935 and it feared that other forms of French aid might prevent Germany obtaining a moratorium on reparations payments under the Young plan. Nevertheless, there was interest in Germany in long-term

---

[73] Minutes of the Reichsausschuß of the DVP, 3 July 1930: Kolb and Richter (eds.), *Nationalliberalismus*, 962–3.

[74] Rauscher too died in December 1930. On the succession to Schubert, see Rödder, *Curtius*, 80–3.

[75] Knipping, *Ende der Locarno-Ära*, 143–8; Rödder, *Curtius*, 104–13.

[76] Knipping, *Ende der Locarno-Ära*, 168–75, 198–205.

loans and that might have led to agreement if there had been a basis of trust.[77] Instead Curtius proceeded with plans for an Austro-German customs union which abruptly ended the French interest in assisting Germany and precipitated the banking crisis in Austria and Germany in the summer of 1931.

Stresemann would have insisted on equality for Germany with as much determination as Curtius or Brüning. He also intended to celebrate the evacuation of the Rhineland as a great national occasion and a personal success.[78] Briand, whose government had fallen in October 1929 but who remained as foreign minister until January 1932, would have liked a joint celebration in the spirit of Locarno. It would have been difficult even for Stresemann to manage the tension between the two concepts.

However, Stresemann would have been receptive to the proposals for economic cooperation which came from the new premier, André Tardieu, despite his reputation as a hardliner in the mould of Poincaré. Stresemann would also have responded to Briand's message that he would understand if the Germans wanted to start with economic cooperation within the proposed European union.[79] The challenge was to find a way of meeting both the German need for capital and the French need for security. It required political will on both sides to present economic cooperation as a step towards a more peaceful Europe. Stresemann and Briand might have been able to supply that leadership. At least Stresemann was most unlikely to have alienated the French by producing without consultation the proposal for an Austro-German customs union which in any case had to be abandoned in the face of French opposition.[80]

The main problem for Stresemann, however, would have been to maintain his political base. The DVP had no sooner joined the Brüning government than the right wing of the party wanted to go further. When

---

[77] Hoesch noted that there was a vicious circle: lack of agreement on political issues led to the attempt to make progress on economic and financial issues, which themselves proved impossible to solve without 'trust', which led back to the political issues. Hoesch to Auswärtiges Amt, 6 Mar. 1931; Rödder, *Curtius*, 122.

[78] It was symptomatic of the change in the political climate that the joint declaration of Hindenburg and the Reich government to mark the occasion made no mention of Stresemann. It was left to Otto Braun to protest against the omission: Braun, *Von Weimar zu Hitler*, 170. Curtius could offer only a lame defence of the decision to the DVP Reich committee. Minutes of the meeting, 3 July 1930: Kolb and Richter (eds.), *Nationalliberalismus*, 970.

[79] Rödder, *Curtius*, 116.

[80] Ibid. 186–226.

Moldenhauer proposed a special tax on those with salaries as part of a programme to fund the continuing budget deficit in June 1930, there was a revolt in the Reichstag party that forced his resignation.[81]

The results of the elections to the Saxon Landtag on 22 June 1930 were alarming: the DVP's share of the vote fell by a third to 8.7 per cent and the NSDAP won 14.4 per cent. Curtius and Scholz were forced to defend the policy of remaining in the Brüning government at meetings of the Reich committee and the national executive.[82] Curtius invoked 'the spirit of Stresemann', claiming that he would have urged them to consider foreign policy and not to destroy 'the last middle-class government' at the very moment when Germany had regained its freedom from foreign controls; he would have reminded them that politics was about power; he would also have asked them to consider what was to happen next: 'Do we as a party want to go to the Social Democrats, to Hugenberg or to the National Socialists?'[83]

The DVP remained in the Brüning government until October 1931 but its presence was a doubtful asset. It insisted on the inclusion of a poll tax in the budget for 1930, making agreement with the SPD—which objected to a flat-rate tax—impossible.[84] That led to the rejection of the budget, Brüning's use of the emergency decree powers to reimpose it, the annulment of the decree by an SPD-led Reichstag majority, and Hindenburg's authorization of new elections to be held on 14 September 1930.

It was a sign of the trend to the right that Curtius was unable to get a reference to Stresemann's policy of peaceful revision into the DVP's election manifesto, which referred instead to 'continuation of Stresemann's policy of national liberation, revision of the treaties of peace and tribute payments'.[85] Scholz attempted to organize a common front of the Protestant bourgeois parties to the left of the DNVP but without success. The DDP leadership did not trust him and refounded itself with Mahraun's Jungdeutscher Orden as the Deutsche Staatspartei. The other

---

[81] Cabinet minutes, 18 June 1930; Tilman Koops (ed.), *Die Kabinette Brüning I und II* (Boppard am Rhein: Harald Boldt, 1982), no. 50.

[82] Minutes of the Reichsausschuß meeting, 3 July 1930, and of the Zentralvorstand, 4 July 1930: Kolb and Richter (eds.), *Nationalliberalismus*, nos. 81–2.

[83] Minutes of the Zentralvorstand, 4 July 1930: ibid. 1011–12.

[84] Winkler, *Weimar*, 379.

[85] Minutes of the meeting of the Zentralvorstand, 24 Aug. 1930: Kolb and Richter (eds.), *Nationalliberalismus*, 1119, 1129. The DVP did, however, combine Stresemann's image with the Rhineland on an election poster; see the jacket illustration.

parties, including splinter groups from the DNVP, were more cooperative, but their efforts failed to achieve practical results.[86]

The elections were catastrophic: the DVP share of the vote fell by
almost a half to 4.5 per cent. It has been calculated that every fourth
DVP voter defected to the NSDAP, helping their breakthrough to 18.3
per cent and 107 seats in the Reichstag.[87] Scholz was forced to stand down
as party chairman but his successor, Dingeldey, was unable or unwilling to
prevent a further drift to the right.[88] In 1931 the DVP supported the
campaign of the radical right for a dissolution of the Prussian Landtag to
destroy the last bastion of SPD power in the Prussian government. When
Curtius resigned as foreign minister, after the abortive attempt at an
Austro-German customs union, Dingeldey led the DVP, against the resistance of a minority of the Reichstag party, into opposition. Some
prominent members associated openly with the right-radical camp at a
rally of the DNVP, NSDAP, Stahlhelm, and others at Bad Harzburg on 11
October 1931. Thereafter the DVP voted against the new Brüning government, expelled Curtius and another dissident (von Kardorff) in 1932,
nevertheless lost the support of the Ruhr faction, and swiftly declined into
irrelevance. In the July and November 1932 Reichstag elections it won
seven and eleven seats respectively and in March 1933 two, before dissolving itself on 4 July 1933.[89]

Whether Stresemann could have done anything to prevent this stam-
pede into self-destruction it is impossible to say. Nevertheless, his absence
left a huge gap. No one else gave the same lead against the radical right.
He would certainly have had more success than Scholz in forming a
common front with the Staatspartei for the 1930 elections since the
alliance would have been a natural extension of the 'patriotic bloc'
which he had discussed with Koch-Weser in 1929.[90] Whether he could
also have united the dissident groups from the DNVP and other middle-
class splinter groups such as the Wirtschaftspartei is more doubtful. The
DVP itself would probably have split, with the right wing defecting to the
DNVP. What the results would have been of a campaign led by Stresemann can only be guessed at. His prestige and ability as an orator,

---

[86] Jones, *Liberalism*, 352–77; Richter, *Deutsche Volkspartei*, 633–6, 651–61.

[87] Jürgen W. Falter, *Hitlers Wähler* (Munich: C. H. Beck, 1991), 110; Richter, *Deutsche Volkspartei*, 673–4.

[88] Hans Booms, 'Die Deutsche Volkspartei', in Erich Matthias and Rudolf Morsey (eds.), *Das Ende der Parteien 1933* (Düsseldorf: Droste, 1960), 529; Richter, *Deutsche Volkspartei*, 676–91.

[89] Richter, *Deutsche Volkspartei*, 692–820.

[90] See above, p. 459.

combined with the evacuation of the Rhineland, would have been assets. But in Baden and Württemberg where as a result of local agreements the DVP and the Staatspartei formed single lists, the results were not encouraging. In both regions their share of the vote fell by over a third compared to their combined vote in the 1928 elections.[91]

Even if Stresemann had been able to bring to the Brüning government a more determined group of Liberal and Conservative supporters, there would still have remained the problem of Hindenburg. Unlike the crisis of 1923 when Ebert worked with Stresemann to preserve parliamentary government, Hindenburg was increasingly arbitrary and determined to govern without the consent of the Reichstag since that meant the consent of the SPD. Stresemann would have been powerless to prevent the dismissal of Brüning in May 1932 or the series of intrigues which led to the appointment of Hitler as chancellor on 30 January 1933.

There is, however, one intriguing might-have-been. Before his death, Stresemann had planned to remain as foreign minister until the evacuation of the Rhineland but then to retire for two years to restore his health, possibly by going to Egypt.[92] He considered thereafter returning to politics and one of the possibilities discussed was for him to stand in the elections for the Reich presidency in April 1932.[93] If Stresemann had been able to take the place in fact occupied by Hindenburg as the candidate supported by the democratic parties to stop Hitler, the course of German and European history might have been different.

That is conjecture. What is certain is that while he was alive Stresemann offered an alternative to Hitler. Hitler was the beneficiary of Stresemann's foreign policy and is said to have acknowledged that 'in that position he could not have achieved more'.[94] But that does not diminish the total opposition that existed between their political ideas.

Stresemann believed that a successful foreign policy required the support of a successful parliamentary democracy. Hitler believed that foreign policy required first the overthrow of the Republic—the 'November criminals' of 1918. Stresemann aimed at an equal status for Germany among the great powers, limited territorial revision, and a stable place

---

[91] Milatz, *Wähler*, 93.

[92] Wolfgang Stresemann, *Mein Vater*, 13; Curtius, *Sechs Jahre Minister*, 87–8.

[93] Wolfgang Stresemann, *Mein Vater*, 13; Hubertus Prinz zu Löwenstein, *Stresemann. Das deutsche Schicksal im Spiegel seines Lebens* (Frankfurt am Main: Heinrich Scheffler, 1952), 333.

[94] A remark attributed to Hitler by Ribbentrop; Joachim von Ribbentrop, *Zwischen London und Moskau. Erinnerungen und letzte Aufzeichnungen* (Leoni am Starnberger See: Druffel, 1954), 44.

in a peaceful Europe. Hitler aimed to overthrow the existing state system and establish a German empire in the east which would provide 'living space' for a century. Stresemann believed that the German economy depended on exports and international trade. Hitler believed in economic autarky. Stresemann, despite occasional anti-Semitism, was not a racist. He respected the intellectual and cultural achievements of German Jews and this respect was reciprocated.[95] Hitler looked to a racial empire where Jews and other subject races would have no rights, an ideology which was to culminate in racial extermination.

By the end of his life Stresemann had come to stand for something in German public life which summed up all these differences—the values of decency and toleration. In his tribute to the meeting of *Länder* representatives on 3 October 1929, Carl Severing—a leading SPD politician—praised Stresemann as someone who had never resorted to making personal attacks on political opponents. He recalled that Stresemann had suggested as public life became more brutal that they should form a 'party of decent people'.[96]

Sebastian Haffner wrote later in similar terms of what Stresemann had meant to young people like himself in Berlin in the 1920s.[97] He described Stresemann strolling through central Berlin without a bodyguard, stopping to admire a flowerbed, doffing his hat to those who greeted him, an inconspicuous presence, who aroused their silent confidence, respect, and gratitude but not stronger feelings. Yet while he was alive Haffner and his friends felt 'a certain safety' from the growing tide of the politicized and disoriented with their ideology of racism. Stresemann's death was 'a sudden cold shock' and, looking back from the perspective of 1939, Haffner saw it as 'the beginning of the end'.

Haffner's description highlights an important aspect of Stresemann's politics. Although a professional politician to his fingertips, he remained a liberal for whom politics was about the competition of different traditions in a free society. Preserving the values of that society was the most important goal of liberalism. That depended on more than politics, indeed it depended on understanding that politics was not the whole of

---

[95] Wright, 'Liberalism and Anti-Semitism in Germany', 120–1.

[96] BH, MA 103239/1.

[97] The account comes from his recently published memoir, first written while living in England as an émigré in 1939. After the war Haffner became a distinguished journalist in Britain and, after his return to Germany in 1954, in the Federal Republic. Sebastian Haffner, *Geschichte eines Deutschen. Die Erinnerungen 1914–1933* (Stuttgart: Deutsche Verlags-Anstalt, 2000), 82–4.

life. In his interest in history, his love of theatre and music, his pleasure in the society of the Bühnen-Klub, his pride in the reception of his ideas about Goethe, his membership of the Freemasons, Stresemann maintained a presence in German, and more especially Berlin society which went beyond politics. And, in his close family life, he showed the importance he attached to maintaining a private sphere free from politics. Stresemann was not only a politician and a politician with a hinterland. The hinterland was part of his political values and that was what made him important to people like Haffner: they felt that so long as he was there they would be free to live their own lives, as he did his. He helped to represent the values of civil society against those who sought to overthrow it.

Stresemann's Jewish physician, Hermann Zondek, left a more personal record. He recalled later that after Stresemann had suffered the first stroke on the night he died, Zondek asked one of his senior colleagues, Professor Friedrich Kraus (a gentile) to come to share the responsibility with him. They both knew that the situation was hopeless. Seeing how deeply moved Zondek was, Kraus said: 'I feel for you. You are losing a great friend. More it is a loss for Germany but most of all for German Jewry. It is dying tonight'.[98] Although these words carry a heavier load of meaning in retrospect than was probably intended at the time, they show how Stresemann had become a symbol for those who valued the survival of a liberal and civilized Germany.

During the 1920s Stresemann became a force for integration in both the unstable world of Weimar politics and in the equally fragile structure of European peace. That was a remarkable achievement for an essentially lonely political leader of a party which never had a major share of Reichstag seats. The instability of Weimar politics with the lack of clear majorities on either right or left making the middle parties essential to government, and similarly the crucial role of Germany to any lasting settlement of European problems, became his opportunity. He showed an unusual ability to cross party divisions and, in time, the divisions between nations. That required imagination, courage, and the ability to compromise—he once said that 'without compromise...nothing great has yet been achieved in the world on a lasting basis'.[99] It also corresponded to his most basic beliefs as a liberal, in the common interests of the

[98] Zondek, *Auf festem Fusse*, 141–2.
[99] Speech to the Association of Saxon Industrialists on being made an honorary member, May 1927: Bernhard (ed.), *Vermächtnis*, iii. 457.

whole nation above sectional interests, and in the possibility of the community of nations. In this political faith he was loyal to the best traditions
of German liberalism from the 1848 revolutions.[100]

His leadership helped Germany to survive the Ruhr occupation and to
benefit from the change in the international climate that followed. He was
not able, however, to build a firm base of support for the Republic among
Protestant middle-class voters: the hoped-for realignment of parties to
produce a Protestant equivalent to the Centre Party eluded him. His
attempt to make foreign policy the bridge across which Protestant support
would rally to the Republic achieved only partial and temporary success.
His efforts to explain his policy in terms the opposition could understand
may even have been counterproductive, serving to maintain expectations
for further revision of the treaty which he could not fulfil. He gave clear
warnings against the danger of the radical right, but they were not sufficient to prevent his party following the trend to disaster after his death.
There was probably no better basis for consolidating the Republic in the
1920s than that represented by Stresemann, but his policies required
reason and patience and never achieved automatic acceptance.

Nevertheless, his foreign policy steered Germany to a remarkable
recovery. The confidence he established among the Western powers
made possible a much more rapid dismantling of the sanctions of the
Versailles treaty than had seemed likely in 1919 or 1923. He also maintained a connection with the Soviet Union which gave Germany the
potential to mediate between West and East. At first he hoped it might
become an instrument of frontier revision against Poland. Later he saw it
rather as a means to the overriding priority of maintaining peace in
Europe. His policy showed an acute sense of the need to reconcile
German interests with the balance of power. No chancellor or foreign
minister had been so successful since Bismarck and none was to be again
until Adenauer, Brandt, and Kohl. And none of the others faced the
problem of conducting foreign policy in a political system as unstable as
that of the Weimar Republic. It is worth remembering that from 1923
Stresemann lived with the risk of assassination and that as late as 1929 he
suspected that his telephone conversations were tapped and his mail
read.[101]

---

[100] The point is well made in Baechler, *Stresemann*, 898.
[101] Stresemann to Kahl, 13 Mar. 1929 (Nl. 104): Harttung (ed.), *Schriften*, 245. Eschenburg,
Also hören Sie mal zu, 222. It is not clear whom Stresemann suspected of interfering with his mail.
In 1926 he had been warned that the Defence Ministry was listening to his telephone conversa-

Stresemann was aware of the problems his policy faced, in particular the growing gap between German expectations and French and Polish fears. He had no solution to that problem other than time. In 1929 it was in any case already becoming clear that the state of the economy and the growing financial crisis would take priority over all other issues. Stresemann was also aware of many other potential threats to European stability: the Soviet Union and its ideology, the growth of protectionism and European dependence on American capital, regional conflicts such as those between Turkey and Greece or Poland and Lithuania, civil conflicts such as those between democracy and authoritarian rule in Greece, Spain, Italy, and Poland.[102] With so many sources of instability there could be no guarantee of peace. He could only emphasize the German interest in cooperation among the great powers and through the League for a more stable international order which would include the recognition of equal rights for Germany.

Despite the contradictions of his career and some remaining tensions in his character, there is a consistency about Stresemann's achievement. After 1923 he stood with increasing conviction for a democratic Germany in a democratic Europe. His death left, as contemporaries realized, a gap that remained unfilled. That was a measure of his achievement. It also showed the dangerous degree to which the Republic and peace had come to depend on his efforts even before the Depression undermined their insecure foundations.

tions. Note by Stresemann, 24 Jan. 1926: *ADAP*, ser. B, ii/i, no. 58, n. 5. The atmosphere of threatened assassination in the early years is well conveyed in John Buchan's novel, *A Prince of the Captivity* (London: Thomas Nelson, 1933), in which Stresemann is portrayed in the character of Hermann Loeffler, a wise and courageous statesman who survives assassination attempts from the extremes of both left and right. (I owe this reference to John Dunbabin.)

[102] Speech to the Reichszentrale für Heimatdienst, 28 Jan. 1927; *ADAP*, ser. B, iv, pp. 585–6. See above, pp. 402–3.

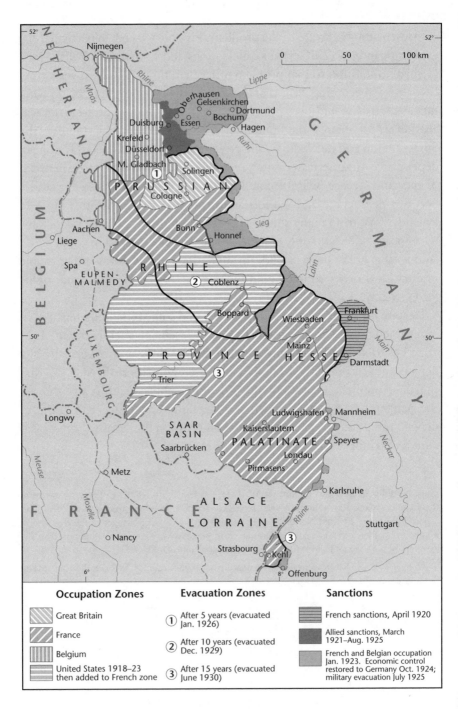

MAP 1.   The Rhine Frontier, 1919–1933

Memel

Annexed by
Lithuania from
Allied control
(1923)

Made a Free City
under League of
Nations control

○ Königsberg

EAST

PRUSSIA

ALLENSTEIN

Stolp

Danzig

POLISH CORRIDOR

MARIENWERDER

Stettin ○

Polish Corridor
and Posen
transferred to
Poland

Schneidemühl

Bydgoszcz
(Bromberg)

Voted to remain
German (1920)

GERMANY

Voted to remain
German (1920)

Berlin
○

POZNANIA

Poznań (Posen)

○ Warsaw

POLAND

Ostrow

Glogau
○

Dresden
○

Breslau
○

Voted to remain
German (1921)

W. UPPER
SILESIA

Beuten

Gleiwitz

Katowice

○Cracow

Prague
○

E. UPPER
SILESIA

Voted to become
Polish (1921)

CZECHOSLOVAKIA

Vienna
○

Territory Germany hoped to recover
from Poland to the north and west
of this line

Territory lost by Germany after her
defeat

AUSTRIA

Territory retained by Germany
following voting by the local
population

Territory retained by Germany, but
within which no fortifications could
be built or soldiers stationed

HUNGARY

0   50   100   150   200 km

MAP 2.   Germany's Frontiers with Poland after 1919

BIBLIOGRAPHY

ARCHIVAL SOURCES

Politisches Archiv, Auswärtiges Amt, Berlin (PA)

Nachlaß Stresemann
  This contains the vast bulk of Stresemann's papers extending from notes he
  made as a schoolboy to his last letters. Most of the collection is also available
  on microfilm, but that does not include personal files and some of the diaries,
  which contain interesting material.

Nachlaß Konsul Bernhard
  An extensive collection of press cuttings about Stresemann from the period
  1916–32. Bernhard was Stresemann's private secretary from 1923 to 1929,
  having earlier worked with him in the Association of Industrialists (1911–14)
  and the Association of Saxon Industrialists (October 1915–June 1916).

Nachlaß Werner Freiherr von Rheinbaben

Auswärtiges Amt Presse-Abteilung

Auswärtiges Amt Büro Reichsminister

Auswärtiges Amt Büro Staatssekretär

Bundesarchiv Koblenz (BAK)

R 45 I Nationalliberale Partei

R 45 II Deutsche Volkspartei

Nachlässe
  Max Bauer, Bernhard von Bülow, Eduard Dingeldey, Alfred Hugenberg, Karl
  Jarres, Siegfried von Kardorff, Katharina von Kardorff-Oheimb, Erich Koch-
  Weser, Hans Luther, Paul Moldenhauer, Hermann Pünder, Arnold
  Rechberg, Hjalmar Schacht, Eugen Schiffer, Paul Silverberg, Friedrich
  Thimme, Theodor Wolff, Albert Zapf

Kleine Erwerbungen
  No. 121 Regierungspräsident Pauly
  No. 339 Felix von Eckardt
  No. 511 Heinrich Ehlers
  No. 549 Jakob Rießer
  No. 557 Theodor Bohm

No. 574 Major Wäninger
Zeitgeschichtliche Sammlung (ZSg)

Bundesarchiv Berlin (BAB)

Büro des Reichspräsidenten
60 Vo1 Deutsche Volkspartei
61 Re1 Reichslandbund Pressearchiv

Bayerisches Hauptstaatsarchiv Munich (BH)

Ministerium des Aeußern
Bayerische Gesandtschaft Berlin
Polizeidirektion München

Archiv für Christlich-Demokratische Politik. Konrad Adenauer Stiftung Sankt Augustin

Nachlaß Stinnes

Friedrich Ebert Stiftung, Bonn

Nachlaß Hermann Müller

Public Record Office, London

FO 371

British Library, London

D'Abernon Papers

University of Birmingham Library

Chamberlain Papers

Universitätsarchiv, Leipzig

Records of Stresemann's doctoral examination

Universitätsarchiv, Heidelberg

Records of Stresemann's honorary doctorate, May 1928

Archives nationales, Paris

Procès verbaux des séances de la Commission des Affaires Etrangères (1925–1927)

PRIVATE COLLECTIONS

Mrs Jean Stresemann, Berlin

Stresemann family papers: mainly letters from Stresemann to Käte, Wolfgang, and Joachim.

Stresemann material: a collection from various sources, including Stresemann papers which remained in the possession of Konsul Bernhard.

(It is intended that both these collections should be transferred to the Politisches Archiv.)

Professor Peter Krüger, Marburg

Nachlaß Carl von Schubert

Jonathan Wright, Oxford

Copies of Stresemann's correspondence with Kurt Himer, November 1896

PRINTED PRIMARY SOURCES

Newspapers and Journals

Allgemeine Deutsche Universitäts-Zeitung, 1898–1900
Archiv der Deutschen Volkspartei, 1920–9
Die Zeit, 1921–5
Deutsche Stimmen, 1915–29
Dresdner Volks-Zeitung, 1895–6
Nationalliberale Blätter, 1907–15
Nationalliberale Correspondenz, 1917–33 (*NLC*)
The Times, 1925, 1929
Veröffentlichungen des Bundes der Industriellen, 1913
Veröffentlichungen des Verbandes Sächsischer Industrieller, 1911
Vertrauliche DVP Mitteilungen, 1919

Works by Gustav Stresemann

'Die Warenhäuser. Ihre Entstehung, Entwicklung und volkswirtschaftliche Bedeutung', *Zeitschrift für die gesamte Staatswissenschaft*, 56 (1900).
Die Entwicklung des Berliner Flaschenbiergeschaefts (Berlin: R. F. Funcke, [1901]).
Wirtschaftspolitische Zeitfragen (Dresden: F. Emil Boden, n.d. [1910]; 2nd expanded edn. 1911).

'Zehn Jahre Verband Sächsischer Industrieller', in *Festschrift zur Feier des zehn-jährigen Bestehens des Verbandes Sächsischer Industrieller Dresden, am 11. und 12. März 1912* (Dresden: F. Emil Boden [1912]).

Deutsches Ringen, deutsches Hoffen (Berlin: Reichsverlag, 1914).

Englands Wirtschaftskrieg gegen Deutschland (Stuttgart: Deutsche Verlagsanstalt, 1915).

Michel horch, der Seewind pfeift...! (Berlin: Reichsverlag Hermann Kalkoff [1916]).

Warum müssen wir durchhalten? (Berlin: Kriegs Presse Amt [1917]).

Macht und Freiheit (Halle: Carl Marhold, 1918).

Von der Revolution bis zum Frieden von Versailles (Berlin: Staatspolitischer Verlag, 1919).

Rede des Abgeordneten Dr. Stresemann zu Magdeburg am 3. November 1919 (Magdeburg [1919]).

Die Märzereignisse und die Deutsche Volkspartei (Berlin: Staatspolitischer Verlag, 1920).

'Bernhard, Henry' [Gustav Stresemann], *Das Kabinett Stresemann* (Berlin: Staatspolitischer Verlag, 1924).

'The Economic Restoration of the World', *Foreign Affairs*, 2 (1923–4).

Nationale Realpolitik. Rede des Reichsaußenministers Dr. Stresemann auf dem 6. Parteitag der Deutschen Volkspartei in Dortmund am 14. November 1924 (Berlin: Staatspolitischer Verlag, 1924).

'Neue Wege zur Völkerverständigung', *Rede bei dem Akt der Ehrenpromotionen des Reichsministers Dr. Stresemann und des Botschafters der Vereinigten Staaten Dr. Schurman in der Aula der Universität Heidelberg 5. Mai 1928* (Heidelberg: Carl Winters Universitätsbuchhandlung, 1928).

Der Schutz der Minderheiten. Rede des Reichsministers des Auswärtigen Dr. Gustav Stresemann in der Sitzung des Völkerbundrats vom 6. März 1929 über die Garantie des Völkerbundes für die Bestimmungen zum Schutz der Minderheiten (Berlin: Reichsdruckerei [1929]).

'Die Minderheitenfrage als Friedensproblem', *Kölnische Volkszeitung*, 582, 20 Aug. 1929, Sonderbeilage.

Other Printed Primary Sources

ABRAMOWSKI, GÜNTHER (ed.), *Die Kabinette Marx I und II* (Boppard: Harald Boldt, 1973).

—— *Die Kabinette Marx III und IV* (Boppard: Harald Boldt, 1988).

Akten zur Deutschen Auswärtigen Politik 1918–1945, series A, viii–xiv; series B, i–xiii (Göttingen: Vandenhoeck & Ruprecht, 1990–5, 1966–79).

BADEN, PRINZ MAX VON, *Erinnerungen und Dokumente* (Stuttgart: Deutsche Verlags-Anstalt, 1927); Eng. edn., 2 vols. (London: Constable, 1928).

BECKER, JOSEF, (ed.), *Heinrich Köhler, Lebenserinnerungen des Politikers und Staatsmannes 1878–1949* (Stuttgart: W. Kohlhammer, 1964).

BEER, MAX, *The League on Trial: A Journey to Geneva*, Eng. edn. (London: Allen & Unwin, 1933).

BERNHARD, HENRY (ed.), *Gustav Stresemann. Vermächtnis*, 3 vols. (Berlin: Ullstein, 1932); Eng. edn. by Eric Sutton (London: Macmillan, 1935–40).

——'Gustav Stresemann. Tatsachen und Legenden', *Aus Politik und Zeitgeschichte*, B 41/59 (7 Oct. 1959), 529–46.

BERNSTORFF, COUNT J., *The Memoirs of Count Bernstorff*, Eng. edn. (London: Heinemann, 1936).

BISMARCK, PRINCE OTTO VON, *Prinz Wilhelm und Napoleon. Neue Bilder aus Preussens Notzeit* (Dresden: Carl Reissner, 1929).

BRAUN, OTTO, *Von Weimar zu Hitler* (New York: Europa, 1940).

BRÜNING, HEINRICH, *Memoiren 1918–1934* (Stuttgart: Deutsche Verlags-Anstalt, 1970).

BUCHAN, JOHN, *A Prince of the Captivity* (London: Thomas Nelson, 1933).

BÜCHER, KARL, 'Karl Viktor Fricker', *Zeitschrift für die gesamte Staatswissenschaft*, 64 (1908), 193–200.

Centralbüro der Nationalliberalen Partei Deutschlands (ed.), *Politisches Handbuch der Nationalliberalen Partei* (Berlin: Buchhandlung der Nationalliberalen Partei, 1907).

CHAMBERLAIN, AUSTEN, *Down the Years*, 4th edn. (Edinburgh: Edinburgh Press, 1935).

COCKBURN, CLAUD, *In Time of Trouble: An Autobiography* (London: Hart-Davis, 1957).

CURTIUS, JULIUS, *Sechs Jahre Minister der deutschen Republik* (Heidelberg: Carl Winter, 1948).

D'ABERNON, VISCOUNT, *An Ambassador of Peace*, i: *From Spa (1920) to Rapallo (1922)*; ii: *The Years of Crisis June 1922–December 1923*; iii: *The Years of Recovery January 1924–October 1926* (London: Hodder & Stoughton, 1929–30).

Das außenpolitische Programm der Deutschen Volkspartei. Vortrag gehalten in Halberstadt am 19. Dezember 1919 bei der Parteibeamtenbesprechung von dem Legationsrat a.D. Freihr. v. Rheinbaben [1919].

DEIST, WILHELM (ed.), *Militär und Innenpolitik im Weltkrieg 1914–1918*, 2 vols. (Düsseldorf: Droste, 1970).

DEUERLEIN, ERNST (ed.), *Der Hitler-Putsch. Bayerische Dokumente zum 8./9. November 1923* (Stuttgart: Deutsche Verlags-Anstalt, 1962).

DIBELIUS, OTTO, *In the Service of the Lord*, Eng. edn. (London: Faber & Faber, 1964).

Documents on British Foreign Policy 1919–1939 (*DBFP*), 1st series: vols. xvi, xxi, xxvi–xxvii; series IA: vols. i–vii (London: Her Majesty's Stationery Office, 1968–86, 1966–75).

Documents diplomatiques belges 1920–1940, ii (Brussels: Palais des Académies, 1964).

DRAGE, CHARLES, *The Amiable Prussian* (London: Anthony Blond, 1958); German edn., *Als Hitler nach Canossa ging* (Berlin: ikoo, 1982).

Dreizehnter allgemeiner Vertretertag der Nationalliberalen Partei am 19. November 1911 in Berlin (Berlin: Buchhandlung der Nationalliberalen Partei [1911]).

Elfter allgemeiner Vertretertag der Nationalliberalen Partei am 3. und 4. Juli 1909 in Berlin (Berlin: Buchhandlung der Nationalliberalen Partei [1909]).

ERDMANN, KARL DIETRICH, *Kurt Riezler. Tagebücher, Aufsätze, Dokumente* (Göttingen: Vandenhoeck & Ruprecht, 1972).

——and VOGT, MARTIN (eds.), *Die Kabinette Stresemann I und II* (Boppard: Harald Boldt, 1978).

ESCHENBURG, THEODOR, 'Stresemann und die Studenten', *Nord und Süd*, 52 (1929), 998–1003.

——*Also hören Sie mal zu. Geschichte und Geschichten 1904 bis 1933* (Berlin: Siedler, 1995).

FRANÇOIS-PONCET, ANDRÉ, *De Versailles à Potsdam: La France et le problème allemand contemporain 1919–1943* (Paris: Flammarion, 1948).

FRÖHLICH, ELKE (ed.), *Die Tagebücher von Joseph Goebbels*, i (Munich: K. G. Saur, 1987).

FRYMAN, DANIEL [Heinrich Claß], *Wenn ich der Kaiser wär—Politische Wahrheiten und Notwendigkeiten*, 2nd edn. (Leipzig: Theodor Weicher, 1912).

GERTH, H. H., and MILLS, C. WRIGHT (eds.), *From Max Weber: Essays in Sociology* (London: Routledge, 1967).

GESSLER, OTTO, *Reichswehrpolitik in der Weimarer Zeit* (Stuttgart: Deutsche Verlags-Anstalt, 1958).

Gestalten Rings um Hindenburg. Führende Köpfe der Republik und die Berliner Gesellschaft von Heute, 2nd edn. (Dresden: Reissner, 1929).

GILBERT, FELIX, *A European Past: Memoirs 1905–1945* (New York: W. W. Norton, 1988).

HAFFNER, SEBASTIAN, *Geschichte eines Deutschen. Die Erinnerungen 1914–1933* (Stuttgart: Deutsche Verlags- Anstalt, 2000).

HARBECK, KARL-HEINZ (ed.), *Das Kabinett Cuno* (Boppard: Harald Boldt, 1968).

HARTTUNG, ARNOLD (ed.), *Gustav Stresemann Schriften* (Berlin: Berlin Verlag, 1976).

HEUSS, THEODOR, *Erinnerungen 1905–1933* (Tübingen: Rainer Wunderlich, 1963).

HIMER, KURT, 'Jugenderinnerungen an Stresemann', *Hamburger Anzeiger*, 7 Oct. 1929.

HOWATSON, M. C. (ed.), *The Oxford Companion to Classical Literature*, 2nd edn. (Oxford: Oxford University Press, 1989).

HÜRTEN, HEINZ (ed.), *Das Krisenjahr 1923. Militär und Innenpolitik 1922–1924* (Düsseldorf: Droste, 1980).

JÄCKH, ERNST, *The New Germany: Three Lectures* (London: Oxford University Press, 1927).

——, *Politik als Wissenschaft. Zehn Jahre Deutsche Hochschule für Politik* (Berlin: Hermann Reckendorf, 1931).

JOHANNESSON, FRITZ, 'Aus Stresemanns Schulzeit', *Mitteilungen des Vereins für die Geschichte Berlins*, 47/4 (1930), 121–32.

Journal officiel de la République Française: Débats parlementaires (Paris: Édition des Débats parlementaires, 1928).

KALKOFF, HERMANN (ed.), *Nationalliberale Parlamentarier 1867–1917 des Reichstages und der Einzellandtage. Beiträge zur Parteigeschichte herausgegeben aus Anlaß des fünfzigjährigen Bestehens der nationalliberalen Partei Deutschlands* (Berlin: Schriftenvertriebstelle der nationalliberalen Partei Deutschlands, 1917).

KARDORFF-OHEIMB, KATHARINA VON, *Politik und Lebensbeichte* (Tübingen: Hopfer [?1962]).

KEMPKES A. (ed.), *Deutscher Aufbau. Nationalliberale Arbeit der Deutschen Volkspartei* (Berlin: Staatspolitischer Verlag, 1927).

KESSLER, CHARLES (ed.), *The Diaries of a Cosmopolitan: Count Harry Kessler 1918–1937*, Eng. edn. (London: Weidenfeld & Nicolson, 1971).

KEYNES, JOHN MAYNARD, *The Economic Consequences of the Peace*, (London: Macmillan, 1st edn. 1919; annotated edn. 1971).

KOLB, EBERHARD, and RICHTER, LUDWIG (eds.), *Nationalliberalismus in der Weimarer Republik. Die Führungsgremien der Deutschen Volkspartei 1918–1933*, 2 vols. (Düsseldorf: Droste, 1999).

KOOPS, TILMAN (ed.), *Die Kabinette Brüning I und II* (Boppard am Rhein: Harald Boldt, 1982).

LEHMANN, MAX, *Freiherr vom Stein*, 3 vols. (Leipzig: Hirzel, 1902–5).

League of Nations Official Journal, 1926-1929 and *Official Journal*, Special Supplements 1926–1929, (Geneva, 1926–9).

LEWINSOHN, RICHARD (Morus), *Das Geld in der Politik* (Berlin: S. Fischer, 1930).

LOCHNER, LOUIS P., *Always the Unexpected: A Book of Reminiscences* (New York: Macmillan, 1956).

LOCKHART, BRUCE R. H., *Retreat from Glory* (New York: Putnam, 1934).

LOWENTHAL-HENSEL, CÉCILE, and PAUCKER, ARNOLD (eds.), *Ernst Feder. Heute sprach ich mit... Tagebücher eines Berliner Publizisten 1926–1932* (Stuttgart: Deutsche Verlags-Anstalt, 1971).

LUTHER, HANS, 'Luther und Stresemann in Locarno', *Politische Studien*, 8/84 (Apr. 1957), 1–15.

——*Politiker ohne Partei. Erinnerungen* (Stuttgart: Deutsche Verlags-Anstalt, 1960).

MACARTNEY, C. A. See under TOYNBEE.

MATTHIAS, ERICH, and MORSEY, RUDOLF (eds.), *Der Interfraktionelle Ausschuß 1917/18*, 2 vols. (Düsseldorf: Droste, 1959).

————(eds.), *Die Regierung des Prinzen Max von Baden* (Düsseldorf: Droste, 1962).

MICHAELIS, H., and SCHRAEPLER E. (eds.), *Ursachen und Folgen. Vom deutschen Zusammenbruch 1918 und 1945 bis zur staatlichen Neuordnung Deutschlands in der Gegenwart* (Berlin: Dokumenten Verlag Dr Herbert Wendler, 1958–64).

MIETHKE, FRANZ, *Dr. Gustav Stresemann der Wirtschaftspolitiker. Eine Skizze* (Dresden: Sächsische Verlagsanstalt, 1919).

Ministerium für Auswärtige Angelegenheiten der Deutschen Demokratischen Republik (ed.), *Locarno-Konferenz 1925* (Berlin: Rütten & Loening, 1962).

MINUTH, KARL-HEINZ (ed.), *Die Kabinette Luther I und II* (Boppard: Harald Boldt, 1977).

MORSEY, RUDOLF, (ed.), *Protokolle der Reichstagsfraktion und des Fraktionsvorstands der Deutschen Zentrumspartei 1926–1933* (Mainz: Matthias Grünewald, 1969).

Neunter allgemeiner Vertretertag der nationalliberalen Partei am 6. und 7. Oktober 1906 in Goslar a./H. (Berlin: Centralbüro der nationalliberalen Partei [1906]).

NIX, CLAIRE (ed.), *Heinrich Brüning: Briefe und Gespräche 1934–1945* (Stuttgart: Deutsche Verlags-Anstalt, 1974).

OLDEN, RUDOLF, *Stresemann* (Berlin: Rowohlt, 1929); Eng. edn. (London: Methuen, 1930).

ONCKEN, HERMANN, *Rudolf von Bennigsen. Ein deutscher liberaler Politiker*, 2 vols. (Stuttgart and Leipzig: Deutsche Verlags Anstalt, 1910).

PAYER, FRIEDRICH, *Von Bethmann Hollweg bis Ebert* (Frankfurt am Main: Frankfurter Societäts-Druckerei, 1923).

POGGE VON STRANDMANN, HARTMUT (ed.), *Walther Rathenau: Industrialist, Banker, Intellectual and Politician. Notes and Diaries 1907–1922* (Oxford: Clarendon Press, 1985).

RADBRUCH, GUSTAV, *Der innere Weg. Aufriß meines Lebens* (Stuttgart: K. F. Koehler, 1951).

Reichsgeschäftsstelle der Deutschen Volkspartei (ed.), *Bericht über den Ersten Parteitag der Deutschen Volkspartei am 13. April 1919 in den Akademischen Rosensälen in Jena* (Berlin: Staatspolitischer Verlag, 1919).

——*Bericht über den Zweiten Parteitag der Deutschen Volkspartei am 18., 19., u. 20. Oktober 1919 im Kristallpalast in Leipzig* (Berlin: Staatspolitischer Verlag [1920]).

——*Die Entstehung der Deutschen Volkspartei*, 3rd edn. (Berlin: Staatspolitischer Verlag, 1920).

——*Grundsätze der Deutschen Volkspartei* (Berlin: Staatspolitischer Verlag, 1920).

——*Die Bemühungen der Deutschen Volkspartei um die Bildung einer nationalen Einheitsfront* (Berlin [1921]).

——*An der Bahre von Gustav Stresemann. Ein Gedenkblatt* (Berlin: Staatspolitischer Verlag [1929]).

REISS, KLAUS-PETER (ed.), *Von Bassermann zu Stresemann 1912 bis 1917. Die Sitzungen des nationalliberalen Zentralvorstandes 1912–1917* (Düsseldorf: Droste, 1967).

RHEINBABEN, ROCHUS VON (ed.), *Stresemann. Reden und Schriften*, 2 vols. (Dresden: Carl Reissner, 1926).

RHEINBABEN, WERNER FREIHERR VON, *Kaiser, Kanzler, Präsidenten. Erinnerungen* (Mainz: Hase & Koehler, 1968).

RIBBENTROP, JOACHIM VON, *Zwischen London und Moskau. Erinnerungen und letzte Aufzeichnungen* (Leoni am Starnberger See: Druffel, 1954).

SAUERWEIN, JULES, 'Bei den Großen der Erde. Was ein Journalist erlebte', v, 'Stresemann', *General-Anzeiger für Dortmund*, 140–1 (23–4 May 1932).

——*30 ans à la une* (Paris: plon, 1962).

SCHACHT, HJALMAR, *The End of Reparations*, Eng. edn. (London: Jonathan Cape, 1931).

——*My First Seventy-Six Years*, Eng. edn. (London: Alan Wingate, 1955).

SCHIFFER, EUGEN, 'Stresemann', in *Deutsches Biographisches Jahrbuch*, ed. Verband der Deutschen Akademien, xi: *Das Jahr 1929* (Stuttgart: Deutsche Verlags-Anstalt, 1932).

SCHIFFERS, REINHARD, and KOCH, MANFRED (eds.), *Der Hauptausschuß des Deutschen Reichstags 1915–1918*, 4 vols. (Düsseldorf: Droste, 1981–3).

SCHMIDT, PAUL, *Statist auf diplomatischer Bühne 1923–45* (Bonn: Athenäum, 1953).

SCHNEE, HEINRICH, *German Colonization Past and Future: The Truth about the German Colonies* (London: Allen & Unwin, 1926).

SCHÜCKING, WALTER, and BELL, JOHANNES (eds.), *Das Werk des Untersuchungsausschusses der Verfassunggebenden Deutschen Nationalversammlung und des Deutschen Reichstages 1919–1928*, 4th series: *Die Ursachen des Deutschen*

Zusammenbruches im Jahre 1918, vol. vii (Berlin: Deutsche Verlagsgesellschaft für Politik, 1928).

Schulthess' Europäischer Geschichtskalender, NS 39 *(1923)*, *ed. Ulrich Thürauf (Munich: Beck, 1928; repr. Nendeln and Liechtenstein: Kraus, 1976).*

SCHULZE, HAGEN (ed.), 'Hans Staudinger, "Wirtschaftspolitik im Weimarer Staat. Lebenserinnerungen eines politischen Beamten im Reich und im Preussen, 1889 bis 1934"', *Archiv für Sozialgeschichte*, Supplement 10 (1982).

SCHULZE-BIDLINGMAIER, INGRID (ed.), *Die Kabinette Wirth I und II*, 2 vols. (Boppard: Harald Boldt, 1973).

SCHWIDETZKY, GEORG, 'Kreise um den jungen Stresemann', *Kölnische Zeitung*, 8 Oct. 1929.

SELF, ROBERT C. (ed.), *The Austen Chamberlain Diary Letters* (Cambridge: Cambridge University Press, 1995).

SEVERING, CARL, *Mein Lebensweg*, 2 vols. (Cologne: Greven, 1950).

SEYDOUX, FRANÇOIS, *Beiderseits des Rheins. Erinnerungen eines französischen Diplomaten* (Frankfurt am Main: Societäts Verlag, 1975).

SÖSEMANN, BERND (ed.), *Theodor Wolff. Der Journalist. Berichte und Leitartikel* (Düsseldorf: Econ, 1993).

STERN-RUBARTH, EDGAR, *Graf Brockdorff-Rantzau. Wanderer zwischen zwei Welten* (Berlin: Reimar Hobbing, 1929).

——*Three Men Tried . . . Austen Chamberlain, Stresemann, Briand and their Fight for a New Europe* (London: Duckworth, 1939).

STILLICH, OSCAR, *Die politischen Parteien in Deutschland*, ii: *Der Liberalismus* (Leipzig: Werner Klinkhardt, 1911).

STOCKHAUSEN, MAX VON, *Sechs Jahre Reichskanzlei. Erinnerungen und Tagebuchnotizen, 1922–1927* (Bonn: Athenäum, 1954).

STRESEMANN, WOLFGANG, *Mein Vater Gustav Stresemann* (Munich: Herbig, 1979).

——*Wie konnte es geschehen?* (Frankfurt am Main: Ullstein, 1990).

——*Zeiten und Klänge. Ein Leben zwischen Musik und Politik* (Berlin: Ullstein, 1994).

STROOMANN, GERHARD, *Aus meinem roten Notizbuch*, 2nd edn. (Frankfurt am Main: Societäts Verlag, 1960).

SUAREZ, GEORGES, *Briand*, vi: *L'Artisan de la paix, 1923–1932* (Paris: Plon, 1952).

TOYNBEE, ARNOLD J. *et al.* (eds.), *Survey of International Affairs*, 1920/23, 1924, 1925 [vol. ii ed. C. A. Macartney], 1926, 1927, 1928, 1929 (London: Oxford University Press, 1925–30).

TREVIRANUS, GOTTFRIED R., *Das Ende von Weimar* (Düsseldorf: Econ, 1968).

VALLENTIN, ANTONINA, *Stresemann. Vom Werden einer Staatsidee* (Leipzig: List, 1930); Eng. edn. (London: Constable, 1931).

Verhandlungen des Reichstags. Stenographische Berichte über die Verhandlungen des Reichstags, vols. 227–37, 258–68, 306–14 (Berlin: Norddeutscher Buchdruckerei, 1908–18).

Verhandlungen des verfassunggebenden Deutschen Nationalversammlung. Stenographische Berichte und Anlagen, vols. 326–33 (Berlin: Norddeutscher Buchdruckerei, 1920).

Verhandlungen des Reichstags. Stenographische Berichte und Anlagen, vols. 344–61, 381, 384–95, 423–6 (Berlin: Norddeutscher Buchdruckerei, 1920–4; Reichsdruckerei, 1924–9).

Vierzehnter allgemeiner Vertretertag der Nationalliberalen Partei in Berlin am 12. Mai 1912 (Berlin: Buchhandlung der Nationalliberalen Partei [1912]).

VOGELSANG, THILO (ed.), *Hermann Pünder. Politik in der Reichskanzlei. Aufzeichnungen aus den Jahren 1929–1932* (Stuttgart: Deutsche Verlags-Anstalt, 1961).

VOGT, MARTIN (ed.), *Das Kabinett Müller II* (Boppard: Harald Boldt, 1970).

—— *Die Entstehung des Youngplans dargestellt vom Reichsarchiv 1931–1933* (Boppard: Harald Boldt, 1970).

WALSDORFF, MARTIN, *Bibliographie Gustav Stresemann* (Düsseldorf: Droste, 1972).

WANDEL, ECKHARD, *Hans Schäffer* (Stuttgart: Deutsche Verlags-Anstalt, 1974).

WEGNER, KONSTANZE, and ALBERTIN, LOTHAR (eds.), *Linksliberalismus in der Weimarer Republik. Die Führungsgremien der Deutschen Demokratischen Partei und der Deutschen Staatspartei 1918–1933* (Düsseldorf: Droste, 1980).

WHEELER-BENNETT, JOHN W., and LATIMER, HUGH, *Information on the Reparation Settlement: Being the Background and History of the Young Plan and the Hague Agreements 1929–1930* (London: Allen & Unwin, 1930).

WOLFF, MAX I., *Club von Berlin 1864–1924* (Berlin: privately printed, 1926).

WULF, PETER (ed.), *Das Kabinett Fehrenbach* (Boppard: Harald Boldt, 1970).

Zehn Jahre Deutsche Geschichte 1918–1928 (Berlin: Otto Stollberg, [1928]).

Zehnter allgemeiner Vertretertag der Nationalliberalen Partei am 5. und 6. Oktober 1907 (Berlin: Buchhandlung der Nationalliberalen Partei [1907]).

ZONDEK, HERMANN, *Auf festem Fusse* (Stuttgart: Deutsche Verlags-Anstalt, 1973).

ZWOCH, GERHARD (ed.), *Gustav Stresemann. Reichstagsreden* (Bonn: az studio, 1972).

Zwölfter allgemeiner Vertretertag der Nationalliberalen Partei am 1. und. 2. Oktober 1910 in Cassel (Berlin: Buchhandlung der Nationalliberalen Partei [1910]).

SECONDARY SOURCES

ALBERTIN, LOTHAR, *Liberalismus und Demokratie am Anfang der Weimarer Republik. Eine vergleichende Analyse der Deutschen Demokratischen Partei und der Deutschen Volkspartei* (Düsseldorf: Droste, 1972).

ARNS, GÜNTHER, *Regierungsbildung und Koalitionspolitik in der Weimarer Republik 1919–1924* (Ph.D., Tübingen, 1971).

BAECHLER, CHRISTIAN, *Gustave Stresemann (1878–1929): De l'impérialisme à la sécurité collective* (Strasbourg: Presses Universitaires de Strasbourg, 1996).

BARIÉTY, JACQUES, *Les Relations franco-allemandes après la première guerre mondiale* (Paris: Editions Pedone, 1977).

—— 'L'Appareil de presse de Joseph Caillaux et l'argent allemand (1920–1932)', *Revue Historique*, 247 (1972), 375–406.

—— 'Finances et relations internationales á propos du "plan de Thoiry" (septembre 1926)', *Relations internationales*, 21 (Spring 1980), 51–70.

BAUMGART, CONSTANZE, *Stresemann und England* (Cologne: Böhlau, 1996).

BAUMGART, WINFRIED, *Deutsche Ostpolitik 1918. Von Brest-Litowsk bis zum Ende des Ersten Weltkrieges* (Munich: Oldenbourg, 1966).

BEITEL, WERNER, and NÖTZOLD, JÜRGEN, *Deutsch-sowjetische Wirtschaftsbeziehungen in der Zeit der Weimarer Republik* (Baden-Baden: Nomos, 1979).

BERDAHL, R. M., *The Politics of the Prussian Nobility: The Development of a Conservative Ideology 1770–1848* (Princeton: Princeton University Press, 1990).

BERG, MANFRED, *Gustav Stresemann und die Vereinigten Staaten von Amerika. Wirtschaftliche Verflechtung und Revisionspolitik 1907–1929* (Baden-Baden: Nomos, 1990).

BERGHAHN, VOLKER, *Der Stahlhelm. Bund der Frontsoldaten 1918–1935* (Düsseldorf: Droste, 1966).

BESSEL, RICHARD, *Germany after the First World War* (Oxford: Clarendon Press, 1993).

BIRKE, ADOLF M., BRECHTKEN, MAGNUS, and SEARLE, ALARIC (eds.), *An Anglo-German Dialogue* (Munich: K. G. Saur, 2000).

BLACKBOURN, DAVID, and ELEY, GEOFF, *The Peculiarities of German History: Bourgeois Society and Politics in Nineteenth-Century Germany* (Oxford: Oxford University Press, 1984).

—— and EVANS, RICHARD J. (eds.), *The German Bourgeoisie* (London: Routledge, 1991).

BROSZAT, MARTIN, *200 Jahre deutsche Polenpolitik* (Munich: Ehrenwirth, 1963).

BRUCH, RÜDIGER VOM, *Wissenschaft, Politik und öffentliche Meinung. Gelehrtenpolitik im Wilhelminischen Deutschland (1890–1914)* (Husum: Matthiesen, 1980).

BRUCH, RÜDIGER VOM, 'Max Lenz', in *Neue Deutsche Biographie*, xiv (Berlin: Duncker & Humblot, 1985).

—— 'Gustav Schmoller', in Wolfgang Treue and Karlfried Gründer (eds.), *Berlinische Lebensbilder. Wissenschaftspolitik in Berlin* (Berlin: Colloquium, 1987).

CAMPBELL, F. GREGORY, *Confrontation in Central Europe: Weimar Germany and Czechoslovakia* (Chicago: University of Chicago Press, 1975).

CARLTON, DAVID, *MacDonald versus Henderson: The Foreign Policy of the Second Labour Government* (London: Macmillan, 1970).

CARSTEN, F. L., *The Reichswehr and Politics 1918 to 1933* (Oxford: Clarendon Press, 1966).

CIENCIALA, ANNA M., and KOMARNICKI, TITUS, *From Versailles to Locarno: Keys to Polish Foreign Policy 1919–1925* (Lawrence: University Press of Kansas, 1984).

COHRS, P. O., 'The Unfinished Transatlantic Peace Order after World War I: Britain, the United States, and the Franco-German Question, 1923–5', unpublished D.Phil. thesis, Oxford, 2001.

CRAMPTON, R. J., *A Short History of Modern Bulgaria* (Cambridge: Cambridge University Press, 1987).

CROZIER, A. J., 'The Colonial Question During the Locarno Conference and After: An Essay on Anglo-German Relations 1924–1927', *International History Review*, 4/1 (1982) 37–54.

DEMM, EBERHARD, *Ein Liberaler in Kaiserreich und Republik. Der politische Weg Alfred Webers bis 1920* (Boppard: Harald Boldt, 1990).

DOHN, LOTHAR, *Politik und Interesse. Die Interessenstruktur der Deutschen Volkspartei* (Meisenheim am Glan: Anton Hain, 1970).

DOSS, KURT, *Zwischen Weimar und Warschau. Ulrich Rauscher. Deutscher Gesandter in Polen 1922–1930. Eine politische Biographie* (Düsseldorf: Droste, 1984).

DOWE, DIETER, KOCKA, JÜRGEN, and WINKLER, HEINRICH AUGUST (eds.), *Parteien im Wandel. Vom Kaiserreich zur Weimarer Republik* (Munich: Oldenbourg, 1999).

EDWARDS, MARVIN L., *Stresemann and the Greater Germany 1914–1918* (New York: Bookman Associates, 1962).

EKSTEINS, MODRIS, *The Limits of Reason: The German Democratic Press and the Collapse of Weimar Democracy* (Oxford: Oxford University Press, 1975).

ELEY, GEOFF, *Reshaping the German Right: Radical Nationalism and Political Change after Bismarck* (New Haven: Yale University Press, 1980).

ENSSLE, MANFRED J., *Stresemann's Territorial Revisionism: Germany, Belgium, and the Eupen-Malmédy Question 1919–1929* (Wiesbaden: Franz Steiner, 1980).

EPSTEIN, KLAUS, *Matthias Erzberger and the Dilemma of German Democracy* (Princeton: Princeton University Press, 1959).

ERDMANN, KARL DIETRICH, 'Das Problem der Ost-oder Westorientierung in der Locarno Politik Stresemanns', *Geschichte in Wissenschaft und Unterricht*, 6 (1955), 133–62.

——*Adenauer in der Rheinlandpolitik nach dem Ersten Weltkrieg* (Stuttgart: E. Klett, 1966).

ERGER, JOHANNES, *Der Kapp-Lüttwitz-Putsch* (Düsseldorf: Droste, 1967).

ESCHENBURG, THEODOR, *Das Kaiserreich am Scheideweg. Bassermann, Bülow und der Block* (Berlin: Verlag für Kulturpolitik, 1929).

——'Gustav Stresemann', in id., *Die improvisierte Demokratie* (Munich: Piper, 1963); repr. in Theodor Eschenburg and Ulrich Frank-Planitz, *Gustav Stresemann. Eine Bildbiographie* (Stuttgart: Deutsche Verlags-Anstalt, 1978).

EYCK, ERICH, *A History of the Weimar Republic*, 2 vols. (Cambridge, Mass.: Harvard University Press, 1962–4).

FALTER, JÜRGEN W., *Hitlers Wähler* (Munich: C. H. Beck, 1991).

FELDMAN, GERALD D. (ed.), *The German Inflation Reconsidered* (Berlin: Walter de Gruyter, 1982).

——*The Great Disorder: Politics, Economics, and Society in the German Inflation 1914–1924* (New York: Oxford University Press, 1997).

——*Hugo Stinnes. Biographie eines Industriellen 1870–1924* (Munich: C. H. Beck, 1998).

FERGUSON, NIALL, 'Public Finance and National Security: The Domestic Origins of the First World War Revisited', *Past & Present*, 142 (1994), 141–68.

FINK, CAROLE, 'Stresemann's Minority Policies, 1924–29', *Journal of Contemporary History*, 14 (1979), 403–22.

——FROHN, AXEL, and HEIDEKING, JÜRGEN (eds.), *Genoa, Rapallo and European Reconstruction in 1922* (Cambridge: Cambridge University Press, 1991).

FISCHER, FRITZ, *Germany's Aims in the First World War*, Eng. edn. (London: Chatto & Windus, 1967).

FLEURY, ANTOINE (ed.), *Le Plan Briand d'Union fédérale européenne* (Bern: Peter Lang, 1998).

FRANZ, OTMAR (ed.), *Am Wendepunkt der europäischen Geschichte* (Göttingen: Musterschmidt, 1981).

FRENTZ, CHRISTIAN RAITZ VON, *A Lesson Forgotten. Minority Protection under the League of Nations: The Case of the German Minority in Poland, 1920–1934* (New York: Lit, 1999).

FREYDANK, RUTH, *Theater in Berlin. Von den Anfängen bis 1945* (Berlin: Argon, 1988).

FRICKE, DIETER, (ed.), *Lexikon zur Parteiengeschichte* (Leipzig: VEB Bibliographisches Institut, 1984).

FROMMELT, REINHARD, *Paneuropa oder Mitteleuropa. Einigungsbestrebungen im Kalkül deutscher Wirtschaft und Politik 1925–1933* (Stuttgart: Deutsche Verlags-Anstalt, 1977).

FULBROOK, MARY (ed.), *German History since 1800* (London: Arnold, 1997).

GALL, LOTHAR, *Bismarck: The White Revolutionary*, i, Eng. edn. (London: Allen & Unwin, 1986).

—— *Bürgertum in Deutschland* (Berlin: Siedler, 1989).

—— and LANGEWIESCHE, DIETER (eds.), 'Liberalismus und Region. Zur Geschichte des deutschen Liberalismus im 19. Jahrhundert', *Historische Zeitschrift*, Supplement, 19 (1995).

GARTON ASH, TIMOTHY, *In Europe's Name: Germany and the Divided Continent* (London: Jonathan Cape, 1993).

GATZKE, HANS W., *Stresemann and the Rearmament of Germany* (Baltimore: Johns Hopkins University Press, 1954; repr. New York: Norton, 1969).

—— 'Zu den deutsch-russischen Beziehungen im Sommer 1918', *Vierteljahrshefte für Zeitgeschichte*, 3, (1955), 67–98.

—— 'Stresemann und Litwin', *Vierteljahrshefte für Zeitgeschichte*, 5 (1957), 76–90.

—— 'Gustav Stresemann: A Bibliographical Article', *Journal of Modern History*, 36 (1964), 1–13.

GEYER, MICHAEL, *Aufrüstung oder Sicherheit. Die Reichswehr in der Krise der Machtpolitik 1924–1936* (Wiesbaden: Franz Steiner, 1980).

GILBERT, MARTIN, *Sir Horace Rumbold: Portrait of a Diplomat, 1869–1941* (London: Heinemann, 1973).

GOETZ, WALTER, *Historiker in meiner Zeit* (Cologne: Böhlau, 1957).

GORDON, HAROLD J., *Hitler and the Beer Hall Putsch* (Princeton: Princeton University Press, 1972).

GÖRLITZ, WALTER, *Stresemann* (Heidelberg: Ähren, 1947).

GORODETSKY, GABRIEL, *The Precarious Truce: Anglo-Soviet Relations 1924–27* (Cambridge: Cambridge University Press, 1977).

GRATHWOL, ROBERT P., 'Gustav Stresemann: Reflections on his Foreign Policy', *Journal of Modern History*, 45 (1973), 52–70.

—— *Stresemann and the DNVP* (Lawrence: The Regents Press of Kansas, 1980).

GRAYSON, RICHARD S., *Austen Chamberlain and the Commitment to Europe: British Foreign Policy 1924–29* (London: Frank Cass, 1997).

GRÜNTHAL, GÜNTHER, *Reichsschulgesetz und Zentrumspartei in der Weimarer Republik* (Düsseldorf: Droste, 1968).

GRUPP, PETER, *Harry Graf Kessler 1868–1937. Eine Biographie*, 2nd edn. (Munich: C. H. Beck, 1996).

HARTENSTEIN, WOLFGANG, *Die Anfänge der Deutschen Volkspartei 1918–1920* (Düsseldorf: Droste, 1962).

HAUENSTEIN, FRITZ (ed.), *Der Weg zum industriellen Spitzenverband* (Darmstadt: Hoppenstedts Wirtschafts-Archiv, 1956).

HECKART, BEVERLY, *From Bassermann to Bebel: The Grand Bloc's Quest for Reform in the Kaiserreich, 1900–1914* (New Haven: Yale University Press, 1974).

HEHL, ULRICH VON, *Wilhelm Marx 1863–1946. Eine politische Biographie* (Mainz: Matthias Grünewald, 1987).

HESS, ULRICH, and SCHÄFER, MICHAEL (eds.), *Unternehmer in Sachsen* (Leipzig: Leipziger Universitätsverlag, 1998).

HETTLING, MANFRED, SCHIRMER, UWE, and SCHÖTZ, SUSANNE (eds.), *Figuren und Strukturen. Historische Essays für Hartmut Zwahr zum 65. Geburtstag (Munich: Saur, 2002).*

HEUSS, THEODOR, *Friedrich Naumann. Der Mann, das Werk, die Zeit,* 3rd edn., ed. Alfred Milatz (Munich: Siebenstern, 1968).

HEWITSON, MARK, *National Identity and Political Thought in Germany: Wilhelmine Depictions of the French Third Republic 1890–1914* (Oxford: Clarendon Press, 2000).

HIDEN, JOHN, *The Baltic States and German Ostpolitik* (Cambridge: Cambridge University Press, 1987).

HIRSCH, FELIX, *Stresemann. Ein Lebensbild* (Göttingen: Musterschmidt, 1978).

HOLZBACH, HEIDRUN, *Das 'System Hugenberg'* (Stuttgart: Deutsche Verlags-Anstalt, 1981).

HÖMIG, HERBERT, *Das preussische Zentrum in der Weimarer Republik* (Mainz: Matthias Grünewald, 1979).

HÖRSTER-PHILIPPS, ULRIKE, *Joseph Wirth 1879–1956. Eine politische Biographie* (Paderborn: Ferdinand Schöningh, 1998).

HUBATSCH, WALTHER, *Hindenburg und der Staat* (Göttingen: Musterschmidt, 1966).

HÜRTER, JOHANNES, *Wilhelm Groener. Reichswehrminister am Ende der Weimarer Republik 1928–1932* (Munich: Oldenbourg, 1993).

JACOBSON, JON, *Locarno Diplomacy: Germany and the West 1925–1929* (Princeton: Princeton University Press, 1972).

JANSEN, CHRISTIAN, *Professoren und Politik. Politisches Denken und Handeln der Heidelberger Hochschullehrer 1914–1935* (Göttingen: Vandenhoeck & Ruprecht, 1992).

JARAUSCH, KONRAD H., *The Enigmatic Chancellor: Bethmann Hollweg and the Hubris of Imperial Germany* (New Haven: Yale University Press, 1973).

——and JONES, LARRY E. (eds.), *In Search of a Liberal Germany* (New York: Berg, 1990).

JASPER, GOTTHARD, *Der Schutz der Republik* (Tübingen: Mohr, 1963).

JEANNESSON, STANISLAS, *Poincaré, la France et la Ruhr (1922–1924)* (Strasbourg: Presses Universitaires de Strasbourg, 1998).

JOHNSON, GAYNOR, '"Das Kind" Revisited: Lord D'Abernon and German Security Policy, 1922–1925', *Contemporary European History*, 9 (2000), 209–24.

——(ed.), *Locarno Revisited: European Diplomacy, 1920–1929* (forthcoming).

JONAS, ERASMUS, *Die Volkskonservativen 1928–1933* (Düsseldorf: Droste, 1965).

JONAS, KLAUS W., *The Life of Crown Prince William*, Eng. edn. (London: Routledge & Kegan Paul, 1961).

JONES, LARRY EUGENE, *German Liberalism and the Dissolution of the Weimar Party System 1918–1933* (Chapel Hill: University of North Carolina Press, 1988).

KAISER, ANGELA, *Lord D'Abernon und die englische Deutschlandpolitik 1920–1926* (Frankfurt: Peter Lang, 1989).

KAMPE, NORBERT, *Studenten und 'Judenfrage' im Deutschen Kaiserreich* (Göttingen: Vandenhoeck & Ruprecht, 1988).

KEETON, EDWARD D., *Briand's Locarno Policy: French Economics, Politics and Diplomacy, 1925–1929* (New York: Garland, 1987).

KERSHAW, IAN, *Hitler 1889–1936: Hubris* (Harmondsworth: Allen Lane, 1998).

KIESERITZKY, WOLTHER VON, and SICK, KLAUS-PETER (eds.), *Demokratie in Deutschland. Chancen und Gefährdungen im 19. und 20. Jahrhundert* (Munich: C. H. Beck, 1999).

KIMMICH, CHRISTOPH M., *The Free City: Danzig and German Foreign Policy, 1919–1934* (New Haven: Yale University Press, 1968).

——*Germany and the League of Nations* (Chicago: The University of Chicago Press, 1976).

——*German Foreign Policy 1918–1945: A Guide to Research and Research Materials*, revised edn., (Wilmington: Scholarly Resources, 1991).

KLEIN, MICHAEL, *Georg Bernhard. Die politische Haltung des Chefredakteurs der Vossischen Zeitung 1918–1930* (Frankfurt: Peter Lang, 1999).

KNIPPING, FRANZ, *Deutschland, Frankreich und das Ende der Locarno-Ära 1928–1931* (Munich: Oldenbourg, 1987).

KOLB, EBERHARD (ed.), *Friedrich Ebert als Reichspräsident* (Munich: Oldenbourg, 1997).

KÖRBER, ANDREAS, *Gustav Stresemann als Europäer, Patriot, Wegbereiter und potentieller Verhinderer Hitlers* (Hamburg: Krämer, 1999).

KOSZYK, KURT, *Geschichte der deutschen Presse*, ii: *Deutsche Presse im 19. Jahrhundert*; iii: *Deutsche Presse 1914–1945* (Berlin: Colloquium, 1966, 1972).

KOSZYK, KURT, *Gustav Stresemann. Der kaisertreue Demokrat* (Cologne: Kiepenheuer & Witsch, 1989).

KREKELER, NORBERT, *Revisionsanspruch und geheime Ostpolitik der Weimarer Republik* (Stuttgart: Deutsche Verlags-Anstalt, 1973).

KRÜGER, GERD, ' "...ich bitte, darüber nichts sagen zu dürfen". Halbstaatliche und private politische Nachrichtendienste in der Weimarer Republik', *zeitgeschichte*, 27/2 (2000), 87–107.

KRÜGER, PETER, *Die Aussenpolitik der Republik von Weimar* (Darmstadt: Wissenschaftliche Buchgesellschaft, 1985).

—— 'Der Deutsch-Polnische Schiedsvertrag im Rahmen der deutschen Sicherheitsinitiative von 1925', *Historische Zeitschrift*, 230 (1980), 577–612.

KÜPPERS, HEINRICH, *Joseph Wirth. Parlamentarier, Minister und Kanzler der Weimarer Republik* (Stuttgart: Franz Steiner, 1997).

LAITENBERGER, VOLKHARD, *Akademischer Austausch und auswärtige Kulturpolitik. Der Deutsche Akademische Austauschdienst 1923–1945* (Göttingen: Musterschmidt, 1976).

LANGEWIESCHE, DIETER, *Liberalism in Germany*, Eng. edn. (Basingstoke: Macmillan, 2000).

LAPP, BENJAMIN, *Revolution from the Right: Politics, Class, and the Rise of Nazism in Saxony, 1919–1933* (Boston: Humanities Press, 1997).

LÄSSIG, SIMONE, and POHL, KARL HEINRICH (eds.), *Sachsen im Kaiserreich. Politik, Wirtschaft und Gesellschaft im Umbruch* (Cologne: Böhlau, 1997).

LAUBACH, ERNST, *Die Politik der Kabinette Wirth 1921/22* (Lübeck: Matthiesen, 1968).

LEE, MARSHALL M., and MICHALKA, WOLFGANG, *German Foreign Policy 1917–1933: Continuity or Break?* (Leamington Spa: Berg, 1987).

LEHMANN, HARTMUT, *Historikerkontroversen* (Göttingen: Max Planck Institut für Geschichte, 2000).

LEHNERT, DETLEV, and MEGERLE, KLAUS (eds.), *Politische Teilkulturen zwischen Integration und Polarisierung* (Opladen: Westdeutscher Verlag, 1990).

LEOPOLD, JOHN A., *Alfred Hugenberg: The Radical Nationalist Campaign against the Weimar Republic* (New Haven: Yale University Press, 1977).

LERMAN, KATHARINE A., *The Chancellor as Courtier: Bernhard von Bülow and the Governance of Germany 1900–1909* (Cambridge: Cambridge University Press, 1990).

LIEBE, WERNER, *Die Deutschnationale Volkspartei 1918–1924* (Düsseldorf: Droste, 1956).

LINK, WERNER, *Die amerikanische Stabilisierungspolitik in Deutschland 1921–32* (Düsseldorf: Droste, 1970).

LÖWENSTEIN, HUBERTUS PRINZ ZU, *Stresemann. Das deutsche Schicksal im Spiegel seines Lebens* (Frankfurt am Main: Heinrich Scheffler, 1952).

McDougall, Walter A., *France's Rhineland Diplomacy, 1914–1924: The Last Bid for a Balance of Power in Europe* (Princeton: Princeton University Press, 1978).

Madajczyk, Piotr, *Polityka i Koncepcje Polityczne Gustawa Stresemanna Wobec Polski (1915–1929)* (Warsaw: Instytut Nauk Politcznych Polskiej Akademii Nauk, 1991).

Marder, Arthur J., *From the Dreadnought to Scapa Flow: The Royal Navy in the Fisher Era, 1904–1919*, iv: *1917: Year of Crisis* (London: Oxford University Press, 1969).

Marks, Sally, 'Mussolini and Locarno: Fascist Foreign Policy in Microcosm', *Journal of Contemporary History*, 14 (1979), 423–39.

Marquand, David, *Ramsay MacDonald* (London: Jonathan Cape, 1977).

Matthias, Erich, and Morsey, Rudolf (eds.), *Das Ende der Parteien 1933* (Düsseldorf: Droste, 1960).

Maxelon, Michael-Olaf, *Stresemann und Frankreich. Deutsche Politik der Ost–West-Balance* (Düsseldorf: Droste, 1972).

Meier-Welcker, Hans, *Seeckt* (Frankfurt am Main: Bernard & Graefe, 1967).

Michalka, Wolfgang. (ed.) *Der Erste Weltkrieg* (Munich: Piper, 1994).

——and Lee, Marshall M. (eds.), *Gustav Stresemann* (Darmstadt: Wissenschaftliche Buchgesellschaft, 1982).

Mielke, Siegfried, *Der Hansa-Bund für Gewerbe, Handel und Industrie 1909–1914* (Göttingen: Vandenhoeck & Ruprecht, 1976).

Milatz, Alfred, *Wähler und Wahlen in der Weimarer Republik*, (Bonn: Bundeszentrale für politische Bildung, 1965).

Miller, Susanne, *Burgfrieden und Klassenkampf. Die deutsche Sozialdemokratie im Ersten Weltkrieg* (Düsseldorf: Droste, 1974).

Missiroli, Antonio, *Die Deutsche Hochschule für Politik* (Königswinter: Friedrich Naumann Stiftung, 1988).

Möllers, Heiner, *Reichswehrminister Otto Geßler. Eine Studie zu 'unpolitischer' Militärpolitik in der Weimarer Republik* (Frankfurt am Main: Peter Lang, 1998).

Mommsen, Hans, *The Rise and Fall of Weimar Democracy*, Eng. edn. (Chapel Hill: University of North Carolina Press, 1996).

Mommsen, Wolfgang J., *Max Weber and German Politics 1890–1920*, Eng. edn. (Chicago: University of Chicago Press, 1984).

——and Jürgen Osterhammel (eds.), *Imperialism and After* (London: Allen & Unwin, 1986).

Morgan, David W., *The Socialist Left and the German Revolution* (Ithaca: Cornell University Press, 1975).

Morsey, Rudolf, *Die Deutsche Zentrumspartei 1917–1923* (Düsseldorf: Droste, 1966).

MÜLLER, HANS JÜRGEN, *Auswärtige Pressepolitik und Propaganda zwischen Ruhr-kampf und Locarno (1923–1925)* (Frankfurt am Main: Peter Lang, 1991).

NIEDHART, GOTTFRIED, *Die Aussenpolitik der Weimarer Republik* (Munich: Old-enbourg, 1999).

NIPPERDEY, THOMAS, *Deutsche Geschichte 1866–1918*, ii: *Machtstaat vor der Demokratie* (Munich: C. H. Beck, 1992).

OESTREICH, BRIGITTA, 'Otto Hintze', in Michael Erbe (ed.), *Berlinische Lebens-bilder. Geisteswissenschaftler* (Berlin: Colloquium, 1989).

ORDE, ANNE, *Great Britain and International Security 1920–1926* (London: Royal Historical Society, 1978).

O'RIORDAN, ELSPETH Y., *Britain and the Ruhr Crisis* (Basingstoke: Palgrave, 2001).

PALMOWSKI, JAN, *Urban Liberalism in Imperial Germany: Frankfurt am Main, 1866–1914* (Oxford: Oxford University Press, 1999).

PAPKE, GERHARD, *Der liberale Politiker Erich Koch-Weser in der Weimarer Republik* (Baden-Baden: Nomos Verlagsgesellschaft, 1989).

PATCH, WILLIAM L. JR., *Heinrich Brüning and the Dissolution of the Weimar Republic* (Cambridge: Cambridge University Press, 1998).

PEASE, NEIL, *Poland, the United States, and the Stabilization of Europe, 1919–1933* (New York: Oxford University Press, 1986).

POGGE VON STRANDMANN, HARTMUT, 'Grossindustrie und Rapallopolitik. Deutsche–Sowjetische Handelsbeziehungen in der Weimarer Republik', *His-torische Zeitschrift*, 222 (1976), 265–341.

POHL, KARL HEINRICH, *Weimars Wirtschaft und die Außenpolitik der Republik 1924–1926. Vom Dawes-Plan zum Internationalen Eisenpakt* (Düsseldorf: Droste, 1979).

—— 'Sachsen, Stresemann und die Nationalliberale Partei. Anmerkungen zur politischen Entwicklung, zum Aufstieg des industriellen Bürgertums und zur frühen Tätigkeit Stresemanns im Königreich Sachsen vor 1914', *Jahrbuch für Liberalismusforschung*, 4 (1992), 197–216.

—— *Adolf Müller. Geheimagent und Gesandter in Kaiserreich und Weimarer Repub-lik* (Cologne: Bund, 1995).

—— 'Sachsen, Stresemann und der Verein Sächsischer Industrieller: "Mod-erne" Industriepolitik zu Beginn des 20. Jahrhunderts?', *Blätter für deutsche Landesgeschichte*, 134 (1998), 407–40.

—— (ed.), *Politiker und Bürger. Gustav Stresemann und seine Zeit* (Göttingen: Vandenhoeck & Ruprecht, 2002).

POST, GAINES, *The Civil–Military Fabric of Weimar Foreign Policy* (Princeton: Princeton University Press, 1973).

PRELLER, LUDWIG, *Sozialpolitik in der Weimarer Republik* (1949: repr. Düsseldorf: Droste, 1978).

PRYCE, DONALD B., 'The Reich Government versus Saxony, 1923: The Decision to Intervene', *Central European History*, 10 (1977), 112–48.

PULZER, PETER, *Jews and the German State: The Political History of a Minority* (Oxford: Blackwell, 1992).

PYTA, WOLFRAM, and RICHTER, LUDWIG (eds.), *Gestaltungskraft des Politischen. Festschrift für Eberhard Kolb* (Berlin: Duncker & Humblot, 1998).

QUATAERT, JEAN H., 'The Politics of Rural Industrialization: Class, Gender, and Collective Protest in the Saxon Oberlausitz of the Late Nineteenth Century', *Central European History*, 20/2 (1987), 91–124.

RAUH, MANFRED, *Föderalismus und Parlamentarismus in Wilhelminischen Reich* (Düsseldorf: Droste, 1973).

RETALLACK, JAMES N., *Notables of the Right: The Conservative Party and Political Mobilization in Germany 1876–1918* (Boston: Unwin Hyman, 1988).

—— 'Society and Politics in Saxony in the Nineteenth and Twentieth Centuries: Reflections on Recent Research', *Archiv für Sozialgeschichte*, 38 (1998), 396–457.

—— 'Saxon Signposts: Cultural Battles, Identity Politics, and German Authoritarianism in Transition', *German History*, 17/4 (1999), 455–69.

RICHTER, LUDWIG, *Die Deutsche Volkspartei 1918–1933* (Düsseldorf: Droste, 2002).

RIEKHOFF, HARALD VON, *German–Polish Relations, 1918–1933* (Baltimore: Johns Hopkins University Press, 1971).

RITTER, GERHARD A. (ed.), *Der Aufstieg der deutschen Arbeiterbewegung* (Munich: Oldenbourg, 1990).

RÖDDER, ANDREAS, *Stresemanns Erbe. Julius Curtius und die deutsche Außenpolitik 1929–1931* (Paderborn: Schöningh, 1996).

RÖHL, JOHN C. G., and SOMBART, NICOLAUS (eds.), *Kaiser Wilhelm II: New Interpretations* (Cambridge: Cambridge University Press, 1982).

ROMEYK, HORST, 'Paul Moldenhauer (1876–1946)', *Rheinische Lebensbilder*, 7 (Cologne, 1977), 253–69.

ROSENBERG, ARTHUR, *Geschichte der Weimarer Republik* (1st edn., 1935; repr. Frankfurt am Main: Europäische Verlagsanstalt, 1961).

RUDLOFF, MICHAEL (ed.), *Erich Zeigner—Bildungsbürger und Sozialdemokrat* (Leipzig: Friedrich Ebert Stiftung [1999]).

RUDOLPH, KARSTEN, *Die sächsische Sozialdemokratie vom Kaiserreich zur Republik (1871–1923)* (Weimar: Böhlau, 1995).

RUPPERT, KARSTEN, *Im Dienst am Staat von Weimar. Das Zentrum als regierende Partei in der Weimarer Demokratie 1923–1930* (Düsseldorf: Droste, 1992).

SALEWSKI, MICHAEL, *Entwaffnung und Militärkontrolle in Deutschland 1919–1927* (Munich: Oldenbourg, 1966).

SCHATTKOWSKY, RALPH (ed.), *Locarno und Osteuropa. Fragen eines europäischen Sicherheitssystems in den 20er Jahren* (Marburg: Hitzeroth, 1994).

SCHEIDEMANN, CHRISTIANE, *Ulrich Graf Brockdorff-Rantzau (1869–1928). Eine politische Biographie* (Frankfurt am Main: Peter Lang, 1998).

SCHOT, BASTIAAN, *Nation oder Staat? Deutschland und der Minderheitenschutz* (Marburg: J. G. Herder Institut, 1988).

SCHUKER, STEPHEN A., *The End of French Predominance in Europe: The Financial Crisis of 1924 and the Adoption of the Dawes Plan* (Chapel Hill: University of North Carolina Press, 1976).

—— 'Bayern und der rheinische Separatismus 1923–1924', *Jahrbuch des Historischen Kollegs 1997*, 75–111.

—— (ed.), *Deutschland und Frankreich. Vom Konflikt zur Aussöhnung* (Munich: Oldenbourg, 2000).

SCHULZ, MATTHIAS, *Deutschland, der Völkerbund und die Frage der europäischen Wirtschaftsordnung 1925–1933* (Hamburg: Dr R. Krämer, 1997).

SCHULZE, HAGEN, *Otto Braun oder Preußens demokratische Sendung* (Frankfurt: Ullstein, 1977).

SCHWABE, KLAUS, *Wissenschaft und Kriegsmoral. Die deutschen Hochschullehrer und die politischen Grundfragen des Ersten Weltkrieges* (Göttingen: Musterschmidt Verlag, 1969).

SCHWARZ, GOTTHART, *Theodor Wolff und Das 'Berliner Tageblatt'* (Tübingen: J. C. B. Mohr, 1968).

SCHWARZ, HANS-PETER, *Konrad Adenauer*, i: *From the German Empire to the Federal Republic, 1876–1952*, Eng. edn. (Oxford: Berghahn, 1995).

SHEEHAN, JAMES J., *German Liberalism in the Nineteenth Century* (London: Methuen, 1982).

SIEBERT, FERDINAND, *Aristide Briand 1862–1932* (Zurich: Eugen Rentsch, 1973).

SÖSEMANN, BERND, *Theodor Wolff. Ein Leben mit der Zeitung* (Munich: Econ, 2000).

SOUTOU, GEORGES-HENRI, 'L'Alliance franco-polonaise (1925–1933) ou comment s'en débarrasser?', *Revue d'histoire diplomatique*, 95, (1981), 294–348.

SPERBER, JONATHAN, *The Kaiser's Voters: Electors and Elections in Imperial Germany* (Cambridge: Cambridge University Press, 1997).

STARKULLA, HEINZ, 'Organisation und Technik der Pressepolitik des Staatsmannes Gustav Stresemann (1923 bis 1929)', unpublished Ph.D., Munich, 1951.

STEGMANN, DIRK, *Die Erben Bismarcks. Parteien und Verbände in der Spätphase des Wilhelminischen Deutschlands. Sammlungspolitik 1897–1918* (Cologne: Kiepenheuer & Witsch, 1970).

STEGMANN, DIRK,'Hugenberg contra Stresemann: Die Politik der Industrieverbände am Ende des Kaiserreichs', *Vierteljahrshefte für Zeitgeschichte*, 24 (1976), 329–78.

STOECKER, HELLMUTH (ed.), *German Imperialism in Africa*, Eng. edn. (London: C. Hurst, 1986).

STÜRMER, MICHAEL, *Koalition und Opposition in der Weimarer Republik 1924–1928* (Düsseldorf: Droste, 1967).

SÜTTERLIN, INGMAR, *Die 'Russische Abteilung' des Auswärtigen Amtes in der Weimarer Republik* (Berlin: Duncker & Humblot, 1994).

SUVAL, STANLEY, *The Anschluss Question in the Weimar Era* (Baltimore: Johns Hopkins University Press, 1974).

SZEJNMANN, CLAUS-CHRISTIAN W., *Nazism in Central Germany: The Brownshirts in 'Red' Saxony* (New York: Berghahn Books, 1999).

TAYLOR, A. J. P., *The Origins of the Second World War* (Harmondsworth: Penguin Books, 1964).

TEWES, HENNING, and WRIGHT, JONATHAN (eds.), *Liberalism, Anti-Semitism and Democracy: Essays in honour of Peter Pulzer* (Oxford: Oxford University Press, 2001).

THEINER, PETER, *Sozialer Liberalismus und deutsche Weltpolitik. Friedrich Naumann im Wilhelminischen Deutschland (1860–1919)* (Baden-Baden: Nomos Gesellschaft, 1983).

THIEME, HARTWIG, *Die nationalliberale Fraktion des Preußischen Abgeordnetenhauses 1914–18* (Boppard am Rhein: Harald Boldt, 1963).

THIMME, ANNELISE, *Gustav Stresemann* (Frankfurt am Main: Goedel, 1957).

THOMPSON, ALASTAIR, *Left Liberals, the State, and Popular Politics in Wilhelmine Germany* (Oxford: Oxford University Press, 2000).

TURNER, ARTHUR, *The Cost of War: British Policy on French War Debts, 1918–1932* (Brighton: Sussex Academic Press, 1998).

TURNER, HENRY ASHBY, *Stresemann and the Politics of the Weimar Republic* (Princeton: Princeton University Press, 1963).

—— *German Big Business and the Rise of Hitler* (New York and Oxford: Oxford University Press, 1985).

ULLMANN, HANS-PETER, *Der Bund der Industriellen* (Göttingen: Vandenhoeck & Ruprecht, 1976).

VASCIK, GEORGE S., 'The German Peasant League and the Limits of Rural Liberalism in Wilhelmian Germany', *Central European History*, 24/2 (1991), 147–75.

VIETSCH, EBERHARD VON, *Arnold Rechberg und das Problem der politischen West-Orientierung Deutschlands nach dem 1. Weltkrieg* (Koblenz: Bundesarchiv, 1958).

VOGT, ADOLF, *Oberst Max Bauer. Generalstabsoffizier im Zwielicht 1869–1929* (Osnabrück: Biblio, 1974).

WALSDORFF, MARTIN, *Westorientierung und Ostpolitik. Stresemanns Rußlandpolitik in der Locarno Ära* (Bremen: Schünemann, 1971).

WANDYCZ, P. S., 'Le Pologne face à la politique locarnienne de Briand', *Revue d'histoire diplomatique*, 95 (1981), 237–63.

WARREN, DONALD, *The Red Kingdom of Saxony: Lobbying Grounds for Gustav Stresemann 1901–1909* (The Hague: Martinus Nijhoff, 1964).

WEIDENFELD, WERNER, *Die Englandpolitik Gustav Stresemanns. Theoretische und praktische Aspekte der Aussenpolitik* (Mainz: Hase & Koehler, 1972).

WEYMAR, PAUL, *Konrad Adenauer*, Eng. edn. (New York: E. P. Dutton, 1957).

WHEELER-BENNETT, JOHN W., *Hindenburg: The Wooden Titan* (London: Macmillan, 1967; reissue of 1936 edn.).

——*The Nemesis of Power: The German Army in Politics 1918–1945*, 2nd edn. (London: Macmillan, 1967).

WILLIAMSON, JOHN G., *Karl Helfferich 1872–1924: Economist, Financier, Politician* (Princeton: Princeton University Press, 1971).

WINKLER, HEINRICH AUGUST, *Arbeiter und Arbeiterbewegung in der Weimarer Republik*, i: *Von der Revolution zur Stabilisierung 1918–1924*, ii: *Der Schein der Normalität. Arbeiter und Arbeiterbewegung in der Weimarer Republik 1924 bis 1930*, 2nd edn. (Berlin: J. H. W. Dietz, 1985, 1988).

——*Weimar 1918–1933*, 2nd edn. (Munich: C. H. Beck, 1994).

——*Der lange Weg nach Westen*, i: *Deutsche Geschichte vom Ende des Alten Reiches bis zum Untergang der Weimarer Republik*; ii: *Deutsche Geschichte vom 'Dritten Reich' bis zur Wiedervereinigung* (Munich: C. H. Beck, 2000).

WINTZER, JOACHIM, 'Deutschland und der Völkerbund 1918–1926', unpublished Ph.D. Heidelberg, 1998.

WITT, PETER-CHRISTIAN, *Die Finanzpolitik des Deutschen Reiches von 1903 bis 1913* (Lübeck and Hamburg: Matthiesen, 1970).

WRIGHT, JONATHAN R. C., *'Über den Parteien'. Die politische Haltung der evangelischen Kirchenführer 1918–1933* (Göttingen: Vandenhoeck & Ruprecht, 1977).

——'Stresemann and Locarno', *Contemporary European History*, 4/2 (1995), 109–31.

WULF, PETER, *Hugo Stinnes. Wirtschaft und Politik 1918–1924* (Stuttgart: Klett Cotta, 1979).

WURM, CLEMENS A., *Die französische Sicherheitspolitik in der Phase der Umorientierung 1924–1926* (Frankfurt am Main: Peter Lang, 1979).

ZEIDLER, MANFRED, *Reichswehr und Rote Armee 1920–1933* (Munich: Oldenbourg, 1993).

INDEX